# 1988 YEARBOOK
## EVENTS OF 1987

*Meeting in Washington, Soviet leader Mikhail Gorbachev and President Ronald Reagan sign a treaty to eliminate their medium-range nuclear missiles.*

# FUNK & WAGNALLS NEW ENCYCLOPEDIA 1988 YEARBOOK

LEON L. BRAM
Vice-President and
Editorial Director

NORMA H. DICKEY
Editor in Chief

## Funk & Wagnalls, Inc.

Publishers since 1876

# CONTENTS

# MEMBERS OF THE STAFF

**SENIOR EDITOR**                     William McGeveran, Jr.

**EDITORIAL ASSISTANTS**              Ingrid J. Strauch
                                      Julia Szabo

**CLERICAL ASSISTANT**                Kay Blake

**STAFF EDITORS**                     Kathy Casey
                                      Mark Curiale
                                      Edward Egan
                                      Inez Salinger Glucksman
                                      Irene Gunther
                                      Archibald Hobson
                                      Lawrence Klepp
                                      Mary A. Morris
                                      Kathryn Paulsen
                                      Dan Wasserman

**INDEXER**                           Jerry Ralya

**ASSOCIATE DESIGN DIRECTOR**         Joan Gampert

**SENIOR DESIGNER**                   Marvin Friedman

**DESIGNERS**                         Marc Sferrazza
                                      Adrienne M. Weiss

**PHOTO EDITORS**                     Joyce Deyo
                                      Margaret McRae
                                      Marcia Rackow

**SENIOR PRODUCTION ASSISTANT**       Mynette Green

**CLERICAL ASSISTANT**                Valerie James

**PRODUCTION EXECUTIVE**              Steven G. Weinfeld

# FOREWORD: THE EVENTS OF 1987

The clandestine U.S. initiative to sell arms to Iran, and the diversion of profits to the Nicaraguan contras, was a major focus of attention during 1987, as key figures in the affair testified at congressional hearings and investigative panels issued reports highly critical of President Ronald Reagan's management of his administration. Reagan, whose popularity was undermined by the Iran/contra affair, also faced an assertive new Congress, with both houses controlled by the Democrats. His vetoes of key bills were overridden, and he lost a crucial battle when the Senate blocked his nomination of conservative Robert Bork to the Supreme Court.

The nation was stunned in October when the stock market took a dramatic plunge that dwarfed even the crash of 1929. The White House and Congress agreed on budget cuts in an effort to allay Wall Street's concern over massive federal budget deficits.

Meanwhile, the Reagan administration finalized an accord with the Soviet Union on intermediate-range missiles, eliminating that whole category of nuclear weapons. The treaty was signed at a December summit between Reagan and Soviet leader Mikhail Gorbachev.

Around the world, tensions heated up in the war-torn Persian Gulf, where the U.S. warship *Stark* was struck by a missile, killing 37 U.S. sailors. Conflict plagued the Central American countries, but a plan proposed by Costa Rican President Oscar Arias Sánchez, for which he won the Nobel Peace Prize, raised hopes for peace in the region. British Prime Minister Margaret Thatcher and Australia's Prime Minister Bob Hawke both won reelection with ease, while in Canada, Prime Minister Brian Mulroney, slumping in the polls, negotiated a new constitutional accord and a controversial free trade pact with the United States.

Other headline-makers ranged from televangelists Jim and Tammy Bakker, whose misdoings caused a scandal in the "electronic church," and Gary Hart, who withdrew from the presidential race in the wake of a scandal (but later reentered), to heavyweight boxing champion Mike Tyson, the Series-winning Minnesota Twins, and a little Texas girl saved from a well in a grueling rescue operation that kept the whole nation in suspense.

The year marked the 200th birthday of the U.S. Constitution; in the first of our three feature articles, a noted historian describes how and why this enduring document was created. A second feature examines a recent creation, the massive James Bay hydroelectric project, and how it has transformed Québec's sparsely populated north. Our third feature looks at the world's oldest domestic animal—the dog—and how dogs have served humans from the Old Stone Age to the present.

THE EDITORS

# THE BIRTH OF THE
# CONSTITUTION

In 1987, as Americans celebrated the 200th birthday of their Constitution, they perhaps became more aware of how it has shaped their history and character as a people. When the Constitutional Convention met in Philadelphia in 1787, the 13 colonies showed signs of going their separate ways. Each was protective of its sovereignty, and together they became quarrelsome, divided over issues such as trade, slavery, and religion. Clearly, an authoritative central government was needed if they were to survive as a nation. The delegates fashioned a pragmatic document that has since proved resilient by adapting to the needs of a changing and developing people.

by JAMES THOMAS FLEXNER

*James Thomas Flexner, a former president of the Society of American Historians, has written over 20 books on American history and American art. In 1973 he received a Pulitzer Prize for his four-volume biography of George Washington and a National Book Award for the fourth volume,* George Washington: Anguish and Farewell *(1793–1799).*

The United States of America, having won a war with the British overlord and established their independence, failed to emerge from the Revolution as a single nation. Nor did it seem likely that the states would draw up or accept a constitution that would join them into a close political entity.

Although by the end of the Revolution settlement had not to any extent crossed the mountains into the Ohio and Mississippi valleys, the area that had won its independence was many times larger than any European nation. From Maine in the north to Georgia in the south was as far as from London to the most distant tip of Italy. And each of the 13 colonies had been from the very start of settlement independent from all the others. The only political connection between them had been the common dependence on the British crown, which was cut in 1776 by the Declaration of Independence.

Inhabitants of neighboring colonies (now become

Celebrations at Philadelphia's Independence Hall,
where a federation of states negotiated its way to nationhood.

states) had down the generations wandered on occasion over their communal borders, but there was almost no contact between widely separated areas. Land transportation for men on horseback or for wagons hauling merchandise was fragmented, irregular, and so slow that it was rarely undertaken for any distance. When sailing ships set out from various ports that dotted the shoreline, they rarely moved along the coast either to the north or to the south: they steered for England or along trade routes to the West Indies.

It was a common fear of British tyranny that drove the 13 colonies to cooperate with each other. In September 1775, for the first time in 150 years of settlement, delegates from all the colonies met face-to-face with each other, at the Second Continental Congress. But they attended the Congress not as compatriots, only as allies. None of the colonies gave up one jot of its individual sovereignty.

## Fragmentation and Rebellion

After two years of debate, in November 1777 the Congress adopted the Articles of Confederation, which gave some order to the states' regional alliance. This

*Visitors at the National Archives in Washington, D.C., line up to glimpse the Constitution, preserved in a sealed glass-and-bronze case.*

*Shays' Rebellion, a revolt by indebted Massachusetts farmers against the confiscation of their lands, spread a fear of civil war through the former colonies and pointed up the need for a strong central authority.*

agreement, ratified by the states in March 1781, established no more than a firm league of friendship. Although General George Washington continued to complain that rivalry between the states made for defeat almost as much as did the military activity of the British, Congress managed to support the war effort as long as danger was imminent. But after British General Charles Cornwallis's surrender at Yorktown, in October 1781, the battle against Britain seemed to be going so well that the states felt further cooperation was no longer necessary. It became impossible even to pay interest on the debts incurred by Congress or to pay even what had been long owed to the army, which could not yet be safely disbanded. A movement was started to have the financiers back the army in terrorizing the civilian governments. Only Washington's personal intervention prevented the loss of any possibility of such a national republican government as the Constitution was to create.

With the return of peace, the United States became increasingly fragmented. The individual states set up customs barriers against each other; made, to the detriment of their neighbors, land-grabbing treaties with

*George Washington, called out of retirement to press for unity among the delegates, addresses the Constitutional Convention.*

the Indians; and refused to obey provisions included in the general peace treaty with England that did not suit them. This created chaos on a continental scale, but on the whole, prosperity reigned, and those who cried "danger" were not listened to. That is, not until a potentially great danger eventuated.

Looking backward, Shays' Rebellion (named for its leader, Daniel Shays) seems no more than a mosquito bite. Small property holders in central and western Massachusetts, because of laws passed over their protests by the more prosperous legislators in Boston, were being sold out of their farms and threatened by county courts with imprisonment for debt. In the fall of 1786, debtors prevented the courts from sitting, and in January 1787 rebels attacked an arsenal in Springfield. Since neither the state nor the central government controlled any funds with which to hire troops that would restore order, the money to do so was supplied by rich citizens. An augury for civil war!

Leaders all over the nation, already queasy about the lack of effective government, were swept with hysteria, as if a deadly epidemic had broken out for which there was no cure. George Washington wrote, "I am mortified beyond expression when I view the clouds that have spread over the brightest dawn that ever dawned upon any country." Was the horrible conclusion being proved, that "mankind when left to themselves are unfit for their own government"? Although the conflagration did not spread, as was feared, and in Massachusetts the crisis was compromised without bloodshed, in all thinking minds the menace remained. Next time?

### Envisioning a New Order

The Continental Congress was still limping along. It was prodded into sanctioning a convention to meet at Philadelphia during May 1787 for a purpose carefully limited to strengthening the Articles of Confederation. That the meeting was not intended as a constitutional convention, that the conception of founding a new government was hidden in a few discreet minds, made the outcome possible. Had the state legislators foreseen such a result, they would have exploded into every kind of divisive debate, and they would surely have tied the hands of their delegates in ways that would contradict the instructions from other states. There was, indeed, doubt among its supporters that the convention would amount to enough to summon from retirement America's great man, George Washington, whose influence for unity was too valuable a trump card to be carelessly played.

But the ghost of Daniel Shays was walking. Although the Continental Congress had become so insignificant that only third-raters were willing to serve as delegates, the major leaders from state after state agreed to answer the new call: James Madison from Virginia; James Wilson, Gouverneur Morris, and the elderly Benjamin Franklin from Pennsylvania; Alexander Hamilton from New York; Rufus King from Massachusetts; Charles Cotesworth Pinckney and John Rutledge from South

*James Madison (left) and Alexander Hamilton were two of the three men (the third was John Jay) whose articles, collected as* The Federalist, *helped sway opinion in favor of the Constitution.*

*John Marshall, chief justice of the Supreme Court from 1801 to 1835, helped establish the Court's enduring role in the constitutional system of checks and balances.*

Carolina; and so on. (Neither John Adams nor Thomas Jefferson could attend, since both were representing the United States in Europe.) Washington was summoned and, reluctantly abandoning his retirement, felt it his duty to attend.

While Washington was still at Mount Vernon, the deepest constitutional thinker in the United States, James Madison, had secured his approval for a radical plan that smashed the new convention's mandate. The Articles of Confederation would have to be scrapped, since they set up the Continental Congress as the only ruling body, which could, without any check, legislate whatever at the moment it pleased, administering its laws through committees made up of its own members.

But advanced political thinkers, such as the Englishman Sir William Blackstone and the Frenchman Montesquieu, had postulated a theory of checks and balances. Tyranny and special privilege could be outlawed by a multiform government made up of a legislature divided into an upper and lower house, an independent executive, and an independent judiciary—all offices to be filled at different dates, for different periods of time, and according to different electoral procedures.

Another fundamental weakness of the Articles of Confederation was, so Madison continued, that the states stood between the Continental Congress and the people. In order to achieve national unity, the central government would have to be enabled to collect federal taxes directly and to enforce federal law everywhere on the continent.

### Meeting of Similar Minds

As the 55 convention delegates straggled in from their often distant states, the seven from Virginia met together to flesh out what became known as the Virginia plan. Their best orator, Edmund Randolph, presented it to the convention. It was clear to all that the plan not only exceeded their given powers but also committed the convention to the awesome task of creating such a government as had never before existed in the world. But small groups of youngish men (the average age was 42, and rarely more than 20 men appeared at a single session) voted resolutely that "a national government ought to be established consisting of a *supreme* legislative, executive, and judiciary."

Before this daring step into the unknown had been taken, Washington had been unanimously elected president of the convention, and the two most

important rules of procedure had been adopted. The first was dictated by the formulation of the convention and what was then universal American usage: every state, whether large or small, would cast an equal, single vote. The second provision was that the proceedings of the convention would be conducted and kept in complete secrecy. As the meetings went on from May to September, even in the hottest days of midsummer, the windows were forever shut against inquisitive ears.

Without secrecy, the Constitution could never have been achieved. Modern enquiring reporters cultivating news leaks would, by pinning delegates to premature statements and stirring up controversy before agreement could be reached, have torn all apart. Fluidity was necessary because in its most creative aspects the convention was an educational institution, where able men rubbed off rough edges, came to know and respect each other, and found paths they could travel together toward what they all agreed was an essential and invaluable goal. As Washington put it, every delegate recognized that "something is necessary because the existing government is shaken to its foundation and liable to be overset by any blast. In a word, it is at an end and unless a remedy is soon applied anarchy and confusion will inevitably be the result."

What was happening Washington had experienced before in the encampments of the Continental Army, when men from all over the land had been thrown together for long passages of time to deal with crises

*Union recruiters in the Civil War made preserving the Constitution their rallying cry (below). Above, President Abraham Lincoln inspects his troops; General George McClellan is sixth from the left.*

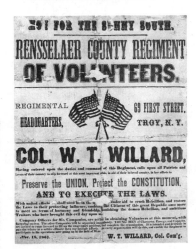

that could only be met by their communal action. The soldiers discovered that whether they came from the semitropical vegetation of Georgia or the pine forests of Maine, they were a common breed of cats, more like one to another than to any Europeans.

To start with, all, whether in person or through their forebears, had been set apart from their neighbors in their countries of origin by having the enterprise and courage to break away from established communities and cross a wide ocean into an unforeseeable environment. When the colonists arrived, they found themselves in a world different from any Europeans had known. Narrow overpopulated areas had given way to vastness. Very important to the Constitutional Convention was the fact that all the delegates were in themselves or in immediate inheritance self-made men, who had profited from a society where opportunity abounded, where there was no royalty or true aristocracy, where no social or economic barriers were so high that they could not be hurdled by the resolute. Furthermore, European wisdom often proved in practice inapplicable to American problems. If Americans were stumped, they did not bleat for precedent but tried this way and then that way until the solution was found. Improvisation was the American way of life, enthusiastically shared by the delegates to the Constitutional Convention. Their thought processes were automatically alike.

This fundamental unanimity was doubly fortunate

*Former Chief Justice Warren Burger, head of a federal commission coordinating official bicentennial events, visits an exhibit of memorabilia at Walt Disney World's Epcot Center in Florida.*

*An American flag made of balloons floats before Independence Hall during bicentennial ceremonies.*

because no decision could be effectively imposed by a majority vote, not even by a vote almost unanimous. The objective being to unify the colonies, if one state refused to accept the ultimate result, a gap that could become a festering wound would be left open. Mutual comprehension, sympathy, and persuasion, a balancing of concession with concession, had to lead to agreement, however grudging, before final action was taken. Whenever possible without weakening the total fabric, contested matters were left undetermined, to be worked out in practice when the government was in motion.

### Key Compromises

The Virginia plan had urged that legislative representation be determined by popular vote. Virginia, Pennsylvania, and Massachusetts had almost half of the population. A counting of heads would give Virginia almost 15 times the voting power of Delaware. But the smaller states, with their history of autonomy, had always cast an equal vote and had no intention of being ground down. As what they regarded as a fair compromise, they suggested that representation in the lower house be by population while all states would have equal representation in the upper house. Madison whipped up vote after vote to knock this down. Finally, a fiery delegate from New Jersey declared that the smaller states would stay out of the union, conscious that, if attacked by the larger states, they could call for

17

help from Europe. The convention seemed on the brink of collapse but was unwilling to give up. A few days' adjournment was voted during which a committee would seek a compromise. This was achieved when the smaller states agreed that all financial bills would originate in the lower house, allowing the numerical majority to control the funds that fueled all branches of the government.

What was basically the most dangerous division—it was eventually to explode into the Civil War—created at the convention no thunderous conflict. The dichotomy between the North and the South, a free mercantile society versus an agrarian society grounded on slavery, impinged in so many particulars that there were endless opportunities for balancing one concession against another. For example, southerners feared regulation of trade lest it make them subservient to the North, but agreement was achieved by postponing the abolition of the slave trade until 1808. Similarly, northerners feared that by including slaves in their population counts, Southern states would be overrepresented in Congress. Delegates agreed on the "three-fifths compromise," which allowed Southern states to count three-fifths of their slave populations for purposes of taxation and representation.

*Thousands of balloons are released at the Capitol in Washington, D.C., honoring the document that defines the role of Congress.*

*Stephanie Petit, a National Spelling Bee winner from Bethel, Pa., and Damien Atkins, an honor student from Washington, D.C., join President Ronald Reagan in the Pledge of Allegiance at the Capitol ceremonies.*

How the executive should be organized (whether consisting of one man or three, each representing a different area) and what powers the executive should be permitted to wield—these questions carried, in a world of kings where no relevant republican government had ever existed, the greatest load of contemporary and historical anxiety. The fundamental dilemma—how to grant adequate authority so that the executive could execute its essential role and at the same time guard against the age-old danger of absolute rule—was deprived of its immediacy by the existence of one man. Washington was certain to become the president and could be trusted. It was easier to envision powers as he would apply them than to preserve alarm at what might happen further down the road. The force of the presidency that still exists is a direct heritage from Washington.

The suggestion that a Bill of Rights be included was not taken seriously. It was considered unnecessary on the grounds that, since all rights belonged naturally to the people, everything not specifically granted to the government was automatically reserved to them. It was feared that such a bill might be interpreted as limiting the people's rights to those listed. (A Bill of Rights was, however, added as the first ten amendments to the Constitution, in December 1791.)

### Gaining the States' Approval

After more than four months of deliberation, the convention ratified its handiwork by a unanimous vote of the 12 states present (Rhode Island had refused to attend). This opened the scene to a more formidable, if

*Twenty-six amendments have expanded the scope of the Constitution over the past 200 years. A proposed 27th Amendment guaranteeing equal rights for women was defeated by state legislatures, but proponents are still active in its behalf.*

less creative, task. Since it would be silly to expect the Continental Congress to vote itself out of existence, it had been stipulated that special ratifying conventions be held in each state and that when nine had ratified it, the Constitution would be held in force.

The strategy urged by Franklin and Washington (and to a major extent followed) was that no delegate would state publicly where, in achieving a necessary compromise, he had been overruled and that necessity rather than perfection be claimed. Washington wrote three Virginia leaders, "Your own judgement will at once discover the good and the exceptionable [open to objection] parts of it, and your experience of the difficulties which have ever arisen when attempts have been made to reconcile such a variety of local prejudices as pervade the several states will render explanation unnecessary. I wish the Constitution which is offered had been made more perfect, but I sincerely believe it is the best that could be obtained at this time and as a constitutional door is open for amendment hereafter the adoption of it is under the present circumstances of the Union, in my opinion, desirable." He added, "If nothing had been agreed on . . . anarchy would soon have ensued, the seeds being richly sown in every soil."

As one state convention after another convened, the stance that had been taken worked admirably. All objections could be met not be denial but by pointing out that if the difficulty proved in practice valid, the

Constitution could be amended. The greatest threat was the suggestion in various state conventions that a new Constitutional Convention should be held to deal with objections raised everywhere. But practical men—and America did not raise visionary theorists—realized that the result would be chaos, since instructions from different states would clash with each other.

Realization of absolute necessity was the driving power. Again and again a majority of the delegates when they first arrived would be opposed, but the educational process that had clarified the Constitutional Convention was repeated again and again. One after another the states came in line.

This process was much assisted in its later phases by the publication in New York City newspapers, beginning in October 1787, of a series of 85 essays signed "Publius." These were also published in book form, in two volumes that appeared in March and May 1788, under the title *The Federalist*. It is a paradox that this contribution to political theory was not an underpinning of the Constitution but a series of commentaries written, after the document was completed, by three individuals, only one of whom, Madison, had played a major role at the Constitutional Convention. John Jay had not even been there, and Hamilton, after making an indiscreet speech advocating what was in effect an elected monarchy, had left the Convention only to return at the very end of it to sign. Washington, who had been at every session, found *The Federalist* enlightening and reassuring, removing his own lingering doubts. "Upon the whole," he wrote, "I doubt whether the opposition to the Constitution will not ultimately be productive of more good than evil. It has called forth in its defense abilities which . . . have thrown new light upon the science of government. They have given the rights of man a full and fair discussion and explained them in so clear and forcible a manner that cannot fail to make a lasting impression. . . . Particularly the pieces under the signature of Publius."

On June 25, 1788, almost an exact month after the appearance of the second volume of *Federalist* essays, Washington was informed that the ninth and tenth states had almost simultaneously ratified. The Constitution was in force! New York came in shortly thereafter. Only North Carolina and Rhode Island lagged, the latter making its belated appearance in May 1790, to complete what Washington hailed as "The New Constellation of this Hemisphere."

# Power From Québec's North

## THE JAMES BAY PROJECT

### by STEVE TURNER

PHOTOS BY LIONEL DELEVINGNE

**S**heer rock cliffs loom above the helicopter, hovering low inside the gorge, and wide waterfalls roar just below. Spray mist rises toward us as the pilot struggles to steady the aircraft in the turbulence. With a side door off for photography, the deep sounds of the huge surging stream below challenge the clatter of the rotor blades. And in this tense and beautiful situation, the immense scope of Québec's subarctic James Bay Hydroelectric Project comes into focus.

The eye helplessly insists that a canyon so stupendously large could only be a work of nature. But in fact, it is the spillway for the dam at La Grande River Complex Number Two, the hydro project's premier installation. It was hewn and blasted out of northern Canada's solid granite just over ten years ago as a safety valve for the LG 2 reservoir, a vast lake created to feed the 16 big turbines of the world's largest underground powerhouse. Now, with two of those enormous generators temporarily down for repairs, the overflowing input of five rivers—La Grande Caniapiscau, Eastmain, Opinaca, and Petite Opinaca—is foaming down the spillway, heading for James Bay. But even with this loss of production, the LG 2 powerhouse is still producing more electricity than five nuclear plants, and sending it down the long swooping power lines to consumers in southern Québec, New England, and New York.

*Steve Turner, a free-lance journalist and member of the National Writers Union, visited the James Bay project in May 1987.*

*Surging toward James Bay, the overflow from the reservoir of the La Grande 2 hydroelectric complex pours into a huge man-made spillway with steep granite walls.*

23

*A Hydro-Québec vehicle perches atop the rocky slope of a dike at the La Grande 2 installation.*

And that's only part of the story. Reservoirs farther upstream in the La Grande watershed, all of which eventually feed into LG 2, turn additional turbines at LG 3 and LG 4 powerhouses that boost the project's installed generating capacity to 10,282 megawatts of power. Moreover, other developments planned for the La Grande and adjoining watersheds all the way to the year 2004 would increase the capacity to more than 22,000 megawatts. This is enough electricity to supply the needs of a city of some 5.5 million people, and it is produced without endangering the biosphere by burning fossil fuels (oil and coal) or creating nuclear wastes and radiation. Even with only one development phase complete, James Bay already supplies 20 percent of Québec's electric energy, besides supplying surplus power to neighboring provinces and to the northeastern United States—all at costs below those of generating electricity from either fossil fuel or nuclear power.

But there are important social and environmental costs. The reservoir system floods vast acreages of the aboriginal lands of the Eastern Inuit (Eskimo) and James Bay Cree and Naskapi Indians, peoples who live principally by hunting, fishing, and trapping. Not only has the flooding significantly reduced the habitats of creatures these native societies harvest, but the decomposition of organic matter in the reservoirs has increased mercury pollution in area waters to dangerous levels. Some species of fish that were formerly staples of the native diet can no longer be eaten. The Inuit particularly are worried that the outflow of mercury also will contaminate the saltwater food chains of James Bay and the larger Hudson Bay of which it is an extension.

The threat to their ancestral way of life galvanized the Crees and the Inuit into resistance that enabled them to negotiate a precedent-setting agreement, covering financial settlement of land claims, recognition of autonomy, and a host of support programs. But the hydroelectric project's huge construction crews, followed by new towns for employees who operate the power plants, have had a fundamental impact on the James Bay region's original people. Television, processed foods, and drugs are altering traditional cultures. Environmental and consumer groups also charge that the project's enormous cost and the power export policies it feeds have adversely affected development of the provincial economy.

24

## A Minimalist Landscape

The James Bay Hydroelectric Project would easily swamp a Guinness-type book of world engineering feats: biggest coordinated hydro development; largest underground powerhouse; second-greatest planned single-site production of electricity (outranked only by the giant Itaipu project on the Brazil-Paraguay border); arguably more dams and dikes than anywhere outside the Netherlands; enough rock and fill moved to rebuild the Great Pyramid of Cheops 80 times; a spillway big enough to handle the combined flow of all the rivers of Western Europe. All these superlatives exist in what could only be described as a minimalist landscape: the glacially scraped, subarctic taiga ranging eastward from the frigid Hudson Bay and its appendix-like extension, James Bay.

The three major watersheds being developed by Hydro-Québec and its subsidiary, Société d'Energie de la Baie James (SEBJ) cover most of the land between the 48th and 56th parallels of north latitude and between the 67th and 78th meridians of longitude: an area the size of England, Ireland, and Switzerland put together, too big to be seen at one time except from space.

Above the 50th parallel, the flora and fauna can

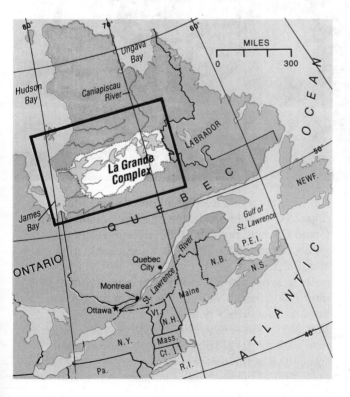

*Sculpted out of forests and scrub in subarctic Québec, hundreds of miles from the province's urban centers, the James Bay Hydroelectric Project has transformed an area the size of several European countries.*

25

*The Cree still hunt and fish in their ancient territory, though some species of fish can no longer be eaten because of pollution. At top, hunters use modern weapons as they pursue a traditional prey, goose; below, a family scene at a hunting camp where game is cooked in tepees over an open fire.*

support only a relatively small population. The Crees, organized in nine bands, the chiefs of which form a Grand Council, number 10,000. The Naskapis, a single group, number 500. The Inuit are estimated to number about 6,000.

These groups range widely over game territory that most outdoorsmen want to see only in the movies. The bay and lake waters hold ice until mid-June. Vast stretches of the gently rolling landscape are covered with dark forests of spindly evergreens: larch and spruce that at the northern edge of the territory (where even a bit of treeless tundra intrudes) may take 100 years to reach their maximum 20 feet of height. Near the coast there is lighter colored muskeg and swamp. In the intermittent areas of open land, often eruptive with bare rock, the best the sandy soil can produce—aside from the blueberry tangles that give the native peoples and wildlife alike a happy summer harvest—are mosses, lichens, scrub willow, and alders.

Summers are short, but they produce mosquitoes so large and ferocious that Inuit ivory carvers expand them to truly mythic proportions in their artwork. Winters are long, with temperatures as low as −54°F. Ice roads built for cold-season transportation may last six months. The powerful frost penetrates 12 feet down, right through the frequently shallow soil layer, into the bedrock granite of the massive Precambrian Shield that underlies the whole region. Most of the area averages around 23 inches of annual precipitation, only half to two-thirds of what Montréal gets. But the diminutive soil layer becomes in effect an endless sponge atop the bedrock. With evaporation reduced by the cold, almost all the water that comes down eventually runs back toward the sea. The flow is so copious and strong, in fact, that even under the thickest winter ice, rivers roll steadily on. Consequently, wherever there are folds and fall lines in the bedrock, the potential for hydroelectric development is great.

To the aboriginal populations this territory is a well-loved homeland, intimately known and used by natives who have probed, tracked, and crisscrossed it for centuries. From the perspective of the south, however, Québec Premier Robert Bourassa described it—in his book *Power From the North*—as a "forbidding and barren land." Bourassa wrote, "It has long been my belief that Québec's economic strength lies in the

*Fort-George, an island in James Bay near the mouth of the La Grande River, was abandoned as a permanent native settlement after water from the power project began buffeting it. The house here, marked by the owner to save it from bulldozers, may hold belongings to be retrieved, or it may be intended for use as a temporary hunting lodge.*

development of its natural resources, the most outstanding of which is its rich hydroelectric potential. And, further, I have always believed that to develop these resources would require conquering and taming the North."

### Bourassa's Vision

In 1971, with words reminiscent of the 19th-century U.S. doctrine of manifest destiny ("'Québec must occupy her territory!"'), the visionary Bourassa started the engines of north-country development in this largest and second most populous of Canada's provinces. Québec was then suffering from unemployment, its labor force at the mercy of slumping national and international markets for the agricultural products and raw materials (chiefly timber and ores) on which its economy was based. But the province was rich in the spirit of reactivated pride in its French heritage. The movement already was building that would reestablish French as Québec's sole official language and seek to make the province independent of the rest of Canada. Québecers were receptive to Bourassa's vision of greatness to be found in this bold venture into energy production, particularly since it promised significant numbers of jobs.

*Hydro-Québec employees are dwarfed by one of the 16 giant turbines at the La Grande 2 generating station, the world's largest underground powerhouse.*

The urgency to move ahead was so strong that construction on the James Bay project began without environmental impact studies and without clearance from the native populations, who claimed aboriginal rights to the land under a federal law construed differently by the provincial government. Soon, significant areas of Cree territory had become monster construction camps: at the peak of the project, some 18,000 workers were on the job, their supplies and equipment pouring northward in a stream of trucks and aircraft.

The result was certainly one of the world's heroic construction projects. To start with, there was not even a road north of Matagami, located down near the 50th parallel: it took two years to build the 375 miles of hard-surfaced highway needed to enable the trucks to reach what became the new town of Radisson, at the site of the LG 2 powerhouse. That road, installed with great hardship through the bug-ridden quagmire of the muskeg, remains the only year-round surface connection with the hydro installations (and with the native communities to which spur roads have been built).

Five airports also were built, and most of the workers were flown in to the construction sites. When they got there, they had more than enough to do. Because so many of the valleys to be flooded were shallow, 215 dams and dikes totaling 75 miles in length had to be built to create and contain the reservoirs at LG 2, 3, and 4. All of these structures were made out of local rock, sand, and glacial moraine. They halt the La Grande River in three places, reroute and dam the Opinaca and Petite Opinaca and most of the Eastmain, and divert up to 45 percent of the Caniapiscau, which flows north through Inuit territory into frigid Ungava Bay. Diverting the other four rivers into the La Grande nearly doubled its hydroelectric potential and made it economically worthwhile to exploit the potentials of some of the other rivers that could not be developed separately.

The reservoirs control the rivers' flow so that the supply of electricity generated can be matched to demand. In northern Québec flow is lowest in winter and heaviest during the spring thaw, whereas demand for electricity in the urban south peaks in the long, cold winters. Thus, from spring through the fall the La Grande reservoirs store up a surplus of water that can be released through the turbines in winter, when the

*Workers in the power plant at La Grande 3, on top of the turbines.*

*James Bobbish, an elected Cree chief from the Chisasiei band and a member of the Grand Council, works with both the federal and provincial governments in matters affecting the people of the James Bay region.*

natural flow would be insufficient. Spillways allow excess water to be drained from the reservoirs during flood periods, mostly during the spring thaw and fall rains.

The first reservoirs began to fill in 1978, and the first two turbines at the LG 2 powerhouse came on line in 1979. By 1984, when the LG 3 and 4 stations were complete, flooding covered about 4,380 square miles, an area just slightly smaller than the state of Connecticut. Completion of LG 4 marked the end of phase one of the La Grande segment of the project. Phase two, scheduled to begin in 1988, will add mainly more powerhouses, although some additional land will be flooded near LG 4. If Hydro-Québec's complete development scheme is carried out, however, damming of the Grande Baleine and Petite Baleine river system to the north and the Nottaway, Broadback, and Rupert system to the south will expand the total flooded territory by two-thirds, to roughly the size of Massachusetts, by the year 2004. In the meantime, the expertise the utility gained in designing and building phases one and two has made it a much-sought-after consultant for giant hydro engineering projects world-wide.

### Accord With the Native Peoples

Among the Indians and Inuit who had subsisted for thousands of years on the resources of untamed rivers and now-flooded wilderness, resentment of the governments that put the hydro project into their lives inevitably lingers. But the outcome of negotiations has included some productive changes for the native peoples. The James Bay and Northern Quebec Agreement (JBNQA), negotiated by the Inuit, the Crees, and the governments of Canada and Québec (and afterward applied to the Naskapis, too), embodies important government concessions. In exchange for the native peoples' abandonment of aboriginal rights to the entire territory, JBNQA established reserved lands for each group and made a settlement of Can $225 million for lands taken. It ceded governmental, economic, and educational autonomy that the native peoples had not had. New housing was provided for many communities, and construction of community centers was authorized. Native-controlled health and education systems were set up. And the Crees negotiated an inspired shift away from the welfare dependency that had begun to plague them. JBNQA established the Income Security Program, in which adult Crees who hunt and trap in the bush for at least 120 days a year are paid a daily stipend for their activity.

Native activists contend that the federal government is not following through on many of its commitments under JBNQA. The government asserts that the unmet obligations are a small proportion of what was promised and that they will be met. In any event, no legal agreement could totally eliminate all of the cultural confusion and social tension the project has brought to the north country. In the Cree communities, still adapting themselves to the new housing provided by JBNQA, a generation gap is growing. Children, who are now required to attend school, spend more time in

*A private store owned and operated by Chisasiei Cree, left, offers an alternative to a nearby Hudson Bay department store. The growing amount of time that young and old spend in front of TV screens in modern housing (below), provided under an agreement with the Québec and Canadian governments, is further evidence of the spread of new life-styles.*

*The control center for the La Grande 2 complex, the first installation of the James Bay project, which began generating electricity in 1979.*

town (and in front of the TV) than out with their families at traditional hunting camps in "the bush"; curfews have been imposed to try to control teenagers and younger children who hang out in the streets until late at night. While deploring the loss of traditional bush skills, the adults have their own troubles adjusting to change. Abuse of alcohol has become a serious problem, even though all nine Cree bands have outlawed its sale (but not possession) in their communities. The project has also disrupted traditional transport routes: Cree trappers can no longer use the lower La Grande as a winter highway because the outflow from the LG 2 reservoir keeps the river from ever freezing.

### Unexpected Mercury Contamination

By contrast with the energy put into development of JBNQA, preparations for dealing with the possible environmental impact of the project were nonexistent. From the outset, some scientists worried that it might cause great ecological upset—that it might trigger earthquakes, for instance, or radically alter the regional climate. Fortunately, none of the more alarming forecasts proved accurate. But the environmental damage that the project did cause—principally the elevation of waterborne mercury contamination—was not foreseen. There were no laws at the time requiring preconstruction environmental impact studies. In fact, according to Hydro-Québec environmental official Robert Lanouette, it was the studies the utility subsequently conducted that led to development of the province's current laws.

Lanouette stresses that after starting construction, Hydro-Québec coordinated a wide-ranging series of environmental studies on the James Bay territory. But the fact remains that when the reservoirs began to fill seven years after the first work began, it still was not understood that the new lakes would also be enormous bowls of methyl mercury soup. Mercury from the bedrock occurs at a naturally high level in the James Bay area's soils (with an added contribution from worldwide airborne pollution), and hence in the vegetation. When organic soil material and vegetation

*Hydro-Québec's research center in Montréal tests the materials used in the new high-voltage transmission technology that brings electricity south from James Bay.*

decompose under water, the mercury binds with methyl compounds and enters the food chain. Browsing species such as whitefish eat it, predator species such as pike and trout concentrate it, and native people who eat significant amounts of fish—as many do—are in danger of being poisoned.

Naturally occurring lakes and streams in the area are contaminated with mercury at a stable level that is about the threshold of medical acceptability. But the new reservoirs drowned and churned vast areas of undecayed plant matter, including millions of acres of trees, causing contamination levels to rise quickly and significantly above the danger point. And the reservoirs contaminate the rivers downstream, which flow into the bay. There is no reasonable way to remedy this contamination once it happens; as the new material decomposes over time, taking perhaps as long as 20 years, contamination will eventually recede to normal levels. In the meantime, medical monitoring and advisory programs on dietary change are under way to prevent serious affliction.

In 1986 the Crees negotiated a ten-year multimillion-dollar environmental monitoring program with Hydro-Québec. The Inuit want that study extended to cover a wider area. There are suggestions that next time the trees should be clear-cut first, or that the reservoirs should be filled more slowly.

### Exporting Energy

If the remaining planned reservoirs are eventually

*Dark forests of larch and spruce blanket much of the James Bay region. The thin layer of soil atop granite bedrock and the cold climate that reduces evaporation help to create a dense network of fast-flowing rivers with immense hydroelectric potential.*

created and filled, the primary markets for the new electricity will be outside of Québec. The New York Power Authority already has one long-term agreement with Hydro-Québec for a firm 3 billion kilowatt-hours a year (the equivalent output of a large power plant), and the New England Power Pool (Nepool), an association of almost all the utilities in that six-state region, is buying even more than New York. An agreement running from 1990 to the end of the century and providing 7 billion kilowatt-hours a year will increase Nepool's present 5 percent dependence on Hydro-Québec electricity to 10 percent, with the bonus of postponing local construction. Both Hydro-Québec and the U.S. utilities are eager to negotiate further contracts.

Economist Elaine LaJambe, who recently founded the Centre d'Analyse des Politiques Energetiques, a joint public-private endeavor based in Montréal, feels that the rosy glow surrounding the massive project and its export flow conceals perils to the Québec economy. Long-term debt for the Can$16 billion development, she points out, already is higher than that of the province, and more than half of Hydro-Québec's gross receipts annually go to debt service. This debt load, LaJambe feels, is a drain on Québec's economy. But the principal problem with the export of electricity, LaJambe argues, is that it continues, rather than changes, the traditional pattern in which Québec ships out raw materials for other provinces and nations to use and—"like a Third World country"—stays in the hinterland of industrial development.

Officials of both Hydro-Québec and the Québec Energy Ministry dispute LaJambe's views. But even if her analysis is correct, another factor may be more powerful than economic considerations in determining the future of the James Bay project. It is the factor of provincial pride, the primal force of an industrial society continuing, as urged by Bourassa, to conquer and tame the North. There is an undeniable excitement in the growling vibration of the world's largest underground powerhouse, the foaming torrent of a spillway big enough to handle all Europe's rivers, the thought of all that power being wrought out of such a cold and challenging place. As an Energy Ministry official put it, "This is a world-class, unique project, designed and built by Québec engineers and construction crews. James Bay is a kind of mythical project in the hearts of Québecers."

*Maintenance work on the power lines running south—in this case, repairs to a shattered glass insulator—must be done 150 feet up, often in temperatures and winds that can freeze exposed skin in two minutes.*

# Dogs at Work

## by ROGER C. CARAS

Roger A. Caras is a correspondent for ABC News, exclusively covering animals and the environment. His writings on these topics have appeared in numerous periodicals and newspapers, and he is the author of more than 50 books. Among his awards is the prestigious Joseph Wood Krutch medal for "significant contributions to the improvement of quality of life."

It is generally believed that the dog was the first domestic animal in most parts of the world. In a few regions goats may have been domesticated a bit sooner, but they would be the only exceptions. The first dogs may have been brought into the human circle as long as 25,000 years ago, in the Old Stone Age, when humans lived by gathering plants and hunting animals with flaked stone implements.

Domestication, of course, does not mean merely keeping wild animals around the cave or hut. It means selectively breeding wild animals until an entirely new descendant species begins to take shape. All known breeds of dogs today are members of one species, *Canis familiaris.* The original ancestor of the dog was almost certainly a smallish subspecies of wolf known as *Canis lupus pallipes,* which is still found in southern Asia, from Israel to India. It was within that area that domestication almost certainly began.

From early times, dogs were used as objects of trade and as special gifts from ruler to ruler, thus spreading far and wide from one society to another. They appeared in Tibet and flourished there thousands of years ago; much later in history, these animals were spread from Tibet across Asia and Europe to the British Isles, and eventually all over the world. People also took dogs with them to Australia and to the islands of the Pacific. If we knew more details about the early movement of dogs we would know a great deal more about the history of early humans.

How did early peoples come to domesticate the dog? In all likelihood it was because they didn't have refrigeration. We know that Stone Age humans ate the meat of wolves. Sometimes, after they drove away a pair of wolves with a shower of stones and sticks, the hunters would probably steal the wolves' cubs and take them back to their cave, campsite, or other shelter for use as food. If the cubs were killed at once, the meat had to be eaten in a day or two, or it would spoil. If the cubs were kept alive, they could be killed and

*At right, Sherlock, a U.S. Department of Agriculture beagle, sniffs out contraband plants and food at San Francisco International Airport.*

The greyhound, a hunting dog (now perhaps better known as a racing breed) whose ancestry has been traced to ancient Egypt, appears here in a 16th-century tapestry, one of a fanciful series depicting "The Hunt of the Unicorn."

eaten as needed. This is done even now in parts of Asia. In time, by keeping cubs around, our early ancestors no doubt developed a new view of the animals, or at least their children did. Wolf cubs, which are easily tamed and often behave like domesticated animals during their first six months, became at least short-term pets.

Since the wolf has shown itself to be genetically flexible, early humans were able to breed these animals, seeking to develop the traits they most prized. By the late Stone Age, a few thousand years B.C., it is believed there were already several different kinds of dogs recognizable. Some would have been companion dogs, others hunting dogs, and others guard dogs. Those distinctions are still very clear today, with a few refinements.

### The Earliest Breeds

About 9,000 years ago, in Sumer at the head of the Persian Gulf, the oldest breed still recognized by us today probably emerged. It is the saluki, a greyhound-like coursing hound of enormous speed but not of great intelligence. (Coursing hounds are used to hunt running game, which they follow by sight rather than smell.) A better-known coursing hound, the greyhound, appeared in Egypt a few thousand years later; it became a pet of Egyptian nobles, was revered by the Greeks as a god or near-god, and is the only breed of dog mentioned in the Old Testament.

In eastern Siberia, the Samoyed peoples developed the dog still called Samoyed, one of the oldest breeds and one which has remained pure from its earliest beginning. It was a multipurpose dog, used for pulling sleds, guarding camps, and helping in the hunt. Today's Norwegian elkhound, Alaskan malamute, Akita, chow chow, and Siberian husky, plus the forerunners of the tiny pomeranian and a number of exotic breeds rarely seen now in North America, all developed in high northern latitudes. Northern European and Asian peoples bred these so-called spitz dogs with timber wolves to increase their stamina.

Other breeds of dogs began to drift back westward from Tibet. Foremost among them was the Tibetan mastiff, which in Rome became what we now call the Neapolitan mastiff. This breed is well-known in Europe but not in the United States. (The America Kennel Club currently recognizes approximately 130 breeds which are common in the United States; there are probably as many as 425 purebred breeds worldwide.)

Mastiffs, as they emerged in the form of different breeds, reflected the various uses to which they were being put. The Tibetan, later Neapolitan, mastiff was used early on in games in the arenas of the Roman Empire. These dogs engaged in combat with one another, with other (often wild) animals, and with gladiators, fighting to the death. When the Roman legions moved north into Germany, they took somewhat subdued versions of the mastiffs with them as cattle drovers and camp guards. The wild tribes encountered by the soldiers often stole dogs from Roman camps; the stolen dogs later developed in Germany into the so-called Great Danes (which had nothing to do with Denmark) and were used to hunt wild boar, very dangerous game. They also evolved into the rottweiler, named for the town of Rottweil (now in West Germany), and into the Saint Bernard and Bernese mountain dogs of Switzerland. When Roman soldiers reached the British Isles, in the first century B.C., they found the wild tribes there already in possession of a form of mastiff, although how that dog got there ahead of the Romans has remained something of a mystery. Once again the dog provides evidence of how ignorant we are of early peoples' movements and commerce.

Mastiffs in England, possibly with some input from the Romans' Neapolitan mastiffs, were bred into dwarf form and became the muscular English bulldog, used in the sport of bullbaiting until that practice became illegal in the early 19th century. Mastiffs were also interbred with the dwarf version to produce what was known as the gamekeeper's night dog and later as the bullmastiff.

This breed was developed in England in the middle to late 1800's in response to rampant lawlessness, when gamekeepers on large private estates were being attacked and even killed by poachers and trespassers. The bullmastiff (then more than now bred to be dark in color) was aggressive enough to attack a poacher, knock him down, grab his arm in its mouth, and hold him, terrified and nearly paralyzed by the pressure the dog's jaws could apply.

The mastiff line, however it got to and from Tibet, has led to many other breeds as well. Mastiff blood appears in the French bulldog, the little Boston terrier, the bullterrier, the so-called pit bulls, and the Doberman pinscher.

Another line of dogs whose earliest ancestral forms are not really known was emerging in the British Isles— the terrier clan. In Scotland, Wales, Ireland, and England and on offshore islands like Skye, these tough little vermin-killers and small hunting dogs appeared and became popular. Seen hundreds of years ago on nearly every farm in the British Isles, they remain quite common today. The two largest types were the Airedale terrier and the Irish version, the Kerry blue terrier. On farms they helped keep down the rat, weasel, and other vermin populations, protected livestock, and were perfect little hunting dogs, besides serving as watchdogs. Terriers were fairly nondescript in the early days; only in recent years have coat style and color been considered very important characteristics of the breeds. There is only one breed in the terrier group in America today that did not originate in the British Isles: the miniature schnauzer, a German breed.

*Guard and herding dogs still have important roles in areas where livestock are raised. Here, a Border collie drives a herd of sheep to a shearing shed in the Australian outback.*

### Hunters, Herders, and Guards

While the British and their nearest neighbors were developing handy little vermin-killing terriers, true hunting dogs were emerging on the European continent. From Spain came the Spanish dogs, or spaniels. Some of these were used to hunt ducks and other waterfowl, others to hunt upland game. The spaniels were bred into large and small versions; the larger dogs eventually became known as setters—because they would "set," or crouch, when locating their quarry. Perhaps around the 17th century, some hunting-dog strains and probably some lighter-boned mastiff descendants emerged as pointers—dogs that freeze in a standing position with nose pointing at the quarry. (Today, setters no longer set, but are trained to point like pointers.) The pointing dogs later came to include the griffons from Holland, the weimaraners from Germany, and the vizslas from Hungary, none very ancient breeds. They are generally multipurpose hunting dogs.

Meanwhile, in eastern Europe, in Hungary and Austria, dogs with possible Tibetan ancestry were developed, some of them to guard sheep, others to herd them. These breeds included the kuvasz, the komondor, and the puli, the latter two with a strange naturally corded coat unlike anything else in dogdom.

In Roman times, perhaps as far back as 2,500 years ago, there were hounds of enormously sophisticated scenting ability throughout the Mediterranean region. They were probably the ancestors of the dogs known in medieval times as Saint Hubert's hounds and, later in England, as bloodhounds. The word "bloodhound" was

*New York State Trooper Jerry O'Hearn with a bloodhound trained to track missing persons. The bloodhound is a gentle dog with an extraordinary sense of smell.*

apparently not used to indicate any savage propensity in the animal. It most probably came about because these highly refined hounds, with the most sensitive nose in the world of dogs, could in the Middle Ages be owned only by noblemen, or people "of the blood." From the bloodhound came another dwarfed dog, the basset hound, and later the various coonhounds of the American South and all of the other scenting (as opposed to sighting, or coursing) hounds.

As for the sight hounds, they were off on a track of their own. The ancient Egyptians had developed a few breeds besides the greyhound, such as the Pharaoh, Ibizan, and Afghan hounds. The greyhound was shrunken in size, by selective breeding, to become the Italian greyhound, a lapdog. Many other hunting dogs also were being reduced in size to become house companions—elegant little playthings for nobility and royalty—and decorative watchdogs. They were status symbols as well as companions.

While several breeds of small dogs developed from sight hounds, the tallest of all dogs—the Irish wolfhound, which stands about 34 inches high at the shoulder—may have developed by mixing greyhound bloodlines with mastiff lines. Another true giant, the Scottish deerhound, also evolved, and in Russia in the early 17th century young noblemen developed the towering Russian wolfhound, known in the United States as the borzoi since 1936, to hunt wolves and other game.

Thus, in their own way, the various lines of dogs spread out across the world and evolved in each new area to fit the needs and tastes of their masters.

### Still on the Job

Dogs today often serve people in ways similar to those for which the breed was originally developed. The komondor and kuvasz that guarded sheep on the steppes of Hungary ten centuries ago are currently being tested in the American West for guarding flocks of sheep against predators. In Australia, where livestock has traditionally been the backbone of the economy, dogs like the Australian cattle dogs and the Australian sheepdogs were developed from breeds (including the collie) that settlers brought in from the British Isles and elsewhere in Europe. They are still very much in use, and some Australian breeds, such as the blue heeler, are now at work in the American Southwest herding livestock. (However, Alsatians, or German shepherds, which were originally bred to herd sheep, came to be used somewhat differently, as Seeing Eye, police, or army dogs. They lead the blind, patrol military installations, and do the kinds of jobs that make people's lives easier and safer.)

The Doberman pinscher, an alert and powerful guard breed developed in Germany by a watchman named Louis Dobermann in the late 1890's, is still a superior guard dog, although modern breeders have worked wonders in calming the animal down and giving it a far softer personality. The rottweiler, which became a cart-puller and guard dog in Germany, continues to serve as a police patrol dog of enormous strength and courage. Over the past ten years the rottweiler's popularity has increased markedly in the United States, with 15 times more dogs registered in 1986 with the American Kennel Club than were registered a decade earlier.

Many farmers still depend on terriers to patrol their barns on the lookout for rats and mice. The fast, feisty little dogs, whose lives seem to revolve around this challenging "game," are as good at their old job as they ever were. Hunters continue to use breeds like the Labrador, golden, and other retrievers for their original tasks—bringing back downed birds from the water and other inaccessible areas. Pointers are still at work locating game, and spaniels still flush out game from cover for hunters. The Brittany, a very popular European dog that looks to be midway between a spaniel and a setter, may be found doing all-around fieldwork.

Though the bloodhound was originally a hunting

*Customs agents use dog "detectives" at international crossing points to speed their searches for contraband. The U.S. Customs Service trains several breeds for the purpose at Front Royal, Va.*

animal, it was weaned away from that task a very long time ago and is used today by police agencies all over the world to track down people, living or dead. Every now and then we hear of escaped convicts or suspected criminals being "nailed" by giant bloodhounds, but the great, gentle dogs have other work they do far more often. About 95 percent of the trails followed by bloodhounds today are so-called mercy runs, looking for lost campers, missing children, confused mental patients, or anyone who can leave a trail and whose life may depend on being found. Bloodhounds are purposely bred to be gentle, since it would be counterproductive to have the dogs track down victims of mischance and then attack them once they found them.

### Man's Best Friend

Some jobs may be less vigorous than hunting and tracking but are nonetheless productive. For example, lapdogs originally from China, such as the Pekingese (considered sacred by the ancient Chinese) and the pug, are familiar companion dogs, meant to provide distractions from daily worries and pressures. Other small breeds, many of them unfamiliar to Americans, serve this function all over the world. The Japanese have their chin (also called the Japanese spaniel), while the Tibetans have the Tibetan spaniel (not a spaniel at all), the Tibetan terrier (not a terrier at all), the Shih Tzu, and the Lhasa apso to amuse and console their owners.

*A U.S. Air Force specialist buying dogs for military service, including possible use against terrorists, tests a German shepherd for aggressiveness.*

*Following Mexico City's devastating 1985 earthquake, dogs were used to locate survivors trapped beneath the remains of toppled buildings.*

Recent medical research has shown that companion dogs may contribute to their owners' physical as well as psychological well-being. Generally speaking, those benefiting from dogs' companionship tend to have lower blood pressure and fewer heart attacks. Studies have also found that severely ill dog-owners tend to have higher survival rates than comparable patients without pets. It could almost be said that while we thought we were selectively breeding dogs, they were selectively breeding us, with dog-lovers outliving people not especially attracted to these companionable beasts.

All kinds of dogs, both purebred and of mixed breed, also are being used to aid the handicapped. Seeing Eye dogs are well-known, but there are other dogs specially trained to serve the hearing-impaired, alerting their owners to sounds at the door, a ringing phone, or perhaps a crying baby. Some dogs have been put to work assisting the physically disabled. People confined to wheelchairs or to bed may have canine servants that bring the phone to them, pick up things that they drop, pull them around in their chairs, and do other work fitted to their owners' needs.

Other dogs labor in the field of crime detection. Beagles are now used by the U.S. Department of

Agriculture to sniff incoming baggage at airports for illegal plants and foodstuffs. With their little green USDA jackets, these government beagles are becoming familiar sights wherever international flights land on American soil. All kinds of dogs with good noses, from German shepherds to hyperactive retrievers to mixed-breed dogs are trained (at Front Royal, Va.) by the U.S. Customs Service to detect drugs in incoming baggage. Billions of dollars worth of illicit drugs have been intercepted because of the enthusiasm of these animals. To them it is a wonderful game, and they go fairly wild whenever they sense the presence of drugs in an innocent-looking piece of luggage.

Also trained at Front Royal are a group of canine detectives who do work at least as vital but must have rather more finesse. They are the bomb detection dogs.

*Assisted by a dog trained to push elevator buttons, a person confined to a wheelchair can travel without a human escort.*

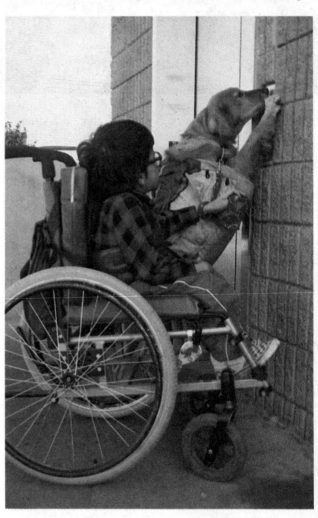

Members of a canine bomb squad fortunately lack the wisdom to be nervous, but they must be taught not to tear and rip excitedly at the cases they pinpoint. Instead, they learn to sit down quietly next to the suspicious object and whine softly. That is the signal for civilians in the area to move away and leave the professionals to their work.

Dogs that help the hearing-impaired and other handicapped people and those that detect drugs and bombs are not necessarily restricted to a few breeds, and they need not be purebred. Intelligence and a certain special temperament to suit the specific case are essential. At one time, just about all dogs leading the blind were German shepherds; now Labrador and golden retrievers are just as commonly used. For most specific tasks, some breeds will do better than others,

*Guide dogs have for decades been used to help the handicapped. Here, two Seeing Eye dogs halt so that their blind owners will know they are at a curb and can feel for it with their feet.*

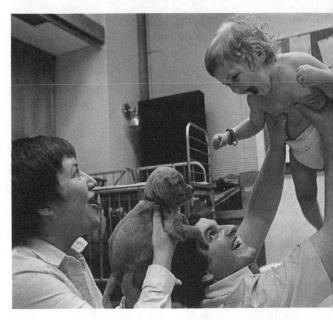

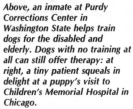

*Above, an inmate at Purdy Corrections Center in Washington State helps train dogs for the disabled and elderly. Dogs with no training at all can still offer therapy: at right, a tiny patient squeals in delight at a puppy's visit to Children's Memorial Hospital in Chicago.*

but it is seldom necessary to have only one particular breed for a job.

### To Err Is Canine

Many amusing or ironic stories have been told involving dogs at work. In one incident a few years ago, authorities suspected that a policewoman who was missing had been murdered and that the body had been buried in a park. A bloodhound was brought in that had been trained to locate bodies hidden in illegal graves. He immediately fixed on a spot in the park, and the police dug in. The bones, although they seemed somewhat large for the missing woman, were dutifully packed off to the coroner. Then the dog found another burying place and another, and a good many more as well. The park had been nearly destroyed, and some police officers were on the disability list with injured backs, before it was discovered that they had unwittingly put the bloodhound to work in a burying ground for old brewery horses.

A few bad days notwithstanding, dogs down through history have succeeded in doing everything from hunting and herding to carrying ammunition to front-line troops, from baby-sitting to sniffing out drugs, from supplying support to the emotionally ill and disabled to guarding livestock and property with their own lives. In all these activities dogs find themselves still doing what they were initially bred to do; faithfully serving their human owners and companions.

48

# 1988 YEARBOOK
## EVENTS OF 1987

# CHRONOLOGY FOR 1987

## January

3 • The year's celebration of the U.S. Constitution bicentennial starts off with ceremonies in Philadelphia.

5 • President Ronald Reagan submits a $1.02 trillion federal budget proposal to Congress.

8 • The Dow Jones Industrial Average climbs over 2,000 for the first time.

9 • Iran mounts a major new offensive against Iraq, in the continuing war between the two Persian Gulf nations.

16 • Hu Yaobang is forced to resign as general secretary of the Chinese Communist Party and is replaced by Prime Minister Zhao Ziyang.

22 • Philippine government forces fire into a surging throng of leftist demonstrators in Manila, killing at least 15 people.

27 • Soviet leader Mikhail Gorbachev charges the Communist Party with stagnation and systematic failures and calls for secret balloting in local, provincial, and republic party elections.

## February

11 • Corazon Aquino is sworn in for a six-year term as president of the Philippines, shortly after voters overwhelmingly approved a new constitution.

26 • A presidentially appointed commission headed by former Senator John Tower criticizes Reagan's management style and faults White House chief of staff Donald Regan and other aides in the Iran/contra affair.

27 • Regan resigns his post as chief of staff and is replaced by former Senate Majority Leader Howard Baker.

## March

19 • At his first news conference in four months, President Reagan denies having known that profits from U.S. arms sales to Iran were diverted to contra guerrillas fighting the Nicaraguan government.

20 • The U.S. Food and Drug Administration for the first time approves a drug for treatment of AIDS.

• Televangelist Jim Bakker resigns as head of the PTL ministry, admitting his involvement in sexual encounters with a church secretary.

27 • Chadian troops retake the town of Faya-Largeau, the last major Libyan military stronghold in northern Chad.

31 • A New Jersey judge awards custody of "Baby M" to the father, William Stern, and denies parental rights to the surrogate mother, Mary Beth Whitehead.

**JAN. 22**

**FEB. 26**

## April

**2** • The U.S. Congress successfully overrides President Reagan's veto of an $88 billion highway and mass transit bill.

**22** • The U.S. Supreme Court upholds the death penalty against the challenge that statistical evidence indicates its imposition is influenced by race.

**30** • Canadian Prime Minister Brian Mulroney and the provincial premiers reach an agreement at Meech Lake, giving Québec special status within the Canadian constitution.

## May

**5** • Congressional special committees begin joint hearings on the Iran/contra affair.

**8** • Former Senator Gary Hart (D) withdraws from the 1988 presidential race after reports that he and model/actress Donna Rice spent part of a weekend together in his townhouse.

**17** • An Iraqi missile attack on the U.S. warship *Stark*, in the Persian Gulf, kills 37 sailors.

**19** • The U.S. Senate confirms William Webster as CIA director, replacing William Casey, who had resigned because of illness and died earlier in May.

**25** • Former U.S. Labor Secretary Raymond Donovan is acquitted of fraud and grand larceny charges.

## June

**1** • Lebanese Prime Minister Rashid Karami is assassinated.

**2** • President Reagan announces that Alan Greenspan will replace Paul Volcker as chairman of the Federal Reserve Board.

**11** • The Conservatives win a large majority in British general elections, giving Prime Minister Margaret Thatcher a third consecutive term in office.

**16** • Bernhard Goetz, who shot four men he claimed were trying to rob him on a New York City subway train, is acquitted of attempted murder and convicted only of illegal weapons possession.

**JULY 4**

25 • Pope John Paul II receives Austrian President Waldheim at the Vatican, despite protests.

26 • The Soviet Communist Party Central Committee endorses Gorbachev's guidelines for economic reform and elevates three Gorbachev allies to full membership in the Politburo.

### July

1 • President Reagan nominates Robert Bork to the U.S. Supreme Court to replace retiring Justice Lewis Powell.

• South Korean President Chun Doo Hwan approves sweeping political changes, including direct presidential elections, in response to three weeks of antigovernment demonstrations.

4 • A French court convicts Klaus Barbie, former Gestapo chief in Lyon, of crimes against humanity.

11 • Labor Party Prime Minister Bob Hawke wins a third term in Australian general elections.

24 • The Kuwaiti tanker *Bridgeton*, newly reflagged to U.S. registry, hits a mine in the Persian Gulf.

• President Reagan nominates federal judge William S. Sessions as FBI director.

29 • India and Sri Lanka sign an accord designed to end the bloody insurgency of Hindu Tamils in Sri Lanka.

• Christian Democrat Giovanni Goria is sworn in as the new prime minister of Italy.

31 • Saudi Arabian police clash with Iranian pilgrims in Mecca, leaving over 400 people dead.

### August

1 • Mike Tyson defeats Tony Tucker to unify boxing's world heavyweight title for the first time since 1978.

7 • Five Central American nations sign a tentative regional peace plan proposed by Costa Rican President Oscar Arias Sánchez.

10 • President Reagan nominates C. William Verity, Jr., as commerce secretary, replacing Malcolm Baldrige, who died in a fall from a horse.

15 • New Zealand voters reelect the Labor government of Prime Minister David Lange.

21 • Marine Sergeant Clayton Lonetree, a former U.S. embassy guard in Moscow and Vienna, is convicted of espionage by a military court.

25 • The Dow Jones Industrial Average peaks at a record 2,722.42.

28 • An unsuccessful military coup attempt in the Philippines leaves over 50 people dead.

### September

11 • East German leader Erich Honecker completes a five-day visit to West Germany.

• The director of the Canadian Security Intelligence Service resigns in a wiretap scandal.

18 • The United States and the Soviet Union

announce an agreement in principle to eliminate their medium-range and shorter-range nuclear missiles.

20 • Pope John Paul II completes a visit to North America in which he stopped at nine U.S. cities and a northern Canadian town.

22 • National Football League players go on strike.

23 • Accused of plagiarism in campaign addresses, Senator Joseph Biden (D) drops out of the 1988 presidential race.

## October

1 • An earthquake rocks Los Angeles; seven people are killed (including one from a subsequent aftershock).

3 • The United States and Canada agree on an extensive free-trade pact.

4 • Mexico's ruling party names Planning and Budget Minister Carlos Salinas de Gortari as its choice for the nation's next president.

8 • U.S. Army helicopters attack Iranian vessels in the Persian Gulf, sinking one.

**OCT. 19**

**SEPT. 23**

• Indian peacekeeping forces in Sri Lanka begin an offensive against Tamil separatist guerrillas.

• President Reagan names James H. Burnley IV as transportation secretary, replacing Elizabeth Hanford Dole, who resigned to join her husband's presidential campaign.

13 • Costa Rican President Oscar Arias Sánchez is named to receive the Nobel Peace Prize.

16 • A Texas girl, 18-month-old Jessica McClure, is rescued after being trapped for 2½ days in an abandoned well.

19 • Wall Street suffers its worse collapse in history, with the Dow Jones Industrial Average falling 508 points, or 22.6 percent, to close at 1,738.74.

• In the Persian Gulf, the United States destroys two Iranian offshore platforms suspected of being used as a base for gunboats.

23 • The U.S. Senate rejects the nomination of Robert Bork to the Supreme Court by a vote of 58-42.

53

**DEC. 3**

## November

1 • A new, younger Communist Party Central Committee is elected in China; paramount leader Deng Xiaoping gives up his seat, though retaining important influence.

3 • President Reagan nominates Ann Dore McLaughlin as labor secretary, replacing William Brock, who resigned.

5 • Reagan accepts the resignation of Caspar Weinberger as defense secretary and names Frank Carlucci to replace him.

• Nicaraguan President Daniel Ortega Saavedra proposes indirect cease-fire negotiations with contra rebels.

6 • Noburu Takeshita becomes prime minister of Japan.

7 • Douglas Ginsburg withdraws as a Supreme Court nominee after admitting to past marijuana use.

11 • Reagan nominates Anthony Kennedy to the Supreme Court.

• Van Gogh's painting *Irises* is sold at auction for a record $53.9 million.

18 • A congressional report on the Iran/contra affair concludes that President Reagan bears "ultimate responsibility" for his aides' wrongdoing and did not fulfill his constitutional duty to uphold the law.

20 • White House and congressional negotiators agree on a $30 billion cut in the fiscal 1988 federal deficit.

29 • A wave of violence in Haiti causes cancellation of the presidential election.

## December

3 • The U.S. government and Cuban detainees negotiate an end to rioting in the second of two U.S. facilities, caused by a U.S.-Cuban pact allowing "undesirables" to be sent back to Cuba.

5 • The Polish government announces it will scale back its austerity plan for 1988, after failure of a referendum.

8 • Launching three days of summit talks in Washington, D.C., President Reagan and Soviet leader Gorbachev sign a treaty to eliminate both sides' medium-range and shorter-range nuclear missiles.

15 • Gary Hart reenters the race for the Democratic presidential nomination.

16 • Roh Tae Woo, candidate of the ruling party, defeats a divided opposition in South Korean presidential elections.

21 • Arabs in Israel stage a general strike, as the death toll rises in clashes between Palestinian demonstrators and Israeli security forces in the occupied territories.

31 • The dollar hits record postwar lows against the yen and the mark.

# A

**ACCIDENTS AND DISASTERS.** The following were among the noteworthy accidents and disasters of 1987:

Jan. 4, Maryland: In the worst accident in Amtrak history, a caravan of three Conrail locomotives crossed into the path of an Amtrak passenger train near Baltimore; 16 passengers were killed and more than 170 injured.

Jan. 13, Ethiopia: An Ethiopian Air Force plane crashed in Asmara, capital of Eritrea, minutes after taking off; all 54 people aboard lost their lives.

Jan. 15, Utah: A Fairchild Metro commuter airliner and a private plane collided over a residential area near Salt Lake City; all ten people aboard the two aircraft were killed.

Feb. 7, Vanuatu: A hurricane with 100-mile-an-hour winds battered the Pacific island of Vanuatu, leaving about 50 people dead and more than $150 million in damages.

Feb. 17, Brazil: Two commuter trains collided on the outskirts of São Paulo, when one switched tracks into the path of the other; more than 150 people lost their lives.

Mar. 5, Ecuador: Two earthquakes, and mudslides and flooding triggered by the quakes, devastated part of northeastern Ecuador, killing at least 1,000 people and causing an estimated $1 billion in damage.

Mar. 6, Belgium: The British ferry *Herald of Free Enterprise*, en route to Dover, capsized off the Belgian port of Zeebrugge after an inrush of seawater flooded through its open front loading doors; nearly 200 passengers and crew members lost their lives.

Apr. 2, Ecuador: As many as 100 people were killed when mudslides triggered by heavy rains buried buses traveling along a coastal highway.

Apr. 5, New York: A bridge collapsed on the New York State Thruway, northwest of Albany, plunging several vehicles into a rain-swollen creek below; ten people died.

Apr. 23, Connecticut: A 13-story high-rise apartment building under construction in

*The British ferryboat* Herald of Free Enterprise, *en route to Dover, England, with over 540 passengers and crew on board, capsized with terrifying suddenness on March 6 in Belgium's Zeebrugge Harbor. Nearly 200 people lost their lives.*

The sole survivor of the Northwest Airlines jetliner crash in Detroit (above) that killed more than 150 people, including her parents and elder brother, four-year-old Cecilia Cichan of Tempe, Ariz., became a national symbol of hope. Her survival was so astounding that investigators at first assumed she must have been a passenger in a car on the highway outside Detroit Metropolitan Airport, where the plane crashed.

Bridgeport collapsed, leaving 28 workers dead.

May 6, China: A fire broke out in a northeastern forest, leaving more than 200 people dead and 50,000 homeless.

May 9, Poland: A Polish Ilyushin 62M jetliner bound for New York from Warsaw developed engine trouble soon after takeoff and crashed into a wooded area; all 183 people aboard lost their lives.

May 22, Texas: A tornado devastated the farming town of Saragosa; 30 people died, and about 150 were injured.

July-Aug., Bangladesh: The worst flooding in decades took the lives of at least 1,600 people, perhaps thousands more, and destroyed millions of acres of grain.

July-Aug., Italy: Fast-melting snow and heavy rains produced floods and landslides in northern Italy, leaving at least 44 dead and cutting off access to many villages.

July 2, Texas: Sixteen Mexican illegal aliens and two apparent smugglers were found dead in a freight train in Sierra Blanca; they had been trapped inside a locked, steel-walled boxcar, as the train was delayed on a siding and temperatures reached 120°F.

July 2, Zaire: At least 125 people lost their lives when a trailer-truck crashed into and partially derailed a moving train at an unguarded crossing near the Zambian border.

July 7, Zaire and Zambia: A barge carrying as many as 550 passengers hit a sandbar and capsized in the crocodile-infested Luapula River along the border; 80 people survived, and about 50 bodies were recovered.

July 14, France: A flash flood ripped through a campsite near Le Grand-Bornand, depositing tons of mud and debris; about 30 vacationers lost their lives.

July 17, Texas: Ten teenagers were killed when the swollen Guadalupe River swept away a church camp bus and van near the town of Comfort.

July 18-27, Greece: A heat wave killed as many as 1,000 people, as temperatures stayed above 106°F and reached 122°F in some areas.

July 30, Mexico: A Boeing-377 cargo plane carrying horses for a U.S. tour crashed onto a crowded Mexico City highway, smashed 26 cars, slammed into buildings, and exploded, killing more than 40 people.

July 31, Alberta: A tornado cut a path of destruction through Edmonton, killing 27 people, injuring 300, and leaving an estimated 750 families homeless.

Aug. 7, Soviet Union: A runaway locomotive smashed into the rear of a passenger train in Kamensk-Shakhtinskiy, southeast of Moscow. Dozens of people reportedly died.

Aug. 16, Michigan: A Northwest Airlines MD-80 jet crashed just after takeoff from Detroit Metropolitan Airport, killing 154 people aboard and 2 on the ground. One passenger, a four-year-old girl, survived.

Aug. 31, South Africa: An elevator fell to the bottom of a 4,600-foot gold mine shaft near Welkom, after an apparent methane gas explosion. As many as 62 workers lost their lives.

Aug. 31, Thailand: A Thai Airways jet crashed into the Andaman Sea near Phuket Island, reportedly after acting to avoid another plane; all 83 people aboard were killed.

Sept. 24-29, South Africa: A record five-day rainstorm led to floods that killed more than 400 people, left at least 55,000 homeless, and caused over $500 million in damage.

Sept. 27, Colombia: At least 175 people were killed, and another 200 injured when a mudslide caused by heavy rains buried a slum area of Medellín.

Oct. 1, Calif.: The state's strongest earthquake since 1971 shook the Los Angeles area, causing six deaths and more than $200 million in damage; another person died later as a result of a strong aftershock.

Oct. 11, Burma: All 49 people aboard a Burma Airways Fokker Friendship 27 died when the plane caught fire and crashed on a flight from Rangoon to the popular tourist center of Pagan.

Oct. 13-16, Venezuela: More than 200 people were killed and over 30,000 were left homeless after torrential rains triggered floods and mudslides.

Oct. 19, Indonesia: Two trains, one jammed with rush-hour commuters, collided head-on 9 miles south of Jakarta, leaving more than 150 people dead.

Oct. 20, Indiana: An Air Force jet crashed into a Ramada Inn near the Indianapolis Airport, killing ten people and injuring five.

Nov. 15, Colorado: A Continental Airlines DC-9 jet crashed on takeoff during a snowstorm, killing 28 people.

Nov. 18, England: Thirty-one people were killed and about 80 were injured when fire that started in a wooden escalator swept through the King's Cross subway station in central London at about 7:50 P.M. An overheated bearing was held responsible.

Nov. 26, Philippines: A typhoon that churned up giant waves and winds of up to 128 miles an hour bombarded the island of Luzon, leaving at least 700 people dead and displacing an estimated 1.3 million.

Nov. 26, Indonesia: An earthquake shook the volcanic island of Pantar, causing landslides and a tidal wave 160 feet high. More than 40 people were killed.

Nov. 28, South Africa: In South Africa's worst air disaster, a South African Airways Boeing 747 crashed into the Indian Ocean about 125 miles southeast of Mauritius. All 159 people on board were killed.

Nov. 30, Southeast Asia: A South Korean airliner crashed near the coast of Burma, killing all 115 passengers. The plane disappeared from radar as it flew across Burma; a North Korean later admitted planting bombs on board.

Dec. 5, Spain: An explosion and fire aboard the Panamanian-registered freighter, *Cason*, two miles off the northwest coast of Spain, left 23 people dead; 8 others were rescued from the water.

Dec. 7, California: A commuter jet crashed midway between San Francisco and Los Angeles, minutes after reports of gunshots in the passenger cabin. A disgruntled former airline employee was suspected of the shooting. All 43 on board lost their lives.

Dec. 8, Peru: A navy plane carrying Peru's top soccer team crashed into the ocean near Lima; of 43 aboard, only the pilot survived.

Dec. 11, Egypt: About 60 schoolchildren on an outing were killed when their bus collided with a train at an unmarked crossing.

Dec. 16-17, United States: A storm raged across the U.S. midsection, bringing heavy snow and tornadoes and causing over 70 deaths.

Dec. 21, Louisiana: A helicopter carrying offshore workers crashed on the deck of an oil rig in the Gulf of Mexico, killing 14.

Dec. 21, Philippines: Over 1,600 people died when the inter-island ferry *Dona Paz* collided with an oil tanker 110 miles south of Manila, causing an explosion and fire. Both ships sank quickly, leaving only 26 survivors.

**ADVERTISING.** Total U.S. advertising expenditures in 1987 were projected to approach $110 billion, with spending on local advertising expected to grow more rapidly than that for national advertising.

**Ad Campaigns.** One of the most talked about advertising campaigns was prepared for the California Raisin Advisory Board. The television commercials featured Claymation (clay animation) raisins, dressed in sunglasses, white gloves, and sneakers, who sang and danced to the 1960's hit "I Heard It Through the Grapevine."

Coca-Cola's computer-animated Max Headroom, who warned the audience not to say "the P word," was seen in the most widely recalled commercial of 1986. Its popularity did not keep sales of New Coke from falling, however. Pepsi-Cola continued its use of celebrities with new ads featuring Michael Jackson and an update of the Pepsi taste test using Bronson Pinchot.

In a year that saw the Iran/contra scandal, the apparent collapse of Gary Hart's presidential campaign after his alleged liaison with actress-model Donna Rice, and charges of sexual and financial improprieties against televangelist Jim Bakker, cynicism appeared to replace patriotism as a theme in advertisements. Isuzu produced commercials that featured an automobile salesman who made outrageous claims and subtitles to refute him. Likewise, a "woman in the street" said that her Seiko watch was more reliable than her husband. Meanwhile, Donna Rice surfaced in print ads and commercials for No Excuse jeans.

IBM retired its Little Tramp character in April, but the company introduced a major campaign for its new Personal System/2 computers. This multimedia campaign featured most of the actors from the *M*A*S*H* television series. Other popular television celebrities appearing in advertisements included Bill Cosby, for Jell-O desserts, and Bruce Willis, for Seagram's wine coolers. Anheuser-Busch created its own celebrity in Spuds MacKenzie, a bull terrier who was called "The Original Party Animal" in spots for Bud Light beer.

**Target Audiences.** The hottest targets for advertisers were the so-called DINK's—couples with double income, no kids. These career-oriented couples were a challenge for advertisers because they had high discretionary income but, in many cases, little time in which to spend it. Advertising directed to the Hispanic market was also on the rise.

**Media.** In September there was a major change in the way television ratings are measured. Prodded by competition from AGB Television Research, A.C. Nielsen dropped its use of household meters (indicating simply whether the TV is on and what the program is) and of viewer diaries in favor of a single sample of homes equipped with people meters. The new technology requires individuals to push a button on a remote control device to signal their presence in the room when the TV is on. A test of the system indicated that ratings would be somewhat lower than under the old system and that there would be changes in the demographic composition of audiences.

**Standards and Practices.** At the request of public health officials, various media began accepting public-service and brand-specific condom advertisements that promoted use of the product for protection against the virus that causes AIDS. Television networks also began to accept ads for bras in which the products were worn by live models.                B.B.R.

**AFGHANISTAN.** In 1987, during the eighth year of civil war in Afghanistan, combat intensified between Soviet forces backing the Marxist government, on the one hand, and Afghan insurgents, the Mujahedeen, on the other.

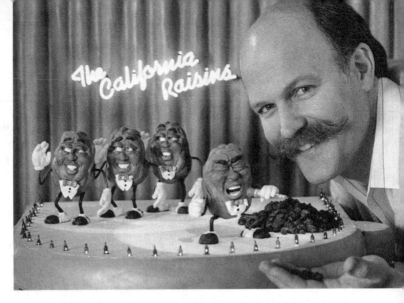

*Stop-motion clay "raisins" singing an old soul music hit made the California Raisin Advisory Board's ads among the most popular on TV. The spots also made a star of Will Vinton, until then an obscure (if critically acclaimed) animator.*

**National Reconciliation Plan.** In January, Secretary-General Najib (later called Najibullah), leader of the ruling People's Democratic Party of Afghanistan, declared a unilateral cease-fire with the Mujahedeen and called for a government of "national reconciliation" in Afghanistan, though indicating that such a regime would remain "loyal to the Soviet Union" and to Communist goals. Najib called upon the 5 million Afghan refugees outside the country to return under amnesty and guarantees of political rights and invited the Mujahedeen to join in the rebuilding of Afghanistan. After some initial disagreement, the Pakistan-based alliance of seven Mujahedeen groups held a joint meeting and firmly rejected the cease-fire proposal as a ruse, offering instead to negotiate directly with the Soviet government.

**The Ongoing War.** As the guerrillas continued to mount attacks on Afghan government strongholds, Soviet troops reportedly continued to carry out major offensive operations, despite the cease-fire. Afghan planes also carried out bombing raids on Pakistani border villages, in an apparent effort to undermine Pakistani support for the Mujahedeen.

Mujahedeen tactics, organization, and training appeared to have improved. But the key military development was the arrival of U.S.-made Stinger shoulder-fired missiles, which became a major factor in the destruction of Soviet aircraft and forced Soviet/Afghan pilots to fly considerably higher or at night, lessening their effectiveness. Resistance forces continued to occupy large sections of Herāt and Kandahar, and Kabul and the major provincial capitals remained ringed with Soviet security posts.

**Peace Talks.** Indirect negotiations between Afghanistan and Pakistan continued, leaving some hope that a political settlement could be reached. In talks held in March and September, under UN auspices, the main issue discussed was the timetable for the withdrawal of Soviet troops. At the end of November, Najib, who had by then resumed his original Islamic name Najibullah, proposed a timetable of 12 months for Soviet withdrawal—a period that Soviet leader Mikhail Gorbachev also proposed at his December summit with U.S. President Ronald Reagan.

With the possibility of a Soviet troop withdrawal in mind, a UN envoy met late in the year in Rome with deposed 73-year-old King Muhammad Zahir Shah, who could play a role in a future broad-based government of national reconciliation. But he was opposed by Afghan fundamentalist insurgents as being insufficiently religious.

**Political Developments.** In late November, a meeting of tribal elders and chiefs, most of them loyal to Najibullah, approved an official constitution that concentrated government power in the new post of president and commander-in-chief of the army. The same group elected Najibullah to the post unopposed.

*See* STATISTICS OF THE WORLD.　　　N.P.N.

# Africa

**The threat of famine intensified in a number of African nations during 1987, and, despite widespread adoption of economic reforms, most countries suffered from serious economic problems. Armed conflicts continued between Chad and Libya and in the Western Sahara, Sudan, and South African-occupied Namibia.**

Governments were overthrown in Burundi and Burkina Faso, and the aging president of Tunisia was deposed. A major political unity accord was reached in Zimbabwe. In the Horn of Africa, continuing war combined with drought to threaten a recurrence of widespread famine in Ethiopia, while in southern Africa a principal cause of famine was the South African-backed guerrilla warfare.

**Economic Crisis.** Over four-fifths of the sub-Saharan African countries had adopted economic reform programs by 1987, stressing price incentives and increased support for agricultural production, and food production was generally increasing. However, in late 1987 the World Food Program said that drought conditions and crop failure were causing renewed crisis in 15 African countries. Ethiopia was the worst affected; also very seriously endangered were Mozambique, Malawi, Angola, Somalia, and Sudan. Ethiopia alone was expected to need over 1 million tons of food aid in 1988.

In 1986, Africa had lost more than $19 billion in export revenues as a result of falling prices, the sharpest drop in nearly four decades; and debt payments of some $15 billion almost equaled new development assistance of $16 billion.

In a dramatic move in May, Zambia's President Kenneth Kaunda repudiated his country's loan agreement with the International Monetary Fund, saying the austerity measures required were impossible to implement. Observers suggested that many of the other 19 countries with IMF standby agreements would find themselves in similar situations.

**Southern Africa.** Because of media restrictions and the apparent success of the government's state of emergency in suppressing large-scale black protest, the continuing conflict in South Africa and the surrounding region attracted less international attention than in 1986. However, in August, in the largest strike in the country's history, over 300,000 of South Africa's approximately 500,000 miners stayed away from work for three weeks.

President P. W. Botha's National Party won 123 of the 166 directly elected seats in the House of Assembly, in all-white elections in May, although its share of the popular vote dropped from 56 percent to 52 percent. The extreme right-wing Conservative Party won 22 seats, replacing the moderate Progressive Federal Party as the official opposition. In November, South Africa released long-term political prisoner Govan Mbeki, a leader of the African National Congress. His release was seen as a test for the possible future release of the ANC's best-known leader, Nelson Mandela. But subsequently, Mbeki's activities were severely limited, and most observers doubted the government would agree to talk to the banned black nationalist organization.

In September, South African air power and artillery, as well as ground troops, were used to aid Jonas Savimbi's rebel Unita army against Angolan government troops, in a series of major battles in sparsely populated southeastern Angola. Unita, which also received Stinger missiles and other military supplies from the United States, retained its control over its base area in this region just to the north of South African-occupied Namibia (South West Africa). Talks continued between Angola and the United States concerning the independence of Namibia and withdrawal of the Cuban troops reinforcing the Angolan Army.

In Mozambique the government, with aid from Zimbabwe and Tanzania, recaptured much of the central Zambezi River area from the South African-backed troops of the Mozambique National Resistance. But from midyear the MNR launched a new series of raids in the south, killing hundreds of civilians.

Zimbabwe's Prime Minister Robert Mugabe reached an accord late in the year with long-time rival Joshua Nkomo, providing for merger of their parties, with Mugabe as head of the merged party and executive president of Zimbabwe, now a one-party state.

**East Africa.** In September, Burundi's President Jean-Baptiste Bagaza was overthrown in a military coup and replaced by Major Pierre Buyoya. Bagaza, who was out of the country attending a summit of French-speaking nations in Québec, had come under strong criticism for his campaign against the Roman Catholic Church in a majority-Catholic country. The government of Burundi is dominated by the ethnic minority of Tutsi, with the majority Hutu severely underrepresented; the coup was considered unlikely to affect this pattern.

In both Sudan and Ethiopia war hindered the distribution of relief supplies. The Sudanese government of Prime Minister Sadiq al-Mahdi imposed a new, more comprehensive state of emergency in July, amid unrest over economic conditions in the capital and the unresolved war in the south. In Ethiopia, drought produced an almost total crop failure in the north and central highlands, and the government of Mengistu Haile Mariam appealed for renewed international aid. The two most severely affected areas were Eritrea, where the Eritrean People's Liberation Front (EPLF) has been fighting a decades-long war for independence, and Tigré, where antigovernment guerrillas are also active. The two areas have a combined population of about 5 million. Relief efforts were threatened in October when EPLF forces destroyed nearly 450 tons of wheat in an attack on a food convoy that they claimed was camouflage for government military activities.

**West Africa.** The military government of Nigeria announced in July a six-year plan for return to civilian rule. President Ibrahim Babangida, the second military ruler since the civilian government of Shehu Shagari was overthrown in 1983, said the transition would include a new census, lifting of the ban on political activities, and a series of elections leading up to national elections in 1992.

The war in northern Chad between the government of Hissène Habré and Libya's Muammar al-Qaddafi escalated significantly during

*A desperate farmer in the northern Ethiopian town of Makelle tries to work his field, transformed by drought into a wasteland.*

the year. With military aid from France and the United States, the Chadian Army took the key Libyan bases of Wadi Doum and Faya-Largeau in northern Chad in March and drove Libyan forces into retreat in the disputed Aozou strip on the Chad-Libya border in August and September, at one point invading Libya itself and destroying a major air base. In September, Libya and Chad accepted a cease-fire mediated by the Organization of African Unity, but the truce was generally regarded as precarious.

In October, President Thomas Sankara of Burkina Faso (formerly Upper Volta) was overthrown in a military coup by one of his deputies, Blaise Compaoré. Sankara and 12 other officials of his government were later killed by troops loyal to Compaoré. Although Sankara had won internal and external praise for his reform programs, his crackdowns on corruption and his iconoclastic style had won him many enemies in his own government. In November, Niger's President Seyni Kountché died in Paris, where he had been undergoing treatment for a brain tumor. Kountché, who

Accused of corruption, murder, and even cannibalism, Jean-Bedel Bokassa stood trial in Bangui, Central African Republic. The court reaffirmed the death sentence imposed in absentia on Bokassa, who ruled the nation from 1965 to 1979.

seized power in a coup in 1974, was succeeded by Army Chief of Staff Ali Seybou.

Jean-Bedel Bokassa, who ruled the Central African Republic from 1965 to 1979 and in 1976 proclaimed himself Emperor Bokassa I, was tried during the first half of the year for murder, embezzlement, and cannibalism. He had voluntarily returned to the country in late 1986, after ten years in exile. Although Bokassa's former cook testified that he had prepared a human body for the emperor's plate, the court found the evidence insufficient to convict Bokassa on the cannibalism charge. He was convicted on the other charges and sentenced to death, but there were indications that the government would commute the death sentence.

**North Africa.** Tunisian President Habib Bourguiba, who had ruled that country for 31 years, was replaced in November by Prime Minister Zine al-Abidine Ben Ali, who had been appointed prime minister the preceding month. Ben Ali charged that the 84-year-old president, who was pressing a crackdown on Muslim fundamentalists, was too ill and senile to continue governing.

Egypt's President Hosni Mubarak won approval in an October referendum for a second six-year term. Libya's Muammar al-Qaddafi, his prestige undermined by military defeats in Chad, successfully sought closer relations with neighboring Algeria.

Despite reports of Algerian-Moroccan talks to resolve the conflict, the war by Saharan guerrillas against Moroccan occupation of Western Sahara continued. In August, Morocco gained U.S. agreement for a new sale of 100 Patton tanks for use in the desert war.

**Organization of African Unity.** The Organization of African Unity summit in Addis Ababa, Ethiopia, in July, attracted only 19 heads of state out of an eligible 50. Chosen as the new chairman was Zambian President Kenneth Kaunda, whose confrontation with the International Monetary Fund and position as chairman of the Southern African frontline states both pointed to key problems for the continent. The summit made plans to call an international conference on the African debt crisis.

See also separate articles on many of the individual countries mentioned.          W.M.

To cut the costs of bringing cattle to market, a Fort Worth, Texas, company was offering a new form of prime time: video livestock auctions, beamed to ranchers, feedlots, and other prospective purchasers via satellite. Bids are phoned in to clerks in such unlikely settings as the Fort Worth restaurant shown above.

**AGRICULTURE AND FOOD SUPPLIES.** World food production in 1987 declined almost 3 percent from the 1986 level. Food production, however, was generally well distributed; sizable carryover stocks of grain, meats, and dairy products eased fear of shortages in most areas. Notable exceptions included Ethiopia, where severe drought posed the threat of massive famine, and Angola, where civil war, politics, and a poor marketing structure hampered the movement of food to the cities.

**World Trends.** World grain production was forecast at 1,614 million tons—a decrease of 4 percent from 1986. (All ton figures are metric tons unless otherwise noted.) Wheat, rice, and coarse grain all were down. World production of red meats (beef, veal, pork, lamb, mutton, and goat meat) was estimated to total 105 million tons, down slightly from 1986. Poultry meat output was estimated at 29 million tons, up about 6 percent. The estimated output of 389 billion eggs represented a gain of 1 percent, with the largest increase in the Soviet Union.

The cow's milk production outlook of 423 million tons was almost unchanged from 1986. Output of butter, cheese, and nonfat dry milk declined, but storage stocks, notably in the European Community, remained relatively large.

World coffee production in the 1987–1988 marketing year was forecast at 27 percent above the 1986–1987 mark. The cocoa bean harvest was projected as slightly larger than in 1986. A record 102 million tons of sugar (raw value) was forecast for 1987–1988, up around 1 percent. The tobacco crop was expected to be 8 percent above 1986. The cotton crop was projected at 77.5 million bales.

**Consumer Food Costs.** A U.S. Department of Agriculture (USDA) survey of retail food prices in 15 world capitals showed that at midyear the total price for a "market basket" of 15 food items was higher than in late 1986 in most cities surveyed. The steepest increases between November 1986 and May 1987 were reported for Mexico City, Tokyo, London, and Paris. Decreases, however, were noted in Pretoria,

63

South Africa; Canberra, Australia; Washington, D.C.; and Ottawa. There was wide variation among the cities studied. For example, foods that cost $45.46 in Washington, D.C., were $136.85 in Tokyo but only $26.08 in Mexico City.

**Food Aid.** U.S. relief shipments of food to Third World countries in the Middle East, South Asia, and Africa were large, totaling more than 8.4 million tons and involving outlays of over $1.4 billion. The United States has been for many years the world's major provider of food relief, although with the European Community's accumulation of large stocks of foods under its price support operations, the Community has been increasingly able to share its abundance through donations or sales.

**United States.** *Land Values, Income.* Farmland values were rebounding modestly during the year, after several years of decline, and net farm cash income was expected to reach a record $57 billion. Part of the reason for the income rise was lower costs for fertilizers, feeds, pesticides, and other items; however, these costs were expected to rise in 1988. Farmers' outstanding debt declined overall. Government payments, which came to $11.8 billion in 1986, comprising about 23 percent of net cash income, continued at about the same level in 1987.

*Soil Conservation.* The soil-saving program advanced. Farmers in the latest 1987 sign-up enrolled 5.8 million acres in the Conservation Reserve Program, bringing the total to 24.7 million—well over halfway toward the U.S. Department of Agriculture's goal of getting 45 million acres of highly erodible land out of production by 1990. Farmers participating in the program agree to plant their land in soil-saving grasses or trees and to keep it out of production for at least ten years. The program, created by the Food Security Act of 1985, pays farmers an annual "rent" to remove their most erosive land from production so as to protect soil and prevent further buildup of commodity surpluses.

*Credit.* Credit problems nevertheless remained. By September, farm acreage taken over by institutional leaders from debt-ridden farmers was approximately equal to the combined area of Maryland and Delaware. The largest lender

to individual farmers, the network of banks and lending cooperatives known as the Farm Credit System, was in difficulty, and in early December the Federal Land Bank of Jackson, Miss., became the first such institution to declare itself insolvent. Congress passed legislation providing up to $4 billion in federally guaranteed bonds to rescue the system.

*Exports and Output.* Agricultural export volume increased in fiscal 1987, with export value up slightly, and the 1987 crop year was fair. In September the USDA's "all-crop" production index (1977 = 100) was forecast at 106, the lowest since 1983 but about equal to the average of the preceding ten years. Wheat was put at 2.1 billion bushels, up 1 percent. Soybeans were forecast at 1.96 billion bushels, down 3 percent, and rice was put at 127 million hundredweight, down 6 percent. Tobacco production was expected to be up 6 percent, however, and the cotton crop was up slightly. The sugarcane crop was up 4 percent and sugar beets up 7 percent. Commercial apple production increased by 22 percent. The grape harvest was off 3 percent from 1986, with California wine varieties forecast to be down 10 percent.

Cattle and calves on farms and ranches on January 1 totaled 102 million head, down 3 percent from a year earlier and the lowest since 1962. The decline was caused in part by prolonged drought in the Great Plains area during the 1982–1984 period and also by the U.S. Department of Agriculture's Dairy Termination Program, which made payments to farmers who would sell their milk cows and get out of dairying for at least five years. Milk production was slightly less than in 1986. The output of butter, cheese, and nonfat dry milk also declined. Red meat production was forecast to be down 2 percent. Poultry meat production was predicted to be up 10 percent, with a further sizable increase expected in 1988. Egg output increased slightly.

**World Output.** Hot, dry weather in Canada's prairie provinces and some reduction in fertilizer use brought Canada's estimated wheat harvest to 25 million tons, 20 percent below the 1986 record crop. Canadian tobacco was down 7 percent, and oilseed output down 9 percent. Coffee harvests in the countries south of the United States were forecast to be more than 60 percent higher than the drought-reduced crop of 1986–1987, and sugar output in Latin America was up slightly.

Grain production in Western Europe was expected to be up 3 percent, but grain output in the Soviet Union was forecast at 205 million tons, down 5 million from 1986. Soviet leader Mikhail Gorbachev stated that within six years the Soviet Union would be an exporter of grain instead of an importer; he set a production goal of 250 million tons of grain annually. However, although the current Soviet intensive technology program could increase agricultural productivity, the major factor in Soviet output will remain the weather. In Eastern Europe grain output was down 6 percent.

In India, production of rice declined by 20 percent and output of coarse grains by 14 percent, largely because of hot, dry weather. China had an above-average agricultural year, with the important rice harvest up 3 percent, the cotton crop up 10 percent, and tobacco up 25 percent. China had drastically reformed its agriculture, which partially explained the recent increase in farm production, but some farmers were beginning to decrease acreage devoted to staple crops—rice, wheat, soybeans, and cotton. Instead, they were planting free-market vegetables and were taking up such "sideline" activities as poultry raising.

Japan reduced its producer rice price 4 percent—the first such reduction since 1956. Australia's wheat harvest for 1987 was forecast to be down 17 percent from the 1986 crop. In New Zealand, beef production was up more than 10 percent from the 1986 level, while cheese output was off 6 percent.

**Hunger in Africa.** In early September, the head of Ethiopia's Relief and Rehabilitation Commission requested 950,000 tons of food aid from the United Nations. Drought was the immediate cause of the emergency. Three years earlier, Ethiopia had suffered 16,000 deaths a day because of famine. In August the Angolan government requested 245,000 tons of food through the United Nations. Farmers were refusing to sell their food for Angolan currency; they preferred to barter their products for such necessities as clothing, soap, and farm tools, which the government lacked the capacity to

In a University of Wisconsin greenhouse, horticulturalist Clinton Peterson (left) and geneticist Phillipp Simon show off the results of four years of work: "supercarrots" with five times the usual amount of beta-carotene, a substance the body converts into Vitamin A.

manufacture, the money to import, or the means to transport. A major cause of the disruption was the 12-year-old civil war in which the Angolan government faced a rebel movement financed by the United States and South Africa. Outside areas suffering from shortages, however, African agriculture generally did well in 1987. Coffee, orange, and tobacco crops all were larger than in 1986.

**Fisheries.** The 1987 world catch of fish was estimated at about 91 million tons, a slight increase over 1986's catch. Developing countries accounted for 52 percent of the 1986 catch, mainly because of more landings by South American countries. In 1986, Chile and Peru, benefiting from a return of anchovy stock, ranked fourth and fifth in total production, following world leaders Japan, the Soviet Union, and China. The United States held the sixth spot.

A strong demand for fish in the main importing countries, together with the weak U.S. dollar, was responsible for substantial price increases in all major types. U.S. commercial landings in 1987 were estimated to be close to the 6.0 billion pounds (2.7 million tons) landed in 1986. U.S. consumption of fish was on the rise, having reached a record high of 14.7 pounds of edible meat per person in 1986.                    D.R.W. (Fisheries) & H.W.H.

**ALABAMA.** *See* STATISTICS OF THE WORLD.

**ALASKA.** *See* STATISTICS OF THE WORLD.

**ALBANIA.** In 1987, in his relations with the superpowers, party and state chief Ramiz Alia held firm to the line fostered by his late predecessor, Enver Hoxha. He accused both the Soviet Union—steeped in "bourgeois-revisionist degeneration"—and the United States of being bent on overthrowing the Albanian Communist regime and subjugating its people. Relations with Yugoslavia remained tense because of chronic friction involving the Albanian majority in Yugoslavia's Kosovo province. In dire need of economic aid, Tirana was more pragmatic in its relations with other nations. Having newly established diplomatic relations with Spain, Jordan, and the Philippines, Albania made moves toward instituting relations with various other countries. Agreements to establish ties were signed late in the year with Canada and West Germany not long after Greece had announced that it was ending the formal state of war with Albania that had existed since World War II.

In national elections held on February 1, 250 parliamentary deputies were reportedly elected unanimously by 1,830,651 votes, with only one spoiled ballot. Of the deputies, 97 were new members, 43 percent were between the ages of 41 and 60, and about 80 percent had higher education. Party leader Alia, chairman of the Presidium of the People's Assembly, and Adil Çarçani, prime minister since January 1982, were both reelected.

The country's principal problem continued to be economic stagnation, attributable to years of rigid "self-reliance" that followed the break with China in 1978. Even the tightly controlled Albanian press—despite official proclamations of no economic difficulties—reported major losses from badly organized production and the use of inadequate technology. In an effort to cope with the problem, the government increased material incentives for workers. Bonuses were to be given to key workers who met or exceeded production targets, and inefficient managers were to be dealt with.

*See* STATISTICS OF THE WORLD.                    R.A.P.

**ALBERTA.** *See* STATISTICS OF THE WORLD.

**ALGERIA.** Economic reform and regional affairs were major preoccupations during 1987, Algeria's 25th year of independence. Concerned over a deficit budget and student riots in late 1986, President Chadli Benjedid initiated an economic reform program stressing "autonomy of the enterprise." New self-financing regulations allowed state-owned companies to raise money or reinvest their earnings without higher approval. Such firms were authorized to contract directly with suppliers for needed materials and to make various marketing decisions. The state also sought to encourage private entrepreneurs.

A continuing slump in oil prices caused a projected budgetary deficit of $2.4 billion for fiscal 1987. Education received the most funding, in the wake of the 1986 student disturbances.

In February elections Algeria's single party, the National Liberation Front, nominated three candidates for each of the 295 seats in the Popular National Assembly. Of 132 incumbents who were nominated, fewer than half won election. In July the assembly passed a law making it easier to form voluntary associations, such as athletic or religious clubs, despite fears of some deputies that greater freedom of association might undermine the country's basic institutions.

In a January shootout, police killed prominent fundamentalist dissident Mustapha Bouiali. When 200 of his followers were tried in June, 4 were sentenced to death and 5 to life imprisonment. The others received lesser sentences. Also in June, 22 people accused of subversive activity on behalf of former President Ahmed Ben Bella were tried. Twelve were found guilty.

Between May and mid-July, Benjedid met with the leaders of neighboring Libya and Tunisia and sent emissaries to Mauritania and Morocco, as part of what appeared to be a major diplomatic initiative. The only concrete outcome was a joint Algerian-Tunisian-Libyan venture to build a new gas pipeline.

Algeria mediated between competing factions in Chad and between Chad and Libya. During April the Palestinian National Council met in Algeria. In July the newly created eight-nation African Petroleum Producers' Association met in Algiers.

See STATISTICS OF THE WORLD.          R.A.M.

**AMERICAN SAMOA.** See STATISTICS OF THE WORLD.

**ANGOLA.** In 1987, fighting apparently stepped up between Angolan government forces and the South African-backed National Union for the Total Independence of Angola (Unita), joined by large numbers of South African troops. Partly as a result of the civil war, food shortages remained acute, and in August the government declared a new food emergency in urban areas.

**Military and Political Situation.** The Unita movement, which claimed a regular force of about 28,000 backed by some 37,000 guerrillas, continued to control the sparsely populated southeast and carried out guerrilla attacks in government-controlled zones, while South African regular troops launched several major raids in the southwest. The Angolan Army was reported to number about 80,000 and to be backed by extensive Soviet aid, Cuban troops estimated by some sources at 35,000 or more, and an estimated 5,000 Eastern-bloc advisers. In September and October intense battles were reported east of Cuito Cuanavale in Cuando Cubango province, on the edge of the Unita zone of control. The Angolan government charged that more than five South African battalions were involved, while Unita claimed that a Soviet general was directing the Angolan attack. Late in the year, South Africa admitted for the first time that its forces were fighting alongside the Angolan rebels. Angolan sources claimed there were 3,000 South African troops in southern Angola and that, by late November, more than 200 had been killed in recent heavy fighting. In December, South Africa said it was beginning to withdraw troops.

The Angolan government continued to stress its policy of clemency, offering to pardon guerrillas and other opponents who gave up their resistance. There were several changes in the Luanda cabinet during the year, apparently connected with the drive to remedy inefficiency and corruption.

**Foreign Relations.** Unita made some attempt to distance itself from South Africa. In June, however, Unita leader Jonas Savimbi made a visit to that country, where he praised South African President P. W. Botha for initiating "change" in apartheid laws. Angolan talks with the United States reopened, with Angola announcing new "flexibility" on the issue of Cuban troop withdrawal. But with the Reagan administration under right-wing pressure to take strong measures against Angola, the prospects for a diplomatic advance seemed bleak. Unita continued to receive covert aid from the United States, and late in the year a captured rebel, interviewed by Angolan government officials, asserted that armed and uniformed Americans were working in a rebel-controlled area to coordinate the delivery of U.S. arms to Unita by way of Zaire.

**Economic Developments.** There was some improvement in oil prices, after a catastrophic drop the previous year, and oil production continued to grow, with output expected to reach 330,000 barrels/day by the end of the year. Austerity measures had, however, reduced imported supplies to industry and agriculture by about 40 percent. Industrial production was expected to decline, and agricultural production was largely paralyzed. The government estimated that $116 million in food aid was necessary for some 690,000 displaced people, as well as for half of the urban population of about 2 million.

In August, President José Eduardo dos Santos announced plans for a major economic restructuring to deal with the crisis and confirmed Angola's intention to join the International Monetary Fund. Angola was also seeking rescheduling on its $4 billion foreign debt, over half of which was owed to the Soviet Union for arms purchases.

See STATISTICS OF THE WORLD.          W.M.

**ANTIGUA AND BARBUDA.** See STATISTICS OF THE WORLD.

Jordan's King Hussein (in suit) welcomes Saddam Hussein (left), president of Iraq, to November's Arab League summit in Amman.

**ARAB LEAGUE.** Several Arab League meetings were held during 1987 to discuss the war between Iran and Iraq, the plight of Palestinians in Lebanon, and the conflict with Israel. Most important was an emergency summit conference, the first since 1985, held in Amman, Jordan, in November.

In April the league sent a delegation to meet with Syrian President Hafez al-Assad for discussions of the conflict between Palestinian and Shiite Muslim Amal militias in Lebanon. As a result of these and subsequent parleys, the fighting that had begun in 1985, and had left some 3,000 dead, was suspended through an agreement signed in November.

Under league auspices, justice ministers from member states, meeting in Amman in April, endorsed an agreement calling for the establishment of an Arab Center for Commercial Arbitration. In June the league protested India's decision to permit Israeli participation in Davis Cup tennis competition at New Delhi.

By far the most important meeting was the November summit in Amman, convened to deal with the Iran-Iraq war. A final resolution issued by the chiefs of state condemned Iran for its "intransigence, provocations, and threats to the Arab Gulf states" and urged the international community to "adopt measures adequate to make the Iranian regime respond to calls for peace." The statement declared Arab "solidarity with Iraq" and demanded that Iran accept the cease-fire called for in UN Security Council Resolution 598. Iran was also labeled the aggressor in recent Persian Gulf confrontations with Kuwait and Saudi Arabia and castigated for its "bloody criminal acts" during July, when Iranian pilgrims in Mecca staged a violent political demonstration.

The Amman conference also reiterated support for the Palestinians and called for an international peace conference under UN sponsorship to resolve the Arab-Israeli dispute. Egypt, suspended from the league since its 1979 peace treaty with Israel, was not restored to full membership, because of Syrian opposition, but the final resolution authorized the Arab states to restore ties with Cairo on an individual basis. The United Arab Emirates and Iraq did so soon after, followed by Bahrain, Kuwait, Mauritania, Morocco, Qatar, Saudi Arabia, and Yemen.                    D.P.

**ARCHAEOLOGY.** In 1987 archaeologists around the world raced to rescue the crumbling heritage of the past, sometimes with the help of space-age technology.

**Urban Archaeology in Paris.** A team of 18 archaeologists worked against time to rescue as much as possible from beneath the Île de la Cité—the island in the heart of Paris—before construction began in earnest on a five-story underground parking garage. While construction workers installed 100-foot-long slabs of concrete above them, archaeologists worked to remove and excavate the remains of thousands of objects dating from as early as the 3rd century A.D. up to the 19th century. The archaeologists, led by Juan Antonio Muñoz Lacasta, were particularly excited about the dig, even under deadline conditions, because it promised to reveal much about a continuous stretch of time in the history of Paris. The site was said to be part of the original settlement of the city, dating to 300 B.C. when the Gallic tribe of the Parisii inhabited the area. Barbarians overran the site in the 3rd century A.D., but archaeologists have recovered enough artifacts from that time and beyond to fill in some gaps in the early history of Paris.

Among the more interesting discoveries were the 261 cat bones from a 12th-century dump, relics of animals that had obviously been skinned. Archaeologist Frédérique Audoin suggested that superstitious Parisians had used the hides for medical cures. Another mystery revolved around some 40,000 sheep anklebones found piled high in what had been a 18th-century cellar. One hypothesis was that the bones were used to reinforce the construction of the cellar.

**A Quest for Egyptian Air.** A pioneer project in remote sensing was developed for an unusual new purpose. Under the direction of Farouk el-Baz, an Egyptian-born geologist who heads the Boston University Center for Remote Sensing, the two-year project planned to explore the ancient air in a sealed chamber near the base of the Great Pyramid of Khufu (Cheops). The purpose was to determine the exact composition of the "ancient air" as an aid to preventing further deterioration of the 4,600-year-old wooden boat that was removed from an adjacent chamber in 1954 and has been on display in a Cairo museum since 1982.

Remote sensing is a technique designed to find out as much as possible on site without costly, time-consuming, possibly impractical excavation. In this case, with the help of space-age technology, a special air-lock drill was developed; plans called for taking air samples without unsealing the chamber. El-Baz believes the pyramid project is an excellent experiment in nondestructive archaeological techniques, which could be applied to Maya tombs, Chinese structures, and other sites as an alternative to excavation.

*Beneath the Île de la Cité in the heart of ancient Paris—and racing against the construction of an underground garage—archaeologists uncovered artifacts from as far back as the third century. Among the more puzzling finds: 40,000 sheep anklebones.*

**Maya Treasure Trove Unearthed.** The ancient Honduran city of Copán yielded fascinating evidence that shed light on the Maya custom of ritual bloodletting. Discovered in March by David Stuart, a sophomore at Princeton University and a recognized expert in Maya hieroglyphs, the find consisted of an unusually well-preserved cache of jade and flint artifacts associated with the dedication of a temple pyramid. According to Stuart and team director William L. Fash, of Northern Illinois University in De Kalb, this temple was dedicated in A.D. 756 by a Maya king called Smoke-Shell. The cache, found in a pot beneath an altar, contained two jade pieces, three flint lance heads, several stingray spines, and a spiny oyster shell coated with a reddish-brown substance. The two jade pieces were heirlooms that can be dated stylistically to the Early Classic Period

*An important carving recently unearthed on the site of a temple pyramid in Copán, Honduras, was this jade figurine dating from the fourth to the seventh century A.D.*

(A.D. 300–600); one was a 7-inch male figure wearing a loincloth and headband; the other, a 10-inch plaque of a Maya god associated with the sun and the jaguar. The spiny oyster shell was perhaps the most exciting discovery because of the reddish-brown substance inside it, perhaps ancient blood drawn by Smoke-Shell himself in an elaborate bloodletting ceremony. Another possibility was that Maya captives were sacrificed with the elaborate flint lance heads and that a still-beating heart was placed in the oyster shell as a ritual offering.

**A Roman Fort in Scotland.** The remains of a first-century Roman fort, discovered in 1979, were excavated to reveal the complete plan of a typical Roman defensive structure. Located about 6 miles southeast of Edinburgh, the site of Elginhaugh was only the third complete Roman fort so far discovered, and the first in Scotland. The excavation, directed by William Hanson of Glasgow University, began in April under the auspices of the Historic Buildings and Monuments division of the Scottish Development Department. The 13-acre site yielded the outline of the fort, major roads represented by stone-lined drains, and the remains of the fort's main timber buildings. All the typical structures were discovered, including the headquarters building (*principia*), the commanding officer's house (*praetorium*), storage buildings, barracks, and defensive ditches. The fort was almost certainly constructed during the governorship of Julius Agricola around A.D. 80, as part of the process of controlling the recently conquered area of lowland Scotland.                                    B.R.

**ARCHITECTURE.** During 1987 new museum buildings stirred public discussion, and the mid-rise office building in the suburbs was establishing itself as an increasingly common fixture on the architectural scene.

**Museums.** The Menil Collection building, which opened in Houston in June, houses works assembled by Dominique de Menil and her late husband, John, and ranging from Cubist and Surrealist paintings to African sculpture and Mediterranean antiquities. Designed by Italian architect Renzo Piano, it is a building that is in essence a "machine" for the perfect lighting and viewing of art. Piano, who is perhaps best known as the architect with Rich-

A "machine" for viewing art: the exterior of the stark, innovative Menil Collection museum in Houston, designed by Renzo Piano.

ard Rogers of the 1977 Centre Pompidou in Paris, designed an elaborate sunlight-control system of ferroconcrete "leaves" suspended from iron trusses in the galleries. These leaves, which protrude beyond the edges of the building, are its only ornament. Combined with simple gray clapboard siding and canvas awnings over conventional windows, they lend the museum the look of a factory. It is this industrial appearance that has generated heated debate between those who believe that a building should reflect its physical function, as the Menil modestly but insistently does, and those who argue for the art in architecture, urging a more monumental expression.

Two museums in London, one completed and the other underway, stirred discussion of a somewhat different order. The Clore Wing of the Tate Gallery, the first major work in that city by British architect James Stirling, demonstrates a kind of "all things to all people" approach to architecture. Like Woody Allen's film character Zelig, the gallery, built to house the J.M.W. Turner collection, changes its appearance to suit its surroundings, which range from the neo-Palladian Tate to a Queen Anne lodge facing the Thames to a 1960's office building at the rear.

The scheduled addition to the National Gallery in London, designed by Venturi Rauch & Scott Brown of Philadelphia, follows a similar strategy, cloaking a well-organized interior with a facade that slips out of one style and into another as it rounds each corner. This so-called contextual architecture, which takes its clues from adjacent buildings, whatever their individual merits, is very much typical of the architecture of the late 1980's. It remained to be seen whether such a method of design, based on association and not on composition, could produce buildings of enduring aesthetic quality. For the moment, however, the National Gallery scheme seemed to have satisfied British critics.

**Suburban Cities.** The biggest newsmakers in architecture, however, were probably not these urban, public buildings but the mid-rise suburban office building. The new dominance of this building type has been attributed to competitive rents, improved telecommunications, and the shift from a manufacturing to a service economy. The suburban office boom has drastically changed the landscape, creating what some authors call "urban villages," or concentrated nodes strung out along interstate highways. The sudden development pressure, which has reached acute proportions in communities such as Princeton, N.J., has forced those hardest hit to institute new, stricter zoning laws. Walnut Creek, Calif., for example, has declared a moratorium on new office construction.

While suburban office parks have long been considered by critics to be architectural graveyards, suburban developers were showing a newfound aesthetic ambition, hiring high-profile firms such as Robert A.M. Stern in New York or Helmut Jahn in Chicago to jazz up what are essentially formulaic boxes built around elevator cores.

**Taxing Architectural Services.** The so-called service tax, adopted by Florida and a few other states, was a source of growing concern to architects and other professionals. Florida's sweeping law required a 5 percent tax on all architectural services supplied to property in the state by local or out-of-state architects. (Services rendered by a Florida architect/engineer outside of the state were tax-exempt, as were the services of design consultants.) The law proved so controversial that it was rescinded late in the year. Other states were nevertheless watching Florida's experience closely to determine if such service taxes are a viable source of income.

**Prizes.** Japanese architect Kenzo Tange won the Pritzker Prize, the most prestigious award in architecture. The septuagenarian Tange is an elder statesman, revered not only for his own work but for his influence on younger Japanese architects such as Fumihiko Maki and Arata Isosaki. Tange is perhaps best known for his 1964 Olympic Complex in Tokyo. Late in 1986, his firm won the competition to design the new Tokyo city hall.

Architects Benjamin Thompson and Associates of Boston won the Firm Award of the American Institute of Architects. Thompson made his mark with urban malls, such as Quincy Marketplace in Boston and Harborplace in Baltimore.

**Obituary.** Critic Henry-Russell Hitchcock died in February at the age of 83. Co-author with Philip Johnson of the International Style, Hitchcock has been credited with introducing modernism to the United States in the 1930's. His own predilections as historian and critic, however, were far more eclectic, and the standards he set for architectural scholarship have remained the guidelines for succeeding generations of American architectural historians.

**Le Corbusier Remembered.** Celebrations and exhibitions were organized from London to Boston to Chandigarh, India, to mark the 100th anniversary of the birth of Le Corbusier, the celebrated French architect and "hero" of the modern movement, who died in 1965. Born at La Chaux-de-Fonds, Switzerland, on October 6, 1887, Charles-Édouard Jeanneret assumed the name Le Corbusier after moving to France as a young man.                    D.D.B.

**ARGENTINA.** The administration of President Raúl Alfonsín was beset by political and economic problems in 1987. Human rights trials resulting from the 1970's "dirty war" on alleged leftists by the military dictatorship continued to occupy the nation's attention.

**Human Rights.** In June, Congress passed legislation barring the trial of military officers who had been "following orders"—after extending the exemption to include not only junior officers (as proposed by Alfonsín) but also colonels and generals not involved in actually planning the dirty war. This legislation reduced the number of officers subject to trial to under 50. The "due obedience" law angered human rights groups, and public opinion polls showed that a majority of Argentines favored continued prosecutions in cases related to torture and disappearances.

**The Military.** The military, meanwhile, remained uneasy with the notion of any further trials, and in April, uprisings of some 400 officers and soldiers took place at several bases. After the Army refused to repress the mutiny, Alfonsín personally negotiated an end to it. Huge rallies indicated massive public support for him, and nine of the ten top generals were retired after the incident.

Plans were developed to use volunteer paid soldiers on an experimental basis, sell off military property, and establish greater civilian control over the intelligence services. Sixteen bomb attacks against offices of the ruling Radical Party on June 25 were linked to disgruntled intelligence personnel. Meanwhile, by 1987 the Army and Navy had been reduced to only about one-third their 1983 size.

**Economy.** Both industry and agriculture lagged, with total growth falling to 2 percent. Floods destroyed about 12 million acres of food crops, damaging grain export levels already hurt by low world prices. In the depressed auto industry, Ford and Volkswagen joined to form Autolatina, Latin America's biggest auto company. Shortfalls in domestic oil production made Argentina a net oil importer, and the foreign debt grew to more than $50 billion; creditor banks agreed to reschedule about $30 billion of this amount over 19 years.

The major economic problems continued to be inflation and lagging wages. A one-day strike was held on January 26 to protest wage levels; in all, there were 683 strikes or other work stoppages in the 12 months ending in August 1987. Inflation, at astronomical levels in 1984 and 1985, was cut to about 80 percent for 1986 by the Austral Plan, which froze prices and wages. When the controls were relaxed, inflation crept up again—to 136 percent for the 12-month period ending in August 1987. New measures announced in July hiked prices for transportation and various fuels, but wage and price freezes were announced in mid-October, after wages were raised and the currency was devalued significantly. At the end of the year the International Monetary Fund gave Argentina renewed access to some $224 million of a new $1.4 billion loan program, which the IMF had shut down in October because of Argentina's failure to meet performance criteria. The agreement also saved a $500 million loan necessary to keep interest payments current on foreign debt.

**Elections.** All these problems added up to gains for the opposition Peronists in the September 6 congressional and gubernatorial elections. The ruling Radicals actually lost their majority in the lower house, leaving the government partly dependent on other parties for support. After the elections, Alfonsín reshuffled his cabinet and announced plans to seek agreement with opposition parties on specific issues, press for a "practical" solution to the debt crisis, and deregulate some public-sector industries. The president was described as deeply depressed over the election losses.

**Papal Visit.** When Pope John Paul II visited Argentina in April, he defended the country's Roman Catholic bishops against accusations that the church had neglected human rights issues during the 1976–1983 military dictator-

*Rebellious soldiers, angered by trials of military personnel for human rights abuses during the 1970's, took over the Infantry School near Buenos Aires in April. President Raul Alfonsín negotiated an end to the uprising; soon after, a law was passed to exempt some officers from prosecution.*

ship. He also spoke against a pending measure to legalize divorce; it nevertheless won passage in June.

**Foreign Affairs.** As both Britain and Argentina continued to claim jurisdiction over the Falkland Islands, off the coast of Argentina, Argentina expressed concern over fishing rights, claimed by Britain for 150 miles around the islands, effective in February. Argentina greatly resented the British move.

Economic integration with Brazil gathered momentum, as duties on capital goods were eliminated and trade increased. Economic ties also grew with Iran; a $31 million arms sale to Iran was arranged in March, and Argentina also agreed to redesign, and supply fuel for, Iran's experimental nuclear reactor.

*See* STATISTICS OF THE WORLD.     J.F., Jr.

**ARIZONA.** *See* STATISTICS OF THE WORLD.

**ARKANSAS.** *See* STATISTICS OF THE WORLD.

**ART.** Highlights of 1987 included theme shows on abstract art and on contemporary art in Berlin, along with exhibitions devoted to Paul Klee, Oskar Kokoschka, David Salle, and other artists.

**Group Exhibitions.** In California the Los Angeles County Museum of Art inaugurated its Robert O. Anderson building for modern art by presenting a theme show entitled *The Spiritual in Art: Abstract Painting 1890–1985.* The exhibition was an attempt to demonstrate that abstract art directly evolved from spiritual ideas current in Europe in the late 19th and early 20th centuries. In contrast to the standard history of modern art propounded by the Museum of Modern Art, this show focused not on the development of formal aspects of abstraction but on a particular kind of content. The Cézanne-Picasso-Matisse stylistic axis was downplayed in favor of an alternate evolution represented by Kandinsky, Kupka, Malevich, and Mondrian—all of whom were involved in various spiritual movements of their time. The show's organizers extended its theme to include a number of present-day artists such as Jasper Johns, Brice Marden, and Sigmar Polke.

In New York the Museum of Modern Art chronicled the postwar resurgence of Berlin as a major center of contemporary art in an exhibition titled *Berlinart 1961–1987.* The show documented the influence this city has exerted on international art since the early 1960's. On view were works by 55 artists from ten countries in a variety of mediums. The work of two postwar generations of expressionist painters dominated the show, especially the powerful art of Georg Baselitz and his contemporaries, including Markus Lüpertz, K. H. Hödicke, and Bernd Koberling.

*The Age of Correggio and the Carracci,* at the Metropolitan Museum, was a fascinating survey of some 200 late Renaissance and baroque paintings from Emilia, the region around Bologna and Parma in Italy. Another noteworthy exhibition, at New York's Pierpont Morgan Library, was *Raphael and His Circle,* a magnificent collection of drawings by this master of the Italian High Renaissance, his students, and his immediate followers.

*A major traveling exhibit of Ottoman art treasures, The Age of Sultan Süleyman the Magnificent, gave Americans a glimpse of Turkey's heritage. Here, a brilliantly illuminated history shows Sultan Süleyman the Magnificent receiving a vassal during a 16th-century military campaign in Transylvania. Other items included sumptuously decorated textiles, jewel-encrusted metalwork, and art combining calligraphy and painting.*

A fanciful work in oil and black paste on newspaper, mounted on burlap, Paul Klee's Insula Dulcamara (1938) was shown in New York's Museum of Modern Art as part of the first major Klee retrospective in decades.

*The Age of Sultan Süleyman the Magnificent,* a dazzling exhibit of 16th-century Ottoman art, traveled from the National Gallery of Art to the Art Institute of Chicago and the Metropolitan Museum. The exhibit showcased precious objects from the treasure rooms of Istanbul's Topkapi Palace (the sultans' residence that is now a museum) and from other museums.

**Individual Retrospectives.** The Museum of Modern Art's Paul Klee exhibition, its first retrospective on the artist since 1949, was a massive assembly of about 300 paintings, watercolors, prints, and drawings, including 100 works on loan from the Paul Klee Foundation in Bern, Switzerland. The show exhibited the complex variety of theories, ideas, and symbols with which this artist was occupied during his career.

*Oskar Kokoschka: 1886–1980,* a centenary retrospective of the great Viennese expressionist, provided a thorough survey of his work and offered ground for reassessing his contribution to modern art. Organized by London's Tate Gallery, the exhibition of 92 paintings and 91 drawings was held at New York's Solomon R. Guggenheim Museum starting in December 1986. Contrary to the traditional view, much of his later work—especially the portraits and pagan reveries—appear here with startling ripeness and vitality. The raw, scraped surfaces of Kokoschka's early portraits, allegories, and landscapes, of course, retain their power.

Another full-scale retrospective of special interest was devoted to 60 oil paintings by the French impressionist Berthe Morisot, as well as selected pastels, watercolors, and colored pencil drawings from her work. This traveling show, which opened at Washington's National Gallery of Art in September, was primarily organized by the Mount Holyoke College Art Museum in South Hadley, Mass.

The Museum of Modern Art presented *Frank Stella: 1970–1987,* featuring his three-dimensional constructivist painted reliefs. The exhibition presented graphic evidence of the daring risks Stella has taken over the years.

**Contemporary Artists in Midcareer.** The Whitney Museum of American Art, in New York, hosted midcareer surveys of the work of David Salle and of Julian Schnabel, the best-known American stars of the emotional, painterly style known as neo-expressionism. The Salle exhibition, organized by the Institute of Contemporary Art in Philadelphia, included 40-odd major paintings executed from 1979 to 1987 by this highly interesting, if controversial, artist. The Schnabel show was the only American appearance of an exhibition co-organized by the Whitechapel Art Gallery, London, and the Centre Georges Pompidou in Paris. It included 35 large-scale works dating from 1975 to 1987.

The first U.S. museum survey of the German neo-expressionist Anselm Kiefer was organized jointly by the Art Institute of Chicago and the Philadelphia Museum of Art. The show included 70 paintings, woodcuts, watercolors, collages, and book constructions, presenting Kiefer's themes of myth and allegory in monumental landscapes and architectural images. **Shift in Contemporary Art.** The gallery spotlight shifted as neo-expressionism, which dominated art for the first half of the 1980's, was replaced by cooler, more intellectual styles derived in part from the minimalist, pop, and conceptual art movements of the 1970's. Also linked to recent critical ideas created by French philosophical theorists such as Jacques Derrida and Jean Baudrillard, this new art explored the relationship of art to advertising, the mass media, and art history. "Simulationism," "neo-geo," "neo-conceptualism," or "smart art" (no one could agree on a label) was declared the wave of the next year or two at least.

Numerous shows at Soho galleries throughout the year focused on the new style. The Whitney Biennial (the regular survey of new art presented every two years by the Whitney Museum) included three of the new "simulationists" in its selections, as well as new work by older masters of abstraction, minimalism, and conceptualism such as Willem de Kooning, Sol Lewitt, and Joseph Kosuth.

**Museums.** In New York the Lila Acheson Wallace Wing for 20th-century European and American art finally ushered the Metropolitan Museum of Art into the modern world. The new facility contained 22 handsomely proportioned galleries ranging from intimate rooms for small-scale works on paper to palatial chambers for the grandiose canvases of the abstract expressionists. Unfortunately, such splendid galleries only tended to highlight the enormous weaknesses of the Metropolitan's permanent modern art collection.

In Houston, the Menil Collection opened its 100,000-square foot, $30 million building designed by Renzo Piano. This private collection, owned by oil heiress Dominique de Menil, includes antiquities and primitive works, as

**Artist Extraordinaire**

One of the most interesting and controversial painters to emerge from the booming art scene of the 1980's, artist David Salle, at 35, courts comparison with such modern giants as Jasper Johns or Robert Rauschenberg. His paintings sell for as much as $85,000, and in 1987 a major exhibition of his works traveled to important museums across the United States. Salle's large works— often diptychs or triptychs—combine drawing, painting, sculpture, photography, and other media in powerfully orchestrated multiple images that seem to resist interpretation. They glean from art history as freely as from today's pop culture (including news photos, magazine ads, and pornographic pictures). Many critics view the enigmatic art of the Oklahoma-born, California-trained Salle as a perfect metaphor for an age in which all values are confused and fact and illusion seem to be one. Others criticize what appears to be a facile avoidance of meaning. But even Salle's detractors praise the elegance and erudition of his style and cannot fail to take note of his continuing productivity.

*David Salle*

*Vincent van Gogh's vibrantly colored* Irises *was sold for nearly $54 million (including the 10 percent sales commission) by Sotheby's in New York City in November—only eight months after one of the artist's famed "Sunflowers" paintings went for $40 million at a rival auction house in London. The lower figure was itself three times the highest price ever before paid at auction for a work of art.*

well as masterworks, of the 20th century. Long acclaimed for its uncompromising quality, the collection now could be housed in a facility of equal architectural merit. The two-story structure, sheathed in gray cypress planks, exhibits a careful selection from the permanent collection on the first floor, while presenting the remainder upstairs, hung salon-fashion on crowded walls, to be seen by appointment only. The simple elegance of the building's exterior disguises a majestic interior with a complex and revolutionary lighting design.

In September the Smithsonian Institution in Washington, D.C., simultaneously inaugurated two new facilities in its underground project on the Mall. The Museum of African Art provided a new home for the Smithsonian's collection of 6,000 African art objects. The Arthur M. Sackler Gallery for Asian and Near Eastern art also opened, with exhibitions displaying 1,000 objects of Chinese, Middle Eastern, and South and Southeast Asian art, donated by Sackler to form the core collection.

In April, the Metropolitan Museum in New York opened its Sackler Galleries for Asian Art. The ten galleries were devoted to Japanese art and artifacts from prehistory to the 19th century. New galleries for Chinese art were expected to open there in 1988. The Met also broke ground for yet another wing, the last in its master plan of expansion, this one dedicated to European sculpture and decorative arts.

# ART

**Restoration.** The ongoing restoration of Michelangelo's 16th-century frescoes in the Sistine Chapel at the Vatican became a subject of intense controversy. Objections by critics focused on two points: whether the Italian Renaissance artist's work was being altered by the cleaning solvent used and whether the frescoes were being exposed to damage after cleaning. In response to criticism from American scholars in particular, the Vatican invited a group of conservators, including top officials from several U.S. museums, to examine progress in the restoration firsthand. The conservators ultimately gave the Vatican unanimous support for its diagnosis of the frescoes' condition and its method of restoring them.

*Andy Warhol, dead at 58, was best known for works like the Campbell's soup can paintings of pop-art fame, which made Americans take a second look at the relationship between their popular culture and art. Warhol's range was wide, from filmmaking to serving as nucleus for the avant-garde artists and actors who gathered at his studio, "the Factory," in New York City.*

**Art Market.** In November, Vincent van Gogh's painting *Irises* was sold at Sotheby's in New York for $53.9 million (including the auction house's 10 percent commission) to an unidentified collector. This was the highest price ever paid at auction for an artwork and $14 million over the previous record of $39.9 million, set in March at Christie's in London for one of van Gogh's "Sunflower" paintings. In September, Sotheby's auction house had announced a record worldwide sales total of $1.3 billion for the 1986–1987 season ending August 31. This represented an 85 percent increase over its international sales for the preceding year. Christie's announced total sales of $954.6 million.

Economic and cultural factors continued to fuel the art market. Art collecting often served as a trendy activity for American businessmen who had accumulated riches in the booming stock market. In addition, the decline of the dollar against other currencies made acquisitions increasingly attractive to European, and especially Japanese, collectors. Art investment specialists reported that Japanese collectors were buying more works in the field of contemporary art, as well as in French impressionism.

**Deaths.** Andy Warhol, 58, the pop-art superstar world-famous for his paintings and prints of soup cans, movie stars, and other icons of American culture, died suddenly in New York in February of a heart attack, following routine gallbladder surgery.

Arthur M. Sackler, 73, research psychiatrist, entrepreneur, and philanthropist, died in May. Sackler was the principal donor of the museum at Harvard University bearing his name, which opened two years ago, as well as chief donor of a new museum at the Smithsonian Institution and of new Asian art galleries at the Metropolitan Museum. B.B.S.

**ASTRONOMY.** The astronomical event of 1987, and perhaps of the century, was the discovery of a supernova, a bright exploding star, in the Large Magellanic Cloud—a companion galaxy of the Milky Way, lying much closer to us than galaxies where supernovas have been discovered in the past. There also was evidence that galaxies in our region of space are being pulled away toward a distant sea of galaxies in the southern sky and that objects, possibly planets, are circling some nearby stars.

**Supernova.** The newly observed supernova was actually visible to the naked eye, though only from locations near and south of the equator. For astronomers it was the chance of a lifetime, as the last supernova so visible appeared in 1604, before Galileo first turned his telescope to the sky. Since then scientists have been limited to observing far-distant, faint-appearing supernovas.

The supernova, officially called SN 1987A, was a variety known as Type II, in which a star perhaps 15 to 20 times more massive than the sun blows up, most likely leaving a tiny, dense neutron star behind as a remnant. When a star becomes a supernova, it expels heavy elements that have been produced in its core, making these substances available for subsequent generations of objects. The iron in our blood, for example, may have been liberated from the center of a long-vanished star by a supernova explosion more than 5 million years ago. Further, our sun and its solar system may owe their very existence to one of these outbursts, which play an important role in triggering star formation.

SN 1987A was discovered on February 24 by Ian Shelton, a Canadian astronomer assigned by the University of Toronto to its southern station at the Carnegie Institution's Las Campanas Observatory in Chile. He noticed it as an unexpected bright star on a new routine photograph of the Large Magellanic Cloud. When the news of the discovery spread, observatories throughout the southern hemisphere were thrown into a frenzy of activity.

The supernova had brightened by a factor of several hundred in the few hours before its discovery but then remained constant for several weeks, just nicely visible to the unaided eye in a clear dark sky. In March, SN 1987A began a slow, steady rise in luminosity, and by late May it had an apparent brightness about that of a Big Dipper star. (At its brightest, the new star actually shone brighter than 100 million suns.) It then began dimming slowly. This complicated behavior was unique among known supernovas. SN 1987A's unusual brightening after the first few weeks was probably powered by the radioactive decay of unstable elements produced at the instant of the explosion or by a rapidly rotating neutron star (pulsar) left behind at the center of the blast. Both causes may have been operating together.

SN 1987A was in fact unusual in many respects. Its most unexpected feature was that it occurred in a hot, blue supergiant star, rather than the larger, cooler red variety previously considered the most likely candidate for such supernovas. The "host" star of the explosion had been catalogued by astronomers a century ago and had evidently shone steadily since then, giving no hint of the fireworks to come. The host's smaller than expected size may account for some of SN 1987A's peculiarities; for example, the supernova changed rapidly at first. Its color turned quickly from white to a rich red as its "surface" temperature plunged in the first few weeks.

**Neutrinos From the Supernova.** The most significant news about the supernova was the detection of neutrinos from the very center of the blast. Enormous numbers of these elusive subatomic particles were produced in the stellar core when it was hottest and densest; in fact, they carried away 99 percent of the explosion energy. Neutrinos can pass freely through enormous thicknesses of matter, and so they escaped from the supernova, bringing astronomers information about conditions at its very heart. But neutrinos' ability to pass largely unimpeded through matter means that these particles are very difficult to observe.

Huge underground detectors in Japan and under Lake Erie caught a combined total of 19 neutrinos over several seconds, starting at 7 hours, 35 minutes, 35 seconds Greenwich time on February 23. This means the actual explosion occurred about 160,000 years earlier—the approximate length of time it would have taken the neutrinos to reach us, traveling at or near the speed of light. The particles' energies indicated that when they escaped, the star's center had a temperature of perhaps nearly 400 billion degrees Fahrenheit. The few supernova neutrinos that were detected represented a tiny fraction of the huge number, some 10 billion, passing through every square centimeter of the Earth—including us, of course—during the few seconds of the neutrino blast.

*Discovering a "naked-eye" supernova made Ian Shelton (right, with his 24-inch telescope) something of a celebrity in scientific circles. Shelton, a Canadian astronomer working in Chile, first noticed the brightest exploding star in nearly 400 years on a routine photograph of the Large Magellanic Cloud. The star was visible only from below the equator.*

**The Great Attractor.** Evidence accumulated during the year to suggest that all the galaxies in our region of space are being pulled toward an enormous concentration of galaxies some 150 million to 300 million light-years away. Much of this grouping is obscured from view by dust in the central plane of the Milky Way. Studies now underway should reveal more about this vast assembly, which contains the mass of more than 10 quadrillion suns.

**Faraway Quasars.** During the year, two quasars a much greater distance from earth than any previously known celestial objects were discovered by a team of British and American astronomers. One of them was 12 billion light-years away. The discoveries were made largely by using improved methods for examining photographic plates. Recent research also indicates that quasars may be found at such great distances more frequently than previously thought.

**Other Jupiters?** A group of Canadian astronomers reported at midyear that they may have detected objects—possibly planets—circling seven nearby stars. The masses of the bodies are no more than eight or ten times that of Jupiter. Bruce Campbell of the Dominion Astrophysical Observatory and colleagues had studied 16 nearby stars from 1981 to 1987. Seven showed variable Doppler shifts in their spectra (changes in the frequency of observed light waves), possibly caused by the gravitational effects of planetary companions. The Canadian study found no evidence of "brown dwarfs," bodies with masses between those of Jupiter-size objects and the faintest known stars. This suggests that there may be a true gap between the masses of planets and of stars.

**Super Telescope.** In December a consortium of European nations agreed to spend about $235 million over 12 years to construct the world's most powerful land-based telescope. The so-called Very Large Telescope would use four mirrors with a total light-gathering power of one mirror 16 meters in diameter and would be built in northern Chile, where conditions for observation are excellent.                R.A.S.

**AUSTRALIA.** Encouraged by disarray in the opposition, Labor Party Prime Minister Bob Hawke (see biography in PEOPLE IN THE NEWS) called an early election in July, eight months before his term was scheduled to expire, and won a third term, with increased parliamentary backing.

**Conservative Infighting.** Sir Johannes Bjelke-Petersen, the National Party premier of Queensland, had made a bid for national leadership early in the year. He demanded that his party's representatives in the federal Parliament pull out of the Liberal-National coalition (which forms the opposition to Hawke's government), proposed a plan for a flat-rate income tax, and spoke of aspirations to become prime minister. His campaign rapidly produced bitterness within the conservative parties. In February, when the National Party in Queensland ordered the state's 12 representatives in the federal Parliament to quit the coalition, federal opposition and Liberal Party leader John Howard claimed the premier was on "a manic power kick."

The first challenge to Sir Joh came when Steve Hatton, chief minister of the Northern Territory, called a snap election in the territory for March 7. Although Hatton's Country-Liberal Party was affiliated federally with the National Party, this did not stop Queensland activists from setting up a National Party organization in the territory with the avowed intention of taking over. But the new party failed resoundingly. On April 4 the Queensland members were authoritatively ordered out of the federal coalition. A week later, after negotiating with Howard, Ian Sinclair, the federal National Party leader, agreed to isolate the Queenslanders from the remainder of his parliamentary party. When Sinclair later attempted to compromise on this deal, Howard responded by announcing the end of the Liberal-National coalition.

The Liberals, too, were suffering from internal conflicts as Howard was forced, partly by Sir Joh's pressure, to abandon his broad-based consumption tax plans. Within the party, his conservative "dry" position aroused opposition from "small-l" or "wet," Liberals.

**Early Election.** At first, Hawke deflated rumors of an early election, but at the end of May he reversed himself and called for an election on July 11. His announcement caught opposition forces off guard. Sir Joh, already having difficulty attracting high-profile candidates to his Joh Nationals ticket, conceded that "time has beaten me," and he renounced plans to run for the federal Parliament. (He later announced he would retire as state premier in 1988.) Liberal leader Howard, who had vowed to campaign on taxation, was caught short, finding himself without a tax policy. When he did unveil one in mid-June, he was further embarrassed by discrepancies it contained.

Hawke's party won 86 seats in the 148-seat House of Representatives, up from 82. The Liberal Party held 43 (a loss of 2 seats), while the National Party held 19 (also a loss of 2). Labor did suffer a slight loss in the Senate, taking 32 out of 76 seats (down 2); Liberals won 27 of the remaining Senate seats.

**Aftermath.** Soon after the election, the Liberal Party confirmed Howard as its leader and elected Andrew Peacock, whom Howard had

*Prime Minister Bob Hawke (shown with his wife, Hazel) benefited from a divided opposition as he led his Australian Labor Party to an election victory, securing his third straight term.*

# AUSTRALIA

## Aussie at the Bat

They may be more familiar with the outback than the outfield, with Canberra than with Yogi Berra, with kookaburras than with the Cardinals, but Australians are showing that they too can play what Americans fondly think of as the greatest game ever invented. Baseball, long seen down under as a game for wimps who couldn't play cricket, is now a big hit there. A good 100,000 baseball players are registered with the Australian Sports Commission, and the Claxton Shield, Australia's equivalent of the World Series, has begun drawing crowds of several thousand spectators. Teams like the Queensland Rams, the Western Australia Brewers, and the Victoria Vics vie for victory. Meanwhile, major league scouts from the United States have signed several Australian prospects; one, shortstop Craig Shipley, played for the Los Angeles Dodgers for parts of the 1986 and 1987 seasons.

deposed in 1985, as his deputy. The opposition coalition with the Nationals was reestablished.

Hawke, who had campaigned on a promise to cut spending, lost no time in launching a major overhaul of the federal bureaucracy. Three days after the election, he announced the reduction of public service departments from 28 to 16 and an increase in the number of ministers from 27 to 30 by creating several new positions known as minister-assisting—a procedure hitherto thought unconstitutional. Within a short time, Hawke called for a debate on possible privatization of government enterprises. He also asked for a review of the distribution of powers and of finances within the Australian federal system. Late in the year, agreement was reached to privatize two government airlines by 1990.

In another new initiative, Hawke proposed a "compact of understanding" between Aboriginal Australians and the majority community when he visited the Northern Territory in September. The proposal—which followed an eight-

Ships reenacting the voyage of the First Fleet to Australia weigh anchor from Portsmouth, England, on May 13, bound for Sydney.

year campaign by Aboriginal groups for a "treaty," or "Makarata," recognizing injustices done to them—caused immediate controversy on all sides.

**Bicentennial.** Preparations continued for the Australian bicentennial in 1988. The plans—more than five years in the making—were particularly elaborate in Sydney, New South Wales, where the so-called First Fleet bearing convicts from Britain had arrived on January 26, 1788. Exactly 200 years later, another fleet from Portsmouth, England, was scheduled to arrive in Sydney Harbor. In July a controversy arose when this "reenactment" First Fleet, put together by a private company with federal and state sponsorship, arrived in Rio de Janeiro on its way to Australia and announced that it needed extensive funding before it could proceed. The Australian Bicentennial Authority was reluctant to oblige. A commercial radio appeal in Sydney raised most of the money, and the fleet continued its voyage.

**The Economy.** The trade deficit for the fiscal year ending June 30 was considerably lower than projected, in part because of improved commodity prices. The proportion of manufactured goods exported rose to about 21 percent of exports. The Australian dollar hovered around 70 U.S. cents, as the Reserve Bank sought to prevent a decline that would add to the foreign debt of US$110 billion at midyear. In September a virtually balanced budget was introduced for 1988.

In January coal-mining companies agreed to reductions of 10 percent in both price and export volume to Japan. The agreement led to the closing of some mines.

**Media Shakeout.** In January, Australian-born Rupert Murdoch (now a U.S. citizen), chief executive of the multinational News International Corporation, purchased Australia's largest media group, the Herald and Weekly Times Ltd. No sooner had he clinched the deal than he began a massive restructuring of Australia's media, which left him in control of about 70 percent of all capital-city newspaper circulation. Subsequently, the country's longest-established television network, the Packer group, was sold to Western Australian brewing, mining, and real-estate tycoon Alan Bond. Also, the Fairfax media group sold all its television

### The Ultimate Weapon

In the escalating war between swimmers and jellyfish, waged summer after summer on the world's beaches, jellyfish may seem to have succeeded in gaining the upper tentacle. Efforts to keep them out, through underwater nets and other devices, have failed dismally. But according to *Discover* magazine, resourceful lifeguards in parts of Australia have developed a new way to defend themselves: pantyhose. Before braving the deep, these hardy souls put on two pairs—one, preferably extra-queen-sized worn upside down over the head, with a hole cut out in the crotch; the other right-side up. The feet are cut off at both ends to keep the outfit from filling up with water. Pantyhose may not do much for the lifeguard image, but, since the Australian jellyfish's stingers are too short to go through the fabric, it does offer protection. And in the waters of northern and northeastern Australia, where deadly varieties of box jellyfish, or sea wasps, can kill with their sting within minutes, this is no laughing matter.

interests, and they became the basis of a new east coast network.

**America's Cup.** Australia's hold on the America's Cup it captured in 1983 proved short-lived, as *Kookaburra III* failed in its defense of the Cup, losing to the U.S. challenger, *Stars & Stripes*, in February. All Australia had been seized with yachting fever, and the defense of the Cup, in Fremantle, Western Australia, was the sporting event of the year.

**Cricket.** In November the cricket World Cup was played in India and Pakistan, outside England for the first time. Australia emerged as the unexpected victor. In a tightly played final match in Calcutta, Allan Border led his team to a seven-run victory over England.

*See* STATISTICS OF THE WORLD.          B.J.

**AUSTRIA.** On January 21, 1987, after lengthy negotiations following November 1986 elections, a coalition government headed by Socialist Chancellor Franz Vranitzky took office in Austria. The second party in the coalition was the People's Party, whose leader, Alois Mack, became vice-chancellor and foreign minister.

The new government announced policy goals which included a reduction of the budget deficit from 5.4 percent of gross domestic product to 2.5 percent by 1992, tax reform designed to reduce rates in the upper brackets, reorganization of state railroads, and partial privatization of selected state-owned industries. The program drew criticism from former Chancellor Bruno Kreisky, who resigned as honorary chairman of the Socialist Party, protesting his party's relinquishment of the Foreign Ministry to the People's Party.

Meanwhile, there was continued controversy over the alleged involvement of President Kurt Waldheim in Nazi atrocities during World War II. (He had been elected to the largely ceremonial post in June 1986, despite such charges.) In April the U.S. Justice Department announced it had placed Waldheim on a "watch list" of 40,000 "undesirables" to be excluded from the United States. In response, Austria recalled its U.S. ambassador. Later, Chancellor Vranitzky paid an official visit to the United States, where he unsuccessfully urged officials to suspend the ban on Waldheim for as long as Waldheim remained president. (Despite this effort on behalf of Waldheim, Vranitzky, and other politicians, also appeared to be attempting to distance themselves from him.) In June, Pope John Paul II, responding to repeated requests by the Austrian government, granted Waldheim a private audience at the Vatican, where he praised his work as UN secretary-general and made no mention of his World War II record. The visit marked Waldheim's first official trip abroad as president. Subsequently, he was invited to several Muslim countries.

See Statistics of the World.          J.O.S.

**AUTOMOBILE INDUSTRY.** Automakers had their third-best sales year, but suffered declines from record sales the previous model year.

**Sales.** U.S. and foreign producers sold 10.5 million cars and 4.9 million trucks in the United States during the automobile industry's 1987 model year. The combined total was 3.7 percent below that of 1986—though it still made 1987 the third-best sales year ever. Imported cars accounted for a record 30.3 percent of the U.S. market. Ford, the sole U.S. automaker to improve on its 1986 performance, sold 2.07 million cars domestically, up 5.5 percent and good for 19.6 percent of the market. General Motors sold 3.7 million cars (35.3 percent of the market), down 18.3 percent from 1986. Chrysler, including sales of newly acquired American Motors, delivered 1.01 million cars, down 17.7 percent and amounting to 9.6 percent of the market. Volkswagen sales were down 20.5 percent, and the company announced plans to close its U.S. assembly plant.

Ford had the year's best-seller, the F Series pickup, as well as the two top-selling cars, the Escort and Taurus. Of the top ten cars, four were foreign—the Accord, Civic, Sentra, and Excel. GM's sales dive was mainly at the expense of its larger, more profitable cars—the Cadillac Seville and Eldorado, Buick Riviera, and Oldsmobile Toronado.

**New Models.** For the 1988 model year, GM introduced only one new model, the front-drive Buick Regal, a family coupe with conventional styling—to be joined by the Pontiac Grand Prix and Olds Cutlass Supreme later in the model year. Chrysler launched the Chrysler New Yorker and Dodge Dynasty. American Motors, now owned by Chrysler, launched its Premier. Ford unveiled a well-styled, front-drive Lincoln Continental.

**Prices, Warranties.** U.S. automakers, benefiting from the low U.S. inflation rates of recent years, raised prices only modestly. Japanese and West German automakers, on the other hand, boosted prices on their cars sold in the United States every few months, reflecting the dollar's fall in value against the yen and the mark, although less than would be required to fully make up for currency exchange rate changes, thereby retaining market share.

On the warranty front, GM and Ford extended the power train guarantees on their North American-made cars to 6 years/60,000 miles, only to see Chrysler push power train warranties to 7 years/70,000 miles, the longest warranty of any domestic manufacturer. Chrysler also matched Cadillac Allanté and several European luxury models by offering a complete-coverage warranty of 5 years/50,000 miles on its three top-of-the-line models.

**Government Regulations and Ratings.** The U.S. Department of Transportation gave automakers until the 1994 model year to install air bags or

Tom Borch, a paint repair specialist at the Ford Motor Company's plant in Wixom, Mich., holds up one of 160,000 profit-sharing checks, with an average value of $2,100, that the company distributed to eligible employees in March.

automatic belts on the front-seat passenger side of their cars. Chevrolet's Japanese-made Sprint headed the U.S. Environmental Protection Agency's fuel economy ratings for the 1988 model year, getting 54 miles per gallon in city driving. The next most fuel-efficient cars were the Honda Civic CRX HF, 50 mpg; Ford Festiva, 38; and Isuzu I-Mark, Chevrolet Spectrum, and Subaru Justy, all at 37.

**Consumer Relations.** Perhaps the most sales-damaging safety problem in U.S. auto history was experienced by Audi of America. Critics contended that sudden and unexplained accelerations by Audi models contributed to hundreds of accidents, resulting in several deaths and hundreds of injuries. Audi in January recalled 250,000 of its 5000 series cars from the 1978–1986 model years. But the company's solution—a special locking device for the automatic transmission gear shifter—was scorned by critics.

In June a division of Chrysler and two company executives were indicted by a federal grand jury for selling as new more than 60,000 vehicles that had been driven up to 400 test miles (the odometers were disconnected or later replaced), and also for selling as just-off-the-line 40 cars that had been damaged, then repaired, after test drives. Under a settlement late in the year the company pleaded no contest to odometer tampering and agreed to pay $16 million in civil damages to settle charges it had sold as new cars that had been test driven with odometers disconnected. Criminal charges were dropped against the two executives.

**U.S. Developments.** U.S. automakers continued to acquire other firms. Chrysler bought American Motors, which had been almost half owned by France's Renault, for $1.2 billion. The chief assets of American Motors were its Jeep, one of the world's best-known nameplates, and a state-of-the-art Canadian plant. Chrysler also bought Electrospace Systems, a supplier of military electronics equipment, for $367 million, and Italy's prestigious Lamborghini, price undisclosed. Ford bought, for an estimated $20 million, Britain's Aston Martin Lagonda, Ltd., as well as United States Leasing International, which leases autos, aircraft, railroad equipment, and electronic hardware, for $512 million.

On September 29, Henry Ford II, grandson of the Ford Motor Company's founder and head of the firm from 1945 to 1979, died in

Detroit. Ford, 70, lived to see his company become the most profitable U.S. automaker ($3.3 billion in sales for 1986) for the first time since 1924.

**Globalization.** Automakers were entering or reentering markets around the world. Chrysler and Ford planned to resume exporting cars to Europe, Ford also to Japan. Chrysler will ship five models to Europe; Ford will offer eight American-made models through 84 Swedish dealers who presently sell European-built Fords. Honda planned to export its Ohio-made Accord to Taiwan, and Mazda and Mitsubishi contemplated the export of American-made vehicles to Japan. The Soviet Union announced plans to export to the United States in 1991 a front-wheel-drive four-door hatchback. Malcolm Bricklin's Global Motors, parent of Yugo America, announced plans to secure U.S. distribution rights for the Feeling subcompact engineered by Nissan and made by Taiwanese automaker Yue Loong. Global also planned to import the Mitsubishi-designed, Malaysian-built Proton. The Chinese government authorized its Second Automotive Works to join with a foreign producer to build 300,000 passenger cars annually.

Japanese firms increased their exports to Europe, raising the ire of that continent's automakers. Meanwhile, foreign producers have penetrated approximately 3 percent of the Japanese home market. South Korea cautiously lifted auto import restrictions, but outsiders had few illusions as to their chances for substantial sales. Because of a 50 percent tariff and a laundry list of excise, defense, and value-added taxes, a Ford Taurus listing for $11,000 in the United States was priced at $42,000.   D.L.L.

# B

**BANGLADESH.** In 1987, President H. M. Ershad had to contend with stepped-up rioting by opposition parties, a weak economy, and catastrophic floods that took more than 1,000 lives according to official estimates.

When Parliament opened on January 24, the eight-party opposition alliance headed by Sheikh Hasina Wazed, daughter of the late Sheikh Mujibur Rahman, first president of Bangladesh, staged a walkout. The alliance contended that since most of the opposition had boycotted the October 1986 presidential election, Ershad, who came to power in a 1982 military coup and sought to legitimatize his rule in 1986, was nothing more than a "self-proclaimed" president. The seven-party alliance led by Begum Khaleda Zia, widow of the late President Ziaur Rahman, staged a violence-marked demonstration in central Dacca (Dhaka) against both Ershad and the Wazed-led group.

In midsummer Parliament passed the Local Government Amendment Bill, which would permit Army representation in the country's 64 district councils. Opposition parties, spearheaded by Wazed, launched antigovernment rallies and work stoppages, claiming the law would allow the Army to expand its alleged diversion of development funds. A general strike in late July, called by Wazed and supported by the Zia faction, paralyzed the country for 54 hours. A number of demonstrators were killed or wounded when they attacked the headquarters of the ruling Jatiya Party.

Added support for the July strike came from public resentment of the government's recent budget cutbacks and price increases, brought on in part by pressure from international lending institutions. Foreign aid continued to bring $1.4 billion annually to the Bangladesh economy, which was hurt by a 15 percent cut in development spending, disappointing industrial growth, and falling prices for jute exports. Food production kept slightly ahead of the 2.6 percent growth in population.

In October, Wazed and Zia agreed to a coordinated series of strikes and roadblocks leading up to a "siege" of Dacca the following month. During the so-called siege, rioters burned cars and buildings, threw bricks and home-made bombs, and clashed with police. Several rioters were killed, and over 1,000 activists were arrested. Wazed and Zia, who called for the government's ouster, were placed under house arrest for a time. In late November the president declared a state of emergency, but protests continued. On December 6, his government dissolved Parliament; new elections were promised for early 1988.

In the summer, Bangladesh was devastated by what were described as the worst floods in 70 years. According to official estimates, the floods killed at least 1,600 people, rendered 5 million homeless, and caused $1.5 billion in damage. The opposition accused the government of mismanagement and demanded its resignation. Disastrous floods in 1970 and 1984 had led to previous political upheavals.

See STATISTICS OF THE WORLD.          R.P.C.

**BANKING AND FINANCE.** In October 1987, Wall Street experienced a worse crash than the one that rocked the nation in 1929. Stock markets in Europe and Asia plunged as well. Earlier in the year, a sharp decline in the value of the dollar against other currencies had finally begun to produce stronger earnings for many American companies, by making U.S. exports more competitive. Investors responded by bidding up U.S. stock prices to record highs. At the same time, however, the falling dollar rekindled fears of inflation. Interest rates rose, producing periods of havoc in the bond market and later contributing to the stock market plunge. Meanwhile, Third World nations continued to be plagued by debt repayment problems.

**The Falling Dollar.** Concern over the falling dollar first became acute in the spring. In late February an agreement was reached among the finance ministers of the United States, Canada, Japan, Britain, France, and West Germany to try to keep major currencies trading at close to their current levels. A dollar was

As the stock market crashed on October 19, bringing the Dow Jones Industrial Average down by a breathtaking 508 points, Terrence J. McManus, a trading specialist on the floor of the New York Stock Exchange, wordlessly summed up the mood among investors.

then worth 153 yen and 1.83 West German marks. Soon after, West Germany agreed to accelerate a tax cut and Japan announced increases in government spending; however, traders were not convinced that the actions would stimulate these countries' economies sufficiently to achieve currency stability.

Currency markets were further shaken when the United States, in April, imposed 100 percent tariffs on selected Japanese electronics products. The dollar plunged, renewing investors' fears of inflation, which began running at an annual rate of about 5 percent. Higher oil prices were a factor in the inflation.

Inflationary fears disturbed investors, who began to demand higher returns on U.S. securities. Yields on 30-year Treasury bonds rose more than a full percentage point, to around 8.6 percent, by the end of April. At that time, the dollar hit a postwar low against the yen of 137 yen to the dollar and also fell below 1.80 marks.

Market sentiment improved when the U.S. Commerce Department reported that the U.S. gross national product had grown at an annual rate of 4.4 percent during the first quarter. There was optimism about the U.S. trade def-

icit, and currency markets enjoyed a period of calm through much of the summer, as the dollar rebounded to close to its late February level. However, in August, with the news that the U.S. trade deficit for June was a record $15.7 billion, the dollar lost 7 percent of its value, plunging to 141.9 yen in a few days.

In September it was announced that the trade deficit for July had surged to a new record of $16.5 billion. By late September, when officials from 151 member nations convened in Washington for the joint annual meeting of the World Bank and the International Monetary Fund, the dollar's value was around 144 yen and 1.8 marks. After the dramatic stock market decline in October, the dollar fell to new record lows against the yen and the mark. In mid-November, the central banks of West Germany, the Netherlands, and France announced coordinated reductions in key interest rates, in another effort to spur their economies and help stabilize the dollar. However, in December, after word that the U.S. trade deficit for October had soared to a record $17.6 billion, the dollar plunged to new postwar record lows. Despite a December 22 pledge by major Western industrial nations to cooperate in stemming the decline, the dollar fell to below 1.6 marks and under 121 yen by year's end.

**Interest Rates.** Inflation fears, combined with growing protectionist sentiment, put upward pressure on U.S. interest rates during the year. In March, for the first time in three years, the prime rate rose by one-quarter of a percentage point, to 7.75 percent. Twice in May major banks raised their prime lending rates again, to 8 percent and then to 8.25 percent.

The specter of rising interest rates triggered one of the severest collapses in the bond market in recent memory. Merrill Lynch & Company announced it had lost some $370 million in bond-trading problems in April. Other large Wall Street firms reported $100-million-plus losses during the spring.

In September leading U.S. banks raised the prime rate to 8.75 percent when the Federal Reserve Board raised the discount rate—the rate charged by the Fed on loans to financial institutions—from 5.5 to 6 percent. The discount rate rise, the first in three years, was viewed as an anti-inflation move. In October

---

### Camp for Young Tycoons

It seems that swimming, baseball, and bug juice just aren't enough to lure some kids to summer camp anymore; they would rather play around with stocks, bonds, and mutual funds. Catering to these fledgling capitalists, two employees at the Shearson Lehman Brothers investment firm created the first money management camp for youngsters aged 10 to 15 years. The five-day summer sessions, held in various Florida hotels and entitled Dollars and Sense, combine theory with hands-on experience: besides being briefed about stocks and bonds and learning to decipher the *Wall Street Journal*, each camper puts together a $100 portfolio, the cost of which is included in the $500 enrollment fee. According to the camp directors, shares in Reebok and Coca-Cola are favorites among the young investors, and the first crop of campers, from the summer of 1986, created their own mutual fund. At least prior to October, it was doing quite well.

**New Fed Chairman**

A few weeks after assuming the post in August, Federal Reserve Board chairman Alan Greenspan pushed through a half-point increase in the discount rate, the interest rate the Fed charges banks for borrowing, to combat inflation and boost a declining dollar. After the stock market drop in October, he quickly moved to discourage a recession by encouraging lower interest rates and making more cash available to the nation's financial system. Decisiveness is vital to a Fed chairman, since financial markets dislike uncertainty in any form. From all indications, Greenspan, 61, has shown he has the right stuff. Before entering government he made his fortune as an economic consultant. Later, as chairman of President Gerald Ford's Council of Economic Advisers, he managed the economy through the 1975 recession. In 1983, as chairman of a national commission, he helped forge a plan to shore up the social security system. Regarded as a pragmatic conservative, he impresses assistants with his quick grasp of numbers and trends. One former Carter administration economist called Greenspan "the best nuts and bolts economist in America."

*Alan Greenspan*

the prime rate was raised to 9.25 percent, and then by a few banks to 9.75 percent, before the stock market plunge resulted in a reduction to 9 percent. A further cut, to 8.75 percent, came in early November.

**Stock Market.** For much of the year, the stock market bounded from one record high to another. The Dow Jones Industrial Average, which hovered at around 1,900 at the beginning of the year, had risen more than 800 points, or about 41 percent, by August—its strongest performance in over 50 years.

Several forces combined to propel stock prices upward. In response to years of takeover threats by corporate raiders, many U.S. companies had restructured their balance sheets and reduced inefficiencies. The decline in the dollar offered an extra boost by making American products more competitive in overseas markets. The prospect of increases of over 20 percent in company earnings proved irresistible to investors. The stock market also benefited

from a surge in interest from overseas investors.

In September, though, continued concerns about the weak dollar and rising interest rates began to take their toll. After peaking at 2,722.42 on August 25, the Dow fell more than 200 points in the next four weeks, dropping below 2,500. A short-lived rally was followed by several days of sharp falls, attributed to lack of sufficient improvement in the U.S. trade balance, inaction over the budget deficit, and U.S.-West German bickering over economic policy.

On Monday, October 19, the stock market went into a free fall. By the end of the day, the Dow had declined 508 points, or 22.6 percent of its value, to 1,738.74. The percentage drop was the worst since World War I, and the 604.3 million shares traded nearly doubled the previous record of 338.5 million set the Friday before. The debacle on Wall Street quickly spread to other equity markets around the world. The Tokyo market lost 15

89

percent of its value the next day, the Hong Kong market took such a beating that authorities there closed the exchange for the rest of the week, and markets in Europe and Australia were also badly shaken.

As Wall Street firms, reeling from losses, struggled to survive the shakeout, the Federal Reserve flooded the nation's financial system with cash to stave off a widely predicted recession. President Ronald Reagan agreed to negotiate with congressional leaders on a package of measures to reduce the budget deficit. A month later, a $30 billion deficit-reduction plan was announced, after much bargaining. A final version was later passed by Congress and signed by the president; in the interim, $23 billion in legally mandated budget cuts automatically took effect.

Extreme volume and volatility characterized the stock market for weeks after October 19. The nation's major stock exchanges closed early each day for about two weeks in an effort to calm the market and enable exhausted employees to catch up on an enormous backlog of paperwork. After staying in the 1,900's for a time, by the first week of December the Dow was back in the 1,700's, barely above the October 19 low. In the following week, however, the Dow rose a record 100.3 points in

all, despite a one-day drop after news of October's trade imbalance. After more fluctuations, it ended the year at 1,938.83.

A *Wall Street Journal* report later described October 20 as the most critical point during the immediate post-crash period, asserting that the financial markets came close to "total meltdown" when trading virtually halted because of a lack of liquidity. Catastrophe was averted partly because the Fed pumped dollars into the banking system; instead, the Dow Jones gained a record 102 points on the day.

With stock prices depressed, investors with the largest cash surpluses were expected to do best. These included not just corporate takeover experts but also Japanese financial institutions. In March, Shearson Lehman Brothers sold a 13 percent stake to Nippon Life Insurance Company for $540 million. In December the Yasuda Mutual Life Insurance Company agreed to pay $300 million for a 25 percent holding in Paine Webber Group Inc. Meanwhile, the 83-year-old brokerage house E. F. Hutton and Company was bought by Shearson Lehman Brothers for $962 million. The merger reflected a retrenchment on Wall Street, where many firms made personnel cuts.

**Banking Industry.** A weak economy in the Southwest caused another year of numerous bank failures. Nearly 40 banks had failed in Texas alone by September, when the Federal Deposit Insurance Corporation pledged almost $1 billion to prevent the collapse of Houston-based First City Bancorporation, reeling from mounting energy and real estate loan losses. In November the largest bailout in U.S. history of a savings institution occurred when the Federal Savings and Loan Insurance Corporation pledged $1.3 billion to solve the financial difficulties of Dallas's Vernon Savings and Loan Association.

Paul A. Volcker left his position as Federal Reserve Board chairman at the end of his term. Alan Greenspan, a well-respected economist and onetime chairman of President Gerald Ford's Council of Economic Advisers, replaced him as chairman on August 11.

In the same month, Congress passed the first major banking legislation in five years, the Competitive Equity Banking Act of 1987. The bill enabled the FSLIC, whose funds were severely depleted, to raise $10.8 billion over three years. Those resources were to be used to close down hundreds of virtually insolvent savings and loan associations in the depressed Southwest. The act placed a moratorium, until March 2, 1988, on the granting of further powers to banks to underwrite securities. In addition, the measure required banks to make funds available to depositors of local checks after two intervening business days starting in September 1988, and after one intervening business day starting in 1990. Banks would be able to hold funds from checks drawn on banks in other Federal Reserve regions for a maximum of six intervening business days starting in September 1988, and for four intervening business days starting in 1990.

**Crime on the Street.** Three major Wall Street figures appeared in the criminal courts. In February, former investment banker Dennis Levine was sentenced to two years in prison after having pleaded guilty to insider-trading charges. His evidence implicated Ivan Boesky, well-known Wall Street speculator, in illegal

*Holding the line on exchange rates proved an elusive goal; the dollar's fall against the yen and other currencies seemed to reflect a lack of coordination among the major industrial countries. Here, currency traders work frantically in Tokyo.*

takeover activities. Boesky in turn provided information against Martin Siegel, a former managing director at the investment banking firm of Drexel Burnham Lambert. Both Boesky and Siegel pleaded guilty to criminal charges. Boesky drew three years in prison; Siegel awaited sentencing. All three agreed to pay large sums to settle civil charges. (*See also* CRIME AND CRIME PREVENTION.)

In November the U.S. Supreme Court upheld, 8-0, the conviction for federal mail and wire fraud of *Wall Street Journal* reporter R. Foster Winans and two co-conspirators. (The Court deadlocked, 4-4, on a separate conviction for securities fraud, leaving the conviction intact but setting no precedent.) The federal government regarded the decision as clearing the way to wide use of mail and wire fraud laws in criminal prosecution of insider-trading cases. Winans, along with a former news clerk and a former stockbroker, had used his knowledge of what was to appear in his influential daily column "Heard on the Street" to deal in stocks likely to be affected by his recommendations.

**Third World Debt.** Third World countries continued to have problems with debt repayment. In February, Brazil's finance minister announced that as a result of plummeting foreign currency reserves, the country was suspending interest payments on $68 billion of its approximately $110 billion in foreign debt (the portion of the debt owed to commercial banks). In September, Brazil asked its bank creditors to extend more than $10 billion in new loans, to enable the country to resume interest payments. The country also asked for a rescheduling of the $68 billion debt at lower interest rates and proposed that the banks convert some of their loans to long-term Brazilian bonds. In November a provisional agreement was reached under which the banks would lend Brazil about $3 billion of the $4.5 billion it needed to meet interest payments and arrears for 1987; at the beginning of 1988, Brazil would resume normal interest payments while a longer-term rescheduling agreement was negotiated.

Mexico and Argentina negotiated new loans with their bank lenders, although in both cases a number of months were required to put the loan packages together, a sign that banks were growing weary of the debt process. Peru's President Alan García Pérez continued to defy his country's creditors by refusing to make anything more than token interest payments, offering instead to repay the banks with export commodities. In September, Britain's Midland Bank agreed to accept iron, copper, and other raw materials from Peru as part payment of Peru's $160 million debt to Midland.

In statements at the opening session of the World Bank-IMF meeting, the heads of both organizations indicated a willingness to provide more money to the world's poorest nations—principally those in sub-Saharan Africa—to help them meet their debt payments and combat poverty.

Third World debt repayment problems generally, and particularly the shock of the February Brazilian moratorium, led Citicorp to announce on May 19 that it was adding $3 billion to its reserve against possible loan losses. Other major banks quickly followed suit. Late in the year, Morgan Guaranty devised a promising plan for Mexico, under which commercial banks would agree to exchange, at a discount, a portion of their outstanding loans for new, marketable Mexican securities backed by U.S. Treasury bonds.

**Safety Net.** To help increase safety in the international banking system, the Federal Reserve and 11 foreign central banks announced a preliminary accord to increase the required capital base of banks to 8 percent of assets by 1992, up from around 4–6 percent. The agreement reflected a response to the problematic Third World debt, as well as to the troubling number of U.S. bank failures and the increasingly global activities of financial institutions.

S.B.

**BARBADOS.** *See* STATISTICS OF THE WORLD.

**BEHAVIORAL SCIENCES.** Among research of interest reported in 1987 were studies suggesting that standards of beauty are partly inborn, that some personality traits have an influence on health, and that marital bliss may be on the decline; there was also evidence that happily married people often come to resemble their spouses over the years.

**Face Value.** Our standards of beauty have been attributed to learned cultural preferences. Now it appears that we may be born with such preferences. Infants as young as two to three months prefer faces judged attractive by adults, reported psychologist Judith H. Langlois of the University of Texas at Austin and her colleagues. The researchers showed color slides of women's faces, previously judged by young adults to be either moderately attractive or unattractive, to 34 infants aged six to eight months. The slides were presented in pairs: half contrasted an attractive face with an unattractive one, while half were similar—the women in both slides attractive or unattractive. To measure which faces the infants preferred, the researchers recorded the amount of time the babies spent looking at each slide.

When presented with contrasting pairs, 71 percent of the infants looked longer at the attractive faces than at the unattractive ones. When attractive pairs of faces were alternated with unattractive ones, 62 percent of the infants spent more time looking at the attractive pairs. And in a second experiment with younger infants—aged two to three months—the babies again preferred attractive faces to unattractive ones when presented side by side.

**The Disease-Prone Personality.** Folklore suggests that certain personality types are prone to specific diseases. Worriers, for example, are supposed to get ulcers, while workaholics develop heart disease, and repressed emotions surface in asthma sufferers. Although research has not tied personality and disease together that neatly, there may well exist a "generic 'disease-prone' personality," reported psychologists Howard S. Friedman and Stephanie Booth-Kewley of the University of California at Riverside.

Friedman and Booth-Kewley performed a sophisticated statistical analysis of 101 studies conducted between 1945 and 1984. At least one of a number of conditions—arthritis, headaches, asthma, coronary heart disease, ulcers, and headaches—was examined in each study. The researchers correlated these diseases with different personality traits: anxiety, depression, anger, hostility, aggression, and extroversion. Although no one trait predicted a single disease, the researchers did find strong links beween personality and illness. The single greatest predictor of disease was depression. All the traits were strongly associated with

At the top, newlyweds; below, the same couple 25 years later. If he married her for her looks, he may have succeeded: there is new evidence that long-married couples grow to resemble each other.

coronary heart disease, and weaker relationships were found between various personality measures and the other conditions.

**Marital Malaise.** Marriage may be "a weakened, declining institution" in the United States, suggested sociologist Norval D. Glenn of the University of Texas at Austin, who found that the reported happiness of married people had decreased in the past decade and a half. From the 1950's through the early 1970's, studies showed that married people were considerably happier than those who had never married or those who had been divorced, separated, or widowed. But Glenn found that things had changed when he and Charles Weaver of St. Mary's University of San Antonio analyzed data collected from 1972 through 1986 by the National Opinion Research Center at the University of Chicago. The nationally representative surveys showed that the proportion of married people who said they were "very happy" declined moderately during the period, from 39 percent in 1972 to 33 percent in 1986.

At the same time, the lives of never-married individuals appeared to have improved, since the proportion of the never-married who said they were very happy rose from 9 percent to 25 percent.

Why the decrease in reported happiness among the married and the increase in happiness among the never-married? Glenn and Weaver speculated that in some sense the lives of these two groups have become more alike. "Many unmarried people now have reliable sources of sexual gratification and companionship," the researchers said, "and marriage no longer provides the security, financial and otherwise, that it once did."

**Wedded Faces.** The long-standing belief that married individuals eventually come to resemble one another was confirmed in a study by University of Michigan psychologist Robert Zajonc. He and his colleagues collected photographs from 12 midwestern couples and presented them to college undergraduates, who were told to match the men and women who most resembled each other. Half the photographs had been shot when the partners first married; the other half were taken some 25 years later.

The judges did no better than chance would predict in correctly matching photos of the partners as newlyweds. But they were significantly more successful in identifying partners when they had aged 25 years. The similarities between partners were subtle but proved to be greater among those who reported higher levels of marital happiness. Zajonc proposed that people unconsciously mimic the facial expressions of their spouses and that, with time, shared expressions modify their faces in similar ways. R.H.C.

**BELGIUM.** On October 19, 1987, the coalition government of Premier Wilfried Martens resigned once again over a long-standing dispute stemming from Belgium's linguistic division between the Flemish-speaking north and the French-speaking south. The disagreement involved the mayor of a mostly French-speaking group of villages who refused to use Flemish in his conduct of official business. Martens had resigned over the issue in 1986, but his resignation had not been accepted. This time, King Baudouin named him to head an interim cab-

inet. Elections, on December 13, resulted in losses for the ruling coalition, making it likely there would be changes in the new government formed after negotiations.

Earlier in the year, the Martens government continued to implement austerity measures aimed at reducing the public sector deficit to 7 percent of gross national product by the end of 1989. Gross domestic product was expected to rise less than 2 percent in 1987. Government efforts to minimize the negative effects of the austerity policies on employment contributed to relatively calm relations with the unions.

Exports were generally strong, and a favorable trade balance was expected. Consumer prices were likely to rise approximately 1.5 percent.

In July, European Community members lifted their ban on high-level contacts with Syria, instituted in 1986 in response to evidence of Syrian involvement in an attempt to plant a bomb on a Israeli airliner. The renewal of contacts followed Syrian actions against terrorism.

In February the government initiated Western Europe's most stringent screening program to detect the AIDS virus among Third World scholarship students. Students who had the disease were offered state-financed medical care. The most controversial part of the plan called for the revocation of state scholarship aid to those students who were found to be carriers of the virus but had not yet fallen ill; the practical effect was to compel such students to return home.

See STATISTICS OF THE WORLD. W.C.C.

**BELIZE.** See STATISTICS OF THE WORLD.

**BENIN.** See STATISTICS OF THE WORLD.

**BHUTAN.** See STATISTICS OF THE WORLD.

**BLACKS IN THE UNITED STATES.** In 1987, Jesse Jackson announced his candidacy for the U.S. presidency, and the power of the black vote was evident in several elections. During the 40th anniversary of Jackie Robinson's entry into the major leagues, the token representation of blacks in management and coaching positions in baseball became an issue.

**Politics.** Jesse Jackson officially announced in October that he would be a candidate for the Democratic presidential nomination in 1988. Polls had him leading the crowded field at that time (Gary Hart was not then running), with support from about 20 percent of his party's voters and a solid base among black Democrats (some 65 percent of whom supported him). Analysts did not expect Jackson to win the nomination but believed he would amass a large bloc of delegates and wield important influence at the convention. In 1984, as a first-time late-entry candidate, he won 11 percent of the delegates, to finish third.

Chicago's first black mayor, Harold Washington, was reelected in April with a comfortable majority that included nearly all black voters. The city was plunged into mourning when he died suddenly of a heart attack in his office on November 25. Washington, 65, was Chicago's most powerful mayor since Richard Daley and was a visible symbol of the rising black political power in the nation's cities. In an acrimonious session, the City Council selected black alderman Eugene Sawyer as acting mayor; he had strong white support, but was strongly opposed by many blacks.

In November elections, W. Wilson Goode was returned to office as mayor of Philadelphia, defeating a white opponent and taking 98 percent of the black vote. Elsewhere, Baltimore elected a black mayor for the first time, and Hartford its first black woman mayor. In Mississippi, strong black support provided the margin of victory to Ray Mabus in the race for governor. The influence of black organizations and voters also emerged as a factor in the failure of Judge Robert H. Bork to win confirmation to the Supreme Court.

**Blacks in Baseball.** A year-long commemoration of the 40th anniversary of Jackie Robinson's debut as the first black to play major-league baseball unexpectedly turned a spotlight on failure to integrate the sport's hierarchy. The furor began in April when Al Campanis, vice president of player personnel for the Los Angeles Dodgers, suggested on the ABC News television program *Nightline*, during a segment planned as a tribute to Robinson, that blacks "may not have some of the necessities to be . . . a field manager or perhaps a general manager." Ironically, Campanis had been invited on the program because he had played minor-league ball with Robinson. His comments came in reply to a question about why

*The first black Miss Mississippi, Toni Seawright, won the title at the Vicksburg pageant in July.*

baseball had had so few black managers or executives. At the time, only three blacks had ever managed major-league teams and only 13 of the current 130 major-league baseball coaches (as opposed to 25 percent of the players) were black.

In the storm that followed, Campanis made a public apology but was forced to resign by the Dodger organization. Meanwhile, the NAACP demanded affirmative action programs in baseball, and Baseball Commission Peter Ueberroth, after meeting with owners, said such programs would be put in place. Harry Edwards, a black sports sociologist, was appointed to assist the leagues in developing a pool of black and Hispanic players who could fill openings at all levels. In the interest of lowering tensions, Edwards named Campanis as a consultant; many black players, in fact, felt Campanis had been unbiased during his long career in baseball, whatever attitudes lay behind his remarks on *Nightline*.

**Death Penalty.** In a significant ruling in *McCleskey* v. *Kemp*, the U.S. Supreme Court upheld Georgia's death penalty law, despite statistical evidence that defendants—especially black defendants—found guilty of killing whites were far more likely to receive the death penalty than were defendants convicted of killing blacks. The Court said there was no

proof in the specific case that willful discrimination had been a factor in the jury's decision.
**Verdict Against Klan.** After Michael Donald was lynched by Ku Klux Klansmen in 1981 in Mobile, Ala., his family filed suit against the United Klans of America, the oldest of various KKK groups, and six current or former members. In February an all-white jury in Alabama awarded the family $7 million in damages; the effect was that the family received title to the group's limited assets. Donald was murdered at the age of 19 by Klansmen seeking a random black victim to avenge the killing of a white police officer.

**Affirmative Action and Voting Rights.** In *United States* v. *Paradise,* the Supreme Court upheld, 5-4, a federal district court's order requiring that Alabama temporarily use a strict racial quota (one black for each white) in promoting state troopers—to make up for past discrimination against blacks. The Court's only Voting Rights Act case during the 1986–1987 term was *City of Pleasant Grove* v. *United States.* In their decision, the justices upheld, 6-3, a lower court's finding that there was racial motivation behind an Alabama city's refusal to annex a black neighborhood. The Supreme Court also said that the city failed to prove that its annexation of a white neighborhood and vacant tract for development did not have the purpose of denying blacks the right to vote.

**Minorities and AIDS.** On August 8 nearly 1,000 black and Hispanic leaders gathered in Atlanta at the federal Centers for Disease Control to address the social implications of a high AIDS incidence for minority communities. Blacks make up 12 percent of the population but 24 percent of AIDS victims; for Hispanics the figures are 7 percent and 14 percent, respectively. Moreover, nearly 80 percent of children with AIDS are members of minority groups and more than half the women with AIDS are black. Black leaders fear an even greater distancing of blacks and Hispanics from the white community, with AIDS used as justification.

*See also* Civil Liberties and Civil Rights; Elections in the United States; *and* United States: Supreme Court.　　　M.Gr. & K.P.

Forty years after he integrated major league baseball, Jackie Robinson was remembered as one of the game's great baserunners. Here, on August 22, 1948, he steals home against the Boston Braves at the Brooklyn Dodgers' Ebbets Field—his fourth such play that season and part of a Dodger triple steal.

**BOLIVIA.** During 1987, Bolivia experienced political shakeups and labor disturbances.

President Víctor Paz Estenssoro called on February 27 for the resignation of his entire cabinet. Four members were replaced. These included Interior Minister Fernando Barthelemy, accused of corruption and protecting drug traffickers, and Agriculture Minister Edil Sandoval, accused of involvement in the drug trade.

Another cabinet crisis occurred 12 days later, when the legislature demanded that five ministers resign. The move followed charges that the government had failed to repay about $150 million in dividends to three oil-producing departments—Santa Cruz, Tarija, and Chuquisaca. That crisis ended after talks had strengthened the ruling coalition.

Early in the year, the Nationalist Democratic Alliance, headed by General Hugo Banzer, split, as members opposed to Banzer's support for the National Revolutionary Movement government formed their own party, the Nationalist Democratic Front. Both leftist and conservative opposition groups did well in municipal elections on December 6.

In August a strike by 70,000 teachers seeking higher salaries was settled after 47 days. Other sectors experiencing stoppages included railways, public health, utilities, and mining. Layoffs were a particular grievance among miners; official policy called for dismantling the publicly owned mining sector and laying off 20,000 of the mines' 26,000 workers, with compensation to those laid off, funded by a World Bank loan.

A three-year, $300 million plan, signed in February by the Paz government and the U.S. Drug Enforcement Administration, called for the destruction of cocaine laboratories, the eradication of coca bushes, and payments to growers switching to other cash crops. It sparked public protests, said to be financed by drug traffickers, and was later modified to make the eradication program a matter of voluntary participation.

Bolivia gained agreement from its creditor banks for permission to buy back debts from individual banks at a discount from the face value. In another innovative arrangement, a conservation group purchased $650,000 in Bolivian debt for $200,000 and donated the purchase to Bolivia, after the government agreed to the establishment of an Amazon nature preserve.

*See* STATISTICS OF THE WORLD. L.L.P.

**BOTSWANA.** *See* STATISTICS OF THE WORLD.

**BRAZIL.** A new austerity program, under a new finance minister, heralded a change in economic policy in Brazil in 1987. But the program floundered, and the minister resigned late in the year.

**New Cruzado Plan.** Luiz Carlos Bresser Pereira, formerly science and technology secretary of the state of São Paulo, was named minister of finance in April to replace Dilson Funaro, whose anti-inflationary Cruzado Plan failed in late 1986, with inflation running at about 400 percent a year. Shortly after taking office, Bresser Pereira devalued the cruzado by 8.5 percent against the U.S. dollar. In June, he announced the New Cruzado Plan, the centerpiece of which was a 90-day wage and price freeze; after the 90 days certain critical prices were to be government-controlled while others would be determined by market forces. Wages would be adjusted quarterly, based on the average inflation rate of the preceding three months. A further 10.56 percent devaluation of the cruzado was aimed at increasing exports and the trade surplus. In addition, some $35 billion in capital projects was abandoned or postponed.

Strikes and demonstrations opposing the program were organized in many cities. An August 20 general strike, however, had little success, partly because of President José Sarney's announcement on August 7 of an increase in the minimum wage.

The New Cruzado Plan appeared to be working when inflation between mid-June and mid-July fell to only 3 percent, compared with 23 percent in May and 21 percent in April. Later on, however, inflation surged, reaching an annual rate of 350 percent by year's end. The public-sector deficit mounted, as state corporations piled up losses. Bresser Pereira sought new spending cuts and taxes on the wealthy, but Sarney vetoed his proposals, and the minister resigned in late December.

**Trade.** The combination of currency devaluations and good rains resulted in increased

In a pit 600 feet deep, in the Brazilian state of Pará, 50,000 men struggle daily to find gold—digging in 20-square-foot concessions, carrying 120-pound sacks of soil up crude ladders to the top, and creating a rough gold rush civilization in the wilderness. The region's gold frenzy began in 1980, when a cowhand discovered a nugget in a stream and sold it in a nearby town; within two weeks, 10,000 "garaimperos," or gold diggers, had arrived in the area.

exports of cocoa beans, orange juice concentrate, and soybeans, which led to a trade surplus projected at around $10 billion for 1987. The rains reduced the likelihood that Brazil would have to import corn, rice, and beans as it did in 1986 and also made it possible that the 1987–1988 coffee crop would reach 29 million 132-pound bags, up from 11.2 million bags in 1986–1987.

In November the United States, angered by regulations that effectively bar foreign participation in Brazil's computer market, announced plans for punitive tariffs covering over $100 million worth of U.S. imports from Brazil. It was the first such U.S. action against a major debtor nation.

**Foreign Debt.** On February 20 the government announced a unilateral moratorium on interest payments on medium-term and long-term loans from foreign commercial banks, to continue

until after a settlement was reached with those creditors. In negotiations beginning in September, Brazil asked its foreign bank creditors for new loans of $10.4 billion to finance interest on debt due from 1987 through 1989. Brazil also asked that bank creditors reschedule their medium-term and long-term loans at an interest rate equal to or less than the banks' own cost of funds. In November, Brazil tentatively agreed to pay $1.5 billion in interest due, in return for refinancing of approximately $3 billion in debt. A first payment on the interest due was made in December.

In January the Paris Club, a group of Western creditor governments, agreed to reschedule some $4.1 billion in Brazilian debt. In July, however, Brazil announced that to defend its international reserves, it was suspending repayment of $1.05 billion of principal due to the Paris Club in 1987.

**Agrarian Reform Slowed.** In late June, Planning Minister Anibal Texeira admitted that the government would not meet its 1990 goal of settling 1.4 million families on unused public and private land. A 1987 target of settling 300,000 families was reduced to 80,000. The program was stymied by the opposition of government officials who were also landowners and by court challenges to government expropriation of unused private land.

**Political Reform.** President Sarney pledged in a nationally televised speech to shake up his cabinet and present a reform plan, but could persuade his coalition partners to accept only a minor reshuffle. Meanwhile, a congressional committee drafting a new constitution voted to change to a parliamentary system of government in March 1988, and called for presidential elections to be held that year—an idea strongly opposed by Sarney.

**Radiation Accident.** One of the world's most serious incidents of radiation exposure occurred in the city of Goiânia in September. A family of scrap metal dealers extracted a capsule containing radioactive cesium 137 from a radiation machine taken from an abandoned medical clinic. Attracted by the glowing bluish dust, they shared it with friends and neighbors. By mid-October, more than 40 people had been hospitalized with radiation sickness, and some 250 more had been contaminated. Soon afterward, four of the victims died.

See STATISTICS OF THE WORLD.          N.J.P.

**BRITISH COLUMBIA.** See STATISTICS OF THE WORLD.

**BRUNEI.** See STATISTICS OF THE WORLD.

**BULGARIA.** In 1987, Bulgaria's longtime party and state leader Todor Zhivkov accommodated himself easily to aspects of the Soviet Union's new policy of *glasnost* (openness). With other high party and state officials, he launched a campaign to root out corruption, crime, alcoholism, and other "negative phenomena" that might affect economic performance. The blame was borne mostly by the rank and file.

Actions against dissidents continued. Six dissidents who appealed to the Helsinki Review Conference in Vienna to monitor the performance of governments that might have signed the Helsinki accords on human rights in bad faith incurred the state's displeasure. One was found to be "mentally unbalanced" and sentenced to a three-year internment; at least three others were also imprisoned. In another incident, ten 14-year-olds who had laid a floral tribute in Sofia to Beatles singer John Lennon in December 1986, on the anniversary of his death, were arrested and placed on probation, and their families were fined about $200 apiece. However, in an unusual reaction, the weekly *Pogled* published a defense of the group.

Zhivkov's New Economic Mechanism was subjected to further revisions. In January, new regulations gave large production complexes a role in planning and financing. Then, in the summer, much of the new structure was swept

*As radiation sickness spread through the Brazilian city of Goiânia, technicians tested the city's children to see who had been exposed to cesium from an abandoned radiation therapy machine.*

away; key ministries were dropped and replaced by newly organized ones. It was doubtful, however, whether the changes would have much practical effect. The Politburo also ended most military parades and called for elimination of the "glorifying" of party leaders by such means as displays of portraits and statues.

The ninth five-year plan, covering 1986–1990, aimed at "qualitative new growth" by stressing high technology fields such as transport systems research, laser technology, and microelectronics.

A visit to Sofia by Italy's foreign minister marked the normalization of relations with Italy, which had been tense since 1981 because of alleged Bulgarian complicity in an attempt on the life of Pope John Paul II. Visits by U.S., West German, and French representatives were proof of growing interest in economic cooperation. But relations with Muslim countries were damaged by Bulgaria's continuing efforts to force the assimilation of 1.3 million ethnic Turks.

See STATISTICS OF THE WORLD.        R.A.P.

**BURKINA FASO.** See STATISTICS OF THE WORLD: *Upper Volta.*

**BURMA.** The Burmese economy continued to flag in 1987, but the government managed to find resources for its continuing efforts to combat opium production, rebellious minorities, and the Burmese Communist Party. In August, Ne Win, head of the country's ruling party, indicated that economic and political changes would be necessary.

While rice production remained high, poor storage, March rains, and inefficient distribution contributed to shortages in the cities. The price of Burmese rice—once the most important foreign exchange earner—was reduced because of the poor quality of the crop. Burma's foreign exchange reserves declined, forcing the government to make drastic cuts in foreign purchases. Consequently, prices rose on the flourishing black market. Oil production also continued to decline. Industry was crippled and private and commercial transportation almost stopped. Burma's foreign debt was estimated to have risen to $4 billion. In the face of these circumstances, the UN General Assembly agreed to designate Burma one of the world's least-developed nations, to make it eligible for special UN assistance.

In September the government took forceful actions, lifting all restrictions on trade in grain and withdrawing from circulation all paper currency of 25-kayat, 35-kayat, and 75-kayat denominations. The latter action, the second such demonetization in two years, provoked unrest and student rioting, which led the government to close down educational institutions.

The military mounted campaigns against various rebel groups during the dry season. But insurgent ethnic minorities continued to hold their territory and to push for negotiations with the government.

See STATISTICS OF THE WORLD.        J.S.

**BURUNDI.** See STATISTICS OF THE WORLD.

# C

**CABINET, UNITED STATES.** See UNITED STATES OF AMERICA: *The Presidency.*

**CALIFORNIA.** See STATISTICS OF THE WORLD.

**CAMBODIA.** "A bit of peace, a bit of war" was how Premier Hun Sen of the Vietnamese-backed government in Phnom Penh described the situation in Cambodia (Kampuchea) in 1987. The number of guerrilla attacks appeared

to drop off, but the war continued to take its toll. Farmland was taken out of production, and thousands of young men were drafted into the army or recruited to clear forests or build defenses along the Thai border.

Vietnamese officials insisted they would withdraw their 140,000 troops from Cambodia by 1990, even if resistance forces stepped up their attacks against the Cambodian government. Tensions continued within the resistance coalition, consisting of the Communist Khmer Rouge and two non-Communist groups, one of them headed by former chief of state Prince Norodom Sihanouk. In May, Sihanouk resigned for one year as leader of the coalition, protesting the killing of two of his soldiers by Khmer Rouge guerrillas.

In July, Vietnam accepted an Indonesian proposal to organize an informal meeting at which the various Cambodian political factions could talk "without preconditions and without political label." But Hanoi later rejected revisions of the proposal.

In early December, Sihanouk and Hun Sen met for three days in a village near Paris, in a first tentative effort to work out a settlement of the guerrilla war. The two parties issued a communiqué promising further meetings, but Sihanouk later vacillated considerably as to his conditions for such talks; at one point, he refused to join in new talks unless the two other antigovernment guerrilla factions agreed to participate.

The Soviet Union, Vietnam's major supplier of economic and military aid, became more active in diplomacy over Cambodia. In March, Soviet Foreign Minister Eduard Shevardnadze toured five Southeast Asian countries; he discussed the future of Cambodia during stops in Thailand and Indonesia.

Cambodia was hit by its most serious drought in more than a decade. Most of the country's short-season rice crop normally harvested in September was lost, and only about 20 percent of the 4 million acres of rice fields targeted for the main crop had been planted by the end of August. The United Nations launched an appeal for international aid, including rice, rice seed, fertilizer, and insecticides.

Amnesty International issued a report in June charging the Phnom Penh regime with detaining and torturing thousands of political prisoners. Phnom Penh immediately rejected the charges. Meanwhile, over 250,000 Cambodian refugees continued living along the Thai border in camps controlled by one of the three resistance groups fighting the Vietnamese.

See STATISTICS OF THE WORLD.     M.H.
**CAMEROON.** See STATISTICS OF THE WORLD.

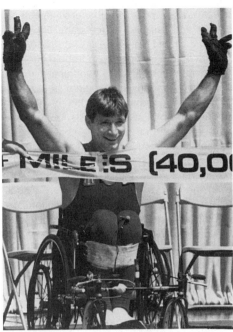

*Over two years and 25,000 miles after setting out on his round-the-world "Man in Motion" wheelchair journey, paraplegic Rick Hansen was back in Vancouver, British Columbia, in May, gliding triumphantly across the finish line. Hansen's marathon raised millions of dollars, mostly from Canadians, for medical research and rehabilitation programs.*

**CANADA.** In 1987, Canada's economy was in its fifth straight year of expansion. Prime Minister Brian Mulroney (see biography in PEOPLE IN THE NEWS) secured a historical constitutional settlement with Québec and an agreement on free trade with the United States. These agreements were controversial, however, and, overall, the Mulroney government, weakened by scandals, appeared unpopular.

**Political Realignment.** Despite some apparent successes, Mulroney's Conservative government was less popular than any Canadian cabinet had been in decades. Odder still, the government's slump in the opinion polls occurred while the Liberals and their leader, John Turner, were themselves held in little favor. Having dominated national politics for half a century, the Liberals were suffering the divisions and self-doubts of a party in opposition. That left the political initiative largely in the hands of the Conservative government, which advanced new policies for defense and the tax system and pursued a free trade agreement with the United States.

With both major parties in trouble, the New Democratic Party (NDP), traditionally ranked third, had by midyear captured both public attention and, temporarily, the number-one position in opinion polls. (Polls in December put it in second or third place.)

Though it has several times formed the governments of three western provinces, the NDP has never formed either the government or even the official opposition in the Canadian Parliament. Over the years it has accumulated a long list of distinctly left-wing policy positions, including nationalization of the Canadian Pacific Railway and withdrawal from the NATO alliance. For the most part, however, the party has stressed mainstream programs. Its current leader was the moderate-sounding, likable Ed Broadbent.

The image of the Mulroney government continued to suffer damage from scandals. In January, Mulroney fired a junior transport minister, André Bissonnette, after it was disclosed that the price of a piece of land in his district had tripled, as it changed hands several times shortly before being bought by a defense con-

tractor, Oerlikon Aerospace. Following a seven-month investigation by the Royal Canadian Mounted Police, Bissonnette was formally charged with corruption, fraud, and breach of trust; it was alleged that he had illegally made a profit from the affair. Another minister, Roch LaSalle, resigned after a number of episodes, including the discovery that he had two convicted criminals on his staff. In September, Mulroney announced the resignation of Thomas D'Arcy Finn, head of the Canadian Security Intelligence Service; the move followed problems in the new federal counterespionage agency, including delays and procedural errors in a case involving the shooting of an Indian cabinet minister who visited British Columbia in 1986.

Later in the year, the government ordered the Intelligence Service to disband the countersubversion unit, which had maintained some 30,000 files on individual Canadians. In December, Ontario Supreme Court Justice William Parker, who had conducted an 18-month inquiry into the conduct of former Industry Minister Sinclair Stevens, reported that while in that office Stevens had violated ethical guidelines on conflict of interest at least 14 times.

*A handshake between Québec Premier Robert Bourassa (left) and Prime Minister Brian Mulroney, as Ontario Premier David Peterson looks on, marks a political watershed. Emerging from meetings at Meech Lake, Québec, on May 1, Canada's leaders announced a tentative accord aimed at making Québec a signatory to the Constitution.*

Such events might have been expected to turn the public to the Liberals as a government-in-waiting. But John Turner, who succeeded the popular Pierre Elliott Trudeau as party leader and, briefly, as prime minister, suffered the inevitable stigma that came from having led his party into defeat in 1984. His 39 fellow Liberal MP's in the Commons divided on several important issues, and the party's failure to capitalize on Conservative unpopularity aroused discontents among Liberal organizers and fundraisers.

In July, by-elections took place in the Newfoundland district of St. John's East, the urban Ontario district of Hamilton Mountain, and the vast Yukon territory, hard by the Alaska border. St. John's East and Yukon had been held for years by Tories, and Hamilton Mountain by a New Democrat who accepted a government appointment from Mulroney. All three sent New Democrats to the Commons. In all such midterm by-elections, local issues and local candidates are important. In addition, it is a Canadian cliché that by-elections give voters the chance to slap the government of the day

without actually knocking it out of office. Nonetheless, the results were ominous for the government.

**Renegotiating the Constitution.** The single most significant achievement of the Mulroney government by the time of the by-elections was undoubtedly the constitutional agreement forged by the prime minister and the ten provincial premiers—subject, however, to ratification by Parliament and the provinces. The agreement, negotiated at a meeting in rustic Meech Lake, Québec, at the end of April, included constitutional changes that would give all provinces additional powers. The changes would also grant particular powers to the government and legislature of Québec to preserve the mainly French-speaking province as "a distinct society" within Canada. Senators and Supreme Court judges, instead of being appointed solely by the federal cabinet, would be named from lists supplied by the provinces. And provinces would have a right to get federal funds if they chose not to take part in federal-provincial social programs.

The accord was signed by national and provincial leaders meeting in Ottawa on June 3. Before taking effect, the constitutional amendments needed approval both by Parliament and by all ten provincial legislatures. Opposition arose immediately, especially from critics who believed the changes would leave the federal Parliament and government far too weak to manage the national economy and keep the country united. Among the harshest of these was Trudeau himself, who called Mulroney a weakling for having conceded so much to the provincial premiers. Despite the dissent, the Commons approved the agreement in October.

**Refugees—Real or Bogus?** For the second summer in a row, a boatload of Asians arrived off Canada's Atlantic coast seeking refugee status under broadly drawn provisions in Canadian immigration law. In 1986 they were Tamils from Sri Lanka; in July 1987, 174 Sikhs landed in Nova Scotia, claiming to be refugees from religious persecution in India. In both cases, it was believed that the Asians had not come directly from these countries but had been transported from Western Europe. These surreptitious arrivals aroused controversy among

Clint Keates shows an insurance adjuster where his home stood before a tornado tore through Edmonton, Alberta, on July 31, reducing a trailer park to rubble.

Canadians. To some, the Asians were cheaters, trying to jump the long queue of prospective immigrants to Canada. To others they were among the wretched of the earth, deserving sympathy if not an unreserved welcome. To the government they were a challenge, both to its public standing and to the immigration processing system, badly in need of repair.

The government had previously introduced a bill to speed the refugee determination process, an unwieldy system of hearings and appeals that commonly take up to five years to reach a final judgment. This measure, however, met stiff opposition on account of the powers it would give officials to turn away applicants without appeal. Immigration Minister Benoît Bouchard responded to the Sikhs' arrival with still tougher legislation, which provided half-million-dollar fines (Canadian dollars used here and throughout) for those who smuggle people illegally into Canada and gave officials the power to detain as security risks all those who arrive without identifying documents. The Commons interrupted its summer recess to debate the new bill, and passed it in September, after which the measure awaited action by the Senate.

Aggravating the problem was the newly enacted U.S. immigration law, which provided tough sanctions against illegal aliens and their employers. The impact of the U.S. law was soon felt in Canada as increasing numbers of aliens, especially from Central and South America, sought entry from the United States into Canada.

**Defense Policy.** In response to another sort of challenge, the government published a white paper on defense policy, the first comprehensive statement on the subject in more than 15 years. In general, it reaffirmed Canada's participation in the NATO alliance and in the North American Air Defense Command (Norad), a joint arrangement with the United States. At the same time, it acknowledged what Defense Minister Perrin Beatty called the "commitment-capability gap" between what Canada had promised to do and what it actually could do in a military crisis.

To close that gap, Beatty proposed both to reduce some commitments and to expand Canada's military capability. The white paper announced the cancellation of the "unsustainable commitment" to send a brigade group and two fighter squadrons to northern Europe; instead, more equipment was to be positioned in Europe for use by troops that in time of crisis would join the brigade group permanently stationed in southern Germany.

Beatty proposed to purchase 10 to 12 nuclear-powered submarines to guard coastal waters. Armed only with conventional weapons, they would be Canada's first nuclear-

104

powered military craft. However, by the end of the year, considerable opposition to the acquisition had emerged because of the cost, estimated at at least $6 billion. The government also faced opposition from the United States, partly because Canada would use the submarines to guard against U.S. as well as Soviet incursions into Arctic waters that Canada claims as its territory.

**Changes in the Tax System.** In still another white paper (and largely in response to changes in U.S. tax law), the Canadian government in June proposed major changes in the federal tax system. Finance Minister Michael Wilson sought both to simplify tax laws and to shift part of the tax burden from individuals to corporations. Wilson's aim was partly to keep Canadians competitive with U.S. taxpayers and partly to redress growing imbalances within the Canadian tax system itself. His major proposals, in brief, involved:

• cutting the number of personal tax brackets to three from ten, while reducing the top federal tax rate to 29 percent from 34 percent;

• replacing a variety of personal deductions and exemptions with tax credits, so as to yield the greatest proportional benefits to the lowest-income earners;

• eliminating some tax deductions, while curtailing others such as entertainment and car expenses;

• lowering the corporate tax rate to 28 percent from 34 percent;

• abolishing or reducing certain business deductions and capital cost allowances.

Wilson left what would potentially be his biggest tax-generator for further public study: a consumption tax allowing the treasury to tap whole new revenue sources. He offered three options: a general goods and services tax, a value-added tax like that imposed in the European Community, and a national sales tax integrated with provincial sales-tax regimes. Meanwhile, many of the changes proposed in June took effect in 1988.

**A Strengthening Economy.** Wilson, meanwhile, could draw comfort (if not credit) from the healthy complexion of the Canadian economy. By December, the unemployment rate had dipped to 8.1 percent, from 11.4 percent in September 1984. Inflation was running at under 5 percent, manufacturing output was increasing, and business confidence was buoyant. Even a slimmer trade surplus (caused mainly by rising imports) was taken as a good sign by Canadian observers: an indication of domestic demand picking up slack left by the slower growth of major trading partners.

*Monique Vezina, Canada's minister of supply and services, ushered in the nation's new $1 coin at Winnipeg's Royal Canadian Mint. The coin, depicting a loon, will eventually replace $1 bills.*

# CANADA

The year saw its share of labor strife, however, including a 19-day national strike by Canada Post letter carriers, a 5-day walkout by the nation's railway workers, and a strike by airline ground workers that closed down Air Canada for over 20 days. Canada's financial markets were jolted by the U.S. stock market crash of October 19, with the Toronto stock exchange dropping 14 percent in one week. The Bank of Canada lowered its lending rate a record 157 basis points, to 8.26 percent, in an effort to restore confidence. For the whole year, the index rose 1.6 percent.

**Regional Review.** As usual, the benefits of economic health were unequally shared among the regions. The chronically poor East had hardly a whiff of the boom; Newfoundland suffered a midsummer unemployment rate of 17.5 percent. In the West, low international prices and lagging demand for grain, oil, and minerals were a deadweight on the regional economy. It was industrial Ontario that enjoyed the strongest growth. A housing boom, a rising population with higher incomes, and business demand for Ontario-made machinery and equipment all helped to trim the province's jobless rate to the 6 percent range.

If anybody won political credit for Ontario's happy economic circumstances, it was not the Conservative government in Ottawa but the Liberal provincial government of David Peterson. Peterson's cabinet had taken office in 1985—the first time in 42 years that Ontario's Conservatives had been out of power. But the Liberals had only a minority in the legislature and governed through an unconventional written accord with the New Democrats. Sensing the prospect of winning his own majority, Peterson called an election for September 10. His chosen issue: defending Ontario interests in any U.S.-Canada trade agreement. The result was a resounding triumph for the Liberals, who won 95 out of the 130 legislative seats. The Conservative leader, Larry Grossman, lost his own seat and announced he would quit the leadership.

In New Brunswick, a month later, the 17-year reign of Conservative Premier Richard

*A national letter carriers' strike led to violence in Edmonton in June. Here, police grab a striker during a scuffle that broke out when pickets attempted to keep a mail truck from entering the downtown post office.*

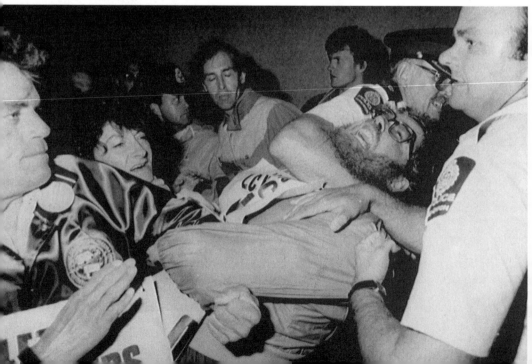

Hatfield came to a stunning end. A provincial election on October 13 gave the Liberals, under Frank McKenna, all 58 legislative seats. Hatfield promptly resigned as party leader.

Québec was shaken by the death on November 1 of former Parti Québécois leader René Lévesque. One of the political ramifications of his death was increased pressure within the party for a more hard-line separatist stance than he had championed. The pressure led the incumbent party leader, Marc Johnson, to announce his resignation as leader and as a member of the provincial legislature. Guy Chevrette was named acting opposition leader.

**Free Trade Agreement.** No one issue had the potential to decide the success or failure of the Mulroney government so sharply as free trade. Mulroney had invested a large part of his political capital in the project when the negotiations with the Reagan administration began in 1986. Historically, U.S.-Canada trade has always touched on sensitive questions of national identity—the survival of Canada as an independent and culturally distinct country next to a neighbor many times wealthier and more populous. In Ottawa, there were loud misgivings about negotiating any deal that would limit Canada's freedom to make its own social welfare policy, for instance, or that would injure Canadian farmers or industry. In Washington, meanwhile, protectionist action against Canadian natural gas, steel, and potash, and other steps along the same line cast doubt on U.S. readiness for free trade of any kind.

However, a tentative agreement was struck in early October. It provided for gradual abolition of cross-border tariffs by January 1, 1999, a bilaterally appointed panel to hear appeals against countervailing duties, the opening of most government procurement to firms in both countries, reduction of barriers to energy imports and exports, and easier terms for foreigners seeking to establish companies to take over existing firms in Canada. Canada's publishing and film industries continued to be protected under the pact's provisions, as did the U.S. maritime industry. After the text of the pact was finalized, it was signed by Mulroney and President Ronald Reagan on January 2, 1988; it still awaited legislative approval in both Canada and the United States.

*René Lévesque, who led the separatist Parti Québécois to power and served as Québec's premier from 1976 to 1985, died at age 65.*

The agreement provoked instant and intense controversy among Canadians. Liberal leader Turner and NDP leader Broadbent condemned it as a sellout of Canadian economic independence, and it also drew opposition from three premiers: Ontario's Peterson, Howard Pawley of Manitoba, and Joe Ghiz of Prince Edward Island. Proponents argued that the accord would give Canadians access to cheaper goods and a better chance at selling in the U.S. market.

**Lévesque Death.** René Lévesque, 65, Québec's premier from 1976 to 1985 and a leader of the Québec separatist movement, died November 1 at his home in Montréal. Lévesque's Parti Québécois had won a landslide victory in Québec in 1976, but four years later his proposal to negotiate virtual independence for the province ("sovereignty-association") was rejected by Québec voters in a referendum. In 1985, with the party's popularity having sharply declined, Lévesque had resigned as premier and party leader.

See STATISTICS OF THE WORLD.                                    J.H.

**CAPE VERDE.** *See* STATISTICS OF THE WORLD.

**CARIBBEAN BASIN.** The overall economic situation of the Caribbean Basin continued to deteriorate in 1987, despite improvements in some areas. There were elections or government changes in several countries.

**Regional Developments.** The region experienced a trade deficit, resulting in part from sharp reductions in U.S. imports of sugar and petroleum products. Increases in exports of winter vegetables, fruits, coffee, beef, textiles, and seafood were not sufficient to offset these cutbacks. Gross domestic product per capita was declining in nearly every country and especially in the oil-producing nation of Trinidad and Tobago. However, some positive economic indicators showed up. Agricultural production increased, despite poor weather. Tourism improved substantially throughout the region. Unemployment declined in many states, most notably Puerto Rico and Jamaica.

**Bahamas.** Prime Minister Lynden O. Pindling won a sixth term in office when his Progressive Liberal Party captured 31 of 49 seats in Bahamian parliamentary elections June 19. The opposition Free National Movement won 16 seats, and independents captured the remaining 2. Pindling's victory came despite new allegations that he and others in the government had taken money from drug smugglers using the Bahamas to bring drugs from South America to the United States.

**Barbados.** Barbados was stunned by the death on June 1 of Prime Minister Errol Barrow, 67, a prominent figure in the political life of the island for more than 40 years. As prime minister from 1961 to 1976, he led his country to independence from Britain. He returned as prime minister in 1986 when his Democratic Labor Party won a sweeping victory in parliamentary elections. Barrow was replaced by Deputy Prime Minister Erskine Sandiford.

**Dominican Republic.** A central political event in the Dominican Republic was the consolidation of power by the country's new president, Joaquín Balaguer, leader of the conservative Social Christian Reform Party. As an ailing octogenarian, Balaguer had been expected by many to serve as a figurehead, while others would formulate policy and reshape the party. Instead, he governed the country energetically, promoting the prosecution of former government officials and seeking to deal with the country's severe economic problems.

In October, at least 50 Dominican "boat people," seeking to enter Puerto Rico illegally, were drowned or killed by sharks when their ship capsized and sank off the Dominican coast.

**Grenada.** The squabbling that characterized the coalition government of Grenadian Prime Minister Herbert Blaize ended with the resignations of three of his cabinet ministers in April. The resignations were triggered by the government's decision to lay off half of the country's civil servants, in a move to reduce to 45 percent the share of the national budget devoted to salaries.

**Guyana.** Responding to Guyana's continuing economic distress and charges of political corruption, President Desmond Hoyte moved toward increased reliance on the private sector and changes in the ruling People's National Congress. Hoyte also reorganized his cabinet.

**Jamaica.** The political scene in Jamaica was dominated by the possibility that Prime Minister Edward Seaga would call for general elections before the constitutionally required date of December 1988. The economy continued to suffer from the fact that its main exports—bauxite, alumina, and sugar—were poor prospects on the world market. By midyear, however, the good news was overtaking the bad. For example, tourism was up for the second consecutive year, despite highly publicized violent attacks on visitors in Montego Bay and elsewhere. International agencies continued to extend loans and to cooperate in rescheduling debt.

**Suriname.** The military dictatorship of Lieutenant Colonel Dési Bouterse received a rebuke in November's elections when a three-party opposition coalition won at least 40 seats in the 51-seat National Assembly. Transition to a civilian government was not, however, assured. In March the National Assembly had approved a draft constitution, which the voters supported in a September referendum, thus paving the way for the elections.

**Trinidad and Tobago.** In its first year in office, the government of Prime Minister A. N. R. Robinson sought to halt Trinidad and Tobago's economic decline with a program of austerity and reform. The government also granted full internal self-rule to Tobago in an effort to stem threats of secession. In February Noor Hassanali was elected president of Trinidad and Tobago by Parliament.

See STATISTICS OF THE WORLD. See also CUBA; HAITI; PUERTO RICO.          F.W.K., L.L.P., P.W.

**CENTRAL AFRICAN REPUBLIC.**    See STATISTICS OF THE WORLD.

**CEYLON.** See SRI LANKA.

**CHAD.** Government forces in Chad scored several dramatic military victories in 1987 and expelled most of Libya's expeditionary force from the northern third of the country before a September cease-fire. The government side was aided by dissension among the rebels and by the defection late in 1986 of many rebels loyal to Goukouni Oueddei, after Libya backed a rival faction loyal to Acheikh Ibn Oumar.

On January 2, about 3,000 of President Hissène Habré's government troops captured Fada, a northern Chad town garrisoned by rebel and Libyan troops. On March 22, Habré's army attacked Wadi Doum, Libya's most im-

portant military base in northern Chad, from which Soviet-made Libyan aircraft frequently bombed government areas. Habré's troops overwhelmed the 3,000 to 5,000 men in the garrison and inflicted the sharpest defeat on Libyan forces since Muammar al-Qaddafi took power in 1969. Afterward, the other Libyan outposts in northern Chad—including the 100-square-mile oasis at Faya-Largeau—were aban-

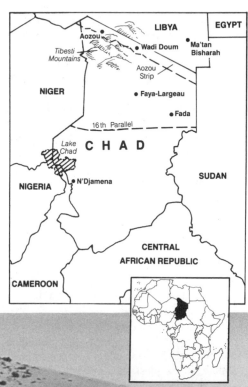

*Chadian government troops, relying on Toyota pickup trucks for mobility in the desert (below), fought a low-tech war but won a string of victories against the forces of Libyan leader Muammar al-Qaddafi, who had been supporting Chadian rebels. Chad's military even made a successful foray into Libya.*

doned by the Libyan Army, which fled into the Tibesti Mountains. On August 8, Habré's forces moved into the Aozou Strip, a band stretching across northern Chad up to the border with southern Libya; the area, which is rich in uranium and other minerals, was annexed by Libya in 1973. The Chadian troops captured Aozou, the only urban center in the area, but Libyan forces recaptured the town on August 28.

On September 5, Chadian forces invaded undisputed Libyan territory for the first time, capturing and demolishing a major air base at Ma'tan Bisharah, 60 miles inside the country. France, which maintained a 1,200-man force in southern Chad to support Habré, urged him to seek a diplomatic solution to the conflict. On September 11, Chad and Libya both accepted a cease-fire. At a special meeting of the Organization of African Unity in Zambia on September 24-25, Chad and Libya both agreed to let the OAU mediate the dispute. Late in the year, the issue remained stalemated, and a number of cease-fire violations were reported.

Negotiations between Habré and Goukouni, still his most significant opponent, were also carried on directly or indirectly, as Habré spent much of the year in Algeria under the protection of that government. Goukouni agreed to recognize Habré as Chad's "supreme authority" but demanded changes in the government that Habré would not accept.

The United States, which was providing military assistance, including advanced Stinger antiaircraft missiles, to Goukouni, found encouraging regional implications in his victories. U.S. support for Habré was emphasized during the Chadian president's first official visit to the United States in June.

An economic policy paper for the period 1987-1989 was presented in June, paving the way for desperately needed development aid. Losses by CotonTchad, the official national cotton company, continued, and the government budget deficit remained large.

See STATISTICS OF THE WORLD.          J.D.

**CHEMISTRY.** New food and environmental health hazards were identified in 1987, while researchers succeeded in creating synthetic bones that can be replaced by living cells.

**Food Hazards.** Potato skins contain naturally toxic chemical compounds called glycoalkaloids, which can cause headaches, nausea, and diarrhea, according to biochemist Nell Mondy, who cautioned that cooking does not destroy these chemicals. In fact, she reported in June, frying the skins more than doubles the concentration of glycoalkaloids. Although a person would have to eat 10 to 50 potatoes at a sitting to actually fall ill, she noted that just a few servings of fried potato skins, a popular snack, can cause ill effects.

Scientists announced in July that a toxic plant seed once commonly eaten by Pacific Islanders appears to be the cause of an unusually high incidence in that region of nervous system disorders similar to amyotrophic lateral sclerosis (ALS), commonly known as Lou Gehrig's disease. During World War II, when rice was difficult to obtain, islanders had regularly used the highly toxic seed of the false sago palm, or cycad, to make flour. Apparently such flour contained an unusual amino acid called BMAA which, when given in large doses to monkeys, caused neurological defects such as tremors, a stooped posture, and a shuffling gait. These findings suggest that environmental factors such as exposure to certain chemicals may play a greater role than previously realized in the development of various neurological disorders.

**Pyramid Cement?** Chemist Joseph Davidovits of Barry University near Miami, contends that the Egyptian pyramids were constructed from synthetic stone that was cast on-site like modern concrete. He reported that a text discovered 100 years ago on an island in the Nile contained a list of 29 minerals that could be processed with crushed limestone and other natural aggregates to produce the synthetic stone, which is extraordinarily durable because the ingredients bind together chemically, as in natural rock, rather than mechanically as in portland cement. Davidovits noted that the pyramid stones contain chemicals not found in stones from Egyptian quarries, as well as microscopic traces of human or animal hairs that could have fallen in while the chemicals were being mixed.

**Synthetic Bone.** A new type of synthetic bone has been developed at the University of Texas

t Austin. Richard J. Lagow of the university announced in June that he had synthesized a orm of hydroxyapatite, a mineral that gives ones strength and rigidity. Tests in animals have show that once the synthetic bone has been implanted, it is slowly broken down by bodily processes and replaced by living bone. xperts predict the new material may be useful n orthodontics and in reconstructing or replacing bones. Tooth enamel is a pure form of he mineral; a Dallas dental surgeon recently mplanted a tooth made of the synthetic substance in his own mouth and hoped to begin using it with patients.

**Anti-rubber.** An unusual material that behaves perversely when stretched or squeezed has been invented by a materials scientist at the University of Iowa. When normal substances re stretched, they get thinner; when squeezed, hey bulge out. But when the new material, a ort of anti-rubber, is stretched in one direction, . bulges out in every other. If it is squeezed om the top and bottom, it shrinks inward from he sides as well. The inventor, Roderic Lakes, hinks the material might be useful for special hock absorbers and Velcro-like fasteners.

**Environmental Hazards.** A new study found hat formaldehyde, a chemical widely used in ertain manufacturing processes, can cause eurological problems at levels as low as 1 art per million to workers exposed to it on the job. The current federal government limit for formaldehyde in the air was set in 1970 at 3 parts per million during an eight-hour workday. In light of the new evidence, the U.S. Occupational Safety and Health Administration proposed a limit of 1 part per million.

A newly developed chemical method uses cyanuric acid, an inexpensive granular chemical used in swimming pools, to remove nitrogen oxide pollutants from the exhaust gases of diesel cars and trucks and from the smokestacks of coal-burning power plants. Nitrogen oxide particles in the air combine with water to form nitric acid, a key component of acid rain, but if cyanuric acid is heated to 675° Fahrenheit, it becomes a gas and reacts with nitrogen oxides to form harmless nitrogen, carbon dioxide, and water vapor. Chemist Robert A. Perry was constructing an emission-control device for trucks, using this technique.     T.H.M.

**CHESS.** In March 1987, Anatoly Karpov defeated 24-year-old fellow Soviet Andrei Sokolov, 7½-3½, without losing a game, to win the right to challenge World Champion Gary Kasparov in Seville, Spain, in the fall. Karpov's victory set the stage for the fourth world championship match between the two "super K's." Kasparov won the last two, 13-11 and 12½-11½. The first match was terminated—after five months of play—by International Chess Federation President Florencio Campomanes.

*Carmen Quintana, 19, who claimed she was set afire by Chilean soldiers during antigovernment protests in 1986, visits the tomb of a friend who died of injuries received in the same incident. Quintana, who received medical treatment in Canada, returned to Santiago to be present during Pope John Paul II's visit to Chile.*

As the 24-game Seville championship approached its end in December, after two months of play, each contender had won three games, with the rest of the games drawn. Since Kasparov as champion would retain his title in the event of a tie, Karpov had to win one more game. He did, when Kasparov suddenly blundered in the 23rd game. But Kasparov mounted a strong attack to defeat his challenger in the final game and retain his title.

Earlier in the year, in April, Kasparov tied for first with Ljubomir Ljubojevic in the S.W.I.F.T. Brussels tournament. Karpov was third in the S.W.I.F.T. tournament. A series of three interzonal tournaments were held during the summer and fall to determine the next challenger for the world championship. The three top players from each interzonal will join the four top players from the last cycle in a candidates' tournament, to be held in Canada in early 1988. Among the interzonal winners, Nigel Short of Great Britain, who is in his early 20's, promised to become the strongest Western challenger for the world championship.

In other events, U.S. champion Yasser Seirawan, who had beaten Kasparov in the 27th Chess Olympiad in late 1986, went on to win first prize in the giant New York Open held in April 1987, with 45 grandmasters competing.

J.T.S

**CHILE.** A visit by Pope John Paul II in April 1987 and the government's preparation for an upcoming plebiscite on its future revealed a Chile that was deeply polarized by underlying political differences.

The major political question mark hanging over the country was the plebiscite, to be held before March 1989, in which voters would be asked to approve or reject a single presidential candidate selected by the ruling junta. President Augusto Pinochet Ugarte indicated that he wanted to be that single candidate. In early July, Pinochet reshuffled his cabinet and the top military posts, making appointments that seemed designed to strengthen his candidacy.

New laws on political parties and voter registration were enacted in March. Parties had been officially banned since the 1970's. The new law governing political parties allowed non-Marxist parties to have legal status by registering with the government, but still prohibited Marxist parties. Voter registration was begun; those registering would be able to vote in the plebiscite. But the new electoral registration law drew heavy complaints because it required people to pay a $1.50 fee (one day's income for a semiskilled worker), and the vast majority of Chile's 8.5 million eligible voters were slow to register.

Some 350 political prisoners staged a hunger strike early in the year, demanding fair trials and an end to torture. The five-week strike ended during the pope's visit after mediation by church leaders. Political violence resumed in June when police killed 12 suspected guerrillas in separate incidents, leading to charges that the victims had been murdered in cold blood. Five young men considered members of the Communist Party disappeared in early October, and three people were killed in clashes with police during an October 7 general strike.

During his visit in April, Pope John Paul II spoke of the need for a prompt return to democracy and human rights, which encouraged the opposition leaders, including Com-

unists and Socialists, with whom he met. He
lso appeared and prayed with Pinochet and
autioned Chilean clergy against taking polit-
al positions. The most serious disturbance in
e pope's visit took place during an outdoor
ass before an estimated 600,000 to 1,000,000
eople; police used tear gas to quell the
emonstrators.

Chile's economy continued to grow. The
ross national product, although still below the
981 level, was expected to rise at an annual
te of 5 percent. Unemployment approached
9 percent, however, and inflation was running
t a 24 percent annual rate during the early
art of the year.

Reacting to instances of alleged repression
Chile, the United States abstained on a
World Bank vote for a $200 million loan to
hile and suspended Chile's limited duty-free
ccess to the American market.

Chile's $21 billion debt was restructured in
ne, and half of it spread out over 15 years.
he 1986 trade surplus of $800 million was
ot enough to cover interest payments. Food
upplies in central Chile were seriously affected
y floods in July and August.

See STATISTICS OF THE WORLD.        J.F., Jr.

**CHINA.** In 1987 continuing conflict over economic and political reform contributed to important political changes in China, including
the fall of Chinese Communist Party Secretary
Hu Yaobang, who was replaced by Zhao Ziyang. Strongman Deng Xiaoping officially retired from the Central Committee but apparently
retained preeminence. In foreign affairs, agreement was reached with Portugal for transfer of
sovereignty over the Portuguese colony of
Macao.

**Reform.** Large-scale protests by students who
were at once stimulated by and dissatisfied
with the country's hesitant movement toward
reform continued during the early part of the
year, highlighting conflict within the party
itself. Although virtually the entire leadership
is committed to reform in principle, it disagrees
significantly over matters of degree and timing.
The "reformers" are relatively pragmatic and
experimental, whereas the "conservatives" put
stress on preservation of the official Marxist-
Leninist-Maoist ideology and on the need for
caution.

The demonstrations in Beijing (Peking) caused
the central Communist Party newspaper, the
*People's Daily,* to publish an editorial on Jan-

Buddhist monks and other Tibetans demanded independence in a
eries of violent outbursts in Lhasa during the fall. The protesters,
who chanted the name of their exiled leader, the Dalai Lama,
ought with Chinese forces; several on each side were reportedly
illed.

*A lull in the Thirteenth Chinese Communist Party Congress found its two most prominent members—Deng Xiaoping, right, and his protégé Zhao Ziyang, the party leader—making informal conversation over tea.*

uary 6, criticizing party members who had been lax in opposing Western influence. The unrest precipitated but did not directly cause the fall of General Secretary Hu Yaobang, who was a leader of the political reform movement. Among those ranged against Hu was the military leadership, which reportedly threatened martial law unless the student demonstrations were stopped and firmer social discipline imposed. Hu was succeeded as acting general secretary by Premier Zhao Ziyang, the major architect of the economic reform program.

In January, three prominent intellectuals were expelled from the Communist Party: Fang Lizhi, a pro-Western scientist and a vice president of the university in Heifi where the first major student demonstrations had occurred; Wang Ruowang, a Shanghai writer; and Liu Binyan, a muckraking reporter for the *People's Daily*. Inevitably, Deng Xiaoping was adversely affected by this conservative backlash, if only because his former protégé Hu Yaobang had been made a scapegoat by the conservatives. But with his usual agility, Deng shifted sufficiently to put himself on the conservatives' side while the backlash lasted.

By about the time the National People's Congress met for its annual session in late March, a working compromise between reformers and conservatives appeared to have been achieved: Students, media, and intellectuals would be firmly disciplined, but punishments would be confined to party members; basic economic reforms, including the "open" policy toward the outside world, would be retained. In December, however, Beijing was again rocked by student protests, occasioned by the fatal stabbing of one student; the protestors demanded better security and other university reforms.

**Party Congress.** The Thirteenth Communist Party Congress, held October 25–November 1, made it clear that the economic reform program would continue, but within a socialist framework. Limited political changes were adopted, stopping well short of a dilution of Communist Party power. Deng Xiaoping retired from the Central Committee—mainly, it appeared, to facilitate the retirement of senior conservatives, including Chen Yun, Peng Zhen, and Li Xiannian; Deng clearly retained paramount influence over policy.

The new Central Committee elected by the Congress named Zhao Ziyang as permanent general secretary. It also named a new Political Bureau and the latter's Standing Committee, both of which were strongly reformist in composition. Soon afterward, Li Peng, 56, a Soviet-educated engineer and newly installed Political Bureau member, was made acting prime minister of China, replacing Zhao Ziyang, who gave up this post to concentrate on his position as general secretary.

**Tibet.** Thousands of Buddhist monks and other Tibetans demonstrated in favor of Tibetan independence on September 27, October 1 (China's National Day), and October 6 in Lhasa and other towns. Chinese troops and police suppressed the demonstrations with considerable force, and several people were killed. Resenting the worldwide sympathy for the Tibetans, Beijing expelled all Western reporters from the region.

**Economy.** The state sector did not do as well as the cooperative and private sectors. Defense industries were operating well below capacity and in many cases were profitably engaged in turning out consumer goods. Poor management of China's scarce forest resources showed up in the form of widespread fires in Heilongjiang and Inner Mongolia during May and June.

Economic figures for 1986 showed an overall growth rate of 9.3 percent. Grain output fell short of targets, and there was a budget and a trade deficit as export prices dropped. In 1987, China had its first trade surplus in four years; however, an accord effective in 1988 sharply curbed exports of textiles and apparel to the United States—a major source of foreign exchange earnings.

**Foreign Affairs.** A major step toward territorial unification was taken in March, when China and Portugal reached an agreement under which sovereignty and jurisdiction over Macao would pass to China in 1999, two years after the United Kingdom was already scheduled to transfer Hong Kong to Chinese control. The Sino-Portuguese agreement provides for a high level of local autonomy under Chinese sovereignty and for a 50-year period during which no major changes are to be made in the existing economic and social systems.

North Korean leader Kim Il Sung visited China in May. Eager to discourage his government from moving unduly close to Moscow, Beijing continued to urge the United States to remove its troops from South Korea and accept the North Korean proposal for three-way talks—to involve the United States, South Korea, and North Korea—on the future of the peninsula.

Sino-Vietnamese relations remained tense, although conflicts along the common border appeared to have declined. Beijing refuses to acquiesce in Vietnamese domination of Cambodia, while the Soviet Union, Vietnam's patron, is reluctant to press Hanoi to withdraw its troops from that country.

While issuing public denials, Beijing—which supports Iran's Khomeini regime—has been selling large quantities of arms, including Silk-

*An army medical officer examines a survivor of a month-long fire in northeastern China that ravaged nearly 1.5 million acres of forest and villages during the spring, killing over 200 people and leaving more than 50,000 homeless. The reported cause: Forest Bureau workers who tossed out lighted cigarettes and used chainsaws improperly.*

worm antiship missiles, to that country. In October the United States responded to the Silkworm sales by suspending consideration of possible exports of some high-technology products to China. China continued to deny that it was selling arms to Iran, but told the United States it would try to block third countries from reshipping Chinese weapons there.

Relations with the United States remained basically good. U.S. Secretary of State George Shultz visited Beijing in March and reaffirmed American interest in a cooperative agreement with China. Shultz made a new policy departure by publicly discouraging contacts between China and Taiwan.

Defense cooperation (the official U.S. term) between China and the United States continued to move ahead. As it has for several years past, the United States supplied equipment manned by Chinese and located in western Xinjiang to monitor nuclear and space developments in Soviet Central Asia. Yang Shangkun, a key party official involved in military affairs, visited the United States in June.

Sino-Soviet relations continued to improve, although slowly; the impetus for the improvement had come from the Soviets, when Moscow abandoned its claim that the Sino-Soviet border ran along the Chinese side of the Amur and Ussuri rivers. The two countries agreed to begin surveying for determination of a new boundary. However, Beijing continued to distrust Moscow's assertiveness in Asia and has canceled or suspended a majority of the 24 industrial projects on which Moscow had agreed to help. Trade has been on the upswing across the common border, but mostly on a barter basis.

Tension was high between China and India during the first half of the year. The causes appeared to arise mainly from Prime Minister Rajiv Gandhi's tendency to compensate for domestic political difficulties by activist behavior toward India's neighbors. Beijing was evidently angered by India's formal integration of Arunachal Pradesh, an area east of Bhutan that China claims, into the Union.    H.C.H.

**CHINA, REPUBLIC OF.** See TAIWAN.

**CIVIL LIBERTIES AND CIVIL RIGHTS.** During 1987 one of the largest national civil rights marches since the 1960's was mounted in Georgia, and some 200,000 gay rights activists demonstrated in Washington, D.C. Testing for AIDS and drugs were important issues. The U.S. Supreme Court decided significant cases involving discrimination against minorities, free speech, women's rights, capital punishment, and other issues. (See also BLACKS IN THE UNITED STATES; UNITED STATES: Supreme Court; and WOMEN.)

**Minorities.** *Demonstration.* One of the largest traditional civil rights demonstrations since the 1960's took place January 24 in Forsyth County, Ga., where an estimated 15,000–20,000 people marched. Forsyth County, a rural district in the northern part of the state, has an all-white population of 38,000. In 1912 black residents were driven out, following the rape of a white woman and the resultant lynching of one black man and the hanging of two blacks after a swift trial. A march, allegedly to show that blacks could visit Forsyth County today, was originally scheduled for January 17, but the 90 persons who arrived to march were rebuffed by about 300 counterdemonstrators. Civil rights leaders, including Coretta Scott King and Andrew Young, then organized the January 24 march, which took place under the surveillance of 1,700 national guardsmen and 500 state troopers. Fourteen people were arrested, but no major disturbances occurred.

*Discrimination.* The Supreme Court held in May that the Civil Rights Act of 1866, enacted to protect the rights of emancipated slaves, is applicable to a wide variety of ethnic groups. One of the cases decided, *Saint Francis College v. Al-Khazraji,* involved a college teacher claiming discrimination because of his Arab origins. The other, *Shaare Tefila Congregation v. Cobb,* involved a Jewish synagogue that was defaced with anti-Semitic slogans. Both plaintiffs won the right to sue under the 1866 law.

**AIDS.** The United States continued to struggle with the alarming threat of AIDS (acquired immune deficiency syndrome). The conflict between the public health implications of this incurable disease and the protection of victims from discrimination challenged public officials. The predominant victims are gay men and intravenous drug users, with a very high incidence among minorities. Hemophiliacs for a time were also a major risk group; in 1987

*Testing positively for the AIDS virus though showing no signs of the disease, the three hemophiliac Ray brothers of Arcadia, Fla. (left), were the focus of protests when they tried to attend school under a court order. After their house was destroyed by a fire of suspicious origin, the family left town.*

family with three hemophiliac children who had tested positive for AIDS were driven out of their home in Arcadia, Fla.

In May, President Ronald Reagan called for mandatory AIDS testing of immigrants and federal prisoners, as well as for "routine testing" of state prisoners, of people seeking marriage licenses, and perhaps of patients in veterans' hospitals. The term "routine testing" has since been widely used but left loosely defined; federal officials said the term indicates testing that is generally carried out but can be declined by individuals. At a conference on AIDS held in Washington, D.C., June 1–5 and attended by over 6,000 scientists, testing for AIDS was the dominant issue.

On June 8, Attorney General Edwin Meese II called for a program to test immigrants overseas and illegal aliens seeking resident status under the amnesty program. As of De-

cember 1, such individuals were required to submit AIDS test results; those testing positive could be denied entry or legal status. The American Medical Association adopted a policy statement in June that endorsed mandatory testing for prisoners and would-be immigrants, and a continuation of such tests for blood, organ, and semen donors and military personnel. Tests were also recommended for patients about to undergo surgery in hospitals in areas with a high incidence of AIDS cases. The AMA called for voluntary testing of high-risk groups. Concern was expressed over the need to protect confidentiality and to avoid discrimination against those who test positive.

In December the U.S. Defense Department said it was removing AIDS-infected military personnel from sensitive posts, on the grounds that the virus could impair mental functioning even in the absence of overt symptoms.

# CIVIL LIBERTIES AND CIVIL RIGHTS

The Supreme Court, in *School Board of Nassau County, Fla., v. Arline,* held that the federal law barring discrimination against the handicapped protects persons with contagious diseases. The case involved a third-grade teacher with tuberculosis but drew wide attention because of the decision's implications for AIDS victims and carriers of the AIDS virus. The first ruling that the law did apply to AIDS victims came in November, when a federal appeals court in San Francisco ordered that a teacher suffering from AIDS be reinstated.

**Gay Rights.** More government money for AIDS research and treatment was one of the major goals of an October 11 demonstration in Washington, D.C., by at least 200,000 homosexuals and their supporters. The demonstrators, who also sought legislation to outlaw discrimination on the basis of "affectional and sexual orientation," marched past the White House to a rally in the Mall. The demonstration was part of a five-day series of political activities that ended with a mass act of civil disobedience on the steps of the Supreme Court building. About 600 people were arrested in a protest of the Court's 1986 decision upholding a Georgia law against sodomy.

**Drug Testing.** In February, President Reagan announced guidelines for drug-testing through urine samples, implementing his 1986 executive order for testing of federal employees in "sensitive posts." The announcement drew sharp criticism from federal employee unions and civil liberties groups such as the American Civil Liberties Union. The first federal agency to act on the president's order was the Department of Transportation. Secretary of Transportation Elizabeth Hanford Dole notified about 30,000 departmental employees in August that their names had been placed in a pool for random testing. Among those to be tested were air traffic controllers, test pilots, aviation inspectors, and railroad safety inspectors. Employees testing positive would be temporarily removed from their positions and given counseling. If drugs were used on the job, the employee would be fired. Court tests of the program were initiated by union officials. Nevertheless, the testing program began.

**Military Justice.** A few court decisions weakened the legal rights of military personnel. The Supreme Court held that the rule that bars service members from suing the government for injuries arising out of the course of military service also bars suits if the injury is caused by the negligence of a civilian agency (*United States. v. Johnson*). The government was held immune from legal action even in the case of

*Flanked by state troopers and national guardsmen, a massive civil rights march wound through all-white Forsyth County, Ga., on January 24. An earlier march had been disrupted when a hostile crowd threw stones and bottles at the demonstrators.*

*Quill pens, one of them in the talons of a stylized eagle, symbolize the Constitution on the $5 gold coin minted by the U.S. government for the document's 200th anniversary.*

an Army sergeant given LSD without his knowledge as part of a CIA "chemical warfare" experiment that damaged his mind (*United States* v. *Stanley*). The Court also decided that soldiers may be tried by military courts for any crime committed while in the military, whether service-connected or not (*Solorio* v. *United States*).

**Free Speech.** The statement made by a clerical employee of a county constable's office after the 1981 assassination attempt on President Reagan, that "if they go for him again, I hope they get him," was held to be protected under the First Amendment and not sufficient cause for discharge in *Rankin* v. *McPherson*. In *Board of Airport Commissioners of the City of Los Angeles* v. *Jews for Jesus Inc.*, the Court struck down a rule barring the religious group from distributing its literature on pedestrian walkways.

**Religious Beliefs and Employment.** In *Corporation of the Presiding Bishop of the Church of Jesus Christ of Latter-Day Saints* v. *Amos*, the Court allowed nonprofit religious organizations to use religious grounds as a basis for employment, even for secular jobs. And in *Hobbie* v. *Unemployment Appeals Commission of Florida*, the Court ruled that a state may not deny unemployment benefits to a person fired for refusal to work on the Sabbath.

**Suspects' Rights.** In a major ruling upholding a controversial provision of the Bail Reform Act of 1984, *United States* v. *Salerno*, the Court approved the pretrial detention of felony suspects if a clear case is made that release would endanger any other person or the community at large. Civil libertarian leaders denounced the decision as contrary to the principle of presumption of innocence. M.Gr.

**COINS AND COIN COLLECTING.** Two unusual coins commemorating the bicentennial of the U.S. Constitution were issued in 1987. A gold coin with a face value of $5 was designed by Marcel Jovine. The obverse displays a highly stylized eagle with a pen quill in its talons, while the reverse depicts the opening phrase of the Constitution, "We the People." The coin contains a quarter ounce of gold and thus has a high intrinsic value. A silver dollar designed by Patricia Lewis Verani shows a pen quill lying across a sheaf of documents and the words "We the People"; the reverse portrays a diverse group of people representing a wide cultural and social spectrum.

With commemorative issues popular, a movement was launched to change the existing designs for all circulating coins of the United States during the next several years. The Lincoln cent was expected to be among the first to undergo revision, with a different portrait of the 16th U.S. president used. Meanwhile, an anticipated change in U.S. paper money, originally scheduled for 1987, was postponed for at least two years. After six years of experimentation, the Treasury Department had hoped to introduce a new paper currency incorporating two novel anticounterfeiting devices: microprinting of the denomination name around the portrait and embedding of a plastic thread into the paper. Problems with the high-speed manufacture of the thread-containing paper led to the postponement.

Canada's first mini-dollar coin was not released on January 1 as planned. The master dies disappeared in transit from Ottawa to the mint at Winnipeg, which delayed the release and also led to complete redesign of the coin. The new coin, depicting a Canadian loon, was introduced in July. In an effort to avoid the fate of America's unpopular Susan B. Anthony mini-dollar coin, which went out of production in 1981, the Canadian piece, though reduced in size, is gold-colored and doubly thick, so as to be easily distinguishable from other coins. The Bank of Canada planned to discontinue printing the dollar bill by the end of 1989.

The British Royal Mint introduced four new coins containing 1, ½, ¼, and ¹⁄₁₀ ounce of gold and having a face value of 100, 50, 25, and 10 pounds respectively. The obverse of each coin carries an effigy of Queen Elizabeth II and the reverse a portrait of Britannia, an allegorical female figure.                E.C.R.

**COLOMBIA.** Colombia moved against poverty and drugs in 1987, as it continued to have problems with human rights violations.

President Virgilio Barco Vargas announced plans in January to spend $1 billion on roads, agriculture, schools, and health clinics in depressed areas. A few months later he announced an $8 billion, three-year development program.

Barco also ordered a crackdown on narcotics activity; he named 39 new judges, gave them protection, and created special tribunals for drug trafficking, terrorism, and extortion. Corrupt police and public officials were replaced, and a 1,500-person antidrug force was created. In February an alleged kingpin of Colombian narcotics, Carlos Lehder Rivas, was extradited to the United States, where he stood trial late in the year on an 11-count indictment involving massive smuggling of cocaine to that country through the Bahamas in 1979 and 1980. Colombia's attack on drugs received a major blow in June, however, when the Colombian Supreme Court annulled the 1979 extradition treaty with the United States. And in December a Colombian judge ordered the release from prison of Jorge Luis Ochoa, sought by the United States and said to be one of the world's leading cocaine smugglers.

A 1985 truce with active guerrilla forces largely unraveled. Six guerrilla groups, including the pro-Soviet Colombian Revolutionary

Armed Forces (FARC) and the nationalist April 19 Movement, united in October to form the Coordinadora Simón Bolívar. As violence broke out again in some areas, security forces found themselves undermanned and underequipped. Guerrillas attacked oil installations and bombed police stations.

The government called for increasing the debt by $9.3 billion (to $23.6 billion), which would cover the social development program. In February the World Bank announced that it would lend $3 billion to Colombia.

Five union officials were assassinated by hired gunmen on May 22, after the officials had negotiated a new contract on pay and working conditions at 260 banana plantations. The workers had gone on strike in March to protest earlier killings.

A dramatic increase in the number of "disappearances" in Colombia (over 900 documented cases between 1977 and 1987) caused international concern. Victims of violence included members of the judiciary, indigenous communities, human rights organizations, unions, churches, and grass-roots groups, as well as at least 800 activists in the Patriotic Union, the political wing of FARC. Most of the Patriotic Union losses, including the party's leader, Jaime Pardo Leal, were attributed to right-wing death squads.

*See* STATISTICS OF THE WORLD.            L.L.P.

**COLORADO.** *See* STATISTICS OF THE WORLD.

**COMMONWEALTH OF NATIONS.** In 1987 the Commonwealth of Nations was confronted by at least two divisive issues: the controversy over economic sanctions against the white-minority government of South Africa (itself a former Commonwealth nation) and Fiji's withdrawal from the Commonwealth after a September coup.

During the Commonwealth's Heads of Government Conference in Vancouver, Canada, in mid-October, attention was focused once again on South Africa and its racial system. Great Britain, which has a substantial trade and investment stake (estimated at $12.5 billion in 1986) in that country, sought to block the Commonwealth's efforts at adopting more stringent economic sanctions in protest against South African racial policy. British Prime Minister Margaret Thatcher argued that those sancions already in place have hurt blacks more than whites and strengthened the minority government's resistance to reform.

Britain came under repeated attacks for its position, perhaps most notably in a joint statement of criticism issued by a group that included Prime Ministers Rajiv Gandhi of India, Bob Hawke of Australia, Robert Mugabe of Zimbabwe, and Kenneth Kaunda of Zambia. The conference's final declaration on South Africa said that, with the exception of Britain, the Commonwealth nations supported "wider, tighter, and more intensified application" of sanctions against South Africa.

The Commonwealth also adopted an aid plan to encourage economic independence among the front-line nations (a group of states bordering or near South Africa). The plan concentrated on rebuilding and protecting transportation and communications links in the region, with the emphasis on the port of Maputo in Mozambique and the Limpopo rail line connecting the port with Zimbabwe.

The 49-nation Commonwealth lost one of its members in September, when the Pacific island nation of Fiji severed its ties with the organization, following a coup. Lieutenant Colonel Sitveni Rabuka, who staged the coup, declared Fiji to be an independent republic and repudiated the authority of Sir Penaia Ganilau as governor general and representative of Queen Elizabeth II. Strong opposition to the coup came from India's Gandhi, who protested the racial components of Fiji's new constitution; it guaranteed control of the government to ethnic Fijians at the expense of ethnic Indians, who comprise 49 percent of the population.                                    M.C.

**COMMUNIST WORLD.** Calls for reform and revitalization were sounded through much of the Communist world in 1987. In both the Soviet Union and China comprehensive plans for economic and political reform were approved, although in some other Communist states the process moved much more slowly.

*Glasnost* and *Perestroika.* Throughout the year Soviet leader Mikhail S. Gorbachev proceeded with his commitment to reform. Vital to his program was the realization that the Soviet Union had to improve its economic and technological performance in order to retain and expand its role as a global power. Economic

*Indian Prime Minister Rajiv Gandhi addresses the opening session of the Commonwealth Heads of Government Conference, held in Vancouver, Canada. At left and behind him are national leaders attending the biennial summit.*

The face of Lenin, leader of the Bolshevik revolution, loomed large as the Soviet Union marked its 70th anniversary with parades in Moscow.

restructuring (*perestroika*) that would reduce the role of the top-heavy central bureaucracy in decision making and management was the key to his proposed economic revitalization; openness (*glasnost*) in public debate over economic and political problems was deemed essential to undermine the opposition of much of the party-state bureaucracy to reform.

Also crucial to Gorbachev's plans was a reduction in tensions in East-West relations that could permit the Soviet leadership to focus on domestic reform. Thus the U.S.-Soviet pact to eliminate short-range and medium-range missiles, signed by Gorbachev on his summit visit to Washington, D.C., in early December, was a major achievement. On his way home after the summit, the Soviet leader met with other Warsaw Pact leaders in East Berlin to brief them on the agreement; as expected, the leaders hailed the treaty in highly favorable terms.

Although the Soviet Communist Party approved the general outlines of Gorbachev's reform program at a Central Committee plenum in June, evidence of widespread resistance to its implementation continued. The sacking of Moscow party chief Boris Yeltsin, a highly vocal advocate of reform, after his criticism of the slow pace of reform later in the year, was viewed as an indication of the opposition strength.

**Reform and Eastern Europe.** Gustav Husák, who presided over the dismantling of liberalization in Czechoslovakia upon coming to power there in 1969, resigned as the country's Communist Party secretary on December 17, though retaining the largely ceremonial office of president of Czechoslovakia. Husák, 75, was the first aging Eastern European leader to step down since Gorbachev took office in 1985. Milos Jukes, Husák's successor as party leader, received a congratulatory message from Gorbachev, urging him to move forward with the "restructuring" of the economy and the "democratization of public and political life." It was uncertain whether he would pursue reforms more vigorously than his predecessor.

Gorbachev's call for reform received a mixed reaction among the various Communist Party chiefs in Eastern Europe. The Polish and Hungarian leaders responded enthusiastically, introducing programs of their own. However, East Germany and Czechoslovakia both had indicated substantial caution over reform, while President Nicolae Ceauşescu of Romania openly resisted. (Ceauşescu also failed to attend the postsummit meeting with Gorbachev in East Berlin, for unknown reasons.)

At his speech on the 70th anniversary of the Bolshevik Revolution, Gorbachev, recognizing the opposition to some of his positions, stated that unity among Communist states did not require identical policies.

Evidence of a shift in Soviet policy toward Eastern Europe could be seen in September, when Erich Honecker made the first trip ever of an East German Communist Party leader to the Federal Republic of Germany (West Germany). Honecker's long-delayed official visit confirmed the durable and growing importance of economic, political, and cultural relations between the two German states, despite existing differences.

**Restructuring and Comecon.** The 43rd session of the trade cooperation bloc known as the Council for Mutual Economic Assistance (Comecon), held in Moscow in October, officially reaffirmed the need for "restructuring" economic relations among the European Communist states. Crucial to these reforms was expanded cooperation in production and research among the Comecon member countries. Negotiations between Comecon and the European Economic Community over establishment of formal relations between the two economic blocs progressed. Late in the year, it appeared that agreements were being worked out to surmount two major stumbling blocks that had prevented agreement in the past—Comecon's refusal to recognize West Berlin as part of the EEC and the European Community's insistence that an agreement between the two economic organizations be supplemented by bilateral accords between the Community and each Comecon member.

**Warsaw Pact.** Warsaw Pact activities focused heavily on support for various arms control proposals made by the Soviet Union and its allies. Warsaw Pact leaders called for consultations with NATO on military doctrine, in line with proposals of Polish leader Wojciech Jaruzelski that both blocs develop strictly defensive military doctrines and armed forces postures, gradually reducing manpower and armaments. The plan received relatively little response from the West. The communiqué issued after a meeting of Warsaw Pact foreign ministers in Prague on October 29 reiterated long-established positions on arms control and regional security.

**Asia.** The 11th round of talks to normalize relations between China and the Soviet Union opened in Beijing (Peking) in October. Despite a lessening of hostility between the two countries in recent years, full normalization of relations still faced serious hurdles. The Chinese remained concerned about what they term the "three obstacles" to improved relations—the Soviet occupation of Afghanistan, the Vietnamese occupation of Cambodia, and Soviet troop concentrations along the Chinese border.

China's 13th Communist Party congress ended with the election on November 2 of Prime Minister Zhao Ziyang to the position of general secretary. Although Deng Xiaoping, China's senior leader and the major architect of reform, retired from both the Central Committee and the Politburo, reportedly to encourage retirement by the oldest political leaders, he continued to head the powerful Central Military Commission. At the end of November, General Secretary Zhao stepped down as head of government in order to devote himself full-time to his party responsibilities; Li Peng was named as acting prime minister. Li, a Soviet-trained engineer, was viewed as a cautious reformer.

In Vietnam, as part of a continuing reform-oriented sweep of an elderly leadership, Pham Hung was appointed prime minister, and Vo Chi Cong became head of state.

**Nonruling Parties.** Although West European Communist parties generally welcomed Gorbachev's reform program, they differed in their openness to reform within their own parties, which have been suffering from both internal fragmentation and declining popular support. In parliamentary elections in March, Finnish Communists won 13 percent of the vote, diluted between two separate groupings, the pro-Moscow Stalinist conservatives, with 4 percent, and the Eurocommunists with the remainder. In the June Italian elections, the Communist Party received only 26.6 percent of the vote for its worst defeat since 1968. This resulted in serious internal disagreements about future party policy. In February former Communist Party leader Santiago Carrillo founded the Workers' Party of Spain-Communist Unity. An adjunct to the "official" Communist Party, headed by Gerardo Iglesias, and the pro-Soviet secessionist Communist Party of the Peoples of Spain, created in 1984 by Ignacio Gallego, this party was the third Communist faction in Spain.

At an informal gathering of foreign Communists on November 4, Soviet leader Gorbachev went a distance toward accepting the

Italian Communist Party position supporting independence of national Communist parties. He noted that the Communist movement required "renewal and qualitative changes," which included independent action of national parties, as well as "joint action in up-to-date forms" and "a more sophisticated culture of mutual relations."

**Other Developments.** In Ethiopia, a reported 96 percent of the electorate approved a constitution that upholds Marxist ideology, effectively joining Ethiopia to the Communist bloc as the People's Democratic Republic of Ethiopia. In Lebanon, the small but active Communist Party was decimated, when many of its leaders and members were reported killed or missing in West Beirut shootouts. Fighting had flared up when Shiite Muslim clerics allegedly issued a religious edict urging the killing of all Communists in the area.   R.E.K.

**COMOROS.** See STATISTICS OF THE WORLD.

**COMPUTERS.** The year 1987 saw the introduction of a dizzying array of new entries by major computer manufacturers. At the same time, 1987 saw the further consolidation of the world of personal computers into two camps: IBM and Apple. Both computer companies consolidated their hold over the personal computing world with new products.

**Apple.** Apple Computer, Inc. made a strong showing with two new machines: the Macintosh SE and the Macintosh II. The SE was an improvement on the company's Macintosh Plus, a compact, graphics-oriented computer based on the Motorola Corporation's 16-bit 68000 microprocessor (capable of processing 16 bits of data at a time) and popular in desktop publishing and other business applications. The Macintosh II had a new 32-bit Motorola 68020 chip, giving it power and speed to match its ease of use. Both machines introduced the first expansion slots for the Macintosh line, meaning that they could be added to in a relatively inexpensive fashion.

**IBM.** The International Business Machines Corporation introduced a new line of computers known as Personal Systems/2, or PS/2. Powered by microprocessors ranging from the Intel Corporation's original 8086 chip to the more recent—and powerful—Intel 80386 (a 32-bit chip), the line provided integrated computing

options with a stronger graphics capability than ever before. The broad array of options presented by the handful of new computers from IBM caused some confusion among institutional hardware purchasers, many of whom took an initial wait-and-see attitude about buying into the new line. Many were waiting to see the new operating system that was to be used with some of the machines. This system, called OS/2, was intended to unlock the power of the advanced 80286 and 80386 microprocessor chips; it came onto the market at year's end. IBM threw the so-called clone makers into a panic with the introduction of its PS/2 line, which would be more difficult to copy than the "open-architecture" IBM PC.

Late in the year, IBM, reversing previous policy, announced that it was joining with supercomputer designer Steven S. Chen to work toward producing and marketing a machine using parallel processing, a radical new technology that dramatically increases computer speed. Chen had recently defected from Cray Research Inc., a top supercomputer maker.

**Software Mogul.** Microsoft Corporation founder William Gates, who had produced the original operating system for the IBM PC and compatibles, expanded his influence in the world of personal computing. Gates was retained by IBM to develop the massive OS/2 operating system for the new PS/2 line. In addition, Gates's company, Microsoft, had the leading word-processing (Word) and spreadsheet (Excel) programs for Apple's Macintosh, and Gates played a role in IBM's decision to follow the Macintosh's easy-to-use graphics interface in its new operating system. In October, Microsoft cemented the links between the competing machines when it introduced an IBM version of its Excel spreadsheet. The product was meant to challenge the near-total dominance of the IBM spreadsheet market by the Lotus Development Corporation's 1-2-3.

**Larger Computers.** It was also a year of expansion in the previously narrow market of workstations. Until recently used by few outside the field of engineering, these powerful, large-screen computing tools began to come within reach of more engineers and designers, along with other buyers, as new products were introduced and some prices were cut. This raditionally expensive market—machines could cost as much as $30,000 or more—has long been dominated by Sun Microsystems Inc. and Apollo Computer Inc. An example of this year's developments was Sun's reduction in April of the price of its entry-level workstation from $7,000 to less than $5,000. IBM's RT Personal Computer workstation saw improvements, including the first use of a one-megabit memory chip (capable of storing 1 million pieces of data) in a desktop machine. Industry analysts suggested that Apple's new Macintosh II was powerful enough to function as a workstation.

**IBM-Fujitsu Fight Settled.** In mid-September an American Arbitration Association panel settled a bitter dispute between IBM and Fujitsu Ltd. of Japan that had originated in the early 1980's. IBM had accused Fujitsu of having "systematically and pervasively" copied IBM operating systems for use in its IBM-compatible mainframe computers. Fujitsu was required by the panel to pay IBM fees for the programs and was allowed to establish a "secure facility" where it could review, under strict supervision, IBM technical data.                    J.R.S.

**CONGO.** See STATISTICS OF THE WORLD.

**CONGRESS OF THE UNITED STATES.** See UNITED STATES OF AMERICA: Congress.

**CONNECTICUT.** See STATISTICS OF THE WORLD.

**CONSTRUCTION.** See ECONOMY AND BUSINESS.

**COSTA RICA.** In 1987, two issues dominated public affairs in Costa Rica: the fallout from the Iran/contra affair in the United States and the peace plan for the Central American region proposed by President Oscar Arias Sánchez, who won the Nobel Peace Prize for his efforts. Indeed, the two were intimately related. President Arias had been instrumental in revealing the full extent of Reagan administration involvement in the contra war against the Sandinista government of Nicaragua. As a consequence of the scandal and the subsequent hearings in Washington, he gained in international credibility.

Arias proposed his peace plan in February at a meeting of Central American presidents, not including Nicaragua's Daniel Ortega, in San José. The plan called for a cease-fire in Nicaragua and amnesty for the contras, followed by free elections. It also called for an end to all conflicts in the region and the

Costa Rican President Oscar Arias Sánchez, shown here speaking at a Unesco meeting in Paris in June, won the Nobel Peace Prize for his efforts to end fighting in Central America.

prohibition of the use of one Central American nation's territory to attack another. Later, Arias included Nicaragua in the peace process, inviting Ortega to a Guatemala peace summit eventually held in August.

On August 7, all five Central American presidents attended the Guatemala meeting and signed a revised version of the Arias peace plan. The signing represented a major personal triumph for Arias, particularly in view of Costa Rica's long-standing differences with Nicaragua. At the invitation of House Speaker Jim Wright, Arias addressed the U.S. Congress in order to build support for the agreement; he received an enthusiastic welcome. Arias's efforts received a major boost in mid-October, with the announcement that he was to be awarded the 1987 Nobel Peace Prize. On November 5 each Central American government announced steps to be carried out to comply with the peace plan; chances of the plan's success remained uncertain.

The presence of over 200,000 Nicaraguan refugees has greatly magnified social and health problems. The quality of the once-vaunted healthcare system has declined precipitously, since it is being forced to deal with diseases that had been conquered but have now been reintroduced by the refugees.

See STATISTICS OF THE WORLD.          L.W.G.

**CRIME AND LAW ENFORCEMENT.** Crime in the streets took a backseat to crime on Wall Street and in government during 1987. The U.S. Supreme Court turned aside the last sweeping constitutional challenge to the death penalty (see UNITED STATES: Supreme Court), and subway "vigilante" Bernhard Goetz got his day in court.

**Wall Street Scandals.** A web of illegal stock-trading schemes was unveiled in civil and criminal charges lodged by the federal government against Wall Street executives. The first major case involved Dennis Levine, a former investment banker, who was sentenced to two years in federal prison and fined $362,000 in February on four felony counts of insider-trading practices. Levine cooperated with authorities in an investigation of other insider-trading activities. His evidence led to the filing of civil and criminal charges against Ivan Boesky, a major Wall Street speculator. Boesky in turn provided information on Martin Siegel, a former head of mergers and acquisitions at the investment house of Drexel Burnham Lambert.

Boesky pleaded guilty in April to one felony count of giving false statements to the federal government regarding his involvement in a takeover bid. He was later sentenced to three years in prison. He had previously agreed to pay $100 million in civil penalties and return of profits for trading abuses.

Siegel pleaded guilty in February to criminal charges involving insider trading. He also paid $9 million to settle—without admitting or denying guilt—civil charges brought by the SEC.

A Merrill Lynch & Company official, Nahum Vaskevitch, was charged by the Securities and Exchange Commission in March with having provided insider information to David Sofer, an Israeli investor, who was also charged. Sofer later agreed to pay $1 million and co-operate with the SEC in exchange for immunity from criminal prosecution. In another case, criminal stock manipulation charges were brought against Boyd Jefferies, a Los Angeles stock trader linked to Boesky; Jefferies pleaded guilty and agreed to stay out of securities activities for five years.

**Espionage.** A 25-year-old U.S. Marine sergeant, Clayton Lonetree, was convicted in August by military court-martial on charges of spying while serving as a security guard at the U.S. embassy in Moscow. He was sentenced to 30 years in prison, fined $5,000, and dishonorably discharged from service. In October his lawyers said Lonetree was cooperating with Marine counterintelligence in return for a five-year reduction in sentence. Another U.S. marine at the embassy, Sergeant Robert Stufflebeam, was convicted of dereliction of duty, for contacts with prostitutes, but acquitted of other charges.

In another case, Jonathan Pollard, a former civilian intelligence analyst for the U.S. Navy, was sentenced in March to life imprisonment for spying on behalf of Israel. His wife was sentenced to five years as an accessory.

**Contra Arms Deals.** In April, Washington fund-raiser Carl Channell pleaded guilty to conspiring to defraud the government by using a tax-exempt organization, the National Endowment for the Preservation of Liberty, to raise money to buy arms for the contra rebels seeking to overthrow the Marxist regime in Nicaragua. Public relations specialist Richard Miller pleaded guilty in May to conspiracy charges in the fund-raising scheme, and both he and Channell implicated a former National Security Council aide, Lieutenant Colonel Oliver North. Special Prosecutor Lawrence Walsh, who was investigating the Iran/contra affair, indicated North also was a target in the investigation that netted Channell and Miller. During hearings before Congress on the Iran/contra affair, North admitted having met with prospective donors but denied having directly solicited contributions.

**White House Officials.** Former White House Chief of Staff Michael Deaver, who left that post in 1985 to start a highly lucrative lobbying business, was convicted in December on three counts of perjury, for lying to a federal grand jury and a congressional subcommittee about his lobbying activities. He was acquitted on two other counts, after a seven-week trial. Deaver was the first person to be indicted under the 1978 Ethics in Government Act,

*Bernhard Goetz is escorted by members of the Guardian Angels, a volunteer group that patrols New York City's subways, after his acquittal on charges of attempted murder; Goetz had shot four black youths threatening to rob him in a subway car.*

which bars high government officials from certain lobbying activities within a set period of time after they leave office. The act also provides for appointing special prosecutors, or "independent counsels." Also indicted by a grand jury, after investigations by a special prosecutor, was former White House aide Lyn Nofziger. He was charged in July with illegal lobbying activities involving, among other clients, Wedtech Corporation, a Bronx military contractor. A number of others involved with Wedtech have been indicted on bribery or influence-peddling charges.

In May, former Labor Secretary Raymond Donovan—the first U.S. cabinet member to be indicted while in office—was acquitted, along with seven others, on charges of grand larceny and fraud in connection with a $186 million New York subway-tunnel deal.

**Organized Crime.** A jury in federal district court in New York convicted 17 men in March on charges involving a $1.6 billion drug smuggling operation. During the 17-month trial the prosecution described an intricate story of cooperation between the Sicilian Mafia and its American counterpart, the Cosa Nostra. After tons of morphine base were smuggled into Sicily from Turkey, they were processed into heroin and distributed through pizza parlors in the northeastern and midwestern United States. Profits went back to Sicily, in a laundering scheme that involved banks in New York, Switzerland, the Bahamas, and Bermuda. During the trial the body of one defendant was found in a trash bag in Brooklyn and another defendant was critically wounded by gunfire on a crowded street. In addition to prison sentences, the judge ordered that four of the defendants contribute a total of $2.5 million to a fund for treatment of drug addicts. Among the four were Gaetano Badalamenti, described as a former leader of the Mafia in Sicily, and Salvatore Catalano, alleged New York boss of the ring, both of whom drew 45-year prison sentences.

In January a U.S. district court judge imposed sentences ranging from 40 to 100 years on eight members of a "commission" of top crime leaders convicted of charges involving murders, labor payoffs, loan sharking, and extortion. Among those sentenced were Anthony Salerno, reputed head of the Genovese family; Anthony Corallo, said to be the boss of the Lucchese group; Carmine Persico, the alleged Colombo family head; and Gennaro Langella, reputed acting boss of the Colombo family.

**Violent Crime.** An unprecedented spree of random shootings and other violence, involv-

A rally in Howard Beach, a mostly white section in the New York City borough of Queens, condemned the December 1986 attack by white teenagers on three blacks who had entered the area.

ing motorists, turned California freeways into concrete lanes of terror during the summer. More than 120 incidents on streets and freeways, most of them in Los Angeles County, had left 5 persons dead and about 20 injured by summer's end. Many attacks were blamed on traffic-related disputes, but a number were without any apparent motive.

In August, Donald Harvey, a former nursing aide at a Cincinnati hospital, admitted killing 24 persons over a period of four years, mostly patients at the hospital. In return for pleading guilty to those murders, Harvey avoided the death penalty; he was sentenced instead to three consecutive life terms. He also admitted responsibility for 30 other murders, dating as far back as the early 1970's.

In what was thought to be the largest mass murder ever in Missouri, seven members of a farm family near the town of Elkland were found slain on September 25. On October 5, police charged the husband of one of the victims, James Schick, with the murders.

In one of the worst mass slaying incidents

in recent decades, R. Gene Simmons, Sr., 47, allegedly murdered 14 relatives who lived at or visited his rural Dover, Ark., home on Christmas weekend; he also allegedly shot 6 others, 2 of them fatally, on a rampage in nearby downtown Russelville. Those killed included Simmons's wife and several of his children and grandchilden. Among other mass murders late in the year, Robert Dressman, 40, apparently killed six relatives before shooting himself to death at the family home in Algona, Iowa.

A three-week trial in federal district court ended on November 17 with the conviction of two white supremacists, and the acquittal of two others, on charges relating to the 1984 murder of Denver talk show host Alan Berg, who had ridiculed their views on his program. The defendants, members of the neo-Nazi Order of the Silent Brotherhood, were already serving terms on racketeering charges.

**Pit Bulls.** In one of the first cases of its kind, a Georgia man was convicted in February of involuntary manslaughter and sentenced to five years in prison after his three pit bulls killed a four-year-old boy; the boy's spine was severed in two places. Although they account for only 1–2 percent of the dogs in the United States, in the past five years pit bulls have been responsible for more than two-thirds of the fatal attacks by dogs on people. Dozens of U.S. communities have proposed ordinances banning the animals, but such laws have been challenged as unconstitutionally vague, because of the difficulty in defining a pit bull, a generic name for usually mixed breed dogs related to the American Staffordshire terrier or the American pit bull terrier. Some breeders maintain that any dog can be trained to be vicious and that the problem lies with owners, not the dogs themselves. Owners include not only persons seeking protection against crime but also drug dealers and other criminals.

A series of fatal attacks on people by pit bulls have turned public opinion against the dogs, which once enjoyed a reputation as gentle pets (Tige in the Buster Brown shoe trademark and Pete in the Our Gang film comedies were pit bulls). There were widespread calls to outlaw the dogs.

**Goetz Acquittal.** Bernhard Goetz, whose shooting of four teenagers on a New York City subway train in December 1984 stirred heated and complex debate, was acquitted on June 16 of all but a misdemeanor charge of possessing a weapon illegally. The jurors grappled with the question of whether Goetz had acted in self-defense or whether, as the prosecution contended, he had acted irrationally in using deadly force against the youths—one of whom, Darrell Cabey, was paralyzed below the waist and brain-damaged in the shooting.

In October, Goetz was sentenced to six months in jail and five years' probation, fined $5,000, and ordered to undergo psychiatric counseling and perform 280 hours of community service. The sentence was appealed.

**Howard Beach Incident.** In February, 12 white teenagers were indicted on various charges stemming from an apparent racial attack the previous December against 23-year-old Michael Griffith and two other black men in the Howard Beach neighborhood of Queens, a borough of New York City. Griffith was allegedly chased onto a highway, where he was struck and killed by a car. A grand jury decided not to bring criminal charges against the driver of the car. Four of the 12 defendants went on trial in September. On December 21, after 12 days of deliberation, the jury convicted Jon Lester, Scott Kern, and Jason Ladone of assault and manslaughter, while acquitting them of

attempted murder. Lester and Kern were also acquitted on second-degree murder charges. The fourth defendant, Michael Pirrone, was cleared.

**Cuban Prisoner Riots.** Fearful of deportation under a newly revived U.S.-Cuban emigration pact, over 2,000 Cuban detainees at a federal prison in Atlanta and a federal facility in Oakdale, La., rioted and held more than 120 hostages in all, for as long as 11 days. The riots led to the death of one inmate and to millions of dollars in damages. However, negotiations at both facilities led to a peaceful release of hostages, under agreements that promised the Cubans case-by-case reviews and a moratorium on deportations.          L.S.G.

**CUBA.** In 1987, Cuban politics combined renovation with retrenchment, and there were mixed signals in the area of human rights. Late in the year, a U.S.-Cuban immigration agreement was revived.

After calling for regeneration of revolutionary idealism, President Fidel Castro had to contend with two major defections in the spring: Air Force Brigadier General Rafael del Pino, a Bay of Pigs hero, and Major Florentino Azpillaga, a senior intelligence officer in Czechoslovakia; both fled to the United States. In the leadership purge that followed, Luis Dominguez lost his position as president of the Institute of Civil Aviation and was arrested on charges of embezzlement.

A different note, however, was sounded with the removal of Jorge Enrique Mendoza, an ideologue and former Castro guerrilla companion, from the editorship of *Granma,* the official Communist Party newspaper. He was replaced by Enrique Roman, a young, sophisticated intellectual—a move that suggested a Cuban version of Soviet leader Mikhail Gorbachev's policy of *glasnost* (openness).

The emigration to the United States of 20 former political prisoners over several weeks in the spring was followed in May by the release of Roberto Perez Rodriguez, Cuba's longest-serving political prisoner, who had been jailed in 1959 for plotting against Castro. However, the new public prominence of the security forces, as well as Castro's stress on revolutionary zeal and ideological orthodoxy, suggested that Havana's liberalization might be more limited than Moscow's.

Cuba's economic problems were due largely to factors beyond Castro's control. Irregular rainfall caused shortfalls in the sugar crop, and low world prices for sugar diminished the value of the crop that remained. A slide in petroleum prices further decreased export revenue. The result was Cuba's most serious economic crisis in two decades. In an effort to spur production and combat materialism, Castro returned to the moral incentives of the 1960's, combined with a 1980's stress on work discipline and pragmatic planning.

The economic crisis led Cuba to suspend payments on its foreign debt, to eliminate nonessential hard currency imports, and to rely more heavily on its socialist (Comecon) trading partners, who already accounted for 85 percent of Cuba's foreign commerce. But above all, Cuba's decreased export earnings reinforced its dependence on Soviet aid and trade subsidies, estimated at $4 billion annually.

Cuba's relations with the United States were poor early in the year, as the Reagan administration tightened its economic embargo and withdrew the head of the U.S. mission in Havana. For its part, Havana began a public campaign against alleged espionage by U.S. diplomats. However, Cuba allowed some 30 political prisoners to emigrate to the United States in August and September, and in mid-September the United States filled its vacant senior diplomatic post in Havana. In November a suspended immigration agreement was revived, allowing Cuba to send 27,000 émigrés

*Ten years after his death, Greek Cypriot leader Archbishop Makarios was a larger-than-life figure. This 30-foot, 11-ton statue of Makarios by Nikos Kotziangis underwent final touches in London before being shipped to Cyprus.*

year and letting the United States return some 2,600 unwanted Cubans. The pact had been suspended in 1985 because of Cuba's anger over U.S. broadcasts to Cuba over Radio Martí. News of the deal sparked rioting by Cuban detainees and prisoners in the United States, arrivals in the 1980 Mariel boatlift, who feared being sent home.

See STATISTICS OF THE WORLD.          P.W.

**CYPRUS.** In 1987 the Greek-Turkish division on Cyprus went unresolved, despite continuing diplomatic efforts.

The 1986 United Nations proposal to reunite Cyprus—which called for a federated republic consisting of a Greek and a Turkish state—remained unacceptable to the Greek Cypriot side, partly because it did not provide a timetable for withdrawal of Turkish troops. In February special UN envoys proposed secret parallel talks between Greek and Turkish Cypriots, but the Turkish side refused unless talks were based on the 1986 UN proposal. The Soviet Union's efforts to promote a settlement also proved fruitless. In June and in December, the UN Security Council renewed the mandate for its multinational, 2,300-man peacekeeping force in Cyprus.

The Greek Cypriot parties began political maneuvering in anticipation of the 1988 presidential election. President Spyros Kyprianou planned to seek reelection, but it seemed unlikely that the Communist AKEL Party would again ally itself with Kyprianou's Democratic Party—as it had in 1983—to help reelect him.

In May the European Community and the Kyprianou government initialed the protocol of a 15-year customs agreement designed to ease trade restrictions between the island state and the 12 EC countries. The agreement took effect January 1, 1988. The Kyprianou government also signed a trade and technical protocol with China, as well as a trade agreement with Czechoslovakia, and it ratified a legal accord with the Soviet Union.

The Greek Cypriot economy continued to perform generally well, while the Turkish sector did poorly.

See STATISTICS OF THE WORLD.          P.J.M.

**CZECHOSLOVAKIA.** The year 1987 saw a change of leadership for Czechoslovakia's Communist Party, the first in nearly two decades. Gustav Husák, 75, who became party secretary in 1969 after a Soviet invasion forced the liberal Alexander Dubček from office, resigned on December 17 and was replaced by Milos Jakes, 65, a prominent member of the party's Presidium, or ruling council. Husák remained as the country's president, a largely ceremonial post. Western observers said Jakes had been considered Husák's likely successor and that his coming to power did not necessarily portend any major change in Czechoslovakia's economic or political climate. Jakes did receive a message from Soviet General Secretary Mikhail Gorbachev urging "restructuring" and "democratization"—an indication that the Soviets may have been impatient with the pace of change in Czechoslovakia.

The Czech leadership in general had shared the reservations of most other Eastern-bloc nations about Gorbachev's reform campaign and had been pursuing a minimalist response to it. In April, Gorbachev himself visited Prague. The visit was the object of high interest, with rumors that he might take some dramatic step. He did not, but on his arrival he was cheered by thousands lining streets which 19 years before had been cleared by Soviet tanks.

In January the tenth anniversary of the Charter 77 movement was noted, though not celebrated in public. Signed at first by a relatively small and loosely organized group of commentators on the political, social, and cultural needs of Czechoslovak society, the charter now has about 1,300 signatories and enjoys international renown as an effective voice of criticism of the Communist regime.

In March the trial of the Jazz Section of the Union of Czechoslovak Musicians took place. The case stemmed from refusal of the accused to disband a club of 5,000 jazz fans. Two of the five leading activists received sentences of 10 and 15 months, while the others received suspended sentences or were placed on probation for up to three years.

In July it was announced that cooperative farms, public organizations, and ordinary citizens "assisted by their family members" would be licensed to open catering establishments. Private individuals would be allowed to "open small stores, particularly in villages."

See STATISTICS OF THE WORLD.          R.A.P.

# D

**DAHOMEY.** See STATISTICS OF THE WORLD.

**DANCE.** In 1987 most dance companies were thinking big, with lavish productions, large-scale projects, and innovative versions of classical ballets.

**American Ballet Theatre.** In February, American Ballet Theatre (ABT), appearing in Chicago, premiered a new production of *The Sleeping Beauty,* paving the way for one of the most successful seasons in its 47-year history. This *Sleeping Beauty,* ABT's third attempt at interpreting Tchaikovsky's masterpiece, was staged by Kenneth Macmillan, after Marius Petipa. Although better danced than its predecessors, it was, however, lacking in theatrical imagination, and the sepia-toned decors of Nicolas Geogiadis created claustrophobic spaces. More successful was the decor for *Giselle,* ABT's second major production, which was first seen in Los Angeles in March. Gianni Quaranta's scenery for this *Giselle* and Anna Anni's stunning costumes were prepared for the 1987 Herbert Ross film *Dancers,* a contemporary drama starring ABT's artistic director, Mikhail Baryshnikov, which incorporated the ballet into its story. Another ABT highlight was *Enough Said,* a sexy number in the Balanchine style by principal dancer Clark Tippet, which showcased Robert Hill and Nora Kimball. Julio Bocca, the exciting new principal dancer from Argentina, provided some of the bravura Baryshnikov used to offer, while Amanda McKerrow established herself as a ballerina with her performances as Aurora in *The Sleeping Beauty,* as Giselle, and in Balanchine's *Theme and Variations.* Baryshnikov himself, nearing 40 and beset by injuries, scarcely danced with ABT in the winter season. He performed with his summer touring group, Baryshnikov & Co., and in a few fund-raising galas, including "Dancing for Life," an AIDS benefit held in New York City in October.

**Joffrey.** In September, in Los Angeles, the Joffrey Ballet launched its 31st year with an eagerly awaited event: the reconstruction by Millicent Hodson and Kenneth Archer of the original *Le Sacre du Printemps,* a collaboration by Vaslav Nijinsky, Igor Stravinsky, and Nicolas Roerich for Diaghilev's Ballets Russes. The original ballet had not been presented since its handful of performances in Paris and London in 1913. But the company's biggest project of the year was its $1.5 million production of *The Nutcracker,* choreographed largely by Robert Joffrey. The ballet opened in Iowa City in December, in a version that shifts the setting of the ballet to America in the late 19th century.

**New York City Ballet.** New York City Ballet, apparently marking time until it celebrates its 40th anniversary in 1988, offered no new ballets by Jerome Robbins. His co-ballet master Peter Martins provided two pleasant, small-scale works—*Les Petits Riens,* set to Mozart, and *Les Gentilhommes,* set to Handel—designed to display the talents of the company's younger dancers. One major but disappointing effort, *Ecstatic Orange,* which was set to music by 26-year-old composer Michael Torke, served as a showcase for Heather Watts and Jock Soto. Some critics saw a decline in City Ballet's creative vigor since the death of artistic director George Balanchine in 1983, including a slippage in the quality of dancing.

**Other American Companies.** The San Francisco Ballet's winter season was distinguished by three new ballets, by William Forsythe (*New Sleep*), James Kudelka (*Dreams of Harmony*), and artistic director Helgi Tomasson (*Intimate Voices*). In May, the Boston Ballet offered an ambitious three-part ballet, *Tales of Hans Christian Andersen.* The Pennsylvania Ballet, which merged with the Milwaukee Ballet during the year, produced *Winter Dreams,* a new three-hour narrative ballet choreographed by its artistic director, Robert Weiss.

The Cleveland Ballet's new *Swan Lake,* by Dennis Nahat, with lavish designs by David Guthrie, was the most ambitious production in that company's 11-year history. In September the Houston Ballet opened its first season at the $72 million Wortham Theater Center with a new *Romeo and Juliet,* and Ballet West gave André Prokovsky's evening-length *Anna Karenina* its first U.S. staging.

**Royal Ballet.** In London, in March, the Royal Ballet produced an ambitious new *Swan Lake*, based on research into the original choreography. It was Anthony Dowell's first production as the company's artistic director. Cynthia Harvey, on loan from ABT, danced the Swan Queen at the premiere.

**Soviet Companies.** The Bolshoi's nine-week summer tour of the United States was its first visit since 1979. The repertory was composed almost entirely of Yuri Grigorovich's simplistic socialist-realist ballets (*The Golden Age* plus substantial chunks from *Spartacus* and *Romeo and Juliet*) and streamlined restagings of *Raymonda* and *Giselle*. However, the dancers, especially the 27-year-old powerhouse Irek Mukhamedov, stirred great enthusiasm. The Moscow Ballet, with guest dancers from the Bolshoi and the Kirov, directed by Bolshoi star Vyacheslav Gordeyev, made a 20-city tour in the fall. In Dallas, one of its dancers, Andrei Ustinov, defected and was granted political asylum; he agreed to perform with the Dallas Ballet for the rest of the year. The Bolshoi's Maya Plisetskaya performed as a guest artist in Ruth St. Denis's *The Incense* at the gala opening of the Martha Graham Company's season in October.

**Other Visiting Companies.** The Paris and Lyon Opera Ballets both came from France to visit the United States. They offered two strikingly different versions of *Cinderella*. The Lyon production, seen in New York and Los Angeles, was choreographed by Maguy Marin and featured a jitterbugging Cinderella who rode a pink convertible and jumped rope at the royal ball. Nureyev's Paris Opera version, seen at the Met, was set in Depression-era Hollywood and ended happily when the ill-treated heroine achieved her dream of becoming a movie star. Among other visitors was the Warsaw Ballet (for the first time).

**Modern Dance.** Martha Graham, well into her 90's, produced her 177th ballet (*Persephone*, set to Stravinsky's *Symphony in C*) and supervised revivals of her *Celebration* (1934) and *Canticle for Innocent Comedians* (1952)—all for her company's fall season at City Center. Merce Cunningham produced three new works for his company, *Points in Space* (adapted from a 1986 BBC-TV production), *Shards*, and *Fabrications*, while Paul Taylor created two—

*Called by some "the greatest dancer in the world," Fred Astaire died in June at age 88. Here, he performs with Ginger Rogers, with whom he costarred in a string of famous movies during the 1930's.*

High-flying Irek Mukhamedov took the spotlight as Moscow's Bolshoi Ballet toured the United States during the summer. The scene is from The Golden Age, a modern ballet by Yuri Grigorovich.

*Syzygy* and *Kith and Kin*—for his troupe. For her four-week stint at the Brooklyn Academy of Music, Twyla Tharp presented an almost entirely new company, in which all the women were ballet-trained. Her two new pieces were *In the Upper Room,* to a Philip Glass score, and *Ballare,* to Mozart.

**Deaths.** Fred Astaire, perhaps the most popular, and critically acclaimed, song-and-dance man of this century, died in Los Angeles on June 22, at age 88. Elegant, graceful, creative, he was considered by Balanchine "the greatest dancer in the world." Other outstanding figures in dance who died during the year included Antony Tudor, 78; Nora Kaye, 67; and Bob Fosse, 60.                              K.F.R.

**DELAWARE.** *See* STATISTICS OF THE WORLD.

**DEMOCRATIC PARTY.** *See* UNITED STATES OF AMERICA: *Political Parties.*

**DENMARK.** The center-right, four-party coalition of Conservative Prime Minister Poul Schlüter lost seven seats in early elections held on September 8, 1987, but retained power for lack of a viable alternative. The morning after the election, Schlüter submitted his resignation as a matter of form, but he reassembled the same coalition and presented his minority government to Queen Margrethe II on September 10.

The governing coalition of Conservatives, Liberals, Center Democrats, and members of the Christian People's Party won a combined total of 70 seats in the vote, compared to 77 in the outgoing Folketing (Parliament) elected in January 1984. With the indirect support of 11 Radical Liberals, to the left, and 9 members of the antitax Progress Party, on the right, Schlüter's government commanded, on paper, a slim majority of 90 votes in the 179-seat Folketing. The Socialist opposition included the fairly middle-of-the-road Social Democrats who also lost ground in the election, falling from 56 to 54 seats), the Socialist People's Party (which picked up 6 new seats for a total of 27), and a new leftist party called Common Cause.

Schlüter had surprised observers by calling the election for September instead of waiting until January 1988, when the current term of the Folketing expired. He acted to maximize support for his Conservative-led government—prior to an anticipated downturn in the economy. Polls showed him winning a decisive victory, as opposed to the marginal victory he actually won.

Schlüter's capacity to remain in office depended, in the short run, on his success in forging a working consensus among his multiple nonsocialist supporters. His most difficult political task was to cultivate the simultaneous backing of the Radical Liberals, who remained highly suspicious of the Progress Party, and of the Progress Party, an unpredictable parliamentary ally in the past.

The long-term prospects of the nonsocialist government hinged to a great extent on Denmark's economic performance. After taking office in 1982, Schlüter pursued restrictive economic and social policies that greatly reduced inflation. Unemployment, however, remained high, and future growth prospects were not considered good.

*See* STATISTICS OF THE WORLD.     M.D.H.

**DISTRICT OF COLUMBIA.** *See* STATISTICS OF THE WORLD. *See also* ELECTIONS IN THE UNITED STATES.

**DJIBOUTI.** *See* STATISTICS OF THE WORLD.

**DOMINICA.** *See* STATISTICS OF THE WORLD.

**DOMINICAN REPUBLIC.** *See* STATISTICS OF THE WORLD. *See also* CARIBBEAN BASIN.

# E

**EARTH SCIENCES.** Earthquakes in Ecuador and California, extreme weather conditions, and an expedition to retrieve artifacts from the *Titanic* attracted attention in 1987.

## CLIMATOLOGY

Extreme weather and the depletion of the ozone layer were major concerns during the year.

**Turbulence in the Midwest.** Periodic flooding and turbulent weather plagued the Midwest. In late May a tornado demolished nearly the entire town of Saragosa, Texas, killing 30 people and injuring about 150 of the community's 350 inhabitants. About half of those killed were inside a community hall attending graduation ceremonies when the building was leveled by the tornado. The same weather system produced extensive flooding along a swath extending from Texas north to Wisconsin and eastward to Ohio.

**Early Snow in the Northeast.** On October 4 the Northeast was struck by its earliest snowstorm on record. There were accumulations of up to 20 inches in upstate New York, 18 inches in western Massachusetts, and 12 inches in

*A street scene in a snowbound Kent village: evidence of the unusually severe winter that disrupted life in many parts of England.*

Vermont. Power was knocked out in more than 340,000 homes.

**Extreme Weather in Europe.** In what was called Europe's most severe winter in decades, low temperatures and snow were blamed for more than 260 deaths during the first two weeks of January. In the Soviet Union, where temperatures in some heavily populated areas fell to $-30°F$, at least 77 deaths related to the cold were reported, not counting 29 deaths from avalanches in the Georgian Soviet Socialist Republic. More than 30 deaths were reported in Poland and at least 37 in Britain. Temperatures of 10°F, the lowest in a quarter-century, were observed in southern England. Snowfall accumulations of 30 inches occurred in some northern areas of Britain. At the same time, Iceland was experiencing elevated temperatures of around 50°F.

A severe heat wave struck Greece, Cyprus, and Turkey in July, lasting more than a week. Temperatures near Athens reached 113°F, and as many as 1,000 deaths were reported in Greece alone.

**Ozone Layer.** Concern about decreasing amounts of ozone in the earth's upper atmosphere continued during the year; ozone in the stratosphere screens out more than 99 percent of the sun's potentially harmful ultraviolet radiation. Emissions of chlorofluorocarbon compounds used as refrigerants, in aerosol propellants, and in foam packaging and insulation tend to deplete the protective stratospheric ozone layer. Though chlorofluorocarbons were banned in the United States in 1978, they remained widely used in many countries.

In August and September, NASA sent two high-altitude aircraft to the Antarctic to take chemical samples and meteorological measurements. Preliminary reports indicated that this spring's ozone declines were the most rapid and extensive ever. In September, 24 nations approved an agreement to limit the use of chlorofluorocarbon compounds on a worldwide basis. The agreement, which must be ratified by at least 11 nations, required gradual reductions in the use of chlorofluorocarbons during the next decade. Earlier in the year, Secretary of the Interior Donald Hodel was criticized for suggesting that hats and sunglasses could be used to safeguard the public

---

**Crystal Magic**

Hardened observers may dismiss them as jazzed-up pet rocks, but more and more people are buying rock crystals, and even toting them to work in briefcases to help the day go smoothly and productively. Long credited with magical powers, these natural gemstones, such as garnet, calcite, and sapphire, supposedly have the "vibes" to heal bodily and mental ills, restore energy, aid concentration, and enhance sleep. According to one theory, interaction between the user's electrical field and the mineral's electromagnetic field is the key to producing the effect. First, however, a crystal must be "programmed" for power. One method is to wash the stone in the ocean, leave it outside to absorb rays from the sun and moon, then hold it in both hands and blow on it while making a wish. Thereafter it may be pressed on areas of the body, rubbed, placed in drinks, slipped under your pillow, chanted to, and admired. Results seemd to depend on the owner. But while skeptics may sneer, vendors of these mystical rocks, with sales and profits soaring, are firm believers in the influence of their product.

---

against the extra ultraviolet radiation resulting from ozone depletion. Hodel responded that he meant for this to represent only one of a range of options for protecting the public if the Geneva agreement was not ratified.

**Great Salt Lake.** Water levels in Utah's Great Salt Lake were receding, after having reached record heights in mid-1986 under the influence of heavy precipitation. The decline was due in part to an elaborate new pumping system that diverted water into a newly formed lake nearby. Because of disagreement over probable future patterns of precipitation in the area, scientists remained split over whether the pumping system was needed and, if so, whether the pumps would be effective over the long term.                                                N.M.R.

## GEOLOGY

In 1987 major earthquakes struck around the world, and scientists analyzed geological data from a deep hole being drilled near the San Andreas fault.

**earthquakes.** Two large earthquakes, of magnitude 6.1 and 6.9 on the Richter scale, struck Ecuador on March 5, killing at least 1,000 people and rupturing the country's economic mainstay, the oil pipeline running from the production center of Lago Agrio to a coastal export terminal. The tremors were centered in mountains east of Quito and near the active volcano El Reventador. Dozens of aftershocks were recorded in the following days. More than 4,000 people were reported missing, and 20,000 left homeless, after the severe mudslides and flooding set off by the quakes.

On March 5 a magnitude 7.3 earthquake centered off the coast of Chile killed one person and damaged buildings; it generated a tsunami (tidal wave) with wave heights of up to 10 feet. On August 8 a magnitude 6.9 quake in the same area killed 4 people; it triggered landslides and destroyed dozens of homes.

California's strongest earthquake in 16 years hit the Los Angeles area on October 1 and was felt as far away as Las Vegas. The 20-second, magnitude 5.9 shock was centered on the Whittier fault, about 10 miles east of downtown Los Angeles. Six deaths and over $200 million in damage resulted; dozens of aftershocks were recorded, including one of a magnitude of 5.3 on October 4 that caused an additional death. Two quakes of magnitudes 6.0 and 6.3 hit a sparsely populated area of the state near the Mexican border later in the year, on November 23 and 24, doing minor damage. Meanwhile

*Many Ecuadoreans, like those at right, saw their homes destroyed in March earthquakes that killed over 1,000 people. An October quake in the Los Angeles area took far fewer lives but still did great damage: below, the remains of an auto repair shop in Pasadena rest atop a row of parked cars.*

a major quake of magnitude 7.4, centered in the Gulf of Alaska, shook south-central Alaska on November 30. That tremor, like a smaller one in the same area on November 16, did little damage.

On March 2 a major earthquake of magnitude 6.8 shook New Zealand's North Island. It caused landslides, buckled rail lines and bridges, and produced a fissure over 3 miles long. One person was killed and 25 injured.

**Volcanic Eruptions.** Lava continued to issue from Hawaii's Kilauea volcano through much of the year, in an eruption that had begun in July 1986. By the end of April, after destroying several houses and starting brushfires, the flow had abated, but several more houses were destroyed by lava flows beginning in late September. Mount Etna in Sicily erupted on April 17, ejecting debris that killed two people and injured about 30.

**Lake Nios Update.** The final report of the U.S. Agency for International Development on the disaster at Cameroon's Lake Nios was released in February. In August 1986 a gas cloud had escaped from the volcanic lake, killing more than 1,700 people. The U.S. report concluded that a small disturbance such as a rock slide or a storm could have been enough to mix the lake's carbon-dioxide-rich lower layer with the layer above and allow the deadly carbon dioxide to bubble out of the lake. French investigators, however, blamed a volcanic explosion.

**Probing the San Andreas Fault.** Work continued at Cajon Pass northeast of Los Angeles on what was to be the deepest hole (over 3 miles) ever drilled in the United States for scientific purposes. The hole, just a few miles from the San Andreas fault, enabled scientists to study the nature of heat and stress resulting from the friction of the North American and Pacific plates that push past each other here. Early results, from partial drilling, indicated there was less stress than expected.     A.C.

## OCEANOGRAPHY

In 1987 an underwater crater was found that may have been caused by an ancient comet, and disagreements continued over exploitation of the wreck of the *Titanic*.

**Underwater Crater.** The search continued for the crater that would have been formed by a huge extraterrestrial object widely thought to

Among the items from the sunken liner Titanic brought to the surface during eight weeks of dives was this metal wall plaque, displayed at a press conference in Saint-Denis, France, by a French specialist in charge of restoration.

have struck the earth about 65 million years ago. According to many scientists, such a colossal impact would explain why the dinosaurs and many other animals, as well as plants, became extinct at that time. The crater would be enormous, but no such crater has been found on land.

Lubomir F. Jansa of the Geological Survey of Canada and Georgia Pe-Piper of St. Mary's University in Halifax reported the identification of a large, well-preserved crater on the shallow continental shelf southeast of Nova Scotia. The size of the crater (about 28 miles across) indicates that the object may have had a diameter as large as 2 miles; in comparison, the object that may have caused the extinction of the dinosaurs is generally estimated to be about 6 miles in diameter. An abundance of iridium—a rare element in surface rocks—in the crater does suggest that the object that caused the crater might have been the head of a comet.

**El Niño.** For over a year, unusually warm waters prevailed in the equatorial Pacific Ocean—a condition known as El Niño. The warm water significantly altered atmospheric circulation, with results felt throughout the world. In the

Atlantic, the effects were apparent in the lower-than-normal number of hurricanes and tropical storms. In the Pacific, island seabirds were decimated when weaker-than-normal winds reduced upwelling and associated fish production along the equator. Drier than normal conditions prevailed throughout the southwest Pacific, and a deficit of monsoon rain caused food shortages in India.

**Titanic Clash.** The ocean liner *Titanic,* which sank in 1912 after striking an iceberg, was again in the news. Despite protests by many scientists and members of the public who wanted the wreck (located in 1985) to remain undisturbed, a French group retrieved hundreds of artifacts from the ship, including dishes, bottles, coins, jewels, and a chandelier. The items were sent to a French laboratory to be cleaned and treated to protect them from damage. In October, on a live television broadcast from Paris, a satchel and safe from the *Titanic* were opened and found to hold money and jewelry. The French answered critics by

---

**Five Fathoms Deep**

If you've decided on a seashore vacation, you might go one step further and try getting your feet wet at Jules' Undersea Lodge, named for the author of *Twenty Thousand Leagues Under the Sea* and located in a made-over marine research center 30 feet down off Florida's Key Largo. This undersea hotel—said to be the only one of its kind in the world—can lodge six at a time, at $295 a night per person, double occupancy. Guests must either be certified divers or take a one-day crash course before descending to the lodge on a 200-foot "hookah" air line. Down below, they can cook food in a microwave oven, listen to recorded music, watch films on a VCR, or gaze through the portholes at triggerfish, parrot fish, lobsters, and a variety of other sea creatures. Pressure, air, and climate control systems are monitored onshore, and telephone and radios provide links to the mainland. Still, watery isolation prevails, which, along with the constant, agreeable temperature and the cylindrical rooms, reportedly makes sleeping feel a lot like an imagined return to the womb.

---

noting that the retrieved items would not be sold, although proceeds from their display would be used to reimburse those funding the expedition.  M.G.G.

**ECONOMY AND BUSINESS.** The U.S. economy rolled into a fifth year of expansion in 1987, making the economic recovery of the 1980's the second longest in post-World War II history. However, the dramatic 508-point dive on the New York Stock Exchange during a single day in October ended a five-year-old bull market and ushered in a period of financial turbulence in markets in the United States and abroad. U.S. trade and budget deficits, as well as the falling dollar, were key factors behind the lack of investor confidence; late in the year, in an effort to allay concern, White House and congressional negotiators agreed on a $30 billion deficit reduction plan. Meanwhile, developing nations, concerned over debt problems, pressed for recognition of their plight at international trade talks in Geneva.

**Economic Growth.** Growth in the U.S. gross national product in the first half of 1987 was generally characterized as sluggish. In the first quarter, GNP growth rebounded from 2.5 percent in 1986 to an annual rate of 4.4 percent, but it fell back in the second quarter to an annual rate of 2.5 percent. Employment nonetheless showed improvement. By December, the jobless rate was at 5.7 percent of the civilian work force, the lowest since 1979. The level of job creation and export increases indicated to some that first-half GNP numbers had not caught the economy's underlying strength. Later figures supported this view: the economy expanded at an annual rate of 4.3 percent in the third quarter and an estimated 4.2 percent in the fourth. However, consumer spending fell rapidly. Leading economic indicators for November (which include stock market prices as a component) were down 1.7 percent, the biggest drop since 1981.

**Inflation.** Before the market's plunge, perhaps the biggest question about the American economy was whether inflation was returning. With oil prices at relatively high levels for much of the year and the value of the dollar falling in relation to other major currencies (making imports more expensive), inflation accelerated, reaching 4.4 percent for the year, the fastest pace in six years. In the minds of many analysts, however, such a rate was not unduly high, and oil price declines late in the year helped calm inflationary fears.

**Interest Rates.** The need for decisions on inflation earlier in the year was a tough challenge for Alan Greenspan, the Wall Street economist who took over the Federal Reserve Board chairmanship in August, when Paul A. Volcker resigned after eight years in the post. Early in September, Greenspan promptly announced a boost in the Fed's key lending rate, the discount rate, from 5.5 to 6 percent. The move showed that Greenspan would act swiftly to establish his inflation-fighting credentials. In response, commercial banks moved their bellwether prime interest rate in increments from 8.25 percent to 9.25 percent by early October, and interest rates picked up throughout the economy. But the Fed changed course after the stock market crisis, and as the central bank pumped money into the financial system to head off recession, the prime dropped back to 8.75 percent by early November. Higher long-term interest rates, prevalent for much of the year, showed up in mortgage rates, which

reached 10.91 percent in September, before dropping below 10 percent. Sales of new and existing homes fell off, with housing starts down 10 percent for the year.

**Turbulent Financial Markets.** After opening the year around 1,900, the Dow Jones Industrial Average soared past 2,700 by late August. Then, a sharp decline set in that saw the Dow drop into the 1,700's in less than two months. On a single day, October 19, the Dow fell more than 500 points, over 600 million shares were traded, and stocks lost over 20 percent of their value. Volatility continued in succeeding weeks, as large advances alternated with sharp declines; volume remained heavy, and investors jittery. The Dow closed a dramatic record-shattering year at 1,938.83.

Mirroring U.S. exchanges, stock markets around the world did exceptionally well prior to the October crash. The Tokyo, West German, British, and French stock markets reached record highs during the summer. The Dow's plunge on October 19 set off alarm bells in Tokyo, where the market fell the next day by 5 percent; in Hong Kong, where the local exchange was shut down for the rest of the

*Surrounded by members of Congress and his cabinet, President Reagan reluctantly signs a revised version of the Gramm-Rudman-Hollings deficit-reduction law. The original version had been ruled unconstitutional.*

week; and in all the major markets of Europe and Australia.

**The Twin Deficits.** America's "twin deficits"—in the federal budget and in international trade—stood behind much of the financial markets' uncertainty. The U.S. trade deficit soared to a record in July, with the month's merchandise imports exceeding exports by $16.5 billion. The deficit shrank in August and September but rose in October to a new record of $17.6 billion.

The trade deficit persisted despite a sharp drop in the value of the dollar. Pressured by its allies, the United States agreed in February to stabilize the dollar, which by this time had already dropped by some 40 percent against other major currencies. But the U.S. currency declined further, and after the stock market crisis, U.S. Treasury Secretary James A. Baker III (as an antirecession measure) sought a still lower value for the dollar. He got it: by December the dollar was trading against the mark and the yen at its lowest level since 1949.

The dollar's long fall did make imports more expensive and also helped exports—the first half of 1987 saw a 17 percent rise in exports of manufactured goods. U.S. manufacturers added some 300,000 jobs during the year, as American companies aggressively sought and regained international market share for their products. But imports remained at very high levels (despite the price increases), and so did the trade deficit.

An important component of the trade deficit was oil imports. The members of the Organization of Petroleum Exporting Countries, by limiting production, were able to keep average oil prices around a targeted $18 a barrel for much of the year, though prices weakened in the fall as some members exceeded their production quotas.

The massive federal budget deficit declined somewhat because of congressional efforts to cut spending in 1986 and because an improving economy brought in higher revenues, but it remained a source of concern. President Ronald Reagan signed a revised Gramm-Rudman-Hollings deficit-reduction bill in September, after months of wrangling with Congress over the budget. The bill set up a new mechanism for making automatic spending cuts to reach prescribed deficit ceilings if Congress and the president could not agree on measures to hold down the deficit. For fiscal 1988, automatic cuts of $23 billion would go into effect unless Congress and Reagan took action to trim the deficit by November 20, 1987.

In a move aimed at restoring the financial markets' confidence, Reagan and congressional leaders began negotiations late in October on a package of deficit-reduction measures that would equal or exceed $23 billion, head off the automatic cuts—and thereby demonstrate the political will to get the federal budget under control. After a month of sometimes stormy bargaining, a $30 billion deficit-reduction plan was agreed upon November 20. Details of the agreement were worked out by congressional committees in the following weeks, and a final package was passed by Congress and signed by the president in late December. Meanwhile, the automatic spending cuts were actually in effect for a time.

**Trade Disputes.** The United States adopted a more aggressive stance toward other countries on trade issues, with Japan being the chief target. Alleging that Japan had violated a 1986 semiconductor agreement by selling computer chips in the United States at below market prices, President Reagan on April 17 imposed 100 percent duties on selected Japanese electronics products, accounting for $300 million worth of imports annually. Two months later, Reagan announced a relaxation of these sanc-

tions, following evidence that Japan had made progress in selling one type of chip at closer to market value. In November, further relaxations of sanctions were announced.

Another dispute arose with the discovery that two foreign firms, Toshiba Machine Company, a subsidiary of the Japanese electronics giant the Toshiba Corporation, and Kongsberg Vaapenfabrikk, a state-owned Norwegian arms concern, had sold sophisticated technology to the Soviet Union that would help that nation develop a quieter submarine. In the uproar that followed the disclosure, the U.S. government canceled some Toshiba contracts, and the Senate included in its version of major trade legislation a ban on imports from both companies for up to five years.

**Trade Bill.** The trade bill, being finalized in a House-Senate conference committee, would require the president to take retaliatory action (for example, imposing tariffs or quotas) against countries deemed to have unfair trade practices and excess trade surpluses with the United States—unless such practices could be ended by negotiation. The measure would also provide financial relief for workers and industries hurt by imports. The House version contained an amendment sponsored by Representative Richard Gephardt (D, Mo.) that would require the president to act to reduce by 10 percent

annually the trade surpluses of countries persisting in unfair trade practices. The trade bill faced a possible veto by President Reagan, who denounced it as overly protectionist.

**Spending and Income.** Strong growth in jobs helped fuel the U.S. economy. However, consumer spending outpaced the growth in income in the first three quarters, and consumers began taking on more debt. From June to October, consumer debt increased by $22 billion. Stripped of a variety of deductions by changes in the tax code, some consumers were using home equity (in essence, mortgage) loans rather than unsecured personal loans (no longer fully deductible) to help fund purchases. Late in the year, consumer spending fell.

**Employment.** Job security was a big issue with workers. In September the United Automobile Workers union signed a contract with the Ford Motor Company in which the firm promised not to lay off any of its UAW workers unless sales dropped. General Motors signed a similar pact the next month.

Civilian employment as a whole was rising, from 110.6 million in December 1986 to 113.7 million in December 1987, and the number of unemployed dropped from 7.9 million to 7.0 million over the same period. A report on payrolls of the nation's business establishments showed that in August, 77.1 million people were working in services-producing jobs while 24.9 million were working in the goods-producing sector of the economy. Manufacturing employment increased during the year as exports rose. Nevertheless, by the fall of 1987 there were still only about 20 million Americans employed in manufacturing—around 2 million fewer than at the beginning of the 1980's.

**Industrial Trends.** The long-term drop in manufacturing employment reflected an industrial sector in the throes of restructuring. Some firms complained that the threat of a takeover forced them to take on more debt and cut their research and development budgets; others found corporate restructuring advantageous. The lean-and-mean image cheered the business community in many sectors, though layoffs and plant closings proved painful.

Industrial production, hurt by the rise in imports in recent years, began staging a comeback in 1987; aided by the falling dollar, output

rose 5.2 percent, the best performance since 1984. But late in the year, unsold inventories were piling up rapidly.

**Mergers and Acquisitions.** Motivated by the declining U.S. dollar during the year and by lower stock market prices after the October crash, European and Japanese companies staked a growing claim in corporate America. By November foreigners had spent $36.7 billion to purchase U.S. companies, compared with $23.3 billion for all of 1986. CBS agreed to sell its records division to Japan's Sony Corporation for $2 billion in cash. British Petroleum paid $7.9 billion for the 45 percent of Standard Oil it did not already own. Among other British companies, Hanson Trust P.L.C. took over Kidde Inc. for $1.8 billion, and Blue Arrow P.L.C. purchased Manpower Inc. for $1.2 billion.

Among U.S. companies themselves, a group backed by Merrill Lynch & Company took industrial conglomerate Borg-Warner private in a leveraged buyout valued at $4.2 billion. National Amusements, a movie-theater chain, paid $3.4 billion for communications company Viacom International. Supermarkets General was taken private by a group backed by Merrill Lynch Capital Partners, for $1.8 billion. And Chrysler Corporation bought American Motors, the fourth-largest U.S. automaker, for some $1.2 billion.

**Battle of the Titans.** The four-year-old dispute between oil giants Pennzoil and Texaco was finally resolved late in the year. In April, Texaco had filed for protection from creditors under chapter 11 of the federal bankruptcy code to avoid enforcement of a $10 billion judgment against it, awarded to Pennzoil by a Texas jury because Texaco's acquisition of Getty Oil Company illegally interfered with a prior Pennzoil pact to purchase part of Getty. The action in April came after the U.S. Supreme Court refused to exempt Texaco from posting a bond for the full amount of the award, pending final appeals. Late in 1987, Trans World Airlines chairman Carl C. Icahn won control of 12.3 percent of Texaco's shares and helped broker an out of court settlement, calling for Texaco to make a $3 billion payment to Pennzoil and another $2.5 billion payment to creditors to bring Texaco out of bankruptcy.

*Ecuadorean President León Febres Cordero and his wife, looking shaken, return to Quito after his kidnapping near Guayaquil, during which two bodyguards were killed.*

**Venice Summit.** The 13th meeting of the major industrial democracies convened in Venice in June. In the shadow of uncertainties due to currency instability and huge U.S. trade and budget deficits, leaders of the United States, Britain, Canada, France, Italy, Japan, and West Germany met to discuss remedies for an ailing international economy, as well as political issues affecting the seven participating nations. A joint communiqué issued at the close of the meeting reaffirmed a commitment to cooperation in redressing trade and other economic imbalances. The conference backed an International Monetary Fund plan to triple its lending to sub-Saharan Africa and endorsed the new round of international trade negotiations under way in Geneva.

**International Trade Talks.** Developing nations, motivated by debt-service problems and heightened self-interest, pushed for a better break in the current round of General Agreement on Tariffs and Trade (GATT) negotiations being held in Geneva. Poorer countries sought stricter curbs on the ability of wealthier industrial nations to unilaterally apply trade restrictions when faced with a surge of imports. They wanted more open trade in raw materials and

relaxation of nontariff barriers that have prolif erated around the world.

In another set of negotiations, the United States and Canada concluded, just before the early October deadline set by the U.S. Con gress, an agreement establishing a free-trade zone between the two countries. The pact signed in January 1988, still required the ap proval of Congress.

*See also* BANKING AND FINANCE; MANUFAC TURING INDUSTRIES; *and separate articles on individual countries.* W.N

**ECUADOR.** There was political turbulence in Ecuador during 1987. President León Febres Cordero was seized at an Air Force base near Guayaquil on January 16 and held for 11 hours by paratroopers loyal to General Frank Vargas Pazos. Vargas had been imprisoned in early 1986 for an attempted military rebellion against the government. Two of the president's body guards were killed and Febres was roughed up also, as a condition for his freedom, he was forced to grant amnesty to Vargas, although many of the paratroopers were later arrested and jailed. The paratroopers' action was fol lowed by an impeachment attempt against Febres in the opposition-dominated Congress but it failed to muster the needed two-thirds majority.

In October, Congress voted to censure In terior Minister Luis Robles Plaza and demand his ouster. When Febres refused to comply, Ecuador's largest union, the Workers' Unity Front, called a one-day general strike for Oc tober 28. On the eve of the strike, the govern ment declared a state of emergency. The fol lowing day, workers firebombed a bank and blocked traffic; some strikers were arrested.

Two earthquakes and a series of aftershocks hit northeastern Ecuador in March, triggering mudslides and flooding. At least 1,000 people were killed and tens of thousands were left homeless. Oil pumping had to be suspended because of the destruction of a pipeline; roads and bridges were wiped out. Febres received new loans to help cover lost oil revenues. Austerity measures introduced after the disaster led to student protests.

The economy was hurt by reduced oil ex ports, lower coffee prices, and a drop in cocoa production. In October a preliminary agree-

ent was reached with commercial banks on
scheduling $5 billion in debt. The following
onth, the World Wildlife Fund announced
lans to buy up to $10 million of Ecuadorean
ebt from banks and use the funds to finance
onservation projects in Ecuador, in a "debt-
r-nature" swap. In December, Febres com-
itted Ecuador to the policy of the so-called
roup of Eight Latin American debtor coun-
ies, including withholding of debt repayments
hen they cannot be afforded.

See STATISTICS OF THE WORLD.          L.L.P.

**DUCATION.** In 1987, the education reform
ovement continued to focus on improving
e teaching profession, and a board was
eated to formulate national standards for
achers.

**eaching Reform.** The education reform move-
ent focused on efforts to make the teaching
rofession more attractive to talented college
aduates and more accountable for results in
e classroom. In May the Carnegie Corpora-
on's Forum on Education and the Economy
nnounced the establishment of the National
oard for Professional Teaching Standards. The
oard, predominantly composed of teachers,

was charged with the task of devising a set of
national standards for teachers and, eventually,
issuing certificates to teachers who meet the
qualifications.

Debate over the national board prompted
the National Education Association, the largest
U.S. teachers' union, to renew its efforts to
establish teacher-controlled standards boards
at the state level. Nevada became the first state
in a decade to create an autonomous licensing
board for teachers; its nine members were to
include four teachers and one practicing school
counselor or psychologist.

Teachers in many school districts invoked
the current debate on professionalization to
win substantial salary increases during contract
negotiations. In one highly publicized case,
teachers in Rochester, N.Y., negotiated a three-
year contract that raised average teacher salaries in the district by more than 40 percent
and created a new category of "lead teachers"
who would earn up to $70,000 a year by the
last year of their contract. While all of the
district's teachers would have a greater say in
decision making at the school level, the lead
teachers were to have additional responsibili-

usinessman Eugene Lang (back row, left) several years ago
romised 61 sixth-graders at his old public school in New York
ity's depressed East Harlem section that if they got their high
hool diplomas he would guarantee their college tuition. Lang
osed in June with 27 of those students, now high school graduates,
ho have taken him up on his promise.

ties, such as assisting teachers experiencing difficulties in the classroom.

**Teacher Testing.** By April all but two states had adopted or were implementing tests for teachers or teacher candidates, according to a Department of Education report. The first analysis of virtual nationwide teacher-testing found that around 80 percent of new teachers passed their certification tests, although minority candidates experienced much lower passing rates. This finding led to charges in several states that the tests discriminated against minorities.

Despite the rapid spread of teacher testing, concerns mounted about the ability of currently used tests to predict teacher performance in the classroom. The Education Department's study said that the examinations might provide some useful information about teacher skills but that there was no proof they accurately predicted classroom performance or improved public confidence in the quality of teachers.

**Reform Controversy.** One cause for concern among educators and policymakers was the lack of uniform criteria for comparing the performance of schools and school districts. The accountability of schools for results was debated at both the national and state levels, and efforts were begun to devise new ways of measuring student achievement.

There continued to be considerable disagreement over methods of reform. In a speech before the Education Writers Association in April, Education Secretary William J. Bennett stated that "the education reform movement being hijacked and held for ransom by education bureaucrats and special interest groups. By September he had narrowed the focus of his attacks, calling the National Education Association the "most entrenched and aggressive opponent of education reform in the nation." Mary Hatwood Futrell, president of the NEA, responded by characterizing the Reagan administration's policies as "voodoo education."

**Humanities.** A series of new books and reports added the humanities to the list of basic subjects such as math, science, and English needing greater emphasis in the classroom. In *What Do Our 17-Year-Olds Know?* education historians Diane Ravitch and Chester E. Finn, Jr., U.S. assistant secretary of education for research and improvement, concluded that students displayed a "shameful" ignorance of history and literature. In *American Memory*, Lynne V. Cheney, chairman of the National Endowment for the Humanities, blamed the negative findings on the decades-old movement to downplay the role of memorization in the schools.

As concern rises over illegal drug use and the spread of sexually transmitted disease, the subjects are finding a greater place in the classroom. At left, a sixth-grade teacher at the Chancellor Avenue School in Irvington, N.J., leads a discussion on AIDS. At right, police present a workshop on drug abuse to young students in Brooklyn, N.Y.

Two books on a related subject were on nonfiction best-seller lists. In *Cultural Literacy: What Every American Needs to Know*, E. D. Hirsch, Jr., a professor of English at the University of Virginia, compiled a list of nearly 5,000 historical events, geographical names, famous people, bits of patriotic lore, words, phrases, and texts. Lack of this common body of knowledge among students, he asserted, was more responsible for literacy problems in the United States than a simple lack of basic skills. Allan Bloom, a professor of social thought at the University of Chicago, took aim at humanities instruction on the college level in *The Closing of the American Mind*. The 1960's movement away from a core curriculum at colleges and universities, he argued, "was an unmitigated disaster."

**Core Curriculum.** In an Education Department report, Secretary Bennett proposed a model high school "core curriculum" with four years of English, three of social studies, three each of math and science, two each of foreign language and physical education/health, and a semester each of art history and music history. The report, *James Madison High School*, also suggested possible course content. Critics said it put too much stress on goals, not enough on means of attaining them.

**At-risk Youth.** Another major topic of the reform debate was the failure of schools to educate or retain students classified as "at-risk," because they come from poor or single-parent families or have other disadvantages.

The Committee for Economic Development, a nonprofit group comprising 225 leaders in business and higher education, concluded in a major report that the cycle of poverty and poor education could not be broken without "early sustained intervention in the lives of young people and their families." The report, *Children in Need: Investment Strategies for the Educationally Disadvantaged,*" recommended ensuring adequate prenatal and postnatal care for all mothers, offering preschool programs to three-year-olds and four-year-olds, educating parents about raising children, and fostering greater parent and community involvement in education.

**College Costs.** To aid parents of future college-age youngsters, at least 19 states either considered or adopted college-savings plans similar to a pioneering program enacted by the Michigan legislature in December 1986. Under these plans, parents contribute a set amount per year to a state account, in return for a guarantee that the accumulated funds will be taken as full payment for tuition in any public college or university in the state, whatever the actual cost then.

**Asbestos Removal.** School districts, with the assistance of state and federal programs, continued their efforts to remove asbestos from school buildings. In March, President Ronald Reagan signed an order allocating $47.5 million for asbestos removal in schools by the Environmental Protection Agency.

**AIDS.** Growing concern over the spread of the AIDS virus caused many school boards and state agencies to overcome their long-standing reluctance to mandate sex education courses in the public schools. The approach to be followed in AIDS education was in dispute, however, with conservatives arguing that sexual abstinence be taught as the best or sole method of preventing infection. In October the U.S. Education Department issued a guide entitled *AIDS and the Education of Our Children,* which urged parents and educators to stress "appropriate moral and social conduct" as the first line of defense and played down the use of condoms as a means of protection.

Controversy over sex education was overshadowed in some communities by debate over enrolling students who have tested positive for the AIDS virus. Although federal courts consistently upheld the right of these pupils to attend school, several communities were rocked by emotional battles on the issue.

**Desegregation and Minorities.** Opposition to mandatory busing dropped considerably over the past decade, according to a poll by Louis Harris and Associates. The poll of 1,250 families found that only 53 percent opposed mandatory busing, a decline of more than 2 percentage points since 1975.

Three studies—the first in this decade to examine the effectiveness of the desegregation plans operating in many U.S. school districts—concluded that such plans, over the long term, had markedly reduced the number of students attending racially isolated schools. Gary Orfield, a professor of political science at the University of Chicago and director of the National School Desegregation Project, found however, that the proportion of blacks who attended racially integrated schools did not increase during the 1980's.

Persistent residential segregation is a major cause of segregation in schools. A settlement in one recent case, brought by Milwaukee public schools against 24 suburban school districts and the state of Wisconsin, called for the state to make major efforts to attract minority families to live in predominantly white neighborhoods. Meanwhile, a series of court orders involving the public schools in St. Louis and Kansas City found the state of Missouri liable for funds to offset costs of desegregating and upgrading district schools.

**Church and State Issues.** Federal appeals courts in Alabama and Tennessee turned back fundamentalist challenges to textbooks, and the U.S. Supreme Court struck down a Louisiana law requiring schools to give equal time to "creation science" (based on the biblical account of creation) when teaching evolution.

*See also* Civil Liberties and Civil Rights.

W.S

**EGYPT.** In October 1987, Egyptian President Hosni Mubarak was returned to a second six-year term in office by a national referendum. Daunting economic difficulties and rising Islamic fundamental opposition presented problems. Abroad, Egypt enjoyed renewed ties with Arab nations.

**Elections.** Egypt experienced significant political activity, much of it generated during the

---

**Back to School**

Pep rallies, track meets, prom night, commencement . . . Nostalgia overflows as you page through your high school or college yearbook, reliving the rituals, and skirt lengths, of yesteryear. But, of course, that was the old way to do it. Nowadays, instead of relying solely on the traditional print yearbook, some schools are capturing the scenes and sounds of school life on videocassette tapes, to be replayed by tomorrow's nostalgia-seekers on their VCR's. Although some tapes are choppy and amateur, put together by enterprising students using simple equipment, entrepreneurs are offering slick productions for a price—possibly $30 to $40 for a 30- to 60-minute saga. The video yearbooks do capture vividly the look and feel of events, but critics cite a major drawback: Where do your friends put their autographs?

irst months of the year by preparations for the April 6 legislative elections. Although open to a more ideologically diverse set of candidates than any others in recent years, the elections were marred once again by numerous acts of violence and widespread allegations of ballot rigging. The violence was said to have accounted in part for the small turnout (50 percent).

Mubarak's National Democratic Party, aided by divisions among the opposition, won a substantial victory, capturing 77 percent of the vote and 346 of the 448 contested seats in the People's Assembly. The Islamic Alliance won 13 percent of the vote and 60 seats, and became the government's major legislative opponent. The center-right New Wafd Party shrank from 57 seats to 35, barely clearing the 8 percent minimum vote required for admission to the assembly. Mubarak easily won renomination to the presidency in July and won reelection in a referendum on October 5.

**Islamic Militancy.** While Mubarak and his party, assisted by military and police forces, retained firm control of the machinery of the state, Islamic radicals apparently engaged in terrorist acts. In early May former Interior Minister Hassan Abu Basha was badly wounded and narrowly escaped death; in June a magazine editor who had criticized the Islamic movement was shot and slightly wounded, as were two American security personnel. Hundreds of suspects were rounded up during this period by Interior Ministry forces.

**Economic Conditions.** The overall economic picture was rather bleak. Food imports were needed to meet more than half of domestic consumption, and government subsidies for food and other basic necessities were estimated to cost some $3 billion annually. The foreign debt reached $40 billion in 1987, necessitating some economic reforms. Subsidies were slashed, and banks were authorized to set the exchange rate for the Egyptian pound at the free market rate. Agreements were reached in May with the International Monetary Fund and other creditors on debt rescheduling and new credit.

**Foreign Affairs.** In January, Egypt attended the Islamic Conference Organization summit, for the first time since the signing of the 1979 Camp David peace treaty with Israel. At the meeting, Mubarak reportedly made progress in repairing relations with Arab nations. Then, at an Arab League meeting in November, a resolution was passed authorizing members to restore diplomatic relations with Egypt. About half of the member nations did so in the next few weeks.

In May, Egypt broke off ties with Iran, following the arrest of Tehran-backed fundamentalists charged with plotting to overthrow the Egyptian government. The month before, Egypt had closed down Palestine Liberation Organization offices in Cairo.

Israeli officials were angered by Egypt's action in inviting Austrian President Kurt Waldheim to visit Cairo, but this flap was offset by the Egyptian foreign minister's trip to Israel in July—the first by an Egyptian official of such rank since Israel's invasion of Lebanon. However, ties were seriously strained late in the year by what Egypt called "brutal, oppressive measures" taken by Israel against Palestinians during disturbances in the occupied territories.

*See* STATISTICS OF THE WORLD.        K.J.B.

**ELECTIONS IN THE UNITED STATES.** The incumbent mayors of Chicago and Philadelphia were among several blacks to win important municipal elections in 1987, but the former died in office in November. Democrats swept the few governorships at stake.

**Municipal Elections.** On April 7, Chicago's first black mayor, Harold Washington, won 54 percent of the vote to become the first mayor reelected in that city in the last 12 years. His closest opponent, Alderman Edward Vrdolyak, a white, received 42 percent. However, later in the year, on November 25, Washington died of a heart attack; the City Council selected Alderman Eugene Sawyer as acting mayor. On October 13, Richard Arrington, Jr., a black, easily won reelection to a third term in Birmingham, Ala.

In the November elections, Philadelphia Mayor W. Wilson Goode, a black, narrowly defeated former Mayor Frank L. Rizzo, who is white, to win reelection, after a bitterly fought campaign that polarized the city along racial lines. Kurt Schmoke, a 37-year-old prosecutor and onetime Rhodes scholar, swamped Republican Samuel Culotta, taking 79 percent of the vote, to become the first black mayor of

*Philadelphia Mayor Wilson Goode gestures "four more years" as he claims victory over former Mayor Frank Rizzo.*

Baltimore. He had edged out incumbent Mayor Clarence Burns, 69, in the primary.

Democrat Carrie Saxon Perry became the first black woman to be elected mayor of a major northeastern city, when she defeated Philip L. Steele (R) to win election in Hartford, Conn. Sue Myrick upset black Mayor Harvey Gantt to win the mayoralty in Charlotte, N.C. Gary, Ind., Mayor Richard Hatcher, elected in 1967 as one of the first black big-city mayors, failed in his bid for a sixth term when he lost the party primary to another black, Thomas V. Barnes, who easily won in November.

In Miami, Mayor Xavier Suarez, a Democrat-turned-Republican, who was the city's first Cuban-American mayor, took 62 percent of the vote in a November 10 runoff to win reelection, defeating a comeback bid by former Mayor Maurice Ferre.

Houston's Mayor Kathy Whitmire won a fourth two-year term, sweeping away six challengers with 70 percent of the vote. Mayor

William H. Hudnut (R) of Indianapolis also secured reelection easily, with 66 percent of the vote, and Raymond L. Flynn won a second term as mayor of Boston, beating City Councilman Joseph M. Tierney by a margin of two to one.

In the San Francisco mayoralty contest, State Assemblyman Art Agnos and Supervisor John Molinari finished first and second in a field of 11 candidates, leading to a runoff election on December 8. Agnos won the runoff with 70 percent of the votes.

**State Elections.** Democrats swept the year's gubernatorial elections with victories in Mississippi, Kentucky, and Louisiana. State Auditor Ray Mabus, a Harvard-educated lawyer, emphasized non-partisan good government in his campaign against Republican businessman Jack Reed, to win Mississippi's governorship with 53 percent of the vote. He had defeated seven competitors in the Democratic primary. Kentucky voters gave the statehouse to 45-year-old millionaire Wallace Wilkinson, in a landslide victory over Republican State Representative John Harper; Wilkinson's 65 percent margin was the highest ever in a Kentucky gubernatorial election. Wilkinson, a virtual unknown, had upset former Governor John Brown in a five-way Democratic primary on May 26.

After an open primary on October 24, in which he came in second in a field of five, Louisiana's incumbent Governor Edwin Edwards, who had been seeking a fourth term, declined to participate in a runoff on November 21. Under the rules, front-runner Representative Charles E. Roemer III, also a Democrat, automatically won election as governor.

**Congressional Elections.** On June 2, Nancy Pelosi (D) won a special election to fill the San Francisco congressional seat left vacant by the death of Democrat Sala Burton, taking 63 percent of the vote over Republican Harriet Ross's 30 percent. In a special election on August 17, in Connecticut, Christopher Shays (R) defeated Christine Niedermeier to win the U.S. House seat left empty by Stewart B. McKinney (R), who died of AIDS in May.

**Referenda.** In a referendum that attracted wide attention, Maine voters defeated environmentalists by rejecting a proposal to shut down the ate's only nuclear plant. Voters in Virginia approved a lottery, and Texans said yes to ace-track wagering; Texans also endorsed a 500 million bond issue to provide and improve site for the federal Super-Conducting Super Collider, if Texas is chosen for the project. In the District of Columbia, a proposal requiring deposits on beverage containers was defeated at the polls. The town of Indian Wells, Calif., near Palm Springs, approved a $1 billion resort development, despite forecasts of increased traffic and crime. The electorate in both San Francisco and New Jersey rejected bond issues to build new baseball stadiums.               I.S.G.

**LECTRONICS.** The U.S. consumer electronics industry in 1987 failed to match the remarkable expansion of the previous few years. Maturing product lines and market saturation for many items kept electronics market growth to an estimated 5 percent for the year, compared to 3.5 percent in 1986.

The entertainment industry and the forces of technological change found themselves at odds over digital audio tape. The concept was not new—it used the same technology that gave compact disk (CD) players their stellar sound. But the digital audio tape player, a cassette version of the CD player, could record as well as play. Some industry groups in the United States opposed its introduction on the ground that it might be used illegally to make copies of compact disks and thus posed a threat of tape piracy. Industry leaders asked Congress to block the introduction of digital audio tape machines unless they could be equipped with a computer chip that would make them unable to record from compact disks. Legal hurdles aside, the market was thought to have strong potential. At the January consumer electronics show in Las Vegas, no fewer than five companies had digital audio tape decks ready for demonstration, at prices in the $1,000 range.

In the absence of much innovation in the adult electronics market, some manufacturers dressed up their existing products with stylish designs and attractive colors, and others sought to explore the youth market. In the realm of child-oriented consumer goods, Fisher-Price introduced a video-recording system for under $300, and Sony marketed rugged versions of its Walkman portable stereos. The year also witnessed the beginning of interactive television, as the first children's product to play directly off a TV set appeared. The Mattel, Inc. toy spaceship was used with a television program called *Captain Power and the Soldiers of the Future.* Children at home pointed their toy spaceships at the screen and fired; light signals encoded into the program allowed the screen to indicate a "hit."

In the spring the United States charged that Japan was violating a 1986 agreement not to "dump"—sell below cost—semiconductor chips and to open its market to foreign companies. The government accordingly imposed a 100 percent penalty tariff on $300 million worth of Japanese electronic goods. However, citing evidence of increased compliance by Japan, the United States later eased the sanctions.

The U.S. semiconductor industry began to pull out of its slump in 1987; forecasters predicted growth of 15-20 percent for the year. Some observers attributed part of the rebound to the U.S. trade sanctions against Japan.

J.R.S.

**EL SALVADOR.** Support for President José Napoleón Duarte showed signs of erosion in 1987 as civil war continued in El Salvador. Duarte endorsed a regional peace plan and met with representatives of the guerrillas fighting to overthrow his government.

**Political Disarray.** Attempts to implement emergency measures to cover the cost of the war—including new taxes, higher interest rates, and currency devaluation—met with widespread opposition. A work stoppage on January 22, organized by business people protesting the additional levies, was 90 percent effective; on the same day, the guerrilla forces halted highway traffic. The Supreme Court declared the new tax law unconstitutional.

Unions also manifested discontent, and confrontations between government and unions became commonplace. On July 8, police fire wounded 15 strikers demonstrating for, among other things, a pay increase of US$30 a month. A week later, police fired on antigovernment demonstrators rioting in San Salvador, wounding three protesters.

**Human Rights.** By midyear the war had taken more than 60,000 civilian lives, and Duarte

*A demonstrator smashes the windshield of a government truck as workers march through San Salvador on July 15 in an antigovernment protest. The march ended when police fired on the crowd, wounding three people.*

was frequently under fire for failing to curb abuses by security forces. Human rights groups strongly denounced an April court decision exonerating three Army officers in the 1983 killings of 76 peasants. The revival of leftist demonstrations led to renewed death squad activity. In October, two gunmen assassinated Herbert Ernesto Anaya, head of the nongovernmental Human Rights Commission, as he left his home in San Salvador. In December an official of the government's human rights commission was murdered.

**Civil War.** The insurgents retained the ability to make war in the countryside. In March rebels destroyed the Army's heavily guarded El Paraíso base, within 40 miles of the capital, and in July and August they blew up nine major bridges. The government also made some gains, establishing greater military control over the strategically vital central provinces.

**Prospects for Peace.** At a summit meeting of Central American presidents held in Guatemala City in early August, Duarte accepted a plan, proposed by President Oscar Arias Sánchez of Costa Rica, for achieving regional peace through negotiation. Duarte accordingly urged Salvadoran rebels to join his government in cease-fire discussions and put all arms aside. The rebels said peace talks would have to embrace issues such as power sharing and incorporation of guerrilla combat units into the Army. Talks did begin on October 4 at the Vatican mission in San Salvador, but failed to produce an agreement. According to diplomatic sources, the government rejected the guerrillas' 18-point plan, while the rebels refused to agree to a cease-fire. A second round of talks was also unproductive. On November 5 the president proclaimed a unilateral cease-fire and an amnesty for both leftist rebels and rightist death-squad members. The guerrillas rejected the cease-fire and staged sabotage attacks on electrical installations around the country.

Later in the month, Rubén Zamora and Guillermo Ungo, leftist rebel civilian leaders, returned to San Salvador after years of exile o attempt political activity under the peace initiative. Soon after, Duarte accused rightist leader Roberto d'Aubuisson and Army Captain Alvaro Rafael Saravia of complicity in the 1980 assassination of Roman Catholic Archbishop Oscar Arnulfo Romero. Legal proceedings were begun in an effort to strip d'Aubuisson of the immunity from prosecution that he enjoyed as a member of the legislature.

A broad amnesty law passed in the fall to comply with the regional peace plan was criticized by human rights advocates as too sweeping, especially after it led to the release of gunmen imprisoned for killings of civilian noncombatants. Among those pardoned were two salvadoran soldiers convicted of killing two American land reform advisers in 1981.

See STATISTICS OF THE WORLD.            L.L.P.

**ENERGY.** A shaky accord among members of the Organization of Petroleum Exporting Countries and mounting tensions in the Persian Gulf combined to stabilize oil prices at about $18 to $20 a barrel for most of 1987, but prices were weakening late in the year. Controversies continued over coastal oil leasing plans. The nuclear power industry faced difficulties.

**Oil.** *OPEC Developments.* As a result of the OPEC accord of December 1986, OPEC production in the first half of 1987 averaged 16.51 million barrels per day, about 1.6 million lower than in the corresponding period of 1986. (World oil production, at 53.94 million b/d, was 1.16 million lower than in the first half of 1986.) Apparently the sharp drop in prices in 1986 persuaded OPEC members for a time to exercise more discipline in adhering to quotas. Nevertheless, Saudi Arabia again had to act as a swing producer (varying production to maintain price stability) in order to restrain total OPEC output. Although Saudi Arabia's quota was set at 4.13 million b/d, its actual output during the first half of 1987 averaged only 3.86 million b/d. In June, OPEC members agreed to raise their production ceiling to 16.6 million b/d. But by then overproduction by OPEC members appeared to be spreading, and it was unclear whether either production restraint by Saudi Arabia or the Iran-Iraq conflict's "tanker war" on Persian Gulf shipping would keep prices from falling.

Total OPEC production reached an estimated 19.9 million b/d in August and was close to

*After a period of lower prices, gasoline rose back above the $1-a-gallon mark around the United States. These numbers went up in July at a gas station in Bloomington, Minn.*

Proposed oil and gas exploration on the coastal plain of the Arctic National Wildlife Refuge—a calving ground for thousands of caribou—pitted the Reagan administration against environmentalists as well as the government of Canada, which is home to the migratory animals for part of the year.

19 million b/d late in the year, with several states exceeding their quotas. When the OPEC ministers met in Vienna in December, agreement was reached extending current production and pricing structures to June 1988. Iraq remained outside the accord, enabling it to maintain its current level of 2.8 million b/d, almost twice the level officially permitted. Iran strenuously opposed the pact but went along to avoid political isolation. It was expected that members would continue to exceed their quotas and that already weakening oil prices would decline.

*U.S. Imports and Production.* The underlying softness in international oil markets over the past few years has led to a potentially dangerous complacency in the United States. Total domestic petroleum consumption increased 3.52 percent in 1986, while domestic crude production fell 3.25 percent. As a result, net imports rose 26.9 percent, so that they accounted for 33 percent of the nation's oil supply. Later statistics indicated that these trends continued in 1987. Domestic petroleum consumption increased 1.8 percent over levels recorded in 1986. Domestic crude production fell by another 4.5 percent, and net imports of petroleum increased during the year by more than 5 percent.

These trends appeared to presage another major oil price shock, perhaps in the early 1990's. The plunge in oil prices in 1986 caused a steep decline in drilling activity in the United States. The number of active rotary rigs dropped from an average of 2,452 in January 1985 to 686 in July 1986. During the first seven months

1987 an average of 812 drilling rigs were operation.

A peak in oil production in the 48 contiguous ates in 1970 was followed by a drop in output om the older fields. The decline in domestic rude production was expected to accelerate hen the oil flow from Alaska's giant Prudhoe ay field started its expected decline in 1988. rudhoe Bay, on Alaska's North Slope, is the 8th-largest oil field in the world in terms of serves. In 1987 it accounted for about 20 ercent of total U.S. crude production. Prud- oe Bay's output was expected to fall at a rate f 10 to 12 percent a year, with a corresponding rop in production from 1.6 million b/d to pproximately 400,000 by the year 2000.

*ew Reserves.* In the ten-year period 1977– 986, reserve additions totaled about 24 mil- on barrels. Of that total, only about 2 billion presented "new field" discoveries, that is, eposits of recoverable oil in new U.S. fields, icluding Alaska. The other 22 billion barrels onsisted of reserve additions in and around xisting oil fields. During the same ten-year eriod domestic production totaled about 30 iillion barrels, and reserves declined by about .3 billion barrels.

Global oil production and reserves data did ot offer much basis for optimism. The dis- overy of new oil in giant fields worldwide eaked at 125 billion barrels in the five-year eriod of 1961–1965. Fortunately for oil-con- uming nations, many of these giant fields were n non-OPEC nations and came into production t a particularly opportune time in the 1970's, o as to moderate the price increases sought y some OPEC members. Unfortunately, pro- uction appears likely to begin declining in lmost all of the non-OPEC producing coun- ies within the next decade.

*)il Leasing.* In April, Interior Secretary Donald lodel sent Congress a final five-year Outer ontinental Shelf (OCS) leasing plan. Congress id not reject the plan within the allowed 60- ay period. But Congress could, as it has in he past, prohibit the expenditure of funds for lanning specific sales. The plan covered OCS ase sales scheduled from August 1987 through 992. Some of the proposed sales—particularly hose off the coasts of California, Washington, )regon, and Florida—were very controversial.

In August, the Natural Resources Defense Council and eight other environmental groups sued in federal court in Washington, D.C., to block the leasing plan on the grounds that it violated federal law by not adequately pro- tecting the coastal environment.

**Natural Gas.** The sharp drop in oil prices in 1986 served to push natural gas prices down. The average wellhead price, which is a com- posite that includes several categories of gas, including old gas still subject to price controls, dropped from $2.28 per thousand cubic feet in January 1986 to $1.66 in January 1987, sinking to $1.40 by August. (By the end of 1987, however, it had rebounded above $1.80.)

Because of the sharp drop in oil prices in 1986, some electrical utilities and industrial users of gas switched to fuel oil. A great surge in gas drilling activity in 1981 and 1982 and declining gas consumption, however, com- bined to create a temporary gas surplus and push gas prices lower. By late 1987 the spot price of gas delivered to pipelines had fallen substantially. Because of depressed prices, some natural gas producers desperately needed to maintain cash flow even though withholding gas from market would ultimately be more profitable. Since the United States was con- suming more gas than it was finding, the gas surplus seemed unlikely to persist.

**Alaskan Debate.** Believing the area might hold as much oil and natural gas as the huge Prudhoe Bay field nearby, Secretary Hodel recom- mended in April that 1.5 million acres in the Arctic National Wildlife Refuge be opened to exploration. The proposal drew opposition from environmentalists, who noted that the area in question, the refuge's coastal plain, is a calving ground for thousands of caribou and a key habitat for other species. There was also con- cern in Canada's adjoining Yukon Territory, where the caribou herd migrates for part of each year. Congress, which had the final say, was considering the plan late in the year.

**Nuclear Power Plants.** By the end of the year there were 110 nuclear reactors licensed for commercial operation in the United States. Construction continued on 14 other nuclear units. Nevertheless, nuclear power faced an uncertain future. Department of Energy pro- jections showed a fairly rapid increase in nuclear capacity through the late 1980's as plants under construction are completed. This rise was expected to be followed by a slow-down; no plans have been announced for new nuclear power plants since 1978.

Huge cost overruns continued to plague some nuclear power plants not yet in operation. In October the board of directors of Public Service Company of New Hampshire voted to suspend interest and principal payments on $800 million of debt. The utility, pushed to the brink of bankruptcy by its 35.6 percent stake in the stalled $5 billion Seabrook plant, was attempting to avoid bankruptcy by exchanging debt for new securities that would pay interest initially in common stock. However, in December trustees representing the company's creditors filed suit in federal court for repayment of over $450,000 in debt.

The Seabrook plant could not be opened because authorities in nearby Massachusetts refused to help prepare the emergency evacuation plan required by the U.S. Nuclear Regulatory Commission. A new nuclear plant at Shoreham, N.Y. (on Long Island), faced a similar problem. In late October, the NRC voted to remove this obstacle, ruling that the participation of state and local governments in preparing an evacuation plan, while desirable, would no longer be required. The rule change was, however, being challenged in the courts.

In early November the Long Island Lighting Company received another setback in its efforts to open Shoreham, when the New York State Public Service Commission refused to grant Lilco any of its requested 5 percent increase in rates. The commission declared that any additional funds granted Lilco would only contribute to a "financially debilitating deadlock" over Shoreham and recommended that the company develop plans to provide adequate electrical service without Shoreham.

In December 1986 the 13-year-old Surrey nuclear plant in Virginia had suffered a break in a high-pressure steam and water pipe. Four workers were killed, and the plant was closed until March 1987. Inspection revealed extensive pipe corrosion in unexpected areas—an indication that nuclear plants were aging in unpredicted ways. Operator negligence was also an issue during the year. In March the

NRC shut down the Peach Bottom nuclea power plant in Pennsylvania; operators ha reportedly been found sleeping, playing vide games, or reading, instead of monitoring th reactor. Meanwhile, criticism of the NRC itse continued, as a congressional subcommitte and the General Accounting Office accuse the agency of lax and inconsistent enforcemer of reactor safety requirements.          D.F.A

**ENVIRONMENT.** The year 1987 began wit national attention focused on water, as th U.S. Congress overrode President Ronald Rea gan's veto of a clean water bill. By the tim the year was nearing its end, attention focuse on air, as the deadline drew closer for citie to meet federal smog standards. In between, wandering ocean barge carrying thousands c tons of refuge from New York became a symbc of the country's garbage glut.

**Acid Rain.** After years of unsuccessful negoti ations between Canada and the United State: President Reagan agreed with Canadian Prim Minister Brian Mulroney in April to consider bilateral resolution to the problem of acid rair An estimated half of the acid rain falling i Canada is created by U.S. sources. Acting o an agreement made with Canada in 1986 Reagan also proposed that the U.S. governmer spend $2.35 billion over five years on th development of clean coal-burning technolc gies. Many believed this would reduce a majc form of pollution linked to acid rain, bu environmentalists argued that clean-coa spending would simply encourage coal prc duction and do little to control acid rain. Th House of Representatives and the Senate bot favored smaller programs; ultimately, $57 million was appropriated over two years.

A July report from the federal government' National Acid Precipitation Assessment Prc gram summarized findings from the first ha of the group's ten-year study. Although it foun that coal consumption had risen by 70 percer since 1975, emissions of sulfur dioxide fror coal-burning plants had decreased by 10 pe cent, and nitrogen oxide emissions staye about the same. (Sulfur and nitrogen oxide are precursors to acid deposition.) U.S. cro yields did not seem to have suffered, but th report concurred with other research indicatin that acid deposition can acidify lakes wit ertain geological characteristics, affecting their sh and plant life.

However, in a September report the same oup concluded that little damage had actually been done to lakes by acid rain and that ttle more would be done in the next few ecades if pollution remained at current levels. Many environmentalists and scientists critized the report, and the National Audubon ociety announced that it would monitor acid in itself because it was dissatisfied with federal efforts.

Congress also considered legislation aimed requiring states to reduce emissions of sulfur nd nitrogen oxides. Meanwhile, testimony efore a Senate subcommittee brought to the ore the potential effects of acid rain and its recursors on health, specifically on the respiratory system.

**ir Pollution.** By December 31, 1987, U.S. ties had been required to bring levels of zone, a major component of smog, in line with a federal standard, but by fall, the U.S. Environmental Protection Agency (EPA) said that about 60 metropolitan areas would not meet the ozone standard and thus could face a federal ban on construction of major new sources of pollution. Because of the number of areas not in compliance with the standard, a number of bills were introduced in Congress that would extend the deadline and at the same time require more rigorous efforts on the part of cities to improve their air quality. Meanwhile, in December the EPA proposed new rules that would delay imposition of sanctions.

**Garbage Barge.** The odyssey of the *Mobro*, a garbage-packing barge from Islip, N.Y., came to national attention during the spring. When the state decided that Long Island was running out of landfill space, the town of Islip sent more than 3,100 tons of mostly paper debris on a seagoing mission. An entrepreneur took the trash to North Carolina, where methane was to be extracted from it, but local officials

*he odyssey of the garbage barge Mobro included a stop in Key /est, Fla., where federal workers wearing elaborate protective ear inspected the refuse to determine if it was hazardous. Governor ob Martinez refused the barge permission to dock in Florida, and plied on, finally returning to New York.*

Among the unique range of landscapes offered by Great Basin National Park, newly created in remote eastern Nevada, is the spectacle of Wheeler Peak towering over a stand of aspen.

there balked when the barge came into view. The *Mobro* moved south, reaching the Gulf of Mexico and the Caribbean without finding a U.S. or foreign site to accept the garbage. It returned to New York, where it sat in the harbor until the garbage was burned at a Brooklyn incinerator, months after the saga had begun. The ashes were finally buried in Islip.

The wandering barge dramatized an EP warning that over half the states would face severe shortage of landfill space in three to t years. A number of environmentalists and oth analysts called for better recycling efforts, a New Jersey became the second state to ena a mandatory recycling law.

**Ozone Layer.** In September international re resentatives, under the auspices of the Unit Nations Environment Program, agreed to free: and eventually reduce production of chlor fluorocarbons (CFC's), a class of industri chemicals associated with thinning of t stratospheric ozone layer. At high altitude ozone acts as a sunscreen, filtering out harmf ultraviolet radiation; loss of ozone could mea damage to crops and an increase in the inc dence of skin cancer. In late September, sc entists who for several years have been mea uring the ozone layer over Antarctica announce preliminary findings that at an altitude of 1 miles, the layer had been depleted by ! percent from the base level of the mid-1970 Then, in December, satellite observatio showed a 5 percent decline in the ozone lay from 1979 through 1986 over nearly the who globe, not just over Antarctica.

The UN agreement called for productic and consumption of CFC's to be held to 198 levels by January 1, 1990. The freeze wou be followed by further cuts in productic through 1999. The pact must be ratified k two-thirds of the nations using CFC's before comes into force.

**Dioxin Report.** In a new draft study, the EP sharply reduced its estimate of the cance causing potential of dioxin, a pervasive chem ical pollutant, to $1/16$ of the agency's estima two years earlier. However, dioxin remaine the most toxic cancer-related substance und regulation. The report struck a balance betwee scientists who regard the alarm over dioxin a exaggerated and those who consider it high dangerous.

**Pesticides.** Researchers uncovered various i stances of pesticide-contaminated fog and rai Fog samples taken from California's San Joa quin Valley and from fields in Maryland showe concentrations of alachlor, malathion, an other chemicals; such toxic fog may be relate to forest decline, according to investigators.

158

In May a committee of the U.S. National Academy of Sciences cited discrepancies in EPA standards for allowable levels of pesticides in fresh and processed foods. Because of a 30-year-old federal law, any amount of cancer-causing pesticide or other substance in processed foods (and thus on any crop destined to be processed) was prohibited, since such chemicals become concentrated in the processing. Meanwhile, certain pesticide residues were allowed to remain on fresh foods, even though there was no scientific reason for the discrepancy. By the committee's analysis, 80 percent of the dietary risk posed by all pesticides comes from only 10 pesticides used on 15 foods—tomatoes, beef, and potatoes being the top three. The committee also found that new pesticides were subject to more stringent rules than old pesticides. To end the inconsistencies, the committee recommended that the EPA allow a pesticide residue only if the risk of causing cancer is less than one in a million. The EPA said it would move to tighten regulation of the pesticides cited in the report.

After four years of study, the EPA announced in December that it would allow continued use of alachlor, perhaps the most commonly used commercial weed-killer in the United States, subject to certain restrictions. The agency said the chemical, banned in Canada and in the state of Massachusetts, offered high benefits to agriculture and did not pose unreasonable health risks. Environmental groups criticized the decision.

Chlordane, the most widely used pesticide for termite control, was taken off the U.S. market in August by its sole producer, the Velsicol Chemical Corporation. The chemical, a suspected carcinogen that had been used in some 30 million homes, was found to leave harmful levels in the air even when properly applied. However, remaining stocks could still be used by termite control companies.

**Public Lands.** The United States gained its first new national park in seven years. The 77,000-acre Great Basin National Park in eastern Nevada contains a complete ecosystem representative of the region, from dry desert flatland to snow-covered mountains.

**Toxic Waste.** In August the EPA added 99 hazardous waste sites to the Superfund program's national priority list of locations eligible for federal cleanup, bringing the list's total to 802 sites. The additions included federal facilities, most of them military installations, for the first time; some of the 32 federal sites, including the Rocky Mountain Arsenal in Colorado and McClellan Air Force Base in California, were among the worst of the sites added to the list.

The EPA also prohibited land disposal of 12 classes of hazardous waste. The wastes on the list included liquids containing cyanides, metals, and PCB's (polychlorinated biphenyls); all corrosive wastes; and liquid or solid wastes containing halogenated organic compounds.

In the largest toxic waste settlement thus far negotiated by the agency, the Texas Eastern Corporation tentatively agreed to a ten-year, $400 million cleanup to remove chemicals along a natural gas pipeline from Texas to New Jersey. Meanwhile, late in the year, Waste Management Inc., the nation's biggest waste disposal company, abandoned plans to burn toxic wastes on incinerator ships off the U.S. coast. No other company has incinerator ships that could carry out such a program.

**Nuclear Waste.** Safety concerns were raised about an underground nuclear waste dump near Carlsbad, N.M., scheduled to begin operations in October 1988. An independent panel of scientists reported in December that water found seeping through salt deposits into the repository, designed to hold plutonium-bearing waste from the production of nuclear weapons, could corrode the steel storage drums, causing radiation to escape and possibly contaminate rivers and aquifers. Federal experts claimed that the threat was not great and that design changes could be made to enhance safety. The repository would be the nation's first permanent underground installation to hold nuclear waste.

At about the same time, Congress settled on Yucca Mountain, Nevada, as the tentative disposal site for even more hazardous nuclear waste, from military and commercial reactors. Legislation called for exploratory drilling to begin at the Nevada site and for an end to work at sites in Hanford, Wash., and Deaf Smith County, Texas, that had also been considered for the purpose.

159

# ENVIRONMENT

**Radon Threat.** During the year, Congress considered providing funds to states to aid them in detecting and controlling radon in homes and schools. In August the EPA released results of a survey covering 11,600 homes in 10 states, showing that more than 20 percent of the homes tested contained unsafe levels of radon. The colorless, odorless radioactive gas greatly increases the chances of developing lung cancer for those exposed to it regularly over a long period of time and may be the principal cause of lung cancer among nonsmokers.

**Lead Poisoning.** The EPA proposed lowering the permissible amount of lead in drinking water, from 50 parts per billion to 20 parts per billion, after releasing a report concluding that children's mental and physical development could be impaired by exposure to lower levels of lead than previously believed. Meanwhile, a study in Maryland found that 52 of 151 schools examined had higher levels of lead in their drinking water than permitted by current federal standards. The lead solder used to connect water pipes in many older buildings was identified as an important source of such contamination.

**Water Pollution.** Congress revived and sent back to the president a clean-water bill that he had pocket-vetoed in late 1986. When Reagan again vetoed the measure, saying it was too costly, Congress overrode the veto, on votes of 401-26 in the House and 86-14 in the Senate. The final bill, identical to the 1986 version, provided $18 billion in funds for states to construct sewage treatment plans and $2 billion for controlling runoff from farmland and city streets and other water pollution.

A report released in March noted a number of positive trends in water-pollution data gathered at 380 nationwide river and stream sampling stations between 1974 and 1981. Lead levels had decreased, and fecal bacteria from sewage pollution had declined. However, levels of such toxic elements as arsenic and cadmium had increased, as had nitrogen levels. Fertilizer runoff and the results of fossil-fuel combustion are thought to contribute to the nitrogen levels.

In June the EPA set new drinking water standards, to take effect in 1988, for eight previously unregulated toxic chemicals: vinyl chloride, benzene, trichloroethylene, carbo tetrachloride, 1,2-dichloroethane, para-dichlo robenzene, 1,1-dichloroethylene, and 1,1,1 trichloroethane. All are volatile organic com pounds used primarily as industrial solvent and, with one exception, are known or likel to cause cancer. About 10 million American were served by the 1,800 public water system that had excess levels of the chemicals.

**Seal Hunts.** In a move that pleased enviror mentalists, Canada banned offshore comme cial hunting of most seal species. The practic of clubbing young seals to death on the ic had aroused indignation and threats of trad retaliation against Canada; a reduced deman for pelts also influenced the decision.    C.M

**EQUATORIAL GUINEA.** See STATISTICS OF TH WORLD.

**ETHIOPIA.** In 1987, Ethiopia adopted a nev constitution and officially joined the ranks c the Communist states, with Mengistu Hail Mariam as president. In preparation for th new political order, the provisional militar government held elections for a people's as sembly and shuffled its economic and militar leadership. It also continued its attempts t deal with the ongoing famine.

On September 12, Ethiopia celebrated it official installation as a member of the Com munist bloc and the 13th anniversary of th 1974 revolution with huge ceremonies at tended by more than 100,000 persons. Th stage for this event was set in February, whe the new constitution was approved by 8 percent of those voting in a national referen dum. Ethiopia had been without a constitutio since the overthrow of Emperor Haile Selassi in 1974. Under the new constitution, th Workers' Party of Ethiopia is the vanguar political party and the predominant structur in the political system. The administration c state power officially lies in the hands of . people's assembly, or Parliament, known a the Shengo, which approves all legislatio shares in initiating it, and selects the presiden prime minister, and cabinet. The president, a head of state and commander-in-chief of th armed forces, may initiate legislation and is i charge of implementing policy. The prim minister supervises the ministries and the re gional or local Shengos.

Elections to the national Shengo were held
n June. Among the victors were the leading
gures of the military government, including
Mengistu, secretary-general of the WPE and
chairman of the Provisional Military Adminis-
ative Council, who was selected by the Shengo
s president.

Clashes with Somalia continued. An Ethio-
ian armored column crossed into Somalia in
ebruary, but the troops were routed and 300
were reported killed. Meanwhile, separatist
ebels continued their struggle against the cen-
al government.

An unexpected drought in June and July led
o fears that famine conditions would be severe,
specially in northern and eastern regions. The
government pushed ahead with its villagization
rogram, whose objective is to relocate isolated
easants into centralized villages. By the end
f the year 7 million peasants were scheduled
o have been relocated; plans call for the
ventual movement of 30 million people. The
rogram to resettle families from the drought-
ricken areas of the north to the south and
outhwest also continued, and 300,000 people
were moved.

In all, some 5 million Ethiopians were still
aid to be in danger of starvation, and the
United Nations, other agencies, and various
ountries (including the United States) pro-
ided emergency assistance. In late October,
ritrean rebels attacked a truck convoy carrying
mergency food aid in Tigre, prompting relief
fficials to suspend further shipments.

*See* STATISTICS OF THE WORLD.          P.J.S.

**UROPEAN COMMUNITIES,** a supranational
rganization comprising the European Eco-
omic Community (EEC), the European Atomic
nergy Community, and the European Coal
nd Steel Community. These may be referred
o jointly as the European Community (EC), or
Common Market. In 1987 the 12 members
were Belgium, Denmark, France, Great Britain,
Greece, Ireland, Italy, Luxembourg, the Neth-
rlands, Portugal, Spain, and West Germany.

Trade relations with the United States were
trained by the sharp rise in Spanish and
ortuguese tariffs on grain imports from the
United States. The January settlement of this
ispute included a European Community as-
urance that Spain would import specified

amounts of corn and sorghum from non-EC
sources, thus enabling continued U.S. exports
to Spain. Another trade dispute with the United
States was resolved in August when the EC
agreed to reduce subsidies on pasta products.
Still unresolved was a dispute over a pending
EC plan to ban imports of all U.S. meat that is
hormone-treated.

In January finance ministers from eight member countries of the European Monetary System
agreed on a currency realignment. They settled
on a 3 percent revaluation of the German mark
and Dutch guilder and a 2 percent revaluation
of the Belgian and Luxembourgian francs. The
currencies of France, Italy, Denmark, and
Ireland were left unchanged.

The Single European Act, a formal agreement
concluded by EC governments in 1986, went
into force in July 1987. Key provisions modified
the 1957 Treaty of Rome which established
the European Community. In particular the act
enabled the Council of Ministers, the EC's chief
decision-making body, to make rules for the
establishment of a barrier-free internal market
(to be achieved by the end of 1992) through
weighted majority voting, rather than requiring
unanimity as before. However, numerous exceptions remained. The act also provided for
a modest strengthening of the role of the
European Parliament in determining EC policy.
A main purpose of the act was to provide a
formal treaty basis for European cooperation
on foreign policy matters.

At the EC summit meeting in June, leaders
failed to reach agreement on a financial reform
program. Britain rejected the plan, approved
by the other members, because it did not
provide firm controls on EC spending. The EC
was expected to incur a $6 billion deficit for
1987, of which about 70 percent was due to
farm subsidy programs. Disagreement on financial reform measures continued to block
adoption of a new EC budget. At a meeting in
Copenhagen in December, EC leaders once
again failed to agree on a financial overhaul
plan or on a budget.

In December, EC transportation ministers
approved a limited airline deregulation package that would lower ticket costs on flights
within Europe by allowing increased competition among carriers.          W.C.C.

# F

**FASHION.** The surprise development of 1987 was the rise in hemlines. Skirt lengths climbed from well below the knee to well above it, revealing an expanse of leg that had not been seen since the 1960's.

**Short and Shorter.** Short skirts began to make headlines in March when, in an across-the-board move, the major European couturiers presented abbreviated lengths in their ready-to-wear collections for fall. The news cheered many males, and the idea was soon endorsed by New York designers at their advance fall showings, held in April. The change was ab-

rupt, but its general acceptance by the mass market was proceeding slowly.

Meanwhile, merchandise in the stores for spring and summer echoed the moods of previous seasons. There were few frills and flounces, but touches of lace gave some clothes a romantic air. Among the continuing styles were roomy cotton knit sweaters patterned with motifs to match printed skirts. Bold stripes and polka dots in black and white, splashy abstracts, and tropical prints in hot colors were prevalent. For business, the coat dress and the loose chemise vied with lightweight tailored sepa-

*French couturier Christian Lacroix won acclaim for theatrical designs combining widely flared dresses, playful patterns, and ruffles—topped by fanciful hats and guaranteed to win attention.*

The miniskirt staged a comeback, in an echo of the 1960's. Left, an outfit by Jean-Charles de Castelbajac has roomy sleeves and bright splashes of color. A long jacket with a bit of skirt showing was one of the most popular looks; right, Angelo Tarlazzi added on gentle gathers, bows, and wide-brimmed hats.

rates. Daytime skirts for the warm weather months were long. The leggy look was restricted to strapless evening dresses with short ballerina, bubble, or pouf skirts.

**The New New Look.** Observers saw the genesis of fall's radical change in the work of 36-year-old Christian Lacroix, the revolutionary new French couturier who was the talk of Paris. As a designer for the house of Jean Patou—which he left early in the year to start his own company—Lacroix had challenged the established order by inventing flirty pouffed-and-petticoated styles and introducing whimsical combinations of colors and materials. At his opening in July, he showed frivolous and feminine clothes that emphasized bosoms, hips, and legs and set the pace for more staid French couturiers, whose new collections had a playful, exuberant spirit.

Despite the analogy with the youthquake of the 1960's, clothes watchers saw the new ultra-short skirts as serious, grown-up fashion. Such American designers as Bill Blass and Oscar de la Renta, whose clothes are worn by the wives of bank presidents and diplomats, were quick to adopt styles that glorified the leg yet managed to combine elegance with a younger, more modern look. Leading furriers, who presented their fall offerings in early summer, underscored the trend by showing short fluffy coats.

The new minis were worn with dark, opaque tights and matching high-heeled pumps, giving a flattering unbroken line to the leg. One such outfit, from the Perry Ellis collection, was topped with a huge black-fox cossack hat.

The concept of long-over-short was also in evidence, exemplified by Geoffrey Beene's hooded ankle-length capes over miniskirts. For women who would be uncomfortable in short skirts, some designers included folkloric looks that covered the leg. Pants were another popular alternative.

**Fabrics and Fit.** An important element in the fall picture was the introduction of stretch fabrics. The addition of 1–2 percent of lycra spandex imparted unusual stretch properties to outerwear fabrics. The springy qualities of stretch cavalry twills and melton cloths allowed for silhouettes that were not possible before. Closely fitted clothes could move with the body without bagging out.

Curvaceous lines were often exaggerated. Besides rounding out the shoulder line, some designers added padding at the hips to stress a well-defined waist, which was sometimes raised to Empire level. Many wrap styles were cinched with high, wide belts. Short swingback coats and cropped jackets over slim shapes were part of the overall picture.

**Colors and Motifs.** Along with the predominant black, brown was exceptionally strong in fall fashions. Charcoal, taupe, loden, camel, oatmeal, and other neutrals also figured in a fall color palette that was brightened with shots of cranberry, violet, cobalt, melon, persimmon, yellow, jade, and other brilliant tones.

Animal prints—the spotted cats particularly—were liberally used. They turned up on suit lapels, cuffs, hats, scarves, and belts. Leopard motifs appeared in intarsia knits and on cotton velvets or satins. Another notable touch was the bow, which marched down fronts of suit jackets, accented hiplines and décolletages, and served as a bustle on evening gowns. In keeping with the season's lavish feeling, fur was generously employed for collars and cuffs and as a banding at necklines, hips, hems, and the tops of strapless evening dresses.

**Roomier, Easier Men's Clothes.** Mobility was the operative word in men's apparel. Tailoring was relaxed, a blend of Italian and British styles. A fuller chest, sloping expanded shoulders, a moderately suppressed waist, and lowered button placement resulted in more comfortable garments. A paring down of superfluous padding also contributed to the sense of ease. Designers used supple fabrics. Suits were cut to make men appear taller and chestier. Big-shouldered, extra-long topcoats were still in style for both dressy and sporty occasions.

Trousers for casual wear had wider legs and jackets, minimal linings. For sportier moments there were burly knits in addition to bold Nordic and Indian-blanket patterned sweaters. Pretreated denims included new acid-washed jeans which looked even more aged than the stone washed types.

The preference for brown in all tones, from tobacco to toast, was attributed to Ronald Reagan's familiar brown suit.                    P.F

**FIJI.** See STATISTICS OF THE WORLD.

**FINLAND.** National elections on March 15-16, 1987, resulted in a shift to the right as the Conservatives (officially the national Coalition Party) enhanced their status as Finland's second largest party after the Social Democrats. Following nearly six weeks of complicated inter party negotiations, the Conservatives and the Social Democrats forged an unprecedented coalition (along with two smaller parties) on April 28. The new government was expected to pursue domestic and foreign policies similar to those of its predecessor. Harri Holkeri, a prominent Conservative, was appointed prime minister, while Kalevi Sorsa, chairman of the Social Democrats and the outgoing prime minister, became foreign minister.

The Conservatives had increased their total representation in the 200-seat Parliament to 53—their largest number ever and only 3 short of the Social Democrats' 56 seats. The Center Party won 2 new seats for a total of 40. The Communists, on the other hand, were badly hurt during the campaign by an open ideological and organizational rupture between the "revisionist" Eurocommunist majority and the hard-line "Stalinist" minority, and the combined strength of the Communist parties fell from 27 seats to 20.

In October, President Mauno Koivisto, a Social Democrat and former prime minister, said he would run for a second term in 1988.

The Finnish economy has generally prospered over the past few years. The average annual growth rate exceeded that of most industrial democracies, while unemployment and inflation were below the European average. However, experts at the Paris-based Organization for Economic Cooperation and Develpment foresaw a decline in Finnish economic performance as a result of a drop in trade with he Soviet Union and reduced domestic investment.

In January, Soviet-Finnish agreements were signed on trade, space research, and exchange of information after nuclear accidents. In February, Finland agreed to share information on nuclear accidents and nuclear safety with Denmark, Norway, and Sweden.

*See* STATISTICS OF THE WORLD.    M.D.H.

**FISHERIES.** *See* AGRICULTURE AND FOOD SUPPLIES.

**FLORIDA.** *See* STATISTICS OF THE WORLD.

**FORMOSA.** *See* TAIWAN.

**FRANCE.** The trial of former Nazi official Klaus Barbie and the ups and downs of relations with Iran brought international attention to France during 1987. The struggling economy was an important issue for the government of Prime Minister Jacques Chirac.

**Barbie Trial.** In May, Klaus Barbie, the former Gestapo lieutenant known as the "Butcher of Lyon" went on trial in Lyon after spending four years in a French prison. Barbie was charged with crimes against humanity, specifically with the deportation to certain death of over 430 Jews (44 of them children) and some 300 French Resistance members. The trial raised disturbing questions about the French Resistance and French collaboration with the Nazis, a subject that Barbie's lawyer, Jacques Vergès, promised to bring up on the grounds that guilt for Nazi crimes was widespread and could not be focused on a Gestapo officer. Vergès also promised to put the entire French nation in the dock as what he called collaborators in brutal colonialism in Algeria.

Barbie's path to Lyon was tortuous. He was arrested by U.S. forces in Germany in 1946 and then put to work for U.S. counterintelligence tracking ex-Nazis and what was believed to be the rudiments of a Soviet intelligence network in Germany. Barbie was arrested again in 1947, was again released, and finally in 1951 traveled to Bolivia with papers reportedly supplied by the U.S. Army. More than 20 years after he settled in Bolivia under a false name, the Nazi hunters Serge and Beate Klarsfeld found him in 1972. But it took another decade,

**Nazi War Criminal**

For eight weeks the eyes of France and much of the world focused on Lyon, where former Gestapo officer Klaus Barbie was on trial for crimes against humanity. From eyewitness accounts and other evidence presented, he emerged as an ambitious officer fully committed to the "final solution to the Jewish problem." He was found guilty on all charges and sentenced to life imprisonment. Born in 1913 near Bonn, Barbie had become a member of the elite Nazi Guard, the SS, in 1935. He participated in the mass deportation of Jews and Resistance members to death camps. After the war he eventually escaped to Bolivia, where he lived safely and prosperously for 32 years. Nazi hunters managed to track him down there in 1972 and waged a long, finally successful effort to have him extradited to France. Although Barbie was twice tried in absentia and sentenced to death, the 20-year statute of limitations for war crimes had run out by 1987. Therefore, he was charged with crimes against humanity, for which there is no statute of limitations.

*Klaus Barbie*

*Blockaded by armed French security forces, employees (center) at Iran's embassy in Paris dealt with the outside world through a doorway. The French government, claiming that a wanted terrorist was holed up in the embassy, had ordered the building surrounded. The incident led to a diplomatic rupture, but France eventually allowed the alleged terrorist to leave without being questioned, reportedly as part of an agreement to "normalize" relations with Iran.*

and the supplanting of the military government in Bolivia, to extradite him to France.

At the trial, the prosecution showed documents that it claimed proved that Barbie was the principal initiator of Jewish deportations from Lyon. Barbie always denied these charges on the grounds that he was too low ranking to have initiated anything of such magnitude. The evidence, however, was against him, and there was nothing that Vergès could do to discredit it, as much as he tried. The fears of some, that the genocide of the Jews would fade into the background of a larger picture of atrocities, did not materialize. Serge Klarsfeld said at the end of the trial that because of the specificity of the verdict, the 44 children of Izieu (a village east of Lyon) who were deported to the Auschwitz death camp on Barbie's orders would not be forgotten.

The judges delivered the verdict in early July. They pronounced Barbie guilty on all 341 counts of the indictment, for which they sentenced him to life imprisonment. Barbie, who was 73 years old at the time of his sentencing, could be paroled in 15 years, but observers suggested that parole was unlikely in his case. Barbie could not be sentenced to death because France's statute of limitations on crimes for which he had been twice tried and sentenced to death in absentia in the 1950's had run out; moreover, France had abolished the death penalty in 1981.

**Relations With Iran.** Relations with Iran deteriorated in June, when French police surrounded the Iranian embassy in Paris in an effort to arrest an embassy employee accused of participating in the Paris bombings of 1986, in which 13 people lost their lives. The embassy refused to give him up, and a standoff between France and Iran resulted.

As French security forces continued to surround the embassy, Iranian revolutionary guards surrounded the French embassy in Tehran; neither government would allow embassy employees to leave the country. On July 17, France broke diplomatic relations with Iran. In response to Iranian threats against French diplomatic and military installations around the world, the French also were forced to tighten security for their ships, planes, and armed forces overseas. What appeared to be France's

wly aggressive stance toward Iran was re-
ected in its decision to join the United States
August in minesweeping efforts in the Persian
ulf region.

In late November, however, two French
ostages in Lebanon were released by a terrorist
rganization with reported ties to Iran and
yria. Barely 48 hours later, the alleged terrorist
the Paris Iranian embassy was allowed to
ave France without being questioned. His
elease was said to be part of an agreement to
normalize" relations with Tehran. Shortly
fter, France expelled to Gabon 17 members
f a leftist anti-Khomeini group, in a move that
as widely criticized.

Meanwhile, previous press reports of illegal
eapons sales to Iran resurfaced in October,
ith new allegations that members of the former
ocialist government had approved the sales—
ade by Luchaire, an arms manufacturer—
nd had diverted some of the profits to their
arty's treasury. President François Mitterrand
ltimately admitted that he had learned of the
rms sales, but said officials had then assured
im falsely that the sales were being stopped.
ress reports later charged that secret arms
ales had continued through summer 1987
nder the Chirac administration.

**errorist Tried.** Georges Ibrahim Abdallah, an
lleged Lebanese terrorist leader, was tried and
onvicted on charges of complicity in the
982 murders of an American military attaché
nd an Israeli diplomat. Given France's con-
ern for its hostages in Lebanon and fears of
ossible renewed bombing attacks in Paris, it
ame as no surprise that the prosecutor asked
or a maximum sentence of only ten years. But
e court instead imposed the maximum sen-
ence allowed by law, life imprisonment.

**he Economy.** The economy continued to
erform sluggishly, despite Chirac's promises
at a strong dose of free enterprise would turn
around. All of the indicators remained dis-
ouraging: the gross national product for 1987
vas expected to grow by a paltry 1.5 percent,
fter rising only 2.2 percent in 1986; France's
rade deficit was expected to reach record
roportions, nearly triple the amount of 1986;
nemployment was close to 12 percent.

Some of the problems derived from Chirac's
olicy of tightening the austerity that President

Mitterrand had introduced before Chirac's conservative government was elected in 1986.
Austerity did not produce lower interest rates
as expected and thereby kept shallow the pool
of capital needed for expansion. Moreover,
after attacking Mitterrand for attempting to keep
so-called inefficient industries—such as steel
and chemicals—afloat, Chirac did much the
same thing. On the labor front, where Mitterrand had attempted to enlist labor unions to
curb inflation and hold down production costs,
Chirac took a confrontational stance, resulting
in repeated work stoppages.

The economy was also suffering because
traditional French industrial strengths and new
developments in transportation and nuclear
energy had not captured export markets as
they were intended to do. Most of this failure
was not France's fault, especially the under-
standable reluctance of other countries to proceed with nuclear power after the Chernobyl
disaster in the Soviet Union.

Chirac's neo-Gaullists came to power with
a promise that by 1991 they would return to
private hands 65 companies that had been
nationalized, many by Mitterrand's Socialists
in 1982 but some as long ago as de Gaulle's
first government in 1946. The denationalization
campaign began in November 1986 and was
led by Finance Minister Edouard Balladur,
considered the number-two man in the Chirac
government. Balladur's efforts at first bore fruit
even more dramatically than expected: a number of the stock offerings put on the market
were many times oversubscribed, raising the
suspicion that the government had deliberately
undervalued major pillars of the French industrial economy by hundreds of millions of francs.
Share prices jumped immediately once they
were offered for sale on the Bourse (the Paris
stock exchange). The privatization program
was seriously threatened, however, by the stock
market plunge that began on October 19.

**Chemical Weapons.** In February the Chirac
government announced plans to develop
chemical weapons. The announcement came
at a time when an international conference on
banning such weapons was making progress
in Geneva and before disarmament negotiations between the United States and the Soviet
Union agreed that French and British nuclear

weapons would not be included in the package of weapons to be dismantled. The French sought to develop new chemical weapons to insure them against a wholesale disarmament process that might leave them vulnerable to increased superpower domination of Europe. The development of new chemical weapons (the French are reported to have stocks left from those developed just after World War II) was part of a general rearmament policy that includes the development of new missiles, a new tank, and a nuclear-powered aircraft carrier and the purchase of Awacs reconnaissance aircraft.

**Attack on Sex Magazines.** In March the government, reviving an obscure 1949 law intended to protect minors, banned the distribution and public advertisement of several sexually oriented magazines, including the French edition of *Penthouse* and a magazine aimed at homosexual men. This move was made by Minister of the Interior Charles Pasqua and supported by conservative forces in the government. Chirac himself approved, in a move to rally conservative and law-and-order forces behind him in preparing for the 1988 presidential election, in which he was expected to be a candidate. Here was a relatively easy way to demonstrate a policy of firmness and toughness against alleged lawbreakers. For those opposed to the ban the issue was simply one of censorship, denounced from within the cabinet by the culture minister and from without by President Mitterrand, who announced his opposition to all forms of censorship. Nevertheless, the ban seemed to be popular with a large segment of the French population.

*See* STATISTICS OF THE WORLD.        S.E

# G

**GABON.** *See* STATISTICS OF THE WORLD.
**GAMBIA, THE.** *See* STATISTICS OF THE WORLD.
**GEORGIA.** *See* STATISTICS OF THE WORLD.
**GERMAN DEMOCRATIC REPUBLIC (EAST GERMANY).** In September 1987, Erich Honecker made the first trip ever of an East German Communist Party leader to the Federal Republic of Germany (West Germany). When he arrived in Bonn to be greeted by West German Chancellor Helmut Kohl, he received a number of honors accorded to foreign heads of state. A military band played the East German national anthem. The similar black, gold, and red flags of the two countries flew side by side. In addition, West German President Richard Von Weizsäcker gave a luncheon in Honecker's honor. At the same time, however, Kohl spoke of a "working visit" rather than a "state visit," and Von Weizsäcker welcomed Honecker as head of the East German state, not nation. In two days of meetings in Bonn, East and West Germans signed agreements to work together for environmental protection, nuclear reactor safety, scientific and technological progress, more contacts between the two countries, and peace.

After Bonn, Honecker visited three cities in the industrial heartland of the Federal Republic and Wiebelskirchen, his hometown in the state of Saarland. He also visited Bavaria.

**Response to Gorbachev Reforms.** East German party leaders took a lukewarm and ambiguous attitude toward the calls of Soviet leader Mikhail Gorbachev for "openness, restructuring, and democracy." The Soviets have 400,000 troops stationed in East Germany and play a major role in policy-making there. Kurt Hager, a 74-year-old Politburo member and the Central Committee secretary responsible for ideology, first put forth the official East German line in an interview with the West German magazine *Stern.* He expressed full support for what the Soviets wished to do in their own country but said the East Germans had already achieved a highly developed economy, a fact that "is internationally acknowledged today." The East German press even went so far as to censor some of Gorbachev's speeches.

**Rock Violence.** The largest confrontation of civilians with police and security forces in the last ten years took place in June, when British rock groups held concerts three nights in a

ow on the West Berlin side of the Brandenburg Gate, adjacent to the Berlin Wall. Young East Germans attempted to eavesdrop on the concerts by coming close to the gate. On the third night, 3,000 to 4,000 youths gathered, but they were stopped about 300 yards before the police barricades by special security strike forces in civilian clothes. The security troops dragged about 50 youths off to police vehicles and also assaulted West German radio and television crews covering the event. The demonstrators, in turn, threw bottles and other objects and shouted in unison, "The wall must go!" and "Gorbachev! Gorbachev!"—an indication of support for his policy of openness.

**Economy.** The strongest economy of the Soviet-bloc states kept to its winning ways in 1987. In the first six months, produced national income rose 3.0 percent over the same period of 1986, a significant achievement in the face of the severe winter weather. All growth was attributed solely to increases in labor productivity. Although party leaders resisted some of the Gorbachev reforms, a significant decentralization had already been instituted in East Germany in the 1960's with the introduction of some 130 semi-autonomous industrial combines.

**Berlin Birthday.** Berlin was 750 years old in 1987, and both East and West parts of the city celebrated accordingly. One June guest to West Berlin was U.S. President Ronald Reagan, who in a speech at the Brandenburg Gate, only a few yards from the Berlin Wall, called upon Gorbachev "to tear down the wall."

See STATISTICS OF THE WORLD.        R.J.W.

**GERMANY, FEDERAL REPUBLIC OF (WEST GERMANY).** In January 1987, West German voters returned to office the three-party coalition government of Chancellor Helmut Kohl, but both Christian Democratic parties in the coalition lost ground.

**Federal Elections.** Kohl's Christian Democratic Union received 34.5 percent of the vote, compared with 38.2 percent in the 1983 elections; the party's loss was proportionally highest among Catholic farmers, a former mainstay, who have demanded greater governmental support for agriculture. The Christian Social Union of Bavaria, led by Premier Franz Josef Strauss, dropped to 9.8 percent of the vote from 10.6 percent in 1983. The two parties combined suffered a net loss of 21 seats, ending up with 223. Much of the Christian Democratic loss benefited the third coalition party, the Free Democrats. Their share of the vote rose to 9.1 percent from 7.0 percent in 1983, and their 46 seats gave the Kohl government the needed majority in the Bundestag. Hans-Dietrich Genscher, as Kohl's foreign minister the leading Free Democrat, had campaigned for a continuation of efforts toward disarmament and friendly relations with the Soviet bloc. He had been heavily attacked by the conservative Strauss.

The opposition Social Democratic Party fielded as its chancellor candidate Johannes Rau, premier of the Federal Republic's largest state, North-Rhine Westphalia. Under Rau, the party continued a voting decline that began after the election of 1972, dropping to 37 percent. The Greens, the second opposition party, boosted their support by half, with 8.3 percent of the vote. They had campaigned strongly against military expenditures and nuclear power.

**Willy Brandt.** One casualty of the campaign was 73-year-old Willy Brandt—the best-known West German internationally—who resigned in March as chairman of the Social Democratic Party, after 23 years. He had been criticized for his lukewarm support of Rau during the campaign and for an increasingly indecisive leadership of the party. Brandt was replaced as chairman by Hans-Jochen Vogel, the party's parliamentary leader, who ran unsuccessfully for chancellor in 1983.

**Spring State Elections.** In February the country's first Social Democratic/Green coalition state government fell in Hesse, when the Social Democratic premier dismissed the Green environmental minister on an issue concerning the production of nuclear fuel. In April elections, the Social Democrats lost control of the state for the first time since 1947; the Christian Democrats and Free Democrats subsequently formed a coalition government with a two-seat majority.

In May the Christian Democrats suffered losses in both Hamburg and Rhineland-Palatinate, while the Free Democrats, previously frozen out of both state legislatures, passed the 5 percent hurdle necessary to gain representation in both states. In Rhineland-Palatinate, where the Christian Democrats' percentage fell more than ten points in many farming districts, the party had to form a coalition

Rudolph Hess, one of Adolf Hitler's closest associates, died at age 93, apparently by suicide, in West Berlin. In custody since his bizarre solo peace mission to Britain in 1941, Hess lived out his last decades as the sole occupant of Spandau Prison, where, at age 90, he was photographed strolling in the garden.

*...six-year-old invitation culminated in September in a historic ...sit. Erich Honecker (walking in front of soldier) became the first ...ader of East Germany's Communist Party to visit West Germany, ...here he was hosted by Chancellor Helmut Kohl (left).*

...overnment with the Free Democrats. In Ham-...urg, the Social Democrats had been governing ...ith a minority since elections in November ...986; they gained 3.3 percentage points in the ...lay vote, largely at the expense of the Greens. ...he Christian Democrats dropped to 40.5 per-...ent from 41.9 percent in 1986. The Social ...emocrats and reinstated Free Democrats then ...egan negotiations to form a coalition govern-...ent. The coalition agreement finally pro-...uced in August included a provision that won ...eadlines nationwide—foreigners who had been ...esidents of Hamburg for at least five years ...ere given the right to vote in city elections.

**...isarmament.** The Free Democratic successes ...rompted Kohl to move the Christian Demo-...rats to their side on the issue of disarmament. ...oreign Minister Genscher and the Free Dem-...crats were fully in support of the Soviet ...roposal that the United States and the Soviet ...Jnion eliminate all their intermediate missiles ...ith ranges between 300 and 3,000 miles. But ...he Federal Republic would then be threatened ...y Soviet nuclear weapons with a range under ...00 miles and by numerically superior Warsaw ...act conventional forces. Conservative Chris-...an Democrats demanded, therefore, that the

missiles eliminated not include 72 older West German Pershing 1A's with a range of about 450 miles. However, Kohl dramatically announced in late August that the West Germans would scrap the 72 Pershings once the two superpowers had fulfilled their missile agreement. The decision exacerbated existing strains among the Christian Democrats.

**September Elections.** Internecine warfare among the Christian Democrats produced heavy losses in Schleswig-Holstein and Bremen in September. In Schleswig-Holstein, the Christian Democrats dropped from 49.0 percent of the vote in 1983 to 42.6 percent, allowing the Social Democrats (45.2 percent) to outpoll them for the first time since 1958. The Christian Democrats were now dependent for assembly majorities on the Free Democrats and the one seat held by a Danish ethnic party.

On the day of the election, the newsmagazine *Spiegel* published an article in which an aide to Christian Democratic Premier Uwe Barschel said the premier had directed him in dirty campaign tactics intended to undermine the reputation of Social Democratic leader Björn Engholm. Barschel was forced to resign, and on October 11, shortly before he was to face a parliamentary inquiry into the charge, he was found dead in a hotel room in Geneva. An autopsy revealed that he had died of an overdose of sleeping pills and tranquilizers.

In Bremen, the Social Democrats, who have governed the city since World War II, retained their absolute majority with 50.5 percent of the vote, down slightly from 1983. The Christian Democrats dropped almost ten percentage points; the big gainers were the Greens and Free Democrats.

**Economy.** After a 2.4 percent rate of growth in 1986, the economy went into a recession in the first quarter of 1987, brought on by halts in construction because of an unusually severe winter and by a rapid upward movement of the mark in relation to the dollar. By midyear, economists were predicting a sluggish 1.5 percent rate of growth for 1987, and they joined U.S. policymakers in urging the Kohl government to take vigorous measures to stimulate domestic demand. In July, unemployment stood at 8 percent, with an inflation rate of only 0.7 percent. The trade surplus for the first half of the year reached a record high.

In October, U.S. Treasury Secretary James Baker threatened to let the dollar continue to fall in relation to the mark if West Germany did not lower interest rates. The threat contributed to the worldwide drop in stock prices in mid-October and to continued turbulence in world financial markets. On November 5 the Central Bank finally lowered one major benchmark lending rate and another minor one, but the dollar continued to fall. In December, with sluggish growth continuing and unemployment rising, Bonn announced a $12.7 billion three-year plan to stimulate the nation's economy; this was promptly followed by a cut in the central bank's all-important lending rate to commercial banks by half a point, to 2.5 percent, its lowest rate ever.

**Rudolf Hess.** The last of the leading Nazis, Hitler's friend and deputy Rudolf Hess, died on August 17 at the age of 93, apparently by suicide, in Spandau Prison in West Berlin. Convicted at the first Nuremberg Tribunal of crimes against peace, he was sentenced to life in prison; since 1966 he had been the sole prisoner in Spandau. After his death, demolition of the building began immediately so that it would not become a shrine for the sma number of Nazis of today.

See STATISTICS OF THE WORLD.        R.J.W

**GHANA.** See STATISTICS OF THE WORLD.

**GREAT BRITAIN.** In general elections on Jur 11, 1987, the Conservative government c Prime Minister Margaret Thatcher (see biog raphy in PEOPLE IN THE NEWS) was returned t office by a comfortable majority.

**Stage Set for Elections.** When Thatcher calle the general elections the omens had bee favorable. Opinion polls showed the Conserva tive Party in the lead. Opposition was almo: equally split between the Labor Party, still i some sense socialist, and the recently forme Alliance, composed of Liberals and member of the Social Democratic Party (SDP). Unem ployment was still exceptionally high, but o a steady decline. Manufacturing had recovere to 1979 levels, after deep recession. Inflatior housing excepted, was down to 4 percent c so and steady.

Revenue was buoyant, and the public bo rowing requirement was running well belov target. This allowed the government to eas up on unpopular spending restrictions withou deviating too obviously from its prescribe course. It also made room for further tax cut: And sure enough, on March 17, in an unmis takably preelection budget, Chancellor of th Exchequer Nigel Lawson lowered the incom tax, reducing the standard rate from 29 percer to 27 percent, while also making a furthe reduction in the borrowing target, to 1 percer of gross national product.

Two foreign engagements took place befor the party leaders were ready for domestic battle Neil Kinnock, the Labor Party leader, travele to Washington to explain his party's antinuclea defense policies to President Ronald Reaga and others, and Margaret Thatcher went t Moscow. Kinnock failed to impress U.S. offi cials, but Thatcher, in Moscow and Sovie Georgia for five days, appeared to good ad vantage, engaging in earnest conversation wit General Secretary Mikhail Gorbachev, lunch ing with dissidents Andrei Sakharov and Yelen Bonner, and signing an accord for diplomatic scientific, and cultural cooperation.

**Election Campaign.** When the campaign opene in May, the Conservatives promised, amon other things, good national housekeeping and lower taxes; more choice and wider ownership; strong national defenses, including submarine-borne Trident nuclear missiles to replace the Polaris fleet; more legislation aimed at weakening the collective strength of trade unions; more sales of state assets; devices for allowing local authority schools to opt for "independence"; and replacement of the unpopular tax on the occupation of houses, which goes to finance local government, by an even more unpopular poll tax.

The Labor Party advocated a massive emergency program to tackle unemployment, poverty, and crime. It promised to slash unemployment, to reverse the recent income tax cut, and to reimpose all taxes of which the wealthiest 5 percent of the population had been relieved in the past seven years. The party also proposed restoration to "social ownership" of the telephone system and gas supply, recently moved to the private sector, as well as cancellation of Trident, scrapping of Polaris, and ejection from Britain of American nuclear weapons.

The Alliance (two parties, two leaders, but one manifesto) promised constitutional reform, a reduction of unemployment, and a large-scale antipoverty program.

The campaign itself struck few sparks. The Alliance leaders—David Steel, Liberal, and David Owen, SDP (the two Davids)—went about in tandem, cryptic about which of them would be prime minister in the unlikely event of its being either, inconsistent about their readiness to cooperate in government with other parties, and handicapped by a manifesto that showed too many marks of compromise. Prime Minister Thatcher started out as the firm favorite. But her party was vulnerable to probes into the details of its proposals for school reform and the poll tax. There was also much popular discontent with the national health service. The Conservative Party's position seemed to slip in the middle of the campaign; then it went on to a new tack, putting across large, simple claims of success and adding, "Don't let Labor ruin it." That struck a chord. Labor was still suffering from the public memory of rampant trade unionism and violence on picket lines. And although Kinnock had successfully

repulsed a challenge from the hard left to dominate his party, that was still perceived as a threat, especially in the area of defense policy.

**Election Results.** It was widely agreed that Kinnock, despite handicaps, fought a strong campaign and showed as never before the makings of a national leader. But it was to no avail. Though the Conservative share of the vote was down a bit from the 1983 election,

*Diana Princess of Wales, right, and her sister-in-law, the duchess of York, made a high-spirited duo at public events during the year. Reports of their antics (for example, jabbing several members of the British gentry in the posterior with their umbrellas at the Derby Day races) had royalty-watchers gossiping furiously and fed rumors of a marital breakdown between Diana and her more restrained husband, Prince Charles.*

and Labor's was up slightly, the government was returned with a substantial majority in the House of Commons. In all, the Conservatives won 42 percent of the vote, Labor 31 percent, and the Alliance 23 percent. The new House of Commons numbered 375 Tories, 229 Laborites, 22 Alliance members, and 24 others. There were marked regional variations in the vote. In Scotland a quarter of a million more people voted for labor than had last time. Rural England remained predominantly Conservative. Labor did well in the industrial north of England, badly in London.

One notable casualty was former Conservative cabinet minister Enoch Powell, who lost his Ulster seat after a 37-year tenure in the House of Commons. Another was Roy Jenkins, former Labor chancellor of the exchequer and first leader of the SDP. He had the compensation of winning a gentler election to become chancellor of Oxford University and of being promoted to the House of Lords. After the election, the Alliance parties moved toward a merger, over the objections of Owens, who resigned as SDP leader.

**The New Government.** Prime Minister Thatcher kept all her principal ministers in the offices they already held, with the exception of the veteran Lord Hailsham, who left the office of Lord Chancellor (this post, the highest judicial office in the land, also carries a seat in the cabinet). Cecil Parkinson, a favorite of the prime minister, and reckoned a "good com-

*Margaret Thatcher (top left, with husband Denis, emerged from the June general election with a solid Conservative majority i Parliament and a third consecutive term as Great Britain's prime minister. The Labor Party, led by Ne Kinnock (left), came in second, while the Alliance, led in uneasy compromise the Social Democrats' David Owen (left, facing page) an Liberal David Steel (right placed third.*

unicator," was brought back into the cabinet s the secretary of state for energy. He had een a chief architect of the 1983 election ampaign, but resigned in embarrassment shortly fterward, amid loudly publicized complaints om a slighted lover, his secretary at the House Commons, who bore his child.

When Parliament met in July the government ave notice of a heavy and contentious pro-ram of legislation; measures envisioned would rovide a right for council tenants to have their wellings transferred to another kind of land-rd (they already had the right to buy them at huge discount); a right for schools to opt out f local control and receive direct government unding; and more curbs on trade unions. The overnment also wanted to levy the notorious oll tax. Many Conservative members of Par-ament already had cold feet about the likely allout of such a tax, but Thatcher was adamant.

In early October, at the annual Conservative 'arty conference in Blackpool, Thatcher spoke f a "national revival" that had come about ince her government took office in 1979 and lescribed the June electoral victory as a "stag-ng post on a much longer journey," as she romised to fight for a dismantling of "munic-al socialism" and a revamping of local gov-rnment and social policy.

**ersian Gulf.** At the end of July, Charles Price, he U.S. ambassador in London, conveyed a equest to the British government to send ninesweepers to the Persian Gulf to help keep international sea-lanes open. Although Prime Minister Thatcher had previously given strong support to President Reagan's controversial decision to accept the reflagging of 11 Kuwaiti tankers and send warships to protect them, the British government declined to send mine-sweepers "in the present circumstances." Within a fortnight, however, the government had judged the circumstances to be different. It decided to dispatch four minesweepers, plus support ships, to the Gulf (it would be five weeks before they arrived). Britain emphasized that the minesweepers were being sent not for general duties but strictly to supplement a patrol of three Royal Navy warships that had been qui-etly accompanying British vessels in those waters; however, as other European states sent minesweepers of their own, the Royal Navy stepped easily into a coordinating role.

In late September, Iranian gunboats fired on the British tanker *Gentle Breeze,* in the Gulf about 20 miles north of Bahrain; one crew member was killed. After the incident Britain closed down an Iranian arms-purchasing office in London and supported a U.S. call for a mandatory United Nations arms embargo against Iran. In late October it was announced that three Kuwaiti tankers would be registered under the British flag.

**Privatization.** It was one of the British govern-ment's proudest boasts that in four years the proportion of people in Britain who owned industrial shares had risen from 7 to 20 percent. The sale to the public of nationalized industries was chiefly responsible.

The telephone system was the first giant to go, then gas supply. In 1987 the national airports followed, as well as British Airways, which promptly made a move to swallow up its only native competitor, British Caledonian. (After a long battle with Scandinavian Airlines System, BA acquired British Caledonian with a sweetened $458 million bid.) On a list for the future were the electricity industry and the regional authorities responsible for the public water supply. But the going was getting harder. The initial plans for water had to be scrapped. Water boards had various regulatory duties that should remain with them but could hardly be allowed to if the boards were transformed into private companies. In the summer pent-up

frustration at the inefficiency of British Telecom burst into the open, as critics cited the unreliability of its domestic telephone service, delays in repairs, lack of international enterprise, and inaccurate billing.

On October 29 the government announced it would proceed with its sale of shares in the British Petroleum Company. The decision, coming about a week after the slump in world markets, was a difficult one. Underwriters had previously agreed to pay a certain price per share; the government now said it would buy back shares from underwriters at the new market price (down about 20 percent), so as to prevent prices from falling further.

**Northern Ireland.** Violence continued in Northern Ireland, with the Irish Republican Army concentrating much of its terrorism on members of the security services, especially the Royal Ulster Constabulary and the locally recruited Ulster Defense Regiment. In May eight IRA guerrillas were killed when police and soldiers intercepted a raid on a police station at Loughgall. On November 9, 11 people were killed when a bomb exploded in Enniskillen, where crowds were gathering for a wreath-laying ceremony to honor Britain's war dead; the IRA later claimed that the detonation had been mistimed and the device intended for security forces.

**Calamities.** As night approached on March 6 the 7,951-ton "roll-on, roll-off" cross-channel car ferry *Herald of Free Enterprise* left Zeebrugge harbor for Dover with more than 500 persons on board. Twenty minutes later, it capsized and sank in shallow water. The ship had sailed with the doors in the bow still open; through them massive quantities of water entered, the shifting weight of which on the car deck turned the vessel over. At least 189 people lost their lives. The crewman who should have closed the doors was asleep on a bunk at the time; the officer who should have checked was performing other duties. An inquest jury later found there had been gross negligence. It was the worse peacetime disaster in the history of English Channel shipping.

On an August afternoon in the quiet country town of Hungerford, about 70 miles from London, a 27-year-old man whose home was in the town—dressed in combat gear and heavily armed—strolled through the streets firing bursts, apparently at random targets. He left 14 dead and 16 wounded, two of them fatally. The shooting spree began when he shot dead a woman having a picnic with her two small children in the woods and ended when, surrounded at last by the police, he also shot and killed himself.

Southern England was raked by winds of over 100 miles an hour on the night of October 15. Power was knocked out in much of the southeast, including London, and at least 14 people were killed. Britain also lost many of its beloved historic trees.

Terry Waite, envoy of the archbishop of Canterbury, on a mission to gain the release of Western hostages held by Muslim factions in Lebanon, was himself abducted in Beirut on January 20. No wholly reliable news of him had reached the West late in the year.

*See* STATISTICS OF THE WORLD.     T.J.O.H.

**GREECE.** In 1987, Greece experienced tensions with other countries; at home, the economic picture was mixed.

**U.S. Relations.** There were strained relations with the United States, partly because of what Greece perceived to be the Reagan adminis-

---

**Tunnel of Love**

Something had to be done, British conservationists agreed, to get thousands of British toads safely across busy highways to their breeding ponds during the mating season. In 1986 they tried bucket brigades. In 1987 the first toad tunnel was opened—with much fanfare and a ribbon-cutting ceremony—in Hambleden, along a major toad migratory route. Clear plastic fences built several hundred yards into the woods guide the toads into the concrete tunnel, which has ventilation slots opening onto the road surface to let in warm air. Similar experiments in West Germany have failed because of cool temperatures in the underground passageways. But Hambleden toad lovers were optimistic, and the project got off to a good start. Within a week of the opening ceremonies, as many as 1,000 toads reportedly had hopped through successfully.

ration's tilt toward Turkey. Problems also arose when the press reported that Washington had accused the Greek government of secret dealings with the Abu-Nidal terrorist group; Premier Andreas Papandreou angrily stated that negotiations on a renewal of military bases could not be held without an apology by the United States. The current agreement was due to expire in December 1988. The United States did apologize, and lease negotiations were begun in November.

**Brush With Turkey.** Greece and Turkey came fleetingly, but dangerously, close to a military confrontation over oil rights and territorial waters in the Aegean Sea. In the spring, Turkey announced that it would start exploring for oil in what Turkey defined as international or Turkish territorial waters (at least 6 nautical miles from Greek island shores), but which Greece regarded as its territorial waters (within 12 nautical miles of its island coasts). When a Turkish prospecting ship, escorted by warships, approached its destination, Greece put its military on alert. However, the crisis was defused by mutual assurances that each country would refrain from drilling in disputed areas, pending possible arbitration.

**Politics.** In September, Premier Papandreou, reversing an earlier move, reinstated three prominent leftists in his cabinet, reportedly in an effort to consolidate the government prior to elections. These need not be held until mid-1989 but could be held before then. Meanwhile, Papandreou was embarrassed by press reports that he was having an affair with a former airlines flight attendant, for whom he was said to have obtained a position as interviewer on the state-run television network. There also were charges, under investigation by a parliamentary panel, that his supporters had ordered the bugging of telephones used by Communist Party politicians, journalists, and others.

On April 3, Parliament voted to expropriate monastic lands belonging to the Orthodox Church of Greece and to place its urban property under lay control. The enactment provided for state distribution of some 350,000 acres of land to agricultural cooperatives, in what was viewed by some as an attempt by the government to retain the backing of farmers.

**Economy.** The gross domestic product for 1987 was expected to decline by 0.75 percent, even though the European Commission in Brussels estimated in midsummer that industrial investment in Greece was increasing strongly. Tourism was up, but declines in employment in the agricultural, construction, and manufacturing sectors continued. A value-added tax went into effect for the first time.

**Heat Wave.** In July, with temperatures reaching above 120 degrees Fahrenheit in some areas, Greece experienced a record-breaking heat wave that killed at least 700 people and perhaps as many as 1,000. The disaster overtaxed the nation's medical facilities and created a water supply problem of major proportions.

*See also* CYPRUS *and* STATISTICS OF THE WORLD.                                                J.A.P.

**GRENADA.** *See* STATISTICS OF THE WORLD.

**GUAM.** *See* STATISTICS OF THE WORLD.

**GUATEMALA.** During 1987, Guatemala's President Marco Vinicio Cerezo Arévalo made various reform efforts but met with resistance from conservatives.

*Bearing a wooden crucifix and religious pictures, Greek Orthodox priests and their supporters from around the country gathered in downtown Athens in April to protest the Greek government's planned expropriation of the church's monastic lands.*

In March he outlined a national reorganization plan, proposing improvements in the country's infrastructure, land reform, improved social services, and inducements to foreign capital. However, the tax reforms Cerezo proposed in September to implement his plan met with solid resistance from a coalition of agricultural, business, and finance associations. Opposition from landowners sharply curtailed land redistribution.

Human-rights activists demanded that the government end a "model village" program, which had been implemented by the armed forces and embraced some 900,000 peasants. However, Cerezo was neither willing to abolish the strategic hamlets nor able to place them under civilian control. Activists also called for the dissolution of civil-defense patrols, made up of peasants forced to guard the villages. The president failed in an attempt to make participation in them voluntary.

Although Cerezo did not seek repeal of his predecessor's amnesty for members of the military and police who were involved in human rights abuses before 1986, he did bow to pressure from the Mutual Support Group (GAM) of relatives of disappeared persons to create a government commission to report on the disappearances of Guatemalans during 30 years of military rule.

A growth rate of 3 percent was forecast for 1987. Demand for petroleum eased as the hydroelectric plant at Chixoy entered into full operation, and in April, Mexico resumed shipments of petroleum at discount prices (suspended in 1986 because of nonpayment).

Labor unions became increasingly active after years of repression by successive military regimes and the decimation of their leadership through murders and disappearances. In spite of a 45 percent unemployment rate, there were 150 labor disturbances during the first half of the year. The largest was a two-week strike by 200,000 public employees, including teachers, but the government refused to grant the strikers any salary increases.

Central American political leaders, meeting in Guatemala on August 6 and 7, reached final agreement on a regional peace pact authored by President Oscar Arias Sánchez of Costa Rica. In October the government, accordingly, held talks with guerrillas, for the first time in Guatemala's 25-year-old civil war. However, after the talks and the accompanying cease fire ended, renewed fighting was reported between rebels and government troops. In compliance with the regional peace accord, an amnesty for political prisoners was enacted in November, and a small group of political exiles was allowed to return. However, government troops had reportedly already killed most prisoners suspected of being rebels.

*See* STATISTICS OF THE WORLD.          L.L.P

**GUINEA.** *See* STATISTICS OF THE WORLD.

**GUINEA-BISSAU.** *See* STATISTICS OF THE WORLD.

**GUYANA.** *See* STATISTICS OF THE WORLD.

# H

**HAITI.** An abortive presidential election in 1987 shook hopes that Haiti could build a democracy in the face of a military government seemingly intent on perpetuating "Duvalierism without Duvalier."

Voting on November 29 was to have been the first round of an electoral process designed to produce a civilian president and legislature by February 1988. The new government would replace the army-dominated provisional government of Lieutenant General Henri Namphy, who had led an interim administration since dictator Jean-Claude Duvalier fled into exile in February 1986. On the day of the election, however, terrorist attacks on polling places, radio stations, and churches in Port-au-Prince killed 34 people, according to official reports, or as many as 200 according to others. Th

In a Port-au-Prince polling station, Haitians view victims of the
carnage that led to cancellation of the presidential election on
November 29.

voting was cancelled, and the government
disbanded the nine-member civilian National
Electoral Council. Several members refused to
accept the government order, calling it unconstitutional. Meanwhile, the United States
suspended nearly all military assistance and,
eventually, most economic aid.

The terrorism was not unexpected since the
Namphy regime had refused to give protection
or administrative support to the polling in the
wake of earlier violence. In fact, many of the
thugs, who were believed to be allies of the
Duvalier dictatorship, were either ignored or
joined in their assaults by soldiers. The military
government had tried to seize control of the
electoral process from the civilian council in
June but had been forced to back down after
a four-day national strike. But the continuing
harassment, murder, and disappearance of
social and political activists reinforced the
belief that government violations of human
rights were continuing under the new regime.

Strikes were also called to protest the cancellation of the November voting, though fewer
workers participated than had been expected.
On December 9, the government announced
that a new election would be held on January
17, 1988. However, four leading presidential
candidates called for a boycott of the elections,
and the government published a law barring
independent observers, but not soldiers, from
polling places and allowing authorities to examine each voter's ballot.

The new populist constitution under which
the election had been scheduled was approved
by a constituent assembly in May. A central
thrust of the new charter was a system of
checks and balances to prevent the concentration of power that had plagued Haiti's political history. Authority would now be shared
by national and local governments and appor-
tioned among a president, prime minister, and
bicameral legislature. The police and army
were divided, the latter made independent of
the executive. Creole, the Franco-African pa-
tois spoken by most Haitians, was made an
official language, and vodun (voodoo), their
popular religion, was legalized. The constitution, providing for the inauguration of a new
president in February 1988, was reportedly
ratified by 99 percent of the voters in a March
29 referendum.

See STATISTICS OF THE WORLD.          P.W.

**HAWAII.** See STATISTICS OF THE WORLD.

# Health and Medicine

**The urgent ongoing battle against AIDS, as well as pioneering surgery, cholesterol-conquering drugs, and the issue of surrogate motherhood, made headlines in 1987.**

During 1987 the assault on AIDS escalated, as scientists sought to develop both effective drugs and a vaccine. Delicate surgery separated Siamese twins joined at the head, and a newborn infant received a heart transplant. A major new drug to lower the cholesterol rate and reduce the danger of heart attack won U.S. government approval. The battle against cancer continued. New evidence emerged suggesting that heredity is a major factor in the development of both Alzheimer's disease and manic-depression.

**AIDS Epidemic.** By year's ends, 50,000 cases of AIDS (acquired immune deficiency syndrome) had been reported in the United States; of those affected, more than 27,000 had died. Health officials estimated that 1.5 million Americans were infected with the AIDS virus and that by 1992 there could be a cumulative total of 270,000 AIDS cases and 170,000 AIDS deaths in the United States. The number of cases diagnosed in Canada as of mid-December reached 1,423; of that number 746 had died. According to a Gallup poll, over 40 percent of American adults were afraid of contracting the disease.

*Heterosexual Spread.* Considerable concern was expressed about whether AIDS was becoming significantly more prevalent in the heterosexual population. In Africa the virus is spread largely through heterosexual contact, but the number of infections in the United States and Canada resulting from heterosexual contact has represented only a small proportion of the total known cases to date.

A study reported from England suggested a genetic factor in AIDS vulnerability. Persons with one of three genetic variants of a certain blood protein appear to have less susceptibility to AIDS infection than those with the other two types. Possibly the proportion of the heterosexual population in the United States with this resistance factor is higher than the proportion in other countries.

Evidence that there has thus far been no significant increase in heterosexual spread of the AIDS virus in the United States was found in the rates of positive blood test results among civilian applicants to the U.S. military and active-duty military personnel; all such individuals have been tested for the virus since October 1985. These rates have remained constant at about 1.5 positives per 1,000 applicants tested and 1.6 per 1,000 active-duty personnel.

The question of heterosexual spread was of particular concern to women. They have accounted for a small share of AIDS cases thus far. However, new studies found evidence that compared with male AIDS patients, women with the disease develop more infections and die sooner. Although some of the researchers believed hormonal differences might be responsible, they were cautious about interpreting their findings at this point.

*"Safe Sex."* How safe is the "safe sex" (particularly sex with the use of a condom) being advised by both government and private organizations? A recent study found that when heterosexual couples with one infected partner were faithful condom users, there was still some transmission of the AIDS virus. Truly "AIDS-safe" sex apparently requires sexual monogamy among uninfected persons who do not use intravenous drugs or receive blood or blood products. It appeared that many sexually active persons, besides using condoms, were being far more cautious in their choice of partners, to minimize the risk of contracting the disease.

*Infection in Healthcare Workers.* New anxieties were produced in May by reports that three healthcare workers had acquired the AIDS virus through contact with blood and body fluids, in the absence of any needle puncture. However, studies of these cases revealed that each of the workers had been exposed to infected human blood that touched either chapped or inflamed areas of skin or, in one case, entered the mucous membranes of the mouth or eyes (when that person's face was splattered with blood). It is now generally agreed that various precautions, such as the use of gloves, should be taken by healthcare workers when there is any chance of being exposed to a patient's blood or mucous membranes.

An increasing number of healthcare workers have refused to treat patients who have AIDS or are carriers of the virus. In response to reports of such refusals, the American Medical Association declared that, in times of medical emergency, physicians have an ethical obligation to care for AIDS patients or carriers of the virus, without regard to their own health.

*Testing Programs.* The question of mandatory screening of large numbers of people for evidence of infection with the AIDS virus is so controversial that it has even split the Reagan administration, with President Ronald Reagan and Secretary of Education William Bennett speaking out for strong screening requirements

and Surgeon General Dr. C. Everett Koop speaking against such requirements. Many medical experts have sided with Dr. Koop. Groups proposed for mandatory testing programs have included all applicants for marriage licenses and all people being admitted to hospitals. The controversy over testing these and other large groups basically concerns a weighing of the benefits of testing against its high cost and the potential for both inaccuracy of results and discrimination against those testing positive. False positive results occur, and (especially in the early months after infection) false negative results.

The Pentagon already screens all prospective recruits for the AIDS virus, rejecting applicants who test positive. Mandatory screening has also been adopted in the United States for would-be blood donors and for State Department and Peace Corps workers. In June, Attorney General Edwin Meese announced that all prisoners entering or scheduled to leave federal facilities would be tested for infection with the AIDS virus. The Reagan administration also issued rules later in the year providing for mandatory testing of all people applying for temporary or permanent residence in the United States; those testing positive could be denied legal status, unless granted a waiver.

*New York City Mayor Ed Koch unveiled an unusually explicit municipal advertising campaign aimed at stopping the spread of the AIDS virus. The ads promoted both sexual abstinence and the use of condoms.*

*AIDS Vaccines.* In August a Connecticut drug company, MicroGeneSys, Inc., became the first to receive permission from the U.S. Food and Drug Administration to begin limited testing of a potential AIDS vaccine. In November the Bristol-Myers Company received permission to test a second vaccine. The first uses a protein, cultured from insect cells, that is identical to one found on the virus's outer coating; the second uses such proteins as well, produced by manipulating a virus that has been used to manufacture smallpox vaccine. In both cases, initial tests were to be performed on small groups of male homosexual volunteers not infected with AIDS, and would determine only whether the vaccines are safe and whether those inoculated actually develop antibodies to fight the virus. (A third vaccine was being tested in Africa by French and Zairean scientists.) U.S. officials cautioned that it would be years before any vaccine could be fully tested and put on the market.

*New Treatments.* Excitement has been generated by the development of the first treatment shown to fight the AIDS virus in patients with active disease: a drug now called zidovudine (formerly AZT). The drug, which was approved for use in the United States by the Food and Drug Administration in March, acts by blocking the virus's ability to reproduce itself. Though far from being a cure, it has been shown to extend the lives and help improve the quality of life of some AIDS patients. However, it initially cost up to $10,000 a year per person and causes side effects so severe that some patients must discontinue its use. (In December the manufacturer announced a 20 percent price cut.)

*Transfusion Recipients.* In March a statement from the U.S. Centers for Disease Control recommended that Americans who received blood transfusions and blood products between 1978 and 1985 (screening of donated blood for the AIDS virus began in 1985) should be tested for infection. The CDC clarified their statement by suggesting that people should decide whether to be tested after consultation with their physicians, who would base their recommendations on how many transfusions the patients had received and on whether they had lived in an area where AIDS was prevalent.

Some concern was raised by a recent study

**Controversial Prescriptions**
As U.S. surgeon general, in charge of the Public Health Service, Dr. C. Everett Koop, 71, has shown that it is not only Supreme Court justices who can confound their original supporters once in office. An accomplished pediatric surgeon, known at the time of his 1981 nomination for his evangelical Christianity and social conservatism, Koop later shocked many on the right with his approach to preventing acquired immune deficiency syndrome. By supporting AIDS education in the early grades, televised advertisements for condoms, and even abortion counseling for pregnant women who test positive for the AIDS virus, Koop has drawn criticism from within the Reagan administration itself. Often seen in uniform—the Public Health Service is made up of commissioned officers, and Koop is a vice admiral—he has used his job to warn of other health problems as well. A former pipe smoker, he has stressed the dangers to nonsmokers of secondhand smoke and advocated restricting smoking in public places.

*C. Everett Koop*

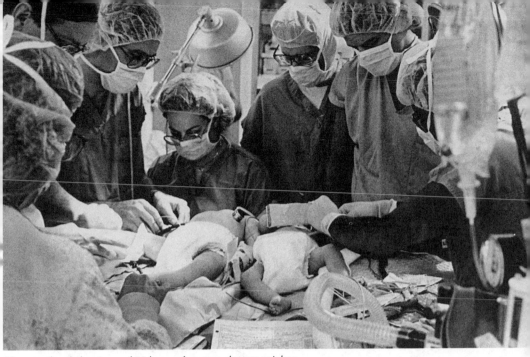

After months of planning and 22 hours of surgery, doctors at Johns
Hopkins Hospital in Baltimore separated seven-month-old Siamese
twins who had been joined at the head.

in Finland suggesting that a significant percentage of sexually acquired AIDS infections
may not produce detectable antibodies until a
year or more after the initial infection. This
preliminary finding suggests that the proportion
of blood donations that are infected may be
higher than the 1 in 250,000 currently estimated.

There has also been concern over the risk—
especially to schoolchildren—of contracting
AIDS from infected hemophiliacs, most of
whom acquired the AIDS virus from a blood
clotting factor (factor VIII) received in transfusions prior to 1985. In one case, an Arcadia,
Fla., family was driven out of their home by a
suspicious fire, shortly after the three hemophiliac children, who tested positive for the
AIDS virus, had been admitted to a local school
under a court order. Health officials, however,
have said that AIDS patients and carriers generally can attend school without special risk
to others. (Although more than half of all U.S.
hemophiliacs have now been infected with the
AIDS virus, the risk of hemophiliacs' infection
today is virtually nonexistent; the donated
blood from which the clotting factor is made

is now screened, and the clotting factor itself
is also pasteurized so as to kill the AIDS virus.)
AIDS Commission. In July, President Ronald
Reagan appointed 12 members to a new national commission on AIDS, incuding an avowed
homosexual, Dr. Frank Lilly, and the Roman
Catholic archbishop of New York, John Cardinal O'Connor. Critics charged that homosexuals were underrepresented on the panel
and that it had no experienced AIDS researchers or doctors who treat AIDS patients. Dr. W.
Eugene Mayberry, the commission chairman,
and one of the other panel members resigned
in October, apparently because of factional
disputes within the commission; Admiral James
D. Watkins, a panelist and former chief of
naval operations, became the new chairman,
and two new members were appointed in
November. The commission was directed to
issue a final report within a year.
**Siamese Twins.** Over Labor Day weekend,
Benjamin and Patrick Binder, seven-month-
old Siamese twins joined at the back of the
head, were separated in an extraordinarily
complex operation at Johns Hopkins Hospital
in Baltimore. Seventy surgeons, doctors, nurses,

183

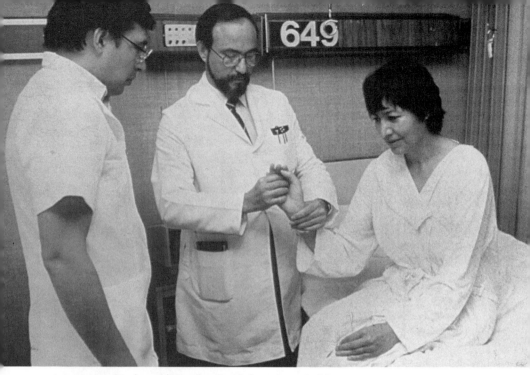

In a Mexico City hospital, Dr. Ignacio Madrazo (center) visits a patient scheduled to undergo his new operation for Parkinson's disease. Early results indicated that transplants of adrenal gland tissue to the brain could reverse the course of the illness.

and technicians took part in the 22-hour-long surgery, which had been planned as carefully as a military operation. The twins, born in Ulm, West Germany, in February, had separate brains but shared an essential vein that draws blood from the brain. Their body temperature was lowered so that their hearts stopped and blood flow nearly ceased, so that bleeding during the operation could be reduced. Despite the low success rate for such operations, doctors were cautiously optimistic about the twins' chances for long-term survival. Three months after the surgery, the twins' medical status was described as stable.

**Infant Heart Transplant.** A four-day-old Canadian boy became the youngest person ever to receive a transplanted heart when he was operated on at California's Loma Linda Medical Center on October 16. The child, known as Baby Paul—who suffered from a fatal heart defect that was diagnosed before his birth— was delivered by cesarean section two weeks early, when a donor heart became available. He was released from the hospital in late November and reported in good condition a month later.

*Anencephalic Organ Donors.* Baby Paul's new heart came from a baby born without most of her brain—a rare condition called anencephaly, which ordinarily causes rapid death. The child had been kept alive on a respirator to preserve her heart for transplant. The case raised troubling moral issues, including that of "organ farming," but growing numbers of couples, learning that their unborn babies were anencephalic, were requesting such procedures so that some benefit could come of their tragedy.

**Heart Disease and Cholesterol.** *Drugs.* In September the U.S. Food and Drug Administration (FDA) approved for marketing a revolutionary drug called lovastatin. The new drug was found in tests to reduce total blood cholesterol levels by 18 to 34 percent. Moreover, it was found to cut levels of the harmful form of cholesterol, low-density lipoproteins, by a higher proportion, while not reducing the level of beneficial high-density lipoproteins. About 20 million adult Americans have blood cholesterol levels that put them at high risk of developing coronary heart disease, the leading cause of death in the United States. Lovastatin inhibits an enzyme in the liver that is needed to make cholesterol; the liver then extracts cholesterol from the blood.

Scientists believe the new drug, sold under the brand name Mevacor, should save lives. However, it could be very expensive, costing patients (depending on dosage and retailers' markup) more than $3,000 a year. Despite widespread optimism about the drug, the FDA also warned that it can cause the liver to become overworked and can affect the lens of the eyes, increasing the risk of cataracts. Lovastatin seems to work best when taken by those already on a low-fat, low-cholesterol diet. The agency approved the drug only for people whose cholesterol count does not respond to diet and exercise.

A study released in November showed that the drug gemfibrozil dramatically reduces the number of heart attacks in men with high blood cholesterol. The drug, sold under the brand name Lopid, works mainly by changing the types of cholesterol in the blood. The effects of gemfibrozil in lowering total cholesterol levels are not as dramatic as those of lovastatin, but side effects are mild, and it is known to be safe for long-term use.

*Cholesterol Guidelines.* The first detailed U.S. guidelines for the identification and treatment of people with high blood cholesterol levels were issued in October, marking the beginning of a nationwide campaign to involve physicians and the public in the effort to reduce such levels. All people aged 20 and above, according to the guidelines, should have their total blood cholesterol level tested. For those with a high level, or with a borderline level and other risk factors for heart disease, further testing (to determine the level of harmful low-density lipoprotein cholesterol) and a strict diet were recommended, with drug treatment to be considered if cholesterol levels do not improve in six months. Restricted diets and annual monitoring were suggested for others with borderline levels.

**Knee Transplant.** An entire human knee, complete with bones, tendons, and ligaments, was transplanted into a 32-year-old New Jersey woman in November at the Hospital of the University of Pennsylvania in Philadelphia. The procedure, the first successful surgery of its kind, was undertaken when the growth of a tumor on the woman's knee threatened to force amputation of the leg.

**Alzheimer's Disease.** Progress toward unraveling the mystery of the origins of Alzheimer's disease was reported recently by U.S. and European scientists working independently. The teams of researchers found on chromosome 21 the gene responsible for manufacturing a brain protein called amyloid. Alzheimer's patients have fibers and plaques in their brains that contain abnormally high concentrations of amyloid. It remained unknown, however, whether amyloid is a cause or effect of Alzheimer's. Moreover, two research reports published later found evidence that the gene that codes for amyloid is apparently a different gene than that responsible for the hereditary form of Alzheimer's. While both genes appear near each other on chromosome 21, they can evidently be inherited independently.

Meanwhile, other scientists studied four large families with a high incidence of Alzheimer's and found an identifiable gene pattern, or "genetic marker," on chromosome 21. But another group of researchers reported no genetic abnormalities in more than 100 Alzheimer's patients studied.

Strong new statistical evidence that the risk of developing Alzheimer's is inherited came in May. Scientists at the Mount Sinai School of Medicine in New York City reported that the risk is four to five times as great for close relatives of Alzheimer's patients as for the general population.

In August the U.S. government announced a two-year trial for a controversial new drug for Alzheimer's that may reduce memory loss caused by the degenerative disorder. The drug, THA, or tetrahydroaminocrydine, appears to inhibit the breakdown of acetylcholine, a chemical involved in communication between nerve cells in the brain. But the tests were halted because of side effects.

**Battle Against Cancer.** *Breast Cancer.* In November the Centers for Disease Control reported that cancer was the principal cause of death among American women under 65 and that breast cancer caused more deaths in this group than any other form of cancer. First Lady Nancy Reagan's surgery for breast cancer in October highlighted the increasingly serious problem. Her cancer was detected in her annual mammogram; publicity surrounding the episode led to increased demand for breast cancer screenings.

Studies published earlier in the year provided new evidence linking alcohol consumption and breast cancer. Researchers at Harvard Medical School concluded that women aged 30 to 59 who have drinks of alcoholic beverages as little as three times a week are 30 percent more likely to develop breast cancer than women who seldom or never drink. Scientists at the U.S. National Institutes of Health reported, overall, a 50 to 100 percent higher risk of breast cancer for women aged 25 and over who drink.

*Interleukin-2.* In April, Steven A. Rosenberg of the U.S. National Cancer Institute published a study tracking a group of patients suffering from advanced cancer (most of them from melanoma, renal cancer, or colon cancer) who were treated with interleukin-2, a substance produced by the body that stimulates the immune system. Rosenberg found that 9

A Harvard researcher sweeps for deer ticks, carriers of Lyme disease, in Nantucket, Mass. The disease, recognized only recently, has become a major public health concern in the United States.

patients went into complete remission after treatment with the drug, while the tumors of 20 others shrank more than 50 percent. However, some patients suffered severe side effects, ranging from fever and nausea to impaired kidney function and paranoid delusions and hallucinations, and 4 patients died from the side effects.

*Parkinson's Disease.* A degenerative disorder that causes the gradual loss of muscle control, Parkinson's disease afflicts as many as 1 million Americans, most of them elderly. The symptoms of the disease—tremors, slurred speech, extreme fatigue, the inability to perform everyday tasks—result mainly from the death of brain cells that produce dopamine, a chemical that helps govern voluntary actions such as walking and speaking. The adrenal glands produce hormones chemically similar to dopamine. In April doctors in Mexico City reported on their success with a new treatment, used on two men in their 30's who suffered from Parkinson's. Dopamine-producing tissue from the patients' adrenal glands was transplanted into the brain. Five months after surgery the men were able to walk without help and to speak clearly. The removal of tissue from one of a person's two adrenal glands destroys the gland, but the person can survive with only the remaining one. An advantage of using the patient's own tissue for a transplant is that the body is less likely to reject it.

**Growing Health Threats.** *Lyme Disease.* Lyme disease—a flu-like illness characterized by a circular rash—is found in many areas of the United States, and public health authorities have become convinced that the disease is spreading rapidly—probably because the ticks that cause it are carried by as many as 30 species of birds, in addition to deer and field mice. Lyme disease was first recognized in the 1970's and by 1987 was endemic to many parts of the Atlantic seaboard; by summer the ticks that transmit the disease had been found in 32 states. Researchers at Yale University determined that the causative agent is a tiny spirochete, or corkscrew-shaped bacterium, which spreads to human beings when they are bitten by ticks carrying the organism. Early symptoms are similar to the flu and are usually accompanied by a rash emanating from the tick-bite center. Later symptoms may involve the heart, nervous system, and joints; they sometimes lead to serious complications. Early treatment with antibiotics usually prevents the more serious symptoms and complications.

*Syphilis.* Major increases in primary and secondary syphilis (the infectious stages of the disease) have been noted recently in the United States. Over 25,000 new cases were reported in the first nine months of 1987, 35 percent more than in the same period of 1986. The increases were almost exclusively in the heterosexual population and were most pronounced among blacks and Hispanics in a few urban areas. One of the big concerns was that rates of congenital syphilis were likely to go even higher and have a further negative influence on infant mortality rates. Also, the risk of AIDS is greater in persons with sexually transmitted diseases like syphilis, perhaps because the lesions provide breaks in the skin through which the AIDS virus can enter.

*Tuberculosis.* Recent studies have indicated that active tuberculosis is up to 300 times more prevalent in selected homeless populations than it is nationally—with rates ranging from 1.6 percent to almost 7 percent. The extent to which homelessness affects tuberculosis transmission (compared to other factors, such as crowding and poor ventilation) is not known.

*Salmonellosis.* For the past ten years, the rates of reported infections of *Salmonella enteriditis* have been increasing in New England and the Middle Atlantic region. These dysentery infections usually result from contaminated foods of animal origin, particularly poultry and poultry products.

**Down's Syndrome Test.** In an August report, a team of scientists suggested that a widely used blood test could help identify up to one-third of pregnant women whose babies will have Down's syndrome. The test checks the mother's blood for abnormal levels of alphafetoprotein, a substance the fetus excretes into the amniotic fluid and that enters the mother's bloodstream. Low levels may indicate a chromosomal defect that may produce Down's syndrome or other (less common) disorders.

**Cosmetic Improvements.** In March an advisory panel reviewing the drug minoxidil recommended that the FDA approve it for use in

*All but routine medically, surrogate motherhood emerged as a legal and ethical minefield. In New Jersey, William Stern, father of "Baby M" (they are shown here), fought and temporarily won a custody battle with Mary Beth Whitehead, who had contracted to conceive and bear the child.*

promoting hair growth. If the drug (to be marketed under the name Rogaine) should gain FDA approval, it would be the first hair restorer to do so. (Minoxidil already had FDA approval for treating high blood pressure.) The advisory panel warned, however, that available data did not show for certain what proportion of users would see enough hair growth to make a visible difference. Experts note that the newly grown hair falls out when minoxidil treatments are stopped, and no one knows if there are any long-term side effects to the drug when applied externally, as in its use for hair restoration.

J.F.J., S.D.H. & K.S.

# HEALTH AND MEDICINE

**Surrogate Mothers.** In March wide attention focused on a New Jersey courthouse where the first American custody case involving a child born to a surrogate mother was being decided. At issue was the fate of "Baby M." The infant was conceived according to a contract under which Mary Beth Whitehead had agreed (for a $10,000 fee) to be artificially inseminated with the sperm of William Stern and then turn the infant she bore over to Stern and his wife, Elizabeth. But shortly after the birth, Whitehead decided she wanted to keep the child. At the end of the landmark nonjury trial to determine legal custody, the judge placed Baby M with the Sterns, holding that the contract should be enforced as long as it was in the child's best interest. Whitehead's parental rights were terminated, and Elizabeth Stern was allowed to adopt the child. Whitehead appealed the ruling and won visitation rights pending outcome of the appeal.

Surrogacy arrangements are occurring more frequently today because of a rise in infertility and a decrease in the number of infants available for adoption. Although most couples who seek surrogate mothers do so because the wife is infertile, some resort to surrogates because the wife has a serious genetic defect or a medical condition that makes pregnancy risky. A variation on the standard procedure is also possible; if the wife can provide an egg though she cannot have a normal pregnancy, her egg can be fertilized with her husband's sperm, with the resulting embryo transferred to a second woman.

Currently, about two dozen surrogate centers operate in the United States, matching couples and surrogates; private arrangements are also sometimes made. In most states, courts must try to fit surrogacy into an existing tangle of statutes and precedents governing such matters as paternity, adoption, or artificial insemination. Among the questions facing courts and legislators today are whether surrogates may be paid, whether for-profit agencies should be permitted to arrange contracts, whether couples who are the intended parents should be recognized as the legal parents, and whether the surrogate should have a grace period after the birth to assert parental rights.

L.B.A. (Surrogate Motherhood)

## MENTAL HEALTH

Two independent research teams offered strong evidence that manic-depression, a serious mental disorder characterized by alternating periods of severely depressed moods and extreme highs, can be inherited. The first report came from psychiatrist Janice A. Egeland of the University of Miami and her colleagues at the Massachusetts Institute of Technology and Yale University. For more than two decades, Egeland has studied families of the Old Order Amish in Pennsylvania, a culturally isolated community of 12,000 descended from thirty 18th-century immigrants. Based on the incidence of manic-depression in three Amish families across three generations, and on chromosomal studies derived from blood samples, Egeland and her colleagues identified a genetic marker on the tip of chromosome 11 that appears to be inherited along with the gene that is believed to cause the disorder. However, even people with the genetic abnormality have at most a 63 percent chance of developing manic-depression.

In separate work, psychiatrist Miron Baron of Columbia University and coworkers at Yale and at Hebrew University in Jerusalem identified two genetic markers on the X chromosome that were associated with manic-depression and other mood disorders in five extended Israeli families comprising 161 adults. Researchers have long suspected a link between manic-depression and the X chromosome because women, who have two X chromosomes, are more likely to develop the disorder than are men, who have only one.

Taken together, the work of both of these groups suggests that at least two genetic abnormalities are responsible for a predisposition to manic-depression. However, because not everyone who inherits these abnormalities becomes manic-depressive, environmental factors must also play a role.

*See also* BEHAVIORAL SCIENCES.

R.H.C. (Mental Health)

**HONDURAS.** In Honduras, 1987 was a year of contrasts. The government pushed for economic growth, as the economy flagged. Relations with the United States remained close but saw strains, as popular sentiment grew against the presence in Honduras of the U.S.-

backed contras, insurgents opposing Nicaragua's Sandinista regime. In January, President José Azcona del Hoyo pledged to implement structural reform, make the public sector more efficient, improve competitiveness, and promote investment. Economic growth, however, continued to lag behind population increase. Coffee and cotton prices dropped sharply, and the United States reduced its import quota for Honduras sugar. Meanwhile, 41 percent of the work force was unemployed, almost as many people were underemployed, and over 200,000 suffered from famine. Despite promises to promote agrarian reform, the government did little, and from February to August landless peasants invaded over 300 farms; on May 20, 100,000 peasants occupied lands in the northeast.

As opposition mounted to the presence of the Nicaraguan contras and the U.S. military in Honduras, critics increasingly became targets of threats and violence. The office of the Committee for the Defense of Human Rights was repeatedly bombed. Dissidents were assassinated or threatened with death, and some simply disappeared. In one notorious case, Supreme Court Justice Mario Reyes Sarmiento was killed by the security police while resisting questioning.

By late 1986 the contra guerrillas controlled perhaps a 200-square-mile area in southern Honduras; there were numerous instances of theft and violence against the local population, as well as reports of terrorism against government critics. Honduran leaders informed the Reagan administration that they wanted the contras out of the country. Early in 1987 most of the contras were sent into Nicaragua; even so, fighting broke out in May between Honduran troops and the guerrillas.

Relations with the United States were complicated not only by Honduran concerns about military activity within Honduras but also by fears that a U.S. withdrawal could lead to loss of economic and military aid. For its part, the Reagan administration maintained an attitude of business as usual. In the spring almost 50,000 U.S. military personnel and 7,000 Honduran troops participated in maneuvers, including a large-scale air and sea assault near Trujillo in Honduras.

In August, Azcona and other Central American presidents met in Guatemala and signed a regional peace accord. The Honduran government reluctantly agreed to appoint a National Reconciliation Commission, as called for in the pact, but its role, at least initially, appeared to be limited. The peace pact called for a halt in outside aid to rebel groups in the region. However, the Honduran government took the position that the contras should not be required to leave Honduras until Nicaragua negotiated a cease-fire with them.

*See* STATISTICS OF THE WORLD.     D.E.S.

**HOUSING AND CONSTRUCTION.** *See* ECONOMY AND BUSINESS.

**HUNGARY.** In 1987 there were signs of political transition in Hungary. Karoly Grosz, first secretary of the Budapest municipal party committee and a Politburo member, became the

*Budapest residents turned out to honor a foreign benefactor at the inauguration of a bronze statue of Raoul Wallenberg, the Swedish diplomat who, before his arrest by the Soviets, helped thousands of Hungarian Jews escape the Nazis.*

chairman of the Council of Ministers—in essence, prime minister—replacing the ailing György Lázár. Karoly Németh, the party's deputy general secretary, became chairman of the Presidential Council and head of state, replacing the ailing Pál Losonczi. Two new members were appointed to the Politburo, and four new members to the Central Committee secretariat. Party chief János Kádár, in his mid-70's and declining in vigor, remained in his post, but he was reportedly becoming less active and influential, as Grosz exercised greater control over state affairs.

The authorities dismissed a number of workers during the year and opened a network of over 400 employment offices and facilities for retraining. In September a more far-reaching program of economic reforms was announced for the period 1988-1990, including strict application of a bankruptcy law that would close many state enterprises, putting 200,000 Hungarians out of work. Many more would be laid off from administrative jobs throughout the economy. To give state companies more incentive for improvement, the tax rate on company profits was lowered. Individuals, on the other hand, were to be assessed both a personal income tax and a value-added tax on most goods and services.

After nine months of negotiation between the Vatican and the Hungarian government, Laszlo Paskai was appointed as the new archbishop of Esztergom and Hungarian primate.

In September, Hungary became the second Eastern European country within a year to announce that it had reestablished (low-level) diplomatic ties with Israel.

*See* STATISTICS OF THE WORLD.　　R.A.P.

# I

**ICELAND.** In general elections on April 25, 1987, the coalition government of the conservative Independence Party and the centrist Progressive Party lost its majority, largely because of a split among the Independents, Iceland's largest party. Albert Gudmundsson, the popular Independent minister of industry and energy, had resigned in March over a tax scandal and formed a new Citizens' Party, which won 7 seats in its first try. The Independents lost 5 seats, leaving them with 18; the Progressives, losing 1 seat, were reduced to 13. The Social Democrats increased from 6 seats to 10, the feminist Women's Alliance doubled its representation to 6, and the Communist-dominated People's Alliance fell from 10 seats to 8; one person was elected as an independent. The new Althing (Parliament) had 63 seats, 3 more than the old.

After two months of discussions about a new government, a three-party coalition cabinet was announced on July 8. Thorsteinn Pálsson of the Independence Party became prime minister, while the former prime minister, Steingrímur Hermannsson of the Progressive Party, was named minister of foreign affairs.

Iceland and Kenya signed an agreement to carry out the first stage of an extensive geothermal development program in Kenya, where Icelandic engineers had already participated in the design and building of Africa's first geothermal power station.

An archaeological dig under Bessastadir, the residence of Iceland's president, unearthed glassware, pottery, and vials of medicine that had been undisturbed for two centuries. Foundations of a 17th-century turf building and a stone floor probably dating to the 13th century were also discovered.

*See* STATISTICS OF THE WORLD.　　E.J.F.

**IDAHO.** *See* STATISTICS OF THE WORLD.

**ILLINOIS.** *See* STATISTICS OF THE WORLD.

**INDIA.** In 1987, with Rajiv Gandhi midway through his five-year term as prime minister of India, the national mood of euphoria that accompanied his election had given way to disillusionment. Gandhi was widely criticized for an alleged arrogance and lack of respect or traditional political norms. His decision-making style weakened support for his government and his ruling party, the Congress-I. By midyear, following a stunning Congress-I defeat in assembly elections in the northern state of Haryana, opposition parties controlled 11 of India's 25 states. Gandhi had reshuffled his cabinet at least a dozen times in less than three years, prompting some of his best ministers to resign.

**Rift With President.** Gandhi failed to consult with President Zail Singh on policy matters, as is customary, and discouraged foreign and domestic presidential travel. Initially, the president had suffered in silence. In early 1987, however, the old-time Congress politician began to counterattack with public comments. With a presidential election scheduled for July, the prime minister and his advisers feared that

Singh might run for reelection, split the Congress-I, and topple the government. Singh decided not to seek reelection, however, and a major threat to Gandhi's tenure as prime minister came to an end. Ramaswami Venkataraman, the Congress-I candidate, was easily elected and was sworn in as president on July 25.

**Corruption Scandals.** Gandhi had given his finance minister, Vishwanath Pratap Singh, a broad mandate to weed out corruption, reduce tax evasion, and prevent foreign-exchange leakage. Singh introduced a series of major tax reforms, and tax raids became the hallmark of his regime, but his rigorous enforcement policies antagonized India's top industrialists, who pressed Gandhi to dismiss him. On January 24, Singh was suddenly removed as finance minister and appointed minister of defense. On

*Deepening troubles for Indian Prime Minister Rajiv Gandhi were manifest in a pointed warning at a demonstration in New Delhi. Tension within the ruling party, corruption scandals, and ethnic violence contributed to a gathering political crisis.*

April 10, Singh announced that he had ordered an inquiry into an alleged kickback paid in connection with the purchase of two submarines from Howaldt Deutsche Werke of Kiel, West Germany. Gandhi's close aides saw Singh's action as an attempt to discredit and topple the prime minister. On April 12, Singh resigned from the cabinet. (In July he was expelled from the Congress-I.)

Another scandal surfaced in April, when a state-owned Swedish radio station revealed that millions of dollars worth of commissions had been paid to an Indian agent on a $1.3 billion contract to purchase weapons from a Swedish firm. Later, Amitabh Bachchan, a boyhood friend of Gandhi, resigned his seat in Parliament when it was disclosed that his brother owned an expensive apartment in Switzerland in violation of Indian foreign-exchange laws.

**Communal Violence.** As ethnic conflict swept key border areas, North India experienced its worst outbreak of communal violence since India achieved independence. The most serious ethnic conflict remained in Punjab, where Sikhs were increasingly alienated. With Sikh moderates withdrawing from the fray, terrorism ruled the state. The number of killings in Punjab rose from 79 in April to 200 in July. In October, more than 250 Sikh militants and others were arrested by government troops near the Sikhs' Golden Temple in Amritsar, prior to a planned rally, and a curfew was imposed on the city. Sikh militants subsequently shot and killed several people in Punjab and threatened further violence.

In Uttar Pradesh, after months of clashes between Hindus and Muslims, provincial police went on a rampage in late May, killing as many as 500 Muslims.

In the northeastern state of Tripura the extremist Tripura National Volunteers (TNV) continued agitation to drive nontribal Indians out of the state. The movement was outlawed by the central government early in the year, after a TNV rampage left 24 people dead.

**Drought-stricken Economy.** Until the monsoon season failed to bring essential heavy rainfall to large parts of rural India in the summer, the performance of the Indian economy was one of the few bright spots of the year. India's gross national product had been growing at an average annual rate of about 5 percent. Industrial production had increased sharply, food stocks were high, prices were under control, and infrastructure bottlenecks had eased. But the worst drought in decades appeared likely to interfere with the achievement of most of the goals of India's current five-year plan (1986–1990). Among the immediate effects of the drought were a decline in food production and a reduction in generation of hydroelectric power. Meanwhile, ironically, severe flooding in some parts of the north and east put further strains on India's already tight financial resources. The World Bank provided $500 million in drought-related aid.

**Foreign Relations.** Skirmishes were reported between India and China, following a buildup of troops in Arunachal Pradesh, a disputed area that became an Indian state in February. By August, however, both sides had pulled back their troops and agreed to negotiations.

On July 29, India signed an accord with Sri Lanka designed to end the insurgency of separatist Hindu Tamils there, and India sent thousands of troops into that country as a peacekeeping force. In Sri Lanka, the accord provoked massive riots among the predominantly Buddhist Sinhalese majority, who called it a sellout of Sri Lankan sovereignty. The Tamil rebel groups accepted the accord but were slow to disarm, and in early October, Tamil rebels attacked civilians and the Indian peacekeeping forces. Weeks of heavy fighting ensued, and over 200 Indians were killed. Meanwhile, in southern India, some 3,000 Indian Tamils were arrested during protests against India's military actions in Sri Lanka.

Relations with the United States were mixed. News of an impending sale of Awacs radar aircraft to Pakistan resulted in the cancellation of a planned U.S. visit by the Indian foreign minister in May. However, relations improved when Prime Minister Gandhi visited Washington, D.C., in October; India was allowed to buy a U.S. supercomputer, and the two countries agreed to jointly construct a new Indian combat aircraft.

In the summer, Gandhi traveled to Moscow to open a year-long Festival of India; while there, he signed a major cooperative agreement on science and technology.

Tamil Leader Dies. On December 24 the chief minister of Tamil Nadu, Marudur Gopalan Ramchandran, died in Madras at age 70. The popular, widely respected former film star was the nation's foremost Tamil leader; his death sparked riots, in which two persons died, and a wave of suicides.

See STATISTICS OF THE WORLD. S.K.

INDIANA. See STATISTICS OF THE WORLD.

INDIANS, AMERICAN. In 1987, Indians won several cases involving treaty or tribal rights and increased their involvement in federal politics.

Treaty and Tribal Rights. At a trial in Florida, James E. Billie, chairman of the Seminole tribe, resisted prosecution for violating the Endangered Species Act by claiming that his right to hunt rare Florida panthers was protected both by treaty and by the American Indian Religious Freedom Act. Following his arrest in 1983, Billie had claimed that hunting the animals was a part of his tribe's religious tradition. The chairman's day in federal court ended in a mistrial in August. In October he was acquitted of similar state charges, and federal prosecutors dropped plans to retry him.

Thirty Vermont Abenaki Indians were scheduled to go on trial for violating that state's fishing and wildlife regulations. At stake was both their right to fish without restrictions and their legal existence as a tribe, as the Vermont Abenakis have never been legally recognized by state or federal authorities. In September the charges were dropped, however, and the state allocated funds to review its policy toward the Indians.

In a Supreme Court case involving Indian bingo, similar issues were at stake because the tribes argued that their status as legitimate governments entitled them to operate games of chance without state regulation. Upholding this claim, the Court's six-justice majority wrote that state regulation would "impermissibly infringe on tribal government." Following the decision, several bills were introduced in Congress to create a federal bingo commission to regulate Indian gambling. A study released later in the year indicated that 113 tribes earn at least $225 million per year from their bingo operations.

At midyear, the Federal Energy Regulatory Commission denied seven Montana power companies a license to construct a hydroelectric dam on the Kootenai River. The dam would have damaged Kootenai Falls, a site sacred to the Kootenai tribe. The commission's action put to rest a nine-year controversy and constituted one of the strongest defenses of Indian religious practices yet on the part of a federal agency.

An Indian group with one of the oldest records of contact with Europeans finally won U.S. government recognition. The Wampanoags of Gay Head, Mass., on Martha's Vineyard, qualified for tribal status under the Bureau of Indian Affairs, thereby becoming eligible for the first time for federal programs to assist native communities. Following recognition, a long-standing effort to settle land disputes between the tribe and property owners on Martha's Vineyard reached fruition. Under an agreement signed in August by President Ronald Reagan, the Wampanoags will receive more than 400 acres of undeveloped land in exchange for dropping all future claims to more than 3,000 acres on the resort island.

People and Politics. Ben Nighthorse Campbell, a Northern Cheyenne from Colorado, took his seat in January as the only American Indian member of the U.S. Congress. Campbell, a Democrat who had previously served two terms in the Colorado state legislature, was elected with financial and organizational support from several Indian organizations and tribal governments but made it clear on taking office that he intended to represent all of his constituents. Increased Indian participation in elective politics was also symbolized by Russell Means's brief run for the Libertarian Party's presidential nomination. Means, a Sioux from South Dakota who came in second in balloting at the party's national convention in September, has been a national leader of the American Indian Movement and other Indian political organizations.

Tribal politics continued to attract wide attention. In January, Verna Williamson became the first woman to serve as governor of the Pueblo of Isleta, 20 miles south of Albuquerque, N.M. She joined Wilma P. Mankiller, who became principal chief of the Cherokees in 1986, as a prominent symbol of political achievement for Indian women. Early in the year, Peter MacDonald, Sr., regained the chairmanship of the country's largest tribe, the Navajos. He vowed to rebuild the reservation and in October announced a joint venture with designer Oleg Cassini to build a resort there.

**Indian Health.** A new federal study covering 1980–1984 reported a sharp increase in American Indian births and surprisingly good health among Indian children, despite delayed prenatal care and a high incidence of premature births. The improvement was attributed to community campaigns focused on better nutrition and the dangers of alcohol and tobacco.

F.E.H.

**INDONESIA.** In 1987, Indonesia's ruling party won its expected majority in legislative elections, and the economy showed continuing weakness, largely because of low oil prices.

April 23 national elections and the preceding campaign period passed almost without incident, in contrast to the 1982 elections, which cost 60 lives. Golkar, the government-sponsored party, captured 299 of the 400 elective seats in the House of Representatives. The Development Unity Party, a coalition of Muslim parties, lost seats, and its share of the vote was down, confirming that President Suharto had succeeded in depoliticizing Islam.

A new development was the revival of attention to the late President Sukarno, both by the government and, during the election campaign, by the small Indonesian Democratic Party (PDI). After years of neglect, Sukarno, who had been deposed by Suharto in 1967, was officially declared a Proclaimer of Independence and accorded hero status. This perhaps set the stage for the PDI's use of Sukarno's image and words at campaign rallies. Ironically, Sukarno and the PDI proved to be especially popular among young people, who were born too recently to know what life under his rule was like. Sukarno's daughter Megawati and her husband campaigned for the PDI and managed to secure parliamentary seats. The PDI won 40 seats in all, up from 24 in 1982 elections.

Although President Suharto hailed the elections as a "festival of democracy," all the competing parties were financed by the government and endorsed Suharto's reelection to a fifth term. The actual presidential election,

scheduled for March 1988, was to be conducted by a consultative assembly, composed of 500 legislators (100 of them appointed by Suharto) and 500 others appointed by political parties and other groups.

The budget announced in January, for the fiscal year beginning April 1, was exceptionally severe—27 percent lower than the previous year's budget, in dollar terms. Spending for development projects, the military, and higher education was cut back sharply, civil service wages were frozen, and taxes were raised. Late in the year, the government announced that nearly all export regulations would be abolished under a new export stimulation program.

Planners appeared to be relying more heavily on borrowing to finance the country's needs; Indonesia's total debt was estimated at $40 billion. Concerns about economic stability encouraged a continuing outflow of capital to foreign banks.

*See* STATISTICS OF THE WORLD        W.F.

**INTERNATIONAL CONFERENCES.** A variety of international conferences were held in 1987. For some not covered in the article below, see AFRICA; ARAB LEAGUE; BANKING AND FINANCE; COMMONWEALTH OF NATIONS; COMMUNIST WORLD; EUROPEAN COMMUNITIES; NORTH ATLANTIC TREATY ORGANIZATION; ORGANIZATION OF AMERICAN STATES; ORGANIZATION OF PETROLEUM EXPORTING COUNTRIES; UNION OF SOVIET SOCIALIST REPUBLICS; UNITED NATIONS; UNITED STATES OF AMERICA.

**Meeting in Venice.** The 13th summit of the seven major industrial democracies took place in Venice during June. Leaders of the attending nations—Britain, Canada, France, Italy, Japan, the United States, and West Germany—reaffirmed the need for international economic policy coordination, warned against rising protectionist trade pressures, and on the subject of the Persian Gulf, endorsed the principle of freedom of navigation. The group also called for worldwide cooperation in the battle against AIDS, among other statements in the communiqué issued at the close of the conference.

**Forum for French.** In September the second annual summit meeting of French-speaking nations took place in Québec City, Canada. Participating were representatives from 41 French-speaking nations and territories where

*Canadian Prime Minister Brian Mulroney (left) and Québec Premier Robert Bourassa smile for the cameras, before the first session of a summit of French-speaking nations and territories, held in Québec City in September.*

French is a primary or secondary language, including Canada and Québec (the co-hosts), France, Belgium, Switzerland, and former French colonies around the world. The community of French-speaking nations, known in French as La Francophonie, hoped to develop into a powerful organization disseminating economic and technical aid and promoting French culture in the member countries. During the meetings human-rights activists demonstrated outside; Amnesty International had charged shortly before that two-thirds of the attending nations were guilty of human-rights violations, a topic that was excluded from the conference's official agenda. French Prime Minister Jacques Chirac pledged $30 million for funding of various French-language projects, including a TV news agency covering French-speaking nations and the first francophone world games, to be held in Morocco in 1989.

**Arusha Conference.** Representatives of government and nongovernmental organizations from nearly 50 nations met in Arusha, Tanzania, in December to mark the 75th anniversary of Africa's oldest liberation movement, the outlawed African National Congress, which is aimed at the elimination of apartheid in South Africa. The conference, hosted by Tanzanian leader Julius K. Nyerere, was aimed in part at consolidating the position of the ANC as the voice of opposition to apartheid, against claims of the rival Pan Africanist Council.

**Asean Summit.** Leaders of the six member nations of the Association of Southeast Asian Nations (Brunei, Indonesia, Malaysia, Philippines, Singapore, and Thailand) gathered in Manila in mid-December for the organization's first summit conference in a decade. They signed a declaration reaffirming principles of cooperation and the political goal of regional neutrality. The leaders also called for an end to the Vietnamese occupation of Cambodia and voiced support for Philippines President Corazon Aquino.                I.S.G.

**IOWA.** *See* STATISTICS OF THE WORLD.

A major export route for the Middle East's oil and a battleground in the Iran-Iraq war, the Persian Gulf drew navies from around the world. As Iranian patrol boats (above) took part in exercises code-named "Martyrdom," warships from the United States, Western Europe, and the Soviet Union cruised the waters to protect civilian shipping. The Gulf's narrow outlet at the Strait of Hormuz, with the presence of Iranian missiles nearby, was a particularly sensitive spot.

RAN. The Iran-Iraq war entered its eighth year in late 1987. Both sides stepped up the "tanker war"—targeting international shipping—in the ersian Gulf.

**War With Iraq.** The largest Iranian offensive f the war began on January 9; it resulted, ccording to some estimates, in 70,000 casalties. Western analysts initially thought the ffensive was an attempt to capture Basra, aq's second-largest city. But the most heavily ortified and defended positions were not atacked, leading analysts to conclude that the ity was not in danger of falling and that the losest the Iranians had come to the city was 0 miles. In February the Iraqis launched nassive counterattacks on Iranian positions utside of Basra and managed to recapture as nuch as one-third of the territory that had been ost.

The Iranians dramatically increased their bility to fight the tanker war in the spring by efitting a number of Swedish-made high-speed abin cruisers for use as patrol boats. They lso obtained Silkworm missiles from China; vith Silkworms installed in the southern Gulf, ran had the capacity to virtually close the Gulf f desired, by making it impossible for shipping o enter or leave through the narrow Strait of Hormuz. Many countries, including Britain, he Soviet Union, the United States, and France, dispatched warships to the Gulf to escort hipping. In addition, the United States in July equested that Western European nations aid t in minesweeping efforts in the Gulf. At the ime the request was denied. But in September, after more ships had been hit by mines, several Western European nations agreed to send ninesweepers.

**Peace Effort.** In July the UN Security Council adopted a resolution demanding that Iran and raq observe an immediate cease-fire. UN Secetary-General Javier Pérez de Cuéllar later raveled to Iran and Iraq seeking a settlement o the conflict. Some analysts suggested that ooth sides might finally be persuaded to hold peace talks. But on September 21, U.S. military nelicopters attacked and disabled an Iranian vessel, the *Iran Ajr*, reportedly found laying nines in the Gulf. The next day Iranian President Sayed Ali Khamenei, in an address to the UN General Assembly, rejected a cease-fire and denied that the vessel has been laying mines (though U.S. Navy personnel reporting finding nine mines on board the ship). Late in the year, UN talks were continuing.

**U.S.-Iran Relations.** The United States accepted Kuwait's proposal to place Kuwaiti ships under the American flag and to have the United States provide a naval escort to the reflagged ships. The program, which began in July, was viewed by Iran as an attempt by the United States to impose itself into the Gulf war more directly. U.S. seizure of the *Iran Ajr* exacerbated tensions; then on October 8, U.S. military helicopters, reportedly responding to hostile fire, attacked a few small Iranian naval craft, killing at least two Iranians. Several days later, Iranian missiles damaged two tankers in Kuwaiti waters, one U.S.-owned and one carrying the U.S. flag. In retaliation, U.S. warships destroyed two Iranian offshore oil platforms regarded as a base for gunboats. The Reagan administration also banned all Iranian imports and further restricted U.S. exports to Iran.

**Other Foreign Relations.** Ties with Syria were seriously damaged in February when Syrian troops in Beirut killed 23 members of the Iranian-backed Shiite Muslim group Hezbollah. In June the Hezbollah retaliated by kidnapping American journalist Charles Glass in Syrian-controlled West Beirut. (Glass later escaped.) In the spring, Tunisia and Egypt both broke diplomatic relations with Iran. Relations with Saudi Arabia reached a low in midsummer after Iranian riots in the holy city of Mecca led to clashes with Saudi security forces and over 400 deaths. Iran responded by urging the overthrow of the Saudi royal family, and mobs stormed the embassies of Kuwait, Saudi Arabia, and France in Tehran. In September, after Iranian missiles were fired at Kuwait, five Iranian diplomats were expelled from that country.

Relations with the Soviet Union were damaged by continuing Soviet aid to Iraq and by such events as Iran's attack on a Soviet vessel in the Persian Gulf in May. Britain expelled most Iranian embassy officials in June, following the arrest and beating of a British diplomat in Tehran, and closed down an Iranian arms purchasing office in London after an Iranian attack on a British tanker.

At the end of June, French police surrounded the Iranian embassy in Paris, where an Iranian suspected of involvement in 1986 terrorist bombings in Paris had taken refuge. Iran retaliated by detaining and interrogating France's consul in Iran and surrounding the French embassy in Tehran with police. On July 17, the two countries suddenly broke diplomatic relations. However, negotiations toward normalizing relations followed; and in November, after the release of two French hostages in Beirut, France let the bombing suspect go free without questioning.

**Oil.** Iran continued to suffer economically from Iraq's attacks on its oil installations and on tankers carrying Iranian oil. Responding to bans by the United States and France on the purchase of its oil, Iran offered large discounts to other customers.

See STATISTICS OF THE WORLD.                J.S.I.

**IRAQ.** The nature of the war between Iraq and Iran changed somewhat during 1987, with increased emphasis placed on attacks on Persian Gulf shipping. Iraqi bombings and Iranian ground offensives continued. An apparently mistaken Iraqi attack on the U.S. warship *Stark* did not damage relations.

**War With Iran.** In January, Iran managed to push closer to Basra, Iraq's second-largest city. To defend it, the Iraqis had flooded huge areas of the countryside and built bunkers and trench systems similar to those used in World War I. During their massive offensive the Iranians found the battleground difficult to take because their tanks were unable to maneuver through the defenses. Iraq launched a counterattack in February and managed to recapture around one-third of the territory near Basra that had been seized by Iran.

Iraq, with almost total air supremacy, repeatedly attacked Iran's cities and oil installations, hoping to force Iran into suing for peace. Particularly frequent were attacks against Khark Island, Iran's largest oil-shipping center. Iraq also bombed large urban centers for the purpose of terrorizing the population. In retaliation, Iran routinely launched missiles at Baghdad. Its ground offensives were also a form of retaliation. In fact, Iranian news reports claimed that Iran's January offensive was called off because Iraq had stopped bombing Iranian

cities. (Iraq resumed bombing Iranian target later on.)

**UN Initiative.** In September, United Nation Secretary-General Javier Pérez de Cuéllar travel to Iran and Iraq, seeking an agreement b both sides to a UN Security Council resolution demanding a cease-fire. Iraq had already in dicated a willingness to accept the proposal but on the condition that Iran also give it ful support. Soon after the secretary-general's visit however, an Iranian vessel was attacked b the United States, and Iranian opposition to cease-fire stiffened.

**U.S. Relations.** Early in the year, Iraq twice asked the United States for a C-130 transpor aircraft and artillery radar, but the request were turned down. Iraq's anger increased when press reports in January revealed that America intelligence agencies had in recent years de liberately given false intelligence information to both Iran and Iraq in order to prevent either from winning the war. After some investigation the Iraqis claimed that they lost the port of Fac (al Faw) in early 1986 because of false intel ligence provided by the United States.

On May 17 an Iraqi warplane attacked the frigate U.S.S. *Stark* in the Persian Gulf, severely damaging the ship and killing 37 of its crew members. However, Iraqi statements and in dependent evidence indicated the attack had been by mistake. President Saddam Hussein expressed deepest regrets and promised to pay whatever compensation the United States deemed necessary.

Only a few days after the attack, President Ronald Reagan publicly stated that Iran "was the real villain in the piece" because of its refusal to negotiate an end to the Gulf war The *Stark* incident and the revelations in March of Iran's installation of Chinese-made Silkworm missiles at the southern end of the Gulf helped trigger increased U.S. naval involvement in the Gulf directed at keeping it open to international shipping. In July the United States began to reflag and escort Kuwaiti shipping through the Gulf. A supporter of Iraq in the war, Kuwait carried some Iraqi goods through its ports.

**Arab Relations.** Iraq's President Hussein and President Hafez al-Assad of Syria met secretly in April to discuss the war and other issues of interest to both countries. At a summit meeting f Arab leaders in November, the two were eportedly reconciled through mediation by ordan's King Hussein and others.

**Oil.** Although Iraq's economy remained weak ecause of the war, it raised its oil output in 987 and was producing 2.7 million barrels a ay by October, having declined to agree to a uota. Iraq benefited from a massive increase n its ability to ship oil through pipelines to urkey and Saudi Arabia.

See STATISTICS OF THE WORLD.          T.I.

**IRELAND, NORTHERN.** *See* GREAT BRITAIN.

**IRELAND, REPUBLIC OF.** Charles Haughey vas returned to power in place of Garret itzGerald in Irish general elections on February 17, 1987. But Haughey's party, Fianna áil, did not win a majority on its own in the Dáil (Parliament), as he had sought. The former, ncreasingly unpopular government had collapsed on January 20, after the Labor Party, he junior partner in the coalition, refused to go along with spending cuts that FitzGerald's ine Gael party deemed necessary. Fitz-Gerald's government had succeeded in reducing inflation and in balancing current revenues and expenditures but had been unable to control the overall budget deficit because of soaring costs for debt servicing. Unemployment was high, and emigration on a large scale had eturned.

In the election campaign, Haughey's strategy vas to let the government stew in its own unpopularity. Promising not to raise taxes, he aid he would reduce the deficit but did not commit himself to any particular action.

The electors punished Fine Gael. The party lost 17 seats in the Dáil, reducing it to 51, its lowest level in 30 years, and its share of the vote dropped by almost a third. Progressive Democrats were returned in 14 seats, to become the third largest party in the Dáil. The pro-IRA Sinn Fein put up candidates for the Dáil for the first time since the war and received barely 2 percent of the vote. Fianna Fáil gained 10 seats, bringing its share to 81, still 3 short of an absolute majority. Nevertheless, Haughey was the victor, and when the Dáil met a month later he was elected prime minister.

The new government's tougher-than-expected retrenchment in the health services brought strong protests and a strike of hospital

*Charles Haughey, a former prime minister of Ireland, again assumed the post after parliamentary elections in February gave the edge to his Fianna Fáil (Warriors of Destiny) party. He inherited an economy suffering from foreign debt and unemployment.*

doctors. All opposition members of the Dáil joined in condemnation, but when Haughey challenged them to a vote in May, Fine Gael abstained. No one wanted another election soon. The 2.5 percent growth rate was elusive; the department of finance was forecasting 1.75 percent for the year. Haughey's first budget was, if anything, more stringent than that proposed by Fine Gael, which, under new leadership, pledged its support, at least in principle.

FitzGerald resigned the leadership of Fine Gael immediately after the election. Alan Dukes, a former finance minister, succeeded him.

Ireland caused a tremor in the European Community when a laboriously negotiated instrument opening the way to closer political cooperation between Ireland and the other member nations was declared unconstitutional by the Dublin supreme court. A hasty referendum was held on May 27 to nullify that decision. All parties urged the voters to oblige. Less than half turned out, but of those 70 percent gave approval.

Late in the year, after France seized weapons—including parts for ground-to-air missiles—said to be destined for use by the Irish Republican Army, and after an IRA bomb killed 11 civilians in Enniskillen, Northern Ireland, Haughey ordered police raids of suspected IRA hideouts and approved a convention making it easier to extradite suspected terrorists to Britain.

See STATISTICS OF THE WORLD.        T.J.O.H.

**ISRAEL.** During 1987, Foreign Minister Shimon Peres sought unsuccessfully to bring down Israel's national unity government over the issue of an international peace conference. U.S.-Israeli relations were somewhat shaky. The Israeli-occupied Gaza Strip and West Bank remained tense, and late in the year, the country was rocked by unprecedented rioting there, leading to clashes that left over 20 Palestinians dead.

**Peace Conference and the Soviets.** Moscow actively sought Israel's agreement for Soviet participation in an international peace conference on the Middle East—a controversial idea that was welcomed by Foreign Minister Peres but sharply opposed by Prime Minister Yitzhak Shamir. As internal debate on this issue raged, Moscow stepped up its signals to Israel demonstrating a desire for improved ties. For example, Soviet Jewish emigration rose from 914 for 1986 to over 8,000 for 1987. On a visit to Rome in the spring, Peres met with two high-ranking Soviet officials, engaging in what he later described as "the first serious direct dialogue between the two nations." The meeting created a major stir in Israel. A Likud spokesman accused Peres of creating the impression that moves toward an international conference were a condition for Jewish emigration from the Soviet Union.

When the deadlocked cabinet failed to endorse the peace conference, Peres threatened to bring down the government, but he lacked the necessary votes. In late September, in a speech before the UN General Assembly, Peres nevertheless outlined an eight-point plan for an international conference. Meanwhile, a

*Members of Peace Now demonstrate in front of the home of Prime Minister Yitzhak Shamir to show their support for an international peace conference on the Middle East.*

*The Lavi jet fighter was a source of national pride to many Israelis; to many others—including the U.S. government, which gives Israel massive military aid—it was an extravagance. After intense debate, Israel's cabinet stopped development of the plane.*

Soviet consular delegation had visited Israel in July, and Hungary, one of Moscow's East European allies, established low-level diplomatic relations on an interests-section basis. In October, Israel rejected a Soviet offer to establish relations on an interests-section basis, maintaining that only full diplomatic ties would be sufficient.

**U.S.-Israeli Relations.** Israel's involvement in the Iran/contra affair became a matter of some controversy. A report issued by the Tower Commission, named by President Ronald Reagan to investigate the affair, indicated Israel had actively encouraged the sale of arms to Iran. During U.S. congressional hearings on the scandal there were periods of tension as the former director general of the Israeli Foreign Ministry, David Kimche, who was alleged to have negotiated arms sales to Iran, was subpoenaed. (He did not testify.) In addition, Lieutenant Colonel Oliver North, the U.S. marine who was a key figure in the affair, claimed that Manucher Ghorbanifar, a middleman in the arms deal, was an Israeli agent—something Ghorbanifar and Israel both denied. Nonetheless, Israel's willingness to provide a detailed chronology of its involvement in the selling of arms to Iran seemed to satisfy the U.S. Congress.

The case of Jonathan Jay Pollard was a more serious blow to relations. Pollard, a former U.S. Navy intelligence analyst, had pleaded guilty to spying for Israel; he was sentenced to a life term in March. His activities were characterized by the Israeli leadership as a "rogue operation," but Israeli insensitivity to U.S. feelings—shown by the promotion to a top command post of Aviem Sella, the Israeli Air Force officer charged by the United States with conspiring with Pollard—caused a near crisis in relations, resolved only when Sella resigned.

**Other Relations.** In April, Israeli President Chaim Herzog made the first visit by an Israeli president to Germany since the founding of Israel in 1948. Meanwhile, Egyptian Foreign Minister Esmet Abdel Meguid made the first visit to Israel by an Egyptian in that capacity since the 1982 Israeli invasion of Lebanon. However, Egypt's official invitation to Austrian President Kurt Waldheim, accused by Israel of complicity in war crimes against Jews during World War II, was a serious irritant.

The long border between Israel and Jordan remained generally peaceful, and there was an increase in de facto cooperation on the Israeli-occupied West Bank, as both Israel and Jordan sought to curb Palestine Liberation Organization influence there. Much of this goodwill was, however, dissipated when Jordan invited Waldheim for an official visit. Relations were further complicated by rioting in the occupied territories late in the year.

**Gaza Riots.** Tension in the occupied Gaza Strip exploded in December as Palestinians clashed with Israeli troops in what a UN relief official there described as "either total lawlessness or a popular uprising." The unrest spread to the West Bank and Jerusalem, and Arabs throughout Israel and the occupied territories staged a general strike to protest Israel's military crackdown in the Gaza. More than 20 Palestinians were reported dead and 170 wounded, and in a massive operation, nearly 1,000 suspected agitators were arrested, to be tried by military courts. The Israeli response to the unrest provoked strong negative reactions abroad. The United States joined in criticizing Israel's security measures as overly harsh and refused to veto a UN Security Council resolution condemning them; it passed, 14-0, with the United States abstaining. Arab lawyers began a boycott of the trials, complaining they were not allowed to interview defendants.

**Other National Security Affairs.** In an agonizing step, Israel decided to cancel production of the Lavi jet fighter, which had become a symbol of Israeli accomplishment. Israel's resources were not up to producing the plane, and the United States, which had funded a large part of the Lavi, opposed the project. After a number of delays, Israel's cabinet voted, 12-11, for termination.

On November 25 an Arab guerrilla landed in a motorized hang glider near an army base in northern Israel, killed six soldiers, and wounded seven others before being shot dead. A Syrian-based Palestinian group took responsibility for the attack. The Israeli Army was sharply criticized for inadequate security provisions.

During the whole year, Israel carried out 23 air, sea, or land attacks against suspected guerrilla bases in Lebanon. Most notable was a September 4 air strike against a Palestinian district outside Sidon, which killed 41 Palestinians.

**Economy.** Israel's economy did well. Unemployment dropped by midyear to 5.6 percent, tourism was up, inflation was held in check,

and the stock of foreign currency rose. However, there was a rash of strikes in various industries, and schools were closed as teachers and students denounced budget cuts for the Ministry of Education.

**Domestic Politics.** Labor and Likud, the two main coalition partners in the national unity government, clashed over policy on the West Bank. While Likud leaders were urging an increase in Jewish settlements on the West Bank, Defense Minister Yitzhak Rabin of the Labor Party used Army troops to turn back bulldozer sent by Likud's Ariel Sharon to start a new settlement. The Likud bloc, beset by severe infighting, regained at least a veneer of unity, and an orderly convention was held. But the Labor Party fell into some disarray. Peres was sharply criticized for, among other things, mishandling the campaign for an international conference. The December violence in the West Bank and Gaza provoked division in the party between hard-liners on this issue led by Rabin and supported by Peres, and a more doveish faction, led by Laborites Ezer Weizman and Abba Eban.

**Demjanjuk Trial.** The trial of John Demjanjuk, a retired American auto worker accused of being the notorious "Ivan the Terrible" who murdered Jews in the Treblinka death camp, opened in Jerusalem. Like the 1961 trial of Adolf Eichmann in Jerusalem, it rekindled memories of the Holocaust for many Israelis.

See STATISTICS OF THE WORLD.            R.O.F.

**ITALY.** Parliamentary elections held in June 1987 brought in a new government under the youngest prime minister in Italian history but did not significantly change the balance of political power.

**Coalition Crisis.** Early in the year there was increasing conflict between the two major parties—Socialists and Christian Democrats—in the five-party coalition government headed for more than three years by Socialist Prime Minister Bettino Craxi. Then Craxi resigned in early March, in accordance with a 1986 agreement, to make way for a Christian Democrat who would head the coalition until scheduled 1988 elections. He stressed that friction between the parties made it impossible to continue, while denying he had firmly committed himself to leave office by this time. After several ttempts to form a viable new government 'ithout elections failed, President Francesco .ossiga dissolved Parliament and, with Chris- an Democrat Amintore Fanfani as head of a aretaker government, called early elections, ɔ be held on June 14–15.

**lections.** Bitterness between Socialists and 'hristian Democrats continued throughout the ampaign. An unusual feature was the Roman 'atholic Bishops' outspoken advice to Cath- lics to vote for the Christian Democrats— heir most blatant support for a party in more han a decade. The small Radical Party enli- ened the generally drab campaign by making pornographic star named Cicciolina one of heir candidates.

The election resulted in a small Socialist ncrease in the Chamber of Deputies, although here was little difference in the makeup of the enate. The Christian Democrats, with 34.3 ercent of the total vote, remained the largest arty, though they increased their vote only narginally. The Communists took 28.3 percent ɔf the total—down 2.5 percentage points. They ɔst votes to the Greens (the new Italian envi- ɔnmental party), the Socialists, and the Rad- cals (who improved their position slightly). he neo-Fascist Italian Social Movement de- lined to below 6 percent.

**Return of the Christian Democrats.** After Par- iament reassembled on July 2, Cossiga went ɔutside the timeworn circle of senior Christian Jemocratic politicians and tapped 43-year- ɔld Giovanni Goria—treasury minister since 982—to form the new government. Goria had teered clear of the tangled webs of Christian Jemocratic factionalism. He formed a five- ɔarty coalition and submitted his cabinet to 'resident Cossiga on July 28. With their im- ɔroved electoral position, the Socialists de- nanded better cabinet posts than they had in he past. They received 8 ministries, while the Christian Democrats got 15. At the last minute, he small Social Democratic Party threatened ɔ sabotage the five-party alliance unless it was ;iven another ministry; it received three min- stries in all, while the Republicans got two nd the Liberals one.

**Crime and Terrorism.** On August 25, in the ɔrison of Porto Azzurro on the island of Elba, ix convicted murderers seized guards and other hostages and demanded a helicopter to take them to the mainland. The new govern- ment decided upon patient negotiations with no concessions, and on September 1 the rebels surrendered.

In February, Parliament passed a law allow- ing large reductions in prison sentences for terrorists who renounced violence and severed links with guerrillas. On March 20, two Red Brigade members shot dead Air Force General Licio Giorgieri as he sat in his car in a Rome traffic jam; responsibility was claimed by the Union of Fighting Communists, the military wing of the new Red Brigades.

The largest Mafia trial ever conducted ended in Palermo, Sicily, on December 16, with 338 of the 452 defendants being convicted of crimes including murder and distributing her- oin to the United States. Nineteen men, in- cluding Michele Greco, leader of the Sicilian mob, received the maximum sentence, life imprisonment. The so-called maxi-trial was widely viewed as a demonstration of the state's determination to strike back at the Mafia.

*Giovanni Goria began the year as Italy's treasury minister; he is shown here in February at a news briefing in Paris during an international meeting of finance ministers. In July, after a drawn-out political crisis, he emerged as the prime minister of Italy's 47th postwar government.*

*Security forces were on alert in Venice, as the leaders of the major industrial democracies gathered in early June for their annual economic summit.*

**Domestic Politics.** In January the Constitutional Court approved a series of referendum measures to be presented to voters. In referenda on nuclear energy and judicial reform, held in November, voters agreed, among other things, to modify the siting procedures for nuclear reactors and to allow magistrates to be sued for wrongful arrests or imprisonment.

A falling-out with the Liberals over a deficit reduction plan led Goria to submit his resignation in mid-November, but he managed to restore the coalition after five days and win a vote of confidence, after promising to restore tax cuts that were delayed under the plan, so long as inflation did not rise unexpectedly. The deficit reduction program remained unpopular with labor unions, which staged a general strike on November 25, the first in six years.

**Economic Trends.** Early in the year, both Prime Minister Craxi and Treasury Minister Goria claimed that statistics showed Italy had surpassed Britain as the Western world's fifth economic power. By mid-1987 inflation had fallen to 4.2 percent (though it later rose slightly), and industrial growth remained steady at around 3 percent. However, the huge budget deficit and the backwardness of the South were continuing problems.

The Italian stock market was shaken by the collapse of stock prices around the world in October; the decline of the U.S. dollar against the West German mark also caused problems for the Italian economy.

**Foreign Affairs.** The Venice summit, a meeting of the seven main industrialized nations, was held on the island of San Giorgio Maggiore from June 8 to 10, presided over by interim Prime Minister Fanfani. Security for the conference was tight, especially after bombing attacks on the U.S. and British embassies in ome on June 9. In addition to accords for conomic cooperation, the summit approved trengthened measures against terrorism.

Following the Western European Union call or a coordinated stance in the Iran-Iraq war, ie Italian cabinet decided on August 27 to end minesweepers to the Persian Gulf if United lations Security Council Resolution 598— alling for a cease-fire—failed to halt the war. )n September 3 an Italian container ship was ttacked in the northern Gulf by Iran. Italy rotested to Tehran, and on September 15 the ;oria government sent an eight-vessel force— icluding three minesweepers—to the Gulf. ater in September, Goria embarked on a tour f European capitals urging a more coordinated fort in the Gulf. In mid-October, Iraqi Kurdish bels announced they had kidnapped three alian engineers.

**Banco Ambrosiano.** On February 25 a Milan court issued warrants for the arrest of Archbishop Paul Marcinkus, chairman of the Vatican Bank, and two other Vatican bankers in connection with possible links of the Vatican Bank to the Banco Ambrosiano. An appeals court ruled in April that they could not enjoy immunity, and in June the findings of the arrest warrants (hitherto kept secret) were published. However, in July the Italian Supreme Court— in a surprising move—canceled the arrest warrants, the legality of which the Vatican had contested. Investigators said they would pursue the case through other means. Licio Gelli, a financier wanted in connection with the collapse of the bank, surrendered to authorities in Geneva in September.

See STATISTICS OF THE WORLD.          M.G.

**IVORY COAST.** See STATISTICS OF THE WORLD.

# J

AMAICA. See STATISTICS OF THE WORLD. See lso CARIBBEAN BASIN.

APAN. In November 1987, after two terms in ffice and a one-year extension, Japanese Prime Minister Yasuhiro Nakasone was obliged to tep aside for another figure; he was succeeded y Noboru Takeshita. The forceful Nakasone ad reached a peak of popularity in 1986. After his success in July parliamentary elections hat year, he felt free to pursue two long-held oals: to increase military expenditures and to evamp the nation's tax system. In the latter ttempt, however, he failed.

**Defense Spending.** The limit of 1 percent of ross national product set on defense spending n 1976 was breached for the first time with arliamentary approval of a fiscal 1987 defense udget (for the 12-month period beginning in April 1987) amounting to 1.004 percent of 5NP. Later, at Nakasone's urging, the cabinet oted to remove the limit entirely, as a matter f policy. The budget for fiscal 1988, passed n December, increased defense spending by .2 percent (and again exceeded the 1 percent imit).

**Elections and Tax Reform.** Nakasone's second major objective had been to revamp the tax system—unchanged since 1950—cutting personal and corporate income taxes while leaving overall government revenues about the same. The cornerstone of the proposal was a new 5 percent national sales tax, included in the tax reform bill submitted to the Diet (Parliament) in January. Because the prime minister had previously promised not to introduce new taxes, opposition to the sales tax was loud and vehement. Also unpopular was the proposal to introduce a 20 percent withholding tax on interest on individual savings accounts. Under existing law, such accounts were tax-free up to about $20,000, and individuals could open multiple accounts. U.S. pressure for a reduction in Japanese savings—in the hope that it would lead to an increase in consumer spending and imports and reduce Japan's trade surplus—was a factor in Nakasone's tax plan.

After the prime minister delivered his policy address to the Diet on January 26, the four major opposition parties led a walkout. Although they returned a few days later, political

The strength of the yen made Japanese goods pricier compared with products from Taiwan, Hong Kong, and South Korea. This Tokyo discount store attracted shoppers with Korean videocassette players, which sold for about 20 percent less than the cheapest Japanese models.

maneuvering continued at high pitch, and passage of the fiscal 1987 budget was stalled over the tax plan, which was widely criticized. When U.S. Secretary of State George Shultz met with Nakasone in Tokyo on March 6, 50,000 people marched in that city's streets in protest against the plan.

In subsequent local elections, Nakasone's Liberal Democratic Party maintained its local government majorities, but by lower margins than before. The results were a blow to Nakasone personally and to the tax reform bill, which was in effect killed in Parliament. The 1987 budget then passed with no debate.

**Nakasone's Successor.** With Nakasone's term as party president set to end October 31, others in his party maneuvered to succeed him. Three major candidates emerged: Noboru Takeshita, Finance Minister Kiichi Miyazawa, and former Foreign Minister Shintaro Abe, each backed by a separate faction. When the three could not agree on who should succeed, they asked Nakasone to decide. He chose Takeshita, a 63-year-old former finance minister, who was officially chosen by LDP members in the Diet and took office as prime minister in early November. Abe became party secretary-general; Miyazawa was named deputy prime minister and finance minister.

**Economic Picture.** The economy was characterized by a strong yen and a large trade surplus, reaching about $90 billion for the year. A supplementary 1987 budget, passed in July as part of a promised package to stimulate the economy and encourage imports, brought the budget deficit to 4.1 percent of GNP. The October crash in world stock markets was relatively mild in Japan, and at year's end the value of shares on the Tokyo exchange was 14.6 percent above levels at the start of the year. Growth for the year as a whole was expected to be slightly under 4 percent. The fiscal 1988 budget provided a 4.8 percent spending increase, cited by the Japanese as evidence they were responding to overseas demands for stimulating the economy.

**Foreign Relations.** Japan's relations with the United States were dominated by trade issues. Through much of 1987 the U.S. Congress worked on a trade bill with tough penalties for nations whose bilateral trade surplus with the United States was high—a measure aimed largely at Japan. (Final action was still pending at year's end.) In April congressional leaders expressed their displeasure over Japanese trade policies by denying Nakasone's request to address a joint session of Congress during his trip to the United States. In the same month, in response to U.S. manufacturers' complaints that Japanese companies were dumping semiconductor microchips at below-production costs, President Ronald Reagan imposed retal atory tariffs of 100 percent on $300 million of lectronic imports from Japan; these affected ertain computers, color television sets, and mall power tools. Reagan subsequently lifted anctions on some items because of indications hat the dumping had stopped. But because of ontinuing restrictions on U.S. access to the apanese market, some goods were still being ubjected to the tariff.

Relations with the United States were also lamaged by press reports of the 1983 sale of ophisticated milling machines by the Toshiba Machine Company to the Soviet Union, where hey were used to produce quieter and less letectable submarines. The head of the Toshiba Corporation resigned to take responsibility for he sale. In June, U.S. Secretary of Defense Caspar Weinberger went to Tokyo for talks concerning the Toshiba case and other defense ssues, including Japan's plans to obtain a new generation of fighter aircraft. Defense Minister

Yukio Kurihara later announced that Japan would buy at least 100 of the aircraft from the United States.

Japan's relations with the Soviet Union worsened. In May, Japan arrested four Japanese on charges of selling secrets concerning U.S. F-16 fighter planes to Soviet diplomats. Four Soviet diplomats were accused and returned home. In August the Soviets accused two Japanese of spying and expelled them.

**Terrorist Arrest.** Osamo Maruoka, 37, said to be second in command of the Japanese Red Army, a terrorist group, was arrested in Tokyo in November after a long manhunt. The organization staged an attack on Lod Airport near Tel Aviv, Israel, in 1972 that killed 26 people; press accounts following Maruoka's arrest said he may have been planning an assault on the 1988 Olympics in South Korea.

**Ailing Emperor.** In September, Emperor Hirohito, 86, underwent surgery for an enlarged

Noboru Takeshita, newly chosen president of Japan's ruling Liberal Democratic Party, leads delegates to a party convention in a cheer. His predecessor, Yasuhiro Nakasone, whom Takeshita succeeded s prime minister, is at right.

pancreas, said to be the first surgery ever performed on a Japanese emperor. Prior to the operation, his son and heir, Prince Akihito, assumed his father's duties for an indefinite period.

*See* STATISTICS OF THE WORLD.　　　M.S.B.

**JORDAN.** King Hussein's continued efforts to find a solution to the Arab-Israeli conflict advanced uncertainly in 1987. The Jordanian king met with Palestine Liberation Organization chairman Yasir Arafat at January's Islamic summit—their first meeting since their joint peace initiative talks collapsed 11 months earlier. Their reconciliation was almost immediately eclipsed when the summit took the position that UN Resolution 242 (which recognized Palestinian rights, but not statehood) was insufficient basis for peace—a position seen as a repudiation of Hussein's approach to negotiations.

In February, European Community foreign ministers voted their support for an international conference, as favored by Hussein, and in April, Jordanian Prime Minister Zaid al-Rifai, visiting Washington, D.C., said that the United States accepted the idea in principle, though there was still disagreement over details. Also in April, there were reports (denied by Israel) that Hussein had met secretly with Israeli Foreign Minister Shimon Peres to work out an agreement for the conference. Meanwhile, Hussein, continuing his efforts to improve relations with neighboring Syria, sought Syrian President Hafez al-Assad's support for the proposed peace conference. To the same end, Hussein helped initiate a reconciliation between Assad and President Saddam Hussein of Iraq.

One concrete result of Hussein's tentative reconciliation with Arafat was the revival of a Jordanian-PLO joint committee to oversee economic aid to Palestinians living in Israeli-occupied territories.

In October the king met with U.S. Secretary of State George Shultz in London. The two reportedly discussed the holding of direct talks between Jordan and Israel under U.S.-Soviet auspices. Palestinians acceptable to Israel would be part of the Jordanian delegation. It was expected that Hussein would discuss the plan at a November summit of Arab leaders in Amman. However, just before the start of the summit, Hussein rejected the proposal, saying he preferred instead a full international conference. The summit participants endorsed Hussein's conference plan, though their attention focused primarily on the Iran-Iraq war.

Revelations that Hawk missiles, which had been denied to Jordan, were secretly sold to Iran damaged U.S.-Jordanian relations. By the end of the summer, though, relations seemed to be improving. The kingdom was pleased by American policy in the Persian Gulf, which was perceived as favoring Iraq.

King Hussein visited the Soviet Union in December, reportedly to pursue an arms embargo against Iran and to discuss the proposed international peace conference.

Campaigning for possible parliamentary elections, the first in 20 years, began during the summer. However, in October the king postponed the elections until 1989.

*See* STATISTICS OF THE WORLD.　　　C.H.A

# K

**KAMPUCHEA.** *See* CAMBODIA.

**KANSAS.** *See* STATISTICS OF THE WORLD.

**KENTUCKY.** *See* STATISTICS OF THE WORLD.

**KENYA.** In 1987, reports of serious human rights violations in Kenya continued to mount. President Daniel arap Moi was forced to defend the country's reputation during a trip to Britain and the United States in March. The Washington *Post* ran a front-page article alleging that dissidents in Kenya were being subjected to illegal detention, torture, and forced confessions. In July, Amnesty International released a 58-page report entitled *Torture, Political Detention, and Unfair Trials,* and the next month a prominent High Court judge resigned over violation of the principle of habeas corpus. In November the government closed down the University of Nairobi after student demonstrations there. Late in the year, the government expelled 15 U.S. missionaries, claiming they were involved in a subversive plot.

The furor over human rights was part of a larger shakeup in the Kenyan political system. Late in 1986 a constitutional amendment had been passed installing the ruling Kenya African National Union (Kanu) as the country's supreme political institution and providing that any Kanu nominee with 70 percent of the party's support be declared elected to office unopposed.

According to the budget presented in June, the gross domestic product rose 5.7 percent in 1986—the highest growth rate in more than a decade—facilitated by a good grain harvest and a decline in world oil prices.

In foreign affairs, relations with Uganda, already uneasy, worsened late in the year, after Kenya charged that 60 Ugandan soldiers had crossed the border and engaged in a gun battle with Kenyan police. Two Ugandan soldiers were reportedly killed in the incident. Kenya subsequently expelled two Ugandan diplomats for making derogatory statements.

In December, Kenya expelled the Libyan chargé d'affaires in Nairobi and closed down the embassy there, charging Libya with spying.

Five other Libyan diplomats were expelled earlier in the year.

In August, Kenya hosted the Fourth All-Africa Games. Kenyan athletes won 63 medals, ranking the country third, behind Egypt and Tunisia. In November a Kenyan runner, Ibrahim Hussein, won the New York City Marathon.

*See* STATISTICS OF THE WORLD.           P.S.

**KHMER REPUBLIC.** *See* CAMBODIA.

**KIRIBATI.**    *See* STATISTICS OF THE WORLD.

**KOREA, DEMOCRATIC PEOPLE'S REPUBLIC OF (NORTH KOREA).** During 1987, North Korea and South Korea made no substantial progress in cooperation. Both countries issued proposals and counterproposals about resuming stalled economic and political talks, and North Korea again called for mutual troop reductions—a suggestion which the South dismissed as propaganda. Continuing North Korean demands to cohost the 1988 Olympics were repeatedly rejected by the International Olympic Committee and by South Korea, the designated host. However, the committee, with the South's consent, proposed one addition to the four events previously offered to be held in the North.

In April the Supreme People's Assembly, in special session, approved a new seven-year plan. During the same month, ground was broken for redevelopment of a gold mine at Unsan, as a joint venture of the North Korean government and a Japanese company formed by North Koreans living in Japan. The gold was expected to help pay North Korea's overdue debt to Japan, part of a larger national debt. North Korea, which formally defaulted on its loan payments, promised in September to start repaying Western creditors, and a rescheduling plan was being worked out.

Kim Il Sung visited China early in the year; the visit was probably intended to offset North Korea's recent tilt toward the Soviet Union and to solicit Chinese aid for the new seven-year plan. In June, North Korea hosted an extraordinary ministerial conference of nonaligned nations. More than 100 delegates from nations and international organizations attended.

The United States announced that its diplomats would be allowed to have substantive discussions with North Korean representatives if initiated by them in neutral settings. It also said it would consider limited trade if the North-South Korean dialogue resumed and the Olympics question was resolved.

See STATISTICS OF THE WORLD.          D.S.M.

**KOREA, REPUBLIC OF (SOUTH KOREA).** A year of unrest and steps toward political reform culminated on December 16, 1987, with the election of the government-favored candidate, Roh Tae Woo, as president of South Korea. He triumphed over a divided opposition (which contested the results), in the country's first genuine presidential elections in 16 years.

**Political Protest and Elections.** A deadlock over constitutional reform continued as the year opened, with opposition forces demanding direct popular election of the president and greater participation in government. There were

*Roh Tae Woo, candidate of South Korea's ruling party, makes a campaign appearance on his way to a victory against a divided opposition in the December presidential election.*

also massive student protests, set off by th death of a student in police custody after h had been tortured. An April directive fror President Chun Doo Hwan, suspending debat on constitutional change until after the 198 presidential election and Olympic Games i Seoul, brought a new surge of demonstration

As the government party moved on June 1 to name Roh Tae Woo, Chun's military-acac emy classmate and associate, as its presidentia candidate, opposition forces staged a natior wide demonstration. Massive numbers turne out or otherwise signaled their support, despi the deployment of 60,000 riot police and th detention of opposition leaders. Demonstra tions and violent protests went on for week University students pelted police with fire bombs and paving stones. Middle-class pro testers—housewives, the elderly, and bus nessmen—took to the streets for the first time Supporting the students, they called for free dom of speech and of the press and proteste the use of the tear gas that hung over downtow Seoul. The government closed the universitie hoping to disperse the students, but turmo spread to some 80 campuses and two doze cities. By late June, police had detained abou 7,000 people (many were quickly released).

On June 29, Roh—the government party chairman as well as its candidate—announce a dramatic reversal of policy. He endorse constitutional change, direct presidential elec tions, and other steps to liberalize politics Chun concurred with Roh in a July 1 statemen By the end of August, government and oppo sition representatives had agreed on the ou lines of a new constitution. Most of those sti detained as a result of the protests were re leased, and opposition leader Kim Dae Jung who had been under a suspended 20-yea sentence for treason, had his full civil right restored. The cabinet was revamped in Ma and again in July.

The National Assembly overwhelmingly ap proved the new constitution, which was ratifie in a popular referendum on October 27. Th document provided for direct popular electio of the president to a single five-year term restoration of the National Assembly's power to inspect and audit the administration, inde pendence of the judiciary, and reinforced civ

...otest marches and riots racked South Korea in ...ne. In one incident (above), demonstrating students ...Seoul overwhelmed police and removed their riot ...ar. When students took shelter in Seoul's cathedral, ...ns mobilized in their support (right).

...ghts (including labor's right to organize and ...ct collectively). The presidential vote was set ...r December. It had been expected that Roh ...ould run against either Kim Dae Jung or Kim ...oung Sam, another prominent opposition ...ader, but after negotiations between the "two ...ms" failed to produce agreement, each de...ared his candidacy. (Other candidates also ...articipated.)

...Following a campaign marked by further ...olence, South Koreans went to the polls on ...ecember 16. Roh emerged the winner with ...7 percent of the vote, about 2 million votes ...nead of Kim Young Sam, according to official ...sults. Kim Dae Jung trailed in third place. ...he opposition charged massive electoral fraud, ...nd students again protested. This time, how...ver, their ranks seemed smaller, and the ...iddle class did not join them in large numbers. ...here were also recriminations within the op...osition over the two Kims' lack of unity; the ...fficial tally showed their combined support ...55 percent of the vote. Roh reaffirmed a ...ampaign promise to hold a plebiscite on his ...onduct in office after about a year and resign ...the vote should go against him.

The U.S. government, which had urged political liberalization, congratulated Roh as the winner, expressing hope that disagreements over alleged electoral fraud would be resolved peacefully. U.S. officials on the scene concluded that whatever fraud may have occurred was not extensive enough to have changed the outcome.

**Economic Developments.** Pent-up labor grievances erupted in a wave of major strikes during the summer. In some cases, the government mediated settlements. However, where violence was involved, riot police were sent in to disperse workers and arrest activists.

Gross national product was projected to grow about 10 percent in 1987, despite labor troubles, and a substantial foreign trade surplus was expected. The United States continued to press South Korea to open its markets more fully to U.S. goods and services. The Koreans loosened import restrictions on some 170 items in July; they remained concerned over the impact of pending U.S. trade legislation.

**Jet Sabotage.** A South Korean jetliner, headed toward Seoul with 115 people aboard, disappeared November 29 near the Burmese coast. Some wreckage was later found, but there was no evidence of survivors. The South Korean government charged that North Korean agents had planted a bomb on the plane. Two suspects seized in Bahrain, where they had disembarked from the plane, swallowed suicide pills, but one, a North Korean woman, survived and admitted responsibility.

*See* STATISTICS OF THE WORLD.          D.S.M.

**KUWAIT.** Kuwait continued to support the Iraqi side in the Iran-Iraq war. Kuwait and Saudi Arabia were donating about $4 million a day in oil revenues from the "neutral zone" between the two countries to the Iraqi war effort.

Frustrated over Iranian attacks on its shipping, and hoping that greater superpower involvement might bring an end to the war, Kuwait in April leased 3 oil tankers from the Soviet Union and later placed 11 of its tankers under the U.S. flag. The United States, which wanted to limit Soviet influence in the Persian Gulf, began escorting Kuwaiti tankers in July. On the first of these convoys, the supertanker *Bridgeton* struck a mine, presumably laid by Iran. After stepped-up Iranian attacks on Gulf

shipping and Iran's firing of missiles at Kuwa during late summer, Kuwait in September e pelled five Iranian diplomats.

In October, Iran began using Silkworm mi siles against tankers in Kuwaiti waters; amor the vessels struck was the *Sea Isle City*, Kuwaiti tanker flying the U.S. flag. Kuwai main offshore oil terminal, Sea Island, w severely damaged in another attack. At the er of October, Kuwait was reregistering 3 of i tankers under the British flag, enabling the to be protected by British warships in the Gu

Domestic tension remained high, stemmir from terrorist attacks and the divisions betwee Sunni and Shiite Muslims. About one-third Kuwait's population is Shiite, mostly of Irania origin, while much of the rest of the populatic and the ruling al-Sabah family is Sunni. January, three oil installations were bombe The government charged 16 Kuwaiti citizen with these bombings; all but 1 of the 16 accuse were Shiites. Six were sentenced to death, or received life in prison, seven received less jail terms, and two were acquitted. The tri led to the removal of Shiites from sensitive jo in the oil industry and military.

In February, Saudi Arabia and Kuwait pledge a total of $14.5 million to a joint Jordania Palestine Liberation Organization fund for aic ing Palestinians on the Israeli-occupied We Bank. The donations were widely viewed as blow to Jordan's King Hussein, who had bee attempting to increase his influence on th West Bank at the expense of the PLO.

*See* STATISTICS OF THE WORLD.          L.A.I

# L

**LABOR UNIONS.** Continued slow economic growth, intense foreign competition, and a large U.S. trade deficit meant another difficult year for unions in 1987. Employers continued to pursue tough bargaining stances, which often resulted in concessionary labor agreements and reduced labor costs. On the brighter side, inflation remained low, and unemployment declined somewhat, from 6.6 percent in

January to below 6 percent later on. Majc private-industry collective bargaining settl ments in the first half of the year provided wag adjustments averaging 2.1 percent in the fir contract year and 2.5 percent annually ov the life of the contract, according to the Burea of Labor Statistics.

**Automobile Industry.** On September 30, th rank and file of the United Automobile Worke

Ford overwhelmingly approved a new three-year contract that emphasized job security. Under the contract, layoffs would be generally prohibited unless there is a decline in sales, and the work force would be reduced by only one guaranteed job for every two lost to attrition. Workers on temporary layoffs would receive payments, possibly equaling their base pay, for as long as two years. The contract also provided pay increases of 3 percent for the first year, with lump-sum payments equal to a 3 percent increase in the next two years. The union consented to the establishment of union-management committees that would explore changes to promote greater productivity.

In February, General Motors hourly workers were upset when they learned that, for the first time since their 1982 profit-sharing plan was negotiated, they would not receive an annual payout. GM reported profits of $2.9 billion for 1986 and paid bonuses to its executives, but it said profits from its U.S. operations were not sufficient to generate a payout to workers under provisions of the agreement. GM's refusal to pay a bonus, on top of its 1986 announcement of mass layoffs and plant closings affecting some 29,000 workers over the next three years, led some observers to expect its bargaining with the UAW to be tougher than Ford's. In October, however, GM and the union reached an agreement closely patterned on the Ford pact, and it was endorsed by an even larger majority of the rank and file. The pact did not cover the plants GM had said it would close.

**Postal Service.** In July negotiators for the U.S. Postal Service and unions representing the postal workers reached agreement on a 40-month contract raising pay by about 7 percent over the term. The pact included an immediate 2 percent increase in base salary, followed by four basic wage increases of $250, $250, $300, and $300 in annual salary, at six-month intervals beginning July 1988. An additional $200 was to be added on July 21, 1990, for the final four months of the contract.

**Steel.** The lockout of the United Steelworkers of America workers by the USX Corporation in 1986 led to a bitter six-month work stoppage, ending in January 1987. The new contract called for wage and benefit concessions modeled after the 8 percent reduction granted by the United Steelworkers to Bethlehem Steel Corporation in 1986, and it provided restrictions on subcontracting that the union insisted upon. The contract also established a profit-sharing plan, eliminated 1,346 jobs in existing plants, permitted the closing of other plants and the termination of up to 4,000 workers, enabled 2,500 workers to take early retirement, and included work rule changes and a commitment to modernize key facilities.

**Other Bargaining.** In February, Deere & Company, a major agricultural machinery maker, reached an agreement with 12,000 United Automobile Workers members after a walkout of more than five months. (In August 1986 the UAW began strikes at three Deere & Company plants and the company shut down the rest of its facilities.) The agreement followed the pattern of a UAW settlement with Caterpillar Tractor Company, which froze pay while providing a one-time bonus of $180, continuing quarterly cost-of-living adjustments, and job training programs. The contract also guaranteed employment to 90 percent of the work force, increased pension benefits, and reduced job classifications.

*A strike by newswriters at CBS was one sign of the relative austerity, including layoffs, that was taking hold at news divisions of the major broadcasting networks. The writers struck ABC as well, while thousands of members of the National Union of Broadcast Employees and Technicians walked out at NBC.*

During March and April members of the Writers Guild of America (television news writers, editors, and other employees) went on strike against CBS and ABC, because of heavy staff cuts. A settlement gave the employees at CBS a 3 percent annual raise for three years and provided arbitration rights for employees who are laid off. The network, for its part, won flexibility in hiring temporary employees, in making some layoffs without considering seniority, and in using managers and on-air employees to write stories. ABC's settlement was similar. In June, 2,800 members of the National Association of Broadcast Employees and Technicians struck NBC over job security issues, because of a demand by management for the right to hire part-time and temporary employees. The walkout ended after 118 days, when the union accepted the company's final contract offer, including the provision to which it had objected.

**Labor and the Law.** In a highly publicized decision, *Johnson* v. *Transportation Agency, Santa Clara County, Calif.,* a 6-3 majority of the Supreme Court upheld the county's promotion of a female employee over a male employee who had received a marginally better rating score. This decision appeared to remove most of the remaining legal obstacles to employers' adopting and implementing affirmative action plans. The Court also affirmed its 1979 ruling in *Weber* v. *Steelworkers* that employers can voluntarily engage in affirmative action even though there has been no legal finding of discriminatory employment practices.

In other cases favorable to unions, the Supreme Court upheld, 6-3, a lower-court ruling that the National Labor Relations Board had properly ordered the Fall River (Mass.) Dyeing & Finishing Corporation to bargain with the United Textile Workers of America. The June decision held that the company was, in effect, the successor to the Sterlingwale Corporation, where the union had represented the workers for 30 years. After Sterlingwale went out of business in 1982, a company vice president and the firm's biggest customer had set up the new corporation and, after a short time, had gone back into business at the company's old location.

In another case decided at the same time,

the Court ruled that state-mandated severanc payments were not preempted by either of tw federal laws—the Employment Retirement I come Security Act or the National Labor Re lations Act—that regulate collective bargainir and employee benefits. At issue was a Mair law which required any company with mo than 100 employees to provide severance pa to departing workers if the firm closed a pla or moved operations more than 100 miles fro the original site.

**Union Organization and Affiliation.** A new a traffic controllers' union was formed in Jun after an election in which nearly 85 perce of the 12,800 eligible controllers participate Of those, 7,494 voted for and 3,275 vote against designating the National Air Traff Controllers Association as the official bargai ing agent for these workers. They had not bee unionized since August 1981, when Preside Ronald Reagan fired 11,500 controllers f joining in an illegal strike led by the nov defunct Professional Air Traffic Controllers O ganization.

In an unprecedented turnabout, the Adolp Coors Company and the AFL-CIO announce an agreement in August resolving their decad long dispute over the Colorado brewer's o position to unionization of its workers. Coors struggle with organized labor began in 196 when the company was accused of forcir many craft unions out of its Colorado brewer Coors maintained it had not tried to illegal block unionization, but the company expresse dislike for unions and insisted that its worke had no need of a union. In 1977 the AFL-CI Directly Affiliated Local 366 went on strik after Coors refused to negotiate a new contrac and the AFL-CIO launched a nationwide bo cott of Coors beer. In 1978, Coors replaceme employees voted by a two-to-one margin oust the union. In the following years, th company and unions sparred frequently, b eventually, as Coors sought to expand its ma ket nationally and began construction of a ne plant in Elkton, Va., the management bega taking initiatives to improve its record c employee rights. Negotiations to end the bo cott were begun by Coors in 1985. Under th settlement, unions were free to seek to organiz Coors workers and any new Coors constructic

## Pork Party

Spam, the luncheon meat for which songs have been written (and that's no bologna), turned 50 in 1987, and the Minnesota town of Austin, where Spam was born, celebrated the event on Fourth of July weekend with fireworks, a big parade, an air show, and fried Spamcakes. By that time, Spam manufacturer George A. Hormel & Co. estimated it had turned out 4 billion cans of the pork loaf, which was served to GI's during World War II and is now produced at a rate of 435 cans per minute. Spam, which is short for "spiced ham," comes in four varieties—regular, smoke-flavored, cheese-flavored, and low-sodium—and its preparation possibilities are said to be endless (is that a turkey on the platter, or is it molded Spam?) Thousands of enthusiastic Spam-lovers attended the festival, which, however, was dimmed by memories of a bitter year-long strike at Hormel that ended in September 1986. Some of the 850 meatpackers who lost their jobs in the strike attended the celebration as a protest, wearing "Cram Your Spam" T-shirts, but no serious disruptions took place.

was to be done under union contract or union conditions."

Two days before the AFL-CIO's biennial convention opened in late October, the body's executive Council voted unanimously to readmit the International Brotherhood of Teamsters to the federation. The Teamsters had been expelled 30 years earlier, when leaders refused to appear before an AFL-CIO ethics committee to answer charges of corruption. Their application for readmission was seen as an effort to gain support in their battle with the U.S. Justice Department, which was preparing to sue them for allegedly being under the influence of organized crime. The 1.7 million Teamsters increased the AFL-CIO's membership by 13 percent and brought to the federation one of the nation's fastest growing political action committees and one of its most aggressive labor organizing operations.

**Reorganization.** Following a pattern of separation that began with the departure of the Canadian Autoworkers Union from the UAW,

the Oregon-headquartered International Woodworkers of America voted to split their union into a 30,000-member U.S. union and a 40,000-member Canadian union. The union said the split was an effort "to resolve a critical financial situation and declining membership." The decision could strengthen the IWA's economic and political action, "undiluted by issues of national identity," according to IWA president Keith Johnson.

**Transitions.** International Longshoremen's Association president Thomas W. Gleason, 86, retired in March after 24 years in office. John M. Bowers, a vice president of the New York State AFL-CIO, was elected at a July convention to replace him as head of the 116,000-member union.

On November 1, William Brock left his cabinet post as secretary of labor to become director of Senator Robert Dole's presidential campaign. In his place, President Reagan appointed Ann Dore McLaughlin, who was a former under secretary in the Interior Department. G.B.H.

**LAOS.** The People's Revolutionary Party, led by General Secretary Kaysone Phomvihan (re-elected in late 1986), continued to exercise firm control in Laos during 1987. In February the Supreme People's Council again set as its main tasks the completion of a long-deferred draft constitution and preparation for national elections.

The number of people in detention, without charges or trial, for "reeducation" apparently declined slightly; Amnesty International reported that 400 out of 6,000 to 7,000 detainees were released. Approximately 80,000 Laotians remained in refugee camps in neighboring Thailand.

In foreign affairs, Laos remained a reliable member of the Indochina bloc, dominated by Vietnam. Vietnam was deploying over 40,000 troops in Laos, some in the northern region to deter a Chinese attack against Vietnam, some to help the Lao Army in fighting insurgents, some to assist in the construction and maintenance of roads and bridges. Nevertheless, late in the year, Laos reached an agreement to restore diplomatic ties with China.

In March, 12 hours before the arrival of Soviet Foreign Minister Eduard Shevardnadze

# LEBANON

for a visit, a bomb exploded in the Soviet cultural center in Vientiane, the capital city. Authorities blamed subversive Lao exiles, trained by Thailand. However, there was a slight warming trend in relations between Laos and Thailand, which share more than 600 miles of frontier along the Mekong River. Lao and Thai technical teams held a five-day conference in Vientiane on measures to prevent Mekong River bank erosion, and a ten-year pilot project was launched.

In November the United States and Laos reached an accord under which Laos would step up the search for Americans missing since the Vietnam war, while the United States would seek to respond "within the limits of its capabilities" to the "needs of Laos for humanitarian aid."

Also in November, Britain's Princess Anne visited the nation in her capacity as president of the Save the Children Fund, a private agency active in Laos. Her entourage was the largest Western group to visit since the 1975 Communist takeover.

See STATISTICS OF THE WORLD.          J.J.Z.

**LEBANON.** As Lebanon entered its 13th year of chaos, efforts to restore peace to the country were frustrated by intractable conflicts. The principal feud pitted Lebanon's Christians, mostly Maronites, against Shiite and Sunni Muslim and Druze. Within the Shiite community there was growing strife between the relatively moderate Amal movement, supported by Syria, and the radical Hezbollah ("Party of God"), backed by Iran. The so-called war of the camps pitted Amal Shiite militia against Palestinian guerrillas. In the southern strip bordering Israel, Israeli forces and their Lebanese surrogates, the South Lebanon Army (SLA), fought constant battle with the Islamic Resistance movement, a coalition of Lebanese Shiite guerrillas assisted by some Palestinian fighters. Finally, another kind of war was directed mainly by Hezbollah and its spin-offs against Western influence, the chief weapon being the taking of hostages.

**Peace Efforts.** In February a preliminary agreement on restructuring the Lebanese government to satisfy sectarian demands was reached in Damascus by representatives of Lebanese Muslims and Druze and the Syrians, but conservative Maronites continued to resist any plan that would diminish their privileged position in the political system or institutionalize Syrian influence in Lebanese affairs. Meanwhile, as the fighting between the Amal militias and a loose coalition of Druze, Communists, and Palestinians intensified, Syria tried to impose order entering West Beirut with 7,000 troops in late February and closing most militia headquarters. But the Syrians refrained from entering the southern suburbs and risking a major battle with the Iran-backed Hezbollah militias dominant there, and the presence of the Syrians in Beirut appeared to reinforce the opposition of the Lebanese Forces, the powerful Christian militia led by Samir Geagea, to the Damascus peace plan.

**Karami Assassinated.** After the Syrian occupation of West Beirut, tensions along the "Green Line" dividing Muslim West and Christian East Beirut grew worse. On May 3 the only road crossing point between the two sections was closed, cutting off supplies of gasoline and flour to the western section. The impasse left Prime Minister Rashid Karami's government of "national unity" unable to meet, let alone make decisions. The next day, Karami, a Sunni Muslim who was bitterly criticized by both militant Christians and by Druze leader Walid

*Anglican Church envoy Terry Waite, visiting Lebanon in an attempt to free foreign hostages, is photographed on January 15 surrounded by Druse militiamen as he leaves the office of a Sunni Muslim leader in West Beirut. Waite disappeared, presumably taken hostage himself, a few days later.*

Mourners streamed toward the coffin of Lebanese Prime Minister Rashid Karami as it was carried through his hometown of Tripoli. Karami (inset), a veteran of Lebanese politics, died on June 1 when a bomb exploded in his military helicopter. Fourteen others were injured in the blast.

umblatt, announced that he would resign. But before President Amin Gemayel could find a replacement, Karami was murdered. On June 1, a bomb placed under his seat in an Army helicopter exploded, killing him and injuring 14 others. The assassins were unknown.

**Death of Chamoun.** In August, six months after surviving an assassination attempt, former President Camille Chamoun died of natural causes. A central figure in Lebanese politics since independence in 1943, he had been president during the 1950's and, since the civil war began in 1975, an ardent champion of the Maronites and a bitter foe of the Syrians and Palestinians.

**War of the Camps.** Of all the Lebanese conflicts, the so-called war of the camps, between Palestinians and Amal Shiites, was by far the bloodiest. Fighting was particularly grim around the Palestinian camps of Shatila and Burj al-Barajneh in the southern suburbs of Beirut. Their 25,000 inhabitants, more than 1,000 of whom were killed, were reduced to eating dogs and cats by the time the Syrian Army began to break the siege in April. The camps remained under intermittent Amal pressure. In September Amal agreed to lift the siege in return for the withdrawal of PLO forces from villages they had occupied east of Sidon. Violence continued, however. Another shaky peace accord was reached late in the year.

**Rise of Hezbollah.** Among the Shiite Muslims, Lebanon's largest and poorest community, Nabih Berri's Amal lost ground to Hezbollah. Syrian support actually weakened Amal, making it look like a Syrian client, while Hezbollah defied the Syrians, clashing with Syrian soldiers and kidnapping American journalist Charles Glass in June. (He later escaped.) The abduction, in a Syrian-patrolled area of Beirut, violated an understanding between Syria and Hezbollah.

**Conflict With Israel.** Hezbollah, supported by Iranian funds, played a major role in the intensifying attacks by the Islamic Resistance and Palestinian guerrillas against the Israeli-controlled security zone in southern Lebanon. In April, after Israel reported killing 18 Lebanese Islamic guerrillas in a major clash in the zone, Palestinian guerrillas infiltrated northern Israel and killed 3 Israeli soldiers. (In return, an Israeli air attack on Palestinian targets near Sidon in September killed 41 people.) In November a Palestinian guerrilla flew a motorized hang glider from southern Lebanon into Israeli territory; he killed one soldier on the road and, entering an Israeli army base, killed five others before being fatally shot.

**Other Violence.** On November 14 a bomb hidden in a box of chocolates blew up in American University Hospital in West Beirut, killing seven people including the bearer. A similar bomb four days earlier killed six people in West Beirut. No group claimed responsibility. During the year several Syrian troops were killed in hit-and-run attacks by unknown gunmen; a Muslim underground group asserted responsibility for certain of these killings.

**Hostage Situation.** The number of Lebanese citizens abducted by one side or another since the civil war began probably exceeded 2,000 by 1987, but it was the plight of the foreign hostages—mostly Americans and Europeans—that drew world attention. Late in the year, there were about 20 foreign hostages, including 8 Americans, 4 Frenchmen (one of whom was believed murdered), and 3 Britons. (Two other French hostages had been released in November, after negotiations involving France, Iran, and Syria.) The Church of England's hostage negotiator Terry Waite was one of ten foreigners apparently kidnapped within a two-week period in January by Islamic revolutionary groups; three others were Americans.

**Economic Collapse.** The economy plunged toward disaster, as inflation approached 300 percent on an annual basis, and the Lebanese pound plunged in value. Workers launched a five-day general strike in early November; the government acceded to various demands, agreeing, among other things, to name a com-

mittee that would try to raise the value of th pound.

See STATISTICS OF THE WORLD.    M.C.H

**LESOTHO.** See STATISTICS OF THE WORLD.
**LIBERIA.** See STATISTICS OF THE WORLD.
**LIBRARIES.** Funding and intellectual freedor were major issues for libraries in 1987.

**Federal Issues.** There were increased pressure on state and local government to pick up greater share of funding for libraries, as th Reagan administration sought to eliminate a most all federal aid to libraries in the fisca 1988 budget and to rescind funding alread appropriated for the 1987 fiscal year. Congres blocked the latter efforts, and the end-of-the year budget compromise in December restore many of the fiscal 1988 library allocations.

There was growing concern over access t government-produced information. Reaga administration attempts to privatize the Na tional Technical Information Service—a self supporting federal agency widely regarded a the most important clearinghouse of technica and scientific information in the United States— met with opposition in Congress. The Hous and Senate passed separate measures that woul prevent the agency from being turned over t private companies; no final action was taken Privatization was opposed by the American Library Association, which feared that thi would drive up prices and narrow the rang of materials available to the public.

In March the administration rescinded government directive allowing the label "un classified but sensitive" to be attached to se lected electronic data available to the public from computer databases and other sources The directive would have restricted access t a wide range of unclassified electronic dat identified by the government as of possible importance to national security.

The Librarian of Congress, Daniel J. Boorstin retired in June at the age of 72. James Hadley Billington, 57, a specialist in Soviet history and culture and director of the Smithsonian Institution's Woodrow Wilson Center, was named to succeed Boorstin. His appointment met opposition from some critics, who argued that a professional librarian should direct the Library. Previous appointees, including Boorstin generally have not been library professionals

To mark its 75th anniversary, the St. Louis, Mo., library baked a cake—a 600-pound model of its central building, with the windows done in chocolate icing. It took two pastry chefs to create the cake and 19 people to lift it.

**Information Technology.** Optical disk information products, including the CD-ROM (compact disk-read only memory) and the laser videodisk, continued to capture interest among librarians. Microsoft's Bookshelf was introduced as the first CD-ROM product to cross all market segment lines; it contains ten different reference works, from a dictionary and thesaurus to a zip code directory, on a single disk, which can be inserted into a special disk drive and connected to a personal computer. The user can call up material from these reference sources and, by pressing a button, insert material into text.

**Renovations, Celebrations, Services.** Restoration of the Los Angeles Public Library, ravaged by fire in 1986, moved forward with the Library Board of Commissioners' approval of $144 million for a 560,000-square-foot building, to be completed in 1991.

Libraries participated actively in celebrating the bicentennial of the U.S. Constitution, with special exhibitions, lectures, forums, and other programs at the New York Public Library, the Free Library of Philadelphia, the Smithsonian Institution, and the Library of Congress, as well as at many local libraries.

Library service programs focused on the reading and information needs of special groups. "Latch-key kids" and various ethnic groups received particular attention. "The Best Gift You'll Ever Give Your Child" was the title of a year-long campaign to put a library card in the hands of every child in the United States.

**Libraries and Politics.** A growing number of municipalities adopted ordinances prohibiting public agencies from purchasing goods from firms with business ties to South Africa. Many librarians complained that they were unable to maintain their collections or that free access to information was threatened; others supported the ordinances as efforts to combat apartheid. University Microfilms International, a major supplier of dissertations and periodicals, halted sales to South African universities, evoking protests from the South African academic community.

In September the New York *Times* reported that the FBI had asked staff members at New York City libraries to report on library users who might be recruiting spies or gathering information harmful to U.S. security. The American Library Association protested that such requests constituted "unwarranted government intrusion" into library users' "First Amendment right to receive information."

219

**Reagan Library.** In November, plans were announced to build a $30 million library facility in Ventura County, Calif., to house Ronald Reagan's presidential documents. The library and affiliated center for public affairs would be built on 100 acres of donated land near Thousand Oaks, Calif., about 30 miles northwest of downtown Los Angeles.          J.M.L.

**LIBYA.** In 1987, Libya suffered from problems at home and reversals abroad.

**Politics.** Libyan leader Muammar al-Qaddafi announced a radical reshuffling of the General People's Committee (cabinet) at the annual gathering of the General People's Congress, where complaints about the economy and other matters were widespread. The appointment of Omar al-Muntasser as secretary-general of the General People's Committee (prime minister) particularly surprised many observers. Muntasser, who comes from an upper-class family and was educated in an English school in Egypt, has excellent contacts with Western businesses as well as a reputation for getting things done. His selection may have reflected Qaddafi's desire to restore Libya's image abroad. Meanwhile, there were reports of a rift between Qaddafi and his second-in-command, Abdul Salam Jalloud.

In February, nine Muslim fundamentalists were executed on national television, presumably as a warning to other opponents of the regime. Nevertheless, in March five Libyan airmen defected to Egypt in a transport plane, followed later in the month by three helicopter crewmen. The defections appeared to reflect mounting opposition in the military to the war in Chad.

**Economic Failures.** The expensive war in Chad, insufficient oil revenues, and bureaucratic mismanagement forced the regime to face up to its economic failures, manifested in growing shortages of staple items and increasing public disaffection. Qaddafi was uncharacteristically frank in admitting the failures. In March he announced that private shops and businesses should be reestablished and markets reorganized to prevent shortages and high prices. In May he called for major changes in industry and agriculture, warning that otherwise Libya's industrial base "will collapse," but he was vague on details.

**Foreign Setbacks.** Qaddafi's policy of extending Libya's influence far beyond the country's borders received numerous setbacks. In March Suriname, where 200 Libyan advisers were reported to be stationed, succumbed to French and U.S. pressure and expelled a Libyan diplomat accused of helping to establish a guerrilla training camp for separatists from the French overseas departments of Guadeloupe and Martinique. The following month, Kenya expelled five Libyan diplomats accused of recruiting Kenyans to convey information about prominent politicians, dissident groups, and student activists. In Malta, a staunch ally of Libya during 16 years of Labor Party rule there, the conservative, pro-Western Nationalist Party was elected to office in May and indicated it would not implement the provisions of a 1985 Libyan-Maltese friendship agreement. Also in May, Australia announced the closing of the Libyan people's bureau (embassy) in Canberra and the expulsion of its two diplomats, charging that Libya had been stirring up trouble in the Pacific region.

**War in Chad.** Qaddafi's greatest humiliation by far occurred in Chad, where the government of Hissène Habré, supported by France and the United States, won several resounding victories in its effort to expel Libyan forces from the country. On March 22, Chadian forces, in a swift surprise attack, captured Wadi Doum, Libya's most important base in northern Chad, killing some 1,200 Libyan troops. A few days later, the Libyans were forced to evacuate the strategic oasis of Faya-Largeau. In August Chadian troops drove the Libyans into retreat in the disputed Aozou Strip between northern Chad and southern Libya, collecting as much as $1 billion worth of abandoned Libyan equipment in the process. In September, Chad invaded undisputed Libyan territory for the first time in the conflict, reportedly capturing and destroying an air base 60 miles inside the country. Libya retaliated with a bombing run on the Chadian capital of N'Djamena, during which French forces shot down a Soviet-made Libyan bomber with a U.S.-made missile. On September 11, Libya and Chad agreed to a cease-fire, letting the Organization of African Unity mediate the dispute over the Aozou Strip, but the situation was precarious.

ter-Arab **Relations.** Libya did manage to reduce its isolation within the Arab world, receiving an aide to Palestine Liberation Organization chairman Yasir Arafat for the first me since 1983, improving relations with unisia, and restoring diplomatic relations with rdan. However, relations between Libya and ost Arab states remained strained, and Libya d not attend the November Arab League ummit in Jordan.

**.S. Relations.** A few days before a rally in ripoli to mark the first anniversary of the U.S. ombing raid on Libya, Qaddafi called for pprochement with the United States and said e expected relations to improve once President Ronald Reagan left office. A spokesman or the U.S. State Department replied that nproved relations were impossible unless Qaddafi demonstrated ''concrete, durable evidence of changes in his policies.

*See* STATISTICS OF THE WORLD.        A.D.

**IECHTENSTEIN.** *See* STATISTICS OF THE WORLD.

**IFE SCIENCES.** Genetic engineering advances nd controversies made headlines in 1987, as lid new drugs, ancient fossils, returning cicadas, and the ever-popular panda.

**BIOLOGY**

cientists made remarkable progress in developing genetically altered bacteria to protect lants and in pinpointing possible genetic causes or disease.

**Biotechnology.** *Agriculture.* Two long-delayed ield tests of genetically engineered microorganisms finally took place. The tests—of an engineered bacterium designed to protect crops rom frost damage—had been delayed since 1983 by court suits and regulatory snafus. They vere done in California on strawberries and potatoes and were conducted by Advanced Genetic Sciences, Inc., of Oakland and the University of California at Berkeley. The bacterium did protect the plants at temperatures two to five degrees below freezing, and the engineered microorganism did not escape from the test plots. Environmental activists vandalized some of these plots.

Several field tests of plants genetically engineered to resist insects or herbicides were also carried out. Many experts believe that the engineered plants hold great potential for reducing farming costs.

Genetically altered bacteria were also being used to fight plant disease. One field test of such bacteria put Montana State University at the center of national controversy. In an unauthorized experiment at first unknown to other university scientists, researcher Gary Strobel injected 14 young elm trees on the university's Bozeman campus with live engineered bacteria. The bacteria had been altered to produce larger amounts of a chemical that can destroy the fungus causing Dutch elm disease, which has come to threaten the very existence of the American elm tree. After learning of the experiment, which had not been approved by the university, the Environmental Protection Agency, or the U.S. Agriculture Department as required, two university committees criticized Strobel's action, and the EPA issued mild sanctions. It was later learned that Strobel had conducted unapproved experiments, introducing altered microorganisms into crop plants, in Montana and three other states back in

*Montana scientist Gary Stroebel hoped to find a cure for Dutch elm disease when he injected 14 young trees with genetically altered bacteria. After the unauthorized experiment caused a furor, a tearful Stroebel destroyed the trees.*

A genetically altered bacterium, designed to protect strawberries from freezing temperatures, made its field test debut as Julie Lindemann, a project leader at Advanced Genetic Sciences, Inc., sprayed over 2,000 plants in California's Central Valley.

1984. These experiments involved the first known release of a genetically altered microbe into the environment. In an effort to calm down the controversy, Strobel terminated his elm experiment, cutting down the trees that had been involved.

The U.S. Patent and Trademark Office ruled in April that genetically altered animals could be patented. Many researchers were working to insert genes into farm animals in order to make them more productive or more resistant to disease. The patent office had previously ruled that genetically engineered microorganisms and plants could be patented, and the new decision was viewed as a logical extension of such a position. The ruling stimulated debate about the ethics of altering animal genes.

*Pharmaceuticals.* A report by the congressional Office of Technology Assessment said that more than 80 different proteins, enzymes, hormones, and other biological products were being developed for human therapy by the biotechnology industry. Virtually all of these were materials that are present in humans in small quantities but can be produced in much larger quantities in bacteria, yeast, or cultured animal cells.

One of the most promising is an enzyme called tissue plasminogen activator (TPA), which dissolves heart attack-causing blood clots.

Studies by the National Institutes of Health and TPA's developer, Genentech, Inc., of South San Francisco, Calif., have shown that the enzyme can dissolve such clots and, presumably, minimize heart damage if it is administered within six hours after the heart attack begins. In May an advisory committee for the U.S. Food and Drug Administration recommended that TPA not be approved right away, arguing that clinical trials of the enzyme had shown only that it dissolved clots, not that it actually saved lives. However, TPA won governmental approval in November.

Another drug that was expected to be approved was erythropoietin (EPO), a kidney hormone that stimulates the production of red blood cells. EPO may be valuable for treating anemia, particularly the severe anemia caused by kidney failure and dialysis.

Atrial natriuretic factor, also known as ANF or auriculin, is a hormone produced by the heart that lowers blood pressure. Discovered only a few years ago, ANF was being studied intensively for the treatment of congestive heart failure, high blood pressure, and kidney failure. Also being studied were a variety of substances obtained from white blood cells, including interferons, interleukins, and tumor necrosis factor. All three looked promising for cancer therapy, and the first two were also being used or the treatment of AIDS (acquired immune deficiency syndrome).

A major new family of biological materials that were being produced by genetic engineering techniques were growth factors and colony stimulating factors—agents that promote the growth of colonies of blood and immune defense cells. These agents are so pervasive throughout the body and so fundamental to all aspects of body function that they may create entirely new forms of therapy for a variety of disorders.

In August the Food and Drug Administration gave permission for the first human trial of a vaccine against AIDS. The vaccine, produced by MicroGeneSys, Inc., of West Haven, Conn., is composed of surface proteins from the virus that causes AIDS. The proteins were produced in bacteria using genetic engineering techniques. Later, Bristol-Myers received permission to test another AIDS vaccine.

**Finding Genetic Defects.** Scientists using the techniques of genetic engineering have made remarkable progress in the past two years identifying genetic markers for various diseases. These markers can be used during pregnancy in a family with a history of a particular disease to show whether or not a fetus will contract the disease. The markers also show researchers where to look in human chromosomes for the defective gene that causes the illness. In October a Massachusetts-based research team reported that it had developed a map of genetic markers covering all 23 pairs of human chromosomes. The map, which will enable scientists to locate defective genes much more efficiently, consists of almost 400 recognizable pieces of the genetic material DNA that occur at known locations on the chromosomes.

Researchers from three U.S. universities reported in February that they had found a marker associated with manic-depression. The study was the first strong proof that psychiatric illnesses can be inherited. A few months later, scientists at St. Mary's Hospital Medical School in London reported the discovery of a genetic marker for cystic fibrosis, the most common fatal hereditary disease among Caucasians in the United States.

Two research teams in May reported the discovery of a genetic marker for the more common form of neurofibromatosis, known as the "elephant man" disease; it occurs once in 3,000 births, with effects ranging from mottled skin to disfiguring tumors. In September, three research teams reported finding a marker for another form of the disease, which occurs in one out of 50,000 births and causes tumors on the cranial and spinal nerves.

*Alzheimer's Disease.* In March, researchers in Bethesda (Md.) and Paris reported that they might have found a genetic defect responsible for Alzheimer's disease. However, two subsequent studies cast doubt on a cause-and-effect relationship between the defect and Alzheimer's. The disease is usually associated with the accumulation in the brain of cement-like plaques. In November 1986, three groups of researchers reported that they had located the gene that codes for the protein that is the principal component of the plaques. The Bethesda and Paris researchers later found that Alzheimer's victims have three copies of the gene, while healthy individuals have only two. They suggested that the extra copy may cause the body to produce abnormal amounts of protein which then accumulates in the brain. The subsequent studies, however, found strong evidence that overproduction of the protein and the hereditary form of Alzheimer's are coded by two different genes on the same chromosome and therefore can be inherited independently.

**Colon Cancer.** Researchers at the Imperial Cancer Research Fund Laboratories near London reported the discovery of a genetic defect that may be responsible for colon cancer. The researchers studied a small group of people who suffered from familial adenomatous polyposis (FAP), which is characterized by the presence of thousands of small tumors called polyps in the colon. The polyps frequently become cancerous. The researchers found that a particular gene was missing or damaged in FAP victims. Healthy individuals have two of these genes, and the pair may prevent the release of growth factors that turn healthy cells into malignant ones. Scientists believe that cancer results in FAP victims when the second gene is damaged or destroyed by viruses or chemicals in the environment.

# LIFE SCIENCES

**Apelike Bodies of Earliest Humans.** The first truly human species—the earliest in the genus *Homo*—is usually said to be *Homo habilis* ("handy man"—it was the first species to make stone tools). For years the only solidly identifiable fossils that scientists had at their disposal were skull fragments and teeth. However, in May a team of scientists, headed by Donald Johanson of the Institute of Human Origins in Berkeley, Calif., published a report on a major fossil find they made in Tanzania's Olduvai Gorge in mid-1986—fossil remains of an adult *Homo habilis* female that included not only a skull but clearly associated arm bones and thigh and shin fragments. The creature, who lived 1.8 million years ago, turned out to have a much smaller and more apelike body than expected. She probably was between 3 feet and 3½ feet tall. Her upper arm bone was nearly as long as her thighbone. The find raised new questions and problems. The body of *Homo erectus,* which appeared only 200,000 years later, is rather modern. How could it have evolved so quickly? If the earliest humans had an apelike body type, does that mean that some fossil bones in existing collections may have been misclassified as nonhuman?

**Return of the Cicadas.** In the spring billions of cicadas, the Rip Van Winkles of the insect world, made their presence heard throughout the eastern United States. Huge colonies of the insects emerged after 17 years underground for a few weeks of raucous courtship. There are many types of cicadas, but the periodic cicada with a cycle of 17 years is found only in the eastern part of the country. Broods emerge almost every year, but the 1987 group was extraordinarily large; the offspring of that cicada crop burrowed as much as 2 feet into the ground, where they will remain, feeding on root juices, until they emerge in the year 2004.

**Natural Wonderland in Peril.** The island of Madagascar, situated in the Indian Ocean off the east coast of Africa, has become one of the world's prime targets for conservation efforts. Over 200,000 square miles in area, it is home to a unique diversity of wildlife that has evolved in isolation for millions of years, but it is threatened especially by poor farmers who destroy habitats to plant crops or obtain fire-

wood. Madagascar's government is working with foreign conservation organizations, such as the World Wildlife Fund in Washington, D.C., to protect the island's natural wealth by, for example, planning the expansion and improvement of nature reserves.

Because of the exceptional number of unique species on the island, the destruction of a few hundred acres could, according to some experts, have far worse consequences than a comparable clearing in other biologically rich areas. Entire species might become extinct before they are even identified. The plant life includes thousands of orchid species. Half of the world's varieties of chameleon live only on Madagascar, and it is the sole home to a large number of frog and bird species and to thousands of species of flowering plants. The island's more than two dozen surviving species of the small, tree-dwelling mammals known as lemurs make up an entire major branch of primates.        T.H.M., L.J.M., M.M., & J.F.

## BOTANY

Botanists in 1987 noted reawakened popular interest in old-fashioned wildflowers and made new studies of plant adaptation to the industrial age.

**Native Plants.** Under the leadership of Lady Bird Johnson, widow of President Lyndon B. Johnson, the campaign to preserve American wildflowers has continued to gain momentum.

This popular movement concerns itself with native plants for the garden as well as those threatened with extinction. People everywhere are becoming aware of the value of wildflowers—even in big cities. In New York, for example, the discovery of some native rose pink plants (*Sabatia*) growing on Staten Island near an expressway recently caused a sensation. The rose pink had not been seen in the city for 100 years; the discovery prompted efforts to protect the flower from expansion of the highway.

**Adaptation to Changing Atmosphere.** Studies of ice cores have shown that the industrial age has increased the amount of carbon dioxide in the air. But at least some plants are responding by reducing the number of microscopic pores—stomata—that control the flow of gas and water into and out of their leaves. This surprising finding was reported in midyear by F. I. Woodward of Cambridge University. Woodward compared the leaves of seven species of trees and one shrub species in the English midlands with herbarium specimens of the species collected over the last 200 years. For that period, there was a steady decline, averaging 40 percent, in the number of stomata per unit area of leaf surface.

This research is part of a growing body of work by scientists investigating the warming and cooling of the planet and the waxing and waning of species. Carbon dioxide in the atmosphere traps heat, and the increasing levels of the gas are expected to raise the earth's temperature in the next few decades. Stomata, which admit carbon dioxide and other gases into the plant, also allow water to evaporate. With fewer stomata, a plant becomes more efficient in using water to draw energy from sunlight and carbon dioxide. At least some plants, then, may be improving their ability to withstand drought as the planet warms.

**Breakup of the Continents.** A recent study of pollen and spores more than 200 million years old suggests that Europe, Africa, North America, and South America began to separate from each other at roughly the same time, and not in stages, as many scientists have believed. Alfred Traverse of Pennsylvania State University reported at midyear on pollen and spores found embedded in shale in rift valleys in eastern North America and the Gulf of Mexico. Such rift valleys had been created in many parts of the world by the forces that eventually tore apart the huge protocontinent from which today's continents are thought to have formed. The spores turned out to have come from particular species that flourished in a relatively short period about 225 million years ago. Similar pollen and spores were known from rift valleys now located across the Atlantic. The fact that the pollen and spores were found in such now far-flung rift valleys indicates that the primeval land mass was still intact when these plants flourished.

L.J.M., M.M., & J.F.

## ZOOLOGY

In 1987 zoological scientists tried to help a pair of giant pandas, visiting the United States

*Proving that New York City isn't just an asphalt jungle, botanist Richard T. Lynch displays rose pinks—a rare species of flower, not seen in the city for over a century—that he stumbled upon while hiking in the borough of Staten Island.*

On loan from China, a pair of giant pandas offered visitors to New York's Bronx Zoo a rare look at the endangered species. Above, the female, Yong Yong, explores her new surroundings after the 20-hour flight from Beijing. The zoo braced for as many as 2,000 panda-watchers an hour; New Yorkers, like the schoolchildren above, responded with—as the newspaper headlines put it—pandamonium.

from China, to breed in captivity; they also sought to reestablish a rare breed of swans in the Great Lakes region.

**Returning the Trumpeter Swan.** The year saw new efforts to reestablish the trumpeter swan in the Great Lakes area, where they had died out after being hunted for their meat, skin, and plumes. In May three eggs donated by the Kansas Zoological Gardens were flown to Michigan and then taken to a marsh 40 miles north of Kalamazoo, where they were placed into the nest of a related bird, a mute swan, who was to serve as a foster mother. Additional eggs were subsequently brought from other areas. To protect the newborn cygnets from predatory snapping turtles, 400 of the turtles were trapped at the marsh before the eggs were brought.

Trumpeter swans were once found in abundance in the marshlands of the Great Lakes region, but today most of the 10,000 birds in the United States live in Alaska. The goal of Michigan's environmentalists is to have two

## Open Wide

It takes a gutsy patient to undergo a root canal, but it takes an even gutsier dentist to perform one on an eight-year-old, 550-pound, male Siberian tiger. Drs. Bert Kaufman and Phil Shindler, who usually perform on people, volunteered their services at the Wildlife Waystation in California's Angeles National Forest, when Reesha, a tiger who lives at the refuge, developed cracked and abscessed teeth from chewing on cage bars and fences. In order to do the root canal work, and also extract one tooth, the dentists used a specially designed 7-foot-long operating table, complete with hydraulic lift. Extra-large dental tools were needed for the tiger's extra-large tooth nerves, eight to ten times the size of a human's. In a postoperative report, dentists and patient seemed to be doing well.

established trumpeter flocks, each 100 strong, by the year 2000.

**Panda News.** Everybody loves the giant panda. That was clear from the enthusiastic welcome New Yorkers gave to Ling Ling and Yong Yong when they arrived at the Bronx Zoo in May. The cuddly black-and-white pair were on loan from China's Beijing Zoo; after six months, they were moved, late in the year, to a Tampa, Fla., zoo.

The giant panda, unfortunately, is an endangered species. Only about 700 are left in the wild, most of them living on reserves in China's Sichuan Province, and attempts to breed giant pandas in captivity have met with only limited success. The National Zoological Park in Washington, D.C., is the only zoo in the United States to have a pair of pandas on permanent exhibit. On June 23 the female panda at Washington's zoo (named Ling Ling, like the male in the Bronx Zoo) gave birth to an apparently healthy cub, as well as to a stillborn infant. The cub was the size of a stick of butter—newborns typically weigh less than 5 pounds. It contracted a bacterial infection and died less than four days after birth. This was Ling Ling's third unsuccessful attempt at motherhood.

L.J.M. & M.M.

**LITERATURE.** Among the major literary developments of 1987 were those that follow.

### AMERICAN

Fiction with a twist of fantasy stood out in 1987. The influence of Latin American magic realism, science fiction, and avant-garde playfulness could often be detected.

**Fiction.** Walker Percy, who adopted science fiction as the backdrop of *Love in the Ruins*, resurrected its psychiatrist-hero, Dr. Tom More, in *The Thanatos Syndrome*. Set in the near future, the novel raises questions about the meaning of moral choice in a technological, bureaucratic society, where the government dopes the drinking water to pacify the citizenry. Joseph McElroy's *Women and Men*—as 19th-century a title as anyone could want—attempts a kind of avant-garde science fiction in its intricate portrait of the world as a vast information network.

John Crowley, Russell Hoban, and Gene Wolfe, three writers best known for their outstanding work in specialized genres, brought out new novels that transcended those genres. Crowley, the author of the fantasy novel *Little, Big*, produced *Aegypt*, a richly textured work in which a young professor moves to a strange country town and finds that the novels of a dead writer contain arcane lore that duplicates his own historical discoveries. Hoban, an esteemed author of children's literature, brought out a brilliant fable, *The Marzipan Pig*, about humankind's longing for love and its failure to find it. Later in the year, he published *The Medusa Frequency*, a tour de force that transposed the Orpheus legend to the world of London publishing. Wolfe, who first achieved fame with the four-volume science fiction novel *Book of the New Sun*, delivered his long-promised "coda" to that work, called *The Urth of the New Sun*, which relies on a fairly conventional science-fiction plot but turns into a novel of, among other things, religious existentialism.

John Barth's new novel, *The Tidewater Tales*, takes the reader pleasantly along Chesapeake Bay, offering reflections on art and life, but it lacks the mischievous narrative playfulness of his best books. The kind of structural experimentation that Barth used to like could be found in James Dickey's *Alnilam*, a long epic

# LITERATURE

set during World War II. In *Alnilam,* each page carries two columns, one presenting straight narrative, the other setting down the thoughts of the blind protagonist.

Among novels more traditional in structure and realistic in content, some were outstanding for their intense ethical concerns. Toni Morrison, the most distinguished black novelist writing in the United States today, examines the burden of slavery in *Beloved,* the tale of a black woman living in post-Civil War Ohio who years earlier had murdered her own daughter rather than send her into slavery. Cynthia Ozick's fable *The Messiah of Stockholm* imagines a small-time man of letters who comes to believe he is the son of the Polish-Jewish author Bruno Schulz, murdered by the

*In his brilliant new novel* The Thanatos Syndrome, *Walker Percy depicts a future society that is irreligious and darkly immoral.*

Nazis in 1942. Reflections on Judaism, the Holocaust, literature, responsibility, and other weighty matters abound, but Ozick's fine, serious prose carries all before it.

Saul Bellow brought out *More Die of Heartbreak,* which takes up an old obsession: intellectuals tortured by love, anxiety, and family problems. Immensely readable, the book was acclaimed as a return to form after the ponderous *The Dean's December.* Equally acclaimed was the new novel by Gail Godwin, *A Southern Family,* which sensitively traces the effects of a death upon a family.

New York has the leading role in Tom Wolfe's *The Bonfire of the Vanities,* the first novel from the apostle of New Journalism. Extensively rewritten after its original serialization in *Rolling Stone* magazine, this Balzac-like story of a wealthy bond trader's downfall in the hopelessly corrupt metropolis was well-received. Kurt Vonnegut's latest novel, *Bluebeard,* is a fictional biography of a New York abstract expressionist; it offers the usual tongue-in-cheek narration, dry wit, and amusing story. So it goes. More ambitious is Harry Mathews's *Cigarettes,* a novel portraying relationships among Greenwich Villagers during the 1960's.

Larry McMurtry's *Texasville* offered some fine moments, picking up the lives of characters from *The Last Picture Show* as they entered middle age. But the novel as a whole was a disappointment to many readers who admired McMurtry's previous book, the Pulitzer Prize-winning epic *Lonesome Dove.* Joyce Carol Oates continued her prolific ways with *You Must Remember This,* a novel about an upstate New York girl in the 1950's who develops a passion for her uncle, a boxer, as well as *On Boxing,* a long, probing essay on the sport, and a suspenseful psychological novel, *Lives of the Twins.*

**Special Areas.** Crime fiction and spy thrillers increasingly have been reaching past genre barriers to become novels about the way we live now. In 1987, for instance, George V. Higgins's excellent *Outlaws* examined the legacy of 1960's terrorism, the machinery of justice, trial by jury, the insanity defense, and much else. Elmore Leonard, who has acknowledged the influence of Higgins's *The Friends of Eddie Coyle* as a model for his own writing,

**And in This Corner . . .**

For Joyce Carol Oates, a prolific writer known for her emotionally charged novels, 1987 was the year for stepping into the ring, sizing up a sport that has inspired literary figures from Hazlitt to Hemingway. Her book-length essay *On Boxing,* a distillation of the "sweet science" flavored with history, philosophy, and anecdote, was soon followed by a novel, *You Must Remember This,* about a young girl's obsessive love for her uncle, a professional boxer; and an anthology of essays, *Reading the Fight,* which she co-edited with Dan Halpern, was due out in 1988. Her abiding interest in the sport may seem surprising, but the fragile-looking 49-year-old author and Princeton University professor has long been known for her stamina and range. Her novels, stories, plays, poetry, and essays amount to some 50 published volumes. One of them, the novel *Lives of the Twins,* caused a mild sensation in 1987 when it was revealed that Oates had originally tried to keep her authorship a secret by publishing the book under a pseudonym.

*Joyce Carol Oates*

brought out *Touch.* This book, actually written a decade ago, possesses his usual virtues: a good ear, sympathetic characters, multiple viewpoints, an economical style. But it also verges on new territory, bringing in television evangelism and a character who appears to possess the stigmata.

The big crime and punishment book of the year was *Presumed Innocent,* a first novel by attorney Scott Turow. In it an erstwhile public prosecutor finds himself accused of the murder of a colleague with whom he had a brief affair; he is soon caught up in the tangles of the law and undergoes a suspenseful and complex trial. Literate and gripping, the book also raises serious questions about legal system.

Andrew Vachss drew great praise for *Strega,* a gritty urban fantasy whose characters live in New York City as though they were guerrillas in hostile territory. The prolific and compelling storyteller Stephen King provided a few more books: *Misery,* the chilling tale of a writer held hostage by a madwoman and forced to compose further adventures for her favorite character; *The Eyes of the Dragon,* a first-rate fairy tale, about a kingdom in the grip of an evil

sorcerer; *The Drawing of the Three,* on the further adventures of Roland, the last gunslinger, in a post-nuclear-war world; and, also another excursion into pure horror, *The Tommyknockers,* in which an ancient ship is dug up, and with it something strange and menacing.

In science fiction, Orson Scott Card won the Nebula and Hugo awards for the second year in a row, this time for *Speaker for the Dead,* a symbolic chronicle of an interspecies war on a distant planet.

**Nonfiction.** Kenneth Lynn's massive biography *Hemingway* made clear that Ernest Hemingway remains the most fascinating and controversial American writer. Lynn, while noting the deep sexual anxieties that lie beneath the exaggerated masculinity of Hemingway's public persona, uses the tools of psychology deftly; the result must be counted as the most satisfying and complete Hemingway biography available.

Some of Papa's contemporaries also earned good biographical studies. *Sherwood Anderson* by Kim Townsend recounts the life of the creator of the classic *Winesburg, Ohio.* Thomas Wolfe's life, writing, and critical fortunes are

*In her book* Beloved, *Toni Morrison, America's most distinguished black novelist, weaves a richly imagined, exceptionally moving tale exploring a black woman's experience in post-Civil War America.*

expertly examined in David Herbert Donald's *Look Homeward,* and John Tytell's *Ezra Pound* takes another look at the perplexing guru of high modernism.

The golden age of Americans in Paris, the 1920's, is vividly re-created in Waverley Root's memoir *The Paris Edition,* which chronicles life on the old Paris edition of the *Chicago Tribune.* The same period in America is evoked in Mary McCarthy's *How I Grew,* a rather disappointing companion to her classic *Memoirs of a Catholic Girlhood.*

**Poetry.** In poetry, it was a year of consolidation. W. D. Snodgrass, Frederick Morgan, Theodore Weiss, Lincoln Kirstein, William Meredith, A. R. Ammons, Gregory Orr, Marvin Bell, and several other poets of the second rank produced retrospective collections. With *Archaic Figure,* Amy Clampitt continued to establish herself as a major voice in the "new formalism," while John Ashbery's *April Galleons* presented his familiar mix of heartbreakingly musical verse and nearly impenetrable meaning.

**Awards.** The Pulitzer Prize in fiction was awarded to Peter Taylor for *A Summons to Memphis.* In poetry the Pulitzer went to Rita Dove for *Thomas and Beulah.* The National Book Critics Circle selected Reynolds Price's *Kate Vaiden* for its fiction award. Edward Hirsch's *Wild Gratitude* won in poetry, and Joseph Brodsky's *Less Than One: Selected Essays* took the award for criticism. The American Book Award in fiction went to E. L. Doctorow for *World's Fair* and in nonfiction to Barry Lopez for *Arctic Dreams.* The National Book Award in fiction went to Larry Heinemann for *Paco's Story* (edging out the favorite, Toni Morrison's *Beloved*) and in nonfiction to Richard Rhodes for *The Making of the Atomic Bomb.*          M.D.

### AUSTRALIAN

The year 1987 was marked by many fine short story collections and some interesting new books on the history of Australia.

**Fiction.** The short story is probably the literary form in which Australians have most consistently excelled. Among the best collections were Tim Winton's *Minimum of Two,* Jessica Anderson's *Stories From the Warm Zone* and *Sydney Stories,* and *Dream People* by Barbara Hanrahan, one of Australia's most original prose writers. The migrant experience pervades Peter Srzynecki's *The Wild Dogs,* while Ninette Dutton's *Probabilities* displays her usual sureness of touch. The prolific Thomas Keneally returns to the early years of white settlement of Australia in a fascinating novel, *The Playmaker,* in which convicts perform a play; Eric Willmot depicts the same period from the Aboriginal perspective in his excellent novel *Pemulwuy: The Rainbow Warrior.* In her last book, *Amy's Children,* Olga Masters, who died in 1986, uses the same spare, lucid prose that characterizes all her work. *Ruth,* Dorothy Johnston's second novel, which treats gender and politics, received critical acclaim for its sensitivity and control of language. Martin Buzacott's exuberant first novel *Charivari* tells the story of two young social dropouts.

**Nonfiction.** Manning Clark concluded his monumental *A History of Australia* with the sixth volume, *The Old Dead Tree and the Young Tree Green, 1916–1935.* Clark has been praised not only for his historical vision but also for his literary style—which has led critics

*Manning Clark published the sixth and final volume in his epic* A History of Australia.

to describe the work as one of Australia's great 19th-century novels. Literary excellence also distinguishes Robert Hughes's *The Fatal Shore,* an internationally popular history of Australia's convict era. Geoffrey Serle's *The Creative Spirit in Australia: A Cultural History* is an excellent guide to the creative arts, while *Yacker 2: Australian Writers Talk About Their Work* introduces the reader to 12 of the nation's best contemporary authors.

**Awards.** The Patrick White Award went to short story writer John Morrison. Elizabeth Jolley won the Miles Franklin Literary Award for her novel *The Well.* Alan Wearne's verse novel *The Nightmarkets* received the National Book Council's gold award and the gold medal of the Association for the Study of Australian Literature. The association's Dame Mary Gilmore Prize for a first book of poetry went to Jan Owen for her collection *Boy With a Telescope,* and the Walter McRae Russell Prize for a first work of literary scholarship was awarded to Graeme Turner's *National Fictions: Literature, Film, and the Construction of Australian Narrative.*

Janine Burke won the Vance Palmer Prize for fiction in the Victorian Premier's Literary Awards, for her novel *Second Sight.* The New South Wales Premier's Literary Award for fiction was withheld; instead Glenda Adams, considered ineligible because she lives in New York, received a medal for *Dancing on Coral.* The poetry award went to Philip Hodgins for *Blood and Bone,* and David Malouf was the recipient of the drama award for *Blood Relations.*                                      I.K.

### CANADIAN

A considerable increase in the number of Canadian books published in 1987 did not reflect an increase in quality. Large English Canadian publishers, many of them under new directors, edged toward the best-seller syndrome, pursuing books with a potential for commercial success. Throughout the country writers expressed deep concern over two measures that the federal government was advocating: free trade with the United States, which appeared to threaten Canada's cultural sovereignty, and federal antipornography legislation that seemed to threaten literary and artistic freedom.

*Canadian writer Michael Ondaatje published* In the Skin of a Lion, *a novel described as a "mural" of diverse, striking scenes.*

**Fiction.** The most impressive novel of the year was Michael Ondaatje's *In the Skin of a Lion,* which follows the intriguing life of Patrick Lewis, a rural Ontario boy who moves to Toronto and joins the continent-wide search for a missing millionaire, Ambrose Small. Along the way he falls in love with Small's mistress, Clara Dickens, as well as with her strange and elusive friend, the former nun Alice Gull. The

plot builds slowly to a frightening climax. *The Honorary Patron,* Jack Hodgins's first novel in eight years, brings a retired art historian and teacher, Jeffrey Crane, home to Vancouver Island from his reclusive life in Zurich. Crane confronts the island world he left behind and the life of the senses he had closed off. The prolific writer Brian Moore published *The Color of Blood,* a rather disappointing melodrama about a cardinal in a contemporary Eastern European country who is kidnapped by a gang disguised as security police.

The short story continued to be a major and popular art form in Canada. Jane Urquhart is intrigued, indeed obsessed, by the past we escape from as well as the past we create for ourselves. Her collection of stories *Storm Glass,* which includes one story that served as the prologue and epilogue to her first novel, *The Whirlpool* (1986), focuses on dreams and memories in a unique style that further confirms the appearance of a major new voice in Canadian fiction. Madeleine Ferron, though not a prolific writer, has earned a reputation as a superb stylist who captures, with arresting simplicity, the joys and pains of the human heart. Her new collection of short stories, *Un amour singulier* ("A Singular Love"), is a series of variations on the theme of lost love.

**Poetry.** Although the number of poetry volumes published increased markedly over 1986, few books stood out. Gérald Godin's *Ils ne demandaient qu'à brûler: poèmes 1960–86* ("They Seek Only Fire: Poems 1960–86") is a retrospective collection that allows a reassessment of a major figure in Québec culture and politics. Godin's early poems now seem curiously dated and simple; his later work balances personal odyssey with some adventurous forays into the complexities of language. Still more powerful in its verbal technique was André Roy's disturbing collection, *C'est encore le solitaire qui parle* ("Still the Voice of Aloneness"). Moving through and beyond his usual thematic focus on the body, passion, and homosexual love, Roy depicts the folly of modern life with a bleak, Kafkaesque intensity. Less adventurous were the many books of English poetry, although new collections by such established poets as Patrick Lane and Don McKay were impressive.

**Nonfiction.** In recent years, Canadian public figures, especially politicians, have captured attention with confessions of their professional and sometimes their personal lives. In 1987 it appeared that the literary community was finally turning to public disclosure. Sylvia Fraser temporarily forsook her fine fiction to write *My Father's House,* an account of the sexual abuse she suffered as a child. Less personal is P. K. Page's *Brazilian Journal,* the distinguished poet's diaries of her years as the wife of the Canadian ambassador to Brazil. *The Russian Album,* journalist and critic Michael Ignatieff's homage to his Russian ancestors, is a beautiful work that might well become a prologue to an autobiography. The second volume of the journals of L. M. Montgomery continued the self-revelation of a major figure in the development of Canadian literature.

**Awards.** The Governor General's Awards for 1986 went to Alice Munro for *The Progress of Love* and Yvon Rivard for *Les silences du corbeau* ("The Crow's Silences") in fiction, to Al Purdy for *The Collected Poems of Al Purdy* and Cécile Cloutier for *L'écouté* ("The Heeded") in poetry, to Sharon Pollock for *Doc* and Anne Legault for *La visite des sauvages* ("The Visit of the Savages") in drama, and to Northrop Frye for *Northrop Frye on Shakespeare* and Régine Robin for *Le réalisme socialiste: une esthétique impossible* ("Socialist Realism: An Impossible Aesthetic") in nonfiction.     D.S.

### ENGLISH

Several distinguished writers published new works in 1987, among them novelists Margaret Drabble, William Golding, and Fay Weldon and playwrights Alan Ayckbourn, Caryl Churchill, and Simon Gray.

**Fiction.** In *Close Quarters,* Nobel Prize-winner William Golding provided a vivid sequel to his *Rites of Passage.* This second volume of a seafaring trilogy set during the Napoleonic War continued the journal kept by a young prospective colonial administrator, sailing among a shipload of emigrants to Australia.

*The Radiant Way,* by Margaret Drabble, presented an ambitious but pessimistic view of Britain in the 1980's, seen through the eyes and lives of three women friends—a psychotherapist, a teacher, and an art historian—from very different social backgrounds. The heroine

of Penelope Lively's *Moon Tiger,* old and near death, also strove to make sense of our century, through reliving her past experiences as war correspondent in the African desert, bereft lover, unmarried mother, and distinguished popular historian; *Moon Tiger* won the 1987 Booker McConnell Prize.

Another novel of fine sensibility was Jennifer Johnston's *Fool's Sanctuary.* Set in her native Ireland, against a 1920's background, it portrayed the dilemma of an ardent young Republican torn between political ideals and loyalty to the Anglo-Irish family of the girl he loved. In *Circles of Deceit,* by Nina Bawden, the painter-hero, a successful copyist of old masters, was in his turn deceived by both his wives and unable to communicate with a loved schizophrenic son.

*English novelist Penelope Lively won the Booker McConnell Prize for* Moon Tiger, *a look back at the modern era through the eyes of a fictional historian.*

*Margaret Drabble's novel* The Radiant Way *views contemporary Britain through the eyes of three women friends of widely differing backgrounds.*

The twin themes of Fay Weldon's *The Heart of the Country* were the "wickedness of men and the wretchedness of women" and the ills of our society. Weldon charted the progress of a helpless young woman who learned to cope in a cold, hard world of predatory men and the welfare state. In *The Book of Mrs. Noah,* by Michèle Roberts, an archetypal everywoman obsessed with the wrongs of her sex conjured up an ark and peopled it with female discontents endlessly debating their grievances. In another fantasy, Nigel Williams's *Witchcraft,* a hack screenwriter was haunted by the ghost of a Puritan witch-hunter.

Malcolm Bradbury's hero in *Cuts* pursued a dual career as don and media man. The novel was a caustic commentary on the state of Britain in the mid-1980's. The central character of Stanley Middleton's 26th novel, *After a Fashion,* was also a lecturer disenchanted with the academic scene.

Two accomplished novelists published read-able volumes of short stories. The recurring theme of those in *Sugar,* by A. S. Byatt, was the pervasiveness of the past. The nine stories in Rose Tremain's *The Garden of the Villa Mollini* subtly explored aspects of man as gardener attempting to civilize unregenerate nature.

**Biography.** In *Thackeray's Universe,* Catherine Peters assembled many of her subject's caricatures, family sketches, and illustrations to his own work. These shed new light on Thackeray's writing. In her candid, sympathetic, and often witty biography, *Rebecca West: A Life,* Victoria Glendinning examined some striking inconsistencies in the career, personality, and relationships of this radical political journalist and battling feminist.

Andro Linklater's entertaining biography *Compton Mackenzie* chronicled the events of

### Elementary, My Dear Watson

The one hundredth birthday of that most famous detective of literature—Sherlock Holmes—was celebrated in 1987 by parties in Britain (in the House of Commons, no less), the United States, Australia, Japan, and points between. The creation of Sir Arthur Conan Doyle (1859–1930), Sherlock Holmes first appeared in a story published in Beeton's Christmas Annual of 1887 and went on to solve mysteries in over 60 stories, all but four of them narrated by his loyal companion, Dr. John Watson. The familiar figure of the great detective—complete with pipe, cape, deerstalker hat (and hypodermic needle)—has been portrayed by such film stars as Basil Rathbone, John Barrymore, and Nicol Williamson, and most recently (in a British television series) by Jeremy Brett, who is a sardonic, super-intellectual Holmes. Such organizations as the 800-member Sherlock Holmes Society in Britain and the Baker Street Irregulars keep alive the Holmes legend, so much so that about 40 letters a week addressed to Holmes arrive at 221B Baker Street, the nonexistent address of the master "private eye." All letters receive a standard reply from the public relations department of the London bank now standing on that site: "Mr. Holmes thanks you for your letter. At the moment he is in retirement in Sussex, keeping bees."

a long and crowded life, including the novelist's intelligence work in Greece during World War I. *Little Wilson and Big God,* the first part of the self-styled "confessions" of Anthony Burgess (born Jack Wilson), portrays the ebullient novelist against backgrounds ranging from Manchester in the 1920's to Malaya in the 1950's.

**Drama.** A new work from playwright Alan Ayckbourn, *A Small Family Business,* depicted the plight of a hapless innocent plunged into a world of fraud and corruption. In *Melon,* Simon Gray's penetrating study of middle-aged marital jealousy, a successful publisher was happy with his "open" marriage until he found himself cuckolded by a friend. The target of Caryl Churchill's hard-hitting *Serious Money* was the tricky, ruthless world of financial speculation. *Fashion,* by Doug Lucie, was an astringent satire on modern electioneering.

In Claire MacDonald's unusual play *The Sleep,* a psychiatrist awakens a woman from 40 years' sleeping sickness. *Portraits,* by veteran dramatist William Douglas Home, was based on the life of Augustus John. The story began in 1944 and ended with the artist's last years, which were marked by despair and diminishing talent. M.W.

## WORLD

Newly translated works by Günter Grass, Louis Aragon, Natalia Ginzburg, and Gabriel García Márquez attracted international attention in 1987, as did novels by the young German writer Patrick Süskind.

**Austrian, German.** On the international scene the sensation of the year proved to be the novel *Perfume: The Story of a Murderer (Das Parfum,* 1984). It is the work of Patrick Süskind, an unknown young German writer who spends most of his time in seclusion in Paris. The book—which has been translated into at least 23 languages and has sold more than 2 million copies—is set in 18th-century France. It is the picaresque story of an orphan who has no bodily odors and who murders people whose odors intrigue him. His ambition is to become the greatest perfume maker in history. Attracting attention at home was Süskind's new work *Die Taube* ("The Pigeon"), in which a common pigeon unsettles the routine life of a Parisian bank doorman.

In *The Rat (Die Rättin,* 1986), Günter Grass assembles many of his earlier fictional characters and introduces in parable form a doomsday figure, a female rat who will, it seems, preside over humanity's demise. From East Germany came a memorable novel by Jurek Becker, *Bronsteins Kinder* ("Bronstein's Children"), which starkly depicts the lingering effects of the Nazi era on the lives of both the older and the younger generations. Similar territory is covered—mainly through the eyes of children—in Gert Hofman's novel *Our Conquest (Unsere Eroberung,* 1984). The dark side of the remarkable German recovery after World War II is depicted in Dieter Wellershoff's much-debated novel *Winner Takes All (Der Sieger nimmt alles,* 1983).

*Die Verzauberung* (1976), the masterpiece of exiled Austrian novelist Hermann Broch, which was published posthumously, has been translated as *The Spell.* An intricate narrative, it probes the mass psychosis in Germany that fostered Hitler's dictatorship. Broch owes much

*Patrick Süskind leaped to fame with* Perfume: The Story of a Murder, *a bizarre novel of 18th-century France.*

of his insight to studies of mob psychology by Elias Canetti, the Bulgarian-born German-language writer who won a 1981 Nobel Prize for literature; his memoirs also were being published. Another important memoir, *T.M.: Tagebücher* ("Diary") *1944-1946*, comes from the posthumous manuscripts of Thomas Mann; it clarifies Mann's pessimism about the possibility of change in the German mentality and explains his preference for living out his days in Switzerland.

**French.** In the late 1920's the surrealist writer Louis Aragon was at work on a gigantic novel, but its parts were distributed among friends and lost or destroyed. Now fragments of the work have been reconstructed and published under the title *La Défense de l'infini et les aventures de Jean-Foutre la Bite* ("In Defense of the Infinite and the Adventures of Jean-Foutre la Bite"). In addition, Aragon's 1924 fiction-sketches *Le Libertinage* have now been translated as *The Libertine*. Both works have stylistic power and embrace large casts of characters whose self-conscious ruminations about the passage of time and about conflicts of identity and sexuality give them poignancy. Novelist Marguerite Duras is again drawing attention with *Les Yeux bleus cheveux noirs* ("Blue Eyes and Black Hair") and *The Sea Wall* (translated in late 1986 from *Un Barrage contre la Pacifique*, 1950). Both novels are semiautobiographical and rely on cinematic techniques to piece together fragmented love affairs and give them retrospective meaning. Louise Colet, the model for Emma in *Madame Bovary*, turned the tables by portraying her lover, Flaubert, in the novel *Lui contemporain* (1859; republished in French in 1973). Now appearing in English, *Lui: A View of Him* gives us an intimate look at the woman Flaubert immortalized.

**Italian.** In *Storia di Casa Leopardi* ("The History of the Leopardi Family"), biographer Mario Picchi unfolds the life of the influential poet Giacomo Leopardi (1798-1837) and gives a brilliant account of the political and social background of the time. The range of the late Italo Calvino's intellect is demonstrated in *The Literature Machine*, a wide-ranging selection of literary and personal essays. The book contains Calvino's unique reading of the works of Homer, Ovid, Voltaire, and Stendhal. The

growing international fame of Natalia Ginzburg, Italy's most prominent woman writer, has prompted the translation of *The Little Virtues* (*Le piccole virtù*, 1972), a memoir that tells of life under fascism and of war and survival.

**Japanese.** The works of two distinguished Japanese novelists, Yasunari Kawabata and Shiga Naoya (who both died in the early 1970's), appeared in translation during the year. Kawabata's *The Old Capital* is a poetic evocation of the old culture-saturated city of Kyoto, and Naoya's *The Paper Door and Other Stories* is a collection of masterful tales about ordinary people who are beset with bizarre psychological problems.

**Latin American, Spanish.** Isabel Allende's novel *Of Love and Shadows* (*De amor y de sombra*, 1984) and Gabriel García Márquez's *The Adventures of Miguel Littin* (*Aventura de Miguel Littin, clandestine en Chile*) take a mordantly satiric and realistic view of contemporary Chilean life.

**Norwegian.** Ibsen aficionados may be surprised to learn that the great playwright was also a poet. John Northam's version of the large number of poems written between 1851 and 1894, entitled Ibsen's *Poems*, and his illuminating commentary introduce us for the first time in translation to an important though neglected part of Ibsen's work.

**Polish.** First commissioned and then suppressed by Polish authorities, *"Them": Stalin's Polish Puppets* (*Oni*, 1985) was published by an émigré group in London. Its author, Teresa Toranska, did extensive interviews with Poland's old-guard Communist leaders of the 1940's and 1950's. She came up with a brutally candid political and social picture of the times that is indispensable to an understanding of the present.

**Russian.** Will the present Soviet policy of glasnost, or openness, change the face of the Soviet Union? In his satirical novel *Moscow 2042* (*Moskva 2042*), the expatriate Vladimir Voinovich does not hold much hope; he believes the effects of glasnost on life and politics will be merely cosmetic. The poet Andrei Voznesensky is as well known in the West as he is in the Soviet Union. But because of the ambiguity of his work, he is neither totally

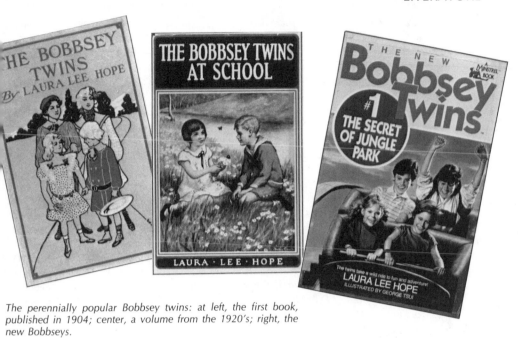

*The perennially popular Bobbsey twins: at left, the first book, published in 1904; center, a volume from the 1920's; right, the new Bobbseys.*

accepted by the one nor totally rejected by the other. A selection of superbly translated poems by Voznesensky, *An Arrow in the Wall*, shows sophistication and emotional power.     S.M.

### BOOKS FOR CHILDREN

In 1987, Caldecott medalist William Steig reached a graceful 80, Margaret Wise Brown's classic *Goodnight Moon* turned a youthful 40, *The Cat in the Hat* took age 30 in stride, and a reprint of *The Poky Little Puppy* became the one billionth Little Golden Book to be printed. (The Golden Book series is credited with launching the mass marketing of children's books in 1942.) Frances Hodgson Burnett's *The Secret Garden* entered the public domain, resulting in a barrage of editions, from knockoff to deluxe. This season also saw the reintroduction of Beatrix Potter's 23 little books; the publisher rephotographed the original art for editions of *The Tale of Peter Rabbit* and other Potter titles. Because of technological advances, the illustrations have a clarity of detail that could not have been envisioned in the author's time.

**Trends in Titles.** The trend toward realism continued, with a dramatic increase in excellent nonfiction for both the picture book set and older readers. Outstanding titles included the astonishing *Being Born* by Sheila Kitzinger, photographed by Lennart Nilsson; the award-winning *Volcano: The Eruption and Healing of Mount St. Helens* by Patricia Lauber; *Foodworks* by the Ontario Science Center, illustrated by Linda Hendry; and *Growing Vegetable Soup* by Lois Ehlert. Other nonfiction notables were *How a Book Is Made* by Aliki; *New Providence: A Changing Cityscape* by Renata von Tscharner and Ronald Lee Fleming, illustrated by Dennis Orloff; *American Heroes: In and Out of School* by Nat Hentoff; *Do Animals Dream?* by Joyce Pope; *Milk: The Fight for Purity* by James Cross Giblin; and *Martin Luther King Day* by Linda Lowery, illustrated by Hetty Mitchell. Among books that marked the bicentennial of the U.S. Constitution were *Shh! We're Writing the Constitution* by Jean Fritz, illustrated by Tomie dePaola, a new collaboration by Betsy and Giulio Maestro called *A More Perfect Union: The Story of Our Constitution*, and Lois Lenski's *Sing a Song of People*, illustrated by Giles Larouche.

Books on AIDS started to show up on children's publishers' lists, as well as books dealing directly and indirectly with apartheid, such as

# LITERATURE

Caroline Meyer's *Voices of South Africa* and Shirley Gordon's *Waiting for the Rain*. *Nettie's Trip South* by Ann Turner, illustrated by Ronald Himler, gave young readers a look at America's own racial injustices. *Flossie and the Fox* by Patrica McKissack, illustrated by Rachel Isadora, was an endearing tale of an ingenious black girl who outwits a fox. In *Nancy No-Size*, Mary Hoffman and illustrator Jennifer Northway recreated the snug world of an urban black family. There were two retellings—received with mixed reviews—of the Uncle Remus tales, which were first told by Joel Chandler Harris: *Jump! The Adventures of Brer Rabbit* by Van Dyke Parks and Malcolm Jones, illustrated by Barry Moser, and *The Tales of Uncle Remus* by Julius Lester, illustrated by Jerry Pinkney.

Virginia Hamilton followed up her highly acclaimed book *The House of Dies Drear* with *The Mystery of Drear House*, which was equally well received. The first title was brought to the small screen on public television, which has become a successful forum for other children's books. Previously, *Anne of Green Gables* was turned into an award-winning series, and Jim Arnosky's books—*Drawing from Nature* and *Drawing Life in Motion*—became the basis for another series, which premiered early in October.

The year produced the usual crop of retold fairy tales and legends. Exceptional among them were James Marshall's wickedly funny *Red Riding Hood*, which took a tongue-in-cheek approach to the Charles Perrault original, and Kate Greenaway medalist Fiona French's *Snow White in New York*, a bright Jazz Age bauble done in dazzling art deco. More imported titles found a niche among American readers, most notably *Miss Fanshawe and the Great Dragon Adventure* by Sue Scullard; *Amazing Maisy's Family Tree* by Lynn Zirkel, illustrated by Peter Bowman; *Bibi's Birthday Surprise* by Michel Gay; *Possum Magic* by Mem Fox, illustrated by Julie Vivas; *Mister King* by Raija Siekkinen, illustrated by Hannu Taina and translated by Tim Stella; and *Bossyboots* by David Cox.

**Prizes.** The Caldecott Medal, awarded to the illustrator of the best American picture book of the year, went to Richard Egielski for *Hey,*

*Al,* written by Arthur Yorinks (Farrar, Straus & Giroux). It told the story of a janitor and his dog, who lead lives of not-so-quiet desperation before they stumble into paradise. The Caldecott Honor Books were *Alphabatics*, illustrated by Suse MacDonald (Bradbury); *Rumpelstiltskin*, illustrated by Paul O. Zelinsky (Dutton); and *The Village of Round and Square Houses*, illustrated by Ann Grifalconi (Little, Brown). The Newbery Medal, awarded for the "most distinguished contribution" to children's literature, went to Sid Fleischman for *The Whipping Boy* (Greenwillow), a rollicking story of Prince Brat and the boy who endures daily beatings on his behalf. The Newbery honor titles were Cynthia Rylant's *A Fine White Dust* (Bradbury), Patricia Lauber's *Volcano* (Bradbury), and Marion Dane Bauer's *On My Honor* (Clarion). Scott O'Dell, a previous Newbery and Hans Christian Andersen medalist, won the Scott O'Dell Award for Historical Fiction (an award he created in 1981) for his well-received *Streams to the River, River to the Sea: A Novel of Sacagawea* (Houghton Mifflin). The Hans Christian Andersen medalists were Robert Ingpen for illustration and Patricia Wrightson for writing. Both are from Australia.

**Old Favorites.** The year saw a flurry of backlist publishing and a reissuance of out-of-print titles. Many of them were in paperback, a form that now dominates bookstore sales. Old favorites could once again be found in bookstores, some for the first time in a generation. They included *What Do You Say, Dear?* by Sesyle Joslin, illustrated by Maurice Sendak; *A Little House of Your Own* by Beatrice Schenk du Regniers, illustrated by Irene Haas; *Phewtus the Squirrel* by V. H. Drummond; the Miss Flora McFlimsey books by Mariana; and *Calico Bush* by Rachel Field, illustrated by Allen Lewis.                    K.O.F.

**LOUISIANA.** See Statistics of the World.

**LUXEMBOURG.** In 1987 the Luxembourgian economy once again performed exceptionally well in most areas. Growth in the construction sector, new industrial ventures, and the dynamic performance of banking activity were particularly noteworthy. The gross domestic product was expected to rise 2.5 percent, as it continued a strong recovery. Industrial production in the steel industry was expected to advance 2 percent. The steel sector continued to be depressed because of slackened global demand. Consumer prices were expected to rise only 1 percent, and unemployment was estimated at a little over 1 percent.

The Christian Social and Socialist coalition government of Prime Minister Jacques Santer won parliamentary approval for a 1987 budget that included substantial personal and business tax reductions. Government policy continued to emphasize and support economic diversification measures to compensate for declining employment in the steel industry. Parliament approved legislation facilitating scientific and technical research in the public sector and the transfer of technology to the private sector. Efforts were intensified to encourage new foreign investment, especially from the United States and Japan. An early retirement program was approved, beginning at age 57, applicable to persons in industries characterized by overemployment, such as steel, or in other areas where unemployed workers were available.

See STATISTICS OF THE WORLD.          W.C.C.

# M

**MADAGASCAR.** *See* STATISTICS OF THE WORLD.
**MAINE.** *See* STATISTICS OF THE WORLD.
**MALAWI.** *See* STATISTICS OF THE WORLD.
**MALAYSIA.** Late in 1987, Malaysia's democratic traditions were challenged when, in an effort to crack down on dissent, the government of Prime Minister Mahathir Mohamed detained opposition leaders without trial and arrested numerous other critics.

In April, Mahathir had narrowly won reelection as president of the United Malays National Organization (UMNO). In order to consolidate his control of the government, the prime minister then removed a number of dissidents from the cabinet, including Abdullah Ahmad Bedawi from the Defense Ministry. Bedawi was the only dissident to win a major office in the party election, as he captured one of the three elected party vice presidencies.

In the days surrounding Malaysia's Independence Day (August 31), five mosques were burned in the state of Pahang. Some Malays, who comprise most of the Islamic population, suspected Christians were responsible for the arson, but no evidence was found to support this suspicion.

Although the Chinese community's main political concern was government plans for continuing the New Economic Policy (aimed at increasing Malay corporate ownership), education issues remained sensitive. The faculty at the University of Malaya required that elective courses in the Chinese and Indian studies departments be taught in the Malay language. Chinese and Indian minorities feared that this action marked a new attack on vernacular education.

Tensions heightened in October after the government assigned administrators not fluent in Mandarin to Chinese-language schools. Following large rallies by Malays and Chinese and a shooting in a racially tense part of Kuala Lumpur, opposition leaders and Chinese politicians and academics were arrested and detained, and the government suspended the publication of three newspapers. Among those arrested were two top leaders of the main opposition party, the Democratic Action Party. As the crackdown continued, by early November about 100 politicians, church workers, consumer advocates, and others were being held without trial. The wave of arrests and the sudden official moves made against dissent shocked observers both inside and outside Malaysia.

Despite renewed economic growth (a 2 percent growth rate was expected), unemployment remained a serious problem, especially among university-educated Malays. A key aspect of government efforts to improve the livelihood of Malays (who make up a majority of the population but are generally less well

On a Kuala Lumpur sidewalk, Malaysians read in the October 28th English-language newspaper The Star about detention of people without trial under the Internal Security Act. As of the next day, the government shut down the Star, along with two other papers.

off economically than the ethnic Chinese) has been support of university education. With a stagnant economy, however, new graduates have encountered saturated job markets.

Since coming to office in 1981, Mahathir has cooled relations with Britain, Malaysia's former colonial ruler (in 1983 he instituted a "buy British last" policy for government contracts). In August 1987, however, he paid his first official visit to Britain and actively courted British investment, promising fair treatment.

*See* STATISTICS OF THE WORLD. K.M.

**MALDIVES.** *See* STATISTICS OF THE WORLD.

**MALI.** *See* STATISTICS OF THE WORLD.

**MALTA.** The Nationalist Party, headed by Eddie Fenech Adami, won a narrow victory in the May 9, 1987, general election. Adami's party, which is linked to the group of European Christian Democratic parties, ended Labor's 16-year rule by taking 50.91 percent of the vote. An exceptionally high 96 percent of Malta's registered voters went to the polls.

To avoid a repeat of the 1981 election outcome, when the Nationalists won a majority of the votes but received a minority of parliamentary seats, two compromise constitutional amendments had been passed in January. One amendment, demanded by the Nationalists, gave the party winning a majority of votes the absolute right to hold a parliamentary majority and form the new government. The other, demanded by Labor, affirmed Malta's neutrality and barred foreign military bases.

Premier Adami spoke of reconciliation with his opponents, a welcome gesture after a heated and occasionally violent campaign that resulted in two deaths and many injuries. During the campaign, Adami and his party promised to improve the welfare program by eliminating alleged waste and corruption, to seek better relations with the United States, and to apply for membership in the European Community. At home, the Nationalists said, they would end bitter feuding between the government and the Catholic Church.

The unemployment rate declined early in the year, thanks to the Labor government's campaign strategy of winning votes by creating more government jobs. Exports and tourist arrivals were running ahead of 1986 rates, and inflation was low.

*See* STATISTICS OF THE WORLD. P.J.M.

**MANITOBA.** *See* STATISTICS OF THE WORLD.

**MANUFACTURING INDUSTRIES.** Manufacturing output increased during 1987, as did employment and productivity. The October tock market decline clouded future prospects but industrial indicators were positive late in he year). Although exports of manufactures ncreased during the year, imports were rising even faster, and a record trade deficit, reaching $17.6 billion in October, contributed to strong protectionist sentiment in Congress. Orders for durable goods were running 7 percent above 1986, according to 11-month figures.

**Overall Trends.** In the third quarter, manufacturing output rose an annual rate of 8.2 percent over the preceding quarter, and productivity was up by an annual rate of 2.6 percent. Factories, mines, and utilities operated at 82.1 percent of capacity in December, the highest level in almost eight years. Employment in factories increased at an annual rate of 2.3 percent in the third quarter, although it was still some 6 percent below the peak of close to 20.7 million workers reached in the summer of 1981. For the whole year, industrial output rose 5.2 percent, the best showing since 1984.

A diminution of workplace quality and an excessive amount of workplace capacity remained causes of concern, and the critical U.S. trade imbalance was being blamed in large part on manufacturers' frequent indifference to product quality. A weak U.S. trade policy, failure to harness technology, and a lack of long-range planning were also blamed.

**Trade and Protectionism.** The U.S. merchandise trade deficit continued to run at slightly above the level of 1986, when the United States imported $169.8 billion more than it exported. It had been expected that the heavy decline in the dollar's value would after a while cause the trade deficit to turn around by making American goods more competitive abroad and imports costlier to American consumers. But economists said many foreign companies were cutting prices and profits in order to maintain their U.S. market share; some Japanese firms were shifting production to plants in Mexico to hold down costs on goods destined for the United States. Prices of some imports, especially from the Far East (not including Japan), were unaffected by the dollar devaluation, since the countries of origin let their currencies rise and fall with the dollar. Also contributing to the high U.S. trade deficit was an increase in oil prices and oil imports.

Congress reacted to the continuing deficit with a wave of protectionist fervor, which led both houses to press for tough trade legislation. The trade bill passed in differing versions by both houses would require the president to take retaliatory action (for example, imposing tariffs or quotas) against countries deemed to have unfair trade practices or excess trade surpluses with the United States—unless such practices or heavy trade imbalances could be ended by negotiation. In September the House passed a separate bill aimed at protecting U.S. manufacturers of textiles, clothing, and footwear—by setting import quotas for those products. All such legislation faced a likely presidential veto if it received final congressional approval.

**Steel.** Production of raw steel amounted to 56,858,890 tons over the first seven months of the year, down from 56,972,239 tons at the same point in 1986. In midyear the steel industry recorded its first six-month profit since 1981, and steel company leaders voiced cautious optimism about the future of the industry. Steel-makers had benefited from capacity cuts of more than 25 percent over the preceding five years, as well as from tax benefits, sales of assets, and other factors. However, the picture in steel, as in other industries, was mixed. Late in the year, three steel-makers—LTV Corporation (the number-two U.S. steel-maker), Wheeling-Pittsburgh, and Sharon Steel—were operating under the strictures of Chapter 11 bankruptcy reorganization. Moreover, Bethlehem Steel (the number-three producer) noted, in a preliminary prospective offering 12 million new common shares, that possible "adverse changes in business circumstances or liquidity" in the future might make it prudent to file for bankruptcy.

The industry leader, USX (formerly U.S. Steel), survived a six-month work stoppage—the longest ever in the industry—that ended in February; it cut its labor costs 15 percent, and had on-stream in Gary, Ind., a year-old continuous caster that was able to sharply cut energy costs and boosted productivity. However, USX was still losing money, and its relations with its employees remained strained in the aftermath of the strike. About 6,000 workers had been cut by the company in the four years before the strike, and some 3,700 out of 22,000 workers were laid off during its aftermath. Union officials claimed that accidents in USX plants were increasing.

With bankruptcies on the rise, those steel companies that escaped bankruptcy were faced with more competitors that had significantly reduced costs and enjoyed special court protection. In particular, bankrupt companies were able to have their pension obligations assumed by the federal Pension Benefit Guarantee Corporation (PBGC), founded in 1974 to ensure that pensions owed by liquidated companies would be paid to employees. By September, the agency was operating with a deficit amounting to $4.1 billion, of which liabilities for underfunded steel-company pensions made

*Continuous casting technology offers steelmakers lower energy costs and higher productivity. In this multistrand continuous casting operation, billets—small, semifinished pieces of steel—are emerging, to be rolled into such shapes as bars and rods.*

up 75 percent; the largest were those for LTV funds—some $2.3 billion. In late September LTV became the first company to have pension obligations returned to it by the PBGC, reducing the agency's deficit to under $2 billion. The PBGC contended that LTV could afford to finance three of its pension plans and had sought a competitive advantage by passing them on to the PBGC. The company was appealing the agency's action in federal court.

In the forefront of improved technology in the industry was the steady growth and adaptation of step-shortening continuous casters that spew out endless slabs of semifinished steel for subsequent rolling. One mini-mill firm, the Nucor Corporation, proposed to pour molten steel into much thinner slabs and hence consume still less energy and manpower while generating less waste. Nucor executives believed it would take just five workers to do what otherwise required 30. A big problem for the innovator will be finding raw material sources capable of meeting major steel-consumer quality standards.

**Paper.** Paper and paperboard production, as reported by the American Paper Institute, set a record high rate of 73.5 million tons per year based on 1987's first-eight-month figures. This was about 5 percent above the high a year earlier and well above the average growth characteristic of the last decade. Forces sustaining this new growth included the rising demand for office-copy and computer printout papers and an ever-expanding need for corrugated shipping containers. Magazines, directories, and catalogues, plus increased orders for commercial printing, have helped boost coated paper demand every year since 1977.

While both imports and exports of paper have responded sharply to gyrations in the value of the dollar, exports appeared to have aligned more closely with dollar-value changes, moving downward in 1984 and 1985, then recovering strongly in 1986. This recovery continued into 1987, hitting a record high for the first seven months of 5.3 million tons per year. Over the long term, paper and paperboard demand tends to move in line with total economic activity measured in terms of real gross national product. In the first eight months of

987, however, the new supply of paper and paperboard rose faster than the GNP. This brought the new supply/GNP ratio to a point somewhat above the average for the past decade, a signal of possible increases of product use within the U.S. economy.

**Textiles.** Much of the textile industry, but not all segments, showed signs of recovery from the mid-1985 low point. At the close of 1987's first half, mill shipments were 4.2 percent over the same point in 1986. Apparel shipments, seasonally adjusted, increased in both first and second quarters. Notwithstanding the industry's 90 percent capacity-utilization score, there was a profit increase in early 1987 of just 12 percent. Cash flow in textile firms has risen steadily, beginning in 1986, encouraging a stepped-up outlay for new plants and manufacturing equipment.

Close to 736,000 workers now are employed in textile-industry plants, a significant rise, and the average work-week has continued to increase. Textile-mill fiber consumption rose through the first half of 1987, with a year-to-date figure 9.9 percent higher than in 1986. The strongest growth rate was in cotton, which climbed 15.5 percent above levels a year earlier. Wool rose 11.8 percent over the previous year; artificial fibers experienced more modest gains.

**Machine Tools.** Tax law changes have had an adverse impact on capital spending for machine tools, but the decline of the dollar may have contributed to a boost in orders for export. For 1987, net new domestic orders were down 2.7 percent over 1986, while foreign orders were up 18.9 percent; overall, orders fell slightly, by less than 1 percent, from the 1986 level.                                    L.R.H.

**MARYLAND.** See STATISTICS OF THE WORLD.
**MASSACHUSETTS.** See STATISTICS OF THE WORLD.
**MAURITANIA.** See STATISTICS OF THE WORLD.
**MAURITIUS.** See STATISTICS OF THE WORLD.

**MEXICO.** The question of who would succeed President Miguel de la Madrid Hurtado when his term ends in 1988 was a major concern in Mexico during 1987. Late in the year, the country faced a growing economic crisis.

**Politics.** Carlos Salinas de Gortari became heir apparent to President de la Madrid in October, when the long-ruling Institutional Revolution-

*Cocaine and heroin go up in smoke as a Mexican soldier stands guard. Mexico's army burned vast amounts of the drugs, confiscated from smugglers during 1987.*

ary Party (PRI) finally named him its candidate for the presidency. Although the formal election was not scheduled to take place until July 1988 and opposition parties were participating the PRI has not lost a major election since it was organized in 1929. The nomination process takes place behind closed doors; generally it is assumed that the sitting president, who cannot run for reelection, makes the choice. In August the party had announced six names as under consideration. Salinas, the secretary of budget and planning in the de la Madrid cabinet, holds graduate degrees in public administration and government from Harvard and would be one of the youngest men ever to hold the Mexican presidency.

**Economy.** While the country remained in the grip of depression, the outlook appeared slightly improved early in the year. Thanks largely to

$12 billion in new foreign credit, negotiated with the aid of the Reagan administration, foreign reserves hit a record high. President de la Madrid announced that for the first time in a decade the foreign debt actually had been reduced, and after years of negative growth the economy once again was expanding. However, in October stocks on the Mexican stock exchange lost over 50 percent of their value; these losses triggered a financial panic, during which the peso nosedived in value against the dollar. Inflation reached a reported annual rate of more than 140 percent by November. On December 14 the peso was officially devalued another 18 percent, in an effort to stabilize the currency.

The next day, the government announced wage increases for unionized workers, to head off a threatened general strike. The government also unveiled a new "economic solidarity pact"; the program included tax rises and budget cuts to stem the large budget deficit, along with plans to raise the price of basic services and to index wages. Late in the year, a plan was proposed by Morgan Guaranty Trust Company under which banks would forgive a large portion of Mexico's $70 billion foreign bank debt in return for U.S.-backed bonds issued by Mexico.

The bureaucracy found itself moving away increasingly from the state capitalism that Mexico had adopted in 1970; by late 1987, the government had reduced by half (to about 750) the number of state-run companies. Private industry, meanwhile, was turning to nonpetroleum exports in order to survive. Exports of manufactured goods were on the increase.

Protests by U.S. organized labor had led to the enactment in the United States of the 1986 Simpson-Rodino immigration act, which penalizes U.S. employers for knowingly hiring illegal aliens. According to some estimates, there are about 6 million Mexicans living illegally in the United States. The availability of jobs north of the border has been regarded both as a safety valve for Mexico, where unemployment is rampant, and as an important source of U.S. dollars. As the year 1987 drew to a close, however, relatively few longtime illegal immigrants in the United States had been forced to return home.

**Relations With the United States.** Relations with Washington improved considerably. Much of the credit went to Ambassador Charles J Pilliod, Jr., a spotlight-shunning former businessman who emphasized the contribution Mexican authorities have made in stemming the flow of drugs toward the border. In November the two governments signed a framework agreement under which mechanisms would be set up for dealing with trade disputes and negotiations would begin on curbing trade and investment barriers. On the negative side Mexico and the United States remained at odds over U.S. policy regarding Central America.

**Latin American Affairs.** In recent years, Mexico has concentrated on closer ties with the rest of Latin America. Mexico, Colombia, Panama, and Venezuela were charter members of the Contadora Group, established in 1983 to seek peaceful solutions to the problems in Central America. The group met in February 1987 and signed a 20-point economic pact promoting regional growth. There were state visits to Mexico by the presidents of Argentina, Brazil, Costa Rica, Peru, and Venezuela. President de la Madrid traveled to Guatemala and Jamaica. In November, Mexico hosted a summit of Latin American leaders, attended by the presidents of Argentina, Brazil, Colombia, Panama, Peru, Uruguay, and Venezuela.

**Education, Culture, and Science.** The government announced that approximately 93 percent of the adult population was literate. Of Mexico's 82 million inhabitants, some 36 million were enrolled in the regular school system or in adult education programs. In spite of the economic crisis, 590 public libraries were opened; now nearly three-fourths of Mexico's municipalities have such institutions. A dozen new museums also were inaugurated during the year. Ecology became a major issue in the country, especially in Mexico City, where smog became so serious that birds were dropping from the sky. No solutions were forthcoming, but the long-ignored problem finally attracted attention. Plans to open the country's first thermonuclear plant in Veracruz state stirred protest, and its future remained in doubt.

See STATISTICS OF THE WORLD.        J.H.B.

**MICHIGAN.** See STATISTICS OF THE WORLD.

**MICRONESIA.** See PACIFIC ISLANDS.

# Middle East

**The escalation of hostilities between Iraq and Iran in the Gulf war and fears that the fighting would continue to spread, drawing in the Soviet Union and Western nations, dominated events in the Middle East during 1987. Because of differences among the Arabs and within the Israeli government over the proper forum for negotiations, little progress was made in the search for peace between Israel and its neighbors.**

Iran's defiance of UN cease-fire resolutions and relentless prosecution of the war with Iraq brought about a major realignment in Middle Eastern politics, as Syria for the first time joined with other Arab states in condemning Iran's belligerence. It was one of several signs that moderate and conservative Arab states, such as Jordan and Saudi Arabia, were in the ascendency in the Arab world and that at least temporarily, the conflict with Israel was no longer the primary concern of the Arab states.

**Iraq-Iran War.** The war between Iraq and Iran along their mutual border intensified early in the year, as Iranian offensives penetrated Iraq

*Iranian mines, shown here aboard the vessel Iran Ajr after it was stormed by U.S. forces in September, were a menace both for civilian shipping in the Persian Gulf and for the Western warships patrolling the waters in force.*

from Kurdistan in the north to the vicinity of Basra in the south and the fighting spilled into the waters of the Persian Gulf. With the help of Kurdish guerrillas inside Iraq seeking an autonomous Kurdistan, Iran captured several Iraqi border towns, but it was unable to overrun Iraqi defenses in its siege of Basra, Iraq's second-largest city. Each country stepped up air attacks on the other's capital and on other heavily populated cities and towns. Each accused the other of using chemical weapons contrary to international law. A United Nation inspection team that visited both countries in April charged that Iraq had stepped up its use of chemical weapons by launching attacks on civilians; while Iraq did not deny using chemical weapons, it maintained that they were no a major factor in the seven-year-old war.

With the spread of the war in the Gulf, scores of neutral merchant ships were attacked by both Iraq and Iran, and Iran's acquisition o Silkworm missiles from China gave it the means

*The deaths of Iranian pilgrims in Mecca strained already tense relations between Saudi Arabia and Iran. At a press conference, Saudi Prince Nayef bin Abdulaziz (far left) said the Iranian Shiite pilgrims had provoked the violence that led to over 400 deaths. Below, defiant Iranians surround the pilgrims' coffins.*

o close Gulf traffic entirely if it chose. The 12-nation European Community, which received over a quarter of its oil supplies from the Gulf, issued a joint declaration in September deploring escalation of the "tanker war" and calling for a cease-fire.

Because of the extensive economic aid and transit facilities it provided to Iraq, Kuwait's shipping was a principal target of Iran. To protect its tankers and other vessels, Kuwait appealed for protection to the Soviet Union, the United States, and China. Moscow responded quickly by agreeing to lease Kuwait three tankers, thus granting it Soviet naval protection. After lengthy discussions and much debate in Congress, U.S. President Ronald Reagan authorized the U.S. reflagging of 11 Kuwaiti tankers, half its tanker fleet. With the transfer of the ships to a U.S. holding company, they received American names and the protection of the U.S. Navy. Late in the year, China was still considering Kuwait's request to register Kuwaiti vessels under the Chinese flag. Meanwhile, China was simultaneously selling arms to both Iran and Iraq.

Reflagging Kuwait's ships and escorting them with American warships, rather than deterring Iranian attacks, led to direct confrontations between U.S. and Iranian forces. In September a U.S. helicopter attacked and disabled an Iranian ship found laying mines in the Gulf, and in October, American warships destroyed two offshore Iranian oil platforms in retaliation for an attack on one of the reflagged ships. An American warship, the *Stark*, was inadvertently hit by an Iraqi warplane in May, leaving 37 American sailors dead and many wounded. (A U.S. team investigating the incident reported that Baghdad had taken steps to prevent similar incidents in the future.)

Despite Kuwait's plea for American protection, it refused to permit U.S. warships to use its port facilities, nor would other Arab Gulf states allow the use of their ports. After some hesitation, the British, French, Italian, Belgian, and Dutch governments began in September and October to escort commercial vessels and to share minesweeping duties with the United States.

**International Reaction.** International concern over the war led to several meetings of the UN Security Council and to unanimous resolutions in July and September demanding an immediate cease-fire. The resolutions called on both sides to "discontinue all military actions . . . and withdraw all forces to the internationally recognized boundaries without delay." They also urged the release and repatriation of war prisoners and requested the UN secretary-general to establish an impartial body to determine responsibility for the conflict. While Iraq agreed to accept the resolutions, Iran insisted that the investigation to determine responsibility for the war precede implementation of the other provisions. The speaker of Iran's Parliament accused the UN of procrastination and deception and threatened to respond with "a resolute blow on the battlefronts" to reaffirm his country's rights in the dispute.

Efforts by the United States to strengthen the UN actions with an arms embargo on whichever side refused to adhere to resolutions were seen as an attempt to pressure Iran. When neither the Soviet Union, Japan, nor any Western power came out in support of the proposed embargo, the United States imposed a unilateral ban in October on all Iranian imports and tightened restrictions on American exports to the country.

Iran's determination to pursue a militant foreign policy was demonstrated in July, when hundreds of Iranian pilgrims staged a political demonstration at the annual pilgrimage in Mecca, contrary to Saudi Arabian law and to established practice. In an apparently premeditated march on the Grand Mosque, the Iranians shouted anti-American and anti-Saudi slogans. When the Saudi police attempted to deter them, a riot erupted in which over 400 people were killed. The event caused consternation throughout the Islamic world; Iranian authorities used the occasion to rally the public against Saudi Arabia, the United States, and Israel. An attack on the Saudi embassy in Tehran by an angry Iranian mob in August left one Saudi diplomat dead.

Efforts by international organizations other than the UN to end or mediate the conflict were fruitless. A January meeting of the Islamic Conference Organization in Kuwait called for an end to the war, but it was boycotted by Iran. The war was also the major item at the

Arab League summit in Amman, Jordan, in November. The final resolution castigated Iran for "intransigence, provocations, and threats to the Arab Gulf states" and appealed to the international community to "exert efforts and adopt measures adequate to make the Iranian regime respond to the calls for peace." Observers were surprised by the nearly unanimous backing for the censure of Iran; only Libyan leader Muammar al-Qaddafi, who stayed away from the conference, refused to support the resolution. It was endorsed even by Syrian President Hafez al-Assad, one of the few Arab leaders who had maintained close ties with Iran. Syria's support was attributed to growing concern over a possible Iranian victory and fears that the extensive economic aid it received from Saudi Arabia would be cut off.

Saudi Arabia brought its denunciations of Iran to a December summit of the six-nation Gulf Cooperation Council, in Riyadh. King Fahd said Iran was trying to "export ideas strange to our Arab Islamic society" by means of the war and accused it of diverting the Arab world from its efforts against Israel. In a statement ending the summit, the nations urged the imposition of sanctions against Iran to induce its support of a truce with Iraq.

**Other Arab League Actions.** The Arab League summit reiterated support for the Palestinians, calling for the recovery of all occupied Arab territories and the restoration of the "inalienable national rights" of Palestinians. Expressing hope for a "just and permanent peace," the Arab leaders backed proposals for an international peace conference under UN sponsorship, with the participation of all five permanent Security Council members and all parties concerned, including the PLO, on an equal footing.

The growing influence of moderate regimes in the Arab world was indicated by the league's support for the reestablishment of relations between its members and Egypt, which had been broken since Egypt's separate peace treaty with Israel in 1979. Only Somalia, Oman, and Sudan among the 21 league members had maintained diplomatic ties with Cairo after the treaty; Jordan and Djibouti had restored relations in 1985. The league now resolved that any member should be free to reestablish ties "in accordance with its constitution and laws."

The wording was a compromise between the majority, which favored readmitting Egypt to the league, and those, especially Syria and Libya, that remained unforgiving. After the summit, a number of Arab countries, including Iraq, Morocco, and Saudi Arabia, renewed relations with Cairo.

**Proposed Peace Conference.** Negotiations over the proposed international peace conference continued throughout the year, but without substantial progress. In Israel, a major dispute within the cabinet was provoked by the issue. Foreign Minister Shimon Peres, striving to get the conference off the ground, called it "an opportunity that we have not had since the creation of the state of Israel." He accepted Jordan's proposal to include the Soviet Union in the conference and to allow Palestinians to participate as part of the Jordanian delegation. Details were allegedly worked out in secret meetings between Peres and Jordan's King Hussein. At the September session of the UN General Assembly, Peres elaborated on his position, proposing the establishment of three committees, allowing Israel to negotiate separately and face-to-face with Syria, Jordan, and Lebanon. No settlement would be imposed by the overall conference, and there would be no veto by the conference of arrangements agreed upon in the three committees. Peres also agreed that the conference would "solve the Palestinian problem in all its aspects." Israeli Prime Minister Yitzhak Shamir, however, adamantly rejected the Peres proposals, describing them as a "perverse and criminal" idea that must be "wiped off" the cabinet agenda.

**Gaza Riots.** Tension between Israel and Palestinians in the occupied Gaza Strip was pointed up in December by repeated clashes between residents and Israeli troops. More than 20 Palestinians died, and demonstrations and unrest spread to Arab communities on the West Bank and within pre-1967 Israel itself. Israel's use of force to quell the Gaza disturbances was condemned by the UN Security Council, with the United States abstaining but adding its own criticism.

**PLO Reconciliation.** In April, five Palestinian factions met in Algiers to discuss their differences. The five, the Democratic Front for the Liberation of Palestine, Al-Fatah, the Palestinan Communist Party, the Arab Liberation Front, and the Palestine Liberation Front, agreed to convene the Palestine National Council, the Palestinian parliament-in-exile, for the first time since 1984.

Since the last meeting of the council, opposition to Fatah leader and PLO Chairman Yasir Arafat had built up among the various factions, several of which called for his removal, citing his willingness to seek a compromise with Israel. As a condition for closing ranks, the opposition demanded that Arafat renounce his February 1985 pact with Jordan's King Hussein and sever all links with Egypt until President Hosni Mubarak scrapped the peace treaty with Israel. At the council meeting, in Algiers, the hard-liners were victorious: The accord with Hussein was rejected, Egypt was harshly denounced, and the PLO reorganized, although Arafat retained his post. Egypt responded by shutting most PLO offices in Cairo and breaking relations with Arafat.

In November, a peace accord was signed by the PLO and Shiite Amal militias, which had been engaged in one of the bloodiest of Lebanon's internal conflicts. It was estimated that about 3,000 Palestinians and Lebanese had been killed and twice that number wounded since the fighting began in 1984. Future prospects, however, remained uncertain.

*See also articles on individual countries mentioned and other Middle Eastern countries.*                                    D.P.

**MILITARY AND NAVAL AFFAIRS.** World military affairs were dominated in 1987 by an escalation of the Iran-Iraq war, which raised the specter of a wider conflict and prompted the United States, the Soviet Union, and several European nations to expand their naval presence in the Persian Gulf. The United States and the Soviet Union signed a treaty to eliminate their intermediate-range nuclear missiles. Talks aimed at reducing strategic nuclear arsenals moved more slowly, however, hampered by a dispute over President Ronald Reagan's space-based missile defense system. U.S. efforts to topple the Sandinista government in Nicaragua showed little progress, but a timetable for withdrawal of Soviet troops from Afghanistan was proposed. Marine guards at the U.S. embassy in Moscow were involved in a major espionage scandal. In the United States, the Reagan administration once again tilted with Congress over the defense budget, and Caspar Weinberger, defense secretary for seven years, resigned his post.

*The Palestine Liberation Organization's most prominent figures attend a meeting of the Palestinian National Council in April in Algiers. From left: PLO Chairman Yasir Arafat, Abu Ayyad, and Georges Habash.*

On May 17 an Iraqi jet fired missiles at the U.S.S. Stark in the Persian Gulf, killing 37 American sailors. Iraq apologized for the tragic incident, which it described as accidental. Above, an honor guard stands by the sailors' coffins at Dover Air Force Base in Delaware.

**Iran-Iraq War.** The war between Iran and Iraq entered its eighth bloody year in September. Despite a major offensive by Iran early in the year, the ground war remained deadlocked, with both sides occupying some enemy territory. Iraq continued its heavy aerial bombing of Iranian cities; Iran launched missile attacks on Baghdad and stepped up air attacks against Arab allies of Iraq, notably Kuwait. However, the most significant development in the conflict was a major escalation of the "tanker war" against enemy and neutral shipping in the Persian Gulf. Scores of oil tankers and other ships were attacked by Iranian and Iraqi jets during the year, causing havoc among oil-producing nations in the region and prompting the United States and several of its European allies to increase their military presence there.

In what was apparently a tragic accident, the frigate U.S.S. *Stark* was attacked by an Iraqi jet on May 17 while patrolling the Gulf. Thirty-seven American sailors were killed. Iraq apologized for the attack and claimed the pilot of the Mirage jet had thought the *Stark* was an Iranian warship when he launched two low-lying Exocet missiles. The captain of the *Stark* and two other officers were relieved of duty, and a naval board of inquiry recommended courts-martial for Captain Glenn R. Brindel, the commander, and Lieutenant Basil Monrief, the officer in charge of the ship's weapons systems. But the Navy announced in July that it would not court-martial the two officers; instead, they were issued letters of reprimand and were permitted to resign from the service.

The centerpiece of the heightened U.S. presence in the region was a decision to "reflag" 11 Kuwaiti tankers to American registry and to provide U.S. naval escorts for the tankers in hopes of halting Iranian attacks against neutral shipping. The new policy was also designed to counter growing Soviet influence in the region and to reassure moderate Arab nations still concerned over the revelations that the Reagan administration had sold arms to Iran. During the first convoy of reflagged tankers, in July, the oil tanker *Bridgeton* struck a mine apparently laid by Iran and was slightly damaged. The incident prompted a further escalation in U.S. military power in the Persian Gulf. By September, the U.S. Navy had deployed 30 warships in or near the Gulf, a force augmented by minesweepers and minesweeping helicopters from Great Britain, France, Italy, Belgium, and the Netherlands, as well as the United States.

On September 21, U.S. Army helicopters operating from the deck of a Navy frigate attacked an Iranian ship caught laying mines in international waters 50 miles northeast of Bahrain. The incident, in which at least 3 Iranian sailors were killed and 26 captured, escalated tensions between the Reagan administration and congressional critics concerned that the buildup in the Gulf might lead to a wider war. Some congressional leaders renewed calls for Reagan to invoke the 1973 War Powers Act, which requires the president to gain approval from Congress, after 60 to 90 days, for sending U.S. forces abroad if those forces are likely to be involved in hostilities. The administration argued that the act did not apply to the U.S. presence in the Persian Gulf and in any case was unconstitutional.

After further clashes between U.S. and Iranian forces, on October 19 four U.S. destroyers shelled two connected Iranian offshore oil platforms, about 120 miles east of Bahrain, that were regarded as a base for Iranian gunboats. A third platform nearby was boarded by a naval commando detachment, which destroyed radar and communications equipment.

Late in the year, attacks on shipping increased in number and severity. On December 6 the Singapore-registered tanker *Norman Atlantic* became the first large merchant ship to be sunk (by Iranian gunboats) in the war; the crew was saved. On December 9–10, Iraqi missiles hit the Iranian supertanker *Susangird*, killing over 20 seamen. On December 12, U.S. sailors rescued the crew of a Cypriot-flagged tanker set ablaze by Iranians.

**Arms Control.** After six years of negotiations, the United States and the Soviet Union in mid-September reached an "agreement in principle to conclude a treaty" that would eliminate all their intermediate-range nuclear force (INF) missiles. The final treaty was signed December 8 at a summit meeting between President Reagan and Soviet leader Mikhail S. Gorbachev in Washington. The treaty was the first between the superpowers to eliminate an entire class of nuclear weapons. A major obstacle to a deal had been removed in late August, when West German Chancellor Helmut Kohl announced that Bonn's 72 aging shorter-range Pershing 1A nuclear missiles would be scrapped, and not modernized, if the United States and the Soviet Union dismantled all their intermediate-range missiles in Europe.

In their September agreement the United States and the Soviet Union also pledged an "intensive effort" to achieve a treaty to reduce their stockpiles of strategic, or long-range, weapons by 50 percent, and Reagan and Gorbachev reported after their summit that they had made substantial progress toward such an agreement. However, the two sides remained deeply divided by the Reagan administration's program for developing a defensive shield against nuclear missiles—the Strategic Defense Initiative (SDI), commonly known as Star Wars. Although the prospect for new initiatives on conventional-arms reductions seemed brighter, another round of the 14-year-old East-West talks on troop reductions in Europe ended in stalemate in December.

# MILITARY AND NAVAL AFFAIRS

**Central America.** The Reagan administration's campaign to overthrow the leftist Sandinista government in Nicaragua became hostage to a region-wide peace plan signed in August by five Central American leaders including Nicaraguan president Daniel Ortega Saavedra. The plan called for a cease-fire between government troops and guerrilla forces in Nicaragua, Guatemala, and El Salvador; the restoration of democratic freedoms in Nicaragua; and a cessation of military aid by the United States and the Soviet Union to their clients in the area. Although U.S. officials were skeptical that the Sandinistas would live up to its terms, the plan temporarily reduced chances that Reagan could obtain approval for more military aid to the contra rebels fighting the Sandinistas. Administration plans to ask Congress for $270 million in military aid for the contras were postponed until 1988, amid indications that the request would be rejected. In December, however, the prospects for renewed aid improved after a senior Sandinista military officer who had defected to the United States revealed that Nicaragua was planning a major military buildup with Soviet arms.

**Afghan War.** The Soviet military occupation of Afghanistan entered its ninth year in December. An estimated 115,000 Soviet troops in Afghanistan continued to control major population centers, but several Soviet offensives failed to crush the insurgency by Afghan rebels. Military analysts believed that the relative strength of the rebels had been improved by the delivery of several hundred American-made Stinger shoulder-fired missiles. In December, Najibullah, leader of the Soviet-backed Afghan regime, proposed a 12-month timetable for the withdrawal of Soviet troops from Afghanistan, but at the Reagan-Gorbachev summit and afterward the United States continued to press for a faster pullout.

**Arms Sales.** The United States was involved in several major arms deals, particularly in the Middle East. The most prominent such transaction was a $1 billion arms package for Saudi Arabia, announced in October. The Reagan administration agreed to sell the Saudis a dozen F-15 jet fighters, plus advanced electronics for F-15's and M-60 tanks already in the Saudi inventory. However, the administration was forced to withdraw plans to sell 1,600 Maverick air-to-ground missiles to the Saudis when it appeared that supporters of Israel in the U.S. Congress had sufficient votes to block the transaction. The United States agreed in January to sell 12 F-16 jet fighters to Bahrain, and in June the Reagan administration agreed to allow Egypt to begin manufacturing the U.S. Army's M-1A1 tank.

Bowing to U.S. pressure, Israel decided in August to scrap development of the Lavi fighter bomber program and instead to purchase American F-16 jets. The United States, which was underwriting the Lavi project, feared that development costs would escalate to a prohibitive $1 billion per year.

A major controversy erupted this year when it was learned that Japan's Toshiba Machine Company and Norway's Kongsberg Vaapenfabrikk had sold sophisticated technology to the Soviet Union, allowing production of submarines that are significantly quieter and consequently more difficult to detect. The incident prompted new regulations tightening procedures for exports of technology by U.S. trading partners.

China expanded its arms sales, supplying a variety of weapons, including lethal Silkworm missiles, to both Iran and Iraq.

**Military Coups.** The most significant military coup attempt of the year failed to topple the struggling democratic government of President Corazon Aquino in the Philippines. Led by Gregorio ("Gringo") Honasan, a popular army colonel, the August 28 mutiny was quickly crushed by troops loyal to army chief of staff Géneral Fidel Ramos. More than 50 soldiers and civilians died in the fighting, the most serious threat to the Aquino government since it came to power in 1986.

Two military coups occurred in Fiji within five months following major gains by an ethnic Indian party in April elections. In May, Army Lieutenant Colonel Sitiveni Rabuka led an uprising that ended inconclusively; in October he seized power again, promising a new constitution guaranteeing political dominance over the Indian population by Fijians of Melanesian descent.

In Africa, the military leader of Burkina Faso, Captain Thomas Sankara, was overthrown in

President Ronald Reagan (right) says farewell to Caspar Weinberger, his defense secretary since 1981, at a White House ceremony announcing Weinberger's retirement.

October by other military officers and executed, along with several of his officials. In September a military committee seized power in Burundi, toppling the government of President Jean-Baptiste Bagaza while he was out of the country. In the South African homeland of Transkei, the army commander in September ousted the family dynasty that had controlled the country's political life; on December 30 he led another coup that ousted the new prime minister, Stella Sigcau, who had been Africa's first woman head of government.

**Base Rights.** Negotiators for the United States and Spain failed to reach agreement on the continued stationing of U.S. forces in Spain, prompting Madrid to give formal notice in November that it would not extend the bilateral defense treaty when it expired in May 1988. The treaty's expiration would force the removal of 14,000 Americans stationed at several air force and naval bases. The talks collapsed over Spanish demands that the United States remove 72 sophisticated F-16 jet fighters from the Torrejón air base near Madrid. However, talks were to resume.

**Canadian Buildup.** In June the Conservative government of Prime Minister Brian Mulroney announced a major 15-year planned expansion of the Canadian armed forces, including the purchase of 10 to 12 conventionally armed nuclear-powered submarines and six frigates, development of a new battle tank, and the addition of 30,000 troops to reserve forces. The defense "white paper" was the first comprehensive review of Canadian defense forces since 1971 and projected an increase of 2 percent annually in defense expenditures over 15 years, plus $13 billion (Canadian) in new spending for weapons systems.

**Other World Developments.** Hostilities waned in the border war between Libya and Chad after a series of impressive military victories by Chadian troops, most notably the recapture in March of Faya-Largeau in Libyan-occupied northern Chad. Chad was supported by both the United States and France.

In September, West Germany and France announced plans to create a joint defense council, as well as an integrated military unit. The move reflected concern that the proposed agreement between the United States and the Soviet Union eliminating intermediate-range nuclear weapons from Europe might result in a reduced U.S. military commitment to its Western European allies. In June, France announced plans to develop and manufacture the Rafale, an advanced jet fighter, for the French navy and air force by 1996. The decision was contrary to a trend among European nations toward greater cooperation in developing weapons systems in order to reduce costs.

In January the Japanese cabinet agreed that Japan's defense spending need no longer be limited to 1 percent of the gross national product. The ceiling had been imposed in 1976 to counter fears that Japan might eventually return to an aggressive military policy. Japanese officials declared that military policy would remain oriented toward self-defense but that defense spending would increase over the next five years. The policy change was designed in part to deal with American concerns that Japan had failed to pay a proportionate share of the cost of defending itself.

**U.S. Developments.** *Star Wars.* Within the United States, the Star Wars program continued to be subjected to the criticisms that it was of uncertain feasibility and would cost too much. For the second consecutive year Congress was unwilling to grant the administration all the funding it wanted for SDI testing and research, and Congress also sought to prevent Reagan from reinterpreting the 1972 anti-ballistic missile treaty with the Soviets in a way that permitted accelerated SDI testing. In a compromise reached in November, the administration received about two-thirds of the SDI funding it had sought for fiscal 1988 and agreed not to act on its broad interpretation of the 1972 treaty during that period.

*Weapons Systems.* The Pentagon went forward with work on a variety of strategic and conventional weapons systems. Testing continued on the MX land-based intercontinental missile, a single-warhead mobile missile nicknamed Midgetman, the Trident II submarine-launched missile, submarine-launched cruise missiles, and the ASAT system for destroying enemy satellites in outer space. In conventional weapons developments, testing continued on a non-

nuclear cruise missile that could be launched from submarines with an accuracy of a few inches, as well as on the "Stealth" bomber able to avoid detection by enemy radar. Rockwell International was awarded a contract in September to develop an experimental jet fighter called the X-31, designed to outmaneuver any other aircraft in existence. The Army began work on a laser pistol that would knock out infrared sensors on enemy tanks and aircraft and approved plans for a new family of armored vehicles expected to cost more than $100 billion.

The B-1B strategic bomber continued to experience various technical problems, causing as many as half of the planes to be grounded at times. A B-1B crashed on September 28 in Colorado, killing three of the six aviators aboard.

*Marine Sergeant Clayton Lonetree, former U.S. embassy guard in Moscow convicted of revealing secrets to the Soviet Union, is led in handcuffs from a courtroom at the Quantico Marine Base in Virginia after being sentenced to 30 years in prison.*

he bomber was on a low-altitude training
ight when it struck a flock of birds, ingesting
ome of them into its engines. In December
ne Strategic Air Command suspended low-
evel flights of the aircraft pending further
nvestigation. A plane that crashed in Nevada
n October 14, killing the pilot, was reportedly
Stealth fighter.

Among other developments, the Army sus-
ended amphibious operations of the Bradley
rmored personnel carrier in April after two
ehicles sank during amphibious maneuvers,
illing one soldier. The Air Force proposed a
3 billion plan to modify 150 of the oldest B-
2 bombers to carry conventional weapons for
se in Europe to fill the gap left by the expected
limination of intermediate-range nuclear mis-
iles.

*spionage.* Early in the year two marine security
uards were accused of permitting Soviet in-
elligence agents into the most sensitive areas
f the U.S. embassy in Moscow in exchange
or sexual favors. In March, Sergeant Clayton
. Lonetree and Corporal Arnold Bracy were
harged with several counts of espionage. All
harges against Bracy, however, were dropped
n June on grounds of insufficient evidence.
onetree was convicted by a military jury in
ugust on 13 counts of espionage and was
entenced to 30 years in prison, a $5,000 fine,
nd a dishonorable discharge. He was later
ffered a five-year reduction in the prison
entence in return for cooperating with inves-
igators.

Government officials said that the Marine
candal had seriously compromised U.S. in-
elligence operations in the Soviet Union. In
n effort to reduce the vulnerability of embassy
uards to entrapment by female foreign agents,
he Marine Corps announced in April that the
tandard tour of duty for embassy guards in 14
ities, most in Eastern Europe, would be re-
uced from 15 months to 12 months.

Jonathan Jay Pollard, a former civilian intel-
igence analyst for the Navy who had pleaded
uilty to selling military secrets to Israel, was
entenced in March to life in prison; his wife
rew five years, as an accessory. The case
trained U.S.-Israeli relations.

In August a court-martial jury convicted
etired Navy radioman Michael Allen of espi-

onage for passing counterintelligence reports
to the Philippine government while working as
a clerk at a naval telecommunications center
in the Philippines. He was sentenced to eight
years in prison and fined $10,000.

The Pentagon revealed that since June 1985
it had cut by 40 percent the security clearances
issued to employees of the Defense Department
and military contractors. The move followed
discovery of a spy ring headed by former Navy
enlisted man John Walker.

*Defense Budget.* On January 5 the Reagan
administration submitted to Congress its proposed budget for the 1988 fiscal year (beginning
on October 1, 1987). Faced with continued
opposition to escalating military spending after
six years of unprecedented peacetime defense
budgets, the administration proposed an increase of only 3 percent, adjusted for inflation,
over the defense budget approved by Congress
for fiscal 1987. The total fiscal 1988 request
for defense, including activities of agencies
other than the Defense Department, was $312
billion. In a departure from the past, a detailed
two-year spending proposal was provided, with
the administration seeking $332.4 billion in
defense spending authority for fiscal 1989. The
administration once again argued that U.S.
defense spending was lagging behind a growing
Soviet military threat. But with the federal
budget continuing to run a huge deficit, Congress made sizable cuts in the defense request.
In June, Congress passed a budget resolution
(which sets spending targets for appropriations
bills) that limited military spending to $289.5
billion, the same as the amount actually appropriated for fiscal 1987. The resolution provided for an additional $7 billion for the Pen-
tagon if Reagan would agree to accept $19.3
billion in various tax increases. After the stock
market plunge in October led to another round
of budget cuts, only $285.4 billion was finally
appropriated for military spending in fiscal
1988.

*Personnel Developments.* The Supreme Court
significantly strengthened the right of the military to prosecute service members in June,
ruling that military personnel could be court-
martialed for crimes unrelated to their military
service or occurring off-base. The decision
overruled a 1969 Court opinion ordering trials

by civilian juries in such circumstances. A separate decision in June forbade military personnel from suing superior officers or the government for damages for alleged violations of constitutional rights. The decision rejected a lawsuit by a former Army sergeant seeking damages for unwitting participation in secret Army experiments with the hallucinogenic drug LSD.

*Command Changes.* Defense Secretary Caspar Weinberger, who had headed the Pentagon since the start of the Reagan administration, announced on November 5 that he was resigning because of his wife's ill health. Frank C. Carlucci, who had replaced Vice Admiral John Poindexter as the president's national security adviser after Poindexter was implicated in the Iran/contra affair, was nominated to replace Weinberger. Carlucci, in turn, was replaced by his deputy, Army Lieutenant Colonel Colin Powell. Admiral William Crowe, Jr., was reappointed in June to a second two-year term as chairman of the Joint Chiefs of Staff. John F. Lehman, Jr., resigned after six controversial years as secretary of the Navy and was succeeded in April by James H. Webb, Jr., an assistant secretary of defense, a highly decorated Marine Corps officer in Vietnam, and the author of several books.

*See also* UNITED STATES: Foreign Affairs, NORTH ATLANTIC TREATY ORGANIZATION, *and articles on individual countries.* T.D.

**MINNESOTA.** *See* STATISTICS OF THE WORLD.

**MISSISSIPPI.** *See* STATISTICS OF THE WORLD.

**MISSOURI.** *See* STATISTICS OF THE WORLD.

**MONACO.** *See* STATISTICS OF THE WORLD.

**MONGOLIAN PEOPLE'S REPUBLIC.** *See* STATISTICS OF THE WORLD.

**MONTANA.** *See* STATISTICS OF THE WORLD.

**MOROCCO.** The focus of the 12-year-old conflict over the Western Sahara—a conflict between Morocco and the guerrilla forces of the Polisario Front seeking independence for the territory—shifted back to the battlefield in 1987. On February 25 the Polisario Front launched its biggest attack since 1983, employing 1,000 troops, over 100 armored vehicles (including Soviet-made tanks), and SAM-6 missiles. The Polisario forces attacked two Moroccan positions, but superior Moroccan air power forced them to retreat. Both sides suffered heavy casualties—an especially important factor for the Polisario Front because of the small size of its army.

The Polisario Front followed this major operation with a series of attacks, from February to April, intended to disrupt the construction of the sixth—and perhaps final—section of the Moroccan wall. The wall extends some 1,20 miles and encloses over two-thirds of the Western Sahara, forcing Polisario guerrillas t cross Mauritanian territory to reach key Moroccan positions.

A leading diplomatic event of the year was a summit meeting on May 4 between King Hassan II of Morocco and Algerian President Chadli Benjedid. The two leaders met, for the first time since 1983, at a neutral site on the Moroccan-Algerian border, and discussed the growing tensions caused by the Moroccan wall. President Benjedid reiterated Algeria's call for direct negotiations between Morocco and the Polisario leadership. King Hassan maintained Morocco's determination not to deal directly with the Front.

Tensions again flared between Morocco and Spain over the Spanish enclaves of Ceuta and Melilla, on Morocco's Mediterranean coast. The crisis began in January when Spanish authorities arrested 27 Muslim leaders; soon afterward a Muslim youth was fatally shot by a Spanish resident of Melilla. In February, Spain rushed police reinforcements to both enclaves in response to demonstrations by the Muslim communities there. Both governments, sensitive to the explosive character of the enclave issue and eager to maintain cooperation, acted with restraint; and tensions gradually subsided.

In July, King Hassan made the first visit ever by a Moroccan head of state to the United Kingdom, meeting with Prime Minister Margaret Thatcher and the British foreign and defense secretaries. The king pressed the Arab case for an international peace conference on the Middle East and for United Nations action to halt the Iran-Iraq war.

A 3 percent economic growth rate was projected for the year, despite depressed prices for phosphates (a key Moroccan export), European trade restrictions, and a $16 billion external debt.

*See* STATISTICS OF THE WORLD. J.D

**MOTION PICTURES.** The year 1987 was notable for the release and popularity of a number of films about the Vietnam war, a topic which had for years been considered bad news at the box office. In all, many films of considerable artistic merit were released.

**Vietnam in Film.** Hollywood's taboo against films about the Vietnam war was shattered by the triumph of *Platoon,* which won four Academy Awards, including those for best picture and best director. The public reaction to *Platoon,* as well as the critical acclaim, indicated that Vietnam could finally take its place with other wars as a movie topic that audiences were ready to face. Stanley Kubrick's *Full Metal Jacket,* subsequently released, also garnered acclaim. Kubrick's vision was more stylized than director Oliver Stone's gritty, realistic approach to *Platoon.* Kubrick was concerned with the dehumanization of war; Stone emphasized the physicality of what the Vietnam fighting experience was really like. Each film had the power to provide an emotional jolt.

*Hamburger Hill,* directed by John Irwin, was another film that sought to capture the Vietnam experience from the viewpoint of the men who fought there. Francis Ford Coppola's *Gardens of Stone* examined the impact of the war at home by focusing on soldiers assigned to burial duty.

**Film Art.** Many of the year's films were of the highest order. Producer Ismail Merchant and director James Ivory, a team that established a remarkable record of independent filmmaking during the past 25 years, were back with another brilliant adaptation—*Maurice,* based on the novel by E. M. Forster, which subtly deals with homosexuality in the face of restrictive laws and social conventions in England before World War I. John Sayles delved into American labor history for the stunning *Matewan,* about West Virginia's coal-mine wars. Paul Newman (*see biography in* PEOPLE IN THE NEWS) brought to the screen Tennessee Williams's classic play *The Glass Menagerie,* in an excellent production starring Newman's wife, Joanne Woodward, as Amanda.

Woody Allen was back with *Radio Days,* a nostalgic look at growing up during the heyday of radio broadcasting. The plight of aluminum-siding salesmen trying to earn a living was comically but earnestly portrayed in *Tin Men,* written and directed by Barry Levinson.

*The Whales of August,* directed by Lindsay

June was the month for weddings in Marrakech, Morocco. A four-day ceremony at the palace of King Hassan II united Hassan's daughter Princess Lalla Asmaa and Khalid Bouchentouf—shown here riding in a specially decorated carriage—along with 250 other couples.

Stanley Kubrick's Full Met.
Jacket was one of sever.
films about America's i
volvement in Vietnam th.
opened after the preceden
shattering success of Pla
toon.

Anderson, paired veteran actresses Bette Davis and Lillian Gish. Denzel Washington played murdered political leader Stephen Biko, and Kevin Kline played journalist Donald Woods, in Cry Freedom, Richard Attenborough's drama about racism in South Africa. The grandeur and entertainment qualities of Hollywood's gangster genre were superbly reprised by director Brian de Palma in The Untouchables. The Dead, the well-received last film directed by the late John Huston, was a family affair. It costarred his daughter Anjelica Huston, and the screenplay, based on a story in James Joyce's Dubliners, was written by his son.

Outside the United States, Soviet director Nikita Mikhalkov cast Marcello Mastroianni as leading man in Dark Eyes, which won praise both for itself and for its durable star. British director Stephen Frears, who had gained attention with My Beautiful Laundrette, was back with the acerbic, perceptive Prick Up Your Ears, based on the life of murdered British playwright Joe Orton, and, later in the year, with Sammy and Rosie Get Laid. Director John Boorman evoked memories of growing up in Britain during World War II in his autobiographical film Hope and Glory.

One of the biggest art-house hits was Jean de Florette, the first of two films that French director Claude Berri made from the late Marce Pagnol's novels. The sequel, Manon of the Spring, while part of the same project, wa withheld to open separately as a feature on it own. A picture of considerable charm was M Life as a Dog, made by Swedish director Lass Hallstrom and structured as a memoir of boy hood thoughts and adventures. From Japa came Tampopo, director Juzo Itami's ger about the sensuous craving for food, exempli fied by the quest for a perfect noodle.

**Light Entertainment.** Among films on the ligh side was The Princess Bride, scripted by Wil liam Goldman from his book; Rob Reine directed this deft spoof. Bette Midler and Shel ley Long were a winsome team in Outrageou Fortune, in which they seek the mysteriou man who has been two-timing them. Richar Dreyfuss and Emilio Estevez made anothe funny duo in Stakeout, director John Badham' comedy about two cops assigned to watch th apartment of a beautiful woman. Steve Marti was immensely entertaining in Roxanne, modern update of Cyrano de Bergerac. Directo Susan Seidelman offered Making Mr. Righ about the innocence of a robot being corrupte by the behavior of humans. Danny DeVito an Billy Crystal shone in the mean-spirited comed Throw Momma From the Train, and Che played a frump-turned-Cinderella in the Norman Jewison comedy *Moonstruck*.

**Out of the Ordinary.** Some of the year's more interesting films were quirky examples of what happens when filmmakers dare to try something different or outrageous. Director Barbet Schroeder came up with *Barfly,* teaming Mickey Rourke as a habitual drunk and drop-out writer with the usually elegant Faye Dunaway as an alcoholic also on the skids. Spalding Gray had a reputation for his stage monologues, and director Jonathan Demme pinpointed the essence of Gray's ability to mesmerize an audience with his witty anecdotes in *Swimming to Cambodia*, the performer's monologue about his Asian exploits.

**Changing of the Guard.** Several of cinema's irreplaceable greats of the past died during the year—including film stars Fred Astaire and Mary Astor and veteran director John Huston. Still, the headway made by new talent promised a fresh supply of artistry and energy. Kevin Costner's star rose with his appearance in two films that showcased his abilities. Playing U.S. Treasury agent Eliot Ness in *The Untouchables,* Costner made a strong impression as a leading man, as he did in *No Way Out,* a thriller about corruption in the Pentagon. Actor Dennis Quaid

Lou Diamond Phillips starred in La Bamba, a film about 1950's rock and roll star Ritchie Valens that made the title song (as recorded by Los Lobos) a hit all over again.

The Untouchables, with (from left) Andy Garcia, Sean Connery, Kevin Costner, and Charles Martin Smith as lawmen fighting Al Capone, drew mobs to the theaters over the summer.

flashed magnetism as a cop in *The Big Easy,* a smartly executed action film set in New Orleans. His costar, Ellen Barkin, portraying an investigating district attorney, also showed why she is considered one of the most promising of rising new stars. *The Secret of My Success* did well at the box office because of star Michael J. Fox, who achieved his fame in television's *Family Ties* (see biography in PEOPLE IN THE NEWS).

Kim Basinger is being increasingly appreciated as a comedienne in the tradition of some of Hollywood's finest; she gave evidence of this in Blake Edwards's *Blind Date* and also in Robert Benton's *Nadine. Hollywood Shuffle,* an effervescent spoof of the plight of the black actor in Hollywood, illuminated the talents of Robert Townsend, who, in addition to acting in the film, wrote, directed, and produced the independent undertaking. David Mamet, celebrated as a playwright, ventured into film by writing and directing his first feature, *House of Games,* starring Lindsay Crouse and Joe Mantegna.

**Potpourri.** One of the year's most successful and talked-about films was the thriller *Fatal Attraction,* starring Glenn Close as a love-crazed, vengeful book editor and Michael Douglas as the Manhattan lawyer and devoted husband whose brief fling with her leads to terrifying consequences. The film was the third highest-grossing movie of 1987. Other noteworthy films included *River's Edge,* a powerful film directed by Tim Hunter, about the aftermath of a teenager's murder of his girlfriend; *Broadcast News,* a look at network television news, starring William Hurt, Albert Brooks, and Holly Hunter, and directed by James L. Brooks; a second Woody Allen movie of the year, *September,* set in a country home in Vermont; Bernardo Bertolucci's *The Last Emperor,* filmed in China; *Ironweed,* based on William Kennedy's novel, starring Jack Nicholson (who also appeared in the popular film *The Witches of Eastwick,* based on a John Updike novel of the same title); *Dirty Dancing,* a Catskill-resort love story directed by Emile Ardolino; *Wall Street,* Oliver Stone's look at

*The immensely popular* Fatal Attraction *took a common premise— a brief affair between a married man (Michael Douglas) and a woman he meets on the job (Glenn Close)—and turned it into a dark tale of fear and vengeance.*

### Director's Breakthrough

After more than a decade of waiting, screenwriter and director Oliver Stone finally achieved a critical and popular success with his Oscar-winning Vietnam war film *Platoon*. Following a combat tour in Vietnam in 1967–1968, during which he won a Bronze Star and a Purple Heart, Stone had attended New York University's film school. Among his instructors was film director Martin Scorsese, whom he credits with helping him to "channel" his anger about Vietnam into creative directions. Stone began the script that eventually became *Platoon* on July 4, 1976. Although Hollywood was reluctant to make Vietnam movies during that era, the script led Columbia Pictures to hire him to write the screenplay of *Midnight Express* (1978), about an American student's hellish imprisonment in Turkey for drug trafficking. Immediately before *Platoon*, Stone directed and cowrote the film *Salvador*, praised as a riveting indictment of U.S. policy in Central America. After *Platoon*, Stone went to work directing *Wall Street*, which he also cowrote, about a money-hungry young stockbroker.

*Oliver Stone*

manipulation in the financial world; Alan Pakula's *Orphans*, from the play by Lyle Kessler; and *Nuts*, with Barbra Streisand as a woman threatened by instability. *Beverly Hills Cop II*, though not critically praised, captivated teen audiences and became the top moneymaker of 1987. (*Platoon* was number two.)

Also attracting attention were *La Bamba*, a recollection of the short but dynamic career of Chicano rock'n'roll singer Ritchie Valens; *Walker*, starring Ed Harris and Marlee Matlin in a story about the life of a 19th-century adventurer who declared himself president of Nicaragua; Taylor Hackford's *Chuck Berry Hail! Hail! Rock 'n' Roll*, a documentary about the life of Chuck Berry; and *Good Morning, Vietnam*, with Robin Williams as a disk jockey broadcasting to the troops.

Late in the year, Steven Spielberg scored with *Empire of the Sun*, the World War II story of an English schoolboy who, separated from his parents by the Japanese invasion of Shanghai, learns to survive. Another latecomer was Bill Forsyth's sensitive adaptation of Marilynne

Robinson's novel *Housekeeping*, starring Christine Lahti as a wayfaring aunt who takes charge of two orphaned nieces.

Hollywood celebrated its 100th birthday in 1987. Although but a shadow of the entertainment capital it once was, Hollywood still symbolizes the movie business and is also the center of television production. Its fortunes grew when filmmakers, at first located in the East, moved to escape patent controls and also take advantage of sunny climes ideal for filming. The anniversary was marked by a series of public events.

Another milestone was the 50th anniversary of Walt Disney's classic *Snow White and the Seven Dwarfs*. The occasion was celebrated with the rerelease of the film, giving yet another generation of youngsters the chance to enter its magical world.

**Color Wars.** Partisans of colorizing old black-and-white movies won a key round against their foes when the Library of Congress decided that a colorized print was worthy of being considered an original work and thereby eli-

*The first animated full-length feature, and to many one of the greatest, Walt Disney's* Snow White *was rereleased to theaters on its 50th anniversary.*

gible for copyright protection hitherto belonging only to the owner of the originally uncolored film. The decision, issued by Ralph Oman, registrar of copyrights, rankled those who see the process as desecration rather than creation. Congressional hearings were held with a view to possibly outlawing the colorization of someone else's work without consent.

**Landis Case.** Director John Landis and four associates were acquitted in a Los Angeles court on May 29 of involuntary manslaughter charges involving the 1982 deaths of three actors on the set of the movie *The Twilight Zone,* after a special-effects explosion caused a helicopter to crash on top of them.

**Business.** Despite the growing videocassette market once feared as fatal competition, box-office business flourished on an overall basis, although there were some memorable flops. Elaine May's *Ishtar,* starring Warren Beatty and Dustin Hoffman, reportedly cost some $51 million, but fizzled. Madonna, starring in *Who's That Girl,* failed to draw an audience even though her stage popularity soared. But costly losses on a grand scale were averted when a settlement was reached between producers and the Directors Guild of America in time to prevent a lengthy strike.

The reign of outspoken producer David Puttnam as president of Columbia Pictures proved to be short lived. Puttnam came to Columbia in a blaze of publicity, but reports were that he alienated key powers in Hollywood. After he had served but half of his three-year contract, his resignation was announced, the latest indication that it is difficult to change Hollywood's traditional way of doing things.

**Milestones.** It was 25 years ago that James Bond first became a movie hero in the film *Dr. No.* Fifteen 007 films later, with the release of *The Living Daylights,* the 25th anniversary of the phenomenal Bond success was marked. The Museum of Modern Art in New York elevated Bond films to the level of pop art, with a retrospective. Meanwhile, in *The Living Daylights,* yet another actor has assumed the starring role; Timothy Dalton followed in the footsteps of Sean Connery, George Lazenby, and Roger Moore as the intrepid secret agent.

**Awards.** In March, *Platoon* received four Academy Awards, including those for best picture and to Oliver Stone as best director; but Stone ost the original screenplay award to Woody Allen, who won for *Hannah and Her Sisters*. After seven nominations, Paul Newman finally won an Oscar—as best actor for *The Color of Money*; Marlee Matlin, who is deaf, signed her acceptance of the Oscar for best actress in *Children of a Lesser God*. Dianne Wiest and Michael Caine received Oscars for supporting roles in *Hannah and Her Sisters*. After being overlooked as a director in 1986, Steven Spielberg became the 27th recipient of the academy's Irving Thalberg Award. Stone was named best director by the Directors' Guild of America, and Allen received the best director award for *Hannah* from the New York Film Critics Circle, which also named *Hannah* as best film.

**Canadian Film.** No single Canadian film attracted as much attention as the previous year's *Decline of the American Empire*. But the 1987 releases showed a greater range of virtuosity. Once again, Canada created a sensation at Cannes, this time with two strikingly original first features by young filmmakers: *I've Heard the Mermaids Singing*, Toronto director Patricia Rozema's whimsical fantasy about a pixieish ingenue (Sheila McCarthy) adrift in the art world, and *Un zoo la nuit* (Night Zoo), Québec director Jean-Claude Lauzon's visceral drama about savagery and tenderness in the Montréal underworld. Both films received worldwide distribution.

Canada's new prominence in the film industry was underlined by the success of Garth Drabinsky, who as chairman of the Toronto-based Cineplex Odeon Corporation presided over an empire of 1,500 Cineplex-owned movie theaters across North America, including a 2-acre, 16-screen complex in Los Angeles that qualifies as the world's largest cinema. With numerous projects in the offing and MCA-Universal, Hollywood's largest studio conglomerate, as a 48 percent shareholder in Cineplex, he has increasingly emerged as a major force in the industry.

B.D.J. (Canadian Film) & W.W.

**MOZAMBIQUE.** In 1987, Mozambican President Joaquim Chissano replaced the military's top leadership in an effort to improve the army's capacity to defend the country against the South African-backed Mozambique National Resistance (Renamo).

In the first half of the year, with the aid of Zimbabwean and Tanzanian troops, Mozambique recaptured most of the central provinces of Zambézia and Sofala, which had been occupied by Renamo in late 1986. The reoccupying troops found extensive destruction; sugar mills, tea plantations, schools, health posts, and entire towns were in ruins. By midyear, however, South Africa had infiltrated into southern Mozambique hundreds of new Renamo troops, who attacked farms and villages. In July, the attackers killed approximately 400 people in the town of Homoine, including hospital staff and patients; in October, at least 264 more reportedly died when Renamo ambushed two convoys of vehicles in the Taninga region, and in November, rebels reportedly killed over 40 travelers in the same area. Renamo denied it was massacring civilians.

Chissano continued his policies of liberalizing the internal economy and cultivating good relations with Western countries as well as with traditional African, Scandinavian, and Soviet-bloc allies.

The United States maintained good relations with Mozambique, and Chissano met with President Ronald Reagan at the White House, during a U.S. visit in October.

The Mozambican government implemented a drastic economic recovery program and gained international support in bolstering the war-crippled economy. However, economic conditions continued to deteriorate in rural areas, where periodic attacks by South African-backed guerrillas destroyed economic targets and drove peasant farmers from their fields. Up to 4 million of Mozambique's 14 million people were estimated to have been affected by acute food shortages resulting from the guerrilla warfare. Marketed production of cereals was calculated at 40,000 tons, leaving a gap of 750,000 tons to be covered by food aid.

International donors and creditors provided economic support on relatively generous terms; external funding increased in 1987 by 40 percent. The International Monetary Fund approved a $36.3 million credit in June, and creditors agreed to reschedule some $400 million in loans.

*See* STATISTICS OF THE WORLD.          W.M.

The fans gave Billy Joel a Western-style welcome as the singer and songwriter toured the Soviet Union.

**MUSIC.** The following is an account of developments in popular and in classical music during 1987.

## POPULAR MUSIC

**Old Faces and New Talents.** In popular music old faces and musical styles returned, while new ideas and talents took hold. Record reissues were rife, especially in the jazz and soul fields. Veteran performers, including Paul Simon, Steve Winwood, Barbra Streisand, and Tina Turner, dominated the Grammy awards, and the Grateful Dead were reborn. Robert Cray scored a Top 40 hit with his revamped version of that hoary yet still vital genre, the blues.

A number of new artists scaled the pop charts. Smooth black pop groups like Levert, badder-than-thou rappers like LL Cool J, and a South African-born crooner named Jonathan Butler appealed to audiences of all races. Meanwhile, mainstream pop rockers like Cutting Crew, T'Pau, and Richard Marx carved out reputations. Los Lobos scored a No. 1 hit with a remake of "La Bamba," from the soundtrack of a popular movie about the life of the late 1950's rock star Ritchie Valens.

Randy Travis's updated rural blues sound and romantic voice gained a wide following, as neotraditional country threw up new stars like Nanci Griffith and Holly Dunn. Trendsetters like Ed Strait and the Judds maintained their popularity, and neo-rockabilly singer Dwight Yoakam crossed over to the rock market. While newcomer Steve Earle garnered acclaim with his brand of hard country, Hank Williams, Jr., the pioneer of the genre, finally began to receive recognition from the country music establishment.

On Paul Simon's *Graceland* album—which won a Grammy as best album this year—and tour, he was accompanied by the South African band Stimela and choral group Ladysmith Black Mambazo. Simon's trail-blazing concert tour showed how richly textured, polyphonic African music could be blended with a Western pop sound and contemporary lyrics.

**Social Concerns.** Social activism was alive among many pop musicians. Concern for America itself was expressed in Willie Nelson's Farm Aid III concert, in September, and a Vietnam veterans' salute on July 4. A number of music stars took part in a trio of concerts in September to raise funds for those opposing aid to the Nicaraguan contras. U2, the socially conscious Irish rock band who began a lengthy tour of America and Europe this spring, released their fifth studio album, *The Joshua Tree*. Among its tracks were songs about drug addiction, the sale of arms to El Salvador, and political prisoners.

In July several American acts, including the Doobie Brothers, James Taylor, Santana, and Bonnie Raitt, performed with Soviet bands at a "peace concert" in Moscow. That show, which capped a Leningrad-to-Moscow "peace walk" by U.S. and Soviet citizens, indicated a greater Soviet openness to Western culture in general and pop music in particular. While the adult audience at the concert was rather stiff and unenthusiastic, the Soviets who turned out for Billy Joel's six concerts in Moscow and Leningrad this year were quite different, shouting and dancing like a typical American crowd. Joel's summer tour was preceded by visits to the Soviet Union by a couple of jazz veterans, Dave Brubeck and Pat Metheny, and by a British rock-reggae outfit named UB40.

**Black Music.** On the talent front, blacks continued to score major successes. Crossover artists like Whitney Houston, Janet Jackson, and Cameo competed strongly in the record marketplace with the leading white acts. Michael Jackson's long-awaited album *Bad* de-buted at No. 1 on the trade charts, and had sold over 5 million copies.

The other leading phenomenon in black music was rap, whose influence spread from the inner city ghettos to the most affluent suburbs. Groups like the Fat Boys, LL Cool J, and Run-D.M.C. broke down racial barriers with propulsive rhythms and streetwise lyrics, and the white Beastie Boys achieved success with their raunchy mixture of rap and heavy metal.

**Tours and Concerts.** It was a big spring and summer for stadium tours, which had been on the decline for several years. Among those who played to giant crowds coast-to-coast were Genesis and David Bowie, as well as U2.

Madonna fever gripped much of the world. Her *True Blue* album was a top seller all year, and her tours of Japan, Europe, and America drew huge crowds wherever she went. In London alone, she performed for 300,000 fans in four concerts. In France, Prime Minister Jacques Chirac himself intervened to allow her scheduled open-air show to go on in a Paris suburb. Local officials had argued that the

*The passage of a decade since Elvis Presley's death didn't dim fans' reverence for the king of rock. Thousands arrived in Memphis for the anniversary, including these visitors to the "Meditation Garden" at Elvis's mansion, Graceland, where the singer and his parents are buried.*

17th-century park that was the concert's intended site was inappropriate.

**Resurfacing of the Past.** The Grateful Dead, a popular group of years past, reemerged on record and on the stage. *In the Dark,* their first new studio LP in seven years, hurtled into the Top 10. Their concert with Bob Dylan was a sellout at New Jersey's Giants Stadium, drawing over 70,000 people—a record for a music event there. Ex-hippies-turned-accountants mingled with young people in tie-dyed shirts as they celebrated the improbable resurgence of the 1960's acid rock group from San Francisco—partly stemming from a rekindled public interest in the late 1960's. Other signs of the trend were the reunion of three of the four Monkees, who also toured and cut a new album, and a summer "Classic Superfest" concert swing featuring the Turtles, the Grassroots, Mark Lindsay, Paul Revere and the Raiders, Herman's Hermits, and the Byrds. At the same time, Capitol Records marked the 20th anniversary of the release of the classic Beatles' album *Sgt. Pepper's Lonely Hearts Club Band,* releasing it on compact disk. Television shows also commemorated the album's anniversary.

The original English version of all 13 of the Beatles' studio albums were issued on compact disks. This followed a bitter legal attack against Capitol by the surviving Beatles, who claimed that the label had held up their CD releases as a maneuver in the continuing litigation over the band's back royalties. Meanwhile, some fans objected to the use of the Beatles' record "Revolution" in a Nike footwear ad. Nike had gotten permission to use the song (as recorded by the Beatles) from Capitol and SBK Songs, which owns the publishing rights on behalf of Michael Jackson. Nike claimed it meant no disrespect, but it did not withdraw the ad.

The biggest rock star before the Beatles, Elvis Presley, received his share of attention. As August 16, the tenth anniversary of his death, drew nigh, there was an avalanche of books and TV shows about the late great singer, and RCA released the cream of his catalog on CD's. During a tourist-targeted Elvis International Tribute Week in Memphis, some 60,000 people descended on the city, 32,000 of whom bought tickets to tour Elvis's Graceland mansion.

The musical past also resurfaced in other ways. The music of the 1950's was reexamined in Atlantic Records' great re-issue series of rhythm and blues and jazz classics from that period through the 1970's. The Beach Boys and the Fat Boys recalled the early 1960's with their joint remake of "Wipeout." Annette Funicello and Frankie Avalon headed "back to the beach" in the film of that name, with music performed by such current stars as Stevie Ray Vaughan and comedian Pee-wee Herman. Aretha Franklin, the queen of soul, went back to her roots by recording a live gospel album in the Detroit church where her late father used to be pastor. Aretha also recorded a hit duet record with British star George Michael, who later created a controversy with his widely banned hit single "I Want Your Sex."

Extra-musical publicity also surrounded the reemergences of David Crosby and Liza Minnelli. Crosby, who had recently served time in a Texas prison for cocaine possession, gave a concert in Houston and later joined former

*The Irish rock band U2 address a variety of social and even spiritual topics in their songs. From left: David ("the Edge") Evans, Adam Clayton, lead singer Bono (Paul Hewson), and Larry Mullen, Jr.*

mates Stephen Stills and Graham Nash for a national tour. Minnelli, who kicked alcohol and drugs at the Betty Ford Center, rewarded her adoring public with three weeks of sold-out concerts at New York City's Carnegie Hall.

**Hammond and Springsteen.** Veteran producer and talent scout John Hammond died in July at the age of 76. Hammond, who discovered Billie Holiday and signed Aretha Franklin, Bob Dylan, and Bruce Springsteen to Columbia Records, also produced sides by many of the great jazz musicians, including Benny Goodman, Benny Carter, Coleman Hawkins, and Teddy Wilson. Meanwhile, Hammond's final discovery, Bruce Springsteen, remained in the news, releasing a studio album, *Tunnel of Love,* in early fall.

**CBS Records Sale.** In November, CBS, Inc. announced plans to sell its record division to the Sony Corporation, the Japanese consumer electronics giant, for $2 billion. Among the performers on the roster of CBS Records, the world's largest record company, were Cyndi Lauper, the Rolling Stones, Springsteen, and Michael Jackson, whose *Thriller* was the best-selling album ever.                        K.T.

## CLASSICAL MUSIC

Experimentation in the staging of standard operas continued, causing more controversy than ever. Many U.S. opera companies and orchestras faced severe financial problems.

**Opera.** In New York, the Metropolitan Opera produced an expensive *Turandot* under the direction and design of Franco Zeffirelli. Some critics were delighted, but New York *Times* critic Donal Henahan said the production had more razzle-dazzle than substance, which prompted an angry response from Zeffirelli. New stagings of *Das Rheingold* and *Il Trovatore* were also put on later in the season.

The most interesting offering from New York City Opera was a double bill, which premiered in November, of Mozart's rarely performed comic opera *The Goose From Cairo* and Oliver Knussen's *Where the Wild Things Are.* The latter was based on the children's book by Maurice Sendak, who designed the sets for both productions.

A *Tristan and Isolde* directed by Jonathan Miller, with sets and costumes designed by artist David Hockney, opened in December at the Los Angeles Music Center Opera. The innovative Opera Theatre of St. Louis presented the U.S. premiere of Stephen Oliver's *Beauty and the Beast,* while Lyric Opera Cleveland offered the first performance of Larry Baker's *Haydn's Head.* A new opera by John Adams, *Nixon in China,* was premiered by the Houston Grand Opera in October; the director was Peter Sellars and the librettist poet Alice Goodman.

PepsiCo Summerfare in Purchase, N.Y., presented a *Don Giovanni* set in contemporary New York City and also directed by Peter Sellars. In an effort to relate the story of the 18th-century womanizer to "sex and death on the streets of New York," Sellars had the Don wear a leather jacket and "shoot up" with drugs.

The San Francisco Opera canceled its summer seasons for financial reasons, and 13 member companies of Opera America responded to a financial crunch by sharing costs and profits of a *Porgy and Bess* that traveled to Omaha; Louisville, Ky.; Minneapolis; Austin, Texas; Detroit, and other cities. On a brighter note, a $5 million opera house, the 920-seat Alice Busch Opera Theater, opened in Cooperstown, N.Y., home of the Baseball Hall of Fame. The Glimmerglass Opera, a company that specializes in English-language productions, inaugurated the new house with *Eugene Onegin.*

In Europe, Strauss's *Salome* was staged at La Scala, Milan, by Robert Wilson. Wilson set the opera on two levels, with one cast acting the roles and another singing them—an innovation that drew more boos than cheers. Bayreuth presented a new *Lohengrin* directed by moviemaker Werner Herzog, and the English National Opera offered a *Carmen* staged by David Pountney as, in the words of one critic, a "soft-porn, 1960's view of lecherous men, available women, and juvenile delinquents aping the adults." Also in London, the Royal Opera's new *Otello* with tenor Placido Domingo was "one of the company's greater nights in a decade," according to *Opera News.*

The Paris Opera presented Lully's *Atys* for the first time since 1760, in a multinational effort headed by American musicologist William Christie. The production, which had an

*Maurice Sendak's fanciful beasts made the transition from children's book to stage as* Where the Wild Things Are, *composed by Oliver Knussen with sets designed by Sendak, premiered at the New York City Opera.*

Anglo-American cast, was coproduced by the Teatro Communale of Florence and the Montpellier Opera; it was a great success. The most spectacular production of the year was undoubtedly the *Aida* staged in the 3,000-year-old temple in Luxor, Egypt, on the site of ancient Thebes. The Arena de Verona production featured a cast of 1,500, and a glittering international audience of some 5,000 attended the opening-night performance, paying up to $750 a ticket. But many were disappointed, in particular by the acoustics and amplification. Placido Domingo sang the role of Radames, and Maria Chiara was Aida.

La Scala and the London Royal Opera joined the ranks of companies using surtitles—captions of the text projected on a screen during performances. Surtitles are now the norm in some 75 American opera companies.

**Instrumental Music.** The Oakland (Calif.) Symphony closed down; the San Diego Symphony ended a long strike by reducing its concert season; and musicians took a pay cut to save the Denver Symphony from bankruptcy, while members of the Detroit Symphony struck for three months to avert a pay cut. The New Orleans Symphony joined forces with a major supermarket for a fund-raising project in which suppliers of products ranging from dog food to paper towels donated a portion of their profits to the orchestra. Music director Maxim Shostakovich starred in a television commercial to advertise the campaign, which brought in more than $20,000.

Philip Glass, a leader of the American musical avant-garde, returned to his classical roots by writing a violin concerto, premiered by the American Composers Orchestra and violinist Paul Zukovsky in New York. Joan Tower's *Silver Ladders* and William Bolcom's *Symphony No. 4* were given premieres by the St. Louis Symphony, and Ellen Taaffe Zwilich's new concert, *Images for Two Pianos and Orchestra,* was performed for the first time in Washington, D.C., for the dedication of the National Museum of Women in the Arts. Also in Washington, Lukas Foss heard the first performance of his latest work, *Tashi,* named after the chamber music group that played it, at the Kennedy Center. On his 60th birthday in March, Mstislav Rostropovich was a guest—not a participant—at a concert given in his honor at the Kennedy Center; at the end of the concert, Nancy Reagan conducted the National Symphony in "Happy Birthday to You," and the audience sang along.

Perhaps the biggest musical event of the New York season was the Vienna Philharmonic's March visit to Carnegie Hall. The orchestra's newly appointed director, Claudio Abbado, conducted the complete Beethoven symphonies, while pianist Maurizio Pollini performed all the Beethoven piano concertos.

In chamber music, the ten-year-old Emerson String Quartet came of age in January by presenting the complete cycle of Beethoven quartets in New York for the first time. Cellist Bernard Greenhouse, a founding member of the Beaux Arts Trio, retired after more than 30 years; he was replaced by Peter Wiley. The Amadeus Quartet decided to disband after the death of violist Peter Schidlof on August 16, at age 65.

**Redgrave Suit.** A federal appeals court ruled in October that the Boston Symphony Orchestra had violated actress Vanessa Redgrave's civil rights in 1982 when it canceled a series of concerts she was to narrate. The orchestra said it had received threats that performances would be disrupted because of her support for the Palestine Liberation Organization, but the court said such a risk was inherent in any public performance. The decision sent the case back to a lower court to consider Redgrave's claims for attorney's fees and damages in addition to the $27,500 she was to have received from the orchestra.

**Awards, Honors, Appointments.** Composer-conductor Leonard Bernstein received the Albert Schweitzer Music Award. The Pulitzer Prize in music went to American composer John Harbison for his cantata *The Flight Into Egypt.* For his opera *The Mask of Orpheus,* Britain's Harrison Birtwistle received the $150,000 Grawemeyer Award for Composition, believed to be the world's largest music prize. Composer Peter Maxwell Davies was knighted by Queen Elizabeth.

The year marked the debut of Spiros Argiris as music director of the Spoleto Festivals in Spoleto, Italy; Charleston, S.C.; and Melbourne, Australia. Sergiu Commissiona began his first season as music director of New York City Opera, and Michael Tilson Thomas was named principal conductor of the London Symphony. Increasingly, conductors juggled positions with several orchestras rather than holding a single full-time position with one. The St. Paul Chamber Orchestra, for example, replaced music director Pinchas Zukerman with three men: conductors Christopher Hogwood and Hugh Wolff, and composer John Adams. R.O.

## CLASSICAL RECORDINGS

The compact disk (CD) continued its steady rise as the medium of choice for classical music, on the part of both record companies and the buying public. The long-playing record (LP) and the tape cassette were by no means dead, but in only the rarest instances were classical recordings released on black vinyl and tape without an accompanying CD. Many of the major labels released a portion of their classical recordings on CD only, and a good many independents, such as Delos, Nimbus, and Denon, held to a policy of CD's only. This was made possible, to a large extent, by the opening of several new CD manufacturing plants in the United States, allowing supply to meet demand on a greater scale than ever before in the short life of the new medium.

**CD Reissues.** With increased production capability, the larger record companies were also able to release on CD the musical treasures they held in their vaults, often digitally remastering the original tapes and restoring the sound that had once been engineered out of them while producing distortion-free long-playing records on vinyl. The classical market, therefore, was virtually inundated, and happily so, by sonically updated re-releases of recordings made as far back as those by Enrico Caruso in the early years of this century. Many, of course, were milestone recordings of the more recent past. Among them, from Angel/EMI, were the celebrated 1958 recording of Richard Strauss's *Der Rosenkavalier* conducted by Herbert von Karajan, with a cast headed by Elisabeth Schwarzkopf, and, over a period of months, what amounted to almost the entire recorded output of operas and solo recitals by Maria Callas, honoring the American diva on the tenth anniversary of her death. RCA Red Seal's centennial tribute to pianist Artur Rubinstein consisted of 34 CD releases, ranging from the popular concertos of Beethoven, Brahms, and Tchaikovsky to the all-but-complete works of Chopin for piano solo.

# MUSIC

A corollary to this stepped-up activity with regard to CD reissues was the introduction by many classical labels of a "mid-price," or lower-priced, line of CD's, some of them bearing rather exotic names like Erato's Bonsai collection or RCA's Papillon series. From Deutsche Grammophon came a budget line under the name Galleria; from Philips, Silver Line Classics; from EMI, Angel Studio; from Denon, Repertoire; and from Harmonia Mundi, the French early-music specialist label Musique d'abord. All of the recordings in these series were drawn from existing catalogs and could be released on CD at reduced cost to the manufacturer, by virtue of lower royalties, less in the way of liner notes, and so forth; they not unexpectedly attracted a whole new audience for the CD and for classical music in particular.

**More Playing Time.** Another reason for the CD's overwhelming acceptance by the classical record buyer, and especially the budget-conscious buyer, was that the record companies began in 1987 to take seriously the often-heard complaints about short shrift on playing time. Consumers who had resisted the idea of paying a good deal more than the price of an LP for an equal number of minutes of music were increasingly won over by CD's that more nearly approached their maximum playing time of some 74 minutes. Record manufacturers went to considerable lengths to find appropriate couplings for classical works lasting only 35 or 40 minutes in order to fill out both new releases and reissues. The total playing time was often conspicuously printed on the front or back covers to assure buyers that they were getting their money's worth. And, for the most part, they were, or were beginning to, not only with well-filled single CD's but also in cases where recordings of operas and sprawling choral and symphonic works occupying three or four LP's could be released on two or three CD's.

**New Recordings.** Outstanding new recordings in this large-scale CD repertory released during the year included the four remaining symphonies in Eliahu Inbal's Mahler cycle, the Sixth through the Ninth (plus the Adagio of the Tenth), with the Frankfurt Radio Symphony (Denon), and a Mahler Eighth from Klaus Tennstedt and the London Philharmonic (Angel). Equally noteworthy were two recordings of Verdi's La forza del destino, one conducted by Giuseppe Sinopoli (Deutsche Grammophon) and the other by Riccardo Muti (Angel). A hit of the 1986 Paris season, Donizetti's The Daughter of the Regiment, with the American soprano June Anderson and the veteran tenor Nicolai Gedda, was recorded by Pathé Marconi. Deutsche Grammophon Archiv released Bach's St. John Passion, conducted by John Eliot Gardiner, while the first recording of Atys, an opera by Jean-Baptiste Lully, performed by Les Arts Florissants under William Christie, was issued on the occasion of the tricentennial of the composer's death by Harmonia Mundi. Three Mozart operas were well served on new CD's—Così fan tutte in a Glyndebourne Festival production conducted by Bernard Haitink (Angel), The Abduction From the Seraglio conducted by Sir Georg Solti (London), and The Marriage of Figaro conducted by Riccardo Muti (Angel). Other notable opera releases included Verdi's Macbeth, drawn from the soundtrack for a feature film featuring Leo Nucci in the title role, with Riccardo Chailly conducting (London), and Strauss's Ariadne auf Naxos, conducted by James Levine (Deutsche Grammophon).

Among the artists who will be remembered for recordings entering the catalog were soprano Kathleen Battle for her Salzburg recital, in which she was accompanied at the piano by James Levine (Deutsche Grammophon), the Spanish pop singer Rocío Jurado for her earthy performance in Falla's El amor brujo, conducted by Jesús López-Cobos (Angel), and Barry Douglas for his recording debut, a performance of Tchaikovsky's First Piano Concerto (RCA). Aldo Ciccolini, who so successfully championed Satie's piano music in the 1960's and 1970's, honored it again in a new CD recording for Angel. Pianist Mieczyslaw Horszowski, now in his mid-90's, recorded a remarkable solo recital for Nonesuch; the young violinist Cho-Liang Lin did a fine album of Mozart concertos for CBS; and also for CBS, Murray Perahia completed his cycle of Beethoven's five piano concertos with Haitink and the Concertgebouw Orchestra of Amsterdam.

C.B.

# N

**NAMIBIA.** *See* SOUTH WEST AFRICA.
**NAURU.** *See* STATISTICS OF THE WORLD.
**NEBRASKA.** *See* STATISTICS OF THE WORLD.
**NEGROES IN THE UNITED STATES.** *See* BLACKS IN THE UNITED STATES.
**NEPAL.** *See* STATISTICS OF THE WORLD.
**NETHERLANDS, THE.** In 1987 the Netherlands was beset by tension with Suriname, a former Dutch colony, as well as by economic and legal problems.

Gross domestic product growth was projected to decline to 1.5 percent in 1987 and to around 1 percent in 1988. Because natural gas prices are set in U.S. dollars, the fall in the dollar's value also meant reduced income from gas sales—a traditional mainstay of the Dutch economy. In January, currency realignments within the European Monetary System included a 3 percent upward revaluation of the guilder, which made Dutch products more expensive in foreign markets. Exports were indeed expected to increase at a slower rate than imports, although the overall trade balance for 1987 appeared likely to remain in surplus. The government deficit, which increased sharply in 1986, reflecting lower gas revenues, was expected to decline slightly in 1987-1988, as a result of new tax measures and planned expenditure cuts. Consumer prices increased only about 0.2 percent, but unemployment was very high—around 13 percent as of September.

In the face of the increasingly open practice of euthanasia in recent years, controversy surrounded the issue of whether, and when, doctors should be allowed to perform mercy killings on hopelessly ill patients in great pain. Passive euthanasia—removing life-support systems to allow natural death, for instance—had long been regarded as acceptable medical practice in the Netherlands. Active euthanasia, involving positive action to cause death, was prohibited by Dutch law. Parliament was considering government-sponsored legislation under which active euthanasia would remain a crime but would not be punishable when doctors observe certain conditions. Also introduced was a measure that would legalize mercy-killing outright.

At the start of 1987, rebel forces controlled much of Suriname, a Dutch colony until 1975, and were drawing financial and logistical support from the large Surinamese community in the Netherlands. The Dutch charged Surinamese government troops with human rights violations, while the military government of Suriname accused the Netherlands of complicity in aiding the rebels, among other charges. The Dutch expelled the Surinamese ambassador from The Hague, but tension eased when a new democratic constitution was approved by a September referendum in Suriname, and elections were held. (*See* CARIBBEAN BASIN.)

In September the Netherlands agreed to send minesweepers to the Persian Gulf in support of U.S. efforts to protect shipping endangered by war, following a refusal of such support in July. Dutch interest in keeping navigation open in the Gulf played a role in the decision—20 percent of that region's oil exports pass through the Dutch port of Rotterdam.

*See* STATISTICS OF THE WORLD.        W.C.C.
**NEVADA.** *See* STATISTICS OF THE WORLD.
**NEW BRUNSWICK.** *See* STATISTICS OF THE WORLD.
**NEWFOUNDLAND.** *See* STATISTICS OF THE WORLD.
**NEW HAMPSHIRE.** *See* STATISTICS OF THE WORLD.
**NEW JERSEY.** *See* STATISTICS OF THE WORLD.
**NEW MEXICO.** *See* STATISTICS OF THE WORLD.
**NEW YORK.** *See* STATISTICS OF THE WORLD.
**NEW ZEALAND.** The Labor government of Prime Minister David Lange won a second term in 1987 with a mixture of left-wing foreign policy and right-wing economic reforms. In foreign affairs Lange maintained his adventurous antinuclear policy. In the domestic sphere, he transformed New Zealand's economy by devaluing the dollar, removing farm and export subsidies, reducing tariffs, and phasing out regulations and controls. The policies of Finance Minister Roger Douglas changed the most heavily regulated economy in the capitalist world into one of the most free.

In June, with the government enjoying an unprecedented 26-point lead in opinion polls, Lange had announced a general election for August 15. The Labor Party, with support from many business leaders, who approved Douglas's free-market policies, retained its comfortable 15-seat majority in the new Parliament. Lange reshuffled his cabinet after the election, but retained Douglas as finance minister. In December the government introduced a new economic package, providing for an increase in the value-added tax, a cut in corporate tax rates, and a new single rate for personal income taxes, among other provisions.

Early in 1985, Lange had announced that New Zealand would forbid nuclear-armed or nuclear-powered ships to enter its waters, and in December of that year he introduced the Nuclear Free Zone, Disarmament, and Arms Control Bill. In June 1987, despite pressures from the United States and Great Britain to renounce Lange's antinuclear policy, the New Zealand Parliament carried the antinuclear measure into law by a vote of 39 to 29. As a result of the growing rift with Washington and London, New Zealand was turning increasingly to Australia for its defense needs. In February, Australia arranged for the sale of army rifles to New Zealand.

On October 2, France was ordered by an international arbitration tribunal in Geneva to pay more than $8.1 million in damages to Greenpeace, the environmental organization whose ship *Rainbow Warrior* had been sunk by French intelligence agents in Auckland harbor in 1985. The ship, used to protest French nuclear testing in the South Pacific, was sunk by an explosion that killed a Greenpeace photographer.

Maori leaders called upon Lange to explain the government's plans for their future, and the prime minister agreed that special steps were necessary to assist Maori development. In June the Maoris won a historic decision when the Court of Appeal upheld their claim to lands administered by the crown as trustees for the native peoples.

In March a powerful earthquake caused widespread damage in parts of North Island and seriously injured 25 people.

*See* STATISTICS OF THE WORLD.          F.D.S.

**NICARAGUA.** President Daniel Ortega Saavedra agreed to a regional peace plan in 1987, leading to some hope that the continuing war with the contra rebels could be ended.

**Peace Plan.** In February, Costa Rican President Oscar Arias Sánchez met with the presidents of Guatemala, El Salvador, and Honduras to discuss a regional peace plan he had devised, calling for a cease-fire, amnesty, and government talks with rebels in each country. Nicaragua was invited to a summit in Guatemala, to discuss the plan.

On August 4, days before the Guatemala summit, U.S. President Ronald Reagan announced his own peace plan, drafted with the assistance of House Speaker Jim Wright (D, Texas). The plan differed somewhat from the Arias plan—it called for more extensive changes in Nicaragua and included a stricter timetable for implementation. The Central American countries instead agreed on an accord in line with the Arias plan.

Under the Guatemala accord, signed August 7, each of the Central American governments would open up a dialogue with unarmed opposition groups and would declare amnesties for and arrange cease-fires with rebel groups. The territory of one country could not be used for attacks on another nation. The plan also called for a cutoff of outside aid to guerrilla groups. In addition, it stipulated that each signatory have a democratic, pluralistic political system, including a free press, and that state of emergency laws be lifted. Each country would organize a National Reconciliation Commission to monitor its compliance. Nicaragua set up such a commission in August, with Cardinal Miguel Obando y Bravo, a government critic, as its head.

In accord with the peace plan's provision on press freedoms, the opposition newspaper *La Prensa* was allowed to resume publication, without government censorship, on October 1. In addition, the Roman Catholic radio station Radio Católica was permitted to resume broadcasting. Later in October, however, the government forbade Radio Católica to broadcast news.

At a meeting with Salvadoran President José Napoleón Duarte on August 21, contra leaders formally accepted the peace agreement but

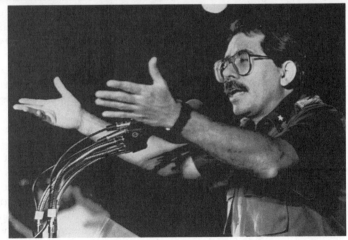

ollowing agreement in Au-
ust by the presidents of five
entral American nations
bove) on a regional peace
lan, world attention fo-
used on the possibility of
n end to the fighting be-
veen the Nicaraguan gov-
rnment and the contra reb-
ls. At right, Nicaragua's
resident, Daniel Ortega
aavedra, tells a November
ally in Managua of his plan
o pursue a cease-fire.

emanded direct negotiations with the Sandi-
istas. Nicaragua continued to refuse, saying
hat direct negotiations would give the contras
egitimacy, and instead declared unilateral
ease-fires in several regions.

In a speech before the Organization of Amer-
can States on October 7, President Reagan
ommended the Guatemala plan but voiced
leep skepticism that the Sandinistas would

honor it. He promised to press the U.S. Congress to approve additional aid for the contras.
The administration contended that without such
continued support for the rebels, the Sandinistas would have no incentive to fully implement
the peace accord.

**War and Peace.** Late in the year, efforts to
implement the peace plan continued, but progress was limited, and fighting continued.

273

# NICARAGUA

On November 5, Ortega agreed to negotiate indirectly with contra leaders on a nationwide cease-fire. Cease-fire talks, involving separate meetings by each side with Cardinal Obando, the mediator, opened in the Dominican Republic in early December. They broke down when Sandinista negotiators rejected a proposal from Obando calling for general amnesty, restoration of press freedoms, and an end to the state of emergency but not including provision for an end to outside support of the contras. New negotiations broke down when the contras refused to meet with representatives of the Sandinista government—an American lawyer and a West German politician.

On December 20, rebels launched one of their most successful attacks of the war, raiding three towns in the northwest. The raids, which showed increased military sophistication on the part of the contras, reportedly inflicted heavy damage and military casualties. Many civilian casualties also were reported. Both sides accepted a brief Christmas cease-fire, but there were charges that contras violated it.

**Outside Aid.** U.S. investigations into the Iran/contra affair—the secret sale of U.S. arms to Iran and the subsequent diversion of arms sale profits to the contras—revealed new information about funding for the rebels. In addition to $10 million to $30 million apparently diverted to the contras from the arms sales, $83 million to $97 million was said to have been raised by the Reagan administration and private supporters between 1984 and 1986. Most of the money came from foreign governments. Despite the Iran/contra scandal and the peace plan, the Reagan administration was able to obtain temporary nonmilitary contra aid in the fall to run through mid-December.

After the Honduran government had asked thousands of contras based there to leave by April, the rebels began infiltrating Nicaragua. By mid-April between 6,000 and 12,000 contras were in Nicaraguan territory, and contra sabotage activity stepped up. Soviet arms shipments to the Nicaraguan government also were increasing. In December a former senior aide to the Nicaraguan defense minister who defected to the United States told American officials there was a major new Soviet-supplied military buildup planned for Nicaragua.

These assertions increased pressure on th U.S. Congress late in the year to continue ai to the contras at least temporarily. In lat December, Congress approved $8.1 million i new nonmilitary aid.

On December 6 an American pilot, Jame Jordan Denby, was shot down over Nicaragua he was accused of engaging in espionage o CIA orders.

**Economic Crisis.** The economy continued t deteriorate. Inflation was expected to excee 1,000 percent for the year, and unemploymer was estimated at 40 percent. Shortages c consumer goods were widespread.

See STATISTICS OF THE WORLD.          J.F.A

**NIGER.** See STATISTICS OF THE WORLD.

**NIGERIA.** In 1987, Nigeria took steps in th direction of major economic and politicε reforms. The country's debt was rescheduled and the military government of President Ibra him Babangida announced plans for a transitio to civilian rule, although at a slower pace tha originally proposed.

**Economic Reform.** Nigeria's Western creditor agreed to reschedule major portions of th country's estimated $18 billion foreign det and, along with the World Bank, to provid new funding, contingent upon approval c Nigeria's adjustment policies by the Interna tional Monetary Fund. IMF approval cam formally in February, and partly as a result c rescheduling, the country was able to reduc its debt service ratio, estimated at about 2 percent for 1987.

The 1987 budget projected increased federε revenues, largely as a consequence of ai improved international petroleum market, an government expenditures were expanded by considerable margin. The budget also reflecte a continuation of wide-ranging economic re forms initiated in 1986. These reforms involve efforts to reorganize Nigeria's foreign debt improve government finances, and transforn incentives and production patterns. The budge also provided for a reduction in personal an corporate taxation and created special allo cations for employment creation and rura development.

**Sectarian Violence.** Religious riots swept acros the northern state of Kaduna in early Marcr Sparked by a dispute between Christian an

Muslim students in the northern town of Ka-fanchan, the unrest spread quickly, eventually reaching the state's capital. During a week of fighting, 19 people were killed and dozens of churches, mosques, and houses were destroyed.

**Program for Transition.** After 15 months of deliberation, a Political Bureau set up to make recommendations for a transition to civilian rule by 1990 delivered its report to the government in March. In July, the government responded to the Political Bureau's report and announced a political program to guide the transition. The new program extended the transition period by two years, so that a full passage to civilian democratic rule would not occur until 1992. The plan provided for a series of elections, beginning with local government contests late in 1987, continuing with state elections in 1990, and culminating in elections for president and the federal legislature in 1992. It also provided for a two-party political system—reduced from the six parties that competed during the Second Republic—and a bicameral legislature modeled after that of the United States. Local elections were held in December as announced but were marred by rioting and irregularities in some areas; as a result, fresh elections were to be held in 14 of the 21 states.

**Foreign Policy.** Nigeria assumed an enhanced West African and international profile. In March a new organization, the Concert of Medium Powers, convened in Lagos. Comprised of 16 countries from the developed and developing worlds, the new grouping was intended to serve as a mediating influence between other major international associations in the resolution of global issues.

Early in the year, all foreign missions in Lagos were told that they would have to transfer their operations by 1989 to Abuja, the new national capital nearing completion in the central part of the country.

*See* STATISTICS OF THE WORLD. P.M.L.

**NORTH ATLANTIC TREATY ORGANIZA-TION.** The U.S.-Soviet treaty eliminating medium-range and shorter-range nuclear missiles was a major focus of discussion and controversy within NATO during 1987. After the treaty was signed in December, NATO mem-

*NATO's highest-ranking military officer, General Bernard W. Rogers, resigned in June, reportedly because of a dispute with the Reagan administration over arms control. Rogers opposed the U.S.-Soviet treaty eliminating medium-range nuclear missiles, saying it endangered the Western allies.*

bers endorsed it, despite private reservations according to some observers; greater attention was then focused on efforts to redress the balance in conventional arms favoring the Soviet bloc.

**NATO and the Arms Treaty.** During the year there was some opposition among NATO members and officials to the planned U.S.-Soviet missile treaty. In June, General Bernard Rogers resigned as Supreme Allied Commander, Europe (NATO's top military leader), to be replaced by General John R. Galvin. The action was widely attributed to Reagan administration displeasure over Rogers's outspoken criticism of the planned treaty, on the grounds that it would leave Western Europe vulnerable to Soviet superiority in conventional arms.

A major sticking point in the negotiations was the Soviet insistence that 72 West German

Pershing intermediate-range missiles, whose nuclear warheads were controlled by the United States, be eliminated. The United States was reluctant to accept this demand since it contravened an existing agreement with West Germany; however, in August, Chancellor Helmut Kohl agreed that the missiles would be eliminated once removal of U.S. and Soviet missiles from Europe was completed. In September the United States and the Soviet Union agreed in principle on terms of a treaty. The NATO countries publicly supported the accord, and in late November the United States and its NATO allies agreed to stop deployment of American missiles in Europe as soon as the treaty was signed, without waiting for U.S. Senate approval. After the signing, by President Ronald Reagan and Soviet leader Mikhail Gorbachev, in Washington, D.C., on December 8, U.S. Secretary of State George Shultz visited NATO allies to brief them. He also issued a strong plea for greater spending by NATO members on conventional weapons. At a NATO meeting in Brussels on December 11, the NATO foreign ministers hailed the accord as a "treaty without precedent in the history of arms control." They also urged efforts toward a new treaty eliminating strategic nuclear weapons.

**Talks on Conventional Forces.** During the year, NATO and Warsaw Pact nations agreed on a new format for negotiating reductions of conventional forces in Europe. The so-called Mutual and Balanced Force Reductions talks, on cutting back conventional forces in central Europe, had been going on intermittently since 1973 without result. New negotiations, planned for 1988, were to be conducted under the auspices of the 35-nation Conference on Security and Cooperation in Europe, but would still include only members of NATO and the Warsaw Pact, excluding neutral nations that make up the rest of the conference. The new talks were expected to cover a wider area from the Atlantic Ocean to the Ural Mountains, and to include participation by France, which is a political member but not a military constituent of the NATO alliance and had not been participating in the MBFR talks.

**Inspecting Military Exercises.** In August, U.S. Army officers carried out an inspection of a Soviet military exercise held in the Soviet Union. It was the first such inspection conducted "on demand" as provided by a 1986 East-West agreement concluded in Stockholm. In September, Soviet-bloc military observers attended a ten-day NATO exercise in West Germany.

**French-German Defense Cooperation.** French President François Mitterrand and West German Chancellor Helmut Kohl announced plans to establish a joint defense council to coordinate defense policies. The council would be open to other European countries as well. The initiative was announced following conclusion of a joint French-German military exercise in which French troops operated under German command in a simulated defense of West German territory. Planning also went forward to create an integrated French-German military unit that would remain outside the NATO command structure, in deference to France's traditional policy on this issue.

Officials stated that the measures were basically intended to strengthen the Atlantic Alliance by improving defense coordination between France and Germany as the core of the alliance's European pillar. The moves were also apparently motivated by concern over U.S. domestic pressures to reduce American conventional troop strength in Europe and by the fear of some that a prospective U.S.-Soviet elimination of intermediate-range nuclear missiles could jeopardize security by leaving the Soviet bloc with a considerable advantage in conventional forces.

**U.S. Bases in Spain.** The United States and Spain continued to engage in difficult negotiations for the renewal of an agreement on U.S. military bases in Spain, which formed part of NATO's southern flank defense. Previously, to secure domestic support for Spain's membership in NATO in a 1986 referendum on the issue, Spanish Prime Minister Felipe González Márquez had pledged that Spain would not join NATO's integrated military structure and that there would be a substantial reduction of the U.S. military presence in the country under any new agreement.

The existing agreement, scheduled to expire in May 1988, provided for three U.S. air bases, a naval base, and nine smaller facilities in pain. Failing a renewal of the agreement, the United States would be required to evacuate the bases by May 1989. The key issue in the negotiations was Spain's demand for the withdrawal of a U.S. tactical air wing stationed near Madrid. Spanish officials rejected U.S. proposals to relocate the air base away from Madrid or to reduce the number of aircraft by one-third. U.S. officials were concerned that the terms of a base renewal agreement with Spain could affect the status of U.S. bases in other key NATO southern flank countries, particularly Greece, Turkey, and Portugal.

**New Secretary-General.** At their December meeting, NATO foreign ministers confirmed the selection of West German Defense Minister Manfred Wörner as the new NATO secretary-general, to succeed Britain's Lord Carrington beginning July 1, 1988. The other main contender for the post, former Norwegian Prime Minister Kaare Willoch, withdrew in the face of sentiment on the part of some members that a West German should be chosen; no West German had previously served in the post.

W.C.C.

**NORTH CAROLINA.** See STATISTICS OF THE WORLD.

**NORTH DAKOTA.** See STATISTICS OF THE WORLD.

**NORTHWEST TERRITORIES.** See STATISTICS OF THE WORLD.

**NORWAY.** The success of the Progress Party and the illegal sale of certain advanced technology to the Soviets made headlines in 1987.

Leaders of Norway's two largest parties, the governing Labor Party and the Conservative Party, were shocked when the Progress Party, which began in 1973 as a protest movement against high taxes, registered striking gains in September's local elections. The Progress Party advanced from just over 6 percent of the vote in 1983 to some 12 percent. Although the outcome had no immediate effect on national policy, it caused concern among leaders of the traditional parties preparing for the next election to the Storting (Parliament) in 1989.

Both Labor and Conservative party leaders admitted that they had failed to take the Progress challenge seriously enough. Labor Party head and Prime Minister Gro Harlem Brundtland was more sanguine about the outcome, mainly because Labor remained Norway's largest party, winning more than 36 percent of the popular vote in the local elections. Moreover, the Progress Party had twice sided with Labor in crucial parliamentary votes during the previous two years.

An increase in the international price of oil made Norwegian officials cautiously optimistic about the immediate economic future. Budget experts foresaw a modest rate of economic growth through the late 1980's, led by a slow but steady increase in North Sea oil and gas production and corresponding sales abroad. They anticipated an accompanying drop in the unemployment rate, to 2.4 percent from 3.5 percent in the mid-1980's.

U.S. government spokesmen irately disclosed in January that a subsidiary of a Norwegian armaments firm, along with the Toshiba Corporation of Japan, had illegally sold sensitive propeller-milling equipment and computer software to the Soviet Union. The United States charged that the advanced technology would enable the Soviets to manufacture a new generation of quieter submarines that would prove more difficult for Western forces to track. Embarrassed Norwegian officials immediately launched a probe of foreign shipments by the state-owned conglomerate, Kongsberg Vaapenfabrikk, and they subsequently confirmed the American allegations. The government indicted one Kongsberg employee and dissolved a trading subsidiary of the company. Kongsberg's Moscow office was also ordered closed. In June, Prime Minister Brundtland announced that the government had initiated stricter controls over export licensing, as well as physical inspections, to help prevent illegal technology transfers in the future.

In October the transfers were found to have been much more extensive than previously thought. Norwegian officials said Kongsberg had sold the Soviets more than 140 computers capable of running sophisticated machine tools and had shipped other high technology equipment to Moscow with the cooperation of other European countries. Additional charges were filed against the already indicted employee and against two technical advisers.

See STATISTICS OF THE WORLD.        M.D.H.

**NOVA SCOTIA.** See STATISTICS OF THE WORLD.

**NUCLEAR POWER.** See ENERGY.

# O

**OBITUARIES.** Each entry below contains the name of a notable person who died in 1987. It also contains a brief description of the accomplishments and events that contributed to making the person notable.

**Abel I(orwith) W(ilbur),** 78, influential American labor leader who, as president of the United Steelworkers of America from 1965 to 1977, added half a million new members and won sharp increases in wages and benefits while avoiding strikes. August 10 in Malvern, Ohio.

**Angleton, James Jesus,** 69, powerful long-time head of the CIA's counterintelligence office. A controversial figure whose efforts ended the careers of many CIA officers suspected of being Soviet agents, he was forced to resign in 1974 by CIA Director William Colby, who apparently considered him over-zealous. May 11 in Washington, D.C.

**Anouilh, Jean,** 77, French playwright who earned a reputation as a master of black comedy for his works, ranging from modernized classics, such as *Antigone* (1944), to historical dramas like *Beckett,* which won a Tony award as best play in 1961. October 3 in Lausanne, Switzerland.

**Astaire, Fred (Frederick Austerlitz),** 88, stylish, graceful American dancer whose seemingly effortless routines, put together with meticulous care, set new standards for movie musicals. Astaire and his sister, Adele, danced to stardom in a dozen Broadway musicals of the 1920's and early 1930's. After she retired, he teamed up with Ginger Rogers and others to star in such films as *Flying Down to Rio* (1933), *Top Hat* (1935), *Follow the Fleet* (1936), *Easter Parade* (1948), and *The Band Wagon* (1953). He also drew praise for dramatic roles, notably in *On the Beach* (1959). His TV special *An Evening With Fred Astaire* won nine Emmy awards in 1957. June 22 in Los Angeles.

**Astor, Mary (Lucile Langhanke),** 81, elegant American actress who began her 45-year career in silent movies and ultimately appeared in more than 100 films. Best known for her riveting

portrayal of a seemingly sympathetic but ev woman in *The Maltese Falcon* (1941), she wo an Oscar as best supporting actress for *Th Great Lie* (1941). September 25 in Woodlan Hills, Calif.

**Awolowo, Obafemi,** 78, Nigerian nationalis leader, chief of the Yoruba tribe, and forme premier of the Western region prior to inde pendence in 1960; he helped draft the consti tution for an independent Nigeria and becam a prominent opposition leader. May 9 in Ikenne Nigeria.

**Baird, Bil (William Britton Baird),** 82, Amer ican puppeteer whose puppets and marionette appeared on Broadway, on television, in film such as *The Sound of Music,* and in perform ance pieces such as Stravinsky's *L'histoire d* soldat. March 18 in New York City.

**Baldrige, Malcolm,** 64, U.S. secretary c commerce since 1981; basically a free-trad

*James Baldwin, who transmuted his anger at Amer ican racism into noteworthy novels, essays, and plays died in his adopted France at age 63.*

Director and choreographer Michael Bennett takes a bow following a special multicast performance of A Chorus Line, *the backstage musical that broke Broadway records.*

advocate, he nevertheless played a strong role in guiding the Reagan administration toward limited protectionist steps. July 25 in Walnut Creek, Calif., after falling from a horse while practicing for a rodeo competition.

**Baldwin, James (Arthur),** 63, expatriate American writer who was an impassioned voice of the civil rights movement. It was his first novel, *Go Tell It on the Mountain* (1953), that catapulted him to literary fame, but he also was esteemed as a playwright (with such dramas as *The Amen Corner* and *Blues for Mister Charlie*) and, perhaps most of all, as an essayist. His eloquent essays are collected in such works as *Notes of a Native Son* (1955) and *The Fire Next Time* (1963). December 1 in St. Paul de Vence, France.

**Barnett, Ross Robert,** 89, former Mississippi governor whose 1962 refusal to comply with a court order and allow a black man to attend the University of Mississippi led to rioting and a confrontation with the federal government. November 6 in Jackson, Miss.

**Barrow, Errol Walton,** 67, prime minister of Barbados from 1961 to 1976 and again since 1986. He led his country to independence from Britain in 1966 and worked to promote economic diversification and strengthen regional ties. June 1 in Bridgetown, Barbados.

**Bennett, Michael (Michael Bennett Di-Figlia),** 44, path-breaking American theater director and choreographer who shaped the backstage musical *A Chorus Line* into Broadway's longest-running show ever. He began as a chorus dancer, made his debut as a choreographer with *A Joyful Noise* in 1966, and went on to direct and choreograph such shows as *Company* (1970) and *Follies* (1971)—both codirected by Harold Prince—*Ballroom* (1978), and *Dreamgirls* (1981). He won 17 Tony award nominations and 8 Tonys. July 2 in Tucson, Ariz.

**Bishop, Jim (James Alonzo),** 79, American newspaperman and author of 21 books, including the pop history best-sellers *The Day Lincoln Was Shot* (1955) and *The Day Kennedy Was Shot* (1968). July 26 in Delray Beach, Fla.

**Bissell, Patrick,** 30, leading principal dancer with American Ballet Theatre; a gifted performer, he was known for his grand leaps, spontaneity on stage, and classical elegance. Found dead, December 29 in Hoboken, N.J.

# OBITUARIES

**Blakely, Colin,** 56, British stage and screen actor who created the role of the husband in Harold Pinter's *Old Times;* his film credits ranged from *A Man for All Seasons* to *The Pink Panther Strikes Again.* May 7 in London.

**Bolger, Ray(mond Wallace),** 83, long-legged and loose-jointed American actor and dancer; in a long, successful career he won widest recognition for his movie role as the Scarecrow in *The Wizard of Oz* (1939) and his rendition of "Once in Love With Amy" in the Broadway hit *Where's Charley?* (1948). January 15 in Los Angeles.

**Brannum, Hugh,** 77, American actor and writer of children's songs who played farmer-handyman Mr. Green Jeans on television's *Captain Kangaroo* (1955–1984). April 19 in East Stroudsburg, Pa.

**Brattain, Walter H(ouser),** 85, American scientist and inventor and senior member of the Bell Laboratories team that won the 1956 Nobel Prize in physics for inventing the transistor. October 13 in Seattle.

**Broglie, Louis Victor de,** 94, French physicist who won a 1929 Nobel Prize for his theory of the wave nature of electrons. He was secretary of France's Academy of Sciences, the author of more than 20 books, and a member of the French Academy. March 19 in Paris.

**Burns, Arthur F(rank),** 83, Austrian-born economist who, as an adviser to President Eisenhower and Nixon and then as chairman of the Federal Reserve Board (1970–1978), played a key role in shaping economic policy. June 26 in Baltimore.

**Butterfield, Paul,** 44, rock musician who began his career playing blues harmonica in his native Chicago; in the 1960's he founded the Butterfield Blues Band, whose music mixed elements of blues, soul, and jazz with rock and roll. May 4 in Los Angeles.

**Caldwell, Erskine (Preston),** 83, American novelist, short-story writer, and social commentator. He wrote more than 50 books, many chronicling rural life in the depression-era Deep South; his novels *Tobacco Road* (1932) and *God's Little Acre* (1933) were best-sellers that won critical acclaim but shocked many readers with language then considered obscene. April 11 in Paradise Valley, Ariz.

**Casey, William J.,** 74, hard-driving, often controversial director of the CIA from 1981 until January 1987, when he resigned because of illness; shortly before his death, his role in the Iran/contra affair came under investigation in Congress, and he was named in testimony as having helped in providing arms to Nicaraguan rebels. Casey served during World War II as chief of secret intelligence in Europe for the Office of Strategic Services; he later was chairman of the Securities and Exchange Commission and was Ronald Reagan's campaign manager in 1980. May 6 in Glen Cove, N.Y.

**Chamoun, Camille Nimer,** 87, president of Lebanon from 1952 to 1958 and a strongly pro-Western Christian leader who survived four assassination attempts during a long political career. August 7 in Beirut.

**Chenier, Clifton,** 62, Louisiana accordionist and singer known as "the king of zydeco," Cajun country music of the bayou, who introduced his Southern sound to a wide audience in the 1970's. December 12 in Lafayette, La.

**Chouinard, Julien,** 58, member of the Supreme Court of Canada since 1979; he had previously been Québec's deputy justice minister and a member of the province's high court. February 6 in Ottawa.

*Song-and-dance man Ray Bolger was indelibly identified with the role of the Scarecrow in the classic 1939 movie* The Wizard of Oz.

**Cochet, Henri,** 85, one of the "Four Musketeers," French players who dominated world tennis in the late 1920's and early 1930's. In 1927 he and the other three captured France's first Davis Cup. April 1 near Paris.

**Coco, James,** 56, American comic actor and television personality who won stardom on Broadway in *Last of the Red Hot Lovers* (1969) and an Emmy for his 1982 appearance on *St. Elsewhere*. February 25 in New York City.

**Cohen, Wilbur,** 73, New Deal Democrat who helped draft the Social Security Act of 1935 and became the first employee of the Social Security Administration, remaining there until 1956. During the Kennedy and Johnson administrations, Cohen helped create important social welfare programs and became secretary of health, education, and welfare. May 18 in Seoul, South Korea.

**Damon, Cathryn,** 56, American television and stage actress who won an Emmy for her role as Mary Campbell on the controversial television comedy series *Soap* (1977–1981). May 4 in Los Angeles.

**Den Uyl, Joop,** 68, Dutch Labor Party politician who served as prime minister of the Netherlands from 1973 to 1977. His government extended social welfare programs and cut the military budget. December 24 in Amsterdam.

**Du Pré, Jacqueline,** 42, brilliant English cellist who was considered one of the world's finest until stricken by multiple sclerosis at age 26, at the peak of her career. October 19 in London.

**Egan, Richard,** 65, American character actor, frequently the tough guy in action films. His credits include *The Damned Don't Cry* (1950), *Demetrius and the Gladiators* (1954), and *A Summer Place* (1959). July 20 in Santa Monica, Calif.

**Feldman, Morton,** 61, American minimalist composer whose music was inspired by the philosophy and techniques of abstract expressionist painting; he credited composer John Cage with encouraging him to create his own style. September 3 in Buffalo, N.Y.

**Folsom, James E.,** 79, colorful two-time governor of Alabama, who was an advocate for the poor and maintained a moderate to liberal stance on racial issues during his tenure

*Henry Ford II poses before a portrait of his grandfather, the founder of the Ford Motor Company.*

in the late 1940's and mid-1950's. November 21 in Cullman, Ala.

**Ford, Henry, II,** 70, grandson and namesake of the famous American automaker and an industrial giant in his own right. When he took control of the Ford Motor Company in 1945, it was losing almost $9 million a month; he turned it around, overseeing creation of the Thunderbird and Mustang, and expanding the company. September 29 in Detroit.

**Fosse, Bob (Robert Louis Fosse),** 60, American choreographer and director of Broadway musicals, movies, and television shows; his choreography was energetic and jazzy, marked by quirky rhythms. His numerous awards included Tonys for *Pajama Game, Damn Yankees, Redhead, Sweet Charity, Pippin, Dancin'* and *Big Deal* and an Oscar for *Cabaret*. September 23 in Washington, D.C.

**Freyre, Gilberto de Mello,** 87, Brazilian sociologist, author, and statesman. He won international acclaim for his 1934 book *Casa grande e senzala* (*The Masters and the Slaves,*

# OBITUARIES

1963), a study of the relationship between Brazil's colonizers and their African slaves. July 18 in Recife.

**Gaines (Otho) Lee,** 73, American singer, lyricist, and founder of the Delta Rhythm Boys, a jazz vocal quartet popular in the 1940's and 1950's. July 15 in Helsinki, Finland.

**Gingold, Hermione,** 89, British-born actress and comedian perhaps best known for her film role as Gigi's grandmother in the 1958 musical *Gigi.* She starred in the long-running London revue *Sweet and Low* and sparkled as a conversationalist on television talk shows. May 24 in New York City.

**Gleason, Jackie (Herbert John Gleason),** 71, rotund American comedian and actor best known for his role as blustery, big-hearted bus driver Ralph Kramden in the classic 1950's television series *The Honeymooners,* which evolved from skits developed on *The Jackie Gleason Show.* Gleason started out as a vaudeville emcee and carnival barker, played movie gangster roles, performed on Broadway and radio, and won early TV stardom in the NBC comedy *The Life of Riley* (1949–1950). He

*Rita Hayworth, star of screen and pinup pictures, in a typically glamorous pose.*

received a Tony award for his role in th Broadway musical *Take Me Along* (1959) an an Oscar nomination for his performance as pool shark in *The Hustler*—one of sever dramatic roles he played. Also a composer an conductor of mellow love tunes, he recorde many albums with the Jackie Gleason Orches tra. June 24 in Fort Lauderdale, Fla.

**Greene, Lorne,** 72, bass-voiced Canadia actor best known as the patriarch Ben Car wright on the television western *Bonanza* which ran from 1959 to 1973. September 1 in Santa Monica, Calif.

**Greenwood, Joan,** 65, husky-voiced Britis stage and screen actress known for such film comedies as *Kind Hearts and Coronets, Th Importance of Being Ernest,* and *Tom Jones* February 28 in London.

**Hardy, René,** 75, French Resistance leade who was sometimes accused of having be trayed the underground and collaborated with Klaus Barbie. Despite his acquittal in two trials the issue remained alive. Hardy wrote sever novels and a war memoir, *Last Words* (1984) April 12 in Melle, France.

**Harlow, Bryce N(athaniel),** 70, top White House staff member under Presidents Eisen hower and Nixon; he held key positions rangin from presidential speechwriter to chief White House lobbyist on Capitol Hill. February 17 ir Arlington, Va.

**Hartman, Elizabeth,** 45, American actress nominated for an Oscar in 1966 for her firs film role, as the blind heroine in *A Patch o Blue.* A possible suicide, June 10 in Pittsburgh.

**Hayes, Woody (Wayne Woodrow),** 74, hard driving Ohio State football coach. He compiled a 205-61-10 record in 28 seasons and earned a reputation as one of the game's greates tacticians. His career ended abruptly after he was seen on national television striking an opposing player during the 1978 Gator Bowl. March 12 in Upper Arlington, Ohio.

**Hayworth, Rita (Margarita Carmen Cansino),** 68, glamorous American actress and dancer whose pinup pictures adorned barracks walls in World War II. Beginning as a dancer at age 12, she made her acting debut in *Under the Pampas Moon* (1935) and starred in such films as *Only Angels Have Wings* (1939), *You'll Never Get Rich* (1941), *Cover Girl* (1944),

John Huston, bearded for his role as Noah in The Bible (1966), a film he directed, was part of a Hollywood dynasty extending from his father, Walter, to his daughter, Anjelica.

Gilda (1946), and *The Lady from Shanghai* (1949). Later, her long bout with Alzheimer's disease drew national attention to the illness. May 14 in New York City.

**Heifetz, Jascha,** 86, Russian-born virtuoso violinist whose name was synonymous with brilliant musicianship. A child prodigy in a poor family, he learned to play the violin at the age of 3 and was the toast of Europe by the age of 12. At his U.S. debut in 1917, critics called him one of the greatest violinists of all time. During a long career, Heifetz traveled widely on concert tours, performing in nearly every corner of the globe. He became a U.S. citizen in 1925. December 10 in Los Angeles.

**Heller, Walter (Wolfgang),** 71, White House economic adviser under Presidents Kennedy and Johnson and a major policy-maker. He pushed for deficit spending and tax cuts in the early 1960's, ushering in a period of economic growth and low inflation, but later pressed for tax increases to counter resurgent inflation and federal deficits. June 15 near Seattle.

**Herman, Woody (Woodrow Charles Herman),** 74, American bandleader who led a succession of ensembles called the Thundering Herd; his music ranged from the blues to bop and rock. Among the Herd's most popular numbers were "Woodchoppers' Ball" and their theme song, "Blue Flame." October 29 in Los Angeles.

**Hess, Rudolf,** 93, Adolf Hitler's close confidant and top deputy in the Nazi party appa-

ratus. In 1941 he parachuted into Scotland, reportedly seeking a separate peace between Britain and Germany, but he was imprisoned and later convicted of war crimes by the Allied tribunal at Nuremberg. Pronounced dead August 17 at a West Berlin hospital, after reportedly strangling himself at the city's internationally administered Spandau war-crimes prison; he had been jailed there since 1947.

**Hitchcock, Henry-Russell,** 83, American architectural historian who, with Philip Johnson, coined the term International Style for the glass-box style of architecture they helped popularize. He wrote on subjects ranging from Renaissance architecture to Frank Lloyd Wright. February 19 in New York City.

**Ho Ying-Chin,** 97, Nationalist Chinese minister of war from 1930 to 1944; he fled to Taiwan in 1949 after the Communist takeover of mainland China. October 21 in Taipei.

**Howser, Dick (Richard A.),** 51, American athlete who as manager of the Kansas City Royals in 1985 led the team to its first World Series crown. During his 25-year major league career, he played for the Kansas City Athletics and Cleveland Indians and played for, coached, and managed the New York Yankees. June 17 in Kansas City, Mo.

**Huston, John,** 81, American filmmaker—also a noted screenwriter, actor, big-game hunter, and raconteur—who directed more than 40 films, beginning with *The Maltese Falcon* (1941). He directed both his father,

*Musical comedy actor Danny Kaye, shown here in a 1946 film, starred in 17 other motion pictures and performed around the world on behalf of Unicef.*

Walter, and his daughter Anjelica to Oscar-winning performances, in *The Treasure of the Sierra Madre* (1947) and *Prizzi's Honor* (1985), respectively; the 1947 film also brought him Oscars for best director and best screenplay. Huston sought to preserve the vision of the author as he made films such as *The Red Badge of Courage* (1951), *The African Queen* (1952), *Moby Dick* (1956), and *Under the Volcano* (1984). His acting roles ranged from the voice of God in his 1966 film *The Bible* to Faye Dunaway's mercenary father in *Chinatown* (1974). He directed his last film, *The Dead*, in 1987. August 28 in Middletown, R.I.

**Jochum, Eugen,** 84, German conductor famous for his interpretations of the classical and romantic German repertoire. He founded the Hamburg Philharmonic and the Bavarian Radio Symphony. March 26 in Munich.

**Johnson, Gus,** 48, American basketball forward who averaged 17.1 points and 12.7 rebounds a game during his career, mostly with the Baltimore (now Washington) Bullets. April 28 in Akron, Ohio.

**Jonathan, Chief (Joseph) Leabua,** 72, prime minister of Lesotho from 1965 until 1986, when he was ousted in a military coup. He suspended the constitution in 1970 and ruled as an autocrat thereafter. At first maintaining close ties with South Africa, he eventually spoke out against apartheid and gave sanctuary to rebels of the African National Congress, fighting South Africa's government. April 5 in Pretoria.

**Jutra, Claude,** 56, Canadian director whose films often portrayed life in rural Québec; his 1971 picture *Mon oncle Antoine* (My Uncle Antoine) was chosen by an international panel as the best Canadian film ever made. Drowned after vanishing from his Montréal home on November 5, 1986; his body was found in April 1987.

**Kabalevsky, Dmitry (Borisovich),** 82, Soviet composer best known for lighthearted works such as his suite *The Comedians* and the overture to his opera *Colas Breugnon*. He won official praise for compositions on patriotic themes, such as his cantata *The Great Motherland*. Death in Moscow reported February 17.

**Karami, Rashid (Abdul Hamid),** 65, prime minister of Lebanon who held that office ten times in 32 years. A Sunni Muslim, Karami was known as a conciliator who favored peaceful relations between Muslims and Christians. Assassinated June 1 in an explosion on a military helicopter en route to Beirut.

**Kaye, Danny (David Daniel Kaminski),** 74, world-renowned American comedian and actor. He first won fame in the 1941 Broadway hit *Lady in the Dark,* in a comic novelty number where he rattled off 57 Russian names in 38 seconds. Kaye starred in 18 films, including *The Secret Life of Walter Mitty* (1947), *The Inspector General* (1949), and *Hans Christian Andersen* (1952), and entertained children around the world as Unicef's ambassador at large. Among honors he received were a special Oscar, a Danish knighthood, and Kennedy Center honors for his lifetime contribution to the arts. March 3 in Los Angeles.

**Kaye, Nora (Nora Koreff),** 67, American ballerina and a longtime principal of American Ballet Theatre, known for her dramatic interpretations of such roles as Hagar in *Pillar of Fire,* Lizzie in *Fall River Legend,* and Novice in *The Cage.* February 28 in Los Angeles.

**Kaye, Sammy,** 77, American bandleader whose "swing and sway" band, often featuring audience participation, achieved fame in the 1930's; the band performed on radio for many years and recorded over 100 hits, including "Harbor Lights." June 2 in Ridgewood, N.J.

**King, Cecil Harmsworth,** 86, British newspaper magnate who built one of the world's largest publishing empires in the 1960's; at one time he controlled over 200 magazines and newspapers, led by the London *Daily Mirror.* April 17 in Dublin.

**Kishi, Nobusuke,** 90, Japanese prime minister from 1957 to 1960. A strong nationalist and an accused war criminal (he was jailed for a time but never tried), Kishi used questionable tactics to win passage of a controversial U.S.-Japanese security treaty, precipitating demonstrations that forced him to step down. August 7 in Tokyo.

**Kolmogorov, Andrei N.,** 84, Soviet mathematician who founded modern probability theory and was one of the leading mathematicians of the century. October 20 in Moscow.

**Kountché, Seyni,** 56, president of Niger who, after seizing power in a 1974 military coup, installed a reformist government and later allied his country with Chad in its war against Libya. November 10 in Paris.

**Lake, Arthur (Arthur Silverlake),** 81, American actor who played the comic strip character Dagwood Bumstead on radio and in more than two dozen *Blondie* films. January 9 in Indian Wells, Calif.

**Landon, Alfred M(ossman),** 100, former governor of Kansas who, as the Republican presidential candidate in 1936, lost by a landslide to Franklin D. Roosevelt; undaunted, he remained influential in Republican politics. October 12 in Topeka, Kan.

**Lash, Joseph P.,** 77, American journalist-turned-historian who won a Pulitzer Prize for *Eleanor and Franklin* (1971),the first half of his vivid biography of Eleanor Roosevelt. August 22 in Boston.

**Laurence, Margaret (Jean Margaret Wemys),** 60, award-winning Canadian novelist and short-story writer. Her works, strongly influenced by her upbringing in a small Manitoba town, included *A Jest of God* (1966), later made into the film *Rachel, Rachel,* and *The Diviners* (1974), which drew controversy for its explicit description of an abortion. January 5 in Lakefield, Ontario.

*Onetime Kansas governor and presidential candidate Alf Landon died in October, a few weeks after his 100th birthday.*

# OBITUARIES

**Leloir, Luis Federico,** 81, Argentine scientist awarded the 1970 Nobel Prize in chemistry for research into the metabolism and storage of sugars. December 3 in Buenos Aires.

**LeRoy, Mervyn,** 86, versatile American director who first gained acclaim with *Little Caesar* (1930) and went on to make such films as *I Am A Fugitive From a Chain Gang* (1932), *Waterloo Bridge* (1940), and *Mister Roberts* (1955). He won a special Oscar in 1945 for the documentary *The House I Live In*. September 13 in Beverly Hills, Calif.

**Lévesque, René,** 65, a founder and president of the separatist Parti Québécois and Québec's premier from 1976 to 1985; originally a journalist, he rose to power with his advocacy of an independent Québec but moderated his stance after a 1980 provincial referendum rejected the idea. November 1 in Montréal.

**Levi, Primo,** 67, acclaimed Italian author, chemist, and Auschwitz survivor. A poet and novelist, he was best known for memoirs of his experiences as a concentration camp inmate, including *Se questo è un uomo* (1947; *If This Is a Man*, 1959), *La tregua* (1958; *The Reawakening*, 1965), and *Lilit e altri racconti* (1985; *Moments of Reprieve,* 1986). April 11, an apparent suicide, in Turin, Italy.

**Levine, Joseph E.,** 81, American movie mogul who produced, imported, or distributed almost 500 films, including *Godzilla* (1956), Fellini's *8½* (1963), *The Graduate* (1967), and *A Bridge Too Far* (1977). July 31 in Greenwich, Conn.

**Liberace (Wladziu Valentino Liberace),** 67, flamboyant American pianist whose classical/pop repertoire, flashy style, dazzling costumes, and trademark candelabra attracted a devoted following and helped him become one of the world's highest-paid entertainers. In the 1950's his widely syndicated *Liberace Show* made him television's first matinee idol, and when the show faded, he survived with panache, grossing an estimated $5 million a year for his live performances. February 4 in Palm Springs, Calif.

**Linnas, Karl,** 67, accused Nazi war criminal who was deported in April from the United States to the Soviet Union; he had been convicted and sentenced to death in absentia there, for commanding a concentration camp in his native Estonia where mass executions took place. Died while appealing for a pardon, July 2 in Leningrad.

**Luce, (Ann) Clare Boothe,** 84, American writer, and public official whose varied achievements won her international fame. She was managing editor of the irreverent *Vanity Fair* from 1932 to 1934; wrote several Broadway plays, including *The Women* (1936), a scathing satire; and was a war correspondent for *Life*, founded by her second husband, publisher Henry Luce. She served in the House of Representatives from 1943 to 1947 and later was U.S. ambassador to Italy. A devout Catholic and staunch anti-Communist, Luce often drew criticism for her sharp tongue. October 9 in Washington, D.C.

**MacLean, Alistair,** 64, Scottish-born author of thrillers and war adventure novels, including *The Guns of Navarone, Ice Station Zebra,* and *Where Eagles Dare,* which he adapted from

*A performance by Liberace, shown with candelabra and glittery suit, was never just a quiet evening around the piano.*

his own screenplay. Some of his international best-sellers were made into popular films. February 2 in Munich, West Germany.

**Marvin, Lee,** 63, American film and television actor. He won an Academy Award for his dual starring role in *Cat Ballou* (1965), played the hard-driving platoon commander in *The Dirty Dozen* (1967), and, in real life, was the successful defendant in a sensational 1979 "palimony" suit brought by former singer Michele Triola Marvin, with whom he had lived. August 29 in Tucson, Ariz.

**Masson, André,** 91, French surrealist painter who was an early exponent of automatism and whose work was characterized by jagged, evocative line; his invigorating presence made him an important part of the international art world for over 60 years. October 28 in Paris.

**McLaren, Norman,** 72, Scottish-born film animator who was director of experimental films at Canada's National Film Board and won international awards for his short films, which made daringly original use of line, color, and motion. January 26 in Montréal.

**Medawar, Sir Peter Brian,** 72, British cowinner of the Nobel Prize for medicine in 1960 for work on the body's rejection of transplanted tissue. In later years he was known for his writing on science and the scientific method. October 2 in London.

**Menten, Pieter Nicolaas,** 88, Dutch Nazi war criminal, also a noted art collector, who was convicted in the killings of dozens of Jews in Poland during World War II. He served eight months in prison in 1949 and again served time from 1980 to 1985. November 14 in Loosdrecht, the Netherlands.

**Murchison, C(lint) W(illiam),** 63, Texas oil financier and founder of the Dallas Cowboys; his fortune reached an estimated $250 million before it collapsed in the early 1980's. March 30 in Dallas.

**Myrdal, (Karl) Gunnar,** 88, Swedish economist, sociologist, pacifist, and reformer whose massive 1944 study, *An American Dilemma,* denounced "separate but equal" racial policy in the United States. Myrdal wrote widely on economic theory and on problems in different parts of the world; he was a cowinner of the 1974 Nobel Prize in economics. May 17 in Stockholm.

**Negri, Pola (Barbara Apollonia Chalupiec),** 88, Polish-born femme fatale of silent films, including the box office hits *Bella Donna* (1923), *The Cheat* (1923), *Forbidden Paradise* (1924), and *East of Suez* (1925); off-screen, she had highly publicized love affairs with Charlie Chaplin and Rudolph Valentino. August 1 in San Antonio.

**Nelson, Ralph,** 71, American director widely credited for his innovative technique in the early years of live television drama and for his artistry in film. Among the more than 1,000 productions he directed were the Emmy-win-

*Geraldine Page capped a distinguished acting career with an Academy Award-winning performance in the film* The Trip to Bountiful.

**Plaza Lasso, Galo,** 80, statesman and diplomat who was president of Ecuador from 1948 to 1952 and secretary-general of the Organization of American States from 1968 to 1975. January 28 in Quito, Ecuador.

**Pottle, Frederick A.,** 89, American scholar who edited the first 17 volumes of the *Boswell Papers,* journals of the 18th-century biographer James Boswell; the first volume, *Boswell's London Journal* (1950), sold more than 1 million copies. May 16 in New Haven, Conn.

**Preston, Robert (Robert Preston Meservey),** 69, brassy American actor who played confidence man Professor Harold Hill in the original Broadway production of *The Music Man* and the film version. His other movies included *The Dark at the Top of the Stairs, S.O.B.,* and *Victor/Victoria.* He appeared often on Broadway, winning Tonys for *The Music Man* (1958)

ning "Requiem for a Heavyweight," on *Playhouse 90,* and the Oscar-winning film *Lilies of the Field.* December 21 in Santa Monica, Calif.

**Nixon, Edgar Daniel,** 87, American civil rights leader who helped organize the Brotherhood of Sleeping Car Porters, America's first successful black union, and chose Martin Luther King, Jr., to lead the famous Montgomery, Ala., bus boycott in 1955. February 25 in Montgomery.

**Northrop, John H.,** 95, American scientist who shared the 1946 Nobel Prize in chemistry for work on the purification and crystallization of enzymes. May 27 in Wickenberg, Ariz.

**Page, Geraldine,** 62, American stage and screen actress, perhaps best known for her performances as Tennessee Williams heroines such as Alma Winemiller in *Summer and Smoke* and Alexandra del Lago in *Sweet Bird of Youth;* she won two Emmy awards and was nominated eight times for an Oscar, finally winning in 1986 for her role in the film version of Horton Foote's *The Trip to Bountiful.* June 13 in New York City.

**Perlmutter, Nathan,** 64, American lawyer who was a longtime director of the Anti-Defamation League of B'nai B'rith and a recipient of the Presidential Medal of Freedom. July 12 in New York City.

288

*Robert Preston in his best known role: The Music Man's Professor Harold Hill, who tries to swindle a small Iowa town into outfitting an entire boys' marching band without benefit of music lessons. The scene is from the 1965 movie version of the musical, costarring Shirley Jones (left).*

*Bayard Rustin was one of the leading figures in the civil rights movement of the early 1960's.*

fast-paced TV comedy show *Rowan and Martin's Laugh-In*, which aired from 1967 to 1973. September 22 in Englewood, Fla.

**Rustin, Bayard,** 75, American civil rights activist who played a key role in the 1963 March on Washington. He was widely respected but lost support among many blacks for his increasing stress on a linkage to liberals and religious groups and to the labor movement. August 24 in New York City.

**Scott, Randolph (Randolph Crane),** 89, Hollywood actor best known as the quiet-talking, fast-drawing hero in some two dozen Westerns; he also played in war movies, light comedies, and musicals during a career that lasted from the 1930's to the early 1960's. March 2 in Los Angeles.

**Segovia, Andrés,** 94, Spanish guitarist who revived interest in the classical guitar, creating for it both a repertory and a public. Not long after his professional debut in Granada at age 16, he became world-famous, touring widely and encouraging leading composers to write music for the guitar. He also recorded extensively, taught, and himself transcribed for guitar the music of classical composers. June 2 in Madrid.

and *I Do! I Do!* (1967). March 21 in Santa Barbara, Calif.

**Rich, Buddy (Bernard),** 69, American drummer who made his vaudeville debut in his parents' act before he was two years old and quickly became a prodigy. He went on to play with many bands, including those of Artie Shaw, Tommy Dorsey, and Harry James, besides leading his own band for a time. April 2 in Los Angeles.

**Rogers, Carl R(ansom),** 85, influential humanistic American psychologist and author. In the 1940's he developed "client-centered therapy," where the patient plays a more active role, in a process aimed at "self-actualization." In the 1960's he helped pioneer what came to be called encounter groups. Among his best-known books was *On Becoming a Person* (1961). February 4 in La Jolla, Calif.

**Rowan, Dan,** 65, American comedian and producer who cohosted and coproduced the

*Playing compositions written especially for him and reviving classical works, Andrés Segovia aroused interest in the classical guitar far beyond his native Spain.*

**Shawn, Dick (Richard Schulefand),** 63, American comedian who played a hippie portraying Hitler in the Mel Brooks movie *The Producers* (1968); besides other film roles, he frequently appeared on Broadway and television. Died April 17, after collapsing on stage during a comedy routine at the University of California at San Diego.

**Singh, Charan (Chaudhuri),** 85, Indian leader in his country's movement for independence from Britain and later president of the Lok Dal, or People's Party; Singh served briefly as prime minister in 1979, before his party was defeated in general elections. May 29 in New Delhi.

**Sirk, Douglas (Detlef Sierck),** 86, German-born director who achieved success in Hollywood with the melodramas *Magnificent Obsession* (1954), *Written on the Wind* (1956), and *Imitation of Life* (1959); after years of obscurity, his films recently won popularity in Europe. January 14 in Lugano, Switzerland.

**Smith, Willi Donnel,** 39, award-winning American designer who marketed his colorful and trendy sportswear under the WilliWear label. April 17 in New York City.

**Soames, Lord Arthur Christopher John,** 66, British diplomat and politician who in 1980 presided as colonial governor of Rhodesia during the months preceding its independence and transition to majority rule; as ambassador to France from 1968 to 1972 he played a vital role in ensuring British entry into the European Community. September 16 in Hampshire, England.

**Stewart, Michael,** 63, American writer and lyricist of Broadway musicals. He won Tony awards for *Bye Bye Birdie* in 1961 and *Hello Dolly!* in 1964; among his other successes were *I Love My Wife* (1977), *Barnum* (1980), and *42nd Street* (1980). September 20 in New York City.

**Sullivan, Maxine, (Marietta Williams),** 75, American folk and jazz singer whose 1937 recording of the Scottish folk song "Loch Lomond" launched a highly successful radio, stage, and film career; she won a Tony in 1979 for her role in *My Old Friends,* a musical about aging. April 7 in New York City.

**Susskind, David (Howard),** 66, American television producer and talk-show host. Susskind won 47 Emmys for his productions, which included *Kraft Television Theater* and other early TV classics. He pioneered the issue-oriented television talk show; his own ran for 28 years, until 1986. February 22 in New York City.

**Taylor, Maxwell D.,** 85, American general, presidential adviser, and military strategist. A decorated battlefield commander, Taylor led the 101st Airborne Division into Normandy on D-day, headed the postwar U.S. military government in Berlin, and commanded U.S. and UN forces in the Korean war. He later chaired the U.S. Joint Chiefs of Staff and was ambassador and presidential envoy to Saigon during the U.S. buildup in Vietnam. In his 1960 book *The Uncertain Trumpet,* Taylor stressed the role of infantry and championed "flexible response" as opposed to nuclear strikes. April 19 in Washington, D.C.

**Taylor, Ralph Waldo,** 105, last survivor of the 27,000 American soldiers who charged up San Juan Hill, Cuba, in 1898, in the best-known battle of the Spanish-American War. May 15 in Pompano Beach, Fla.

*From World War II battlefields to the American embassy in Saigon during the Vietnam war, General Maxwell Taylor was a major voice in U.S. military and strategic policy.*

**Teichmann, Howard M.,** 71, American playwright, biographer, and master storyteller who coauthored the 1953 comedy hit *The Solid Gold Cadillac.* July 7 in New York City.

**Tomás, Américo Deus Rodrigues,** 92, president of Portugal from 1958, when he was chosen to run by dictator Antonio Salazar, until 1974, when he was ousted in a leftist military coup. September 18 in Cascais, Portugal.

**Tosh, Peter (Winston Hubert McIntosh),** 42, Jamaican reggae star who in 1963 with musician Bob Marley founded the popular group the Wailers; his lyrics were often political, condemning injustice and poverty. September 11 in an apparent robbery at his home in St. Andrew, Jamaica.

**Trapp, Maria Augusta von,** 82, Austrian baroness whose life story inspired the stage and screen musical *The Sound of Music.* While a novice at a Salzburg convent, she was sent to serve as governess to the seven children of widower Baron Georg von Trapp; she married him in 1927, and they had three children. The family toured Europe as a choral group, fleeing to the United States after the 1938 Nazi occupation of Austria. March 28 in Morrisville, Vt.

**Trifa, Valerian,** 72, Romanian-born archbishop and former head of the U.S. Romanian Orthodox Episcopate; in 1984 he agreed to deportation on charges of having been a Nazi supporter who incited violence against Jews. January 28 in Cascais, Portugal.

**Tsatsos, Constantine,** 88, president of Greece from 1975 to 1980 and the author of more than 20 books on history, law, and philosophy. October 8 in Athens.

**Tudor, Antony (William Cook),** 78 (?), influential British-born dancer and choreographer who transformed classical ballet with his introduction of psychological themes; his works include *Pillar of Fire, Dark Elegies,* and *Romeo and Juliet.* A founder of the London Ballet in the 1930's, he later served for over 40 years as choreographer with American Ballet Theatre. April 20 in New York City.

**Unruh, Jesse M.,** 64, California state treasurer. As speaker of the state Assembly from 1961 to 1968, Unruh, a Democrat, was an important force in national, as well as state, politics; he was credited with winning the

*Harold Washington, the first person to win reelection as mayor of Chicago in 12 years, was several months into his second term when he died suddenly of a heart attack.*

passage of major liberal legislation in California and was an early key political ally of John F. Kennedy. August 4 in Marina del Rey, Calif.

**Vernon, Jackie,** 62, American television and nightclub performer popular for his self-mocking style of delivery. November 10 in Los Angeles.

**Warhol, Andy (Andrew Warhola),** 58 (?), world-famous American pop superstar and fixture on the celebrity nightclub scene. He gained notoriety in the 1960's for reproducing commercial images such as Campbell's soup cans and Brillo soap pad boxes in his art and for his portraits of such celebrities as Marilyn Monroe and Elizabeth Taylor. At his Manhattan studio, "the Factory"—a legendary gathering place for artists and hangers-on—he made many experimental films, including *The Chelsea Girls,* the most notorious underground film of its day. He also started *Interview,* a celebrity-oriented magazine, and in recent years vigorously promoted the work of younger artists. February 22 in New York City.

**Washington, Harold,** 65, Democratic mayor of Chicago. The first black to hold the post, won in a tight election in 1983, he battled City Council opponents for most of an acrimonious first term but was easily reelected in April. November 25 in Chicago.

**Williams, (George) Emlyn,** 81, Welsh actor, playwright, and director who frequently starred in his own works; he first won recognition for his role as a psychopathic bellhop in his play *Night Must Fall* (1935), his success continuing with *The Corn Is Green* (1938). Playing Charles Dickens, he toured the world in a one-man show. September 25 in London.

**Wilson, Earl,** 79, Broadway and Hollywood gossip columnist whose "It Happened Last Night" columns, written from 1942 to 1983, ran in as many as 175 newspapers nationwide. January 16 in Yonkers, N.Y.

**Wittig, Georg,** 90, West German scientist who shared the 1979 Nobel Prize in chemistry; his process for regulating the regrouping of atoms in a molecule, called the Wittig Synthesis or Wittig Reaction, made possible the mass production of many important drugs and industrial chemicals. August 26 in Heidelberg, West Germany.

**Yourcenar, Marguerite,** 84, Belgian-born author and classical scholar who wrote novels, essays, memoirs, and plays in her native French, winning international renown. Her novel *Memoirs of Hadrian* (1951) was the best known to English-speaking readers. In 1981 she became the first woman inducted into the French Academy, France's most prestigious language and literary society. December 17 in Northeast Harbor, Me.

**Zorinsky, Edward,** 58, conservative U.S. senator from Nebraska. As mayor of Omaha in 1976 he switched parties to run as a Democrat for the Senate, becoming the first Jew to win a statewide election in Nebraska. March 6 in Omaha.

**OHIO.** See STATISTICS OF THE WORLD.

**OKLAHOMA.** See STATISTICS OF THE WORLD.

**OMAN.** See STATISTICS OF THE WORLD. See also PERSIAN GULF STATES.

**ONTARIO.** See STATISTICS OF THE WORLD. See also CANADA.

**OREGON.** See STATISTICS OF THE WORLD.

**ORGANIZATION OF AMERICAN STATES.** Deliberations of the Organization of American States were dominated in 1987 by the peace process in Central America.

In January, João Baena Soares, secretary-general of the OAS, was authorized to travel with the foreign ministers of the four Contadora Group nations—Colombia, Mexico, Panama, and Venezuela—in a diplomatic mission to bring peace to war-torn Central America. This effort did not bear fruit. However, a new peace initiative spearheaded by Costa Rica President Oscar Arias Sánchez began to gain acceptance. It called for cease-fires with rebels, amnesty for political prisoners, steps to increase freedom and democracy, and other measures in each of the five Central American nations. The accord, signed by five Central American nations in August, later garnered the Nobel Peace Prize for Arias.

In November, as the Arias plan began to take effect, the 1987 session of the OAS general assembly opened in Washington. Addressing the foreign ministers in attendance, President Ronald Reagan announced a readiness to resume high-level peace talks with the Nicaraguan regime once it began indirect negotiations with the U.S.-backed contras. In a speech to the assembly, Nicaraguan President Daniel Ortega Saavedra promised full compliance with the peace accord. He accused the United States of meddling in the Central American peace process, while demanding direct talks with the Reagan administration.

Later in November, presidents of the eight Latin American OAS nations met in Acapulco, Mexico, in a conference that, for the first time, did not include the United States. They called for an overhaul of the OAS, as well as for a ceiling on repayment of their foreign debt and for reintegration of Cuba into regional organizations. L.L.P.

**ORGANIZATION OF PETROLEUM EXPORTING COUNTRIES.** While oil prices held fairly steady—between $18 and $20 a barrel—during most of 1987, disagreements persisted within OPEC over pricing policies and methods to prevent prices from falling. By year's end, no seemingly effective agreement had been reached.

The 12-member organization was divided among three perspectives. Saudi Arabia, Kuwait, and the United Arab Emirates preferred to see gradual increases above the official price of $18. They feared that too rapid a rise would stimulate world inflation and disrupt the international economy. All in this group had massive petroleum reserves and were concerned about long-term supply and demand; if prices were to increase too rapidly, they believed, non-OPEC members would intensify their search for oil, eventually leaving OPEC to face a shrinking market. The OPEC "hawks," Iran, Libya, and Algeria, wanted a rapid price increase; because of their smaller reserves and urgent need for immediate capital, they were less concerned about the long-term consequences of escalating prices. Iran, the leader of this group, was especially eager for immediate income to finance its costly war against Iraq. Finally, a middle group, including Nigeria, Venezuela, Indonesia, and Ecuador, had a need for immediate capital but did not urgently advocate a rapid price rise.

These differences were debated by the ministers attending the plenary OPEC session, the 81st, held at Vienna during June, where it was agreed to keep the official price at $18. A compromise on production quotas established a total of 16.6 million barrels a day (b/d) for the second half of 1987, despite opposition from Iran, which wanted to maintain the 15.8 million b/d quota for the first half of 1987, as agreed at the organization's December 1986 meeting.

At a subsequent meeting in December, six days of difficult negotiations ended in an agreement to extend the $18-a-barrel price and current production quotas through mid-1988. An official ceiling of 15.06 million b/d was adopted for the total output of 12 members, excluding Iraq. Over strong objections from Iran, Iraq was allowed to remain outside the agreement and thus to continue producing nearly twice the amount OPEC theoretically set for it. It was expected that other members as well would exceed their production quotas, as they already had been doing, while also continuing to offer cut-rate prices and discounts below the $18 price. These expectations helped drive already weakening prices downward on the world markets.           D.P.

# P

**PACIFIC ISLANDS.** In 1987 a pair of coups in Fiji reversed the results of April elections and Palau voters approved a new relationship with the United States.

April elections in Fiji provided an unexpected victory for the coalition of the ethnic Indian-dominated National Federation Party and the multiracial Fiji Labor Party, headed by Timoci Bavadra. But groups of ethnic Fijians then protested what they felt was a takeover of political power by the Indian community. On May 14 the new Bavadra government was ousted in Fiji's first military coup, led by Lieutenant Colonel Sitveni Rabuka and other indigenous Fijians. Fiji's governor-general, Sir Panaia Ganilau, refused to recognize the takeover; he appointed a temporary Council of Advisers, which included the ousted Bavadra. By September 23, agreement had been reached on a new multiracial "caretaker" Council of State and a process of constitutional review.

But two days later, Rabuka staged another coup, and abolished the office of governor-general. Rabuka declared Fiji a republic and in early December appointed Ganilau as president, while naming Sir Kamisese Mara prime minister; Mara had held that post for 17 years prior to the April elections.

Voters in Palau (Belau) finally approved a compact of free association with the United States, after voting for a referendum measure that reduced the required margin of approval to a simple majority. One effect of the compact was to ban nuclear weapons testing within the island's territory, but it permitted visits by nuclear-armed or nuclear-powered ships. In return, Palau was to receive payments of approximately $1 billion over 50 years.

In July, Sir Peter Cook lost office as prime minister of the Cook Islands after a vote of no confidence in which members of his own party joined. He was succeeded by Pupuke Robati.

Vanuatu signed an agreement with the Soviet Union granting fishing rights and port access to Soviet ships for $1.5 million.

In Papua New Guinea's elections, 47 members of the 109-seat parliament lost their seats and no party emerged with a clear majority. Later, Prime Minister Paias Wingti was returned to office as head of a new coalition.

Membership in the South Pacific Forum increased to 15 with admission of the Republic of the Marshall Islands and the Federated States of Micronesia. The organization welcomed a fisheries treaty with the United States allowing U.S. vessels to fish in member nations' waters for licensing fees.

See STATISTICS OF THE WORLD.          R.J.M.

**PACIFIC ISLANDS, TRUST TERRITORY OF THE.** See STATISTICS OF THE WORLD.

**PAKISTAN.** As President Muhammad Zia ul-Haq celebrated his tenth anniversary as Pakistan's leader in mid-1987, grave threats to national unity remained.

**Domestic Unrest.** In the Northwest Frontier Province, where Pathans have long pined for their own independent state and more than 3 million Afghans have fled since the Soviet invasion of Afghanistan in 1979, acts of violence increased markedly. Pakistan authorities blamed Afghan agents living among the refugees. Meanwhile, the Sindhis were perhaps the most outspoken ethnic minority, strongly criticizing Punjabi monopolies in the government, the armed forces, and the economy. The Sindhis launched repeated street demonstrations, and the government countered with broad-scale arrests and detentions.

Sporadic clashes between Pathans, joined by Afghan refugees, and Muhajirs (Muslim refugees from India and Bangladesh) continued, following the fierce communal rioting that broke out in Karachi late in 1986. In February the government began moving the Afghan refugees to a tented area where they could be better monitored. However, ethnic fighting erupted again in Karachi in July. After four days of strife and several deaths, the army was called upon to restore law and order.

Popular support for the opposition parties grew, but neither Benazir Bhutto nor any other leader seemed able to rally the support needed to challenge President Zia, who celebrated the tenth anniversary of his seizure of power on July 5. On the same day, small protests were mounted, and bombs exploded at the central railway and bus stations in Lahore, killing 7 people and injuring 50. On July 14, car bombs were detonated in a crowded bazaar and at the city bus station in Karachi. More than 70 people died and at least 300 were injured. Zia again blamed Afghan agents.

An arranged marriage according to Muslim tradition was announced for Benazir Bhutto (left), Pakistan's most prominent dissident, and Asif Zardari (center)—like her, the scion of a wealthy family. For Bhutto, marriage would mean freedom of movement to pursue her political career. At right is her mother.

*New accusations that Panama's strongman, General Manuel Antonio Noriega, had engaged in crimes ranging from corruption to murder brought thousands into the streets of Panama City to demonstrate against him. The government clamped down on dissent by declaring a "state of urgency."*

**Foreign Affairs.** The year began with the threat of a new war between Pakistan and India. Late in 1986 the two countries had massed troops on their mutual frontier. High-level talks eased the tension, and in February, Zia met with Indian Prime Minister Rajiv Gandhi to discuss the border situation. Subsequently, the forces of both countries were systematically withdrawn. In September, however, Pakistani and Indian troops clashed in Kashmir. Indian military officials characterized the fighting as the most serious clash with Pakistan in three years and claimed that 150 Pakistani soldiers were killed.

The civil war in Afghanistan continued to spill over the Pakistani border. Afghan warplanes and artillery bombed and shelled Pakistani towns along the frontier, killing close to 100 people in one instance. Pakistan reported shooting down an Afghan warplane in March, and the following month Afghan warplanes shot down a Pakistani fighter for the first time.

The Zia government repeated its pledge not to construct nuclear weapons and also declared its willingness to sign the Nuclear Non-

Proliferation Treaty if India would do so. Nevertheless, rumors were unabated concerning Pakistan's nuclear weapons program. The U.S. government criticized Islamabad in July after a Pakistani-born Canadian businessman was arrested in Philadelphia and charged with trying to obtain restricted nuclear materials for a Pakistani bomb program. He was later convicted. The U.S. Congress, which had suspended new aid because of controversy over Pakistan's nuclear program, nevertheless backed off and approved a $480 million package late in the year.

In December, Saudi Arabia, reportedly irate over Pakistan's failure to condemn Iran for the summer riots in Mecca, canceled its security contract with Islamabad and expelled Pakistani military personnel.

*See* STATISTICS OF THE WORLD. L.Z.

**PALESTINE LIBERATION ORGANIZATION.**
*See* MIDDLE EAST.

**PANAMA.** During 1987, Panama's strongman and Defense Forces commander, General Manuel Antonio Noriega, encountered increased protests at home and was embroiled in controversy with the United States. The protests started on June 9, a day after Colonel Roberto Díaz Herrera publicly charged that Noriega had rigged the 1984 national elections, was involved in drug operations, and played a role in the 1981 death of General Omar Torrijos, the former Panamanian leader, and in the 1985 death of government critic Hugo Spadafora. Díaz Herrera, who had been forced to retire on June 1 as second in command in the military, was arrested on July 27. After judicial proceedings behind closed doors, he was sentenced in December to five years in prison for crimes against state security.

On June 11, after protests turned violent, the government imposed a "state of urgency," suspending civil and political rights. Five newspapers, three radio stations, the national university, and high schools in Panama City were closed for a time. Noriega sought popular backing by lowering some food prices, approving a new hospital, and replacing the military heads of three agencies by civilians. The opposition was unable to generate widespread support for a protest march and general strike in October, but the government did suffer from the decision of Vice President Roderick Esquivel to withdraw his faction of the Liberal Party from the governing coalition.

A Supreme Court justice who had been a frequent critic of the government was shot and killed in late October; police claimed that the killing had no connection with politics.

The U.S. State Department and U.S. Senate in June called for free elections, the military's withdrawal from political appointments, and an independent investigation of charges against Noriega. Panama's Legislative Assembly, for its part, asked the government to declare U.S. ambassador Arthur Davis persona non grata, and thousands of Noriega supporters—including eight cabinet ministers—pelted the U.S. embassy with bottles, paint, and rocks. Subsequently, the United States suspended economic and military aid. In retaliation, Panama ordered the Agency for International Development in Panama closed, expelling the U.S. employees and their dependents. By December, Noriega was openly courting the Soviet Union, further eroding any U.S. support.

See STATISTICS OF THE WORLD.            N.J.P.

**PAPUA NEW GUINEA.** See STATISTICS OF THE WORLD. See also PACIFIC ISLANDS.

**PARAGUAY.** In 1987 pressure from the United States and the approach of a presidential election led to the relaxation of some political restrictions in Paraguay. However, President Alfredo Stroessner continued to maintain a tight grip on the country.

In April the government lifted the decades-old state of siege in preparation for the presidential elections of February 1988. The government also released some political prisoners. Meanwhile, Stroessner sought to resolve divisions within his ruling Colorado Party, to clear the way for his anticipated bid for an eighth consecutive five-year term. The two major factions in the party, the *militantes* and the *tradicionalistas*, both professed loyalty to Stroessner, but they squabbled with each other. In April noted opposition figure Domingo Laíno was finally allowed to return to the country after five unsuccessful attempts to do so. In June, 30,000 people came to hear Laíno speak at what was the largest opposition demonstration in 20 years. The labor movement was also permitted to hold its May Day rally for the first time since 1958. However, repressive actions reportedly continued.

On the economic front, a business federation report estimated that two-thirds of Paraguay's foreign trade consisted of uncounted, untaxed contraband, much of which is widely believed to be controlled by high-ranking army officers and others close to Stroessner. Foreign debt continued to grow.

In January, Paraguay had its preferential trade status with the United States suspended because of its poor human rights record and its actions against trade unions. The interior minister threatened to declare outspoken American ambassador Clyde Taylor persona non grata if he continued to "interfere" in Paraguayan affairs. In February police teargassed a crowd attempting to get into a reception at which Taylor was an honored guest. Two Paraguayan apologies and a guarantee of Taylor's future security were required before relations returned to normal. The suspension of preferred trade status continued, however.

See STATISTICS OF THE WORLD.            J.F.,Jr.

**PENNSYLVANIA.** See STATISTICS OF THE WORLD.

# People in the News

**The biggest newsmakers during 1987 ranged from world leaders and their families, royalty, and the usual media superstars to a woman sailor who circumnavigated the globe and a little Texas girl whose rescue from a well drew national attention.**

The foibles, follies, and failings of politicians, preachers, and media celebrities made headlines in 1987—a year when America flirted with "Olliemania" and "Gorby fever." **Gary Hart** bowed out of the presidential sweepstakes, then in again, and the bloodhounds of the British press relentlessly tracked the scent of royal scandal.

This was a difficult year for the first family. On January 5, President **Ronald Reagan,** 75, underwent surgery to relieve an enlarged prostate and two noncancerous polyps were excised from his colon during a checkup in June. On October 17, surgeons removed the cancerous left breast of First Lady **Nancy Reagan,** 66, who suffered the loss of her mother, **Edith Luckett Davis,** 91, only nine days later. Meanwhile, a close adviser and friend, U.S. Commerce Secretary **Malcolm Baldrige,** 64, died in a rodeo accident. **Michael Deaver,** a longtime family friend and adviser, was convicted of lying to Congress and a federal grand jury. Another former Reagan White House aide, **Lyn Nofziger,** was indicted for influence peddling. Finally, the Iran/contra scandal cast the president and some present and former members of the administration in a poor light.

Not all the White House news was doleful. Although Reagan's first two Supreme Court nominees, **Robert Bork** and **Douglas Ginsburg,** both stumbled, the president's third choice, **Anthony M. Kennedy,** seemed well on the way to winning Senate confirmation. Another cause for celebration was the acquittal in May of **Raymond J. Donovan,** who had resigned as Reagan's secretary of labor in 1985 following his indictment on larceny and fraud charges.

Moreover, the visit to Washington in December of **Mikhail** and **Raisa Gorbachev** was a triumph for both the president and the Soviet leader—who appeared to have developed a warmer relationship than did their first ladies. While the husbands were able to relate on a first-name basis, the wives appeared locked in a verbal cold war, with no détente in sight. Meanwhile, Raisa's role was a matter of controversy in the Soviet Union, where many thought she should be considerably less visible

*Raisa Gorbachev (right), wife of the Soviet leader, escorts First Lady Nancy Reagan to dinner in the Soviet embassy during the December superpower summit in Washington. In contrast to the summit's official tone, relations between the two women were widely believed to be frosty.*

# PEOPLE IN THE NEWS

*A political activist by inheritance, Amy Carter was acquitted of charges relating to a 1986 protest against CIA recruiting at the University of Massachusetts. Carter, shown here with fellow-protester Abbie Hoffman, is the daughter of former President Jimmy Carter.*

in public. The Soviet leader, in answer to a question by interviewer **Tom Brokaw,** told American television audiences he discussed important affairs at home with his wife, but Soviet censors toned down his answer on the taped version shown in the Soviet Union. Americans in any event took a liking to "Gorby," who emerged from his limousine to press the flesh of Washington pedestrians like a seasoned American political pro—and was even named *Time* magazine's Man of the Year. Honoring the Reagan-Gorbachev summit at a White House dinner were such diverse notables as former Secretary of State **Henry Kissinger,** nuclear scientist **Edward Teller,** evangelist **Billy Graham,** and sports greats **Meadowlark Lemon, Mary Lou Retton,** and **Joe DiMaggio,** with pianist **Van Cliburn** providing musical entertainment.

Other Reagan family members also made news. In January the president's daughter **Maureen Reagan,** 46, became cochairperson of the Republican National Committee. **Michael Reagan,** 42, the adopted son of Ronald Reagan

and his first wife, **Jane Wyman,** launched a Canadian-produced syndicated TV game show. Also, in an autobiography slated for publication, he revealed he had been sexually abused by a day-camp official at the age of seven—and had never told his family. Moscow vetoed a request by **Ron Reagan, Jr.,** 29, to film a series of reports on Soviet life for ABC's *Good Morning, America;* the president's son then turned to the lighter side of international politics, filming a cable-TV comedy special. The young Reagan also spoke up for safe sex in a 30-minute documentary on AIDS, which, in addition, featured model **Beverly Johnson** and Panamanian salsa superstar **Rubén Blades.**

AIDS continued to strike down figures in the arts and entertainment world. Among them were flamboyant pianist **Liberace,** 67, author and illustrator **Arnold Lobel,** 54, and theatrical pioneers **Charles Ludlam,** 44, and **Michael Bennett,** 44. Performers as diverse as **Madonna, Leonard Bernstein,** and **Luciano Pavarotti** appeared in benefit concerts to support AIDS treatment and research, and actress **Elizabeth Taylor** made the winning bid ($500,000) for a diamond clip from the Duchess of Windsor's fabled jewelry collection, auctioned in Geneva for a record $50 million; the proceeds went to the Pasteur Institute in Paris, for AIDS research.

Slimmed down and radiant, Taylor made a dazzling impression at the Cannes Film Festival in May. Other celebrities at Cannes included **Prince Charles** and **Diana, Princess of Wales,** who later appeared together at a Swiss ski resort, on a royal visit to West Germany, and on various other occasions. For the most part, however, they went their separate ways, prompting dire predictions about their marital future. Another storm raged around **Prince Edward,** 22, fifth in line to the British throne, who broke tradition early in the year by quitting the Royal Marines after only four months' training.

**Jimmy Carter,** 63, and his wife, **Rosalynn,** 60, published a retirement manual, *Everything to Gain: Making the Most of the Rest of Your Life.* It was a difficult collaboration, according to the exasperated former president. "If she wrote something, it was sacred," he complained, "as though she received it from God on Mount Sinai, and nobody could modify a word of it." In April their daughter **Amy,** 19, was acquitted along with 14 other protesters (including **Abbie Hoffman**) of charges stemming from an anti-CIA demonstration in November 1986. Amy, a sophomore at Brown University, left the school a few months after her acquittal.

The spotlight repeatedly fell on another former president, **Richard Nixon,** whom the French Académie des Beaux-Arts honored as one of 15 foreign associate members. Nixon even appeared as the subject of a new opera, *Nixon in China,* by composer **John Adams.** Also loosely depicted in the opera, which premiered in Houston, were former First Lady **Pat Nixon** and Chinese leaders **Mao Zedong** (Mao Tsetung) and **Zhou Enlai** (Chou En-lai). In November, Hofstra University held a retrospective conference on the Nixon presidency; in attendance were such Watergate principals as **H. R. Haldeman, John Ehrlichman, Charles Colson,** and **Jeb Stuart Magruder.** (Nixon himself was invited, but declined to attend.)

There was good news for 1984 Democratic vice-presidential nominee **Geraldine Ferraro.** The U.S. Justice Department dropped an investigation of alleged irregularities in financial-disclosure statements filed while she was a member of Congress, and a New York jury acquitted her husband, **John Zaccaro,** in a bribery and extortion case. Retired House Speaker **Thomas P. ("Tip") O'Neill, Jr.,** 74, published his autobiography, *Man of the House,* and even played a bit part in a beer commercial before undergoing surgery twice—for rectal cancer and for removal of an enlarged prostate.

In November, **Betty Ford,** 69, had quadruple-bypass surgery to relieve a heart problem, and she had minor follow-up surgery in December. Earlier in the year, she published a frank memoir, *Betty: A Glad Awakening;* her struggle to overcome her dependence on alcohol and prescription drugs was also recounted in a television special. Another former first lady to tell her story in print was **Jihan Sadat,** widow of Egyptian President **Anwar al-Sadat,** in *A Woman of Egypt.*

Also taking up the pen was U.S. Supreme Court Chief Justice **William H. Rehnquist** (*The Supreme Court: How It Was, How It Is*), one of several Supreme Court justices who shed

their customary cloak of institutional anonymity. The resignation of 79-year-old **Lewis F. Powell, Jr.,** focused attention on the age and health of the remaining justices: Harry A. Blackmun, 78, was treated for a recurrence of prostate cancer, and **Thurgood Marshall,** 79, was hospitalized for a blood clot in his right foot. Marshall—the only black ever to sit on the Court—also made headlines when he told an interviewer that of all the presidents in his lifetime, Ronald Reagan ranked at "the bottom" on civil rights. Entering a somewhat less inflammatory controversy, Associate Justices **William J. Brennan, John Paul Stevens,** and Blackmun ruled, in mock court proceedings in September, that **William Shakespeare**—and not **Edward de Vere, the 17th Earl of Oxford**—was most probably the real author of the plays long attributed to the immortal bard.

The acknowledgment by Supreme Court nominee Douglas Ginsburg that he had smoked

*Fawn Hall—Oliver North's secretary at the National Security Council—came to national prominence during the Iran/contra hearings with her spirited defense of her boss's activities. Here, she confers with her lawyer while giving testimony.*

marijuana as a Harvard law professor in the 1970's put him under fire and led him to remove his name from consideration. It also set off a wave of secret-baring by politicians of both parties. Among those who admitted they had tried pot in their younger years were Democratic presidential hopefuls **Bruce Babbitt** and **Albert Gore, Jr.** (along with his wife Tipper); Senators **Claiborne Pell** (D, R.I.) and **Lawton Chiles** (D, Fla.); and Representatives **Connie Mack** III (R, Fla.) and **Newt Gingrich** (R, Ga.). In May far more serious allegations, about a fling in his Washington townhouse with **Donna Rice,** led **Gary Hart** to bow out of his presidential campaign. Rice, a Miami model, actress, and sales representative, soon surfaced for a while in ads for "No Excuses" jeans.

*Bess Myerson, ex-Miss America and former New York City commissioner of cultural affairs, arrives at federal court in Manhattan for arraignment on charges of improperly influencing the judge who was hearing her companion's divorce case.*

Somewhat more unexpectedly, Hart (offering few excuses) reentered the primary race in December, saying he would "let the people decide" his fitness for office. Another Democratic candidate, Senate Judiciary Committee Chairman **Joseph R. Biden, Jr.,** dropped out of the race, presumably for good, after admitting he had pinched part of a speech by British Labor Party leader **Neil Kinnock.**

The "character" issue struck two other campaigns. In response to a reporter's query, Reverend **Jesse Jackson** revealed that his wife was pregnant with their first child when they married; it also emerged that former TV evangelist **Pat Robertson** had misrepresented his marriage date to hide the fact that his first child was born only ten weeks after the wedding.

Television evangelist **Oral Roberts** drew fire from fellow religionists for telling his followers that God would call him "home" if they did not donate $8 million for a medical missionary school. And a serious sex and money scandal forced **Jim** and **Tammy Bakker** to resign their PTL ("Praise the Lord" or "People That Love") ministry in March. As for **Jessica Hahn,** the church secretary whose sexual encounter with Jim in 1980 led to his downfall, she bared body and soul in a *Playboy* article. In October the Bakkers' successor at PTL, the **Reverend Jerry Falwell,** quit the post after a prolonged controversy with Jim and Tammy; later, Falwell announced he was stepping down as head of the Moral Majority and quitting politics for the pulpit.

The Iran/contra scandal created its share of media stars—most notably charismatic Lieutenant Colonel **Oliver North,** whose unapologetic testimony during televised hearings outdrew soap operas and unleashed a flurry of "Olliemania" that sellers of Ollie dolls, T-shirts, buttons, books, stickers, and videos found all too brief. North's most loyal and spunky supporter was his secretary, **Fawn Hall,** who staunchly defended him in testimony before a congressional committee. She later signed with a talent agency to cash in on her summer celebrity—but rejected a reported six-figure offer to appear unclothed in *Playboy*.

Another overnight sensation was **Vanna White,** *Wheel of Fortune*'s generally mute letter-turner extraordinaire, who published her autobiog-

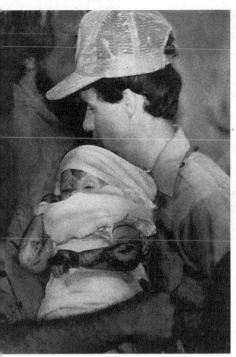

or two days in October, TV viewers around the United States followed efforts to rescue 18-month-old Jessica McClure, trapped 22 feet below ground after falling into an abandoned water well. Finally pulled to safety, Jessica was alert and, considering her ordeal, in rather good shape.

aphy, *Vanna Speaks,* and appeared in a *Playboy* spread. Actress-model **Brooke Shields,** 22, received her baccalaureate from Princeton, while former starlet **Brigitte Bardot,** 52, auctioned off jewelry and other personal belongings to raise $500,000 for animal protection.

The years were less kind to a former Miss America, **Bess Myerson** (62); a longtime confidante of New York's Mayor **Ed Koch,** Myerson was forced to resign as the city's cultural affairs commissioner and was later indicted on charges of trying to influence a judge in a spousal support case. More positive accomplishments were recorded by **Ann Dore McLaughlin,** sworn in as U.S. labor secretary and the only current woman cabinet member; by the **Reverend Patricia Ann McClurg,** the first woman minister to head the National Council of Churches; by **Molly Yard,** the new leader of the National Organization for Women; and by Norwegian

Prime Minister **Gro Harlem Brundtland,** Soviet refusenik **Ida Nudel,** and saucy actress-singer **Bette Midler,** three winners of *Ms.* magazine's Women of the Year awards.

The year's splashiest wedding took place in India, where, before 20,000 guests (including **Birendra Bir Bikram Shah Deva,** the king of Nepal), **Chitrangda Scindia,** 20, and **Vikram Singh,** 23, the daughter and son of two former maharajahs, were married at Jai Vilas Palace. **Benazir Bhutto,** 34, Pakistan's most prominent opposition leader, wed Karachi building contractor **Asif Ali Zardari,** 34, in an arranged marriage. The 230-IQ author **Marilyn Vos Savant,** 40, and artificial heart pioneer Dr. **Robert Jarvik,** 41, also exchanged wedding vows. Among show business marriages, TV actor **Mark Harmon,** 35, wed *My Sister Sam* star **Pam Dawber,** 36(?); *Dynasty's* **Diahann Carroll,** 51, married singer **Vic Damone,** 58, in

*Her marriage torn apart, she said, by pressures of the fight for custody of Baby M, surrogate mother Mary Beth Whitehead (left) announced plans to wed accountant Dean Gould (right), by whom she was to have a child.*

Woody Allen and Mia Far row show off their newbor son, Satchel O'Sullivan Far row, who weighed in at pounds, 4 ounces, on De cember 19. In Woody's arm is the couple's two-year-ol adopted daughter.

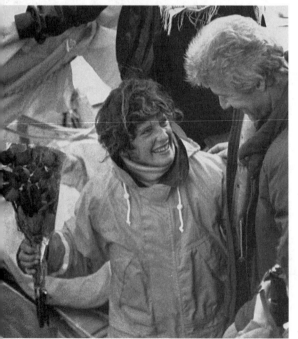

Tania Aebi (left), a world circumnavigator at age 21, is greeted by friends at New York's South Street Seaport after a 2½-year solo sail.

the fourth marriage for each; and **Johnny Car son,** 61, took the plunge for the fourth time with **Alexis Maas,** said to be 35. Among thos in the family way was actress **Cybill Shepherd** 37, who gave birth to twins (told she wa expecting, she married their father, chiroprac tor **Bruce Oppenheim,** 38). Longtime compan ions **Mia Farrow** and **Woody Allen** added son, Satchel, to her brood of three natural an five adopted children (two of whom had als been adopted by Allen).

Personally and professionally, 1987 was dreadful year for **Joan Rivers,** formerly he apparent to Carson's *Tonight Show.* Her ow competing late-night TV show was cancele and her husband, **Edgar Rosenberg,** committe suicide. Rivers also launched a $50 millio libel suit against *Gentleman's Quarterly* fo what she claimed was "a total pack of evi vicious, sick lies" about her marriage.

Calling it quits during 1987 were actres **Joan Collins** and her fourth husband, **Pete Holm** (who unsuccessfully sought a $2.3 mi lion settlement after their 13-month marriage **Madonna** filed for a divorce from hot-tempere actor **Sean Penn,** but she had a change of hea around holiday time late in the year. Surrogate mother **Mary Beth Whitehead** and husband **Richard** split in November, less than eight months after they lost their bid to regain custody of 12-month-old **Baby M,** the girl she bore for the child's biological father, **Richard Stern,** and his wife, **Elizabeth.** Whitehead also revealed that she was pregnant by another man; she later married the father, accountant **Dean Gould**.

Another toddler, 18-month-old **Jessica McClure** of Midland, Texas, captured nationwide attention in October. As the whole country waited in suspense for two days, an army of dedicated volunteers slowly managed to extricate the brave little girl from an abandoned well shaft 22 feet below ground, where she had fallen while playing in her aunt's yard. The shocking case of **Lisa Steinberg,** 6, allegedly beaten to death by her adoptive parents (who had never adopted her legally, it turned out), led Manhattan disc jockey **Scott Shannon** to play a song about child abuse by nine-year-old **Sharon Batts.** The record, "Dear Mr. Jesus," originally recorded in 1985, became the most requested song of the 1987 Christmas season.

On a happier note, Sir **Georg Solti** celebrated his 75th year by winning his 25th Grammy award and conducting the Chicago Symphony in a gala concert that included **Placido Domingo** and **Kiri Te Kanawa.** That multimillion-dollar one-man entertainment industry named **Bill Cosby** marked his 50th year by starring in America's top-rated TV series, publishing a new best-seller (*Time Flies*), recording an album of jazz tunes, and appearing in a feature film, *Leonard Part 6* (which, however, he himself panned). The summer brought not only a new Bond film, *The Living Daylights,* but a new 007—**Timothy Dalton. Garrison Keillor,** popular chronicler of mythical Lake Wobegon, Minn., dropped his *Prairie Home Companion* radio program, published the best-selling *Leaving Home,* and moved to New York City. Actress **Shirley MacLaine,** author of *It's All in the Playing,* made a cross-country lecture tour preaching the gospel of New Age consciousness and self-exploration to acolytes willing to pay $300 a head.

In the world of pop music, **Michael Jackson** made his first solo world tour and released a new album, *Bad,* but media attention centered on his eccentric personal habits and his bid to purchase the skeleton of the deformed "Elephant Man" of the 19th century, **Joseph Carey Merrick,** from the London Hospital Medical College. (No sale.) A new book and film

*Humorist Garrison Keillor rolled up the sidewalks of his mythical Lake Wobegon, Minn., after 13 years of recounting its happenings on the radio variety program* A Prairie Home Companion. *On stage for the final broadcast with Keillor (left) are performers Kate McKenzie, Leo Kottke, Chet Atkins and Stevie Beck.*

*Having shelved his presidential ambitions to take Donald Regan's place as White House chief of staff, ex-senator Howard Baker was no less the subject of controversy as he tried to steer President Reagan between a Democratic Congress and conservative activists in and out of the administration.*

celebrated the career of veteran rock 'n' roller **Chuck Berry,** while former Beatle **George Harrison** and ex-Band member **Robbie Robertson** made vigorous comebacks. *A Very Special Christmas,* an album sold to benefit the Special Olympics, featured such unlikely carolers as **John Cougar Mellencamp, U2, Eurythmics,** and **Bon Jovi.**

**Richard Wilbur** became America's poet laureate, **James H. Billington** replaced the retiring **Daniel J. Boorstin** as Librarian of Congress, and French historian **Emmanuel Le Roy Ladurie** was appointed director of the Bibliothèque Nationale.

Soviet émigré pianist **Vladimir Feltsman** made his Carnegie Hall debut, and ballet star **Rudolf Nureyev** returned to the Soviet Union for the first time since his defection in 1961. Soviet authorities gave a less cordial welcome to **Mathias Rust,** 19, who made an unscheduled landing in his single-engine Cessna only yards

from the Kremlin wall; the West German pilot received a four-year term in a Soviet labor camp.

Completing another newsmaking journey, 21-year-old **Tania Aebi** sailed into New York harbor after a 2½-year solo voyage around the world on her 26-foot sloop *Varuna,* a gift from her father in lieu of a college education.

Reaching their 100th birthdays in 1987 were Broadway director-producer **George Abbott** and 1936 Republican presidential candidate **Alf Landon,** the father of Senator **Nancy Landon Kassebaum** (R, Kans.). Landon died a month after his birthday party, which was attended by President Reagan and other notables.

G.M.H.

### BAKER, HOWARD (HENRY), JR.

White House chief of staff, born November 25, 1925, in Huntsville, Tenn. A widely respected moderate Republican and former Senate majority leader, Baker in February took on a daunting task when he replaced the embattled Donald Regan as chief of staff and sought to bolster an administration badly damaged by the Iran/contra affair. Complicating Baker's assignment was the fact that he was disliked by many conservative Reagan supporters—for having sided with President Jimmy Carter in the Panama Canal Treaty debates of the 1970's and for his starring role in the 1973 Senate Watergate hearings, where he raised the famous question about the scandal: "What did the president know and when did he know it?"

Baker plunged into his new job with enthusiasm. Determined to avoid his predecessor's much criticized mistake of sharply restricting access to the president, he called for regular meetings between Ronald Reagan and his most ardent right-wing supporters. However, Baker achieved limited success with Congress. In April he urged Reagan to sign an $88 billion highway bill rather than face an embarrassing veto override in Congress. Reagan vetoed the bill anyway, and Baker's prediction came true. Worst of all was the defeat of Judge Robert Bork's nomination to the Supreme Court. Conservatives accused Baker of fumbling the White House campaign and appeared to triumph when Reagan then nominated Douglas Ginsburg to the Supreme Court, against the advice of Baker, who reportedly favored the more moderate Anthony Kennedy. Days after the selection, however, Ginsburg withdrew amid controversy over his admitted past marijuana use, and Reagan nominated Kennedy to the Court.

Baker had some success in his plan to help Reagan deflect the political damage of the Iran/contra affair by focusing on arms control. The resulting agreement with the Soviets to eliminate all intermediate-range nuclear missiles was Baker's victory as well as the president's.

G.D.L.

### BAKKER, JIM, and TAMMY (TAMARA FAYE)

Television evangelists. Jim was born January 2, 1940, in Muskegon, Mich.; and Tammy, March 7, 1942, in International Falls, Minn. Before leaving Christian television in a blaze of notoriety, the Bakkers had created a ministry—PTL, whose initials stand for Praise the Lord or People That Love—that generated $129 million in income in 1986. More than a quarter of a million U.S. households tuned in daily to the couple's television show, and many thousands had visited PTL's Heritage USA theme park in South Carolina.

When Jim, the son of a machinist, was 18, he ran over a child while driving his father's car. The child survived, but the incident shook Bakker, causing him to take more seriously his roots in the Assemblies of God church. He enrolled in North Central Bible College in Minneapolis, where he met his future wife, Tammy. In her autobiography, *I Gotta Be Me,* Tammy describes her family as poor, living without indoor plumbing, and her father, who left home when she was three, as abusive. The oldest of eight children, she had a severe religious upbringing.

After their marriage in 1961, the Bakkers dropped out of school and spent five years as traveling evangelists. In 1965 they went to work for TV preacher Pat Robertson at the Christian Broadcasting Network, hosting a puppet show for children. Jim later cohosted (with Robertson) *The 700 Club* talk show. Between leaving CBN and starting PTL in 1974, he spent some time at the fledgling Trinity Broadcasting Network.

Resentful of his humble beginnings, Jim Bakker became convinced that poverty was not God's will for Christians. He preached a Christianity that went hand in hand with material success, and the Bakkers themselves lived in lavish homes and acquired, among other things,

*Toppled from the leadership of the PTL Ministry by a series of sexual and financial scandals, Jim Bakker and his wife, Tammy, struggled to regain control in a story that had elements of a corporate takeover battle.*

a 55-foot houseboat, two Mercedes-Benzes, a Rolls-Royce, and considerable diamond and gold jewelry. In March, however, their empire began to crumble. First came the announcement that Tammy was undergoing treatment for drug dependency. Then Jim resigned from PTL, admitting an adulterous episode in 1980. Examinations of PTL's finances later revealed that $92 million in revenues could not be accounted for. None of it seemed to matter to Bakker loyalists, who talked of forgiveness and supported the return of Jim and Tammy to PTL.                                                                  R.L.F.

### BORK, ROBERT H(ERON)

U.S. appeals court judge, born March 1, 1927, in Pittsburgh. Bork became perhaps the best-known conservative jurist in the United States, after being nominated to the Supreme Court in July by President Ronald Reagan. His qualifications for the post were the subject of two weeks of televised hearings before the Senate Judiciary Committee (including his own five days of testimony). In the end, the committee voted, 9-5, against recommending his confirmation, and an acrimonious floor debate culminated in the defeat of his nomination, by a 58-42 vote.

*Robert Bork's three decades as lawyer, scholar, Justice Department official, and federal judge went under the microscope as a Senate committee argued over his fitness to serve on the Supreme Court.*

The son of a businessman who believed in unions and the labor movement, Bork, as a teenager, described himself as a socialist. In law school at the University of Chicago, he converted to free-market conservatism and gained the respect of antitrust scholars with a paper arguing that vertical integration of businesses is not necessarily anticompetitive. After beginning in private practice, he joined the Yale Law School faculty and began a teaching and writing career that brought him both prominence and notoriety. In various journals he challenged civil rights laws and Supreme Court decisions in sensitive areas, including abortion and contraception, and stressed his belief that the concept of a right of privacy—on which many contemporary Supreme Court rulings relied—had no basis in the Constitution.

As U.S solicitor general during the Watergate era, Bork obeyed President Richard Nixon's order to dismiss Watergate special prosecutor Archibald Cox, after his superiors had refused to do so and were fired or resigned. (Bork has said he acted to prevent chaos at the Justice Department.) He continued as solicitor general under President Gerald Ford. When Jimmy Carter was elected president in 1976, Bork returned to Yale; after Reagan's election, he was nominated to serve on the U.S. Court of Appeals for the District of Columbia Circuit and was confirmed to that position by the Senate with little opposition.

Despite Reagan administration attempts to portray Bork as a moderate during his Supreme Court confirmation hearings and despite his own testimony asserting he had modified many of his controversial views, Bork was widely considered an extremist, and he was strongly opposed by labor and civil rights groups, which mounted a massive lobbying campaign against him.                                                                  C.J.S.

### BUSH, GEORGE H(ERBERT) W(ALKER)

U.S. vice president, born June 12, 1924, in Milton, Mass. After seven years as a loyal subordinate to Ronald Reagan, Vice President George Bush set in motion a campaign that he hoped would catapult him to the presidency in the 1988 elections. He officially announced his candidacy in October, by which time he was already considered the front-runner among Republican contenders.

*'ice President George Bush occupied the often perilous front-runner spot among the Republican presidential hopefuls. His organization and financing were impressive, but not since 1836 had a sitting vice president (Martin Van Buren) been elected president.*

Although Bush maintained his record of support for Reagan, he began to stake out some independent positions. In July he had called for an increase in federal student loan programs—programs the Reagan administration had sought to curb. And though the administration hesitated to reopen the tax code so soon after the sweeping changes made in 1986, Bush proposed sharp reductions in the capital gains tax for individuals.

The vice president's fortunes were complicated somewhat by the Iran/contra scandal. Bush's contention that he was aware of the Iranian arms sales but knew nothing about the diversion of funds to the contras was supported by both a congressional investigation and a bipartisan presidential commission; still, critics said he had failed to speak out forcefully against the arms sales. A New York *Times*/CBS News national poll in July found that Bush was

regarded as "dependable but not exciting." His persistent image problem was dubbed by some political analysts as the "wimp factor."

During a ten-day visit to Poland and Western Europe in the fall, Bush angered American autoworkers when he praised the ability of Soviet mechanics and suggested it might be a good idea to "send them to Detroit." Despite image problems and gaffes, Bush nevertheless remained a formidable candidate, with extensive government experience—as congressman, UN ambassador, envoy to China, and CIA director. He also had sizable funds and a sophisticated campaign organization; at year's end he remained the front-runner among Republican candidates.                    T.D.

### FOX, MICHAEL J.

Actor, born Michael Andrew Fox on June 9, 1961, in Edmonton, Alberta. A star in two realms, Fox is the mainstay of NBC's comedy *Family Ties,* the second-highest-rated television series of the 1986–1987 season, and also a fixture on the motion picture screen, with starring roles in two movies out in 1987 alone.

On *Family Ties,* Fox plays Alex Keaton, the ultra-conservative son of 1960's liberal parents. When the series premiered in the fall of 1982, Meredith Baxter Birney, who plays his mother, was intended to be the star. But soon, Alex became the program's dominant character, in large part because of Fox's acute sense of timing and dry natural wit. He received Emmy Awards as best actor in a comedy series in 1986 and 1987.

Fox's brightest moment in films thus far was probably the blockbuster hit *Back to the Future,* in which he played a high school student who travels back in time to 1955, meets his parents as teenagers, and must play matchmaker for them. In *Light of Day,* released in February 1987, the actor took on his first dramatic role, as lead guitarist in a rock band. Although the film did poorly, Fox got generally good reviews. Then, in April, he came back with *The Secret of My Success,* a wry comedy about a go-getter from Kansas who comes to New York and hustles his way to the top of a giant corporation. In the offing were a sequel to *Back to the Future;* the starring role in the movie *Bright Lights, Big City,* scheduled for release in 1988; and a film Fox will direct for Steven Spielberg.

The star of one of television's most popular situation comedies, Michael J. Fox of NBC's *Family Ties*, was making a steady sideline out of movies, where he was a major box-office attraction.

Fox, who dropped out of high school and moved to Los Angeles in 1979, was unemployed and deeply in debt when he was cast in *Family Ties*. He now reportedly receives more fan mail than any other current television star, and a fee of $2 million per film.     J.L.G.

### GORBACHEV, MIKHAIL S(ERGEEVICH)

General Secretary of the Soviet Communist Party, born March 2, 1931, in Privolnoe, southern Russia. Perhaps the world's most visible and active leader in 1987, Gorbachev worked at home to build support for his reform programs of political and social *glasnost,* or "openness," and economic *perestroika,* or "restructuring." Abroad, his success in projecting a dynamic image was reflected by several West German opinion polls in the spring that rated him as more popular and more concerned about peace than President Ronald Reagan. He gained new respect and even admiration from Americans during his three-day visit to Washington in December for a summit meeting with Reagan, where the two signed a historic arms control treaty.

To promote his policies, Gorbachev made a speaking tour of the Baltic countries early in the year and went to Czechoslovakia and Romania in the spring. His disappearance from

Far from being incapacitated, as midyear rumors had it, Soviet leader Mikhail Gorbachev spent the year promoting Soviet economic change, preparing to meet U.S. President Ronald Reagan, and displaying an un-Soviet flair for public relations.

view for more than seven weeks beginning in August led to rumors of ill health or an assassination attempt, but in October it was announced he had been working on a book, *Perestroika: New Thinking for Our Country and the World,* which was released simultaneously in the Soviet Union, the United States, and Great Britain.

When the United States and the Soviet Union reached an agreement in September to dismantle their intermediate-range nuclear missiles, it was announced that Reagan and Gorbachev would sign the pact at a summit meeting. In October, after temporarily refusing to set a date for the summit until progress had been made on other weapons systems, Gorbachev finally agreed to come to Washington on December 7. A week before the trip, he was interviewed by NBC anchorman Tom Brokaw on U.S. television; his mixture of toughness and conciliation was widely praised and he continued to draw favorable notices in Washington, where he stopped his motorcade to shake hands with passers-by and charmed even conservative Republicans at meetings with members of Congress and other prominent Americans. At the end of their talks, Gorbachev and Reagan said they had made substantial progress toward a treaty to reduce U.S. and Soviet strategic nuclear arsenals, and Reagan agreed to come to Moscow in 1988. Later, *Time* magazine recognized the Soviet leader as "man of the year."

Amid foreign acclaim, Gorbachev still faced domestic political challenges. During his absence from public view, *glasnost* was criticized by two top Soviet officials, and at a party Central Committee meeting in October, Boris Yeltsin, a onetime ally, dissatisfied with the slow pace of change, accused Gorbachev of developing a cult of personality. Yeltsin was later removed, in an action that raised questions about the reform process. But Gorbachev pressed on: at the Communist Party congress marking the 70th anniversary of the Bolshevik Revolution, he declared that Joseph Stalin had committed "enormous and unforgivable crimes" during his leadership of the Soviet Union and praised two other former Soviet leaders, Nikita Khrushchev and Nikolai Bukharin, who had been in official disgrace.

*Bob Hawke won a third consecutive term as Australia's prime minister—a first for a Labor Party leader.*

### HAWKE, BOB (ROBERT JAMES LEE)

Prime minister of Australia, born December 9, 1929, in Bordertown, South Australia. On July 11, Prime Minister Bob Hawke won a third consecutive term in office—becoming the first head of the Australian Labor Party ever to do so. Three days later, bolstered by his victory, he launched a drastic reorganization of the government, trimming the number of departments from 28 to 16. He also broadened the geographic base of his cabinet and increased the number of women ministers from one to three. Within a month of his reelection, challenging a Labor Party sacred cow, Hawke was advocating the sale of major government assets—two airlines and Australia's largest bank.

Such bold moves would have been expected of the "old" Bob Hawke, who, as leader of the Australian Council of Trade Unions in the 1970's, was noted for his beer drinking and maverick behavior. But since becoming prime minister in 1983, Hawke (now a teetotaler) had begun taking a more cautious approach.

Raised in Australia, Bob Hawke began his

political career after completing graduate work at Oxford, where he had been awarded a Rhodes scholarship in 1953. Returning to Australia, he joined the ACTU, becoming its president in 1969. During the next ten years, as a rising star in the Australian Labor Party, he became known for his ability to effect last-minute compromises in major industrial disputes. In 1982 he made an unsuccessful bid for the party leadership. The next year, when Liberal Prime Minister Malcolm Fraser announced a snap general election, the charismatic Hawke won the leadership post, and Labor was swept into office.

An accord on wages and prices with the ACTU has been a cornerstone of Hawke's prime ministership. It has produced unprecedented wage restraint in spite of a major decline in Australia's balance of payments and falls in the exchange rate that damaged government attempts to reduce inflation. Also a supporter of economic deregulation and a strong advocate of the alliance with the United States, Hawke has sometimes been accused of being more conservative than the conservative Liberal Party opposition.                                    B.J.

## JOHN PAUL II

Pope of the Roman Catholic Church, born Karol Wojtyła, May 18, 1920, in Wadowice, Poland. With the completion of his 11-day trip to North America in September, John Paul II could claim to have covered 334,952 miles during almost nine years as pope. His travels have revolutionized the conduct of the papacy.

In Chile, on a Latin American trip in 1987, the pope lent support to church leaders who criticize the government of President Augusto Pinochet Ugarte for human rights violations. In his native Poland, John Paul challenged the Communist regime to respect human rights. The pope was the stern theological traditionalist during his visit to North America. He did praise those who help Latin American refugees and, in Canada, spoke on behalf of Indian rights. But, in doctrinal matters, he repeatedly stressed that adherence to the church's prohibitions of such practices as abortion, artificial birth control, and divorce and remarriage was not optional.

There appeared to be a duality in the pope's attitudes toward Jews. In talks and letters, he has used the word *Shoah,* which is Hebrew for Holocaust, underlining Jewish claims that the Holocaust was a uniquely Jewish tragedy. However, this year, on a visit to a former Nazi death camp in Poland, he failed to mention that its victims were mostly Jewish. More startling was the pope's decision to receive Austrian President Kurt Waldheim on an official visit to the Vatican in June, despite accusations of Waldheim's involvement in Nazi atrocities. Moreover, the pope made no mention of Waldheim's Nazi war record.

In an apparent effort to repair damages to Catholic-Jewish relations, there was a historic 75-minute, give-and-take meeting between the

*On his visit to nine U.S. cities in September, Pope John Paul II warned a diverse flock that Catholicism required obedience to church doctrine.*

pope and Jewish leaders September 1 at the papal summer residence outside Rome. The exchange seemed to ease tensions considerably. Ten days later, at a public meeting with American Jewish leaders in Miami, John Paul spoke movingly of the horrors of "*Shoah,*" but he also surprised his audience with a strong defense of Pope Pius XII, who has been accused of "silence" and inaction during the Holocaust.                                          J.G.D.

## KNIGHT, BOBBY (ROBERT MONTGOMERY)

Head basketball coach, Indiana University; born October 25, 1940, in Massillon, Ohio. On a clutch basket with five seconds remaining, Bobby Knight's Indiana Hoosiers won the 1987 NCAA championship on March 30, edging Syracuse, 74-73. It was the third NCAA title in 11 years for Knight, one of the most successful—and controversial—coaches in college basketball.

The disciplined play Knight fosters was one of several deciding factors in that game. The presence of Keith Smart, a junior college transfer ("juco") who made the winning shot, attested to a new flexibility in a coach long accused of being unyielding; he had previously dismissed jucos as problem students who would not do well in Indiana's athletically and academically rigorous program. Knight has also begun using the zone defense on occasion—as opposed to his traditional man-on-man—to keep his opponents guessing.

Knight made the basketball team himself as a student at Ohio State University, but spent most of his time on the bench. After college, as assistant and then head coach at West Point, his style quickly became infamous: he kicked chairs, threw coats, and screamed at referees and at his own players. But he won games, and in 1971 he moved to Indiana, where he compiled a 366-119 record through the 1986–1987 season. He was chosen to coach the U.S. men's basketball team in the 1984 Summer Olympics, and his team took the gold medal; but then, exhausted, Knight had the worst season of his career. During one nationally televised game, he threw a chair across the gym floor during an opponent's foul shot.

On the night Indiana won the NCAA final, a movie entitled *Hoosiers,* about high school basketball in Indiana, was up for two Oscars;

*Bobby Knight, one of big-time sports' more temperamental coaches, remained one of the most successful as well, guiding the Indiana Hoosiers to their third NCAA championship in recent years.*

the coach who was the main character bore more than a slight resemblance to Knight. First place on that same week's New York *Times* best-seller list was held by *A Season on the Brink,* an account of Knight's 1985–1986 season. The Knight legend was growing, and the public, it seemed, shared the love-hate relationship he establishes with his players.

## MEESE, EDWIN, III

U.S. attorney general, born December 2, 1931, in Oakland, Calif. Never far from controversy during seven years as a top Reagan administration official, Edwin Meese III was besieged by new difficulties in 1987.

# PEOPLE IN THE NEWS

Meese's main problem centered on his ties to several figures linked by federal investigators to the Wedtech Corporation, a Bronx, N.Y., firm that in 1982 won a $32 million no-bid contract to manufacture engines for the Army. In December, with corruption charges already facing several former Wedtech officials and New York politicians, two of Meese's associates were charged with racketeering, conspiracy, and fraud in promoting the company's interests: E. Robert Wallach, Meese's personal attorney, and W. Franklin Chinn, who placed a blind investment by Meese into Wedtech in 1985, shortly after the firm hired him as a consultant. Meese, who was not accused in the indictment, had acknowledged that he and members of his staff intervened with Army officials to plead Wedtech's case while he was counselor to the president. He steadfastly denied doing anything improper, however, and predicted he would be vindicated by an independent counsel appointed to look into Wedtech and other matters.

*Between allegations of unethical conduct, criticism of his role in investigating the Iran/contra affair, and unsuccessful efforts to name a new Supreme Court justice, it was a rocky year for Attorney General Edwin Meese III, long one of President Ronald Reagan's closest associates.*

Meese also came under assault during the Iran/contra hearings, as critics maintained he had bungled the Justice Department investigation of that affair. In two days of testimony in July, he acknowledged having failed to ask pertinent questions of senior government officials but angrily denied he had tried to cover up evidence to protect President Reagan from political damage.

The nomination of Judge Robert Bork, a strong exponent of judicial restraint, to the Supreme Court typified Meese's effort to promote a more conservative judicial philosophy on the federal bench. After the Bork nomination was defeated in the Senate, Meese successfully pressed Reagan to name another pronounced conservative, Judge Douglas Ginzburg; but his nomination collapsed, after which the president named Judge Anthony Kennedy, regarded as more moderate.                     T.D

## MULRONEY, (MARTIN) BRIAN

Prime minister of Canada, born March 20, 1939, in Baie-Comeau, Québec. By his own measure, Brian Mulroney's greatest achievement in 1987 was the agreement he won in April with the provincial premiers for a sweeping amendment of the Canadian constitution. Québec had never assented to the constitutional compromise reached by former Prime Minister Pierre Elliott Trudeau and the nine other premiers in 1981. Winning his native province over tested all Mulroney's old skills and best instincts—the mediating skills of a former labor lawyer and the inclination of a consensus politician to seek compromise. The accord, giving Québec a particular mandate to preserve its distinctive culture and granting certain other powers to all the provinces, gained approval by the House of Commons in October. Approval of the provincial legislatures was also needed.

The negotiation of a free trade treaty with the United States was another important achievement. The pact, signed by Mulroney and President Ronald Reagan in January 1988, fulfilled a major goal of Mulroney's first term, but it produced enormous debate; a key issue was whether Canada's economic and cultural independence would be threatened.

Through all this, the opinion polls showed low popularity ratings both for the Conservative

*Canadian Prime Minister Brian Mulroney helped produce two agreements of historic proportions— one renegotiating the nation's constitution, the other revamping trade relations with the United States— and faced criticism over whether they were in Canada's best interests.*

tion, due by September 1989. He could also take heart from end-of-year opinion polls showing a modest gain in popularity—to some extent, analysts speculated, a result of the trade agreement. J.H.

### NEWMAN, PAUL (LEONARD)

Actor, born January 26, 1925, in Cleveland. In 1986, Newman had been presented with Hollywood's equivalent of a gold watch—an honorary Oscar—and he joked that he was glad he had not also been given a gift certificate to Forest Lawn cemetery. But in 1987, after nearly 50 films and seven Oscar nominations, the hard-working Newman finally received his first Academy Award for best actor.

He has also proved that his career is far from dead by taking on highly challenging parts during the last decade. In 1977 he played a foul-mouthed hockey coach in *Slap Shot*. A few years later he was a compassionate policeman in *Fort Apache, The Bronx*. He then made *Absence of Malice*, about a businessman who is ruined by a journalist's erroneous story.

government and for Mulroney himself as a leader—at a time when the main opposition party, the Liberals, commanded no great support themselves. Among the factors hurting Mulroney was a series of embarrassments. One minister (Sinclair Stevens) was the subject of a judicial inquiry into alleged conflicts of interest, while another (André Bissonnette) was formally charged with corruption. There were smaller events as well: Mulroney's wife, Mila, was accused of instigating favorable treatment from the Immigration Department for a French-born teacher at her children's school.

During the year Mulroney played host to two large international summits—first, a conference of some 40 French-speaking countries and regions; then the biennial Commonwealth Conference. These may have helped polish up his image as he looked toward the next elec-

*Superstar Paul Newman not only continues to play leading movie roles (as in* The Color of Money, *shown here)—he sells the popcorn, too. The proceeds from Newman's Own food business, which also encompasses spaghetti sauce and salad dressing, are donated to a variety of charities.*

313

And in *The Verdict* Newman played an alcoholic lawyer redeemed by his sense of justice.

In 1986 he faced the challenge of reprising the role that 25 years earlier had defined his screen image—pool shark Fast Eddie Felson in *The Hustler.* In *The Color of Money,* Newman played a middle-aged, more human and vulnerable Eddie; the part won him his long-deserved Oscar.

After serving in the Navy in the mid-1940's, Newman first took up acting at Kenyon College, then studied at the Yale Drama School and under Lee Strasberg at the Actor's Studio in New York. He began his career with a beefcake image but quickly convinced critics that he had real talent. His portrayal of the bitter alcoholic Brick in the film adaptation of Tennessee Williams's *Cat on a Hot Tin Roof* earned him his first Oscar nomination. The following year he starred on Broadway in Williams's *Sweet Bird of Youth.* In the 1960's, Newman made his so-called lucky "H" films—*The Hustler, Hud, Harper,* and *Hombre.* Along with *Cool Hand Luke* (1967), these films delineated the character with which he became associated: cool, rebellious, cynical, irresistible: more antihero than hero. Newman then teamed up with Robert Redford to make two classic films, *Butch Cassidy and the Sundance Kid* (1969) and *The Sting* (1973).

Newman is a politically active liberal and has strong convictions about the arms race and the environment. In 1982 he launched a food company, Newman's Own, which sells popcorn, salad dressing, and spaghetti sauce from his own recipes. All profits are donated to charities, among them The Hole in the Wall Gang, a camp for terminally ill children. He has been married to actress Joanne Woodward for 30 years.

### NORTH, OLIVER (LAURENCE)

Marine lieutenant colonel, born October 7, 1943, in San Antonio. Formerly an obscure if highly influential staff member of the National Security Council, Oliver North became a national celebrity in 1987 as star witness in televised congressional hearings probing the Iran/contra scandal. North—described by President Ronald Reagan as "a national hero" for his work in combating international terrorism and supporting the cause of the contra rebels

fighting the Sandinista government in Nicaragua—impressed many viewers of the hearings, particularly for his earnest demeanor and engaging style. However, some of his activities at the NSC may have been illegal, and it was widely expected that he would ultimately be indicted by an independent counsel examining the U.S. sale of weapons to Iran and the diversion of resulting profits to the contras.

A decorated Vietnam veteran, North had been assigned in 1981 to the staff of the NSC, where he was involved in a variety of highly sensitive operations. He was instrumental in planning the 1983 U.S. invasion of Grenada, the 1985 capture of the hijackers of the cruise ship *Achille Lauro,* and the 1986 U.S. bombing raids against Libya. A passionate defender of

*In his nationally televised testimony before a congressional committee looking into the Iran/contra affair, Marine Lieutenant Colonel Oliver North declared he would not accept the role of scapegoat, saying his actions had been approved farther up the chain of command.*

the contra cause, North was also deeply involved in running a clandestine network to supply the contras and in encouraging private contributions to keep the rebels in the field during a period when Congress had cut off government funding.

North was dismissed from the NSC in November 1986, when his role in the Iran/contra scandal was revealed. Later, during six days in July, he testified at joint hearings of special congressional committees, under an agreement that gave him limited immunity—meaning he could not be prosecuted on the basis of the testimony he gave. North admitted shredding documents detailing the arms transactions, deceiving Congress about the extent of administration involvement in supporting the contras, and misusing some funds generated by the Iranian arms sales. But he asserted that all his activities had been explicitly authorized by his superiors and strongly maintained that he had acted in the national security interests of the United States. North said that he had been prepared to be the political scapegoat for the Reagan administration if word of the arms sales and diversion of funds became public, but had changed his mind when it became clear that he might be liable to prosecution.    T.D.

*Benefiting from a reviving economy and a divided opposition, Margaret Thatcher won her third term as Great Britain's prime minister.*

## THATCHER, MARGARET (HILDA ROBERTS)

Prime minister of Great Britain, born October 13, 1925, in Grantham, England. As late as 1986, retirement seemed fairly imminent for Margaret Thatcher. She had lost two cabinet ministers—one storming out with angry accusations, the other a reluctant scapegoat for a major political bungle. Many Conservative MP's were discontent, and the economy remained in recession. The centrist Liberal-Social Democratic Alliance was eating into the Conservative vote. In June 1987 general elections, however, Thatcher easily won a third successive term of office—a feat unequaled by any British prime minister in over 150 years—with the second-largest Tory majority in Parliament since World War II.

After seven lean years, there had been something of a lift-off in the British economy in 1986—part cyclical, part luck, part good management by Thatcher's government. It was enough to give electoral underpinning to the revolution of attitudes for which she takes credit: a change from dependency to self-reliance, from confrontation at the workplace to cooperation, from socialism to sturdy independence, as her friends see it. Others blame her for division where consensus was sought, pursuit of private interest at the expense of public service, an emerging underclass, and a willingness to accept 3 million unemployed as the price of efficiency.

Abroad, Thatcher, the longest-serving major Western leader, was considered the most assertive and influential voice in Western Europe. She was seen in action in Moscow in the spring, establishing a rapport with Soviet leader Mikhail Gorbachev without any hint of weakness. In mid-July, she was at the White House, praising President Ronald Reagan (lamed by the Iran/contra affair) as a great leader. A few months later, at a Commonwealth of Nations conference in Canada, she asserted another familiar view of hers—that economic sanctions against South Africa had not been productive—

*Relying more on ferocity than finesse, Mike Tyson became the first undisputed (or nearly so) world heavyweight boxing champion in nine years by defeating Tony Tucker (left) on August 1 for the International Boxing Federation title.*

and firmly refused to go along with wider sanctions, to the anger of many fellow Commonwealth members.                     T.J.O.H.

### TYSON, MICHAEL (GERALD)

Heavyweight boxing champion, born June 30, 1966, in Brooklyn, N.Y. Within little more than eight months in 1986 and 1987, Mike Tyson won a handful of decisive bouts and became the first heavyweight champion in nine years to be acknowledged by all of boxing's major governing bodies.

Prior to Tyson's takeover, the World Boxing Council (WBC), the World Boxing Association (WBA), and the International Boxing Federation (IBF) had each recognized a different champion. Then Home Box Office (HBO) put together a series of bouts in Las Vegas in an effort to unify the title. During the $22 million series, Tyson beat Trevor Berbick late in 1986 to capture the WBC crown. At the age of 20 years, 4 months, he was the youngest ever to hold such a title. On March 7, he outpointed James "Bonecrusher" Smith for the WBA title; in May he retained both titles by knocking out

Pinklon Thomas. Finally, on August 1, Tyson beat Tony Tucker to clinch the IBF title.

That made Tyson the first widely recognized champion since Leon Spinks in 1978. It also boosted his professional record to 31 victories (27 by knockout) in 31 bouts and pushed his professional earnings past $11 million. On October 16, Tyson added another victory and retained his title with a seventh-round knockout of Tyrell Biggs. He was scheduled to meet Larry Holmes in January 1988.

Tyson is a devastating, relentless brawler in the style of Rocky Marciano and Joe Frazier. Though his height is listed at 5'11½", he looks at least an inch shorter. He weighs 220 pounds and has a blocky build, thick legs, and a barrel chest. Trained by veteran manager and trainer Constantine "Cus" D'Amato (who eventually became Tyson's legal guardian), he became a leading heavyweight contender by 1985; the year before, he won the Golden Gloves national amateur championship as a 17-year-old. Tyson won his first 19 professional fights by knockouts and soon became a celebrity.             F.L.

**PERSIAN GULF STATES.** In 1987, the Iran-Iraq war continued to threaten the stability of the small Persian Gulf states (Bahrain, Oman, Qatar, and the United Arab Emirates). Those states preferred to keep foreign powers out of the conflict, but Kuwait, a strong supporter of Iraq, encouraged superpower involvement by requesting Soviet and American protection of its oil tankers in the Persian Gulf. The U.S. Navy began escorting Kuwaiti tankers in July. Late in the year, the U.S. Congress approved the sale of 70 shoulder-fired Stinger missiles to Bahrain.

In late December, the members of the Gulf Cooperation Council—Saudi Arabia, Kuwait, Oman, the United Arab Emirates, Qatar, and Bahrain—meeting in Riyadh, called for a cease-fire in the Iran-Iraq war and sanctions against Iran.

During the year Oman and South Yemen agreed to exchange ambassadors. Libya severed diplomatic relations with the United Arab Emirates, in response to Egyptian President Hosni Mubarak's official visit there. However, the United Arab Emirates, Bahrain, and Qatar all restored relations with Egypt late in the year, after an Arab League resolution authorizing such action. (Oman had not severed its ties in the first place.)

Because of relatively low oil revenues, all of the small Gulf states faced soaring deficits and declining gross domestic products. Contracts with foreign companies were deferred, and the use of foreign labor was reduced.

For the first time in recorded history, snow fell on the United Arab Emirates. The snow, which fell over an area of approximately 24 square miles in February, reached depths of up to 20 inches.

See STATISTICS OF THE WORLD. See also IRAN; IRAQ; KUWAIT; MIDDLE EAST.     L.A.K.

**PERU.** In 1987 the administration of President Alan García Pérez continued to be plagued by two chronic problems—the unrelenting terrorism of the Maoist Sendero Luminoso (Shining Path) guerrillas and an unmanageable foreign debt. In addition, the domestic economy deteriorated significantly, eroding the once broad base of popular support enjoyed by the charismatic García.

The war between the government and the Sendero Luminoso insurgents, which has cost 10,000 lives since it began in 1980, continued. Terrorist assassinations, bombings, and other major incidents occurred at an average rate of almost 200 per month. Breaking a time-honored tradition, police on February 13 raided three university campuses, searching for terrorists. But of the nearly 800 persons arrested during the operation, fewer than 100 were formally charged with crimes. A week of student protest demonstrations followed the raids.

Peru's external debt grew to $15 billion, with back interest representing a third of the total. The García administration continued to limit debt service payments to 10 percent of Peru's export earnings, and it sought better terms from the nation's creditors. In September, Britain's Midland Bank became the first commercial creditor to agree to accept payment in Peruvian commodities, rather than cash.

Although the year began with a big drop in the inflation rate, a strong increase in the gross national product, and a rise in worker purchasing power, these trends appeared to be reversing as the year progressed, with private investment and industrial capacity insufficient to sustain the rate of growth. The government acted to nationalize private banks so as to stem the flight of capital from the country, but the move was under challenge in the courts.

In March and April the government secured some noteworthy reforms. The basic agrarian law was changed to facilitate subdivision of large cooperative farms into small private parcels. Peru was divided into 12 administrative regions, in which locally elected officials would assume some powers previously held by national authorities. And despite opposition from the military, ministries for the army, navy, and air force were combined into one.

See STATISTICS OF THE WORLD.     D.P.W.

**PETROLEUM AND NATURAL GAS.** See ENERGY; ORGANIZATION OF PETROLEUM EXPORTING COUNTRIES.

**PETS.** In 1987 there was accelerating controversy over the ownership of pit bulls. The cocker spaniel retained first place in the hearts of dog-loving Americans, while fighting fish and ferrets enjoyed growing popularity.

In the past five years American Staffordshire terriers and similar breeds vaguely referred to as pit bulls accounted for over two-thirds of all fatal attacks on people, while comprising only a tiny percentage of the U.S. dog population. Several vicious attacks on small children—the most frequent victims of pit bulls—made headlines in 1987. In one case a Georgia man was sentenced to five years in prison after his three pit bulls killed a four-year-old boy. In the wake of such attacks, municipalities across the nation introduced laws restricting possession and sale of the breed, to the dismay of legitimate pit bull breeders, who insist that these animals make gentle pets if properly bred and handled. A major problem in framing or implementing legislation against pit bull ownership has stemmed from the loose definition of pit bull, and some laws designed to control ownership of these dogs have been challenged successfully on the grounds that they are too vague.

In other developments, the top ten dog breeds registered in 1987 showed little change from the previous year. The cocker spaniel was king, with over 98,000 registered with the American Kennel Club. Other highly popular breeds included the poodle varieties, Labrador retrievers, golden retrievers, German shepherds, chow chows, beagles, miniature dachshunds, schnauzers, and sheepdogs.

A German shepherd—Ch. Covy Tucker Hill's Manhattan—became the first of that breed to win Best in Show at the Westminster Kennel Club since 1907, the year the award was introduced.

The domestic ferret, or polecat, continued

Ch. Covy Tucker Hill's Manhattan became the first German shepherd to be named "Best in Show" at the Westminster Kennel Club since the award was introduced in 1907.

to enjoy a rapid rise in popularity among pet owners. The American Ferret Fanciers Association says that the ferret, fully domesticated for about 3,000 years (mostly for vermin control), is now so docile and people-oriented that it can be a desirable pet even for the apartment-bound animal lover. However, some states currently prohibit the possession of ferrets on the grounds that, if liberated, the animals would

A stable home environment was just what some residents of Thousand Oaks, Calif., said didn't belong in the suburbs—at least in the case of Ragtime, a 28-inch-tall miniature pinto who, as a virtual housepet of Patty and Richard Fairchild, found himself at the center of a zoning dispute. Here, Ragtime (housebroken, if a messy eater) snacks with one of the Fairchilds' two dachshunds.

establish wild populations that could pose a threat to native wildlife. The AFFA contends that the domestic ferret could not survive if liberated.

Tropical fish fanciers were showing increased interest in the more aggressive aquarium fish. Pet shops in some areas reported growing sales of piranhas, snakeheads, wolffish, and large, combative cichlid species. Also showing marked growth were marine fish, despite the relative complexity and expenses of maintaining a tropical saltwater aquarium.

Among pet birds, parrots and their relatives retained strong attraction. The budgerigar was still the front-runner. Other popular parrot-like birds included the cockatiel, the African gray parrot (the best talker), various Amazon parrots, and the large, flashy cockatoos.　　　J.Q.

**PHILIPPINES.** In 1987, after her fairy-tale ousting of Ferdinand Marcos in a nearly bloodless revolt the year before, Philippine President Corazon Aquino faced harsh reality in the form of repeated coup attempts, a failed cease-fire with Communist insurgents, and serious political and economic problems.

**August Coup Attempt.** Early in the morning of August 28, renegade troops under Colonel Gregorio ("Gringo") Honasan attacked the presidential palace and seized key broadcast facilities and military camps. The mutiny came close to overthrowing Aquino, but loyal troops under the command of General Fidel V. Ramos, the armed forces chief of staff, launched a counterattack that forced the rebels to surrender or to retreat with Honasan, who went into hiding after the government ordered that he be shot on sight. The coup attempt left 53 people dead, including 22 civilians, and at least 300 injured, including Aquino's son Benigno.

As an aide to Juan Ponce Enrile, Honasan had been a key strategist in the military rebellion against Marcos and was implicated in the November 1986 plot against Aquino that led to Enrile's dismissal as her defense minister. Enrile, elected an opposition senator in May, continued to attack Aquino for being soft on Communism. In September, Vice President Salvador Laurel broke with Aquino and resigned his cabinet post as secretary of foreign affairs. In December, Honasan was captured in a raid on a Manila townhouse and was

expected to face "due process of law," according to military authorities.

**New Constitution.** The August mutiny took the government by surprise, for Aquino's position had seemed strong after a series of stunning victories earlier in the year. In February a new constitution, restoring the civil liberties suppressed by Marcos and providing a six-year presidential term for Aquino, was approved overwhelmingly in a national plebiscite. The constitution also authorized the first free elections since 1972, which took place in May and gave Aquino-backed candidates huge majorities in both houses of the new bicameral Congress.

**Communist Insurgency.** In January soldiers outside the presidential palace opened fire on peasant farmers demanding land reform, killing 17 and dooming Aquino's cease-fire with Communist rebels, which had been in effect for six weeks. During that time there had been no progress in achieving a negotiated end to the insurgency, which began in 1969. The estimated 23,000 troops of the New People's Army resumed the battle for the countryside in February, blowing up bridges and power installations and ambushing military convoys. The number of insurgents was reportedly growing.

**Growing Unrest.** With guerrilla strength growing, the military had become increasingly restless. Many soldiers felt that Aquino was not dealing forcefully enough with the insurgency and that she had an insufficient appreciation of their role in overthrowing Marcos. A January assault on a Manila television station by Marcos loyalists was comic opera compared to the August mutiny under Honasan, who was not a Marcos loyalist but represented a group of young officers with an apparent political agenda of their own.

In September, Aquino was further weakened when right-wing pressure forced her to dismiss her executive secretary and chief adviser, Joker Arroyo. A human-rights lawyer during the Marcos years, Arroyo had sharply criticized military and business leaders.

Meanwhile, the growing influence of the left was manifested by a paralyzing transportation strike, called by a coalition of unions in August. Another sign was the outpouring of 100,000 people for the funeral of the leftist leader

Leandro Alejandro, who was murdered in September, allegedly by the military.

On August 2, Jaime Ferrer, Aquino's secretary of local governments and a vocal proponent of anti-Communist vigilantes, was murdered by unknown assailants. The New People's Army denied killing Ferrer, but leftist urban guerrillas known as "sparrow units" were moving aggressively into Manila, targeting police informers and military officers for assassination.

**Economic Problems.** Although Aquino promised a bold land redistribution program after the January massacre of peasant activists, the plan she eventually came up with was opposed by landlords as too much and by peasant rights advocates as too little. The economy, after years of decline, grew 5 percent from 1986 to 1987, but the country's $28 billion external debt remained a crushing burden.

**U.S. Relations.** Friendship with the United States proved valuable during the August mutiny, when a pledge of U.S. support apparently helped turn the tide against the rebels. Mean-

*An attempted coup by Philippine soldiers in August was crushed after the bloodiest fighting Manila had seen since President Corazon Aquino's election. Above, Aquino pays her respects to five members of her bodyguard killed in the rebel attack; below, government troops disarm insurgent soldiers.*

while, the U.S. military presence was a continuing target of violence. On October 28, three U.S. Air Force sergeants and a Filipino bystander were shot and killed outside Clark Air Force Base, apparently by leftist guerrillas.

See STATISTICS OF THE WORLD.        A.L.N.

**PHOTOGRAPHY.** Photography of the 19th and 20th centuries was the subject of several important museum exhibitions in 1987. Other shows highlighted the interrelations between photography and the other visual arts.

**Major Exhibitions.** The 125 rare vintage prints shown in "Masterpieces of 19th-Century French Photography: Gustave Le Gray and Henri Le Secq" at New York's Metropolitan Museum of Art provided an opportunity to compare the development of two of the finest French photographers of the 1850's. Whereas Le Gray's pictures are filled with light and atmosphere, Le Secq's studies of landscape, still life, and medieval architecture focus closely on surface, texture, and shadow. The complete exhibition of Le Gray's work traveled on to the Art Institute of Chicago, which had organized the show originally. The full Le Secq show, organized by the Musée des Arts Décoratifs of Paris from a recently uncovered archive, was shown at the Boston Museum of Fine Arts.

"Photography and Art: Interactions Since 1946" was a massive survey focusing on long-term interrelations between modern photography and the other visual arts. Mounted at the Los Angeles County Museum of Art, with over 300 images by more than 100 photographers and other artists who use photographs (including Robert Rauschenberg and Andy Warhol), this wide-ranging exhibition provided a lively revision of photographic history.

"Alvin Langdon Coburn: A Retrospective," mounted by the International Museum of Photography at the George Eastman House in Rochester, N.Y., provided a rare look at the vintage prints of this important turn-of-the-century photographer. The 100 photographs, drawn from the archive of the museum, traced Coburn's career from early pictorial work to his revolutionary 1917 "vortographs," perhaps the first abstract photographs ever made.

"Henri Cartier-Bresson: The Early Work," at the Museum of Modern Art, provided the first major reassessment of this famous photographer's achievement. Cartier-Bresson is generally thought of as a photojournalist of extraordinary lyrical power, but this show, consisting of 90 images taken between 1929 and 1934, revealed him as an artist deeply influenced by Surrealist ideas.

**Mid-Career Retrospectives.** An extensive, if not flattering, look at 15 years of work by Jan Groover was provided by the Museum of Modern Art in March. The show opened with Groover's seldom-seen color diptychs and triptychs of moving cars and trucks, building facades, and suburban landscapes, which displayed a rich vitality. It moved on quickly to her most famous work, the color still lifes of kitchen utensils, plants, and vegetables, but then bogged down in large numbers of unconvincing pictures.

In the spring, the International Center of Photography in New York had a survey of Ellen Carey's work, which documented her evolving investigation of "self as idea." Large-scale images, mainly of her own face or body, were camouflaged with geometric designs to suggest both primitive body decoration and transcendent psychic states.

*Realism and abstraction meet in* Untitled *(1986), part of the Ellen Carey show at the International Center of Photography in New York City.*

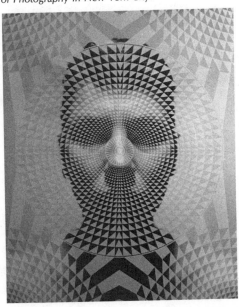

*An 1856 glass negative photograph of the imperial yacht* La Reine Hortense *docked in Le Havre was among the works of Gustave Le Gray on display in an exhibit organized by the Art Institute of Chicago.*

**Gallery Shows.** Nan Golden's "Ballad of Sexual Dependency" was an exhibition of 75 prints at the Burden Gallery in New York. A powerful, often offensive exploration of the failure of human intimacy, sexual or otherwise, Golden's work was widely acclaimed.

Andy Warhol's last show before his death on February 22 was his first as a pure photographer. In the more than 60 black-and-white photographs shown at the Robert Miller Gallery, he turned the repetitious grids of his silk screens into repetitious grids of photographs. The images had little meaning, but the presentation was, as usual, full of wit.

**The Whitney Biennial.** The Biennial of the Whitney Museum of American Art in New York presented photographic work on an equal footing with painting and sculpture for the first time. Many nonphotographic artists featured in the Biennial, such as Ross Bleckner or Annette Lemieux, incorporated photography in their works to point up the central role of the reproductive image in contemporary thought

and vision. In addition to such familiar names as Barbara Kruger and Richard Prince, several new photographers captured the spotlight.

**Art Market.** Like prices in the rest of the art world, prices for photographs were soaring. At Christie's in May, Clarence White's 1903 *Boy With Camera Work* sold for $50,000, the third highest auction price thus far paid for a photograph; other pictorial works established new records for the artists.

**New Technology.** Fully automated single-lens reflex (SLR) cameras, with autofocus and autoexposure, continued to flood the market. The newly released Nikon N4004 made the special benefits of an SLR—interchangeable lenses, an accurate viewfinder, and through-the-lens exposure control—available in what is virtually a point-and-shot camera. The Contax 167 MT took automation one step further by offering an automatic exposure-bracketing control. This enables the user to make a series of three rapid-fire pictures in which the exposure setting is automatically varied by fixed increments.

322

In the race for higher-speed color print films, the Konica SR-V3200 set new records. The film is twice as fast as the previous leaders, Fujicolor Super HR 1600 and Konica's own SR 1600. Although very grainy and soft in color, the pictures produced by the new film when used at normal exposure or under-exposed at 1600 are vastly superior to those produced by the slower films.          B.B.S.

**PHYSICS.** The discovery of ceramic oxide compounds that remain superconductive at temperatures much higher than had previously been thought possible created tremendous excitement among both physicists and the public in 1987. Two scientists who made key discoveries in this field won special recognition when they were awarded the 1987 Nobel Prize in physics. Also in the news was the proposed Superconducting Super Collider.

**Superconductors.** Superconductors are materials with two unique properties. First, they can carry a constant electrical current with no resistance or friction and, consequently, no loss of energy—so that their use in electric motors, generators of electric power, or electric power transmission lines would in theory make these systems considerably more efficient and less costly. The second unique feature of superconductors is the expulsion from their interior of lines of magnetic flux (the lines of force constituting a magnetic field). This property makes possible transistor-like devices that could be the basis of ultrahigh-speed, miniaturized supercomputers and gives rise to the fabled levitation effect, in which a magnet will float over a superconductor or vice versa. An experimental frictionless high-speed railroad train has been built in Japan using this principle.

Until 1986 the highest temperature at which any superconductor kept its remarkable properties was 23 degrees Kelvin, or $-418$ degrees Fahrenheit, a temperature so cold that systems employing superconductors were too costly to compete with ordinary technologies. But a 1986 report by two scientists at the IBM research laboratory in Zurich, Switzerland—Karl Alexander Müller and Johannes Georg Bednorz—disclosed preliminary evidence for superconductivity at temperatures up to $35°K$ ($-397°F$) in a ceramic oxide compound. The report attracted little notice until it was con-firmed by independent groups of researchers in the United States and Japan; it then generated wide attention and won for Müller and Bednorz a Nobel Prize (see PRIZES AND AWARDS).

An important new step was made in February 1987, when researchers at the University of Houston and the University of Alabama in Huntsville, working under the direction of Paul C. W. Chu, announced finding a second family of ceramic oxides that remained superconductive at an even higher temperature—above $90°K$ ($-298°F$). This discovery opened the way to possibly achieving superconductivity by using liquid nitrogen, a common, inexpensive, conveniently usable refrigerant.

Nearly everyone agrees that difficult technical problems need to be overcome before it is possible to make these brittle ceramic materials in useful forms—such as flexible wires. Experimentation along such lines was continuing. Scientists were also seeking new superconducting materials that might retain their properties at still higher temperatures, possibly even at room temperature. Also under study was the question of why certain ceramic materials are high-temperature superconductors.

In general, the ability to carry electric current with no resistance, friction, or energy loss derives from the current-carrying electrons' all being in a special quantum state in which they move together without suffering collisions as they go. In ordinary electric conduction, individual electrons are constantly losing energy by colliding with anything that disturbs the perfect periodicity of the crystal lattice (the orderly geometric arrangement of atoms). Vibrations of the atoms on their lattice sites, impurity atoms (atoms of other substances), and other electrons that are not localized at the lattice sites all cause collisions. According to the 1957 Bardeen-Cooper-Schrieffer (BCS) theory that correctly describes ordinary superconductors, electrons must overcome the natural repulsive force between them that results from their electrical charge and form pairs of linked electrons in order to enter this special quantum state. Somewhat paradoxically, in the BCS theory the lattice vibrations that give rise to electrical resistance at high temperature also provide a way to accomplish this pairing at low temperature.

Most theorists do not believe that the pairing force due to lattice vibrations is strong enough to explain the high-temperature superconductors. There is no paucity of alternate explanations, and several Nobel laureates are in the hunt.

**Super Accelerator.** Superconductors also figured in an unfolding drama of extreme importance to elementary particle physicists, who want the U.S. government to build a mammoth new accelerator, at a cost probably exceeding $5 billion. Scheduled for completion in 1996, the Superconducting Super Collider (SSC) would hurl two beams of protons in opposite directions around the 53-mile circumference machine. At selected points, the beams would intersect, allowing the protons to collide at an energy of 40 trillion electron volts, more than 20 times higher than any accelerator today can produce. Scientists hoped that use of the device would help answer fundamental questions about elementary particles. Superconductors figure in the SSC because high-strength electromagnets are needed to guide the proton beams around the accelerator and to keep the beam tightly focused; such magnets would be built from coils of superconducting wire.

In January, Secretary of Energy John Herrington announced that President Ronald Reagan had approved construction of the SSC. Herrington's announcement set off a race among the states to see which would receive the economic boost in jobs, new business, and income that is expected to benefit the home of the SSC. Final site selection was not expected to be announced until January 1989. Actual construction depends, of course, on congressional approval, and many senators and representatives share budget officials' concern over costs.

A further note of uncertainty was cast by the discovery of the ceramic oxide superconductors, which offer the possibility of a considerably less expensive accelerator because of operation at higher temperature and because of stronger magnets. Since the technology of superconducting magnets for accelerators is the most difficult of all applications for superconductors, most superconductor scientists and engineers do not believe that magnets built of ceramic oxides could be ready in time for

*Paul C. W. Chu, a University of Houston physicist, displays an experimental ceramic superconductor—one of several new materials which, when cooled with an inexpensive refrigerant, offer no electrical resistance.*

the SSC. But opponents of the accelerator have argued that it is worth putting the project on hold until more information is available.

A.L.R.

**POLAND.** In October 1987 the government of General Wojciech Jaruzelski announced plans for a "radical program of economic reform," along with political reforms aimed at a "deep democratization of political life." However, the government failed to win support for its plans in a November 29 referendum; as a result, economic austerity measures were scaled back.

**Initial Changes.** The policy changes originally set forth in October sought to make Poland's economy work more efficiently by eliminating subsidies that had kept prices of basic commodities artificially low and by linking wage levels to company profits. To improve productivity in large state enterprises, the government called for such measures as selling company shares to workers and allowing unprofitable businesses to go bankrupt or be bought out by profitable ones. The government also opened he doors to market forces by proposing simplification of procedures for establishing private business and creation of competitive commercial banking systems, among other steps.

On October 24, at the end of the parliamentary session where the reforms were announced, the government's structure was overhauled. Twelve of the ministers were dismissed, the number of ministers was cut from 26 to 19, and the number of senior government agencies was cut in half, to eight. Leading industrial managers and economists (rather than party politicians) were promoted to a number of major posts.

The government hoped these changes would help it obtain credit from the International Monetary Fund and the World Bank, of which it became a member in October. Nevertheless, there was public opposition. The government scheduled a referendum on its plan; the outlawed Solidarity labor movement called on Poles to boycott the referendum, saying that it proposed no "concrete democratic reform projects."

**Referendum.** In the referendum on November 29, a reported 66 percent of those voting, but only 44 percent of all eligible voters, supported the economic austerities. The political liberalization plan was backed by a reported 69 percent of voters and 46 percent of the total electorate. Since Polish law requires backing by a majority of the total electorate, the referendum did not pass. It appeared to be the first public vote of no confidence ever handed to an Eastern-bloc country on a major program. Citing the results, which were not binding, the government said there would be some "downward revision" of the economic program but no change in direction. On December 15 the government announced that prices would rise an average of 27 percent in 1988, rather than 40 percent as planned, and would be cushioned by higher wages and other compensation.

**Pope's Visit.** In June, Pope John Paul II made his third official pilgrimage to his native land since 1978. He was more outspoken than ever in criticizing government policy and called for greater respect for human rights in Poland. In one incident, workers and security forces clashed after an open-air mass said by the pope

before as many as 1 million people in Gdańsk, Solidarity's birthplace.

**Foreign Relations.** The Polish leadership was among the most supportive in Eastern Europe of Soviet leader Mikhail Gorbachev's calls for openness; one important aspect of this openness in Soviet-Polish relations was the public airing of differences in past relations between the two countries.

Poland's relations with the United States improved measurably. In February the United States removed the last of the economic sanctions it had imposed following the regime's introduction of martial law, and in September, immediately prior to a visit by Vice President George Bush to Poland, the two countries agreed to restore ambassadors to each other's capitals after a four-year absence.

See STATISTICS OF THE WORLD.          R.E.K.

**PORTUGAL.** In elections held on July 19, 1987, Portuguese voters gave the Social Democratic Party of Prime Minister Anibal Cavaco Silva 149 of the 250 seats in the unicameral Assembly of the Republic. It was the first time a party had won an absolute parliamentary majority since the 1974 revolution.

The elections, which occurred two years earlier than required, were prompted when Socialist President Mario Soares dissolved the Assembly on April 28, following a vote of censure that led to the resignation of Cavaco Silva and his minority government. The censure vote was precipitated by a motion from the center-left Democratic Renewal Party, a political vehicle for former President Antonio Ramalho Eanes. The Socialists, Communists, and Christian Democrats joined with Eanes, who sought a leftist coalition. Eanes and his party were the big losers in the elections, falling from 45 seats to 7. (Eanes later resigned as party leader.)

The Social Democrats' victory and Cavaco Silva's reelection were widely viewed as a result of Portugal's steady economic growth—4.6 percent in 1986—under the austerity policies begun by the previous prime minister, Mario Soares, and maintained by Cavaco Silva. Inflation was cut to 10 percent, foreign investment increased, and the nation's runaway foreign debt was curbed. Portugal's January 1986 entry into the European Community helped further stabilize the nation's politics and steady the economy.

During the electoral campaign Cavaco Silva promised to continue the economic policies that brought Portugal a measure of prosperity and stability. These included liberalization of the economy, the privatization of some companies, and tougher control over those industries that remained in the public sector. More flexible labor laws and a simplification of the tax code were also promised. It was also announced that efforts would be made to strengthen Portugal's unproductive agriculture.

Negotiations with China on the fate of the Portuguese territory of Macao concluded in March with a Sino-Portuguese declaration that control would revert to China on December 20, 1999, under arrangements similar to those devised for Hong Kong.

After a trial, Lieutenant Colonel Otelo Saraiva de Carvalho, a hero of the 1974 revolution that toppled the Salazar dictatorship, was found guilty of running the secret left-wing terrorist organization Popular Forces of the 25th of April (FP-25). He was sentenced to 15 years in prison. Nearly 50 other codefendants were also convicted and sentenced to prison.

*See* STATISTICS OF THE WORLD.          J.O.S.

**PRESIDENT OF THE UNITED STATES.** *See* UNITED STATES OF AMERICA: *The Presidency.*

**PRINCE EDWARD ISLAND.** *See* STATISTICS OF THE WORLD.

*Anibal Cavaco Silva (arms raised) became the first Portuguese prime minister since the 1974 revolution to govern with a parliamentary majority. His Social Democratic Party took 149 of 250 seats in July's national elections.*

Susumu Tonegawa of MIT, who helped explain the adaptability of the immune system, won the Nobel Prize in physiology or medicine.

**PRIZES AND AWARDS.** The following is a selected listing of prizes awarded during 1987 and the names of the persons who received them. For some awards given in specific fields, see the appropriate subject entry, such as MOTION PICTURES.

## NOBEL PRIZES

In 1987 the Nobel awards focused to an unusual degree on recent achievements—including the regional peace plan for Central America, devised by Nobelist Oscar Arias Sánchez, president of Costa Rica. The awards, carrying with them approximately $340,000 prize money in each category, were presented on December 10.

**Chemistry.** For their research in the field of "host-guest," or supramolecular, chemistry, including work leading to the creation of synthetic molecules that mimic the action of natural proteins:

*Donald J. Cram* (1919- ), professor at the University of California at Los Angeles. Born in Chester, Vt., he received a Ph.D. from Harvard University in 1947 and shortly after joined the faculty of UCLA.

*Jean-Marie Lehn* (1939- ), who has been called the leading chemist in France. Born in Rosheim, France, he received a doctorate in chemistry at the University of Strasbourg in 1963 and became a professor at the Collège de France in Paris and the University of Strasbourg.

*Charles J. Pederson* (1904- ), retired research chemist. Pederson was born in Pusan, Korea, to a Norwegian father and a Japanese mother.

After studying at the University of Dayton and the Massachusetts Institute of Technology, he worked for E. I. Du Pont de Nemours & Company from 1927 until his retirement in 1969.

**Economics.** For his studies of growth in industrialized economies, which show that, contrary to the traditional view, increases in capital and labor are not necessarily the vital factors in economic growth:

*Robert M. Solow* (1924- ), professor at MIT. Born in Brooklyn, N.Y., Solow received his doctorate from Harvard University in 1951 and joined the MIT faculty in 1949. He has served as a consultant for the RAND Corporation, a director of the Boston Federal Reserve Bank, and a staff member of the Council of Economic Advisers. His economic philosophy is described as tending toward Keynesianism.

**Literature.** For works that displayed "an all-embracing authorship imbued with clarity of thought and poetic intensity":

*Joseph Aleksandrovich Brodsky* (1940- ), a Soviet exile living in the United States. Born in Leningrad, the son of a commercial photographer, he learned Polish to translate Czeslaw Milosz, and English to translate John Donne. His own poems often express sadness and despair, and he has expressed aversion to the Soviet Union's "shabby materialist dogma." Brodsky's independent spirit made him enemies; in 1964 he was sent to a labor camp, but he was released the next year after protests from Soviet and foreign writers. "Invited" to

327

leave the Soviet Union in 1972, he later settled in the United States and taught at such institutions as the University of Michigan, New York University, and Columbia University. Translations of his poetry include *Selected Poems* (1973) and *A Part of Speech* (1980). A collection of essays, *Less Than One,* and another collection of poems, *History of the Twentieth Century,* were published in English in 1986. Little of his work has been published in the Soviet Union.

**Peace.** For his outstanding contribution toward the possible return of stability and peace in a region long torn by strife and civil war:

*Oscar Arias Sánchez* (1941- ), president of Costa Rica and chief architect of a peace plan for Central America. On August 7, Arias signed the initial accord—aimed at ending civil wars and promoting democracy in the region—along with the presidents of El Salvador, Guatemala, Honduras, and Nicaragua. The chairman of the Norwegian Nobel Committee noted that the prize was intended not only to honor peacemakers but also to encourage peace efforts and contribute to peace. Efforts to bring the accord into play were in progress when the award was announced in October; on November 5, as provided in the pact, each of the Central American presidents did take steps toward its implementation. Accepting the prize in Oslo on December 10, Arias asked that the superpowers "leave the interpretation and implementation of our peace plan to us" and that they "send our people plowshares instead of swords."

Arias was born in Heredia, Costa Rica, to a prosperous coffee-producing family. He studied in Costa Rica, the United States, and England. A professor in the political science school of the University of Costa Rica from 1969 to 1972, he served in the 1970's first as a member of the president's economic council and then as minister of national planning and political economy. In 1979 he became general secretary of the National Liberation Party, and he won its nomination to run for president in the 1986 election. Arias won that election and was sworn in as the country's youngest president ever. Arias said the prize money would be used to establish a foundation for the Costa Rican poor.

**Physics.** For their work in producing superconductivity—the absence of resistance to electricity—at higher temperatures than had been believed possible, thus opening up a wide range of possible applications:

*Karl Alex Müller* (1927- ), scientist at IBM's research laboratory in Zurich, Switzerland. Müller was born in Switzerland and earned a doctoral degree in physics from the Swiss Federal Institute of Technology in 1958. He went to work at the IBM facility in 1963.

*Johannes Georg Bednorz* (1950- ), researcher at IBM's laboratory in Zurich. Born in West Germany, he graduated from the University of Muenster and the Swiss Federal Institute of Technology in Zurich. He joined IBM in 1982 and was known as a specialist in making ceramics. He and Müller tested numerous materials before finding a ceramic compound in which superconductivity was achieved at the then-unheard of temperature of about $-400°F$.

**Physiology or Medicine.** For proving "in a convincing and elegant manner" that bits of genetic material controlling antibody production are repeatedly shuffled and reshuffled over time to produce the various genetic sequences and, ultimately, the multitude of antibodies needed to protect the body against foreign substances:

*Susumu Tonegawa* (1939- ), a molecular biologist at MIT. Born in Nagoya, Japan, he took his bachelor's degree in chemistry from Kyoto University in 1963 and his Ph.D. in biology from the University of California at San Diego in 1969. In 1971 he joined the Basel Institute for Immunology in Switzerland, where he launched his Nobel-winning research. Tonegawa became a professor at MIT in 1981. His findings may contribute to the development of vaccines and immunological therapies for various diseases, as well as to progress in organ transplant surgery, where the body's tendency to reject foreign tissue is a major concern.

## PULITZER PRIZES

The winners of the 1987 Pulitzer Prizes were announced on April 16. The drama award went to August Wilson for *Fences,* a play about black American life. David K. Shipler received the nonfiction award for *Arab and Jew: Wounded Spirits in a Promised Land,* and Memphis-born writer Peter Taylor won the fiction prize for *A Summons to Memphis*. The music award went to John Harbison for his 13-minute cantata *The Flight Into Egypt*. Rita Dove's *Thomas and Beulah* won the poetry prize, and the history award went to Bernard Bailyn for *Voyagers to the West: A Passage in the Peopling of America on the Eve of the Revolution*. The national reporting award in journalism was shared by the Miami *Herald* (for coverage of the Iran/contra affair) and the New York *Times* (for covering the aftermath of the *Challenger* explosion).

Other Pulitzer Prizes in letters and journalism included the following:

**Biography.** David J. Garrow for *Bearing the Cross: Martin Luther King, Jr., and the Southern Christian Leadership Conference.*

**Commentary.** Charles Krauthammer, Washington *Post* Writers Group.

**Criticism.** Richard Eder, Los Angeles *Times*.

**Editorial Cartooning.** Berke Breathed, Washington *Post* Writers Group.

**Editorial Writing.** Jonathan Freedman, San Diego *Tribune*.

**Explanatory Journalism.** Jeff Lyon and Peter Gorner, Chicago *Tribune*.

**Feature Writing.** Steve Twomey, Philadelphia *Inquirer*.

**Photography, Feature.** David Peterson, Des Moines (Iowa) *Register*.

**Photography, Spot News.** Kim Komenich, San Francisco *Examiner*.

**Reporting, General News.** Staff of the Akron (Ohio) *Beacon Journal*.

**Reporting, International.** Michael Parks, Los Angeles *Times*.

**Reporting, Investigative.** Daniel R. Biddle, H. G. Bissinger, and Fredric N. Tulsky, Philadelphia *Inquirer*.

**Reporting, Specialized.** Alex S. Jones, New York *Times*.

*David Peterson, a photographer at the Des Moines Register, won the Pulitzer Prize for feature photography for his studies of families caught up in America's farming crisis.*

# PRIZES AND AWARDS

## OTHER PRIZES AND AWARDS

Among the many other awards made in 1987 were the following:

**Academy of American Poets.** Fellowships to Josephine Jacobsen and Howard Moss. Walt Whitman Award to Judith Baumel for *The Weight of Numbers.*

**Albert and Mary Lasker Foundation.** $15,000 (shared) to molecular biologists Susumu Tonegawa, Philip Leder, and Leroy Hood, for research into development of the immune system. $15,000 to Dr. Mogens Schou for work in psychopharmacology.

**American Academy and Institute of Arts and Letters.** Award for Distinguished Service to the Arts to Isaac Stern. Gold medals to Isabel Bishop (painting) and Jacques Barzun (belles lettres and criticism). Arnold W. Brunner Memorial Prize in architecture ($1,000) to James Ingo Freed. Charles Ives Fellowship in music ($10,000) to Russell F. Pinkston. Richard and Hilda Rosenthal Foundation award ($5,000 each) to Chris Martin (painting) and Norman Rush (fiction). Award of merit for drama ($5,000) to A. R. Gurney, Jr. Jean Stein Award for literature ($5,000) to Wendell Berry. Harold D. Vursell Memorial Award for literature ($5,000) to Stephen Jay Gould. Goddard Lieberson Fellowships in music ($10,000 each) to Robert Beaser and Lee Hyla.

**American Film Institute.** Life achievement award to Barbara Stanwyck.

**Bristol-Myers Award.** $50,000 cancer research award to Dr. Donald Metcalf of the Walter and Eliza Hall Institute of Medical Research, Melbourne, Australia.

**Franklin D. Roosevelt Freedom Medal.** Awarded to Thomas P. O'Neill, Jr., Herbert Block, Reverend Leon B. Sullivan, Mary Lasker, and George F. Kennan.

**General Motors Cancer Research Foundation.** $100,000 awards to Dr. R. Palmer and Dr. Jesse W. Summers (shared), Dr. Basil Hirschowitz, and Dr. Robert Weinberg.

**Kennedy Center Honors.** For outstanding achievement in performing arts, awarded to singer Perry Como, actress Bette Davis, entertainer Sammy Davis, Jr., violinist Nathan Milstein, and choreographer Alwin Nikolais.

**MacArthur Foundation.** MacArthur Awards to "outstandingly talented and promising individuals," ranging from $150,000 to $375,000, based on the age of the recipient. Awarded to 32 persons ranging in age from 82 (art historian Meyer Schapiro) to 27 (free-lance journalist Tina Rosenberg).

**National Medal of Arts.** Awarded to Romare Bearden, painter; J. W. Fisher, opera patron; Ella Fitzgerald, singer; Dr. Armand Hammer, art patron; Sydney and Frances Lewis, art patrons; Howard Nemerov, writer and scholar; Alwin Nikolais, choreographer; Isamu Noguchi, sculptor; William Schuman, composer; and Robert Penn Warren, poet and novelist.

**Onassis Foundation.** Gold medal to King Juan Carlos of Spain for his aiding Spanish democracy; $100,000 awards to former Italian President Alessandro Pertini, to the Pugwash Conference on Science and World Affairs and the Archaeological Society of Athens (shared), and to Archbishop Arturo Rivera y Damas of El Salvador and Amnesty International (shared).

**Presidential Medal of Freedom.** Highest U.S. civilian honor, awarded to Republican Party activist Anne Armstrong, the late industrialist Justin Dart, Judge Irving R. Kaufman, the late comedian Danny Kaye, retired General Lyman Lemnitzer, former CIA Director John A. McCone, United Negro College Fund founder Frederick D. Patterson, conductor Mstislav Rostropovich, Project Hope founder Dr. William Walsh, and the late composer Meredith Willson.

**Samuel H. Scripps-American Dance Festival Award.** $25,000 to Alvin Ailey.

**Templeton Foundation.** $330,000 Templeton Prize for Progress in Religion to Reverend Stanley L. Jaki.

**Tyler Foundation.** For research in environmental science, $150,000 (shared) to botanist Richard Evans Schultes (for cataloging plants used in the tropics for various purposes) and geographer Gilbert F. White (for devising ways to cope with recurring floods and storms).

**Wolf Foundation.** $100,000 each to Theodore O. Diener (agriculture), Sir David C. Phillips and David M. Blow (chemistry; shared), Kiyoshi Ito and Peter D. Lax (mathematics; shared), Pedro Cuatrecasas and Meir Wilcheck (medicine; shared), Herbert B. Friedman, Bruno B. Rossi, and Riccardo Giacconi (physics; shared), and Isaac Stern and Krzysztof Penderecki (arts; shared).

*Peter Wright, a retired British counterintelligence official living in Australia, charged in* Spycatcher *that his former boss, Sir Roger Hollis, had been a Soviet agent. The British waged a legal battle to prevent the book's publication at home and abroad, but it was a best-seller in the United States, and copies were flowing freely into Britain.*

**PUBLISHING.** In 1987, history rose to the top of the best-seller lists as readily as celebrity memoirs, and the book publishing industry was swept by a wave of takeovers. There was less excitement in the newspaper and magazine field, where total circulation remained stable and the industry seemed to be on firm economic ground.

**Books.** *Best-sellers.* Books with a historical slant did well during the year. New York *Times* columnist William Safire produced an impressive 1,100-page novel about Abraham Lincoln and the Civil War, called *Freedom.* *Time* magazine art critic Robert Hughes offered a

history of the early settlement of his native Australia in *The Fatal Shore.* In *Life and Death in Shanghai,* Nien Cheng recounted her chilling experiences during China's Cultural Revolution. Other personal encounters with 20th-century history could be found in memoirs by former House Speaker Tip O'Neill (*Man of the House*), industrialist Armand Hammer (*Hammer: A Witness to History*), TV White House correspondent Sam Donaldson (*Hold On, Mr. President!*), and journalist George Seldes (*Witness to a Century*). In the fall, Bob Woodward's *The Veil: The Secret Wars of the CIA 1981–1987* grabbed headlines with disclosures of illegal CIA activities and a purported deathbed interview with CIA Director William J. Casey. Former British spy Peter Wright told his story of skullduggery in *Spycatcher;* the book, temporarily banned in Britain pending the final outcome of legal action, identified an ex-head of Britain's Secret Service as a Soviet mole.

Celebrity biographies and autobiographies were never far behind, with memoirs by such Hollywood figures as Bette Davis (*This 'n' That*), Katharine Hepburn (*The Making of the African Queen*), Myrna Loy (*Myrna Loy: Being and Becoming*), and Patty Duke (*Call Me Anna*). East and West met—at least on best-seller lists—with Mikhail S. Gorbachev's blueprint for change in the Communist world, *Perestroika,* and Donald Trump's *Trump: The Art of the Deal,* a celebration of capitalism.

Two books by university professors attacking American educational shortcomings did surprisingly well. In *Cultural Literacy,* E. D. Hirsch, Jr., supplied a list of historical facts, scientific concepts, and literary allusions that, he argued, anyone who purports to be educated should be familiar with. Allan Bloom's *The Closing of the American Mind* offered a philosophical analysis of American cultural decline. Another pessimistic best-seller addressed the economy: *The Great Depression of 1990,* by Ravi Batra, predicted a severe worldwide depression unless extraordinary measures were enacted.

Self-help books, particularly those about personal relationships, continued to win readers' hearts. Among them: *How to Marry the Man of Your Choice* by Margaret Kent; *Men Who Can't Love* by Steven Carter and Julia Sokol; *Women Men Love, Women Men Leave* by

# PUBLISHING

Connell Cowan and Melvyn Kinder; and *Men Who Hate Women and the Women Who Love Them* by Susan Forward and Joan Torres.

In fiction, prolific author Stephen King scared readers again with *Misery, The Eyes of the Dragon, It,* and *The Tommyknockers.* Tom Clancy demonstrated that his military thrillers were not flukes as readers thronged to buy his *Red Storm Rising* and *Patriot Games.* Lawyer Scott Turow offered a gripping murder mystery set in a fictional midwestern city in his first novel, *Presumed Innocent.* Among other best-selling authors and their novels: Sidney Sheldon *(Windmills of the Gods),* Dick Francis *(Bolt),* Colleen McCullough *(The Ladies of Missalonghi),* Jack Higgins *(Night of the Fox),* Pat Conroy *(The Prince of Tides),* Louis L'Amour *(The Haunted Mesa),* Robin Cook *(Outbreak),* Lawrence Sanders *(The Timothy Files),* Elmore Leonard *(Bandit),* Danielle Steel *(Fine Things),* and Janet Dailey *(Heiress).*

*Business News.* The kind of takeover battles rampant on Wall Street in recent years also erupted in the book business. Early in the year, the board of directors of Harper & Row adopted "poison pill" provisions designed to thwart hostile takeovers. But before shareholders could enact the changes, Theodore L. Cross, a private investor, offered $190 million for the company, touching off a bidding war. Harcourt Brace Jovanovich offered $220 million, and Rupert Murdoch, whose media empire encompasses Britain and the United States as well as his native Australia, offered $300 million. The Harper & Row management finally chose Murdoch, believing that he would keep the house intact and that the British house William Collins, which he also owned, would mix well with Harper.

In the spring, British publishing tycoon Robert Maxwell offered $1.7 billion for Harcourt Brace Jovanovich. Calling Maxwell "entirely unfit" to control Harcourt, company chairman William Jovanovich enacted a $3 billion recapitalization plan to block Maxwell, who brought suit but eventually had to concede defeat. After the dust settled, Harcourt began implementing strict austerity measures to pay the increased debt resulting from its recapitalization costs.

**Bloodcurdling for Fun and Profit**
Stephen King is in the business of scaring people, and business is good. Since 1974, he has written some 20 books, which have sold more than 60 million copies worldwide, besides spawning a dozen films and a TV miniseries. His knack for making people's hair stand on end has earned him over $20 million. Born in 1947, King was a lonely child who amused himself by going to science fiction and monster movies. After college, he began writing part-time and hit it big with the novel *Carrie* (1974), about a girl who uses telekinetic powers to incinerate her classmates at a senior prom. In early 1987 his 1,100-page blockbuster *It* lingered at the top of best-seller lists, where it was soon joined by two new King novels, an epic called *The Eyes of the Dragon* and *Misery,* a thriller about a best-selling author held captive by an insatiable fan. Yet another horror novel, *The Tommyknockers,* showed up in the fall. There were no signs at all that King's strange and prolific imagination was about to let up or loosen its hold on the public.

*Stephen King*

In other acquisitions, Random House bought both Schocken Books, known for its Judaica, psychology, and art lists, and the highly regarded British literary publishing group Chatto, Virago, Bodley Head & Jonathan Cape. Virago, a feminist publisher, was later bought back by its management. Macmillan bought Laidlaw Educational Publishers (textbook publishers) from Doubleday, and Price/Stern/Sloan purchased HP Books, which specializes in practical and self-help books, from Knight-Ridder.

*Litigation.* The U.S. Supreme Court, in a decision hailed by publishers, struck down a Louisiana state law that required public schools teaching evolution to devote equal time to "creation science." The law would have forced textbooks to include creationism or to exclude coverage of the theory of evolution. In another ruling, the Court established a national standard, as opposed to local community judgment, for one of its three tests to determine obscenity—whether a work has serious literary or artistic value.

In a major case involving the issue of fair use as applied to unpublished materials, the Supreme Court let stand a federal appeals court ruling barring publication of an unauthorized biography of reclusive writer J. D. Salinger by Ian Hamilton. Hamilton had used quotations from unpublished Salinger letters available in libraries around the United States. After failing to persuade Random House to eliminate all of the quotations from the manuscript, Salinger copyrighted the letters and filed suit to block publication.

Archbishop Paul Marcinkus, the head of the Vatican bank and former unofficial bodyguard to Pope Paul VI, filed suit to halt sales of *In the Name of the Father* by A. J. Quinnell. The novel—prefaced with a note stating that real individuals are shown in "entirely fictitious" circumstances—portrays the archbishop as having ordered the assassination of the late Soviet leader Yuri Andropov so as to protect Pope John Paul II.

Federal courts ruled in favor of publishers' interests in two cases involving fundamentalist groups. In Tennessee, an appeals court overturned a lower-court ruling allowing parents to remove their children from a class if they disagreed with what was being taught. At issue was a Holt, Rinehart and Winston reading series for elementary school students. In Alabama, an appeals court overturned a federal judge's decision to ban 44 elementary and high school textbooks from use in public schools because they promoted the "religions of secularism, humanism, evolution, materialism, agnosticism, and others."

**Newspapers.** The trend toward group ownership of newspapers continued, though slowed somewhat by the increasing scarcity of desirable independent papers and the high price they commanded. Newspaper groups by 1987 controlled nearly 75 percent of all U.S. daily newspapers, with more than 80 percent of the total circulation.

In Houston, both daily papers changed hands. In June the Hearst Corporation bought the Houston *Chronicle,* the largest daily in the southwest, bringing the total number of Hearst's dailies to 15. In September an affiliate of the Dallas-based MediaNews Group, Inc. bought the morning Houston *Post* from the Toronto Sun Publishing Corporation. In the same month another MediaNews affiliate acquired the Denver *Post* from the Los Angeles-based Times Mirror Company. That left the MediaNews group with 28 daily papers in the United States. In April a subsidiary of the Canadian-based Thomson Newspapers Inc. agreed to buy the Charleston (W. Va.) *Daily Mail* and three smaller West Virginia and North Carolina dailies from Clay Communications, giving Thomson 102 U.S. dailies, more than any other company, though all of them were small. The 18-month-old proposed merger of Detroit's two dailies—Gannett's Detroit *News* and Knight-Ridder's Detroit *Free Press*—was rejected by an administrative law judge, leaving a final decision to the attorney general.

United Press International, the second-largest U.S. news agency, continued to struggle for survival, afflicted by the defection of half a dozen major clients, including the New York *Times,* the New York *Daily News,* and the *Wall Street Journal.* UPI aroused controversy in October when it signed a $2.5 million contract with the U.S. government to transmit government press releases and publications of the U.S. Information Agency to news organizations in six European cities. The deal was criticized

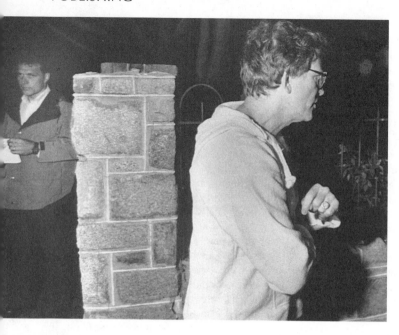

The stakeout as a form of political coverage, and sexual behavior as a criterion for judging candidates, were hotly debated after a Miami Herald team observed Gary Hart's Washington, D.C., townhouse in May and reported that model/actress Donna Rice had spent part of a weekend there. Here, Hart walks away from a Herald reporter who had asked about Rice's presence in the house.

by many journalists. In November three top editors at UPI resigned, saying the quality of the service's reporting was in jeopardy.

The newspaper industry as a whole remained profitable, and the American Newspaper Publishers Association celebrated its 100th anniversary in May on an upbeat note. While production costs continued to rise, so did ad revenues, and newspaper companies were investing heavily in new printing equipment to improve quality and production. On the other hand, daily circulation, almost static for a decade, remained close to the 1986 total of 62,489,630.

*Gary Hart and the Press.* A front-page story in the May 3 issue of the respected Miami *Herald* that linked Democratic presidential candidate Gary Hart to a 29-year-old model and actress named Donna Rice set off a major controversy over journalistic ethics. A few days later, after unprecedented media coverage of a politician's private life, Hart angrily withdrew from the race for his party's nomination, implicitly blaming the press for forcing him out. The *Herald* story, which reported that Hart had spent part of a weekend with Rice in his Washington, D.C., townhouse while his wife, Lee, was home in Colorado, had been based

on a stakeout of the house by several *Herald* reporters. Many journalists, as well as a majority of the public, according to polls taken after the events, believed that it went beyond the bounds of journalistic propriety for reporters to spy on politicians and dig deeply into their private life. *Herald* editors defended their actions, stating that there had long been rumors about Hart's infidelities, raising questions about his judgment and character. In December, Hart made a surprise announcement that he was resuming his presidential campaign so as to "let the people decide" his fitness for office.

**Magazines.** Revenue growth in the magazine industry was relatively slow, partly because cigarette, liquor, and computer advertising was not up to expectations. Total magazine circulation remained almost constant, with an increase in subscriptions offsetting a continued decline in single-copy sales. Publishers tended to be cautious, and some reduced their staffs— among them *Time* magazine, which also disbanded its magazine development group.

In July, Time Inc. gave up on *Discover,* after having poured a reported $30 million into the magazine on popular science since launching it in 1980. For $26 million it sold the 925,000 circulation monthly, whose ad revenues had been disappointing, to Family Media.

The Hearst Corporation acquired *Esquire,* a 53-year-old men's monthly with a circulation of 700,000. *Ms.* magazine was sold to John Fairfax Ltd., one of Australia's largest publishers. The deal ended a search by *Ms.* cofounders Gloria Steinem and Patricia Carbine for an infusion of new capital for the feminist monthly, which had experienced increasing operating losses.

Comic books, which flourished from the 1930's to the early 1950's, before television distracted the attention of children, appeared to be making a comeback. Marvel Comics, the leader in the field with about half the total market, reportedly doubled its sales over the past eight years, and the industry as a whole was expected to do even better than the 150 million copies that, according to one estimate, were sold in 1986.                J.M. & J.L.

**PUERTO RICO.** Preelection activity and relations with the United States were the principal concerns in 1987 for Puerto Rico. As the 1988 gubernatorial election approached, incumbent Governor Rafael Hernández Colón looked much stronger politically than he had previously. He kept his ruling Popular Democratic Party tightly disciplined, and his economic policies began producing satisfactory results.

The debate continued over the status of the island vis-á-vis the United States—an issue that has been a constant of modern Puerto Rican politics. Within the Popular Democratic Party, which is pro-autonomy (other parties are pro-statehood or pro-independence), some members wanted to see the commonwealth gain greater control over migration and broadcasting, as well as gain the ability to enter independently into bilateral agreements with foreign states. Many members wanted Puerto Rico to be free to articulate an independent foreign policy. Prospects for some modification of commonwealth status brightened, as a number of U.S. congressmen appeared more willing to support the island's position on independent economic ventures.

By mid-1987 the Puerto Rican economy was on the upswing. Unemployment was down to 16.7 percent, compared to about 23 percent when Hernández Colón took office. More tourists were visiting Puerto Rico than in 1986, and the cruise ship business was booming. Several new hotels were under construction, and old ones such as the Hyatt Regency Cerromar and the Hyatt Dorado Beach were revamped. Coffee production soared.

Three hotel workers charged by the federal government with arson and conspiracy for involvement in the 1986 New Year's Eve fire at the Dupont Plaza Hotel in San Juan pleaded guilty and drew prison terms of 75 to 99 years. Two of the workers—and eventually the third worker—also pleaded guilty to commonwealth murder charges, on which they were sentenced to concurrent terms.

*See* STATISTICS OF THE WORLD.        F.W.K.

# Q

**QATAR.** *See* STATISTICS OF THE WORLD. *See also* PERSIAN GULF STATES.

**QUÉBEC.** *See* STATISTICS OF THE WORLD. *See also* CANADA.

# R

**RADIO.** *See* TELEVISION AND RADIO. BROADCASTING.

**RAILROADS.** *See* TRANSPORTATION.
**RECORDINGS.** *See* MUSIC.

# Religion

In 1987, scandal enveloped one of the major Protestant television ministries in the United States, even as a former TV preacher launched his bid for the presidency. Tension between Roman Catholics and Jews heightened. Differences within Islam led to bloody violence in the holy city of Mecca.

The "electronic church" was torn by scandal involving the PTL ministry of Jim and Tammy Bakker, and Southern Baptists were divided by internal opposition. Meanwhile, three major U.S. Lutheran denominations merged into one. An important event for Catholics was the visit to North America of Pope John Paul II, who issued a strong call for fidelity to church teachings. Jews were encouraged by increased Jewish emigration from the Soviet Union. In Tibet, Buddhist monks led calls for independence from China. In Sri Lanka, violence continued between two major ethnic-religious communities.

## PROTESTANT AND ORTHODOX CHURCHES

Revelations of sexual and financial misconduct within the PTL ministry and subsequent struggles for control of PTL stained the reputation of television evangelism. Evangelist Pat Robertson announced his candidacy for the Republican presidential nomination and gave up his ministerial ordination; evangelist Jerry Falwell, on the other hand, announced he was giving up political activism. Three Lutheran churches merged, and two Protestant denominations issued statements aimed at improving relations with Jewish groups.

**PTL Scandal.** On March 19, Jim Bakker, founder and head of the PTL (Praise the Lord or People That Love) ministry, announced he was turning control of PTL over to fundamentalist TV preacher Jerry Falwell. Bakker admitted having had sexual relations in 1980 with Jessica Hahn, at the time a church secretary in New York, and said Hahn received $265,000 over a period of years in exchange for her silence about the incident. (The figure was later put at more than $360,000 by the Internal Revenue Service.) Hahn claimed Bakker and a PTL colleague had raped her. In resigning from PTL, Bakker accused fellow TV preacher Jimmy Swaggart of orchestrating an attempt to take over the ministry. Swaggart denied any intentions of taking control but did say that he, along with Falwell and Christian television talk-show host John Ankerberg, had looked into allegations of financial and sexual misconduct at the highest levels of PTL. Tulsa, Okla., evangelist Oral Roberts entered what became known as the Holy War by publicly denouncing Swaggart and declaring Bakker a "prophet of God."

In May the Assemblies of God, the 2.1-million-member denomination to which Swaggart also belonged, revoked Bakker's ministerial credentials, citing his admitted adultery and alleged homosexual behavior. Bakker publicly denied that he is homosexual but declined to meet his accusers before Assemblies of God authorities.

Investigations later revealed severe financial mismanagement within Bakker's PTL. The new PTL administration reported a $67 million debt, attributable largely to exorbitant salaries. Bakker and his wife, Tammy, had received $1.6 million in 1986 and $640,000 in the first three months of 1987. Despite Falwell's urgent pleas for emergency funds to save PTL, the ministry was forced to file for protection under federal bankruptcy laws in June. In October, Falwell and the entire PTL board of directors resigned because of concern that the ministry's creditors would seek to have the Bakkers return as part of a reorganization plan; the federal bankruptcy court then appointed an official of the rival Christian Broadcasting Network as trustee of PTL. A financial reorganization plan was approved in December.

As a result of the PTL scandal, Congress launched an investigation into the finances of television ministries. Also, the 1,300-member National Religious Broadcasters, an organization to which many TV preachers belong, passed a stricter code of ethics that among other provisions requires full disclosure of salaries and special privileges. (*See also* PEOPLE IN THE NEWS: Jim and Tammy Bakker.)

**Roberts Plea.** Roberts had made headlines prior to his involvement in the PTL debacle. In January he told his television congregation and those on his mailing lists that God had told him he would be "called home" if he was unable to raise $8 million by March 31. Roberts claimed the money was needed to finance missionary work in underdeveloped countries. The evangelist was accused of emotional blackmail, but the appeal succeeded: a $1.3 million donation late in March from Florida racetrack owner Jerry Collins put Roberts over his $8 million goal. In June he stirred yet more negative reaction by claims that he had raised many people from the dead.

**Robertson Campaign.** Marion G. (Pat) Robertson, founder of the Christian Broadcasting Network, had said in 1986 that he needed 3 million petition signatures before he would run for president, and in September he announced he had 3.3 million. He won a Republican straw poll in Iowa, beating out presumed front-runners Robert Dole and George Bush. Later in the month he resigned his ordination as a Southern Baptist minister and severed his ties with the Christian Broadcasting Network, explaining that he felt such formal religious roles are inappropriate for a political candidate. In October, Robertson formally declared his candidacy, stressing a return to family values, economic renewal, and a limited reliance on government.

Shortly afterward, it was disclosed that Robertson had been misrepresenting the date of his marriage, because his first child had been born only ten weeks after the real wedding date. Robertson said that he had been trying to protect his family from embarrassing publicity and that the out-of-wedlock conception had preceded his religious conversion. The disclosure did not seem to affect his campaign, but

*Prayers by three Lutheran bishops marked the merger of their denominations into the Evangelical Lutheran Church in America, the nation's fourth largest Protestant church. From left: Will Herzfeld of the Association of Evangelical Lutheran Churches, David Preus of the American Lutheran Church, and James Crumley, Jr., of the Lutheran Church in America.*

he continued to be accused of having misrepresented details of his background.

**Falwell and Moral Majority.** In November, Falwell announced he was giving up the presidency of Moral Majority, the organization he had founded in 1979 to encourage political activism by conservative Protestants. He said he wanted to devote full time to his 22,000-member Thomas Road Baptist Church in Lynchburg, Va., and his TV ministry. Falwell, whose support had sometimes proved a liability for candidates in recent years, said he would continue to speak out on political issues but would no longer campaign for candidates or lobby for legislation.

**Lutheran Merger.** The Evangelical Lutheran Church in America came into being in April with the official merger of the American Lutheran Church, the Lutheran Church in America, and the Association of Evangelical Lutheran Churches. With over 5.3 million members, it became the country's fourth largest Protestant denomination. Herbert W. Chilstrom, the new church's first presiding bishop, described himself as a "theological centrist" who is "left of center on social issues."

**Jewish Relations.** The 1.7-million-member United Church of Christ became what was thought to be the first major U.S. Protestant denomination to officially declare that Judaism has not been superseded by Christianity. While various churches have strongly denounced anti-Semitism, none had gone so far as to assert that the Jewish and Christian faiths have equal validity. The 3-million-member Presbyterian Church (U.S.A.), in a more limited action, adopted a study paper stating that Christians have not replaced Jews in God's favor but have been "engrafted into the people of God established by the covenant with Abraham, Isaac, and Jacob."

**Southern Baptist Discord.** More than 25,000 delegates to the annual meeting of the Southern Baptist Convention, held in St. Louis, overwhelmingly approved a report of the denomination's Peace Committee, which had been created to seek an end to the internal political and theological strife between fundamentalists and moderates. Two years in the making, the report generally sided with the fundamentalists.

The report did little to quell underlying tension in the 14.6-million-member body. A dispute between fundamentalists and officials at the Southeastern Baptist Theological Seminary, one of the SBC's six seminaries, over alleged heresies led to threats of resignation there. The Georgia Baptist Convention defeated a fundamentalist move to cut off another seminary's funding and also killed a reelection bid by the convention president, a fundamentalist who was replaced by a moderate.

**United Methodist Controversy.** A United Methodist Church court in New Hampshire suspended lesbian minister Rose Mary Denman in August, stating she had violated a church rule banning practicing homosexuals from the clergy. Denman had requested a church trial in order to challenge the rule, established in 1984. The suspension was considered a lenient verdict, since she could have been expelled.

**Charismatics.** More than 35,000 charismatic Christians met in New Orleans in July at the North American Congress on the Holy Spirit and World Evangelism. The meeting—which

*The Reverend Jerry Falwell assumed control of the PTL Ministry in March as scandal enveloped fellow TV evangelist Jim Bakker, the founder of PTL, and Bakker's wife, Tammy.*

*Preaching orthodoxy to his American flock, Pope John Paul II was greeted by admiring crowds (right, a motorcade in San Antonio) but encountered protests as well. In addition to reaffirming doctrine on such matters as the unmarried priesthood, the pope spoke out for various minority groups.*

drew Roman Catholics, Protestants, Orthodox Christians, and messianic Jews—signified growing unity in the 27-year-old American charismatic renewal movement, whose leaders believe their approach will be the predominant form of Christianity by the year 2000. R.L.F.

## ROMAN CATHOLIC CHURCH

Strains in Catholic-Jewish relationships were a major concern in 1987; also a matter of concern, especially during the pope's visit to the United States in September, was the issue of dissent within the church.

**Relations With Jews.** Tensions in Catholic-Jewish relations quickened in May, when Pope John Paul II beatified Edith Stein, a German Jew who converted to Catholicism, became a Carmelite nun, and died in the Nazi prison camp in Auschwitz. The action was opposed by some members of the Stein family and by Jewish officials, who regarded it as an effort to claim for Roman Catholicism a woman who was killed because of her Jewish origins. Relations were further strained when, during a visit to the Maidanek death camp in Poland in early June, the pope failed to mention that the camp's victims were overwhelmingly Jewish.

The most serious breach in Catholic-Jewish relations occurred later in June when the pope received Austrian President Kurt Waldheim on an official visit at the Vatican. Jewish objections were based on charges that, as a German Army lieutenant, Waldheim had participated in the deportation of Greek Jews to death camps and in reprisals against partisans in Yugoslavia. The papal audience broke the diplomatic isolation that had surrounded Waldheim since his election as president of Austria in 1986.

After this episode, some major American Jewish organizations threatened to boycott a scheduled meeting between the pope and Jewish leaders during the pontiff's visit to the United States. An informal meeting was arranged between nine Jewish leaders and the pope at the papal summer residence in Castel Gandolfo, Italy, shortly before his departure. The meeting, the first of its kind in history, lasted 75 minutes and seemed to ease discord considerably. Afterward, the Vatican announced intentions to prepare a major document on the Holocaust and other manifestations of anti-Semitism.

At the Miami meeting on September 11, John Paul spoke of the suffering of the Jewish people at the hands of the Nazis. However, the pope also asserted the rights of the Palestinian people to a homeland and favorably referred to efforts on behalf of Jews made by Pius XII, who has been widely criticized for his alleged silence in the face of Nazi atrocities. John Paul's defense of him at this occasion surprised many Jews and caused some ill feeling.

**Papal Trips.** On March 31, John Paul began a two-week visit to Uruguay, Chile, and Argentina. The pope bluntly characterized the Chilean government of President Augusto Pinochet as "dictatorial" and challenged the church there to help bring democracy to the country. In Argentina, where democracy was reestablished in 1983 under President Raúl Alfonsín, several cultural leaders declined to attend a meeting with the pontiff, in protest against the Argentine church's silence during the military repressions of the 1970's.

On a spring visit to West Germany, the pope presided at the beatification of Edith Stein. Also beatified was Father Rupert Mayer, a Jesuit who was imprisoned three times during the Hitler era for resisting Nazi rule but was spared death when church leaders arranged for him to be interned in a Benedictine monastery. During his German visit, the pope vehemently condemned abortion and mercy killing, comparing such acts to the killing of invalids and the terminally ill by the Nazis.

A June trip to Poland was John Paul's third visit to his homeland since becoming pope. He repeatedly invoked the name of Solidarity, the outlawed Polish labor movement, and visited the grave of Father Jerzy Popieluszko, a pro-Solidarity priest killed by Polish secret police in 1984.

The pope's visit to North America, beginning September 10, took him from Miami to Detroit by way of Columbia, S.C., New Orleans, San Antonio, Phoenix, Los Angeles, San Francisco, and Monterey, Calif. Before returning home he also made a stopover in Canada's Northwest Territories. The visit coincided with observances marking the bicentennial of the U.S. Constitution, but though the pope praised the ideals of freedom and pluralism enshrined in the document, he made it plain that they had limited application within Catholicism itself. When the open and democratic traditions of American society were raised at a meeting in Los Angeles with the U.S. hierarchy, John Paul responded with a reaffirmation of orthodoxy, calling it a "grave error" to believe that one could pick and choose among church teachings. He criticized dissent from church doctrine and, time and again, reiterated the church's opposition to abortion, contraception, divorce and remarriage, the ordination of women, homosexuality, and a married priesthood.

**Other U.S. Developments.** A compromise was reached in May in the four-year dispute concerning Seattle Archbishop Raymond G. Hunthausen's orthodoxy on issues of sexual morality and clerical discipline. Under a settlement worked out in May by a special bishops' commission, the archbishop's authority, pre-

A meeting at the Vatican between Pope John Paul II and Austrian President Kurt Waldheim (left) was widely criticized, particularly by Jewish leaders upset over Waldheim's alleged participation in Nazi war crimes. His wife is at right.

viously delegated in part to an auxiliary bishop, was substantially restored.

Father Charles E. Curran was formally suspended from teaching at the Catholic University of America. The Vatican had previously revoked Curran's license to teach as an official theologian, because of his views on matters of sexual morality.

In a major case, the Second U.S. Circuit Court of Appeals upheld a 1986 federal district court decision fining the U.S. Catholic Conference-National Conference of Catholic Bishops $10,000 a day until it produced extensive church records on antiabortion strategies. The ruling was the latest development in a seven-year effort by Abortion Rights Mobilization, a pro-choice organization, to have the existing tax-exempt status of the Catholic Church revoked for engagement in political activities. The fines were suspended pending further appeals. In December the U.S. Supreme Court agreed to consider whether the suit should be killed on the grounds that the abortion rights group lacked standing to sue.

Some 1,500 black Catholics, including all 11 black bishops, gathered in Washington, D.C., in May. Delegates from 110 of the nation's 184 Catholic dioceses urged that the church be clearer in its affirmation of black culture and identity.

**European Developments.** The delicate coexistence between church and state in Hungary produced agreement in March on the new primate to replace Cardinal Laszlo Lekai, who had died nine months earlier. Named archbishop of Esztergom and primate of Hungary was Archbishop Laszlo Paskai.

In October the Vatican announced steps toward restoring the standing of suspended Archbishop Marcel Lefebvre, the French prelate who rejected the reforms of the Second Vatican Council and established an ultratraditionalist religious order. Final reconciliation would still require study.

**Vocations.** Religious vocations showed remarkable growth in the Third World, according to a Vatican study released in July. The number of seminarians in Africa and South America reportedly increased 88 percent between 1970 and 1985, while Asia registered a 55 percent growth. However, the number of young men studying for the priesthood in North America dropped 44 percent.

*Birth Technologies.* A sweeping condemnation of new biomedical technologies was issued in March by the Vatican's Congregation for the Doctrine of the Faith. The document condemned virtually all artificial methods of human reproduction, and governments were urged to enact laws barring genetic counseling, surrogate motherhood, embryo and sperm banks, various forms of artificial insemination, in-vitro fertilization, and experimentation on embryos. It evoked some negative reaction.

**Synod of Bishops.** A month-long Synod of Bishops was convened in Rome in October to consider the role of the laity in the church. The bishops condemned discrimination against women but defeated a proposal that all non-ordained ministries be opened to them.

J.G.D.

## JUDAISM

The number of Soviet Jews permitted to emigrate increased noticeably in 1987, a development attributed to Soviet leader Mikhail Gorbachev's program of *glasnost,* or openness. Pope John Paul II became embroiled in controversy with American Jews as a result of his meeting with Austrian President Kurt Waldheim.

**World Jewry.** Early in the year, prospects of Jewish emigration from the Soviet Union were discouraging. A U.S. congressional resolution criticized new Soviet regulations governing emigration that significantly tightened existing restrictions. The U.S. State Department in its annual survey on implementation of the Helsinki accords noted the Soviet Union's lack of compliance with human rights provisions.

Some encouraging signs began to appear, however. In February Soviet dissident Iosif Begun, imprisoned since 1983, was granted an unconditional pardon and release, along with more than 140 other dissidents. In April and May, delegations of American Jewish leaders returning from Moscow announced that the Soviet Union would ease emigration restrictions and liberalize policies toward Jews internally. The flow of emigration increased, and later in the year, several prominent Soviet Jewish refuseniks, among them Begun and Ida Nudel, were given permission to leave. Soviet

*Standing trial in Israel, John Demjanjuk, a 66-year-old retired autoworker from Cleveland, Ohio, was charged with being "Ivan the Terrible," a notoriously brutal guard at the Treblinka death camp in Poland during World War II.*

diplomats also announced that certain restrictions used to prevent émigrés from leaving were to be eased and that amnesty was possible for some political and religious prisoners.

For the first time a representative of Soviet Jewry, Moscow Chief Rabbi Adolph Shayevich, was permitted to attend an international Jewish conference. The World Jewish Congress met in Budapest, Hungary, in May in the first such gathering in a Communist country since 1967.

**Nazi War Criminals.** In May, former Gestapo officer Klaus Barbie, who had been extradited from Bolivia after a long legal battle, went on trial in Lyon, France, for crimes against humanity committed during World War II. The eight-week trial ended in July with the French court's conviction of Barbie on all counts. He was sentenced to life in prison. In February, John Demjanjuk, accused of crimes against humanity and of being the sadistic Nazi death camp guard "Ivan the Terrible," went on trial in Jerusalem. Demjanjuk, a retired Cleveland auto worker, was the first suspected war criminal ever extradited to Israel.

Karl Linnas, deported from the United States to the Soviet Union in April to face a death sentence as a Nazi war criminal, died in July in a Leningrad hospital before Soviet authorities could decide whether to retry him or confirm the death sentence passed in absentia by a Soviet court in 1962. In January, Romanian Orthodox Archbishop Valerian Trifa died in Portugal, where he had fled in 1984 under threat of deportation from the United States as a suspected war criminal. In November the Netherlands' most notorious Nazi war criminal, wealthy art collector Pieter Menten, died in a nursing home at age 88.

On August 17, Rudolf Hess, onetime deputy to Adolf Hitler and sole survivor of the leading Nazi officials convicted in the Nuremberg war crimes trials, died in prison at age 93, an apparent suicide.

Josef Schwammberger, 75, described as a particularly brutal Nazi labor camp commandant, faced deportation to West Germany after his arrest in Argentina in November. Schwammberger, an Austrian who escaped Allied detention in 1945, was accused of torturing and killing hundreds of Jews and stealing their valuables.

**Waldheim Controversy.** In April, Austrian President Kurt Waldheim, who has been accused of complicity in Nazi war crimes, was barred from entry to the United States. In June controversy broke out over Pope John Paul II's 35-minute audience with Waldheim at the Vatican. The situation escalated when, as a result of the Waldheim visit, representatives of American Jews announced that they would refuse to meet with the pope during his September visit to the United States without prior discussions of the Waldheim affair and other issues. On September 1 the pope met with nine Jewish leaders at his summer residence outside Rome, where he reiterated his rejection of anti-Semitism but made no change in the Vatican's long-standing position not to grant official recognition to the state of Israel. Later in the month, the pope did meet with American Jewish leaders in Miami. He spoke in defense of Pope Pius XII's conduct during World War II; Jewish leaders again expressed their pain over the Waldheim visit.

**Culture and Religious Life.** In March the U.S. Navy launched an education campaign for Navy chaplains on the Holocaust, in response to a request for such programs by Secretary of Defense Caspar Weinberger. The world's oldest continuing Yiddish newspaper, *Der Forverts (Forward)*, celebrated its 90th year in May.

In July a center for Jewish studies was dedicated in Budapest, the first ever in a Communist country.

In the summer, a "para-rabbi" program was established in Vermont. It will attempt to meet the religious needs of Jews living in remote rural areas lacking established communities, by offering courses in Jewish religious observance and training lay people to perform rituals.                                                L.G.

## HINDUISM

On September 4 the traditional Hindu ritual of sati, in which a widow commits suicide by throwing herself on the funeral pyre of her husband, was performed in Deorala, a village in Rajasthan, India, by 18-year-old Roop Kanwar. Outlawed since 1829, sati is still occasionally observed, most often in Rajasthan, where it is revered by the warrior caste to which her family belonged. The site of the immolation immediately became a shrine, attracting tens of thousands of pilgrims for the final ceremony, at which the flames were quenched. Women's groups in India condemned the rite as barbaric. There were later reports that members of the husband's family may have coerced Roop Kanwar into performing the ritual suicide; eventually the father-in-law was arrested on murder charges, while others in his family were arrested on lesser charges. Meanwhile, India's Parliament passed a law imposing a maximum penalty of death for abetting sati.

Recent surveys of the major world religions have indicated that Hinduism alone is declining in numbers of adherents. In India there has been a growing concern over the conversion of Hindus to Christianity and Islam. As the ancient Hindu social order has eroded, traditional religious observances have fallen off as well. In response, a number of militant Hindu groups have arisen, such as the Rastriya Svayam Sevak Sangha ("India for the Hindus"), advocating the establishment of Hinduism as the state religion and the imposition of Hindu tenets—the prohibition against killing cattle, for instance—on Indian society by law.

One group, the Bajrang Dal, advocated "liberating" former Hindu shrines that were converted to Muslim use. In Ayodhya, Uttar Pradesh, where a 16th-century mosque occupies a site venerated by Hindus as the birthplace of the god Rama, continuing conflict between Hindus and Muslims over ownership of the site erupted into riots in May. The rioting spread to the city of Meerut, where more than 100 Muslims were killed.

## BUDDHISM

Buddhist monks, calling for Tibetan independence and the return of the Dalai Lama, the exiled spiritual leader of Tibetan Buddhism, were conspicuous participants in demonstrations in Tibet against the Beijing (Peking) government during late September and early October. According to some reports, at least eight Tibetans, including three monks, were killed in clashes with police, and Chinese authorities said six Chinese policemen were killed. The Chinese, who have occupied Tibet since 1950, acted harshly, beating demonstrators and arresting large numbers of monks and other Tibetans. Armed Chinese police also occupied part of the Jokhang Temple, Tibetan Buddhism's holiest place. The Beijing government blamed the unrest on the Dalai Lama, who has advocated independence since fleeing to India in 1959 and who, during a six-city tour of the United States in September, told a congressional caucus that China should withdraw from Tibet, allowing the country to become a "zone of peace." He later urged his followers in Tibet to avoid violence and to engage in peaceful civil disobedience. The Chinese, who had destroyed most Tibetan Buddhist monasteries during the Cultural Revolution in the 1960's, more recently began allowing some religious freedom and showing greater respect for Tibetan culture. Tibetan resentment nevertheless remained strong.

Buddhist monks also were among the Sinhalese demonstrators who rioted in Sri Lanka during protests against a July accord between Sri Lanka and India that allowed Indian troops to temporarily occupy northeastern Sri Lanka. Tamil-speaking Hindus have been conducting a violent separatist campaign there against rule by the Sinhalese Buddhist majority. The accord stipulated that the Tamil areas were to be given a degree of local autonomy if the separatist groups gave up violence and laid down their arms. (See INDIA; SRI LANKA.)

## ISLAM

The tensions generated throughout the Middle East by the Iran-Iraq war erupted in violence during the annual Muslim pilgrimage to Mecca on July 31. Iranian Shiite pilgrims reportedly began demonstrating outside the Grand Mosque against Saudi Arabia, a major supporter of Iraq, as well as against Israel and the United States, and the demonstration quickly turned into a riot that left over 400 people dead, including 275 Iranians and 85 Saudi security police. The Saudis said the police had fired in self-defense when the mob charged them. The event increased the fears of Iranian Shiite fundamentalism felt by Sunni Muslim Arab leaders in the region.

## MORMON CHURCH

A bizarre case of murder, fraud, and forgery came to an end in January when Mark Hof-

Mark Hofmann, shown arriving at court in Salt Lake City, Utah, with his wife, pleaded guilty to two bomb murders—attempts, he said, to cover up his forgeries of Mormon historical documents. Hofmann was injured when one of his bombs exploded in his own car.

mann, a former Mormon missionary, pleaded guilty in a Utah court to second-degree murder, fraud, and theft by deception. The charges stemmed from the 1985 bombing murders of Steven Christensen and Kathleen Sheets in Salt Lake City. Hofmann had been involved in an elaborate scheme to defraud investors by taking their money to purchase purported historical documents (which he forged) discrediting the official Mormon version of the church's founding. Hofmann killed his associate Christensen with a shrapnel bomb to keep him from disclosing the scheme. He then killed Sheets, whose husband had been a business partner of

Christensen's, in an attempt to divert suspicion. Hofmann received one term of 5 years to life and three of 1 to 15 years.　　C.S.J.W.

**REPUBLICAN PARTY.** See UNITED STATES OF AMERICA: *Political Parties.*

**RHODE ISLAND.** See STATISTICS OF THE WORLD.

**RHODESIA.** See ZIMBABWE.

**ROMANIA.** In 1987, Romanian party and state chief Nicolae Ceauşescu resisted the idea of reform implicit in Soviet leader Mikhail S. Gorbachev's proposals for economic and social "restructuring." Depicting himself as a national Marxist leader defending Romanian social and political patterns, Ceauşescu professed to see the proposals primarily as a scheme for the integration of the economies of the Eastern European bloc. He opposed this, he said, out of fear of losing control over the Romanian economy.

In May, Gorbachev visited Romania to present his "restructuring" in person. He implied criticism of Romania's handling of its ethnic minorities and urged Romania to consider the Soviet model. Ceauşescu resisted the notion that he should reform his system, but in the end he apparently gave at least lip service to part of the Gorbachev program.

Vocal dissidents in Romania remained few in number. Perhaps best known was Mihai Botez, an authority on mathematical methods of planning and management and a high-ranking economic adviser to the government until he quit in protest over policies. His continued criticism led to his being ordered to leave Bucharest to direct a computer center in the Danube delta. Also of note was Karoly Kirali, an ethnic Hungarian who resigned in 1972 as a candidate member of the party Central Committee's Political Executive Committee in protest at the regime's treatment of the Hungarian minority in Transylvania; he became the director of a meat-canning factory. Another prominent critic, Ioan Puiu, was arrested when security police found him with a memorandum he had hoped to convey to Gorbachev during the latter's visit.

Young adherents of Romania's outlawed National Peasant Party who formed a Romanian Association for the Defense of Human Rights were subjected to police and judicial reprisals. Selective punishment on an individual basis broke up the group.

The winter of 1986–1987, like the two before it, played havoc with Romania's ailing economy. Excessive export of agricultural products and industrialization beyond the country's domestic energy supply made it certain that even moderately severe winter conditions would bring a crisis. Low reserves and outmoded equipment also ensured chronic shortages in industry, agriculture, and water supply. In November 1987, workers in the industrial city of Brasov, facing continued austerity as well as pay cuts imposed as a penalty for not meeting production quotas, staged a march on the city hall that developed into a riot.

See STATISTICS OF THE WORLD.　　R.A.P.

**RUSSIA.** See UNION OF SOVIET SOCIALIST REPUBLICS.

**RWANDA.** See STATISTICS OF THE WORLD.

# S

**SAHARA, WESTERN.** See AFRICA. See also MOROCCO.

**ST. KITTS-NEVIS (ST. CHRISTOPHER AND NEVIS).** See STATISTICS OF THE WORLD.

**ST. LUCIA.** See STATISTICS OF THE WORLD.

**ST. VINCENT AND THE GRENADINES.** See STATISTICS OF THE WORLD.

**SAMOA, AMERICAN.** See STATISTICS OF THE WORLD: *American Samoa.*

**SAMOA, WESTERN.** See STATISTICS OF THE WORLD: *Western Samoa.*

**SAN MARINO.** See STATISTICS OF THE WORLD.

**SÃO TOMÉ AND PRÍNCIPE.** See STATISTICS OF THE WORLD.

**SASKATCHEWAN.** See STATISTICS OF THE WORLD.

**SAUDI ARABIA.** Oil policy, better relations with the United States, and the conflict in the Persian Gulf were major issues in 1987.

**Petroleum Affairs.** With Hisham Nazer as the new minister of petroleum and mineral resources, Saudi Arabia agreed in late 1986 to support oil production cuts of about 7 percent by OPEC nations, so as to encourage an $18-per-barrel price level. In June, with prices holding at the $18-per-barrel range, OPEC oil ministers agreed to raise the production ceiling to 16.6 million barrels per day (b/d). Six months later, the ceiling was, in effect, extended through mid-1988, as prices appeared to be weakening.

**Regional Affairs.** A late April reconciliation meeting in Jordan between Presidents Hafez al-Assad of Syria and Saddam Hussein of Iraq was attended by Saudi Crown Prince Abdallah bin Abdul Aziz. King Fahd hosted May talks between King Hassan of Morocco and President Chadli Benjedid of Algeria on the war in the Western Sahara. Saudi Arabia wielded major influence at the November Arab League summit, held in Amman, Jordan. The meeting issued a communiqué upholding Iraq in the Persian Gulf war and agreed that members should be free to reopen relations with Egypt. Days later, Saudi Arabia and Egypt resumed full relations.

The war between Iran and Iraq had an increasingly negative effect on relations. Among other incidents, Iranian gunboats in March attacked a Saudi-owned vessel off the coast of Dubai. On August 15 a Saudi frogman died while detonating a mine in the Persian Gulf.

On July 31 violence erupted during the Muslim pilgrimage in the Saudi city of Mecca, when Iranian Shiite pilgrims demonstrated against the United States, the Soviet Union, and Israel outside the Grand Mosque. Saudi officials—blaming the riot on the Iranians—said that 402 people (275 Iranians, 85 security police, and 42 others) were killed and 649 injured in clashes between protesters and security units. Iran claimed that the Saudis had provoked the conflict and had fired on the crowd with machine guns; the Saudis said only tear gas and clubs had been used. The tragedy was followed by bombings of Saudi business and government offices in Beirut and an attack on the Saudi embassy in Tehran by an angry mob of Iranians; one Saudi diplomat was killed in the violence.

**Relations With the United States.** Saudi Arabia surpassed both Mexico and Venezuela as principal oil supplier to the United States. Saudi officials were, however, infuriated by revelations of secret U.S. arms sales to Iran, especially as some of the same arms had previously been denied to the Saudis. U.S. congressional hearings on the Iranian arms sales subsequently revealed that Saudi businessman Adnan Khashoggi had played a prominent role and that Saudi Arabia had donated some $32 million to the anti-Sandinista guerrillas (contras) in Nicaragua.

Congressional opposition to arms sales to Saudi Arabia heated up in mid-May when two Saudi F-15 jet fighters, operating in the vicinity of the U.S. warship *Stark* in the Persian Gulf, failed to intercept and force down an Iraqi jet that had fired missiles at the ship, killing 37 U.S. sailors. In June, the Reagan administration temporarily set aside a planned $1.4 billion arms package for Saudi Arabia; in late October, a scaled-down $1 billion package was ultimately agreed upon. Meanwhile, Saudi Arabia actively, if not openly, supported the U.S. naval operation aimed at protecting oil tankers in the Persian Gulf.

**Industry.** Stabilizing oil prices gave a welcome boost to the economy during 1987, as the kingdom began the second stage in its industrialization program, with the emphasis shifting from basic industries to high tech communication and defense-related industries. Several new agreements with Boeing were announced early in the year. They included a $300 million-$500 million, ten-year agreement to build military radios in Saudi Arabia and four other joint-venture projects, worth $250 million, involving aircraft repair, manufacture of advanced electronic systems, and computer engineering.

See STATISTICS OF THE WORLD.    C.H.A.

**SENEGAL.** See STATISTICS OF THE WORLD.

**SEYCHELLES.** See STATISTICS OF THE WORLD.

**SIERRA LEONE.** See STATISTICS OF THE WORLD.

**SINGAPORE.** In 1987, Singapore experienced incidents involving political subversion, corruption in government, and freedom of the press; at the same time its economy experienced improvement.

In May and June the Singapore government arrested 22 persons whom it described as members of a "clandestine Communist network." Fourteen were later released, but the rest were held without trial under one-year and two-year detention orders. (Under the National Security Act, trials are not required for detention.)

In January the death of National Development Minister Teh Cheang Wan on December 14, 1986, was declared a suicide, from an overdose of barbiturates. Teh's death brought to light the fact that he was under investigation for allegedly accepting bribes from government contractors. Singapore has long prided itself on the honesty and efficiency of its government. In defending its image, the government has closely monitored regional and international media, attempting to correct any coverage with which it disagrees. Because of such disagreements, Singapore circulation of the Hong Kong-based *Asian Wall Street Journal* was drastically reduced, as was that of *Time* in late 1986. The latter restriction was lifted in June. However, in December circulation of the *Far Eastern Economic Review* was severely restricted.

Rebounding from an economic slump, Singapore showed increased industrial activity, especially in the electronics sector. Economic growth was projected at 4 percent for 1987 and even more for 1988. Unemployment fell to under 5 percent, and wage restraints introduced in 1986 continued.

See STATISTICS OF THE WORLD.          K.M.

**SOCIAL SECURITY.** See UNITED STATES OF AMERICA: *Congress.*

**SOLOMON ISLANDS.** See STATISTICS OF THE WORLD.

**SOMALIA.** Pro-Islamic and antigovernment activity in Somalia was on the rise in 1987, and fighting continued between Somalia and Ethiopia. Economic activity remained weak, and drought and famine continued to ravage the country.

Political opposition to President Muhammad Siad Barre continued to grow, and fear of Iranian-type radicalism caused the government to crack down hard on Islamic fundamentalism. In April the National Security Court sentenced to death ten sheikhs who were also teachers of Islam. The sheikhs were members of the Somali Islamic Movement, a political and religious organization seen as threatening to the political order.

The presence of over half a million Ethiopian refugees put a severe strain on the economy, already suffering the effects of drought. More than 5 million people were affected by the drought, and of these over a million were said to be in danger of starvation. In addition, the country suffered the worst concentration of locusts since 1978. The swarms were capable of consuming enough sorghum and maize in a day to feed 40,000 people for a year.

Although the revolutionary regime in Ethiopia has in the past negotiated with Somalia over border disputes, Ethiopia attempted to exploit the political weakness of Siad Barre's regime, and Somalia continued to consider itself threatened by its neighbor. Tens of thousands of Somali troops faced more than 25,000 Ethiopian troops and 3,000 Cuban advisers stationed in the Ogaden border region. In February, Ethiopia sent an armored column into northern Somalia; its troops were routed, and 300 Ethiopian soldiers were reported killed.

Saudi Arabia remained a major supporter and trading partner, and Somalia supported the Saudis in their dispute with Iran over the rioting in July by Iranian pilgrims in Mecca.

See STATISTICS OF THE WORLD.          P.J.S.

**SOUTH AFRICA.** The ruling Nationalist Party, under State President Pieter W. Botha, won reelection in voting for the white chamber of South Africa's Parliament on May 6, 1987. Black protest was more peaceful than during 1985 or 1986, as the government continued to arrest large numbers of anti-apartheid activists and used army units to supplement its expanding police force in patrolling the black townships. In June the government strengthened the year-old state of emergency that granted wide latitude to the security forces to arrest and detain persons, conduct searches without warrants, and control information in the media.

**Divisions Among Whites.** In the May election, the Nationalist Party took 123 seats, an increase of 6 from its pre-election strength, out of a total of 166 directly elected seats. The right-wing Conservative Party won 22, a gain of 5, and the Progressive Federal Party took 19, a loss of 7. The ascendancy of the Conservative

He would not be rushed into reforming apartheid, South African President P. W. Botha (left) told supporters at Johannesburg's city hall before May's general election. At right is Foreign Minister "Pik" Botha.

Party over the PFP as the official opposition indicated the growing resentment by some Afrikaners of the government's limited racial reforms. In another expression of dissent, some 3,000 conservatives formed their own all-white Afrikaans Reformed Church to protest the Dutch Reformed Church's increased distancing of itself from apartheid. Within the government and academia, on the other hand, some influential *verlightes* ("enlightened ones," or liberals) protested the slowness of governmental reform, and several noted politicians resigned from the Nationalist Party and ran as independents in the May elections.

In July, 61 leading Afrikaner opponents of the government and 17 officials of the anti-government African National Congress (ANC) held talks in Dakar, Senegal. The South African government, which considers the ANC a terrorist organization, verbally attacked the meeting but took no legal action against the participants.

**Labor Activism.** As the government cracked down on opposition political organizations, trade unions became generally more militant. In August the 300,000-strong National Union of Mineworkers (NUM) staged a three-week strike that was joined by most gold and coal miners and resulted in the firing of 36,000 employees. The most expensive labor action in South Africa's history, the strike halted production at 44 out of 99 mines and cost the economy up to $15 million a day. The NUM subsequently rejected a $240 million stock offer by the Anglo American Corporation, a giant mining conglomerate, calling it a maneuver to weaken the union.

**Government Negotiations.** In May, Botha for the first time offered to participate personally in political power-sharing negotiations with blacks. He subsequently visited several black townships outside Johannesburg and created a new post, deputy minister of constitutional development, to pursue contacts with black leaders.

On November 5 the government released ANC leader Govan Mbeki, after 24 years in jail. The move was described as a "trial run" for the possible release of jailed ANC leader Nelson Mandela. However, a few weeks later Mbeki's freedom of travel and speech was severely restricted.

**Violence.** Violence against the government was at significantly lower levels than during the previous two years. In January, Oliver Tambo, president of the ANC, publicly criticized "necklacing"—the practice of killing alleged government collaborators and informers by igniting a fuel-soaked tire placed around the victim's neck—while calling on South Africa's blacks to carry the fighting beyond their townships.

South African troops continued to raid Zambia and Mozambique in pursuit of ANC guerrillas based there. In July, South Africa reported that in two major clashes in southern Angola, its troops had killed 190 Angolans and other fighters for the South West Africa People's

Organization (Swapo), which seeks independence for the South African-administered territory of South West Africa (Namibia). In November the government said that 21 South African soldiers had died in fighting in southern Angola between Angolan troops, supported by Soviet and Cuban forces, and rebels seeking to overthrow the leftist Angolan government and supported by South Africa and the United States. It was the first time Pretoria had acknowledged its troops had aided the Angolan rebels.

Differences between black groups within South Africa continued to turn violent. By late in the year more than 170 people had been killed near Durban; the United Democratic

*Workers at the Anglo American Corporation's East Rand Gold and Uranium plant, near Johannesburg, were among the many black miners who joined in a massive strike in August, disrupting South Africa's mineral production.*

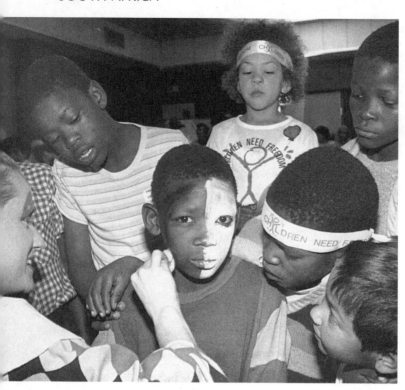

"Free the Children" was the theme of a June rally in Johannesburg calling for the release of children detained in prison under South Africa's state of emergency. Hundreds of children, like those shown here, joined the protest, including some who had been freed the previous week.

Front, a multiracial alliance of groups seeking nonviolent change, blamed Chief Mangosuthu Buthelezi's Inkatha movement. Rivalry between the UDF and black-consciousness organizations claimed fatalities in Johannesburg and the Eastern Cape.

**Transkei Coups.** In late September, Major General Bantu Holomisa led a military coup in the nominally independent Transkei black homeland, overthrowing the long-dominant Matanzima family dynasty. Subsequently, Stella Sigcau was installed as prime minister. However, on December 30, Holomisa ousted Sigcau and obtained the forced resignations of her cabinet. He cited governmental corruption as justification for both coups.

**Economic Developments.** South Africa's economy began a limited recovery from its worst crisis since the Great Depression. The economy benefited from a rise in the world price of gold; each rise of $1 per ounce in its market price meant an extra $20 million annually to South Africa.

In June the Reverend Leon Sullivan, author of the Sullivan Principles (a set of fair-labor guidelines for U.S. corporations employing blacks in their South African subsidiaries), changed his position on the benefits of Western investment. He called for a near-total U.S. economic embargo of South Africa and a withdrawal of U.S. businesses. Late in the year, the Ford Motor Company completed its disinvestment from South Africa.

**Foreign Relations.** Western governments distanced themselves from Pretoria while according more legitimacy to the ANC. In January, U.S. Secretary of State George Shultz met with Oliver Tambo in Washington. It was the first time a U.S. secretary of state had met with an ANC leader. Late in the year, the U.S. Congress passed a measure that would end tax credits for U.S. companies operating in South Africa. In March the Israeli government announced a phasing out of existing agreements with South Africa on arms sales and military technology transfers; Israel later imposed economic and cultural sanctions.

*See* STATISTICS OF THE WORLD.　　H.H.

**SOUTH CAROLINA.** *See* STATISTICS OF THE WORLD.

**SOUTH DAKOTA.** *See* STATISTICS OF THE WORLD.

**SOUTH WEST AFRICA (NAMIBIA).** The 21-year guerrilla war between the South West Africa People's Organization (Swapo), the guerrilla organization fighting for the independence of Namibia from South African control, and South African troops showed no signs of abating. Since 1966, 20,000 Namibians have been killed in the conflict.

In April the United States and Great Britain vetoed a United Nations Security Council resolution calling for broad sanctions against South Africa for refusing to grant Namibia true independence. Vernon Walters, U.S. ambassador to the UN, contended that such sanctions would "seriously limit" mediation attempts by Western nations.

Relations were strained between the South African government and the Namibian government, whose proposed constitution called for universal suffrage and omitted any specific reference to minority rights (whites comprised 7 percent of Namibia's population). In the June budget, Pretoria cut its financial contribution to Namibia by 40 percent.                H.H.

**SOVIET UNION.** *See* UNION OF SOVIET SOCIALIST REPUBLICS.

**SPACE EXPLORATION.** The Soviet Union took the lead in space during 1987 with a record-breaking Mir space station flight, while the U.S. space program, left in disarray after the *Challenger* explosion, continued to flounder.

**United States.** *Successes and Failures.* The U.S. space program appeared to be getting back on track as the year began. On February 11 the Air Force successfully launched a military Satellite Data System Communications spacecraft into orbit on board a small Titan 3B rocket. NASA also started off well. On February 26 a Delta booster fired from Cape Canaveral, Fla., placed into orbit the GOES-7 geosynchronous operational environmental satellite. A few weeks later, another Delta rocket was launched, carrying the Indonesian Palapa B 2P communications satellite, originally planned for launch on the space shuttle.

However, on March 26 a NASA Atlas-Centaur rocket carrying a Navy Fleet Satellite Communications spacecraft was struck by lightning and broke up 50 seconds after launch from Cape Canaveral. A review board found that NASA managers in the blockhouse had launched the Atlas into weather conditions that violated safe launch limits. On June 9, lightning struck again, igniting three rockets on a NASA pad and causing them to blast off and crash in the Atlantic.

On May 15 the Air Force successfully launched, from Vandenberg Air Force Base in California, an Atlas carrying a secret military satellite; on June 19 it put into orbit a Defense Meteorological Satellite. But in July, technicians at Cape Canaveral accidentally ruptured a thin-skinned fuel tank on an Atlas-Centaur booster, rendering the vehicle unsalvageable. The planned launch of a military communications satellite had to be canceled.

On October 27 the Air Force successfully launched a Titan 34D from Vandenberg. The rocket carried a secret payload believed to be a KH-11 reconnaissance satellite, the most advanced U.S. spy satellite and one crucial to monitoring Soviet compliance with nuclear arms agreements. Another Titan 34D with a military reconnaissance satellite was launched from Cape Canaveral on November 28.

**Space Shuttle.** The redesign program to correct the space shuttle solid-fuel booster problems that caused the *Challenger* accident had limited success. The first full-scale test of a totally redesigned booster was delayed for a few days by technical problems with instrumentation not associated with the rocket, but the booster was fired successfully on August 30. NASA scheduled resumption of space shuttle flights for June 1988, but late summer or early fall of 1988 was more likely, according to shuttle engineers. Moreover, in December the space agency announced that the failure of a rocket nozzle component could mean further delay in relaunching the shuttle.

**Future Missions.** December saw a step toward deployment of the first permanent U.S. space station with the award of design and construction contracts having an initial value of $5 billion. The station, to be launched piecemeal by space shuttles and put together in orbit, was to be operational by 1996. NASA also announced that a probe to Jupiter, delayed since 1982 by a variety of problems, would be

# SPACE EXPLORATION

launched from the shuttle *Discovery* in 1989. **Soviet Union.** *Setbacks.* Although the Soviet Union dominated the space scene, it began the year with two major failures. On January 30 the Soviets' largest operational booster, the 187-foot-long SL-12 Proton, failed during the launch of a communications satellite, leading to the largest space vehicle accident since the U.S. loss of the *Challenger* and a Titan vehicle in early 1986. The Soviets blamed new guidance components in the booster's fourth stage. A day earlier, the Soviets were forced to explode a military reconnaissance satellite because it also was malfunctioning.

**Mir Saga.** The Soviets' record-setting manned space flight began on February 6 with the launch of cosmonauts Yuri V. Romanenko and Aleksandr Laveikin toward the Mir space station on board the Soyuz TM-2 spacecraft. Mir is the world's first space station capable of being enlarged, by means of docking additional space station modules at a docking hub. The crew flew a two-day rendezvous chase to catch up with Mir, then docked their Soyuz to Mir's forward docking port.

On March 31 the Soviets took the first step in a program to gradually enlarge the space station, by launching the 22-ton Kvant module (containing a laboratory, scientific instruments, and more than 2 tons of other equipment), which linked up with the orbiting Mir. Laveikin and Romanenko then began weeks of work with the Kvant module's instruments. Laveikin had to return to earth prematurely because of

*Western European and Soviet rockets loomed larger in satellite deployment as the U.S. civilian space program continued to falter. The European Space Agency's Ariane 3 (left) was launched successfully after a failure had forced a redesign, while the Soviet Union introduced the powerful Energia booster rocket (below).*

*The successful stationary test of the redesigned space shuttle booster (at right) near Brigham City, Utah, in August was at least one piece of good news for NASA, which was still reeling from the 1986* Challenger *disaster and a subsequent string of failures. December brought new problems, however, with word that a faulty rocket nozzle component would apparently delay the first post-*Challenger *shuttle launching.*

heart irregularities, but Romanenko returned on December 29 after a record 326 days in space.

With the cosmonauts in orbit, meanwhile, the Soviets mounted an impressive series of unmanned launches.

*Booster Problems.* A second SL-12 Proton booster failed on April 24 during launch, placing three large military navigation satellites into useless orbit. The accident hurt Soviet space capability and also impeded Soviet commercial launch marketing activities. In June the Soviets sent marketing teams to several countries to seek commercial launch users for the Proton and other boosters.

*Energia.* One of the Soviet Union's significant technological achievements in many years occurred on May 15 with the successful launch of the new Energia booster. The vehicle was the most powerful booster ever launched by the Soviets, with a capability similar to that of the U.S. Saturn 5 moon rocket, no longer operational. The new Soviet booster rocket provided nearly 7 million pounds of liftoff thrust and could place a 220,000-pound payload into space. It would probably be used to launch the Soviet space shuttle, expected to be flown by the end of 1988.

*Other Soviet Launches.* The Soviets launched the largest satellite studying earth resources that was ever put into space. The Cosmos 1870, launched on July 25, carried a large radar that could obtain images of more terrain features than conventional photography and operate even through clouds. The craft, with a weight of 15-20 tons, was a type of satellite the United States could not duplicate until the mid-1990's.

In April the United States and the Soviet Union signed a new agreement to foster cooperative space programs between the two countries.

In late September a research satellite carrying two monkeys, along with other experimental animals, was launched by the Soviets. A special problem arose five days into the flight when one monkey called Yerosha, or Troublemaker, freed its left arm from a restraining cuff and tinkered with everything in reach. However, Soviet scientists reported that since Yerosha was isolated in a sealed chamber, there was

*Space-traveling monkeys, like this one being sealed in a flight simulator by a Soviet technician, are valuable for experiments but can present problems. A monkey named "Yerosha" (Russian for "troublemaker"), launched aboard a Soviet research satellite in September, freed an arm and began tinkering happily with the equipment—but no real harm was reportedly done.*

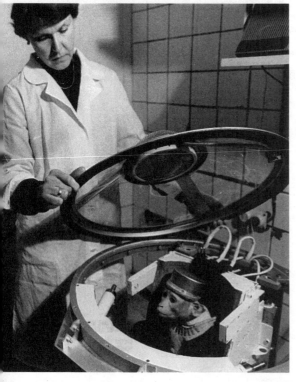

no real danger to the 12-day mission studying the effects of weightlessness. On October 12 the satellite's descent capsule landed in the city of Mirny, thousands of miles from the planned site; the Soviet news agency did not say whether Yerosha was responsible for the off-course landing.

The Soviets had plans to send an unmanned craft to Mars in 1992, as part of the buildup to an eventual manned landing there. In addition, they formally requested that the United States modify one of its own unmanned Mars missions to help relay data from another Soviet probe scheduled for 1994.

**Other Nations.** The European Space Agency successfully launched its redesigned Ariane 3 rocket on September 15. (An Ariane failure in May 1986 had forced major design changes.) The Japanese space program made major progress, starting with the launch on February 4 of the Astro-C X-ray spacecraft on board a Japanese M-3S-2 booster fired from Kagoshima Space Center; as the only X-ray satellite operating in space, it provided data of international importance. The Japanese later put into orbit their first earth-resources spacecraft.

China's major achievement was the launch on August 5 of a Long March 2 booster carrying a spacecraft with a French Matra materials-processing payload. The satellite, China's 20th successful satellite launch, also took earth-resources photographs.                    C.C.

**SPAIN.** In the spring of 1987, the Socialist government of Prime Minister Felipe González Márquez contended with waves of demonstrations and strikes that had begun at the end of 1986. Negotiations with the United States over the future status of U.S. military forces in Spain reached a stalemate. ETA, the extremist wing of the Basque separatist movement, continued its terrorism.

**Strikes and Unrest.** In response to students' demands for improved and more widely available education, Education Minister José María Maravall met with protest leaders on January 28 and promised increased funding for education and a voice for students in the making of educational policy. The chief student demands—elimination of college entrance examinations and free admission to universities—were not, however, met. The disturbance ended on February 16. Soon afterward, workers from key sectors—railroad and airline employees, teachers, farmers, coal miners and steelworkers—took to the streets to protest limits on wage increases, adopted by the González government as part of its economic austerity program. Both the major Communist trade union group and the Socialist General Union of Workers (UGT) backed the strikes. The prime minister insisted that no government had done more for workers than his and pointed to Spain's economic growth rate of 3 percent in 1986—one of the highest in Europe. But, with unemployment high, public opinion polls showed that the government's popularity had declined, although the charismatic González remained a popular figure.

**Elections.** Elections in June for local, regional, and European Parliament positions resulted in a slippage of support for the Socialists. But they remained the dominant party, as the Popular Alliance opposition fared poorly.

**U.S. Relations.** In negotiations with the United States over renewal of the military agreement, the González government sought substantial U.S. troop reductions at four bases the United States shares with Spain—especially at the Torrejón Air Base, located just outside Madrid. Spain also sought the removal of F-16 jet fighters from Torrejón, a base that was considered vital to NATO's Mediterranean strategy. The military treaty expires on May 13, 1988, and González set a deadline of November 13, 1987, for reaching a new agreement. The deadline passed with an impasse especially over the F-16's, which Spain was determined to bar, but both sides were open to further negotiations.

Catalan separatist groups claimed responsibility when an American sailor died and nine other sailors were wounded in the bombing of a U.S.O. club in Barcelona on December 26. It was the fourth bombing attack of the year against American targets in Spain.

**Summit Talks.** French Prime Minister Jacques Chirac and President François Mitterrand visited González for summit talks in March. The talks resulted in a pledge by Spain to join the seven-member European Union defense group and to bring the peseta into the European Monetary System.

*A Spanish student, his identity card in his mouth, was led away after being arrested by a riot policeman in February, when students tried to march illegally on the offices of Prime Minister Felipe González. The protesters demanded unrestricted access to university education.*

**Terrorism and the Basques.** ETA continued its terror campaign. On June 19 a bomb set off in a parking garage in Barcelona killed 17 people and injured 40 more, leading to a public outcry. The French agreed to step up the extradition of suspected ETA members, and in October, French police arrested the suspected military commander of the ETA and about 150 alleged members of the group. In November massive police raids on ETA hideouts were thought to have crippled the organization. However, in the following month an ETA car bomb killed 11 people and wounded 34 in Zaragoza.

See STATISTICS OF THE WORLD.                    J.O.S.

355

# Sports

**In 1987, professional football players launched a 24-day strike, and controversy erupted over the role of blacks in baseball. It was a year of triumph for hockey's Edmonton Oilers, basketball's Los Angeles Lakers, and baseball's Minnesota Twins, as well as for many other brilliant teams and stars.**

Alysheba failed to win the Triple Crown in horse racing, but Mike Tyson finished taking all three heavyweight titles to reign as the youngest heavyweight champ in boxing history. Steffi Graf emerged as the number-one woman player in tennis, while Ivan Lendl easily retained top ranking among the men. These and many other sports highlights are recorded in the pages that follow.

## AUTOMOBILE RACING

Al Unser won the Indianapolis 500 for the fourth time, driving as a last-minute replacement in a year-old car. Unser, who started the season without a team even though he had won the 1985 driving championship, filled in for the injured Danny Ongais on the three-car Roger Penske team. The Penske crew had to resurrect a 1986 March-Cosworth that was being used as a show car in a shopping mall to replace Ongais's demolished car. Five days shy of his 48th birthday, Unser replaced his brother Bobby as the oldest driver to win the Indianapolis 500.

Bobby Rahal, 34, of Dublin, Ohio, became the first driver since 1982 to win back-to-back titles in the Championship Auto Racing Team (CART) PPG Cup series for Indy cars; he also won in 1986.

Dale Earnhardt, 35, of Kannapolis, N.C., drove to victory in his second consecutive National Association for Stock Car Auto Racing (Nascar) championship at the wheel of a Chevrolet owned by Richard Childress. It was the third championship overall for Earnhardt.

Nelson Piquet, 35, of Brazil and Nigel Mansell, 33, of Britain, teammates in identically prepared Williams-Honda machines, waged a season-long battle for the world Formula One championship before Piquet broke away with three wins—in West Germany, Hungary, and Italy—in four races. Piquet, who won the championship in 1981 and 1983, had seven second-place finishes that more than offset Mansell's six wins. The performance by both drivers brought Frank Williams his fourth consecutive world constructors' championship.

One of racing's most cherished records fell when Alan Prost, 32, of France won his 28th Grand Prix in Portugal, to break the record of 27 set in 1973 by Jackie Stewart of Britain.

Porsche won the 24 Hours of LeMans for the seventh straight year, with defending champions Al Holbert of Warrington, Pa., Hans Stuck of West Germany, and Britain's Derek Bell bringing the winning 962-C home 168 miles ahead of the next car for Bell's fifth LeMans win. The first-place car covered 2,977 miles, averaging 124 mph.          S.G.

## BASEBALL

Controversies over free agency, possibly livelier bats and balls, and the unfulfilled aspirations of blacks in the major leagues highlighted the 1987 season but did not eclipse the drama of the Minnesota Twins' victory over the St. Louis Cardinals in the World Series.

**Season Highlights.** In a year notable for power hitting, the American League set records when 51 players reached the 20-home-run mark (10 more than in 1986) and 21 players reached 30. There were suspicions that bats hollowed out and filled with cork were contributing to some players' prowess. No evidence turned up when several bats were confiscated and x-rayed, but one incidence of corking did surface—when the bat in question shattered on contact and revealed its hidden secret. Other observers insisted that the ball was livelier this season, but scientific tests failed to show any significant difference between the 1987 ball and the ones used in previous years. Pitchers

356

were suspected of transgressions as well, with a few suspended for doctoring the ball.

Don Mattingly of the New York Yankees set a major league record with six grand slams in a season and tied a major league record by homering in eight straight games in July. After the season, the Yankees named Billy Martin manager for the fifth time, replacing Lou Piniella, who became general manager. Minnesota was able to win its first AL West division crown in 17 years, primarily because of its dominant play in the Metrodome. The Twins were 56-25 at home, the best home record in baseball, but wound up with only an 85-77 overall mark.

The New York Mets, the 1986 World Series winners, had all five of their starting pitchers on the disabled list at one point or another. Still, Darryl Strawberry and Howard Johnson both joined baseball's exclusive 30-30 club—two of only ten players ever to hit 30 home runs and steal 30 bases in the same season. Mike Schmidt, of the Philadelphia Phillies, hit his 500th career home run in April and finished the year with 35 homers on the season and 530 in his career. The pitching-rich San Francisco Giants won 90 games, with a team earned run average of 3.69—best in the National League. The Houston Astros fell dramatically after winning the NL West division crown in 1986; nevertheless, Nolan Ryan won the major league strikeout crown with 270 and the ERA crown with 2.76.

Paul Molitor rode a 39-game hitting streak

Al Unser holds up four fingers to signify his fourth victory at the Indianapolis 500, winning by five seconds over Roberto Guerrrero. He was the oldest Indy winner ever.

With over 55,000 fans in the Metrodome roaring their support and waving white handkerchiefs, the Twins' Frank Viola (right), on his way to becoming the World Series MVP, led his team to victory over the St. Louis Cardinals in the seventh game of the World Series.

through July and August for baseball's longest streak in a decade. George Bell was named Most Valuable Player in the American League, and Roger Clemens won the league's Cy Young Award for the second year in a row. In the National League, Steve Bedrosian, with 40 saves, became the third relief pitcher in history to win the Cy Young Award. Andre Dawson led the league with 49 home runs and 137 runs batted in; he was the first member of a last-place team (the Chicago Cubs) to be named MVP. Reggie Jackson retired after a historic 21-year career. Other stars ending careers in the sport included Steve Carlton and Phil Niekro.

**Playoffs.** In the American League playoffs, the Twins took a two-game lead with victories of 8-5 and 6-3 in what turned out to be an upset against the Detroit Tigers. The Tigers won Game 3, by a score of 7-6, but the Twins came

right back in the next game with a 5-3 win. The Twins finished the Tigers off in the fifth game with a 9-5 victory, to take Minnesota's first pennant in 22 years.

In the National League, the Cardinals had to fight and scratch their way through a seven-game playoff with the San Francisco Giants to get a berth in the World Series. The Cards took the first game, 5-3, but the Giants won Game 2, 5-0. St. Louis then stunned the Giants by taking the next game, 6-5, at San Francisco's Candlestick Park. The Giants tied the series at two all with a 4-2 win and followed up by taking Game 5, by a score of 6-3. But, amazingly, the Cardinals combined for back-to-back shutouts to take the playoffs.

**World Series.** Game 1 of the World Series was played at Minnesota's Metrodome—the first time a Series game was played indoors. It may also have been the loudest game ever. With a sellout crowd screaming excitedly, the Twins scored seven runs in the fourth inning and beat the Cardinals, 10-1. In the next game, the Twins scored six runs in the fourth en route to an 8-4 win. The Cards, back in the friendlier confines of St. Louis for Game 3, cut their deficit to 2-1, thanks to John Tudor's strong pitching. The Cardinals tied the Series at 2-2 with their first real offensive outburst against the Twins; Tom Lawless's three-run homer in the fourth keyed St. Louis's 7-2 win.

The Cards ended the three-game Busch Stadium meet with a 4-2 win in Game 5 that put them within a game of the championship. Then, in Game 6 back at the Metrodome, St. Louis lost a heartbreaker, 11-5, that tied the Series at three all. For Game 7, a record crowd of 55,376—the largest one-game draw in Minnesota history—watched the Twins squeeze out a 4-2 victory and, with it, the World Series. Twins' pitcher Frank Viola was named Series Most Valuable Player.

**All-Star Game.** The National League won the All-Star game, beating the American League by a score of 2-0 on June 14 in Oakland. Superb pitching kept both sides scoreless until the top of the 13th, when Montréal's Tim Raines unloaded a triple with two on and two out for the game's only scoring.

**Off-the-Field Events.** In a decision on the long-running free-agency issue, arbitrator Thomas Roberts ruled in September that the owners had acted in collusion after the 1985 season to block the movement of free agents, thus violating their labor agreement with the players. Roberts ordered the players and owners to work out a compensation plan but threatened to impose one of his own if they did not. A different arbitrator was considering a case brought by players who were free agents after the 1986 season.

The season was dedicated to the late Jackie Robinson, the Hall-of-Fame second baseman who broke baseball's color barrier in 1947 when he joined the Brooklyn Dodgers. But what many will remember is the furor that broke out when Los Angeles Dodgers Vice President Al Campanis told a television audience that blacks did not have the "necessities" to become managers and general managers. Campanis was forced out of his job, and baseball soon adopted its own affirmative action program.

New York Mets' pitching star Dwight Gooden missed the first two months of the season, spending a month in a rehabilitation center, following the disclosure that he had tested positive for drug use. He returned to the Mets on June 5 and finished with a respectable 15-7 record.                                              B.K.

## NATIONAL LEAGUE

**Eastern Division**

| | W | L | Pct. | GB |
|---|---|---|---|---|
| St. Louis Cardinals | 95 | 67 | .586 | — |
| New York Mets | 92 | 70 | .568 | 3 |
| Montréal Expos | 91 | 71 | .562 | 4 |
| Philadelphia Phillies | 80 | 82 | .494 | 15 |
| Pittsburgh Pirates | 80 | 82 | .494 | 15 |
| Chicago Cubs | 76 | 85 | .472 | 18½ |

**Western Division**

| | W | L | Pct. | GB |
|---|---|---|---|---|
| San Francisco Giants | 90 | 72 | .556 | — |
| Cincinnati Reds | 84 | 78 | .519 | 6 |
| Houston Astros | 76 | 86 | .469 | 14 |
| Los Angeles Dodgers | 73 | 89 | .451 | 17 |
| Atlanta Braves | 69 | 92 | .429 | 20½ |
| San Diego Padres | 65 | 97 | .401 | 25 |

## AMERICAN LEAGUE

**Eastern Division**

| | W | L | Pct. | GB |
|---|---|---|---|---|
| Detroit Tigers | 98 | 64 | .605 | — |
| Toronto Blue Jays | 96 | 66 | .593 | 2 |
| Milwaukee Brewers | 91 | 71 | .562 | 7 |
| New York Yankees | 89 | 73 | .549 | 9 |
| Boston Red Sox | 78 | 84 | .482 | 20 |
| Baltimore Orioles | 67 | 95 | .414 | 31 |
| Cleveland Indians | 61 | 101 | .377 | 37 |

**Western Division**

| | W | L | Pct. | GB |
|---|---|---|---|---|
| Minnesota Twins | 85 | 77 | .525 | — |
| Kansas City Royals | 83 | 79 | .512 | 2 |
| Oakland Athletics | 81 | 81 | .500 | 4 |
| Seattle Mariners | 78 | 84 | .481 | 7 |
| Chicago White Sox | 77 | 85 | .475 | 8 |
| California Angels | 75 | 87 | .463 | 10 |
| Texas Rangers | 75 | 87 | .463 | 10 |

**PENNANT PLAYOFFS**

**American League**—Minnesota defeated Detroit, 4 games to 1.

**National League**—St. Louis defeated San Francisco, 4 games to 3.

**WORLD SERIES**—Minnesota defeated St. Louis, 4 games to 3.

*Indiana's Keith Smart (left) launches the 16-foot jump shot that won the Hoosiers the NCAA championship in their series with Syracuse.*

## BASKETBALL

In a season in which the pros and cons of the three-point goal were constantly debated, Indiana won the 1987 National Collegiate Athletic Association championship. The Los Angeles Lakers won their fourth National Basketball Association title in seven seasons.

**College.** For the longest time Bobby Knight's law on recruiting read: "No junior college transfers." But before the start of the season, the Indiana coach relented and recruited Keith Smart, a lightning-quick point guard, as well as center Dean Garrett. On March 30 in the Superdome in New Orleans, Smart hit a 16-foot jump shot from the left baseline with five seconds remaining that enabled the Hoosiers to beat Syracuse, 74-73, for the NCAA title. The game was played before a crowd of 64,959, which equaled the college-game attendance record just set in the semifinal round.

When the championship game was on the line, it was the 6'1" Smart—voted the Final Four's Most Valuable Player—who turned almost certain defeat into victory. With Syracuse ahead, 61-56, and 7 minutes and 22 seconds remaining, Smart scored 12 of the Hoosiers' final 15 points. Then he intercepted Derrick Coleman's length-of-court pass to ensure Indiana's fifth national title, the third under Knight. Only John Wooden and Adolph Rupp have won more titles than Knight.

Indiana reached the final by defeating Nevada-Las Vegas, which shared the No. 1 ranking at various times during the regular season with North Carolina. The other semifinal featured Syracuse and Providence. No team in the nation adapted better and faster to the three-point shot than did Providence, which came out of the Big East Conference with a 10-6 record to reach the Final Four for the first time in 14 years. But the Friars were no match for Syracuse, which also plays in the Big East and had defeated Providence three times during the regular season. Syracuse, which finished the season with a 31-7 mark, extended its dominance over the Friars to 16 straight games since 1980 with a 77-63 victory.

In a move designed to bring out the zone defenses jammed around the basket, the NCAA adopted the three-point shot, with a boundary line of 19 feet, 9 inches—4 feet shorter than in the NBA.

In women's play, Tennessee combined superior rebounding with a tenacious defense and triumphed over Louisiana Tech, 67–44, also ending Louisiana's 19-game winning streak. It was the second worst defeat ever handed the 30-3 Lady Techsters. In winning their first women's national title, the Lady Volunteers had earlier ended Texas's 40-game winning streak. Tonya Edwards, who scored 13 points for the Lady Vols, was named the tournament's Most Valuable Player.

Dick Baldwin of Broome County Community College in Binghamton, N.Y., won his 876th game on February 14, to become the all-time winningest coach in college basketball history. Kevin Houston of Army became the first player to win both the Division I national scoring and free-throw shooting titles.

Acting on a lawsuit brought by two Stanford

University athletes, a California judge ruled in November that NCAA drug testing at the school was unconstitutional. An exception was made to allow limited testing of the men's football and basketball teams.

**Professional.** Described by rival coaches as a team "close to perfection," the Los Angeles Lakers defeated the Boston Celtics four games to two in their best-of-seven championship

series. The pairing of the Lakers and the Celtics for the NBA championship has become a familiar springtime event. But instead of the usual predictions of a close series, the injury-ridden Celtics had emerged in the unfamiliar role of underdog. They entered the series with only two days' rest, after a tough series in which they beat the Detroit Pistons, four games to three, for the right to meet the Lakers. The Lakers, for their part, entered the championship round after a sweep of Seattle and nine days off.

The Celtics kept their championship hopes alive until game six, when the Lakers used an 18-2 scoring burst at the start of the second half as the springboard to a 106-93 victory and the series clincher. The Celtics scored only 37 points in the second half. Kareem Abdul-Jabbar

*Surrounded by Celtics, the Los Angeles Lakers' Earvin "Magic" Johnson displays the form that made him the NBA's most valuable player and helped win the championship for Los Angeles.*

### NATIONAL BASKETBALL ASSOCIATION
1986–1987 Regular Season

**EASTERN CONFERENCE**

| Atlantic Division | W | L | Pct. | GB |
|---|---|---|---|---|
| Boston Celtics | 59 | 23 | .720 | — |
| Philadelphia 76ers | 45 | 37 | .549 | 14 |
| Washington Bullets | 42 | 40 | .512 | 35 |
| New Jersey Nets | 24 | 58 | .293 | 35 |
| New York Knicks | 24 | 58 | .293 | 35 |

| Central Division | W | L | Pct. | GB |
|---|---|---|---|---|
| Atlanta Hawks | 57 | 25 | .695 | — |
| Detroit Pistons | 52 | 30 | .634 | 5 |
| Milwaukee Bucks | 50 | 32 | .610 | 7 |
| Indiana Pacers | 41 | 41 | .500 | 16 |
| Chicago Bulls | 40 | 42 | .488 | 17 |
| Cleveland Cavaliers | 31 | 51 | .378 | 26 |

**WESTERN CONFERENCE**

| Midwest Division | W | L | Pct. | GB |
|---|---|---|---|---|
| Dallas Mavericks | 55 | 27 | .671 | — |
| Utah Jazz | 44 | 38 | .537 | 11 |
| Houston Rockets | 42 | 40 | .512 | 13 |
| Denver Nuggets | 37 | 45 | .451 | 18 |
| Sacramento Kings | 29 | 53 | .354 | 26 |
| San Antonio Spurs | 28 | 54 | .341 | 27 |

| Pacific Division | W | L | Pct. | GB |
|---|---|---|---|---|
| Los Angeles Lakers | 65 | 17 | .793 | — |
| Portland Trail Blazers | 49 | 33 | .598 | 16 |
| Golden State Warriors | 42 | 40 | .512 | 23 |
| Seattle SuperSonics | 39 | 43 | .476 | 26 |
| Phoenix Suns | 36 | 46 | .439 | 29 |
| Los Angeles Clippers | 12 | 70 | .146 | 53 |

**PLAYOFFS**

**First Round**
Boston defeated Chicago, 3 games to 0
Milwaukee defeated Philadelphia, 3 games to 2
Atlanta defeated Indiana, 3 games to 1
Detroit defeated Washington, 3 games to 0
Los Angeles defeated Denver, 3 games to 0
Golden State defeated Utah, 3 games to 2
Seattle defeated Dallas, 3 games to 1
Houston defeated Portland, 3 games to 1

**Second Round**
Boston defeated Milwaukee, 4 games to 3
Detroit defeated Atlanta, 4 games to 1
Los Angeles defeated Golden State, 4 games to 1
Seattle defeated Houston, 4 games to 2

**Conference Finals**
Boston defeated Detroit, 4 games to 3
Los Angeles defeated Seattle, 4 games to 0

**Championship Finals**
Los Angeles defeated Boston, 4 games to 2

led Los Angeles, and with 32 points Earvin "Magic" Johnson—already named the National Basketball Association's MVP—was unanimously chosen series MVP.

Michael Jordan, the 6'6" guard for the Chicago Bulls, became the second player in NBA history ever to score over 3,000 points in a season. On a sadder note, Lewis Lloyd and Mitchell Wiggins, both of the Houston Rockets, were banned from the NBA after testing positive for cocaine.

A moratorium designed to hasten contract negotiations between the NBA and the players' union expired on October 1 with no settlement in the offing. In the new negotiations, the National Basketball Players Association sought to eliminate the college draft, the salary cap, and the right of first refusal for free agents—that is, the right of a player's team to match any offer another club might make to him. The owners adamantly opposed these changes. On October 1, after the moratorium expired with no new agreement having been reached, nine players filed a federal class-action suit on behalf of all the players against the NBA and its 23 franchises. The suit charged that the college draft, the salary cap, and the right of first refusal for free agents violated federal antitrust laws.

Five players were named to the Hall of Fame: Walt Frazier, versatile New York Knicks guard; Pete Maravich, high-scoring college and NBA ace (who died suddenly in early 1988); Rick Barry, University of Miami and pro star; Bobby Wanzer of the Rochester Royals; and Bob Houbregs of the University of Washington and the NBA.

Julius Erving, the 6'6" star known as Dr. J, announced his retirement. In his 16 pro seasons, he scored 30,002 points, the third highest in pro basketball history.                    S.M.G.

## BOWLING

Many of the leading women bowling pros separated from the Ladies Pro Bowlers Tour (LPBT) in January and formed the Ladies Touring Players Association (LTPA). The LTPA dissidents were unhappy because the men on the Professional Bowlers Association (PBA) tour were playing for purses of close to $6 million a year, while the women's total was less than $1 million. The new group included all five women on the Bowlers Journal 1986–1987 All

America team. The LPBT ran 14 tournaments, with total prizes of $819,000; the LTPA had 10, with close to the same total. All of the top pros competed in the United States Open. Carol Norman took the $40,000 winner's purse, the highest ever for women.

All three major tournaments on the PBA tour were won by bowlers under 25. Del Ballard took his first tour title in the United States Open, gaining $100,000, the richest prize ever. Randy Pedersen won the PBA championship. Pete Weber captured first place in the Tournament of Champions, raising his career earnings to $733,331.                    F.L.

## BOXING

In 1987, retired welterweight champion Sugar Ray Leonard returned to boxing and outpointed Marvelous Marvin Hagler for the world middleweight title. Meanwhile, Mike Tyson (see biography in PEOPLE IN THE NEWS) reigned as the youngest heavyweight champion in boxing history.

Hagler had long wanted to fight Leonard to gain more public recognition, and Leonard finally agreed to return for one fight only, scheduled for April 6 in Las Vegas. By this time only Hagler's World Boxing Council (WBC) title was at stake. The World Boxing Association (WBA) had stripped Hagler of that title because he failed to defend it against the first-ranked contender, Herol Graham of Great Britain, and the International Boxing Federation (IBF) refused to sanction the Hagler-Leonard fight. Although Hagler was a 3½ to 1 favorite, Leonard won the 12-round fight by a split decision. Hagler wanted a rematch, but Leonard, having achieved his goal, was content to retire. On October 12, also in Las Vegas, Thomas Hearns, of Detroit, knocked out Jose Roldan of Argentina for the vacant WBC middleweight title.

On March 7, Mike Tyson, by then the WBC heavyweight champion, outpointed James "Bonecrusher" Smith for Smith's WBA crown; on May 30 he defended the WBC and WBA titles with a sixth-round knockout of Pinklon Thomas; and on August 1 he beat Tony Tucker for his IBF title. At that point, Tyson became the first universally recognized heavyweight champion since 1978.

There was still one important rival—Michael

*On his way back to a world title, underdog Sugar Ray Leonard throws a looping right at Marvelous Marvin Hagler. Their Las Vegas showdown for the WBC middleweight championship grossed more money than any other boxing match in history.*

Spinks. He had taken the IBF heavyweight title in 1985. But he lost it when, instead of defending his title against Tucker as required, he fought—and defeated—Gerry Cooney, in a big-money match in Atlantic City on June 15. A Tyson-Spinks match now seemed logical, but an agreement proved elusive. Meanwhile, on October 16, Tyson successfully defended his crown in Atlantic City against Tyrell Biggs of Philadelphia. He was scheduled to fight Larry Holmes in January 1988.

Lloyd Honeyghan, of Jamaica, defended his WBC and IBF welterweight titles against Johnny Bumphus in February and Gene Hatcher in August. The match against Hatcher lasted only 40 seconds; it was the fastest knockout ever in a world title fight. But on October 28 in Wembley, England, Jorge Vaca of Mexico took Honeyghan's WBC title in a split decision.

F.L.

## FOOTBALL

The National Football League's 1987 season had barely begun when the players launched a 24-day strike. The team owners pressed ahead with games using replacement players and concluded on schedule, although one weekend of games was lost to the walkout.

The playoffs were held as planned, and in Super Bowl XXII, on January 31, 1988, in San Diego, the Washington Redskins demolished the Denver Broncos.

College football's regular season ended with Oklahoma generally ranked No. 1 and Miami of Florida No. 2. They met on January 1, 1988, in Miami for the Orange Bowl; the victory went to Miami, which was then named as unofficial national champion, for the second time in the decade.

**NFL Strike.** On August 31 the existing collective bargaining agreement between the NFL club owners and the players expired. The players' bid for free agency was rebuffed, and they struck after the season's second weekend. The next weekend's games were canceled; the three after that were played by fill-ins, along with regulars who either refused to strike or came back before the strike ended. The strikers finally returned without an agreement, and negotiations had not resumed by the end of the year.

Over the objection of the striking players, the games between replacement teams counted in the standings. One major loser was the New York Giants, who had won Super Bowl XXI in January 1987, but lost all three replacement games and did not qualify for the playoffs.

During the strike, attendance dropped 60 percent and television ratings 35 percent. The low ratings particularly upset the league, because six months earlier it had negotiated a three-year, $1.428-billion television contract. The agreement kept games on CBS, NBC, and ABC and awarded a 13-game package to ESPN, the league's first venture into cable television.

**NFL Season.** Ten of the 28 NFL teams qualified for the playoffs. The National Conference play-off teams were the San Francisco 49ers (13-2), the Chicago Bears (11-4), and the Washington Redskins (11-4) as division champions and the New Orleans Saints (12-3) and the Minnesota Vikings (8-7) as wild cards. The American Conference qualifiers were the Denver Broncos (10-4-1), the Cleveland Browns (10-5), and the Indianapolis Colts (9-6) as division champions and the Houston Oilers (9-6) and the Seattle Seahawks (9-6) as wild cards.

The year before, New Orleans (7-9), Indianapolis (3-13), and Houston (5-11) had finished last in their divisions. New Orleans had never before had a winning season.

Indianapolis helped its climb in the standings by trading in midseason for Eric Dickerson of the Los Angeles Rams, the league's leading running back in 1986. Dickerson became the American Conference's leading rusher with 1,288 yards; Charles White, who had been Dickerson's backup on the Rams, led the league with 1,374 yards.

*Quarterback Steve Walsh completed 18 passes for 209 yards and two touchdowns, helping Miami trounce top-ranked Oklahoma in the Orange Bowl and emerge as unofficial national champions.*

San Francisco was favored to win the Super Bowl. It led the league in points scored (399) and fewest points allowed (273). Its quarterback, Joe Montana, led the league in passing efficiency. Its star wide receiver, Jerry Rice, set NFL records with 22 touchdown catches in one season and 13 consecutive games with at least one touchdown catch in each.

The playoffs began on January 3, 1988, with the wild-card games. Both produced surprises, as Minnesota trounced New Orleans, 44-10, and Houston upset Seattle, 23-20, in overtime. In conference semifinals, Minnesota defeated San Francisco, 36-24; Cleveland beat Indianapolis, 38-21; Washington pushed aside Chicago, 21-17; and Denver crushed Houston, 34-10. In the finals, Denver defeated Cleveland, 38-33, and Washington knocked out Minnesota, 17-10. In the Super Bowl the underdog Redskins, powered by quarterback Doug Williams (who threw for four touchdowns), exploded with 35 points in the second quarter and beat the Broncos by a score of 42-10.

**Canadian.** The Canadian Football League was threatened by continued financial problems that forced the Montréal Alouettes out of business the day before the season began. The eight remaining teams negotiated salary cuts with the players, centralized their marketing, and established spending limits for 1988.

The Winnipeg Blue Bombers (12-6) and the British Columbia Lions (12-6), the division champions, were eliminated in the division playoff finals. The teams that beat them, the Edmonton Eskimos and the Toronto Argonauts, advanced to the Grey Cup championship game November 29 in Vancouver, British Columbia, in which Edmonton scored a 38-36 last-minute victory.

**College.** Oklahoma was the preseason favorite to become national champion, and almost succeeded. Its wishbone offense led all major colleges in total offense, rushing, and scoring, while its defense led in total defense, pass defense, and scoring.

Oklahoma, Miami, and Syracuse finished the regular season with 11-0 records, with Florida State, Nebraska, and San Jose State at 10-1. On the afternoon of January 1, 1988, when Syracuse played a 16-16 tie with Auburn in the Sugar Bowl in New Orleans, it lost its

Early in the 1987 season, National Football League players launched a 24-day walkout. The main issue in the strike, which marked the second time players had walked out during a regular season, was free agency. Above, a fan protests the owners' decision to field teams made up of replacement players.

only hope for the unofficial national title. That would go to the winner of the night's Orange Bowl game in Miami between Oklahoma and Miami. Miami won, 20-14, holding Oklahoma's powerful offense to 255 yards.

It was a good year for Tim Brown, Notre Dame's wide receiver and kick returner, who was voted the Heisman Trophy as the outstanding college player. It was a bad year for Earle Bruce, Ohio State's coach, who was dismissed despite a nine-year record of 81-26-1 and a 1987 record of 6-4-1.

It was a terrible year for Southern Methodist, which suffered the stiffest penalty ever levied by the National Collegiate Athletic Association against a football program. The school, which had been on NCAA football probation six previous times since 1958, was found guilty of making $61,000 in monthly payments to players. The NCAA canceled Southern Methodist's 1987 season and so restricted its 1988 season that the school canceled that season itself.                    F.L.

365

*Larry Mize exults after sinking a 140-foot chip shot on the second hole of sudden-death play to win the Masters, his first major championship.*

## GOLF

Several bright new stars emerged on the Professional Golfers' Association tour, including Paul Azinger, Curtis Strange, and Larry Mize. Veterans like Jack Nicklaus and Raymond Floyd had few bright moments, although Tom Watson broke the longest slump of his career by winning the Nabisco Championship, taking home a record individual prize of $384,000.

Among the highlights of the regular tour season was the emergence of Azinger, who finished second in the British Open and won the Phoenix Open, Panasonic Las Vegas Invitational, and Greater Hartford Open. Other multiwinners included Corey Pavin, in the Bob Hope Classic and Hawaiian Open; Curtis Strange, in the Canadian Open, St. Jude Classic, and World Series of Golf; and Scott Simpson, in the U.S. and Greater Greensboro opens.

For pure dramatics, nothing could match the finish of the Masters in April. Mize edged out Greg Norman during a sudden-death playoff (only the third in Masters history) by sinking a seemingly impossible 140-foot birdie for a one-stroke win. Strange won a record $925,941

for the year, and Azinger took Player of the Year honors. Larry Nelson staged a comeback to win the PGA championship.

For the first time in the 27-year history of the biennial Ryder Cup matches, the Europeans won on American soil, in Dublin, Ohio. It was their second consecutive Ryder Cup.

Betsy King, Jan Geddes, and Japan's Ayako Okamoto dominated the Ladies Professional Golf Association season and tied for Player of the Year. Geddes won the LPGA Championship, King the Dinah Shore, and Okamoto the Nestle World Championship.          T.McC.

## GYMNASTICS

In the 1987 biennial championships, held in Rotterdam, the Netherlands in late October, the Soviet Union won the men's team competition but lost the women's team competition to Romania. In the men's individual all-around competition, Soviets Dmitri Bilozerchev, Yuri Korolev, and Vladimir Artemov placed one-two-three. Bilozerchev regained the title despite a leg injury two years earlier that had threatened to destroy his career. Aurelia Dobre, a virtually unknown 14-year-old Romanian, was the surprise winner of the women's all-around, upsetting 1986 winner Elena Shoushounova of the Soviet Union. (Shoushounova had previously taken six gold medals at the World University Games in Yugoslavia.)

The leaders in total medals at Rotterdam were the Soviet Union with 17 and Romania with 10. Bilozerchev won four gold medals and two silvers. Shoushounova took two golds, three silvers, and one bronze; and Dobre won three golds and a bronze. The United States did poorly and won no medals.

The United States won both team titles in the Pan American Games in August in Indianapolis. Sabrina Mar of Monterey Park, Calif., was the women's all-around champion, with Kristie Phillips of Baton Rouge, La., second. Until then, the 15-year-old Phillips had enjoyed a highly successful year. She won the women's all-around titles in the American Cup, held in March in Fairfax, Va.; the U.S.-U.S.S.R. McDonald's Challenge, held in April in Denver; and the U.S. championships, held in June in Kansas City, Mo. Scott Johnson of Lincoln, Neb., won the U.S. men's all-around title in that competition.          F.L.

## HARNESS RACING

In 1987, it seemed as though Mack Lobell was going to capture trotting's first Triple Crown since 1972. After commencing his three-year-old season by winning the June 28 Yonkers Trot, he moved on to New Jersey's Meadowlands to take the prestigious $1,046,300 Hambletonian on August 8. Mack beat Napoletano (a son of Super Bowl) and set a two-heat total time record of 3:47⅗. It was driver John Campbell's first Hambletonian win after five losing tries. Two weeks later, Mack lopped 1⅕ seconds off the trotter's mile record by taking the Review Stakes at the Illinois State Fairgrounds in 1:52⅕. But Napoletano took the final leg of the Triple Crown by beating Mack Lobell at the Kentucky Futurity at the Red Mile in Lexington, Ky. The loss was softened just a bit when, on November 14, Mack beat Napoletano by 12¾ lengths at the Breeders Crown Trot for three-year-olds at Pompano Park in Florida.

In pacing, Righteous Bucks took the Cane Pacer, Jaguar Spur the Little Brown Jug, and Redskin the Messenger Stakes.          W.L.

## HORSE RACING

Unexpected developments and the heavy hand of racing luck combined to make the 1987 racing season a fascinating one.

On April 4 three major Kentucky Derby preps were run: the $500,000 Florida Derby at Gulfstream Park; the $503,250 Santa Anita Derby in Arcadia, Calif., and the $317,000 Gotham Stakes at Aqueduct in New York. Cryptoclearance defeated long shot No More Flowers by a head in Florida. Temperate Sil ran off from a small field of five others to win the Santa Anita Derby. Capote, expected to be a major Triple Crown contender, made his first start of the year in the Gotham, catching a sloppy track and little else as he wobbled home fourth behind Gone West. Meanwhile, running at Oaklawn Park in Hot Springs, Ark., Demons Begone crushed his opponents in the Southwest and Rebel Stakes by a total of 12 lengths, then went on to win the $500,000 Arkansas Derby.

Demons Begone became the Derby favorite, but it was not to be his day. In a race later called the "Demolition Derby," with ³⁄₁₆ mile left, the leader, Bet Twice, drifted out and bumped Alysheba, nearly knocking Jack Van Berg's colt to his knees. Somehow Alysheba recovered and went on to win by ¾ of a length, with Bet Twice second and Avies Copy third. The running time of 2:03⅖ was dull, but the race itself was exciting. Demons Begone bled from the lungs on the backstretch and had to be eased home last. The total purse for the Derby was a record $793,600, and Alysheba took $618,600 of it.

At the Preakness on May 16, Van Berg's Alysheba captured the second leg of the Triple Crown by catching Bet Twice in the run to the wire, winning by a half-length in 1:55⅘. Then came the third leg of the Crown: the Belmont Stakes. In winning both the Derby and the

*Recovering from near disaster when he was bumped by Bet Twice, Alysheba, with Chris McCarron up, won the 113th Kentucky Derby by three-quarters of a length.*

Preakness, Alysheba had raced on Lasix, a drug used to aid horses that bleed while running. Legal in both Kentucky and Maryland, Lasix is banned in New York State, where the Belmont is held. Van Berg showed little concern over not being able to use Lasix. However, Bet Twice took the lead approaching the stretch in the 1½-mile race and virtually cantered home a 14-length winner, with Alysheba fourth.

In an attempt to squelch questions about his colt's ability, Van Berg also ran Alysheba without Lasix in the 1⅛-mile Amory Haskell Invitational at Monmouth Park, N.J. Bet Twice beat Alysheba by a neck. Another meeting between the two horses came at Saratoga Springs, N.Y., in the $1 million Travers Stakes. But this time Bet Twice came in fifth and Alysheba sixth, as Java Gold took the honors.

W.L.

### ICE HOCKEY

The Edmonton Oilers, after a year's absence atop the National Hockey League, regained the Stanley Cup for the 1986–1987 season by defeating the Philadelphia Flyers. The Oilers thus captured their third Stanley Cup in four years.

In a hard-fought championship series, the Oilers and Flyers split the first six games, and then met for the climactic seventh game at Edmonton on May 31 before a crowd of 17,502. Despite Murray Craven's power-play goal for the Flyers early in the first period, the Oilers calmly and convincingly shot their way to a 3-1 victory.

Ron Hextall, the outstanding rookie goalie for the Flyers, was voted the Conn Smythe trophy winner as the Most Valuable Player in the playoffs. He was a mainstay for the Flyers, who played a record 26 playoff games. Hextall, however, was guilty of a stick-swinging incident against Edmonton's Kent Nilsson in Game 4 of the Stanley Cup finals. As a result, Hextall was suspended for the first eight games of the 1987-1988 NHL regular season.

In the regular season, the Oilers won 50 of 80 games and tied 6 to amass 106 points in the standings, the most in the league. In the Norris Division, the St. Louis Blues edged the upstart Red Wings, 79 points to 78, only to be knocked off by the fourth-place Toronto Maple Leafs in the playoffs. The Hartford Whalers, who beat out Montréal, 93 points to 92, to capture the Adams Division, suffered a similar fate. The Whalers lost their first playoff series to the Québec Nordiques. Philadelphia, with 46 victories and 8 ties, totaled 100 points, enough to win the Patrick Division by 14 points over the Washington Capitals.

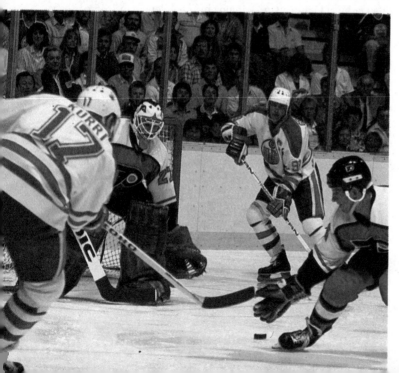

A pass from Jari Kurri (17) to Wayne Gretzky (99) and the resulting Gretzky goal foiled the efforts of Philadelphia Flyers goalie Ron Hextall and Ron Sutter (right) and helped the Edmonton Oilers take the second game of the Stanley Cup finals, 3-2.

Wayne Gretzky, the magnificent center for the Oilers, collected 62 goals and 121 assists for 183 points and a record seventh straight scoring title; he was named the league's MVP for the eighth consecutive season.

At the start of the 1987-1988 season, the NHL adopted tougher penalties for violence, but many observers were disappointed with the mild 15-game suspension handed the Flyers' Dave Brown for cross-checking Ranger Tomas Sandstrom in the face from behind, sending Sandstrom to the hospital overnight with a concussion.                                    B.V.

**NATIONAL HOCKEY LEAGUE**
**1986–1987 Regular Season**

### PRINCE OF WALES CONFERENCE

| Patrick Division | W | L | T | Pts. |
|---|---|---|---|---|
| Philadelphia Flyers | 46 | 26 | 8 | 100 |
| Washington Capitals | 38 | 32 | 10 | 86 |
| New York Islanders | 35 | 33 | 12 | 82 |
| New York Rangers | 34 | 38 | 8 | 76 |
| Pittsburgh Penguins | 30 | 38 | 12 | 72 |
| New Jersey Devils | 20 | 45 | 6 | 64 |

| Adams Division | | | | |
|---|---|---|---|---|
| Hartford Whalers | 43 | 30 | 7 | 93 |
| Montréal Canadiens | 41 | 29 | 10 | 92 |
| Boston Bruins | 39 | 34 | 7 | 85 |
| Québec Nordiques | 31 | 39 | 10 | 72 |
| Buffalo Sabres | 28 | 44 | 8 | 64 |

### CAMPBELL CONFERENCE

| Norris Division | W | L | T | Pts. |
|---|---|---|---|---|
| St. Louis Blues | 32 | 33 | 15 | 79 |
| Detroit Red Wings | 34 | 36 | 10 | 78 |
| Chicago Black Hawks | 29 | 37 | 14 | 72 |
| Toronto Maple Leafs | 32 | 42 | 6 | 70 |
| Minnesota North Stars | 30 | 40 | 10 | 70 |

| Smythe Division | | | | |
|---|---|---|---|---|
| Edmonton Oilers | 50 | 24 | 6 | 106 |
| Calgary Flames | 46 | 31 | 3 | 95 |
| Winnipeg Jets | 40 | 32 | 8 | 88 |
| Los Angeles Kings | 31 | 41 | 8 | 70 |
| Vancouver Canucks | 29 | 43 | 8 | 66 |

### STANLEY CUP PLAYOFFS

**Division Semifinals**
Québec defeated Hartford, 4 games to 2.
Montréal defeated Boston, 4 games to 0.
Philadelphia defeated N.Y. Rangers, 4 games to 2.
N.Y. Islanders defeated Washington, 4 games to 3.
Toronto defeated St. Louis, 4 games to 2.
Detroit defeated Chicago, 4 games to 0.
Edmonton defeated Los Angeles, 4 games to 1.
Winnipeg defeated Calgary, 4 games to 2.

**Division Finals**
Montréal defeated Québec, 4 games to 3.
Philadelphia defeated N.Y. Islanders, 4 games to 3.
Detroit defeated Toronto, 4 games to 3.
Edmonton defeated Winnipeg, 4 games to 0.

**Conference Finals**
Philadelphia defeated Montréal, 4 games to 2.
Edmonton defeated Detroit, 4 games to 2.

**Championship Finals**
Edmonton defeated Philadelphia, 4 games to 3.

*Skating flawlessly, Jill Trenary took the women's title from defending champion Debi Thomas at the U.S. Figure Skating Championships in Tacoma, Wash.*

### ICE SKATING

Upset victories sparked the 1987 figure skating season. In the U.S. championships in Tacoma, Wash., Colorado's Jill Trenary turned in a glittering performance to wrest the gold medal and ladies' title from defending champion Debi Thomas. A second upset occurred in the pairs competition, when 1985 champions Jill Watson and Peter Oppegard defeated reigning Gillian Wachsman and Todd Waggoner, becoming the first pair to regain a national title in 52 years. In yet another upset, Suzanne Semanick and Scott Gregory edged out ice dancing champions Renee Roca and Donald Adair for the 1987 gold medal and title. Brian Boitano of California retained the men's title.

In the World Figure Skating Championships in Cincinnati, Olympic and three-time world

Pirmin Zurbriggen of Switzerland took two gold and two silver medals at the International Ski Federation World Championships, held at Crans-Montana early in the year.

silver medalist Brian Orser of Canada prevailed to win the men's title, and Katarina Witt of East Germany regained the world title she had lost in 1986 to Debi Thomas. Soviets Ekaterina Gordeeva and Sergei Grinkov successfully defended their pairs title. Another Soviet, Nikolai Gulyayev, captured the men's title at the World Speed Skating Championship in the Netherlands. In the women's competition, East Germany's Karin Kania again raced off with the gold.                                                             D.M.

### SKIING

Swiss skiers dominated the Alpine World Championships and the entire Alpine World Cup season.

In the International Ski Federation World Championships at Crans-Montana, Switzerland, Swiss women won all 5 gold medals and 8 of the 15 medals awarded for the women's events; Swiss men captured 3 of the 5 golds and 6 of the 15 medals. The Swiss had the first sweep by one nation in 56 years, in the men's downhill, with Peter Mueller, Pirmin Zurbriggen, and Karl Alpiger finishing one-two-three. Besides the silver in the downhill, Zurbriggen

himself won another silver and two golds. Maria Walliser earned two golds and a bronze. Erika Hess took golds in the combined and the slalom; the latter triumph was particularly stirring since it was Hess's last major race before her retirement.

In the men's World Cup season, Zurbriggen thrashed the field, winning three out of four individual cups (downhill, Super G, and giant slalom). On the women's side, the high-flying Swiss captured the first five spots in the overall standings, with Walliser retaining her overall crown—the first woman to do so in 11 years. The Swiss contenders also won all the individual titles.

With Sweden's Gunde Svan out for much of the season because of a rib injury, his teammate Torgny Mogren captured the overall men's World Cup title in Nordic skiing, despite winning only one race all season. Marjo Matikainen of Finland took the women's title. In the Nordic World Championships, the once-dominant Swedes won eight medals, but the Norwegians led with ten. Sweden's Thomas Wassberg took two golds.                                       S.C.

## SOCCER

In 1987, two world championship tournaments were organized by the Fédération Internationale de Football Association (FIFA), the governing body of world soccer, and in both of them the controversial penalty kick shoot-out had to be used to decide the champions. In the world championship for boys under 17 years of age, staged in Canada, Nigeria and the Soviet Union played to a 1-1 overtime tie before the Soviets triumphed, 3-1, in the shoot-out. In the final of the world youth championship (for players under 20), held in Chile, Yugoslavia and West Germany also played to a 1-1 overtime tie. Yugoslavia won the subsequent shoot-out, and the title, by a score of 5-4.

Brazil, Argentina, and China became the first countries to gain berths in the 1988 Olympics in South Korea.

**South America.** The 26th edition of the South American Championship—the Copa America—was staged in Argentina. The host country, though favored, finished an embarrassing fourth, and the tournament was won by Uruguay, with a 1-0 victory over Chile in a rough final that saw four players ejected. The South American Player of the Year award went to the Uruguayan forward Antonio Alzamendi of the Argentine club River Plate.

**Europe.** Although the ban imposed in 1985 on English club teams playing in Europe was extended, the English national team was allowed to enter the European Championship, to be staged in 1988. Fan violence, however, proved contagious; serious incidents were reported from Italy, West Germany, the Netherlands, and the Soviet Union.

Everton won the English First Division, and in Italy, Napoli—captained by the Argentine star Diego Maradona—won the First Division for the first time. Soviet forward Igor Belanov, of Dynamo Kiev, was European Player of the Year. French star Michel Platini announced his retirement.

**North America.** The United States Soccer Federation's under-20 and under-17 teams were engaged in the world championships, but were eliminated early on. Things were brighter in qualifying games for the 1988 Olympics; the U.S. team, having eliminated Canada and Trinidad and Tobago, and beaten El Salvador in one game, 4-2, only had to tie El Salvador in a May 1988 game to ensure a berth. The Major Indoor Soccer League championship was won by the Dallas Sidekicks; the MISL's MVP was the Sidekicks' Tatu.           P.G.

## SWIMMING

In 1987 the United States and East Germany dominated international swimming. World records were broken in 4 of the 17 events for men and 4 of the 17 for women.

Tamas Darnyi, a 20-year-old from Hungary and a newcomer to the top ranks, lowered the records in the European championships in August to 4:15.42 for 400 meters and 2:00.56 for 200 m. Another newcomer, 15-year-old Janet Evans of Placentia, Calif., won three titles in the United States short-course championships at Boca Raton, Fla., in March. In the long-course championships a few months later, she broke the world freestyle records for 800 m (8:22.44) and 1,500 m (16:00.73), only to lose the former less than a month later to Anke Moehring of East Germany (8:19.53) in the European championships.

Those championships produced six world records in all. The East German women won 14 of their 16 finals, while in the men's events, East Germany and West Germany won four gold medals each. The Pan Pacific Games, also in August, attracted more than 300 swimmers from 14 nations. Of the 32 gold medals, the United States won 24, Australia 4, Canada 3, and China 1. At the Pan American Games, the United States excelled again, winning 27 out of the 32 golds.

Greg Louganis, of Boca Raton, the world's outstanding diver, won two titles each in the U.S. outdoor championships, the Pan American Games, and the U.S. Olympic Festival. He also won the men's springboard title in the World Cup competition; the other titlists, all from China, were Tong Hui (men's platform), Xu Yanmei (women's platform), and Cao Min (women's springboard).           F.L.

## TENNIS

West Germany's young Steffi Graf was the big story in tennis, as she usurped Martina Navratilova's number-one ranking. She earned a 75-2 record for the season, losing only at Wimbledon and the U.S. Open. In men's play, Ivan

It was her first singles crown in a Grand Slam event.

**Men's Tour.** Early in the year, Boris Becker was upset in the Australian Open's quarterfinals by low-ranked Wally Masur; Becker lost control of his game and his emotions in the match, and his longtime coach resigned. Through Wimbledon, the West German managed only three titles. Lendl was also sidetracked in the Australian Open, with a semifinals loss to Pat Cash. Sweden's Stefan Edberg, going strong, beat Cash to win the tournament.

At the French Open in May, Lendl beat Miloslav Mecir in straight sets in the semifinals. Number-two seed Becker reached the semifinals only to have Sweden's Mats Wilander aggressively defeat him, 6-4, 6-1, 6-2. However, Wilander abandoned his aggressive game

*Pat Cash of Australia stoops to conquer at Wimbledon. Cash lost only one set en route to the men's singles title, overcoming top-ranked Ivan Lendl in straight sets in the final.*

*Steffi Graf seesawed through the French Open finals (shown here), ultimately triumphing over Martina Navratilova, whom she replaced during the season as top-ranked woman player in tennis.*

Lendl's top ranking was never seriously threatened, partly because Boris Becker of West Germany had a disappointing year. However, Pat Cash of Australia denied Lendl the chance of a Grand Slam by knocking him out of competition in both the Australian Open and Wimbledon.

**Women's Tour.** Hana Mandlikova got off to a fast start by taking the Australian Open in January. (Graf did not participate.) Her 7-5, 7-6 win in the final ended Navratilova's 58-match winning streak. Navratilova then began a losing streak. By the time the French Open arrived in May, Graf, then 17 years old and seeded number two, was her main challenger. Navratilova and Graf lost but one set each moving up to the final. In that spirited contest, Graf took the first set, 6-4, but Navratilova captured the second by the same score. In the third set, Martina was up, 5-3, but Graf broke her serve, to win the set, 8-6, and the match.

*Bulgaria's Stefka Kostadinova raises her own world record in the women's high jump to 6'10¼" at the world outdoor championships, held in Rome during the summer.*

in the final against Lendl, who took the title, 7-5, 6-2, 3-6, 7-6. It was Lendl's second consecutive French Open crown.

**Wimbledon.** Cash made the most of Becker's early elimination at Wimbledon and rose to the final brilliantly, losing only one set, while Lendl had to struggle to the championship match. There Cash shocked Lendl, 7-6, 6-2, 7-5, to win the singles crown. Navratilova overcame Chris Evert in the semifinals; then, in the finals, her determination and heavy slice serves to Graf's weaker backhand side won her the singles crown, 7-5, 6-3.

**Later Events.** At the U.S. Open, Wilander lacked the power to contain Lendl, who captured his third consecutive U.S. Open title, 6-7, 6-0, 7-6, 6-4, in the final. Navratilova proved once again that her game was far from washed up; she won the Open with 7-6, 6-1 in the final against Graf. However, at the Virginia Slims tournament in November, Navratilova, hoping for a successful showdown with Graf, was upset in the quarterfinals, 6-4, 7-5, by 17-year-old Gabriela Sabatini of Argentina, who ended up battling Graf in the finals. Graf held her off, 4-6, 6-4, 6-0, 6-4, to end the season as a clear number one. In December, Lendl

defeated Wilander, 6-2, 6-2, 6-3, to take his fifth Nabisco Masters title, and Wilander and Joakim Nystrom defeated Anand and Vijay Amritraj of India, 6-2, 3-6, 6-1, 6-2, to help clinch the Davis Cup for Sweden.      R.J.L.

### TRACK AND FIELD

Nothing in track and field in 1987 had more impact than Ben Johnson's 100-meter world record. On August 30, during world outdoor championships in Rome, the muscular 25-year-old Jamaica-born Canadian ran 100 m in 9.83 seconds, eclipsing Calvin Smith's 1983 mark of 9.93 seconds, which had been set in the thinner air of Colorado. Also in Rome, Bulgaria's Stefka Kostadinova raised her own world record in the women's high jump to 6'10¼". Jackie Joyner-Kersee of Long Beach, Calif., confirmed her standing as the world's best all-around woman athlete, easily winning the heptathlon with 7,128 points, and upsetting Heike Drechsler of East Germany in the long jump to win with 24'1¾". The East Germans still came out on top, winning 31 medals, followed by the Soviet Union with 25 and the United States with 19.

Among outstanding individual performances during the year, Said Aouita of Morocco kept

373

breaking distance records. He posted the fastest time ever for 2,000 m (4:50.81) on July 16 in Paris and for 5,000 m (12:58.39) on July 22 in Rome. He also set a world record for 2 miles (8:13.45) on May 28 in Turin and ran the second fastest mile ever (3:46.76) on July 2 in Helsinki. Other world records were set by Patrik Sjoberg of Sweden in the high jump (7'11¼" outdoors and 7'10¾" indoors) and Sergei Bubka of the Soviet Union in the pole vault (19'9¼" outdoors and 19'7" indoors). Harry (Butch) Reynolds of Ohio State University ran the three fastest 400-m low-altitude races ever—44.10, 44.13, and 44.15 seconds.

Another stunning individual event was a loss: Starting in 1977, Edwin Moses had won 122 consecutive races in the 400-m hurdles, but on June 4 in Madrid he lost to Danny Harris

of Ames, Iowa, by 1 meter, ending one of the most remarkable streaks in sports.

The first world indoor championships were held March 6–8 in Indianapolis, with 490 athletes from 90 nations participating. In total medals, the leaders were the Soviet Union with 15, the United States with 11, and East Germany with 9. World indoor records were set by Johnson in the men's 60-m dash (6.41 seconds), Greg Foster of the United States in the men's 60-m hurdles semifinals (7.46 seconds), Drechsler in the women's 200-m dash (22.27 seconds), and Kostadinova in the women's high jump (6'8¾").                    F.L.

### YACHTING

Dennis Conner ended his three-year pursuit of the America's Cup in triumph on February 4, skippering the 12-meter yacht *Stars & Stripes*

Canada's Ben Johnson (right) heads for victory over Carl Lewis of the United States in Rome's Stadio Olimpico, with a record 9.83-second time in the 100-meter race.

to a fourth straight victory over the Australian defender *Kookaburra III* in their best-of-seven series off the coast of Western Australia. Conner, who in 1983 had been the first American to lose the Cup, thus became the first to win it back, triumphing over a tough field.

Conner was backed by the San Diego-based Sail America syndicate, which raised more than $15 million for the effort. Of that sum, $3.4 million went into putting some of the leading U.S. experts in aerodynamics and hydrodynamics to work on boat design. Changes to the yacht's rig, keel, and rudder, the plastic coating applied to the hull to reduce friction, and a vastly improved sail inventory played a key role in the victory.

French sailor Philippe Jeantot lowered his previous record by almost 25 days as he won the BOC Challenge round-the-world race for the second time. His elapsed time for the solo race was 134 days, 5 hours, 23 minutes, and 56 seconds. Philippe Poupon of France lowered the transatlantic sailing record to 7 days, 12 hours, and 50 minutes in a west-to-east passage.

In the Admiral's Cup big-boat series, New Zealand, Britain, and Australia placed first, second, and third among 14 teams competing in British waters.                                    D.M.P.

*Reclaiming the America's Cup for the United States,* Stars & Stripes *leads the Australian defender* Kookaburra III *in the fourth and final race.*

### The Quest for the Cup . . . Completed

Dennis Conner's three-year campaign to win back the America's Cup was rewarded on February 4 in the waters off Fremantle, Australia, when his yacht, *Stars & Stripes,* ended the 26th America's Cup match with his fourth straight win over the Australian defender, *Kookaburra III,* in the best-of-seven series. The victory almost washed away the burly Californian's bitter memories of the 1983 day when he became the first U.S. skipper to lose the Cup trophy, which the United States had kept for 132 years. (Conner had successfully defended the Cup in 1980.) Conner also found time in 1987 to race a 72-foot sloop on the Southern Ocean Racing Circuit and to compete in the 12-Meter World Championship, after enjoying a New York City ticker-tape parade in his honor.

*Dennis Conner*

**SRI LANKA.** In July 1987, Sri Lanka and India signed an agreement designed to end Sri Lanka's civil war between the largely Hindu separatist Tamils, living mainly in northern and eastern Sri Lanka, and the primarily Buddhist Sinhalese, the majority of the Sri Lankan population. The peace pact, however, provoked violent reactions among the Sinhalese, and in the autumn fighting broke out between militant Tamils and Indian peacekeeping forces attempting to implement the accord.

Early in the year, Indian-mediated negotiations had stalled over the issue of provincial councils, when Tamil leadership insisted that the Northern and Eastern provinces be united in any provincial-council system. Tamils dominate the Northern Province, Sinhalese and Muslims the Eastern Province; if both provinces were united under a single council, the Tamils would prevail. Meanwhile, the Liberation Tigers of Tamil Eelam (the largest rebel group) announced they were taking civil control of the Jaffna Peninsula. The government imposed an economic embargo on the peninsula and in February launched a major offensive, with mixed results. On April 17 the Tigers set up

*Soldiers in Sri Lanka display piles of weapons turned over by some Tamil rebels after the signing of a peace accord in the summer. Despite such actions, fighting broke out anew.*

roadblocks in the Eastern Province and slaughtered 127 civilians. Four days later a car bomb exploded in Sri Lanka's capital, Colombo, killing over 100 people. The government responded with a massive assault on rebel strongholds on the Jaffna Peninsula.

India's 50 million ethnic Tamils pressured Prime Minister Rajiv Gandhi to intervene. In early June the Indian government broke the economic blockade of the Jaffna Peninsula by airlifting supplies into the area. It then pressured Tamil leaders to accept a compromise offer from the Sri Lankan government.

The July 29 accords called for the creation of provincial councils with administrative control over a wide variety of local affairs. The Northern and Eastern provinces initially would be united under a single provincial council; after one year, the issue of union would be put before the voters. India took responsibility for policing the accords and sent more than 10,000 peace-keeping troops to Sri Lanka to close down guerrilla bases.

President Junius R. Jayewardene was widely condemned for signing the pact, and Gandhi himself, who had flown to Colombo to sign it, was struck by a Sri Lankan sailor while inspecting an honor guard. Sinhalese rioting broke out in several cities. On August 18, grenades were thrown in the Parliament building in Colombo in an attempt to kill the president. He escaped injury, but two people were killed.

The Tigers and other rebel groups began surrendering some of their weapons in compliance with the peace plan. But in September rival factions began fighting among themselves, with heavy casualties resulting. India responded with more troops, and its negotiators worked out a plan for the Tigers to dominate the interim administration in the Northern and Eastern Provinces, if the Tigers would cease fighting. However, a new wave of Tamil violence was touched off in early October, and fighting between Tamil and Indian forces escalated. On November 21 a unilateral Indian cease-fire was declared for 48 hours. Tensions continued, and on December 27, more than 20 people were killed when Tamil rebels clashed with police and Indian soldiers in Batticaloa.

*See* STATISTICS OF THE WORLD.     R.C.O.

**STAMPS, POSTAGE.** In 1987, for the second successive year, an international exhibition dominated North American philately. Meanwhile, special issues marked the bicentennial of the U.S. Constitution and commemorated noted Americans.

**Capex 87.** An international exhibit, called Capex 87, was held in Toronto in June to honor the centennial of organized philately in Canada. Historic Canadian post offices was the theme of a four-stamp set issued to publicize it; the souvenir sheet itself featured two undenominated partial designs showing stages in the stamp printing process. The U.S. Postal Service participated in the event with a first-day sale of a sheet of 50 different stamps picturing American wildlife.

**Special Issues.** The Postal Service marked the bicentennial of the U.S. Constitution with a five-stamp booklet featuring quotations from the Preamble. Singles were also issued; they featured the actual signing ceremony as well as statehood anniversaries of Delaware, New Jersey, and Pennsylvania. A pictorial 14-cent postal card noted the convening of the Constitutional Convention.

A new booklet with reproductions of historic locomotives of the 1829-1839 period was issued to celebrate National Stamp Collecting Month in October. A block of four se-tenant sheet stamps honored lacemaking as an American folk art. A commemorative of Jean Baptiste Point du Sable, founder of the first permanent settlement in Chicago, was added to the Black Heritage series. William Faulkner joined Literary Arts; Enrico Caruso, Performing Arts. New faces in the Great Americans series were social reformer Julia Ward Howe, educator Mary Lyon, author Bret Harte, and Oglala Sioux chief Red Cloud. Collector enthusiasm also greeted five new designs in the Transportation Series of coil stamps.

**CIA Intrigue.** In August the Bureau of Engraving and Printing revealed that several CIA employees had sold 85 misprinted stamps—unwittingly bought by the agency—reportedly for thousands of dollars, presumably dividing the proceeds among themselves. The $1 stamps, which featured an upside-down picture of a vintage candleholder and inverted lettering, were among 400 misprints out of the more

*Opposite page: some notable stamps of 1987. Vertical column at left, from top: historic locomotives, from a U.S. booklet honoring National Stamp Collecting Month; U.S. issues recalling Sioux Chief Red Cloud and an early racing car; and three from Canada, showing historic post offices, to mark Capex 87. Top horizontal row: Britain depicts stages in the life of Queen Victoria. Second row, from left: joint U.S.-Moroccan issues marking 200 years of friendship; the United States honors Jean Baptiste Pointe du Sable, a founder of Chicago. Center: four designs from the American wildlife sheet; below these, the United Nations warns against drug abuse, promotes shelter for the homeless, and honors its first secretary-general, Trygve Lie. Center right: U.S. issues marking Pennsylvania's ratification of the Constitution and the bicentennial of the document itself; below, the five designs from the U.S. Constitutional Bicentennial booklet.*

than 28 million stamps with the candleholder design that were printed in November 1985. The rarity proved valuable—one stamp brought $17,000 in a later sale; another, $21,000.

**Tampering Investigation.** Also in August, the Treasury Department began a review of every stamp produced over the last ten years to determine if unauthorized markings may have been secretly engraved into the master dies. The action followed reports that two recently issued U.S. postage stamps may have contained secret markings. In one instance, a Star of David, invisible to the naked eye, was found etched into the die of the $1 postage stamp issued in September to mark the 100th anniversary of Yeshiva University.

**International Commemoratives.** The international scene was quiet, highlighted by modest commemorations of the America's Cup competition in Australia and the Europa 87 series featuring modern architecture. Britain noted the sesquicentennial of Queen Victoria's accession to the throne. The United Nations concentrated on social themes, such as drug abuse and shelter. B.R.M.

**STATE GOVERNMENT REVIEW.** During 1987, state governments dealt with such issues as budget problems, prison overcrowding, AIDS prevention, and surrogate parenthood. Three states elected new governors; in another, the controversial governor was the object of a recall drive.

**Finances.** Overall, states, under growing economic pressure, raised taxes by about $1 billion

more than in 1986. States in the Southwest and Midwest were especially affected, and tax hikes in Florida and Texas alone accounted for about half of the more than $6 billion in total new taxes. Still, a few states actually lowered taxes, and taxpayers in California and Massachusetts could look forward to refunds because of revenues that exceeded state-allowed ceilings.

As a result of linkages between state tax provisions and federal income tax law, many states stood to gain revenue from federal tax reform measures enacted in 1986. States returned to taxpayers most of the anticipated windfall, by such changes as dropping lower-income persons from their tax rolls and increasing standard deductions and personal exemptions. Still, more than a dozen states kept all of the federal tax windfall.

In the spring, Florida, which does not have an income tax, imposed a 5 percent tax on advertising and professional services, becoming the first state to tax services on such a scale. The measure went into effect July 1, but out-of-state advertisers and affected businesses mounted an intense public campaign against it, and Governor Bob Martinez called a special legislative session to consider an alternative. After long and heated debate, legislators agreed to rescind the tax in early 1988, instead increasing the sales tax on goods.

Alaska, Texas, and Louisiana, which depend heavily on oil tax revenues, reported deficits,

**Bambiscam**

The hefty white-tailed buck in full view of the road seemed too easy a target for passing motorists to resist. That's how 11 hapless hunters got nabbed early this year, in a sting operation devised by law enforcement officials to catch poachers in rural Virginia. The officers simply set up the stuffed animal in a strategic spot, then closed in on any rifle-toting motorist who succumbed to temptation. While the game plan was right on target, so, usually, were the poachers, and the buck, affectionately dubbed Sucker by his co-conspirators, soon had to visit the taxidermist to have his bullet wounds patched up.

*After 13 years of a nationwide 55-mile-per-hour speed limit, Congress voted in March to let states raise the maximum on rural sections of interstate highways. On May 29, as drivers waved and honked, California's first 65-mph sign went up, about 20 miles east of San Diego on Interstate 8.*

caused primarily by declining world oil prices. Texas Governor Bill Clements was forced to accept a major tax increase, despite a campaign pledge. Industrial midwestern states also were hurt by economic slowdowns.

**Wins for State Lotteries.** In November, Virginia voters gave the state authority to run a lottery, due to start in 1988. Also scheduled for 1988 was the nation's second multistate lotto game, involving the District of Columbia, Iowa, Kansas, Oregon, Rhode Island, and West Virginia. Pennsylvania awarded a $46 million lottery prize in October, the largest ever given.

**Automobiles.** A total of 29 states and the District of Columbia had mandatory seat belt laws, and a study by three University of North Carolina researchers, released in December, estimated that these laws had saved 1,300 lives since the first such law went into effect in New York in 1981. However, the success of these laws, and the degree of enforcement, varied widely from state to state.

Early in the year, Congress gave its approval to states to raise the speed limit on rural interstate highways to 65 miles per hour, and more than three dozen states adopted the higher limit. The National Traffic Safety Administration reported substantial increases in fatalities on highways where the limit was raised. Late in the year, a little-noticed measure passed by Congress as part of the omnibus spending bill allowed up to 20 states to increase speed limits to 65 mph on certain rural roads.

**Crime and Punishment.** Institutions in half the states were under court order to reduce prison overcrowding, and many states provided more money to expand facilities. The U.S. Supreme Court upheld Georgia's capital punishment law, clearing the way for executions there and in several other states. The age for those subject to capital punishment was raised to 16 in Indiana and to 18 in Maryland.

**Education.** State spending on education continued to rise. Among states appropriating major funding increases for schools were Indiana and North Carolina—both of which increased taxes to do so—and Mississippi. Indiana added five days to the school year and established a new system for evaluating teachers and a new accreditation system. Vermont funded education for preschoolers. California and New York adopted new curriculum guidelines.

Mississippi announced it would deny certification to graduates of teacher training colleges if 75 percent of the graduates failed a standardized test for teachers. Nevada created a nine-member teacher licensing board independent of the state board of education and composed in large part of teachers or school counselors.

**Health and Welfare.** Legislatures considered more than 400 AIDS-related measures, but only a few passed. Illinois enacted a broad package of bills, including provisions for mandatory testing of those wishing to marry and mandatory AIDS education in public school starting at grade 6. Also included was a strict measure governing confidentiality of AIDS test results. Louisiana already mandated AIDS tests for those wishing to marry. A handful of states required AIDS tests for prison inmates and convicted prostitutes. Idaho and Florida set criminal penalties for AIDS carriers who know-

"Mecham for Ex-Governor" was the slogan adopted in Arizona by Evan Mecham's foes as they collected signatures (above), eventually totaling almost 390,000, on a recall petition that could force him from office. The new Republican governor (left) had angered many in the state by canceling a recently proclaimed holiday honoring Martin Luther King, Jr., and by making comments considered offensive by women, blacks, and homosexuals.

ingly infect others. Over half the states had some form of AIDS education program in schools, and some had funded public education campaigns.

A few states took the innovative step of requiring employers to offer leave to new parents or parents of seriously ill children. More states offered facilities or income tax reductions to their employees for child care, while Maine and Rhode Island offered tax credits to private employers who provide day care services. Major welfare reform in Washington state provided jobs, training, and child care incentives for those receiving public assistance. Several states restricted smoking in public places.

Louisiana became the first state to ban surrogate parenting arrangements, in the wake of the highly publicized Baby M custody battle in New Jersey. In that case, a New Jersey superior court awarded custody to the father of the child born as a result of a surrogacy contract, rather than the surrogate (natural) mother, Mary Beth Whitehead. (The ruling was appealed.) Bills to regulate, ban, or examine surrogacy were introduced in more than two dozen other states.

**Mecham Faces Recall.** Arizona's Republican governor, arch-conservative Evan Mecham, was subjected to a recall campaign and to a grand jury investigation, as a result of alleged corruption and incompetence in office. By November the recall drive had collected enough signatures—including those of former Republican Senator Barry Goldwater and Democratic presidential contender Bruce Babbitt—to force a new election in 1988. Mecham had offended blacks by using derogatory language and by rescinding the holiday commemorating Martin Luther King. He also offended homosexuals, women, and other groups, and was broadly criticized for ill-chosen political appointments. The governor denied any wrongdoing and blamed his troubles on the press and on left-wing radicals.

**Elections.** In state elections, State Auditor Ray Mabus, a Democrat, was elected governor of Mississippi, and another Democrat, businessman Wallace Wilkinson, won the governorship of Kentucky. Edwin Edwards, Louisiana's Democratic governor, declined to take part in a runoff, leaving Representative Charles E. Roemer III, the front-runner, as winner of the gubernatorial election in Louisiana. (See also ELECTIONS IN THE UNITED STATES.)          E.S.K.

**SUDAN.** Sudan's first civilian government since the 1985 coup was dissolved in May 1987 and there was another government crisis in August, but each time only minor reshuffling of the cabinet resulted. The civil war showed no sign of abating, and food supplies were scarce.

In mid-May the Sudanese government was dissolved when Prime Minister Sadiq al-Mahdi announced that he and his cabinet could not solve the nation's principal problems. On June 3 a new cabinet, again headed by al-Mahdi, was sworn in. Like the one it replaced, it was a coalition of al-Mahdi's Umma party and the Democratic Unionist Party (DPU). In August the leader of the DPU withdrew support from the coalition. However, a new government consisting of the same coalition was formed late in the year.

The civil war between the Muslim north and the mainly Christian secessionist south became more bitter as atrocities mounted and military conflict continued at full force. In March a large number of Dinkas—the group that forms the core of the southern rebel strength—were slain in southern Darfur province. In May, elements of the rebels' 20,000-strong Sudanese People's Liberation Army (SPLA) claimed to have shot down a Hercules C-130 plane carrying two platoons of government troops, as it was about to land in the city of Wau.

The war has become more internationalized, with Ethiopia, Israel, Kenya, and Uganda supporting the SPLA forces; Ethiopia has provided them with an external base and recruiting facilities close to its border with Sudan. On the other side, Libya and the United States were both supplying weapons to the Sudanese Army. Government forces were inflicting heavy casualties and damage. Nevertheless, the south, except for the largest towns, was still essentially controlled by SPLA forces. In December the government held talks with SPLA representatives in London, but no agreement was reached.

Between 2 and 5 million Sudanese were reportedly in danger of starvation. The efforts of relief agencies to get supplies to the south have been hampered by civil war, and by the presence of more than 1.5 million refugees fleeing political and military havoc in Chad, Uganda, Zaire, and Ethiopia. The United Nations High Commissioner for Refugees reported that more than a million Ethiopian refugees were living in Sudan in abysmal conditions.

The worsening economic situation was a primary reason for the government's resignation in May. In an attempt to boost the economy, efforts were made to increase production in the Gezira district, where half the Sudan's cotton is grown, as well as one third of its groundnuts and most of its wheat.

See STATISTICS OF THE WORLD.

**SUPREME COURT OF THE UNITED STATES.**
See UNITED STATES OF AMERICA: *Supreme Court.*
**SURINAME.** See STATISTICS OF THE WORLD.
**SWAZILAND.** See STATISTICS OF THE WORLD.
**SWEDEN.** In 1987, Sweden was troubled by arms sale scandals, the escape of a Soviet spy, and continuing investigation into the 1986 assassination of Olof Palme, Social Democratic prime minister of Sweden.

Since Palme was shot to death on a Stockholm street on February 28, 1986, police reportedly had opened files on at least 28,000 people and pursued an estimated 40,000 tips. Conspiracy theories abounded. The most prominent, linking Palme's murder to hostilities between Iran and Iraq, was nourished by revelations that the Swedish firm Bofors, a subsidiary of Nobel Industries, had made surreptitious arms sales to Iran through third parties after Swedish arms exports to Iran were suspended by the government following the Iranian revolution of 1979. It was theorized that Palme, who served as a United Nations-appointed mediator in the conflict, could have been targeted by either Iraq, angry over the continued arms sales, or Iran, angry because the government was trying to stop them.

Allegations of a conspiracy were strengthened in mid-January by the death of Carl-Fredrik Algernon, head of Sweden's arms export office, who fell in front of a subway train on the eve of his scheduled testimony before an investigation of the Bofors operations. (However, no evidence of foul play was found.) Two months later, the chief of the Stockholm county police force, who had initially led the official investigation of Palme's murder, angrily resigned from the force, charging that prosecution authorities had hindered his investigatory efforts. Government spokesmen, however, heatedly denied charges of a high-level cover-up.

Justice Minister Sten Wickbom, already under fire for lack of progress in the Palme case, resigned in October after convicted Soviet spy Stig Bergling, a former Swedish intelligence agent, fled while unguarded during a visit he had been granted to his wife at her suburban Stockholm apartment.

The arms scandal deepened when two Swedish businessmen were indicted on charges of secretly exporting explosives and gunpowder to Iran and other countries blacklisted by Sweden. Such operations were under investigation by a police prosecutor and by a government commission. Also investigated were reports of bribes paid by Bofors to the Indian government for a $1.3 billion field artillery contract awarded to the company in 1986.

See STATISTICS OF THE WORLD.    M.D.H.

**SWITZERLAND.** Concerns about the environment and developments involving banking and finance dominated the news in 1987.

The Sandoz chemical plant fire of November 1986, which led to the release of 30 tons of chemicals into the Rhine River, left a legacy of hostility toward both the Swiss government and the Sandoz Corporation. This year, the government ordered dredging operations, which removed over a ton of insecticide-laden silt from the waters near the site. Meetings of environmental ministers from Switzerland, West Germany, France, and the Netherlands resulted in an agreement to establish better warning systems in case of a similar incident and a plan to clean up the Rhine by the year 2000. Sandoz set up a $6.6 million foundation to be used for research and purification, and by October it had begun to reimburse West German fishermen for about $1.7 million in losses.

Heightened awareness of the environment led to gains for Switzerland's various Green (ecology-oriented) parties in cantonal elections in Basel in February and in Zurich and Geneva in April. However, the Greens did not do as well as expected in national elections in October, in which the four-party center-right coalition that has governed Switzerland for nearly 30 years retained its substantial parliamentary majority. In April voters overwhelmingly approved a referendum to tighten restrictions on immigration and political asylum.

Switzerland's Bank Leu was implicated in the scandal associated with British brewing company Guinness P.L.C.'s $3.74 billion takeover of the Distillers Company. Bank Leu denied any wrongdoing.

A July decision by the Federal Tribunal (Switzerland's highest court) held that Swiss bank secrecy laws did not bar Swiss authorities from aiding the Philippine government's probe of former Philippine President Ferdinand Marcos's reputed $1.55 billion fortune frozen in Swiss bank accounts, so long as Philippine authorities clearly established intent to bring criminal charges against Marcos.

Swiss financial institutions figured prominently in the Iran/contra scandal. The Geneva-based finance firm Compagnie des Services Fiduciaires S.A. was linked to various stages in the sale of U.S. arms to Iran and the transfer of the resulting funds to antigovernment guerrillas (contras) in Nicaragua. Crédit Suisse, Switzerland's third largest bank, held accounts belonging to or controlled by major figures in the scandal. In November, after Switzerland's Federal Tribunal had ruled in favor of U.S. special prosecutor Lawrence E. Walsh's request for the secret Crédit Suisse banking records, they were turned over to him.

See STATISTICS OF THE WORLD.                    J.S.

**SYRIA.** Syria, often accused of involvement in terrorist activities, made an effort in 1987 to convince the West that it was seeking to prevent them; it also sought to strengthen its relations in the Arab world.

*Syria got credit for helping free Charles Glass (left), an American journalist held hostage in Lebanon, though Glass insisted he escaped without outside assistance. Here, he leaves the home of a U.S. diplomat in Damascus on his way to London and a reunion with his family.*

**Shift on Terrorism.** In February, Muhammad al-Kholi, head of Air Force intelligence and a close associate of President Hafez al-Assad, was demoted, and some of his associates were demoted or dismissed. Kholi had been implicated in terrorist plots during trials in Great Britain and West Germany in late 1986. In June the government closed the Damascus offices of the Palestinian terrorist organization headed by Abu Nidal, which had been linked to a 1985 attack that killed 13 people at Rome's Leonardo Da Vinci Airport. Syria also attempted to prevent further kidnappings and bombings by Lebanese Shiite groups when its troops occupied West Beirut in February.

As a result, Syria's relations with both the United States and the European Community improved. In July, Vernon Walters, the U.S. ambassador to the United Nations, arrived in Damascus for a meeting with Assad. The visit followed a letter to Assad from U.S. President Ronald Reagan proposing discussion of U.S. hostages in Lebanon and other mutual concerns. Also in July the European Community lifted a ban on high-level diplomatic contacts it had imposed in 1986, after revelations of Syrian involvement in terrorist activities.

**Arab Meetings.** At a summit conference of Islamic leaders in Kuwait in January, Assad spoke with Egyptian President Hosni Mubarak, in their first meeting since Mubarak took office in 1981. The meeting did not amount to a genuine rapprochement, however, since the countries remained divided over Egypt's separate peace treaty with Israel. Assad also met in April with another old antagonist, President Saddam Hussein of Iraq, at a remote air base in Jordan. The meeting was arranged by Jordan, Saudi Arabia, and the Soviet Union, all of whom had a strong interest in healing the bitter quarrel between the two countries and ending the Iran-Iraq war. A second meeting took place in November at the Arab League summit meeting in Amman, where Syria, in a departure from previous policy, supported a resolution condemning its ally Iran for continuing the Gulf war with Iraq.

**Intervention in West Beirut.** Much of the tension with Iran was a result of Syria's occupation of West Beirut. Syria, with 25,000 troops in northern and eastern Lebanon, was asked to intervene by Lebanese Muslim and Druze leaders during some of the bloodiest factional fighting of Lebanon's 12-year civil war, and in February 7,000 Syrian troops moved into Muslim West Beirut. The Syrians demanded that the warring militias disband.

The Syrian presence in Beirut led to a confrontation with the Iranian-backed militant Shiite group Hezbollah ("Party of God"), which favored the establishment of a Lebanese Islamic theocracy and was viewed by Syria as a growing threat to its position in Lebanon. Although Syria refrained from entering the southern suburbs of Beirut where the Hezbollah militias were dominant, Syrian troops in West Beirut killed 23 Hezbollah militants in late February. Iran denounced the killings. Syria, which had warned Hezbollah to release all foreign hostages and had guaranteed the safety of foreign residents of Beirut, was further provoked in June when an American journalist was kidnapped by Shiites probably connected with Hezbollah (he later escaped, after Syria had worked to win his release).

**Domestic Problems.** The nation continued to suffer from severe economic difficulties. Military expenditures were heavy, and many basic goods were in short supply. One bright spot was the increased production from domestic oil fields. In November the Syrian prime minister and four other ministers who had been censured by Parliament for incompetence were replaced.

See STATISTICS OF THE WORLD.        A.D.

# T

**TAIWAN.** In 1987, Taiwan took significant steps toward democracy. The 38-year-old martial law was lifted in July, and mass rallies were permitted to commemorate the uprising of February 28, 1947, in which Chinese Nationalist troops massacred more than 10,000 Taiwanese—an incident that had been virtually unmentionable for 40 years.

Drastic political change in the neighboring Philippines and South Korea brought pressure on the ruling Kuomintang party to broaden political participation in Taiwan. Pressure also came from the new opposition party—the Democratic Progressive Party—which was established in defiance of a government ban, and which, in the December 1986 elections, had taken 12 of the 73 open seats in the Legislative Yuan, or national legislature.

The proposed reorganization of the Legislative Yuan and two other national bodies was a topic of strong debate. About two-thirds of the Yuan's 320 members were elected before 1947 from provinces of mainland China, which they still claimed to represent. The Democratic Progressive Party and most native Taiwanese favored pensioning off these "life members," while the Kuomintang wnated to keep power in the hands of these mainlanders. President Chiang Ching-kuo faced a dilemma, having pledged broad reforms in order to increase support for his Kuomintang party.

Indirect, and clandestine direct, trade with China was growing, and Taiwanese were secretly traveling back to the mainland to visit relatives. Given this situation, the regime decided late in the year to lift the ban on travel to China, for those who could prove they had relatives there.

Taiwan's export-driven economy remained strong. During the year, Taiwanese authorities relaxed foreign exchange controls and were preparing to lower tariffs further and eliminate nontariff trade barriers.

See STATISTICS OF THE WORLD.        P.H.C.

**TANZANIA.** In 1987 there were signs that Tanzania's African socialist policy could be reaching an end, even as leaders of Chama Cha Mapinduzi (CCM), the ruling party, celebrated the 20th anniversary of the Arusha Declaration. That declaration inaugurated former President Julius Nyerere's ambitious program of nationalization and state control. In the course of time, the system came to be regarded as a failure by some observers.

385

The frank and critical assessments of African socialism at the CCM's annual conference in January 1987, the goals set by the government in the five-year plan for 1987-1991, and the direction of the 1987-1988 budget all reflected a movement away from orthodox socialism. Also, Nyerere indicated he would step down as chairman of the CCM, thus presumably leaving more independence to President Ali Hassan Mwinyi, who succeeded Nyerere in 1985 and was moving in the direction of a free-market economy. In October, however, Nyerere allowed himself to be reelected as chairman of the CCM. This step was widely seen as an effort to keep Mwinyi from veering too far from socialism, and it left the future course of events in doubt.

The new five-year plan was essentially an extension of Mwinyi's blueprint to rehabilitate the economy and promote free-market policies. The 1987-1988 government budget was designed to attract added foreign aid and to meet some of the changes urged by the International Monetary Fund. Revenue was projected to increase 4 percent over the previous year. In April the government levied additional taxes on beer, cigarettes, and soft drinks, to make up for anticipated shortfalls.

*See* STATISTICS OF THE WORLD.          M.E.D.

**TECHNOLOGY.** *See* COMPUTERS; ELECTRONICS; LIFE SCIENCES; SPACE EXPLORATION.

**TELEVISION AND RADIO BROADCASTING.** The year 1987 was one of turmoil for the three major television networks. As Laurence A. Tisch, the president and chief executive officer of CBS, put it, "A once unified and coherent industry seems to be splitting down further and further into separate components." About 2 million Americans had satellite dishes in their yards, allowing them to pick up signals directly from orbiting satellites. Moreover, 59 percent had videocassette recorders. With the alternatives offered by VCR's, cable television, and independent stations continuing to nibble away at the market, the networks suffered further erosion of audiences.

Network revenues, which had fallen by about 3 percent in 1986, were projected to rise by about 5 percent in 1987. With the presidential election and Olympics to spur viewership, revenues were expected to increase by about 11 percent in 1988. For the long term, however, analysts were predicting a decline of network audience shares in the early 1990's. They estimated as well that the network share of the advertising dollar would fall below 50 percent (it had been above 60 percent in the 1970's).

**People Meters.** Television changed its long-standing method of collecting ratings. On September 1 the A. C. Nielsen Company and a rival ratings service, AGB Television Research, began compiling national prime-time ratings based on information from so-called people meters instead of the audimeter/diary system that had been in use, in one form or another, for 30 years. Under the old system, a device attached to the TV sets in "Nielsen households" recorded the channel selected, and people wrote down the names of programs they had seen. People meters are intended to give the industry and advertisers more reliable and precise information on who is watching what. Each family member in a sample home is supposed to log in with a personal identification number on a remote control-type device every time he or she begins watching TV and to log off after finishing; the data thus collected are fed to a central computer.

There were worries about the effect the new system would have on sales of commercial time, in part because gadget-loving yuppies were expected to take to the new devices more readily than others, biasing the ratings in favor of shows watched by young, affluent city dwellers. Underreporting was also a concern. Nielsen numbers using the new system were somewhat lower than those from the past, despite some program-by-program variances, and AGB numbers were slightly lower than those of Nielsen.

**The 1986-1987 Season.** Judging by the Nielsen ratings for the 1986-1987 season, situation comedies were the preferred prime-time entertainment in the United States—particularly NBC sitcoms. For the second year in a row, NBC's *The Cosby Show* was the nation's most popular series. Also for the second year in a row, NBC was the most popular network, with CBS second and ABC third. The rest of the top ten regularly programmed shows were: *Family Ties*, NBC; *Cheers*, NBC; *Murder, She Wrote*,

CBS; *The Golden Girls*, NBC; *60 Minutes*, CBS; *Night Court*, NBC; *Growing Pains*, ABC; *Moonlighting*, ABC; and *Who's the Boss*, ABC. NBC continued to dominate late-night programming, as *The Tonight Show Starring Johnny Carson* celebrated its 25th year on the air.

CBS succumbed to a trend away from hard news in the morning and inaugurated *The Morning Program*, anchored by actress Mariette Hartley and newsman Rolland Smith, in January 1987. The ratings and critics were less than kind, and the program was canceled by fall. The network filled the time slot with a news show, *CBS This Morning*, anchored by Kathleen Sullivan, formerly of ABC News, and CBS correspondent Harry Smith.

Public broadcasting won acclaim for *Eyes on the Prize*, a six-part series on the civil rights movement from 1954 to 1965. Despite protests from liberals, ABC went ahead with the broadcast in February of a $30 million, seven-part, 14-hour series called *Amerika* that depicted a military defeat and occupation of the United States by the Soviet Union. Its ratings failed to live up to expectations, as did those for miniseries in general. Only one, *I'll Take Manhattan* on CBS, was a big winner.

**Fall Season.** NBC's *L.A. Law*, on the air since 1986, was widely credited with opening prime time to yuppies; dealing with the staff of a high-powered California law firm, it featured a blend of drama and offbeat comedy similar to what its executive producer, Steven Bochco, had brought to the departed *Hill Street Blues*. Still, the new rating system also probably played a role in the large number of fall 1987 shows geared toward those demographically choice viewers. ABC's drama *thirtysomething* featured a prosperous young couple coming to grips with the changes in their lives caused by a new baby. Yuppie characters also populated such shows as the NBC sitcom *My Two Dads*, the CBS comedy *Everything's Relative*, and even a CBS private eye show, *Leg Work* (both CBS shows were later canceled). Aimed at the same generation, but more serious, was CBS's *Tour of Duty*, about American soldiers in Vietnam. Other new shows ran the gamut from sober family drama (*A Year in the Life* on NBC) to fantasy (CBS's *Beauty and the Beast*, in which a young female lawyer teams up with a deformed recluse who lives underground).

ABC canceled *Max Headroom*, but not before the show had established itself as bizarrely

**The Talk of Daytime TV**
Would Phil Donahue ever tell viewers about the trouble he's had sticking to his latest diet, or ask diminutive actor Dudley Moore about the technical difficulties of sleeping with tall women? Oprah Winfrey, whose nationally syndicated daytime TV talk show is giving Donahue stiff competition, would and did. Brassy, vulnerable, and spontaneous (she once dramatically admitted on the air to having been sexually abused as a child), she has drawn on these assets in film roles as well, winning an Oscar nomination for *The Color Purple* (1985). Winfrey, 33, was a champion orator in high school and worked as a radio and TV newswoman while in college. She had trouble reporting sad stories without crying, and later on switched from anchoring the news on a Baltimore TV station to cohosting a morning talk show there—"what I was born to do," in her words. She moved to Chicago to host what grew into today's popular *Oprah Winfrey Show*.

*Oprah Winfrey*

*L.A. Law was about lawyers, though not of the Perry Mason mold. In one episode, an attorney played by Harry Hamlin (right) represented a TV newswoman (Barbara Bosson, left) fired for undressing on camera to illustrate a medical story.*

innovative. Headroom—previously incarnated as a movie hero and (on British television and U.S. cable) a talk show host—was literally a "talking head": a wisecracking face on a video screen (played by actor Matt Frewer). Set in the near future, the show offered flashy video tricks mingled with satire of the television industry.

Vanna White was a phenomenal success. As the lavishly outfitted "hostess" of the game show *Wheel of Fortune,* her job was to spin letter-clues into view for the contestants (and a home audience of 43 million). Bemused as she went from anonymity to national renown, White appeared on posters and magazine covers and published her autobiography, *Vanna Speaks.*

**News.** Americans clustered around television sets during the summer to watch the congressional hearings into the Iran/contra affair. The testimony of Marine Lieutenant Colonel Oliver North was particularly closely watched and helped make North a national celebrity, although "Olliemania" faded in a few weeks. Television coverage played a key role in other major stories as well, particularly the Senate Judiciary Committee's hearing on the nomination of Judge Robert Bork to the Supreme Court. (He was rejected by the committee and the Senate.)

Network news divisions faced a barrage of budget cuts. At NBC, members of the National Association of Broadcast Employees and Technicians returned in the fall from a four-month strike to word that 200 of them, half in the news operation, were to be laid off. Longer-range plans to cut 500 more jobs at NBC were under discussion. At CBS the news division underwent restructuring that included the layoffs of 215 people and a $30 million budget cut. (Some jobs were later restored.)

Harmed by a long writers' strike and increasing disharmony after the budget cuts forced widespread layoffs and bureau closings, the *CBS Evening News With Dan Rather* fell for a short period to third place in the ratings. (Subsequently, with people meters gathering the Nielsen data, the program recovered.

**A Fourth Network.** In April, with a $150 million investment by owner Rupert Murdoch and with 108 affiliates enrolled, the Fox Broadcasting Company began introducing its prime-time lineup with the debut of five Sunday night shows; four others on Saturday night were introduced in July. Bargain rates attracted advertisers, but viewer response was lukewarm. Fox's flagship program, *The Late Show Starring Joan Rivers,* drew disappointing ratings, and Rivers was replaced, at least initially, by a series of substitute hosts and reruns.

**Awards.** Among winners of the George Foster Peabody Awards were NBC for *The Cosby Show,* ABC for *This Week With David Brinkley,* and CBS for *Newsmark: Where in the World Are We?,* for *CBS Reports: The Vanishing Family—Crisis in Black America,* and for *Sunday Morning: Vladimir Horowitz.* WQED-TV, Pittsburgh, and the National Geographic Society were recognized for *The National Geographic Specials.* MacNeil Lehrer Productions and the British Broadcasting Corporation won a Peabody award for *The Story of English.*

*Promise,* a CBS special about schizophrenia, won several major Emmy awards, including best special, best actor in a miniseries or special (James Woods), and best director (Glenn Jordan). Among other Emmy winners, *L.A. Law* was chosen as best dramatic series, with Bruce Willis (*Moonlighting*) and Sharon Gless (*Cagney and Lacey*) winning the top acting awards in this category. *The Golden Girls* was chosen as best comedy series, with the show's Rue McLanahan winning as best actress in a comedy series; Michael J. Fox (*see biography in* PEOPLE IN THE NEWS) was named best actor in a comedy series. The Emmy awards presentation, broadcast over Fox, lasted four hours and attracted the lowest ratings in its history.

**Federal Regulation.** With both houses of Congress under Democratic control and with the House Telecommunications Subcommittee chaired by a liberal activist, Representative Edward Markey (D, Mass.), Congress moved toward increased control over the communications industry and greater oversight of the Federal Communications Commission. Meanwhile, at the FCC, Mark Fowler, chairman since 1981, stepped down and was replaced by another advocate of less regulation, Dennis Roy Patrick.

A move was under way in Congress to establish a fee on the sale of radio and television station licenses, the income to be used to establish a fund beginning in 1991 to aid public broadcasting. The Fairness Doctrine, a rule requiring broadcasters to air diverse views on controversial issues, was also the subject of congressional action, as a bill to codify the regulation into law was vetoed by President Ronald Reagan in June. In August the FCC did away with the regulation entirely, though congressional efforts to put it on the statute books continued.

**Offensive Material.** Prompted by complaints about off-color radio broadcasts, the FCC tightened its standards on program content. The basis for its action was a nine-year-old Supreme Court decision involving the broadcast of comedian George Carlin's recorded monologue on the so-called "seven dirty words" that could not be uttered over the air. In that ruling, the Court had empowered the FCC to regulate the broadcast of sexually explicit material and punish violators; by a unanimous vote, the agency now put the industry on notice that it would become more aggressive on the matter. Shortly afterward, in a ruling arising out of complaints against three radio stations, it decided that both television and radio broadcasters could air "patently offensive" material, though not obscenity, between midnight and 6 A.M., when children were unlikely to be in the audience.

*Jackie Gleason died at age 71, but his comedy series* The Honeymooners *seemed immortal, flourishing in reruns three decades after the original broadcasts. From left: Gleason, Art Carney, Audrey Meadows, and Joyce Randolph.*

**Radio.** Westwood One, the network radio company based in Culver City, Calif., completed its $50 million acquisition of the NBC Radio Network from General Electric. The sale did not include the eight radio stations owned by NBC, a division of General Electric. Humorist Garrison Keillor discontinued his popular public-radio program *A Prairie Home Companion,* to the consternation of some 4 million fans.

**Canadian Broadcasting.** The future of the Canadian airwaves remained in limbo, as the federal government made no move to implement the wide-ranging recommendations—including increased funding of the Canadian Broadcasting Corporation (CBC) and the creation of a new, independent commercial-free network called TV Canada—that its own task force on broadcasting had made in 1986. CBC programming suffered from government budget cuts. Lacking even the funds to properly celebrate its 50th anniversary, the CBC paid only lip service to the occasion on its TV network. But CBC Radio, which remained the heart and soul of public broadcasting in Canada, marked the anniversary with a generous schedule of special broadcasts and archival compilation,

and its standard of regular programming remained high.

CBC-TV offered a season short on innovation. Its hockey soap opera, *He Shoots, He Scores,* produced in both French and dubbed English versions, was a sensational hit in Québec, but fared poorly with English Canadian viewers, who tend to have low tolerance for dubbed dialogue. In a spirit of national compromise, it was renewed for a second season. With its 1987 fall lineup the network put the accent on improving existing programs, rather than creating new ones at greater cost. *Street Legal,* the CBC's answer to *L.A. Law,* came back for a retrial, as did its Disney coproduction *Danger Bay.* One of the few new shows, *Not My Department,* satirized Ottawa mandarins—but without the punch of its inspiration, Britain's *Yes, Minister.*

B.D.J. (Canadian Broadcasting) & J.T.

**TENNESSEE.** *See* STATISTICS OF THE WORLD.

**TEXAS.** *See* STATISTICS OF THE WORLD.

**THAILAND.** Thai politics in 1987 were marked by internal controversies, while tensions continued along the border with Cambodia. The Thai economy appeared to be doing well.

A major controversy arose in February, when

**The Smartest Man on Television?**

When a major story breaks, millions of Americans tune in to *ABC News Nightline,* seeking more information than they can get from standard news broadcasts. Since 1980, Ted Koppel, 47, has anchored the late-night show, deftly juggling discussions among guests with conflicting views, asking probing questions, and earning a reputation as one of the best serious interviewers— some say the smartest man—on television. Born in England, of Jewish parents who fled Nazi Germany, he came to New York in 1953 and worked in radio before moving to ABC-TV, where his jobs included Vietnam correspondent and chief diplomatic correspondent. *Nightline* guests in 1987 included former National Security Adviser Robert McFarlane, shortly after the latter's attempted suicide; TV evangelists Jim and Tammy Bakker, in an hour-long interview; and Al Campanis, whose statements on *Nightline* about blacks in baseball led to his ouster as Los Angeles Dodgers vice president.

*Ted Koppel*

Prime Minister Prem Tinsulanonda reorganized the military-affiliated Internal Security Operation Command (ISOC) and took over its direction, replacing General Chaovalit Yongchaiyut. The reorganization, said to have been advocated by Chaovalit, was apparently aimed at countering the increasingly political activity of the Communist Party of Thailand. Subsequently, General Chaovalit, widely assumed to be a possible successor to Prem, made controversial speeches calling for a "peaceful revolution" in Thailand.

Former Prime Minister Kukrit Pramoj criticized the restructuring program, charging that the ISOC had been infiltrated by Communists and that Chaovalit had been "brainwashed." Kukrit's criticisms prompted paramilitary and army demonstrations in support of Chaovalit. In Parliament, a no-confidence motion was introduced against Prem's cabinet, but it did not win passage. Around the same time, police arrested 18 suspected members of the Communist Party, reportedly including four members of its Politburo.

Thailand's economy emerged as one of the most dynamic in Southeast Asia, in part because of low oil prices, falling local interest rates, and the decline of the Thai baht against the Japanese yen and European currencies. Economists expected Thailand's gross national product to grow 5 percent or more a year for the next three years.

Thai and Vietnamese troops engaged in a protracted battle in the spring when the Thais tried to oust Vietnamese soldiers dug into a cluster of hills in the northeast. The Thai troops suffered heavy casualties.

For unexplained reasons, Thailand faced a heavy new influx of asylum-seekers, mostly ethnic Vietnamese. More than 11,000 boat people arrived during the year, a 165 percent increase over 1986. Meanwhile, over 250,000 Cambodian refugees continued living along the Thai border, in camps controlled by resistance groups fighting the Vietnamese in Cambodia.

The United States and Thailand signed an executive agreement, approved by Congress, to set up a war-reserve stockpile in Thailand, composed of weapons supplied by both countries. In the spring, a Thai Army delegation visited China and negotiated a deal for $10 million worth of military supplies, marking a significant improvement in relations between the two nations.

See STATISTICS OF THE WORLD.   M.H.

**THEATER.** A resurgent Broadway provided one of the bright spots of the American theater in 1987. New productions in 1986–1987 increased 24 percent over the previous season, and box office receipts were up.

**Broadway.** Broadway's first straight play of 1987, *Sweet Sue*, by A. R. Gurney, Jr., starred Mary Tyler Moore and Lynn Redgrave in a gift-wrapped comedy whose substance did not quite match its packaging. In Richard Harris's *Stepping Out*, a collection of British urban types came together to learn tap routines and unscramble their lives. Author-director John Bishop spoofed whodunit clichés in *The Musical Comedy Murders of 1940*, which reopened on Broadway after its successful Off Broadway run. Earle Hyman gave a powerful performance in *Death and the King's Horseman*, Nobelist Wole Soyinka's drama about a British colonial officer's blundering attempt to interfere with native African customs. Farcical absurdities ran wild in the late Larry Shue's *The Nerd*.

The season's standout drama was August Wilson's *Fences*, which probed with eloquence and power generational conflicts in a family of blue-collar black Americans in the pre-civil-rights era. Its fine cast was headed by James Earl Jones and Mary Alice. Harvey Fierstein wrote and starred in *Safe Sex*, which examined homosexual life-styles and sensibilities, particularly as related to the AIDS crisis. Charles Marowitz earned mixed reviews for *Sherlock's Last Case*, starring coproducer Frank Langella and Donal Donnelly. John Malkovich and Joan Allen headed the cast of *Burn This*, Lanford Wilson's new play about a dancer's personal tragedy. Late in the year, Joseph Papp presented Caryl Churchill's *Serious Money*, an angry political satire about financial wheeler-dealers.

Britain's Royal Shakespeare Company contributed a glittering production of Christopher Hampton's *Les Liaisons Dangereuses*, adapted from the novel by Choderlos de Laclos. Derek Jacobi recreated the role of mathematician Alan Turing, who deciphered a vital German World War II code, in *Breaking the Code* by Hugh Whitemore.

# THEATER

Also crossing the Atlantic from Britain—and becoming a smash hit—was *Les Misérables*, a musical version of the Victor Hugo classic, by Alain Boublil (book), Claude-Michel Schönberg (music), and Herbert Kretzmer (lyrics). The Royal Shakespeare Company spectacular, staged by Trevor Nunn and John Caird, with Colm Wilkinson as Jean Valjean, opened with an advance sale of $11 million. And *Starlight Express*, by composer Andrew Lloyd Webber and lyricist Richard Stilgoe, was a rollerdome fantasy about railroads, for wide-eyed children and susceptible grown-ups.

Writer-director James Lapine and composer-lyricist Stephen Sondheim drew upon the Grimm brothers and other folklore sources for *Into the Woods*, put on by a cast headed by Bernadette Peters. Richard Kapp shared composing honors with John Philip Sousa in *Teddy and Alice*, in which Len Cariou portrayed President Theodore Roosevelt.

Revivals on the Broadway calendar included Arthur Miller's *All My Sons*, from the Long Wharf Theater, with a cast headed by Richard Kiley; George Bernard Shaw's *Pygmalion*, with Peter O'Toole, Amanda Plummer, and a splendid supporting cast; and, among musicals, a revamped *Dreamgirls*, Cole Porter's *Anything Goes*, and *Cabaret*, with Joel Gray repeating his award-winning role.

Lincoln Center's Vivian Beaumont Theater was the scene of *The Comedy of Errors*, in which the Flying Karamazov Brothers, the Vaudeville Nouveau, Avner the Eccentric Eisenberg, and other crazies juggled Shakespeare's comedy of mistaken identities.

**Off Broadway.** In *North Shore Fish*, Israel Horovitz dramatized the predicament of the staff of a failing Gloucester (Mass.) fish-processing plant. In *My Gene*, Colleen Dewhurst portrayed Eugene O'Neill's wife Carlotta in Barbara Gelb's one-woman drama about the

*Victor Hugo's novel* Les Misérables, *a sprawling tale of poverty and revolution in 19th-century Paris, came to Broadway (via Paris and London) as an outsize, dazzling musical. The climactic scene shows Parisians at the barricades, with hero Jean Valjean (Colm Wilkinson, forefront left) confronting his implacable pursuer, Inspector Javert (Terrence Mann).*

### Master of the Spectacular

With his melodic cats dancing around the globe and his roller-skating trains whizzing by in London and New York, British composer Andrew Lloyd Webber, 39, was undisputed king of the musical theater in 1987. Born into a musical family, Lloyd Webber met aspiring lyricist Tim Rice at Oxford—and dropped out of college to team up with him. The pair's first success came in 1968 with the offbeat musical entitled (in its original form) *Joseph and the Amazing Technicolor Dreamcoat.* But it was the highly controversial "rock opera" *Jesus Christ Superstar,* which opened on Broadway in 1971, that made their name. They also teamed up to make the musical *Evita,* which garnered seven Tony awards, and Lloyd Webber (without Rice) wrote the music for the extravaganza *Cats,* which won another seven Tonys in 1983 and was still going strong four years later. The spring of 1987 saw the New York opening of Lloyd Webber's $8 million spectacular *Starlight Express,* in which the cast performs on roller skates. His latest London smash, *Phantom of the Opera,* was scheduled to open on Broadway in January 1988.

*Andrew Lloyd Webber*

O'Neills' often stormy relationship. Clarice Taylor starred in *"Moms,"* Alice Childress's tribute to the legendary black comedienne, Jackie ("Moms") Mabley. Eric Overmeyer's *On the Verge* was a comically cosmic fantasy about the world and time travels of three intrepid American women.

*The Lucky Spot,* Beth Henley's latest, assembled an assortment of waifs, strays, misfits, and losers for a celebration of Christmas, 1934. Robert Harling's *Steel Magnolias* was a comedy about life and gossip in a New Orleans beauty salon. For mellow humanity, nothing touched *Driving Miss Daisy,* in which Alfred Uhry traced the role of human kindness and tact in the relationship between a formidable Atlanta widow (Dana Ivey) and her black chauffeur (Morgan Freeman).

Eric Bogosian's *Talk Radio* was a timely comedy about the foul-mouthed host (Bogosian) of a radio call-in show. Scenarist and short story writer David Shaber made his stage debut with *Bunker Reveries,* a satirical drama with post-Watergate overtones. Actors Dan

Gerrity, Gerrit Graham, Anthony M. La Paglia, and Adrian Paul played all 30 roles in John Godber's *Bouncers,* a frenetic, rawly explicit comedy about four unemployed working-class Britons. The Lincoln Center Theater Company presented *Sarafina!,* an all-South African musical by Mbongeni Ngema and Hugh Masekela, in which high school students create their own play to honor jailed black South African leader Nelson Mandela. Pamela Reed played the title role in the world premiere of Ezra Pound's version of *Elektra,* staged by Carey Perloff at the CSC Repertory.

The Roundabout Theater Company inaugurated the year's Off Broadway revivals with Robert Bolt's *A Man for All Seasons,* in which Philip Bosco portrayed Sir Thomas More. La Mama E.T.C. celebrated its 25th year of avant-garde experimentalism with *Fragments of a Greek Tragedy (Medea, The Trojan Women, Electra)* as conceived and staged by Andrei Serban with music by Elizabeth Swados. The year also saw the return of Jules Feiffer's *Little Murders,* Samuel Beckett's *Happy Days,* and

Bob Fosse, Broadway's master choreographer, died on September 23, just as the lights were going up on the opening of his revival of Sweet Charity in Washington, D.C. (above, a performance on the road). Fosse, who also won fame as a theater and film director, drew from vaudeville, jazz, and modern dance to create his energetic, sexually charged dances.

Jamaican playwright Trevor Rhone's *Two Can Play*.

**Regional Theater.** Although operating deficits continued, regional theater, helped by increased attendance and higher contributions, seemed to be adapting to the country's changing economic climate. A sampling of schedules and announcements showed a growing venturesomeness with respect to new plays. In one of several joint ventures, the Studio Arena Theater of Buffalo, N.Y., and the Actors Theater of Louisville, Ky., introduced Jon Klein's *T Bone 'N' Weasel* to their respective publics. Philadelphia's Walnut Street Theater gave its first world premiere, John McNicholas's *Dumas,* a drama about the French father-and-son novelists. The Yale Repertory Theater of New Haven premiered Lee Blessing's *A Walk in the Woods,* Athol Fugard's *A Place With the Pigs,* Dario Fo's *Almost by Chance a Woman: Eliz-*

abeth, Bernard Pomerance's *Melons,* and August Wilson's *The Piano Lesson.* Yale Rep shared with the Los Angeles Theater Center the premiere of Vladimir Gubaryev's *Sarcophagus,* based on the Chernobyl nuclear accident and its aftermath. The Los Angeles Center also premiered *The Unified Field,* a musical about Albert Einstein, and Darrah Cloud's *The Stick Wife,* a drama about race hatred.

The Long Wharf Theater of New Haven began its 23rd season with *The Downside,* author Richard Dresser's seriocomic view of executive suite struggles. British playwright Alan Ayckbourn visited Houston to stage the U.S. premiere of his *Henceforward . . .* at the Alley Theater.

South African actress Yvonne Bryceland, a longtime interpreter of Athol Fugard roles, appeared at the Spoleto Festival U.S.A. in Fugard's *The Road to Mecca.* Another Antigone, by A. R. Gurney, Jr., received its first performance at San Diego's Old Globe Theater, where Ayckbourn's *Intimate Exchanges* had its U.S. premiere in the same season. Adrian Hall's adaptation of Robert Penn Warren's novel *All the King's Men* opened at the Trinity Repertory Theater in Providence, R.I., and was later mounted by the Dallas Theater Center.

The theater community celebrated George Abbott's 100th birthday in June with affectionate tributes, and Abbott himself staged a revival of his 1926 hit *Broadway* at the Great Lakes Shakespeare Festival in Cleveland. One of the year's most ambitious events was the Los Angeles Festival, which presented the U.S. premiere of *The Mahabharata*, Peter Brook's nine-hour marathon based on classic Indian sources.

**Awards and Honors.** August Wilson's *Fences* garnered all the major play awards, including the Pulitzer Prize for drama, the New York Drama Critics' Circle Award for best American play, and the Tony for best play. *Fences* also won Tonys for James Earl Jones, Mary Alice, and director Lloyd Richards. The Critics' Circle chose *Les Liaisons Dangereuses* as best foreign play and *Les Misérables* as best musical. *Les Misérables* also won Tony awards for its book,

score, direction, scenery, and lighting and for performers Frances Rufelle and Michael Maguire. John Napier received Tonys for his *Misérables* sets and his *Starlight Express* costumes. Robert Lindsay and Maryann Plunkett, both of *Me and My Girl*, were honored as best actor and actress in a musical, and Linda Lavin and John Randolph won Tonys for their performances in *Broadway Bound*. The Tony ceremony included a tribute to the late Robert Preston, who received the Lawrence Langner Award.

**Deaths.** Geraldine Page, one of the major actresses of her generation, died on June 13 at 62. Michael Bennett, best known for his long-running hit *A Chorus Line*, died July 2 at age 44. Director/choreographer Bob Fosse died September 23 at 60. Among other leading theatrical figures who died were librettist-lyricist Michael Stewart, 63; Charles Ludlam, 56, guiding spirit of the Ridiculous Theatrical Company; and rotund character actor James Coco, 56. Noted Welsh actor and playwright Emlyn Williams, perhaps best remembered for his play *The Corn Is Green*, died at 81.

**Canadian Theater.** In Toronto, David Mirvish's ambitions for his Royal Alexandra Theater in-

**A Larger-Than-Life Actor**

James Earl Jones says he entered acting with no ambition except to do the best he could. His riveting performance in August Wilson's play *Fences*, which won him a Tony award, proved that Jones's best is more than enough. In this drama, about generational conflict in a black family, he portrays a character of almost mythic proportions, an embittered former baseball player in the Negro leagues who has become a garbageman in the industrial north. Born in rural Mississippi and raised in Michigan, Jones himself was the first member of his family to earn a college degree. He later studied acting at the American Theater Wing and slowly built a career on the New York stage. Fame—and his first Tony—came in 1968 when he starred on Broadway in *The Great White Hope*. Besides many fine Broadway roles, Jones played the voice of Darth Vader in films and was seen on TV by over 100 million Americans as Alex Haley in *Roots: The New Generation*.

*James Earl Jones*

cluded coproductions with subsidized theaters (*I'm Not Rappaport*) and with fledgling local producers (Brian MacDonald's *H.M.S. Pinafore*). The show *B-Movie*, a satire of filmmaking, drew large crowds in Edmonton and Toronto, but its commercial possibilities were not exploited.

It was a weak year for established playwrights. Exceptions included Michel Tremblay's *Le Vrai Monde?* for Le Theatre Français, which looked at how a writer uses his life in his work, and Margaret Hollingsworth's *War Babies,* for the Nightwood Theatre, an elegant examination of the violence in intimate relationships. Hollingsworth recently moved to Toronto from Vancouver—an example of the continuing drift of the country's best theater talent to Canada's acknowledged theater capital.

Minority groups gained a stronger voice in Canadian theater. Tomson Highway, a highly talented native writer, won a Dora award for *The Rez Sisters,* a stunning work about women on a native reservation. The Japanese-Canadian voice continued to develop with a strong Toronto production of the American play *Song of a Nisei Fisherman.*

R.C. & J.B. (Canadian Theater)

**TOGO.** *See* STATISTICS OF THE WORLD.

**TONGA.** *See* STATISTICS OF THE WORLD.

**TRANSPORTATION.** Travel delays and safety were leading issues in transportation in 1987. Trucking companies and railroads appeared to be performing sluggishly.

## AVIATION

The U.S. air transportation system was plagued by a rising chorus of consumer criticism and by airline disasters and near-disasters.

**Travel Problems.** The number of U.S. airline passengers for 1987 was estimated at a record 450 million, with 650 million annually expected by 1997. But the increase in travelers seemed to be overwhelming the system. By midsummer the stress exerted on airport facilities and on movement within the national air space seemed to have reached crisis proportions. In June, then U.S. Transportation Secretary Elizabeth Hanford Dole warned the airlines to improve services or face stricter scrutiny by her department and possible fines. In September she announced a rule requiring the 14 largest U.S. airlines to submit their on-time performance records, along with statistics on lost, delayed, or damaged baggage, which would be made available to the public at travel agencies and airline ticket offices. The department subsequently issued its first comprehensive monthly ranking of major airlines' performance.

Meanwhile, in another controversial area, Congress enacted legislation late in the year to ban smoking in all domestic flights of two hours or less—about 80 percent of all domestic flights.

**Safety Concerns.** According to U.S. government data, in the first nine months of 1987 there were over 850 reported cases of planes coming within 500 feet of one another. In August the Federal Aviation Administration proposed legislation requiring all large airliners to be equipped within four years with an anticollision device warning pilots of an approaching aircraft. Concern continued for the situation of the air traffic controllers, whose burden was growing heavier because of increased airline operations.

Delta Air Lines suffered an embarrassing series of mishaps during June and July. In one instance, a Boeing 767 taking off from Los Angeles dropped to within a few hundred feet of the Pacific when the pilot inadvertently shut down the plane's two engines. One crew landed on the wrong runway in Boston, and another, scheduled to land at Lexington, Ky., landed 30 miles away in Frankfort instead. A subsequent FAA safety report found Delta's policies on crew training and coordination insufficiently clear and called for improvements.

**Major Crashes.** On August 16 a Northwest Airlines twin-engine MD-80 jetliner crashed and burned just after takeoff from Detroit Metropolitan Airport, killing all but 1 of the 155 people on board, as well as 2 people on the ground. The lone survivor from the plane was a four-year-old girl. The crash was the second deadliest in U.S. history. A key factor in the disaster, according to preliminary findings, was that the aircraft's wing flaps, which produce additional lift when extended, were apparently not in the proper position for takeoff. On November 15 a Continental Airlines DC-9

*A well-publicized string of near collisions in midair raised new questions about the U.S. air traffic control system.*

taking off in a heavy snowstorm from Denver's Stapleton International Airport skidded out of control, flipped over on the runway, and broke up, leaving 28 dead. A buildup of snow and ice on the wings may have been a major factor in the crash. On December 7 a commuter plane crashed in California killing 43 people; the accident was believed to have been caused by a former airline employee who boarded the plane with a pistol. The Federal Aviation Administration subsequently ordered that all airport and airline employees, including flight crews, undergo security screening before boarding planes.

### RAILROADS

For the 12 months ending June 30, 1987, the Interstate Commerce Commission (ICC) reported that operating revenues of the major U.S. railroads fell to $26 billion, from $26.8 billion for the same period during 1986. However, net income rose a slim 3 percent (after allowing for certain accounting changes).

**Fatal Crash.** A caravan of three Conrail freight locomotives ran through slow and stop signals and collided with a northbound Washington-to-Boston Amtrak passenger train on January 4, killing 16 passengers and injuring 175. The accident, which occurred outside of Chase, Md., was the worst in Amtrak's history. Safety devices had been disabled in the Conrail locomotive driving the caravan, which was manned by an engineer and brakeman. Tests after the accident found traces of illicit drugs in both men's blood, but it was unclear whether they were under the influence of drugs at the time of the crash. In May the Conrail engineer was indicted on 16 counts of manslaughter.

**Tracking Business.** Conrail was transferred to the private sector from U.S. government ownership, as a result of legislation passed by Congress in 1986. The 85 percent of Conrail's stock owned by the government was sold to the public, in one of the largest such offerings in U.S. history.

# TRANSPORTATION

The ICC refused to review its 1986 decision rejecting the proposed merger of the Atchison, Topeka, and Santa Fe Railway Company and the Southern Pacific Transportation Company—a merger that would have created a 25,000-mile system in the Southwest and Midwest. As a result, Santa Fe Southern Pacific Corporation (SFSP), which owned both railroads, was required to divest itself of Southern Pacific. SFSP announced in December the sale of Southern Pacific to Rio Grande Industries for $1.8 billion. In September the ICC approved the Union Pacific Corporation's $1.2 billion purchase of the Richmond, Va., based Overnite Transportation Company, the largest nonunion motor carrier in the United States. Union Pacific intended to combine some operations of its railroad unit with Overnite's, offering a new combination rail-truck service.

**Victory for Unions.** In a major court victory for railroad unions, the U.S. Supreme Court ruled in April that unions on strike against one railroad cannot be enjoined by federal courts from picketing connecting carriers. The ruling could be an important factor in nationwide negotiations on labor contracts in 1988.

**Magnetic Levitation Train.** A major commercial application of magnetic levitation for railroad passenger service was announced in October by HSST (High-Speed Surface Transport) Corporation, a Japanese company that said it would build a 4.4-mile magnetic-levitation train system in Las Vegas by 1989 for about $40 billion. In this system, electric magnets lift a wheelless passenger car a fraction of an inch above a single rail. Linear induction motors provide propulsion, producing a smooth ride, little noise, and no pollution.

## SHIPPING

United States Lines filed for protection from its creditors under chapter 11 of the federal bankruptcy code in late 1986, after losing $237 million in the first nine months of the year. The line temporarily continued some services but ceased all operations by mid-1987. The ICC in February approved the $800 million purchase by CSX Corporation of Sea-Land Corporation, owner of Sea-Land Service, the largest U.S. shipping company. CSX owns a major railroad operating in the East, Midwest, and South. The approval marked the first railroad purchase of a major steamship line in U.S. history.

## MOTOR TRANSPORT

ICC statistics for the 12 months ending June 30, 1987, indicated that operating revenues for the 100 largest trucking companies rose to $18.4 billion, about 4 percent higher than for the same period in 1986. However, profits were expected to be low.

Torn apart by the force of a collision with three Conrail locomotives, an Amtrak coach straddles the tracks outside of Chase, Md. The January accident left 16 people dead and 175 injured.

## Identified Flying Object

Pilots on northern-based airlines are understandably alert to the danger of hitting a moose on the runway or a seagull on takeoff. But a midair collision with a fish? Not possible, but it was the only explanation for the thud heard by the crew of an Alaska Airlines jetliner above the Juneau airport on March 30. When the plane was inspected at the next stop in Yakutat, there were decidedly fishy scales on a greasy spot above the cockpit. An airline spokesman claimed that a bald eagle had been seen soaring in the vicinity with a fish in its talons, and the law of the jungle had apparently prevailed. The bird of prey dropped its dinner when a bigger bird appeared.

**Truck Safety.** The Department of Transportation on July 1 implemented rules that prohibited truck drivers from holding driver's licenses from more than one state. (With numerous licenses, drivers could spread out the recording of traffic violations, thus avoiding penalties for multiple violations on a single license.) The trucking industry asked the federal government to also end the so-called commercial-zone safety exemption. Certain trucks, such as construction and waste-removal vehicles, are exempt from federal safety requirements when they operate solely in ICC-defined metropolitan commercial zones. The industry, reacting to several fatal accidents involving such trucks, wanted all commercial vehicles to be brought under federal safety rules.

**Bus Industry.** A major development in the bus industry was the $80 million purchase by Greyhound Lines of the financially troubled Trailways Corporation, leaving the United States with only a single nationwide bus company. Earlier in the year, Greyhound Lines itself was purchased for $350 million from the Greyhound Corporation by a group of investors. In July the ICC issued Greyhound a temporary permit to operate its lines and the Trailways lines as one company, pending a final decision.

## DEPARTMENT OF TRANSPORTATION

Secretary of Transportation Elizabeth Hanford Dole resigned effective October 1 to assist in the presidential campaign of her husband, Senator Robert Dole (R, Kan.). President Ronald Reagan nominated James Burnley IV, deputy transportation secretary, to succeed her in the top post. During the year, the department began random drug testing of those employees involved in safety-related jobs.

R.E.B. (Aviation) & R.J.K.

**TRINIDAD AND TOBAGO.** See STATISTICS OF THE WORLD.

**TUNISIA.** The major news of 1987 was the ouster from power of President-for-Life Habib Bourguiba. On November 7 newly appointed Prime Minister Zine al-Abdine Ben Ali took over the government, stating that Bourguiba, 84, had become too ill and senile to handle affairs of state. Bourguiba had governed Tunisia since the country gained its independence from France in 1956. He and four of his ministers were placed under house arrest, but there were no immediate plans to bring criminal charges against them.

In seizing power, Ben Ali had the backing of many leaders of the ruling Destour Socialist Party, as well as many government officials and the military chief of staff. He assumed the title of president and appointed Hebi Baccouche as prime minister. The new leadership promised to bring greater openness and democracy to Tunisia. Major foreign powers and other Arab countries immediately recognized the new regime.

Before the coup, the principal adversary of the government was the Islamic Tendency Movement (ITM), an Islamic fundamentalist organization led by Rachid Ghannouchi. Violent opposition—highlighted by arrests of ITM militants and clashes between demonstrators and riot police—culminated in bombings of four tourist hotels in Monastir and Sousse in August. Although ITM officials denied involvement, nearly all of the 90 Islamic militants brought to trial were ITM members. Ghannouchi was sentenced to a life of hard labor, and seven others were condemned to death; most defendants received sentences of from 2 to 20 years. Fourteen were acquitted.

Amid severe economic difficulties, a new five-year (1987–1991) plan for the economy was initiated. Economic problems were exacerbated by lagging tourism, low oil-export earnings, and a winter drought.

*See* STATISTICS OF THE WORLD. K.J.B.

**TURKEY.** In 1987 elections, Prime Minister Turgut Özal was returned to power and his Motherland Party increased its majority in the newly expanded Parliament.

In a referendum on September 6, voters had narrowly approved amending the Turkish constitution to lift the ban on political participation for over 100 politicians who had held office before the 1980 military coup. The vote restored political rights to two ex-premiers, rightist Suleyman Demirel and leftist Bülent Ecevit. On the same day, Premier Ozal called the election for November 1, a year ahead of schedule. Political analysts believed Özal had set an early election date to deny Demirel and Ecevit enough time to organize an effective campaign. But because new candidate selection procedures had alienated many Motherland Party deputies by excluding them from running for election, the premier was forced to call a special session of Parliament to settle the election date issue. The assembly approved legislation scheduling the election for November 29 and expanding the membership from 400 to 450 seats.

Özal's party ended up with 292 seats in Parliament—well over 50 percent—with only about 36 percent of the vote. The result reflected changes in the election laws that favored the larger parties at the expense of the smaller ones.

In response to escalating attacks by Kurdish separatists, the government created a special unit to combat terrorism in the southeast. It also acknowledged the need to improve economic conditions for Kurds in that area. In March, Turkish warplanes raided nine Kurdish separatist bases in Iraq.

A six-year trial of Alparslan Türkes, a deputy premier in rightist coalition governments prior to the 1980 military takeover, and 380 members of his defunct right-wing Nationalist Action Party concluded in April; of the defendants, who were accused of political violence, 5 were sentenced to death and 230 drew prison terms of varying length. (Türkes received an 11-year sentence.) A five-year trial of 43 leftist intellectuals ended in April with 12 convictions and 31 acquittals.

The Turkish-Greek dispute over oil drilling rights on the Aegean continental shelf erupted again, bringing the two countries close to military confrontation (see GREECE).

In March the United States and Turkey re-

Turkish President Kenan Evren (right), who led a 1980 military coup, votes in the September referendum on the political future of over 100 banned politicians.

newed a defense and economic cooperation agreement, allowing the United States to continue operating its 27 air, naval, and intelligence facilities in Turkey until 1990 in exchange for a Reagan administration promise to press for increased aid. However, the Özal government postponed ratification because of U.S. congressional actions unfavorable to Turkey. (U.S. use of the facilities continued.)

The Özal government continued moving toward a free-market economy and applied for membership in the European Community.

See STATISTICS OF THE WORLD. P.J.M.

**TUVALU.** See STATISTICS OF THE WORLD.

# U

**UGANDA.** Uganda, under the leadership of President Yoweri Museveni, experienced internal unrest, tensions with Kenya, and economic problems.

Although Museveni's National Resistance Army had control over central and southern Uganda, armed resistance in the north persisted. In January remnants of former President Milton Obote's Uganda National Liberation Army and of the Uganda People's Democratic Movement struggled unsuccessfully against government troops. In June, Ugandan troops killed more than 200 rebels of the Holy Spirit Movement, led by Alice Lakwena, whose followers believe she has magical powers. Later in June the government offered a three-month amnesty to rebels in the north, and nearly 8,000 former soldiers surrendered before it expired; the government then vowed to crush all remaining resistance.

Differences between Museveni and Kenyan President Daniel arap Moi continued to arise. When the Ugandan government announced that it would use the less expensive railway instead of trucks to move its imports and exports to and from the Kenyan port of Mombasa, the Kenyan government interpreted the decision as a threat to its trucking industry. In May, Kenya closed the border with Uganda and instituted strict immigration controls. Uganda later announced it was stationing troops along the border to prevent any guerrilla incursions from Kenya.

With inflation running at around 200 percent and unemployment at unmeasurable levels, Uganda had difficulty attracting private investment but was able to win aid from foreign governments and international organizations. In April, for example, a group of Afro-Arab aid organizations pledged nearly $500 million in assistance. The following month, Uganda devalued its currency by over 75 percent.

Uganda continued to have one of the highest incidence rates of AIDS on the African continent. The government, with international assistance, established a five-year program aimed at fighting the epidemic.

See STATISTICS OF THE WORLD. M.E.D.

**UNION OF SOVIET SOCIALIST REPUBLICS.** In 1987, Soviet Communist Party leader Mikhail Gorbachev (see biography in PEOPLE IN THE NEWS) actively pursued his two related goals of glasnost, or "openness," and perestroika, a radical restructuring of the Soviet economy. The Soviet Union reached an agreement with the United States on a treaty to eliminate their intermediate-range nuclear weapons; it was signed at a December summit meeting in Washington between Gorbachev and President Ronald Reagan.

**The New Openness.** The effects of glasnost were perhaps most obvious in the intensive reexamination of the period of Joseph Stalin's rule (1924–1953). The most dramatic development came in a speech by Gorbachev in November marking the 70th anniversary of the Bolshevik Revolution. Gorbachev said Stalin had been guilty of "enormous and unforgivable crimes"; he also praised two former Soviet leaders who had been in official disfavor: Nikita Khrushchev, the country's leader from 1953 to 1964, and Nikolai Bukharin, an associate

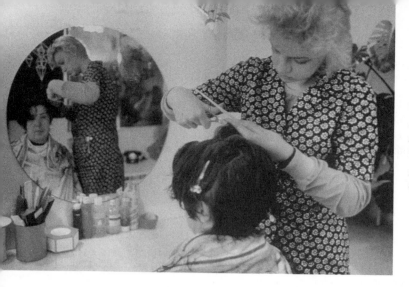

A law enacted in May allowed Soviet individuals and families to operate small service businesses. By July, 137,000 such enterprises had been registered, from carpentry and plumbing businesses to taxi services to the "Number 59" hairdressing salon in Tallinn, Estonia, shown here.

of Lenin who was executed by Stalin in 1938.

The revised view of Stalin could also be seen in the treatment of literary works dealing with the Stalin era. Anatoly Rybakov's anti-Stalin novel *Children of the Arbat,* written in the 1960's, was published serially beginning in April, and it caused a sensation. Set in the 1930's, the book, in which Stalin himself was a major character, described the atmosphere in Moscow at the start of the great purges. Judging by readers' letters, public reaction was mixed. In the theater, Mikhail Shatrov's political drama *The Dictatorship of Conscience,* which criticized the terror of Stalin's regime and raised other questions unusual and disturbing to a Soviet audience, played to packed houses in Moscow.

*Glasnost* led to the publication of major literary works that had long been suppressed, such as the poem "Requiem" by Anna Akhmatova. The government announced that Boris Pasternak's novel *Doctor Zhivago* would be published for the first time in the Soviet Union in 1988, and a Soviet magazine announced plans to publish works of Soviet-born poet Joseph Brodsky, who won the 1987 Nobel Prize for literature.

**Increased Tolerance for Dissent.** The year saw increased tolerance of political dissent, and some dissidents who had been exiled from Moscow were permitted to return. Nuclear physicist Andrei Sakharov, the most famous of the dissidents, who had been allowed to return to Moscow in late 1986 after seven years of

exile in the city of Gorky, continued to criticize certain government policies, although he was himself criticized by some dissidents for supporting Gorbachev's initiatives. In February more than 140 political prisoners were pardoned and released. Some of the returnees acknowledged that they had signed a pledge not to resume their "anti-Soviet" activities. A new underground journal, with the title *Glasnost,* appeared in June under the general editorship of Sergei Grigoryants, one of the dissidents released in February. For a while the government appeared to tolerate this new challenge to the party line. In October, however, police confiscated copies of one issue and several times detained editors, including Grigoryants.

**Glasnost and Domestic Politics.** Gorbachev's policies won enthusiastic support from most of the Soviet intellectual and scientific community but ran into some opposition from the political leadership. Politburo member Yegor Ligachev, generally regarded as the Kremlin's number two man, criticized *glasnost* (although not Gorbachev) on several occasions. KGB chief Viktor Chebrikov also criticized *glasnost* indirectly.

Nonetheless, Gorbachev continued to consolidate his position by bringing in supporters. These included Viktor Nikonov, Nikolai Slyunkov, and Aleksandr Yakovlev, promoted to full (voting) membership in the Politburo in June. Gorbachev also succeeded in removing some older Politburo members associated with former party chief Leonid Brezhnev. Dinmukhamed Kunayev, who had been dismissed in late 1986 as party head in the Soviet republic of Kazakhstan, lost his Politburo membership in January 1987. At a Central Committee meeting in October, Geidar Aliyev, another senior Politburo member who was said to have voiced opposition to Gorbachev's policies, was removed.

At the same meeting, Moscow party chief Boris Yeltsin, known as a key Gorbachev supporter, made an unexpected speech criticizing the Soviet leader for not pressing reforms fast enough and for developing a cult of personality. A short time later, Yeltsin was removed from office. The Yeltsin affair created a considerable stir both in the Soviet Union and abroad, and its implications for Gorbachev's reform program were not immediately clear.

**Emigration.** Jewish emigration from the Soviet Union increased substantially from the 1986 total of 914. Protests in Moscow in February for the release of Iosif Begun, an imprisoned leader of the Jewish emigration movement, may have helped win his release; Begun received an exit visa in September. Other notable emigrés included pianist Vladimir Feltsman and his family, Vladimir Slepak and his wife, and Ida Nudel.

*Mathias Rust, a West German teen, penetrated Soviet air defenses to land his single-engine plane in Moscow's Red Square in May. The incident was an acute embarrassment for the Soviets; for Rust, who claimed he was trying to promote peace, it brought a sentence of four years in a labor camp.*

*After signing the nuclear arms reduction treaty with President Ronald Reagan, Soviet General Secretary Mikhail Gorbachev holds a press conference at the Soviet embassy for reporters covering the summit in Washington, D.C.*

**Ethnic Nationalism Revived.** Encouraged by *glasnost,* several ethnic nationalist groups aired their grievances through demonstrations. The Russian nationalist organization Pamyat, which had originally dedicated itself to preserving historical monuments, became an openly political movement in 1987 and appeared to have been taken over by anti-Semites. In the spring it criticized the government's plan to build a World War II monument on Poklonnaya Hill in Moscow. Pamyat also demanded official recognition for itself. The government arranged a well-publicized meeting between Pamyat leaders and then-Moscow party chief Yeltsin. The designs for a victory monument were rejected, but Pamyat did not achieve its goal of legal recognition.

In July a group of Crimean Tatars staged a small demonstration in Moscow demanding to be allowed to return to their traditional homeland on the Crimean Peninsula. The government took no harsh reprisals, and the Tatar leaders were allowed to meet with chief of state Andrei Gromyko. In August, thousands of people demonstrated in the Baltic republics, protesting the 1939 Hitler-Stalin pact that opened the way for the Soviet occupation and annexation of Lithuania, Latvia, and Estonia.

**West German Lands in Red Square.** In May, Mathias Rust, a West German teenager, flew a single-engine plane from Finland to Moscow and made a spectacular landing in Red Square. He was arrested and, in September, sentenced to a four-year term in a labor camp. The Soviet military's decision not to intercept or shoot down Rust provided Gorbachev with an unexpected opportunity to replace Defense Minister Sergei Sokolov with Dmitri Yazov, who was expected to be more supportive of Gorbachev's policies.

**Economic Reform.** Gorbachev left no doubt that his primary goal was to restructure the Soviet economy to make it more productive, more adaptable to high technology, and more able to compete with the West. In a remarkably frank article appearing in the literary journal *Novy Mir* (New World) in June, economist Nikolai Shmelyov stated that the economy was ontrolled by bureaucrats who were stifling efforts at reform. Shmelyov called for introducing elements of a free-market economy into the Soviet Union, including allowing Soviet firms to sell securities to individuals and permitting some measure of unemployment. (The Soviet Union prides itself on having eliminated unemployment.) Gorbachev, while conceding that Shmelyov's diagnosis was basically sound, reacted to public concern by reasserting that unemployment was not acceptable.

In June the Central Committee approved a broad range of reform proposals aimed at making state-owned enterprises competitive and reducing central control over management, prices, and distribution. Later, the Supreme Soviet (Parliament) enacted a law allowing state-owned factories and farms to retain some of their profits.

**Social Policy.** *Glasnost* made it possible for the press to cover previously ignored social problems such as drug abuse, prostitution, alcoholism, and juvenile delinquency. In June a decree was published that made prostitution—which, according to previous official claims, had disappeared from the Soviet Union—an administrative offense subject to a fine, though not a crime.

**Foreign Policy.** The Soviet government sought the restoration of détente with the United States, in part to further economic reform by opening up opportunities for foreign trade. The major breakthrough in U.S.-Soviet relations was the successful negotiation of an arms control treaty that would dismantle all of the two countries' medium-range and shorter-range nuclear missiles over a five-year period. In February, Gorbachev indicated that Moscow was willing to consider these missiles independently of the U.S. Strategic Defense Initiative (SDI), aimed at building a space shield against nuclear missiles. Earlier, Moscow had insisted on keeping the United States from moving ahead with SDI, so as to be spared from diverting scarce resources to match the U.S. effort.

In September, Foreign Minister Eduard Shevardnadze visited Washington and reached an agreement in principle with Secretary of State George Shultz on the missile treaty. The two sides also agreed to work toward reducing strategic, or long-range, nuclear arms by 50

percent and to begin negotiations on nuclear testing before the end of the year. After conflicting signals from Moscow in the next few weeks, it was announced in October that Gorbachev would sign the treaty at a summit meeting with President Ronald Reagan in Washington beginning December 7. At the end of the three-day summit, he and Reagan reported that they had made significant progress toward a strategic arms treaty, and Reagan accepted an invitation to Moscow in 1988.

In a shift in policy toward the United Nations, Gorbachev gave his approval in September to multinational peacekeeping forces organized under UN auspices. Following his statement, the Soviet Union made a surprise announcement that it would pay the large sum of money it owed to the UN, including support for peacekeeping forces, which it had withheld.

In Afghanistan, Moscow appeared to be looking for a solution to the eight-year conflict that would allow it to withdraw its troops without a shattering blow to its prestige. But resistance leaders in Afghanistan refused to accept a settlement that would leave the pro-Soviet government in control.

**Chernobyl Trial.** Several former officials of the Chernobyl nuclear power plant, where the worst accident in the history of nuclear power occurred in April 1986, were tried in July. Three senior officials, including Chernobyl's former director, were found guilty of grossly violating safety regulations and were sentenced to ten years each in labor camps; three others received lesser sentences.

*See* STATISTICS OF THE WORLD.          D.H.

**UNITED ARAB EMIRATES.** *See* STATISTICS OF THE WORLD.

**UNITED NATIONS.** The long decline in the prestige of the United Nations showed signs of abating in 1987. In his annual report, Secretary-General Javier Pérez de Cuéllar noted occasions of "greater solidarity in addressing global problems." In the Security Council a unanimous agreement was reached to seek an end to the seven-year Iran-Iraq war. Elsewhere, the Soviet Union adopted more cooperative policies on a range of UN issues.

**Financing and Restructuring.** The United Nations began the year without financial reserves and with a balance of only $10 million, enough for less than a week of operations. However, in December 1986, the General Assembly had adopted a resolution to meet the emergency; among many changes, a radically revised budget-making process was approved, giving major financial contributors greater influence. The new procedure required members of a Committee for Program and Coordination to reach consensus on budget priorities and a spending ceiling before sending a budget to the General Assembly for approval.

The secretary-general's budget proposals for 1988, as submitted to the 21-member committee, were $30 million below the 1987 budget. In June the committee accepted most of his recommendations but broke up in disagreement over the budget ceiling and over a contingency fund for meeting unexpected costs. As a result, the General Assembly was again left to decide the budget itself.

The shortfall in paid assessments remained a major problem. By fall $997 million was still due, more than $400 million of which was owed by the United States. Good news came in October when the Soviet Union paid its debt for regular contributions and announced that it would pay its outstanding debt of $197 million since 1975 for peacekeeping operations. By year's end the United States had also paid $100 million, to help the UN avoid insolvency.

**Peace and Security Issues.** *Middle East.* Iran continued to resist the Security Council's efforts to obtain a cease-fire in the Iran-Iraq war and withdrawal of forces, because of the Council's refusal to condemn Iraq as the initial aggressor (which Iraq denies). In April a UN team of medical specialists visiting Iran and Iraq found that chemical weapons had been used by Iraq against military and civilian targets in Iran. Some Iraqi forces were also injured in April by chemical weapons, though the team could not determine a source for the chemicals.

Tensions in the Persian Gulf escalated in May after a U.S. warship was attacked by Iraqi missiles, and again in July when the United States began reflagging and escorting Kuwaiti oil tankers. Discussions among the five permanent members of the Security Council on ways to end the conflict resulted on July 20 in a unanimously approved resolution demanding

an immediate cease-fire and withdrawal of forces to internationally recognized borders. Iraq accepted the resolution conditioned on Iran's doing the same, and its attacks on Iranian oil installations and shipping temporarily ceased. Iran, however, delayed a definite response while protesting the U.S. naval buildup in the Gulf. The "tanker war"—attacks on international shipping in the Gulf—resumed in late August, but the six-week pause found the United States no longer alone in attempting to keep sea lanes open. The British, French, Belgian, Dutch, and Italians were escorting commercial vessels or sharing minesweeping duties.

With Security Council approval, the secretary-general visited Tehran and Baghdad in September for discussion on the cease-fire resolution. He requested an informal cease-fire while responsibility for starting the war was determined. Iraq, however, insisted on an immediate and unconditional cease-fire, a position supported by President Ronald Reagan in his address to the General Assembly on September 21. The U.S. attack on an Iranian vessel allegedly laying mines in the Gulf, on the day of Reagan's speech, was denounced by Iranian President Ali Khamenei in the Assembly the next day. Despite Khamenei's seeming rejection of the peace effort, permanent members of the Council, except the United States and Britain, insisted on further negotiations on the secretary-general's proposals before considering an arms embargo against Iran. Late in the year, after these new efforts reached an impasse, the Council members appeared ready to impose an embargo.

The possibility of the UN's convening an international peace conference on the Middle East came up again. In May the secretary-general reported that none of the five permanent Security Council members were opposed in principle to participation; there were, however, deep differences over procedures. Elsewhere in the Mideast, mandates of the two peacekeeping forces, Undof (UN Disengagement Observer Force) in the Golan Heights and Unifil (UN Interim Force in Lebanon), were renewed. In December a UN Security Council resolution "strongly deplored" Israeli use of force in controlling widespread disturbances in the occupied West Bank and the Gaza Strip, during which more than 20 Palestinians were killed. The vote was 14-0; the United States abstained, having itself publicly criticized Israel for "harsh security measures."

*Southern Africa.* UN efforts to implement the plan approved by a 1978 Security Council resolution calling for the independence of South West Africa (Namibia) were stalled, as South Africa and the United States continued to insist that independence be conditional on the prior withdrawal of all Cuban troops from Angola. On April 9, a Security Council draft resolution branding South African administration of Namibia as a breach of international peace and security and demanding compre-

hensive mandatory trade and other sanctions against South Africa was vetoed by the United States and the United Kingdom. In late August, however, Angolan President José Eduardo dos Santos announced economic and diplomatic initiatives, including a new plan for Cuban withdrawal, that opened the way to new talks on Namibia with the United States. Later in the year, the General Assembly passed a package of resolutions again calling for sanctions against South Africa to pressure it to end apartheid.

*Cyprus.* The impasse in negotiations between Greek and Turkish Cypriots continued despite the efforts of a mission sent to the island by the secretary-general in February. The Security

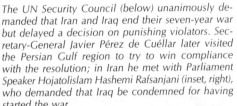

*The UN Security Council (below) unanimously demanded that Iran and Iraq end their seven-year war but delayed a decision on punishing violators. Secretary-General Javier Pérez de Cuéllar later visited the Persian Gulf region to try to win compliance with the resolution; in Iran he met with Parliament Speaker Hojatolislam Hashemi Rafsanjani (inset, right), who demanded that Iraq be condemned for having started the war.*

Council acted in June and again in December to renew the mandate of the UN peacekeeping force (Unficyp) on the island.

*Environment and Development.* Negotiations on protection of the earth's ozone layer, conducted under the auspices of the UN Environment Program, were concluded in Montréal on September 16. Over 40 countries agreed to limit and eventually halve the use of industrial chemicals such as chlorofluorocarbons that damage the ozone layer.

The UN Conference on Trade and Development (Unctad) met in Geneva from July 9 to August 3. Seeking to avoid the confrontational character of the sixth Unctad conference in 1983, the secretariat prepared an agenda less focused than in the past on redistributing resources from rich countries to poor ones. The conference's theme was the revitalizing of global development, economic growth, and international trade through multilateral cooperation. At the conference the Soviet Union announced it would sign a pending agreement establishing an international fund to be used to help stabilize commodity prices.

A UN-sponsored 21-member World Commission on Environment and Development ended its mission in April with the publication of its report. The commission concluded that while economic growth is necessary to development, it is equally essential that growth not deplete natural resources. The report called for a radical change in attitudes toward the use of natural resources.

The first International Conference on the Relationship Between Disarmament and Development, postponed since 1984, met in New York City from August 24 to September 11. The United States refused to participate because it viewed the two topics as distinct, not interrelated. The members focused on the relationship between what each spends on armaments and on development, the effect of military expenditures on the world economy, and ways in which resources saved through disarmament measures might be made available to assist with Third World development. The Soviet Union proposed an international fund to channel money saved by disarmament to the less developed nations, but the motion was defeated.

**Nuclear Power.** The first UN Conference for the Promotion of International Cooperation in the Peaceful Uses of Nuclear Energy met in Geneva from March 23 to April 10. Disagreement over the principles that should govern international cooperation prevented the adoption of a final document.

The Board of Governors of the International Atomic Energy Agency, meeting in June, voted to recommend that South Africa be suspended from membership in the IAEA because of its failure to reach agreement with the agency on safeguards at its nuclear facilities. However, Western countries opposed the move. In September, South African President Pieter W. Botha indicated a willingness to begin negotiations leading to a possible signing of the 1968 Nuclear Non-Proliferation Treaty and to allowing the IAEA to inspect its nuclear facilities. At the meeting it was decided to defer action on suspending South Africa.

**Drug Abuse.** An International Conference on Drug Abuse and Illicit Trafficking met in Vienna from June 17 to 26. It was attended by 138 countries and 200 non-governmental organizations, with a mandate to generate universal action to combat the drug problem at the national, regional, and international levels. The conference adopted by consensus a handbook that lists possible actions to resolve problems related to drug demand, supply, trafficking, treatment, and rehabilitation. For the first time in the 16 years since the UN Fund for Drug Abuse Control was established, the Soviet Union and Eastern bloc nations offered cooperation.

**Elections.** In November, Spain's former education minister, Federico Mayor Zaragoza, was confirmed as the new director general of Unesco (the United Nations Educational, Scientific, and Cultural Organization) by a vote of that body's 158-member General Conference. The previous director general, Amadou-Mahtar M'Bow of Senegal, had served two terms that saw conflict over the agency's alleged waste, poor management, and anti-Western bias and the resulting withdrawal from Unesco of the United States, the United Kingdom, and Singapore. Also in November, the UN Food and Agriculture Organization reelected Edouard Sauma of Lebanon to a third term as director general.                                         I.C.B.

# United States of America

During 1987, President Ronald Reagan had to contend with an assertive Democratic-controlled Congress and with the devastating fallout from the Iran/contra affair. Late in the year, he signed a historic arms accord with the Soviet Union, while meeting with Soviet leader Mikhail Gorbachev in Washington, D.C.

The U.S. economy was shaken by a record-setting stock market crash, partly brought on by massive U.S. trade deficits (see ECONOMY AND BUSINESS). As the president and Congress grappled over such domestic issues as the fiscal 1988 budget and the choice of a new nominee to the Supreme Court, turmoil in the Persian Gulf and in Central America were among the dominant foreign policy concerns. Meanwhile, the nationally televised Iran/contra hearings claimed a major part of public attention, as did the early stages of the contest among Democrats and Republicans for their party's presidential nomination in 1988.

## THE PRESIDENCY

President Ronald Reagan had his most turbulent year in the White House in 1987, seeing his credibility and political standing tumble as a result of the Iran/contra affair and a series of other setbacks. Late in the year, however, Reagan's popularity received a boost when he and Soviet leader Mikhail Gorbachev signed a historic treaty to eliminate all U.S. and Soviet intermediate-range nuclear missiles. The signing came at the two leaders' third summit meeting, held in early December in Washington, D.C.

As he entered the next-to-last year of his presidency, Reagan witnessed an increasing turnover in his cabinet and senior staff. He also for the first time faced a Congress with both houses controlled by Democrats. In domestic policy, he battled with Congress over the federal budget and his controversial nominees to the Supreme Court; in foreign affairs, clashes came over the increased U.S. naval presence in the Persian Gulf, which led to hostilities with Iranian forces, and over aid to the Nicaraguan contra rebels (see MILITARY AND NAVAL AFFAIRS and UNITED STATES: Congress and Foreign Affairs).

**Iran/Contra Scandal.** Reagan's presidency had been clouded by the Iran/contra scandal since it was first revealed in November 1986 that the administration had sold arms to Iran while negotiating with Iranian officials to free Americans held hostage by pro-Iranian Shiite Muslims in Lebanon, and that some profits from the sales had been delivered to the contra rebels fighting Nicaragua's leftist Sandinista regime. On February 26, a board of inquiry headed by former Senator John Tower of Texas, which Reagan had established to investigate the role of the National Security Council staff in the affair, issued a report severely criticizing the president for a "hands-off" management style that it said had allowed him to be deceived by dishonest staff members. House and Senate select committees investigating the affair, which held joint public hearings during the spring and summer, issued their report on November 18; it said Reagan had failed to carry out his constitutional responsibilities to uphold the law, and had "created or at least tolerated" the atmosphere in which the diversion of funds to the contras could take place. Although the hearings failed to uncover any evidence that Reagan knew of the diversion, public opinion polls indicated that most Americans did not believe Reagan's denial of such knowledge.

In March and August, Reagan delivered two nationally televised speeches on the Iran/con-

Howard Baker (far left), former Senate majority leader and potential presidential candidate, took the top White House staff job instead when chief of staff Donald Regan resigned. Regan, criticized for his handling of the Iran/contra affair, shows his credentials (below) as he enters the White House the next day to clean out his office.

tra affair. He did not apologize for either the decision to sell arms to Iran or the effort to aid the contras. But he did assume personal responsibility for the scandal and admitted that "mistakes were made" that allowed the dealings with Iran to become an arms-for-hostages swap.

See also UNITED STATES: Iran/Contra Affair.

**Cabinet and Staff Changes.** A key figure in the Iran/contra affair, CIA Director William Casey, resigned in January, after surgery for brain cancer, and died in May. At first Reagan picked Casey's deputy at the CIA, Robert Gates, to succeed him. But Gates withdrew from consideration after Senate critics questioned his role in the Iran/contra affair. Reagan then named William Webster, the veteran director of the Federal Bureau of Investigation, to succeed Casey. Webster, in turn, was succeeded

at the FBI by U.S. District Court Judge William Sessions of Texas.

In February, White House chief of staff Donald Regan resigned under fire after the Tower board accused him of being responsible for the "chaos" that enveloped the White House after the Iran/contra scandal broke into public view. Reagan replaced him with former Senate Majority Leader Howard Baker, who quickly brought in a new team of aides, marking the third complete overhaul of the White House staff since Reagan took office.

In July, Commerce Secretary Malcolm Baldrige was killed in a riding accident. Reagan replaced him with businessman C. William Verity, Jr. In the fall, two cabinet members resigned to join the presidential campaign of Senator Robert Dole. Transportation Secretary Elizabeth Dole resigned October 1 to campaign ull-time for her husband, and two weeks later Labor Secretary William Brock announced he was leaving to become chairman of the campaign. Deputy Transportation Secretary James H. Burnley IV succeeded Dole, and Ann Dore McLaughlin, who had held a number of public-relations and other posts in the Nixon and Reagan administrations, replaced Brock.

Also in early November, Caspar Weinberger, who had served as defense secretary during Reagan's entire period in office, announced his resignation for personal reasons. National security adviser Frank Carlucci was named to replace Weinberger, and Carlucci's deputy, Lieutenant General Colin Powell, was chosen as national security adviser (the first black to hold the post).

**Supreme Court.** For the second year in a row, Reagan moved to ensure that the Supreme Court would retain a conservative cast well beyond the end of his presidency. After the unexpected retirement in June of Justice Lewis Powell, who had often provided the "swing vote" in the court's 5-4 decisions, Reagan nominated conservative U.S. Appeals Court Judge Robert Bork to fill the vacancy. After an intense and bitter confirmation battle, however, Bork's nomination was decisively rejected by the Senate. Reagan's second choice, another appeals court judge, 41-year-old Douglas H. Ginsburg, withdrew from consideration after it emerged that he had smoked marijuana during the 1960's and 1970's. Reagan then turned to a third appeals court judge, Anthony Kennedy, who was thought likely to win confirmation.

**Legislative Proposals and Budget.** Early in the year, Congress overrode Reagan's vetoes of two major bills, one providing $20 billion for water pollution control projects and the other allocating $88 billion for highways and mass transit. Reagan had little more success in his own new legislative initiatives, partly because the Democrats controlled Congress and partly because he was widely perceived as having entered the "lame-duck" phase of his presidency. In his State of the Union address on January 27, Reagan unveiled "new competitiveness" proposals that he asserted would help the nation improve its productivity, strengthen its educational system, and regain its competitive edge in world trade. The legislative pack-

age generated little enthusiasm in Congress, however. Reagan's proposals to reform some aspects of the nation's welfare system spent most of the year bogged down on Capitol Hill.

Although he had insisted that Democrats could obtain a tax increase only "over my dead body," Reagan was forced late in the year to agree to consider tax hikes in order to restore confidence in the U.S. economy after the stock market plunge in October, which was partly the result of growing worldwide concern about the ever-increasing federal budget deficit. In September, Reagan had reluctantly signed legislation restoring a mechanism for automatic across-the-board cuts in spending for each of the next six fiscal years if the president and Congress failed to reach deficit-reduction goals. After the stock market drop, however, congressional and administration negotiators agreed on a plan to reduce the fiscal

## Cabinet of the United States

**Vice President**  George Bush

**Secretary of State**  George Shultz
**Secretary of the Treasury**  James Baker
**Secretary of Defense**  Frank Carlucci
**Attorney General**  Edwin Meese III
**Secretary of the Interior**  Donald Hodel
**Secretary of Agriculture**  Richard Lyng
**Secretary of Commerce**  C. William Verity, Jr.
**Secretary of Labor**  Ann Dore McLaughlin
**Secretary of Health and Human Services**  Otis Bowen
**Secretary of Housing and Urban Development**  Samuel Pierce, Jr.
**Secretary of Transportation**  James H. Burnley IV
**Secretary of Energy**  John Herrington
**Secretary of Education**  William Bennett

**Director of the Office of Management and Budget**  James Miller III
**Director of the Central Intelligence Agency**  William Webster
**U.S. Representative to the United Nations**  Vernon Walters
**U.S. Trade Representative**  Clayton K. Yeutter

1988 deficit by more than the targeted amount, partly through increases in various taxes.

**Arms Control.** After months of intensive negotiations, on September 18 the United States and the Soviet Union announced a historic "agreement in principle" on a treaty to eliminate all of their intermediate-range nuclear-force missiles in Europe and Asia. Reagan also announced that he and Gorbachev would sign the treaty at their third summit later in the year. After the three-day meeting, the two leaders reported that they had also made considerable progress toward an agreement for a major reduction in their countries' strategic (long-range) nuclear arsenals.                    G.D.L.

## IRAN/CONTRA AFFAIR

The year was shadowed by continuing investigation into a major scandal. In November 1986 the Reagan administration confirmed reports that it had secretly sold arms to Iran, despite an official policy against dealing with terrorists and a U.S. campaign urging other nations not to sell arms to either side in the Iran-Iraq war. President Ronald Reagan said the sales had been authorized to open dialogue with moderates in Iran. On November 25, 1986, he announced that Lieutenant Colonel Oliver North had been fired as a National Security Council aide and that his superior, Vice Admiral John Poindexter, had resigned as national security adviser; Attorney General Edwin Meese III then reported having discovered an unauthorized operation to divert profits from the arms sales to contra rebels fighting the Sandinista regime in Nicaragua, in apparent violation of congressional restrictions.

From May to August 1987, a joint congressional committee held televised hearings on the affair, with testimony from North, Poindexter, and others. That panel and two others issued fact-finding reports, and a special prosecutor, Lawrence E. Walsh, was probing possible criminal wrongdoing.

**The Iranian Initiative.** During the year, most of the principal figures talked to investigators, and a basic chronology of events emerged. The affair apparently had its origins in July 1985, when Reagan's national security adviser at the time, Robert McFarlane, met with an Israeli official; the latter said certain Iranians were interested in opening a dialogue and might release U.S. hostages being held by pro-Iranian terrorists, in return for arms. Later in 1985, Israel sent arms to Iran with tacit U.S. approval. Reportedly at the urging of North, Poindexter, and then-CIA Director William Casey, plans were then made to send U.S. arms directly to Iran. Reagan authorized the sales, at least by January 1986, when he signed a directive approving them. Deliveries were made on several occasions in 1986. McFarlane, by then out of office, flew to Iran as an emissary but was unable to meet with senior officials. By the time the operation was exposed, three U.S. hostages had been released, but two remained in captivity, two had apparently been killed, and three new hostages had been taken.

**Contra Connection.** The diversion of funds to the contras arose as part of an ongoing attempt to bypass congressional restrictions on contra aid. North had recruited Major General Richard Secord to put together a network of agents to deliver contra aid and Iranian-born businessman Albert Hakim to handle financial arrangements. North worked with fund-raiser Carl Channell, who solicited money from wealthy conservatives (in the spring Channell and public relations executive Richard Miller pleaded guilty to use of a tax exempt organization to raise funds illegally). Funds were also obtained from Saudi Arabia, Brunei, and other countries. North testified that Poindexter had approved his activities. According to North, the use of Iranian arms sale profits was a "neat idea" first suggested by Manucher Ghorbanifar, a key Iranian middleman in early phases of the affair. Poindexter said he himself had authorized the diversion and had not told the president, so as to protect him, but believed he would have approved.

**Key Figures.** The colorful Colonel North appeared in July before the joint congressional committee, under limited immunity (meaning he could not be prosecuted on the basis of his testimony). To many he conveyed the image of a "can-do" marine intent on aiding "freedom-fighters" and rescuing hostages. But critics accused him of reckless disregard for the Constitution and the will of Congress.

Major General Secord, an experienced covert operator, testified without immunity before

the committee. He described the arms ship-ments and the bank accounts used to handle the money. The question about Secord ulti-mately became whether he was basically a patriot or a profiteer. Other figures in the affair ranged from Casey, who became ill and died before his role in the affair could be thoroughly examined, and McFarlane, who made an ap-parent suicide attempt in his depression over the affair, to Fawn Hall, North's attractive NSC secretary, who defended herself and North while admitting she helped to shred sensitive papers and smuggle files out of the White House.

**Panel Reports.** Aside from the criminal inves-tigation, three fact-finding investigations were conducted. The Senate Select Committee on Intelligence issued its findings in January, por-traying in detail the clandestine operation in which arms sales were laundered through Swiss bank accounts. A three-member panel ap-pointed by Reagan and headed by Senator John

*Above: a flow chart displayed at congressional hear-ings into the Iran/contra affair tracks the flow of money through bank accounts controlled by contra leader Adolfo Calero. Below: Oliver North testifies.*

413

Tower (R) reported in February. Though handicapped, like the Senate committee, by refusals of key figures to testify before it, the Tower Commission pieced together a strong indictment of the president, who "did not seem to be aware of the way in which operations were implemented and the full consequence of U.S. participation." The panel also found that, "whatever the intent," the Iranian initiative became "a series of arms-for-hostages deals."

The joint congressional committee, drawing on earlier probes and testimony from major figures, released a report on November 18. It found that Reagan had failed to fulfill his constitutional duty to see that the laws are faithfully executed; he did not make clear that aides should advise him of their activities, made some false public statements, and allowed "a cabal of zealots" to take over key areas of foreign policy. A dissenting report was issued by eight Republican panelists.     R.T.

## CONGRESS

Democrats were in control of both houses of Congress for the first time since 1980, and, with the aid of Robert Byrd (D, W.Va.) as Senate majority leader and Representative Jim Wright (D, Texas) as the new House speaker,

they hoped to direct the legislative agenda for the 100th Congress. However, they still lacked the votes needed to end a filibuster or override a veto without GOP cooperation and were unable to convert their advantages into substantial political gains. President Ronald Reagan's vetoes of highway and water project bills were overridden early in the year. But Democrats failed to complete passage of such key measures as catastrophic health insurance, welfare reform, and trade legislation, while campaign finance reform legislation was blocked by Senate Republicans. Passage of fiscal 1988 budget legislation dragged on until the final day of the session. The nomination of Judge Robert Bork to the Supreme Court triggered acrimonious Senate confirmation hearings that divided the nation (see UNITED STATES: Supreme Court), and the congressional Iran/contra hearings were a major focus of attention.

**Iran/Contra Affair.** The dominant issue for much of the session was the administration's involvement in the Iran/contra scandal. Two select committees investigating the affair held nearly 12 weeks of joint hearings and listened to dozens of witnesses. In November the congressional committees issued a report on

*Representative Jim Wright (D, Texas) accepts congratulations after his first speech as speaker of the House in January.*

# MEMBERSHIP OF THE 100th CONGRESS IN 1987

## Senators — Term Expires

### ALABAMA
Howell T. Heflin (D) . . . . . . 1991
Richard C. Shelby (D) . . . . . . 1993

### ALASKA
Ted Stevens (R) . . . . . . . . 1991
Frank H. Murkowski (R) . . . . . 1993

### ARIZONA
Dennis DeConcini (D) . . . . . . 1989
John McCain (R) . . . . . . . 1993

### ARKANSAS
Dale Bumpers (D) . . . . . . . 1993
David H. Pryor (D) . . . . . . 1991

### CALIFORNIA
Alan Cranston (D) . . . . . . . 1993
Pete Wilson (R) . . . . . . . 1989

### COLORADO
William L. Armstrong (R) . . . . 1991
Timothy E. Wirth (D) . . . . . 1993

### CONNECTICUT
Lowell P. Weicker, Jr. (R) . . . . 1989
Christopher J. Dodd (D) . . . . 1993

### DELAWARE
William V. Roth, Jr. (R) . . . . 1989
Joseph R. Biden, Jr. (D) . . . . 1991

### FLORIDA
Lawton M. Chiles, Jr. (D) . . . . 1989
Bob Graham (D) . . . . . . . 1993

### GEORGIA
Sam Nunn (D) . . . . . . . . 1991
Wyche Fowler, Jr. (D) . . . . . 1993

### HAWAII
Daniel K. Inouye (D) . . . . . . 1993
Spark M. Matsunaga (D) . . . . 1989

### IDAHO
James A. McClure (R) . . . . . 1991
Steven D. Symms (R) . . . . . 1993

### ILLINOIS
Alan J. Dixon (D) . . . . . . . 1993
Paul Simon (D) . . . . . . . . 1991

### INDIANA
Richard G. Lugar (R) . . . . . . 1989
Dan Quayle (R) . . . . . . . . 1993

### IOWA
Charles E. Grassley (R) . . . . . 1993
Tom Harkin (D) . . . . . . . . 1991

### KANSAS
Robert Dole (R) . . . . . . . . 1993
Nancy Landon Kassebaum (R) 1991

### KENTUCKY
Wendell H. Ford (D) . . . . . . 1993
Mitch McConnell (R) . . . . . . 1991

### LOUISIANA
J. Bennett Johnston (D) . . . . 1991
John B. Breaux (D) . . . . . . 1993

### MAINE
William S. Cohen (R) . . . . . . 1991
George J. Mitchell (D) . . . . . 1989

### MARYLAND
Paul S. Sarbanes (D) . . . . . . 1989
Barbara A. Mikulski (D) . . . . 1993

### MASSACHUSETTS
Edward M. Kennedy (D) . . . . 1989
John F. Kerry (D) . . . . . . . 1991

### MICHIGAN
Donald W. Riegle, Jr. (D) . . . . 1989
Carl Levin (D) . . . . . . . . 1991

### MINNESOTA
David F. Durenberger (R) . . . . 1989
Rudy Boschwitz (R) . . . . . . 1991

### MISSISSIPPI
John C. Stennis (D) . . . . . . 1989
Thad Cochran (R) . . . . . . . 1991

### MISSOURI
John C. Danforth (R) . . . . . . 1989
Christopher S. Bond (R) . . . . 1993

### MONTANA
John Melcher (D) . . . . . . . 1989
Max Baucus (D) . . . . . . . . 1991

### NEBRASKA
John James Exon, Jr. (D) . . . . 1991
David K. Karnes (R) . . . . . . 1989

### NEVADA
Chic Hecht (R) . . . . . . . . 1989
Harry Reid (D) . . . . . . . . 1993

### NEW HAMPSHIRE
Gordon J. Humphrey (R) . . . . 1991
Warren B. Rudman (R) . . . . . 1993

### NEW JERSEY
Bill Bradley (D) . . . . . . . . 1991
Frank R. Lautenberg (D) . . . . 1989

### NEW MEXICO
Peter V. Domenici (R) . . . . . 1991
Jeff Bingaman (D) . . . . . . . 1989

### NEW YORK
Daniel P. Moynihan (D) . . . . . 1989
Alfonse M. D'Amato (R) . . . . . 1993

### NORTH CAROLINA
Jesse Helms (R) . . . . . . . . 1991
Terry Sanford (D) . . . . . . . 1993

### NORTH DAKOTA
Quentin N. Burdick (D) . . . . . 1989
Kent Conrad (D) . . . . . . . . 1993

### OHIO
John H. Glenn, Jr. (D) . . . . . 1993
Howard M. Metzenbaum (D) . . 1989

### OKLAHOMA
David L. Boren (D) . . . . . . . 1991
Donald L. Nickles (R) . . . . . 1993

### OREGON
Mark O. Hatfield (R) . . . . . . 1991
Robert W. Packwood (R) . . . . 1993

### PENNSYLVANIA
H. John Heinz 3rd (R) . . . . . 1989
Arlen Specter (R) . . . . . . . 1993

### RHODE ISLAND
Claiborne Pell (D) . . . . . . . 1991
John H. Chafee (R) . . . . . . 1989

### SOUTH CAROLINA
Strom Thurmond (R) . . . . . . 1991
Ernest F. Hollings (D) . . . . . 1993

### SOUTH DAKOTA
Larry Pressler (R) . . . . . . . 1991
Thomas A. Daschle (D) . . . . . 1993

### TENNESSEE
James R. Sasser (D) . . . . . . 1989
Albert Gore, Jr. (D) . . . . . . 1991

### TEXAS
Lloyd Bentsen (D) . . . . . . . 1989
Phil Gramm (R) . . . . . . . . 1991

### UTAH
Edwin J. "Jake" Garn (R) . . . . 1993
Orrin G. Hatch (R) . . . . . . . 1989

### VERMONT
Robert T. Stafford (R) . . . . . 1989
Patrick J. Leahy (D) . . . . . . 1993

### VIRGINIA
John W. Warner (R) . . . . . . 1991
Paul S. Trible, Jr. (R) . . . . . 1989

### WASHINGTON
Daniel J. Evans (R) . . . . . . . 1989
Brock Adams (D) . . . . . . . . 1993

### WEST VIRGINIA
Robert C. Byrd (D) . . . . . . . 1989
John D. Rockefeller IV (D) . . . 1991

### WISCONSIN
William Proxmire (D) . . . . . . 1989
Robert W. Kasten, Jr. (R) . . . . 1993

### WYOMING
Malcolm Wallop (R) . . . . . . 1989
Alan K. Simpson (R) . . . . . . 1991

## Representatives

### ALABAMA
1. Sonny Callahan (R)
2. William L. Dickinson (R)
3. William Nichols (D)
4. Tom Bevill (D)
5. Ronnie G. Flippo (D)
6. Ben Erdreich (D)
7. Claude Harris (D)

### ALASKA
At large: Donald E. Young (R)

### ARIZONA
1. John J. Rhodes III (R)
2. Morris K. Udall (D)
3. Bob Stump (R)
4. Jon L. Kyl (R)
5. Jim Kolbe (R)

### ARKANSAS
1. William V. "Bill" Alexander, Jr. (D)
2. Tommy F. Robinson (D)
3. John P. Hammerschmidt (R)
4. Beryl F. Anthony, Jr. (D)

### CALIFORNIA
1. Douglas H. Bosco (D)
2. Wally Herger (R)
3. Robert T. Matsui (D)
4. Vic Fazio (D)
5. Nancy Pelosi (D)
6. Barbara Boxer (D)
7. George Miller (D)
8. Ronald V. Dellums (D)
9. Fortney (Pete) Stark (D)
10. Don Edwards (D)
11. Tom Lantos (D)
12. Ernest L. Konnyu (R)
13. Norman Y. Mineta (D)
14. Norman D. Shumway (R)
15. Tony Coelho (D)
16. Leon E. Panetta (D)
17. Charles Pashayan, Jr. (R)
18. Richard H. Lehman (D)
19. Robert J. Lagomarsino (R)
20. William M. Thomas (R)
21. Elton Gallegly (R)
22. Carlos J. Moorhead (R)
23. Anthony C. Beilenson (D)
24. Henry A. Waxman (D)
25. Edward R. Roybal (D)
26. Howard L. Berman (D)
27. Mel Levine (D)
28. Julian C. Dixon (D)
29. Augustus F. Hawkins (D)
30. Matthew G. Martinez (D)
31. Mervyn M. Dymally (D)
32. Glenn M. Anderson (D)
33. David Dreier (R)

34. Esteban Edward Torres (D)
35. Jerry Lewis (R)
36. George E. Brown, Jr. (D)
37. Alfred A. McCandless (R)
38. Robert K. Dornan (R)
39. William E. Dannemeyer (R)
40. Robert E. Badham (R)
41. Bill Lowery (R)
42. Dan Lungren (R)
43. Ron Packard (R)
44. Jim Bates (D)
45. Duncan Hunter (R)

**COLORADO**
1. Patricia Schroeder (D)
2. David E. Skaggs (D)
3. Ben Nighthorse Campbell (D)
4. Hank Brown (R)
5. Joel Hefley (R)
6. Dan Schaefer (R)

**CONNECTICUT**
1. Barbara B. Kennelly (D)
2. Samuel Gejdenson (D)
3. Bruce A. Morrison (D)
4. Christopher Shays (R)[2]
5. John G. Rowland (R)
6. Nancy L. Johnson (R)

**DELAWARE**
At large: Thomas R. Carper (D)

**FLORIDA**
1. Earl Hutto (D)
2. Bill Grant (D)
3. Charles E. Bennett (D)
4. Bill Chappell, Jr. (D)
5. Bill McCollum (R)
6. Buddy MacKay (D)
7. Sam Gibbons (D)
8. C. W. Bill Young (R)
9. Michael Bilirakis (R)
10. Andy Ireland (R)
11. Bill Nelson (D)
12. Tom Lewis (R)
13. Connie Mack (R)
14. Dan Mica (D)
15. E. Clay Shaw, Jr. (R)
16. Lawrence J. Smith (D)
17. William Lehman (D)
18. Claude Pepper (D)
19. Dante B. Fascell (D)

**GEORGIA**
1. Robert Lindsay Thomas (D)
2. Charles Hatcher (D)
3. Richard Ray (D)
4. Patrick L. Swindall (R)
5. John Lewis (D)
6. Newt Gingrich (R)
7. George Darden (D)
8. J. Roy Rowland (D)
9. Ed Jenkins (D)
10. Doug Barnard, Jr. (D)

**HAWAII**
1. Patricia F. Saiki (R)
2. Daniel K. Akaka (D)

**IDAHO**
1. Larry E. Craig (R)
2. Richard H. Stallings (D)

**ILLINOIS**
1. Charles A. Hayes (D)
2. Gus Savage (D)
3. Martin A. Russo (D)
4. Jack Davis (R)
5. William O. Lipinski (D)
6. Henry J. Hyde (R)
7. Cardiss Collins (D)
8. Daniel Rostenkowski (D)
9. Sidney R. Yates (D)

10. John Edward Porter (R)
11. Frank Annunzio (D)
12. Philip M. Crane (R)
13. Harris W. Fawell (R)
14. J. Dennis Hastert (R)
15. Edward R. Madigan (R)
16. Lynn Martin (R)
17. Lane Evans (D)
18. Robert H. Michel (R)
19. Terry L. Bruce (D)
20. Richard J. Durbin (D)
21. Melvin Price (D)
22. Kenneth J. Gray (D)

**INDIANA**
1. Peter J. Visclosky (D)
2. Philip R. Sharp (D)
3. John P. Hiler (R)
4. Dan Coats (R)
5. Jim Jontz (D)
6. Dan Burton (R)
7. John T. Myers (R)
8. Frank McCloskey (D)
9. Lee H. Hamilton (D)
10. Andrew Jacobs, Jr. (D)

**IOWA**
1. James A. S. Leach (R)
2. Thomas J. Tauke (R)
3. David R. Nagle (D)
4. Neal Smith (D)
5. Jim Lightfoot (R)
6. Fred Grandy (R)

**KANSAS**
1. Pat Roberts (R)
2. Jim Slattery (D)
3. Jan Meyers (R)
4. Dan Glickman (D)
5. Robert Whittaker (R)

**KENTUCKY**
1. Carroll Hubbard, Jr. (D)
2. William H. Natcher (D)
3. Romano L. Mazzoli (D)
4. Jim Bunning (R)
5. Harold Rogers (R)
6. Larry J. Hopkins (R)
7. Carl C. Perkins (D)

**LOUISIANA**
1. Bob Livingston (R)
2. Lindy Boggs (D)
3. W. J. Tauzin (D)
4. Charles Roemer III (D)
5. Jerry Huckaby (D)
6. Richard H. Baker (R)
7. James A. Hayes (D)
8. Clyde C. Holloway (R)

**MAINE**
1. Joseph E. Brennan (D)
2. Olympia J. Snowe (R)

**MARYLAND**
1. Royden Dyson (D)
2. Helen Delich Bentley (R)
3. Benjamin L. Cardin (D)
4. C. Thomas McMillen (D)
5. Steny H. Hoyer (D)
6. Beverly B. Byron (D)
7. Kweisi Mfume (D)
8. Constance A. Morella (R)

**MASSACHUSETTS**
1. Silvio O. Conte (R)
2. Edward P. Boland (D)
3. Joseph D. Early (D)
4. Barney Frank (D)
5. Chester G. Atkins (D)
6. Nicholas Mavroules (D)
7. Edward J. Markey (D)
8. Joseph P. Kennedy II (D)

9. Joe Moakley (D)
10. Gerry E. Studds (D)
11. Brian J. Donnelly (D)

**MICHIGAN**
1. John Conyers, Jr. (D)
2. Carl D. Pursell (R)
3. Howard Wolpe (D)
4. Frederick S. Upton (R)
5. Paul B. Henry (R)
6. Bob Carr (D)
7. Dale E. Kildee (D)
8. Bob Traxler (D)
9. Guy Vander Jagt (R)
10. Bill Schuette (R)
11. Robert W. Davis (R)
12. David E. Bonior (D)
13. George W. Crockett, Jr. (D)
14. Dennis M. Hertel (D)
15. William D. Ford (D)
16. John D. Dingell (D)
17. Sander M. Levin (D)
18. William S. Broomfield (R)

**MINNESOTA**
1. Timothy J. Penny (D)
2. Vin Weber (R)
3. Bill Frenzel (R)
4. Bruce F. Vento (D)
5. Martin Olav Sabo (D)
6. Gerry Sikorski (D)
7. Arlan Stangeland (R)
8. James L. Oberstar (D)

**MISSISSIPPI**
1. Jamie L. Whitten (D)
2. Mike Espy (D)
3. G. V. Montgomery (D)
4. Wayne Dowdy (D)
5. Trent Lott (R)

**MISSOURI**
1. William Clay (D)
2. Jack Buechner (R)
3. Richard A. Gephardt (D)
4. Ike Skelton (D)
5. Alan Wheat (D)
6. E. Thomas Coleman (R)
7. Gene Taylor (R)
8. Bill Emerson (R)
9. Harold L. Volkmer (D)

**MONTANA**
1. Pat Williams (D)
2. Ron Marlenee (R)

**NEBRASKA**
1. Douglas K. Bereuter (R)
2. Hal Daub (R)
3. Virginia Smith (R)

**NEVADA**
1. James H. Bilbray (D)
2. Barbara F. Vucanovich (R)

**NEW HAMPSHIRE**
1. Robert C. Smith (R)
2. Judd Gregg (R)

**NEW JERSEY**
1. James J. Florio (D)
2. William J. Hughes (D)
3. James J. Howard (D)
4. Christopher H. Smith (R)
5. Marge Roukema (R)
6. Bernard J. Dwyer (D)
7. Matthew J. Rinaldo (R)
8. Robert A. Roe (D)
9. Robert G. Torricelli (D)
10. Peter W. Rodino, Jr. (D)
11. Dean A. Gallo (R)
12. Jim Courter (R)
13. Jim Saxton (R)
14. Frank J. Guarini (D)

**NEW MEXICO**
1. Manuel Lujan, Jr. (R)
2. Joe Skeen (R)
3. Bill Richardson (D)

**NEW YORK**
1. George Hochbruekner (R)
2. Thomas J. Downey (D)
3. Robert J. Mrazek (D)
4. Norman F. Lent (R)
5. Raymond J. McGrath (R)
6. Floyd H. Flake (D)
7. Gary L. Ackerman (D)
8. James H. Scheuer (D)
9. Thomas J. Manton (D)
10. Charles E. Schumer (D)
11. Edolphus Towns (D)
12. Major R. Owens (D)
13. Stephen J. Solarz (D)
14. Guy V. Molinari (R)
15. Bill Green (R)
16. Charles B. Rangel (D)
17. Ted Weiss (D)
18. Robert Garcia (D)
19. Mario Biaggi (D)
20. Joseph J. DioGuardi (R)
21. Hamilton Fish, Jr. (R)
22. Benjamin A. Gilman (R)
23. Samuel S. Stratton (D)
24. Gerald B. H. Solomon (R)
25. Sherwood L. Boehlert (R)
26. David O'B. Martin (R)
27. George C. Wortley (R)
28. Matthew F. McHugh (D)
29. Frank Horton (R)
30. Louise McIntosh Slaughter (D)
31. Jack F. Kemp (R)
32. John J. LaFalce (D)
33. Henry J. Nowak (D)
34. Amo Houghton (R)

**NORTH CAROLINA**
1. Walter B. Jones (D)
2. Tim Valentine (D)
3. H. Martin Lancaster (D)
4. David E. Price (D)
5. Stephen L. Neal (D)
6. Howard Coble (R)
7. Charles Rose (D)
8. W. G. Hefner (D)
9. J. Alex McMillan (R)
10. Cass Ballenger (R)
11. James McClure Clarke (D)

**NORTH DAKOTA**
At large: Byron L. Dorgan (D)

**OHIO**
1. Thomas A. Luken (D)
2. Willis B. Gradison, Jr. (R)
3. Tony P. Hall (D)
4. Michael G. Oxley (R)
5. Delbert L. Latta (R)
6. Bob McEwen (R)
7. Michael DeWine (R)
8. Donald E. Lukens (R)
9. Marcy Kaptur (D)
10. Clarence E. Miller (R)
11. Dennis E. Eckart (D)
12. John R. Kasich (R)
13. Donald J. Pease (D)
14. Thomas C. Sawyer (D)
15. Chalmers P. Wylie (R)

16. Ralph S. Regula (R)
17. James A. Traficant, Jr. (D)
18. Douglas Applegate (D)
19. Edward F. Feighan (D)
20. Mary Rose Oakar (D)
21. Louis Stokes (D)

**OKLAHOMA**
1. James M. Inhofe (R)
2. Michael Lynn Synar (D)
3. Wes Watkins (D)
4. Dave McCurdy (D)
5. Mickey Edwards (R)
6. Glenn English (D)

**OREGON**
1. Les AuCoin (D)
2. Robert F. Smith (R)
3. Ron Wyden (D)
4. Peter A. DeFazio (D)
5. Denny Smith (R)

**PENNSYLVANIA**
1. Thomas M. Foglietta (D)
2. William H. Gray III (D)
3. Robert A. Borski (D)
4. Joe Kolter (D)
5. Richard T. Schulze (R)
6. Gus Yatron (D)
7. Curt Weldon (R)
8. Peter H. Kostmayer (D)
9. Bud Shuster (R)
10. Joseph M. McDade (R)
11. Paul E. Kanjorski (D)
12. John P. Murtha (D)
13. Lawrence Coughlin (R)
14. William Coyne (D)
15. Don Ritter (R)
16. Robert S. Walker (R)
17. George W. Gekas (R)
18. Douglas Walgren (D)
19. William F. Goodling (R)
20. Joseph M. Gaydos (D)
21. Thomas J. Ridge (R)
22. Austin J. Murphy (D)
23. William F. Clinger, Jr. (R)

**RHODE ISLAND**
1. Fernand J. St Germain (D)
2. Claudine Schneider (R)

**SOUTH CAROLINA**
1. Arthur Ravenel, Jr. (R)
2. Floyd Spence (R)
3. Butler Derrick (D)
4. Elizabeth J. Patterson (D)
5. John M. Spratt, Jr. (D)
6. Robin Tallon (D)

**SOUTH DAKOTA**
At large: Tim Johnson (D)

**TENNESSEE**
1. James H. Quillen (R)
2. John J. Duncan (R)
3. Marilyn Lloyd (D)
4. Jim Cooper (D)
5. William Hill Boner (D)[3]
6. Bart Gordon (D)
7. Don Sundquist (R)
8. Ed Jones (D)
9. Harold E. Ford (D)

**TEXAS**
1. Jim Chapman (D)
2. Charles Wilson (D)

3. Steve Bartlett (R)
4. Ralph Hall (D)
5. John Bryant (D)
6. Joe Barton (R)
7. Bill Archer (R)
8. Jack Fields (R)
9. Jack Brooks (D)
10. J. J. Pickle (D)
11. Marvin Leath (D)
12. Jim Wright (D)
13. Beau Boulter (R)
14. Mac Sweeney (R)
15. E. de la Garza (D)
16. Ronald D. Coleman (D)
17. Charles W. Stenholm (D)
18. Mickey Leland (D)
19. Larry Combest (R)
20. Henry B. Gonzalez (D)
21. Lamar S. Smith (R)
22. Tom DeLay (R)
23. Albert G. Bustamante (D)
24. Martin Frost (D)
25. Michael A. Andrews (D)
26. Richard K. Armey (R)
27. Solomon P. Ortiz (D)

**UTAH**
1. James V. Hansen (R)
2. Wayne Owens (D)
3. Howard C. Nielson (R)

**VERMONT**
At large: James M. Jeffords (R)

**VIRGINIA**
1. Herbert H. Bateman (R)
2. Owen B. Pickett (D)
3. Thomas J. Bliley, Jr. (R)
4. Norman Sisisky (D)
5. Dan Daniel (D)
6. James R. Olin (D)
7. D. French Slaughter, Jr. (R)
8. Stanford Parris (R)
9. Frederick C. Boucher (D)
10. Frank R. Wolf (R)

**WASHINGTON**
1. John R. Miller (R)
2. Al Swift (D)
3. Don Bonker (D)
4. Sid Morrison (R)
5. Thomas S. Foley (D)
6. Norman D. Dicks (D)
7. Mike Lowry (D)
8. Rod Chandler (R)

**WEST VIRGINIA**
1. Alan B. Mollohan (D)
2. Harley O. Staggers, Jr. (D)
3. Robert E. Wise, Jr. (D)
4. Nick Joe Rahall II (D)

**WISCONSIN**
1. Les Aspin (D)
2. Robert W. Kastenmeier (D)
3. Steve Gunderson (R)
4. Gerald D. Kleczka (D)
5. Jim Moody (D)
6. Thomas E. Petri (R)
7. David R. Obey (D)
8. Toby Roth (R)
9. F. James Sensenbrenner, Jr. (R)

**WYOMING**
At large: Richard Bruce Cheney (R)

---

[1] Elected June 2 to fill vacancy due to the death of Sala Burton, February 1.
[2] Elected August 18 to fill vacancy due to the death of Stewart B. McKinney, May 7.
[3] Resigned October 5.

*A champion of the elderly, Representative Claude Pepper (D, Fla.) advocates the broadest long-term medicare coverage. Pepper, himself 87, is shown visiting nursing home patients.*

the scandal, sharply criticizing the president and holding him responsible for the misdeeds of subordinates. The affair served to diminish Reagan's stature on Capitol Hill, while diverting congressional attention from other issues. It also led to renewed demands for presidential consultation with Congress on covert operations; in August, Reagan sent a letter to committee leaders promising to inform Congress of any future covert activities within 48 hours of approving them.

**Budget Package.** The budget the president submitted to Congress in January, for fiscal year 1988 (beginning October 1, 1987), called for expenditures of $1.02 trillion and revenues of $916.6 billion, with a deficit of $107.8 billion. Congressional critics quickly claimed that the deficit had been underestimated and would run closer to $160 billion. In June, Congress voted in favor of a trillion-dollar budget that projected a deficit of $133.9 billion; it included over $19 billion in tax increases and no increase in military spending.

Unable at the time to draw the administration into serious budget negotiations, Congress on September 23 passed legislation that required automatic spending cuts—with equal amounts to come from domestic and defense programs—if other deficit-reduction legislation

could not be approved by November 20. The measure was a rewrite of the 1985 Gramm-Rudman balanced-budget law, a major part of which—the system for automatic spending cuts—had been declared unconstitutional by the Supreme Court. Congress tried to address the Court's concerns by requiring the president's Office of Management and Budget, not an arm of the legislative branch as mandated by the original law, to implement the automatic cuts. The new law also called for the budget to be balanced in fiscal 1993, instead of fiscal 1991, and required reducing the deficit by $23 billion in fiscal 1988.

Reagan reluctantly signed the measure, attached to legislation raising the federal debt ceiling, but he vowed to fight any tax increases or cuts in defense spending. Then, with the stock market crash on October 19, the situation changed. Administration and congressional negotiators vowed to work together to calm the market frenzy and agreed on a $30-billion-plus deficit reduction plan; the $23 billion in mandated cuts went into effect temporarily until the new plan could be worked out. A series of four stopgap spending measures also were enacted. The final budget package, passed by Congress just before adjournment on December 22 and signed by Reagan on the same lay, provided $604 billion to finance government operations through fiscal 1988 and called for $9.1 billion in new taxes in fiscal 1988 and $14.1 billion in fiscal 1989, mostly affecting corporations and the wealthy. User fees were increased, certain government assets were to be sold, and fiscal 1988 cuts were made in both military spending ($5.1 billion) and non-military spending ($7.8 billion), including cuts in medicare reimbursement as well as in farm programs.

The overall spending bill passed easily in the Senate but was only narrowly approved, 209-208, in the House; many Republican votes were needed to offset defections by liberal Democrats, over a provision of $8.1 billion in interim aid to the Nicaraguan contras. The final budget package also allowed continued aid to Pakistan, despite Pakistan's failure to meet U.S. conditions to ensure it was not developing nuclear weapons. The bill cut off most aid to Haiti and Panama and barred U.S. companies from U.S. tax deductions for taxes paid to South Africa.

**Defense.** Congress and the president were at loggerheads over the issues of arms control and nuclear testing. Both the House and the Senate passed defense authorization bills that would require compliance with certain limits in the unratified 1979 Strategic Arms Limitation Treaty (SALT II) with the Soviet Union. The Senate measure passed only after being blocked for four months by a GOP filibuster. Both bills also included provisions to prevent the administration from broadly interpreting the 1972 U.S.-Soviet antiballistic missile treaty so as to permit testing in space as part of the Strategic Defense Initiative (SDI), or "Star Wars." Reagan and Congress eventually agreed on a compromise measure, signed by the president, that in effect kept SDI at the planning stage and required dismantling of a nuclear submarine in partial compliance with SALT II.

**Central America.** Despite the furor over the Iran/contra affair, President Reagan was determined to press forward in his support of the contra rebels, but he delayed efforts to win $270 million in fiscal 1988 aid because of congressional resistance and a new regional peace plan signed in August by Nicaragua and four other Central American countries. As a

temporary measure, Congress in September approved $3.5 million in humanitarian aid for the contras to tide them over past November 5, the day implementation of a region-wide cease-fire was to begin. Shortly after the plan nominally went into effect, Congress approved another $3.2 million in nonmilitary aid through mid-December, and the final budget bill allowed continued nonmilitary funding until early 1988, when a more decisive showdown between the president and Congress was expected.

**Catastrophic Health Insurance.** The year's major social welfare initiative was medical insurance for the elderly to cover costs of catastrophic illness. In July the House approved legislation to provide medicare protection for up to 365 days' hospitalization annually to some 31 million aged or disabled Americans who receive medicare benefits. Out-of-pocket expenses would not exceed $1,700 a year, and the program would be financed by a monthly surcharge, based on income, over the regularly monthly premium. In October the Senate passed similar legislation. Final action on the measure remained pending.

**Highways and Mass Transit.** Under intense pressure from state officials and the construction industry, Congress in April overrode President Reagan's veto of a bill the legislators had easily passed to provide $88 billion in highway and mass transit aid over the next five years. The bill, which had strong bipartisan backing, also provided funds for some 120 special "demonstration" projects in individual congressional districts. And it allowed the states to raise the speed limit on rural interstate highways from 55 to 65 miles per hour. The veto was overridden by 350-73 in the House, but by only 67-33 in the Senate, exactly the number needed.

**FSLIC Aid.** Congress in August approved a plan to provide $10.8 billion in new borrowing authority over three years for the troubled Federal Savings and Loan Insurance Corporation. The administration had wanted at least $15 billion for the FSLIC—to enable it to pay off depositors in insolvent savings and loans that would be closed—but accepted the lower figure when it became apparent that a threatened veto could not be sustained.

**Clean Water.** Congress began the year by quickly reenacting a $20 billion water pollution control bill and overriding President Reagan's veto of the measure. Reagan had pocket-vetoed an identical bill after the 99th Congress had adjourned, saying it was too expensive, but the measure was extremely popular with members, largely because it provided funds to state and local governments to build much-needed sewage plants.

**Airlines.** Amid widespread complaints about air traffic safety and flight delays, the House and Senate both passed legislation that would require airlines to post various statistics on performance. Final action on this legislation remained pending. Both houses cleared leg-islation to reauthorize federal programs to ex pand the nation's airports and to moderniz the air traffic control system. Late in the year Congress imposed a ban on smoking on mos domestic flights.

**Homeless Aid.** Congress readily approved $50 million measure, signed into law by Pres ident Reagan in February, to fund emergency food and shelter for the homeless during the waning winter months. Also easily passed wa a $1 billion two-year plan to provide the homeless with temporary housing, health, food and other assistance; Reagan signed it into law in July.

**Housing.** Despite a veto threat, the House anc Senate initially overwhelmingly voted to au thorize public housing and community devel opment programs for the first time since 1980 The House passed a one-year, $15.9 billior bill, and the Senate approved a similar measure With the administration criticizing the legis lation as too expensive, however, Congres eventually passed a compromise. The $3C billion two-year program authorized interest free housing loans in low income areas bu also made permanent the rent voucher progran favored by the administration as an alternative to construction of new federal housing.

**Trade.** Both houses passed broad legislation tc overhaul the nation's trade laws. The measure: would require retaliation against unfair trade practices by foreign countries, where negoti

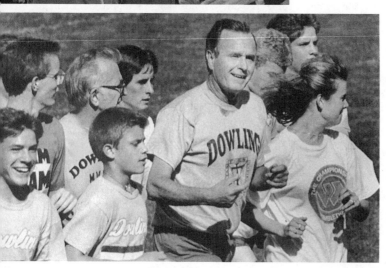

*Above: Senator Robert Dole en listed a high-powered aide ir his race for the GOP presiden tial nomination: his wife, Eliz abeth, who resigned as U.S transportation secretary to help Left: Vice President George Bush may or may not be the front runner as he works out with a high-school cross-country team in Des Moines in preparation for the Iowa caucuses.*

*Paul Kirk (center), chairman of the Democratic National Committee, poses in October with the current field of Democratic presidential aspirants (Gary Hart had withdrawn but not yet reemerged). From left: Albert Gore, Richard Gephardt, Jesse Jackson, Kirk, Bruce Babbit, Michael Dukakis, and Paul Simon.*

ations failed, and provide relief to those U.S. businesses and workers harmed or displaced by imports. The administration opposed both houses' bills as too protectionist. Final action was pending. Meanwhile, at year's end, Congress passed a provision banning participation by Japanese companies in U.S. public works projects until Japan opens its projects to U.S. companies.

**Farm Credit.** Facing possible collapse of the Farm Credit System (a network of banks and lending cooperatives), legislators tried to agree on whether and how to provide the $4 billion to $6 billion officials said was needed to keep the system afloat over the next five years. Ultimately, a $4 billion rescue plan was approved, which the president signed into law in early 1988.                    P.M.F.

## POLITICAL PARTIES

For both the Republican and the Democratic parties, 1987 was marked by painful adjustments. The Republicans were faced with a lame-duck president in Ronald Reagan and a House and Senate controlled by the opposition, as well as the aftermath of the Iran/contra affair and other Reagan administration problems. As

for the Democrats, the collapse of the presidential candidacies of former Colorado Senator Gary Hart and Delaware Senator Joseph R. Biden left them without a clear front-runner for 1988; then Hart scrambled the picture further by rejoining the race. The GOP chose New Orleans as its 1988 national convention site, while the Democrats decided on Atlanta.

**Republican Party.** A poll conducted for *Time* magazine in September showed that when Republicans were asked to name their top choice among declared or likely presidential candidates, Vice President George Bush (*see biography in* PEOPLE IN THE NEWS) emerged as the clear leader, with 45 percent; the runner-up was Senate Minority Leader Robert Dole (Kan.), with 21 percent. Trailing with 10 percent or less were former Secretary of State Alexander M. Haig, Jr., Representative Jack F. Kemp (N.Y.), the Reverend Marion G. (Pat) Robertson, and former Delaware Governor Pierre S. du Pont IV.

Pat Robertson resigned his ordination as a Southern Baptist minister just before formally declaring his candidacy in October. At that time his campaign reported having already raised and spent over $11 million (Bush had raised $12.7 million, Dole $7.9 million). Robertson made strong showings in caucus votes and straw polls in Iowa, Michigan, South Carolina, and Virginia; Bush won a straw poll in Florida.

**The Democrats.** Front-runner Gary Hart withdrew from the Democratic presidential race May 8, after the Miami *Herald* reported at the beginning of May that he had apparently spent part of a weekend at his Washington home with actress-model Donna Rice, while his wife, Lee, was in Colorado. Following Hart's withdrawal, seven candidates remained in the Democratic field: Biden, the Reverend Jesse Jackson, Representative Richard A. Gephardt (Mo.), Governor Michael S. Dukakis (Mass.), Senators Albert Gore, Jr. (Tenn.), and Paul Simon (Ill.), and former Governor Bruce Babbitt (Ariz.). Of these "seven dwarfs," as critics dubbed them, Jackson was the only one who consistently rose above 20 percent in the polls, but few party professionals believed the civil rights activist could actually win the nomination. Among the others, Dukakis was the leading fundraiser, but there was no clear front-runner by late in the year.

In September, just as Biden was gaining wide public exposure by presiding over the confirmation hearings of Robert H. Bork for Supreme Court justice, a series of news stories revealed that he had quoted the speeches of other politicians without proper attribution, plagiarized parts of a law school paper, and exaggerated his academic record. On September 23, Biden dropped out of the race. A few days later, Dukakis campaign manager John Sasso resigned after admitting he had given journalists the videotape that started the news stories about borrowed passages in Biden speeches.

On December 15, Democrats received another shock when Hart unexpectedly announced that he was reentering the race because the other candidates were not dealing with the issues he had stressed. Although a New York *Times*/CBS poll showed that he then had the support of more Democratic voters than any of the other candidates, many party officials called the move selfish and arrogant and said it would hurt Democratic chances in 1988.

If the Democratic presidential field seemed weak, one reason may have been that several popular Democrats had declined to make the race—among them, Senator Bill Bradley (N.J.), Governor Mario Cuomo (N.Y.), and Senator Sam Nunn (Ga.). Cuomo, clearly the "front-runner" noncandidate, said he would not enter the primaries but refused to rule out a draft.

*See also* ELECTIONS IN THE UNITED STATES.

G.M.H.

## SUPREME COURT

A vacancy on the Supreme Court in 1987 raised the prospect of an appointment that could turn the Court sharply to the right, and the nomination of judicial conservative Robert Bork for associate justice touched off one of the most heated confirmation battles in the nation's history. Among important decisions, the Court turned back a major constitutional challenge to the death penalty and ruled on cases involving separation of church and state, affirmative action, and free speech.

**Bork Battle.** In June, Justice Lewis F. Powell, Jr., unexpectedly announced his retirement from the Court; the next month, President Ronald Reagan nominated Robert Bork, a well-known conservative federal appeals court judge (*see biography in* PEOPLE IN THE NEWS), to replace him. Bork was an outspoken advocate of judicial restraint—allowing the legislative and executive branches freedom to make and carry out laws with minimal judicial interference—and of original intent, which holds that judges should be faithful to the words of the Constitution and the perceived intentions of the framers.

An intensive and well-organized campaign against Bork's confirmation by the Senate was mounted by groups including the American Civil Liberties Union, the NAACP, and the AFL-CIO. By the time televised hearings on the nomination by the Senate Judiciary Committee began in September, the Bork confirmation had turned into a highly political battle, and in part a test of power between a Republican administration and a Democratic-controlled Senate. The committee voted, 9-5, to recommend against Bork's confirmation. Although defeat on the Senate floor appeared all but certain, Bork carried on the fight to the end, losing in a 58-42 vote on October 23.

**Ginsburg and Kennedy Nominations.** Less than a week after Bork's defeat, Reagan nominated U.S. Appeals Court Judge Douglas Ginsburg to fill the Court vacancy. Once again, it was a controversial selection: Ginsburg, 41, had been on the bench less than a year and was one of the youngest and least experienced nominees in the Court's history. He was the choice favored by Meese and other right-wing voices within the administration, and another bruising confirmation battle was generally expected. However, Ginsburg's admission that he had smoked marijuana on "a few occasions" in the 1960's and 1970's, added to other controversies surrounding him, led him to withdraw his name only days after it had been presented.

Administration embarrassment over the Ginsburg nomination may have influenced the choice of the next candidate—U.S. Appeals Court Judge Anthony Kennedy—who was considered more moderate than the previous nominees, and also highly experienced. Kennedy received the top rating of the American Bar Association by a unanimous vote; he testified before the Senate Judiciary Committee on December 14 and 15, encountering a generally amicable reception.

**Court Decisions.** William H. Rehnquist's style as chief justice contrasted sharply with that of Warren Burger. He spent less time than his predecessor on administrative matters like court reform and on nonjudicial issues, such as work programs for prisoners. He moved business more rapidly—the 1986–1987 term ended on June 26, the earliest in 14 years. The chief justice wrote 20 opinions, more than any of his colleagues. There were an extraordinary number of 5-to-4 decisions—with Powell usually the "swing vote." Associate Justice William J. Brennan, Jr.—as the ranking liberal on the Court—ended up writing key majority rulings, mainly in the area of civil liberties. (*For some decisions not covered below, see* BLACKS IN THE UNITED STATES; CIVIL LIBERTIES AND CIVIL RIGHTS; WOMEN.)

*Church and State.* In *Edwards* v. *Aguillard*, a decision that may have broad implications for future cases involving religion and schools, the justices struck down a Louisiana law that would have required the teaching of "creation science"—based on the biblical account of the origin of the universe—alongside evolution in public school science classrooms. A 7-to-2 majority said that the Louisiana law's real purpose was "to advance the religious viewpoint that a supernatural being created humankind."

*Death Penalty.* In a major death penalty decision, the justices rejected, 5 to 4, the argument that statistical evidence of racial discrimination in capital cases is sufficient to declare the practice of capital punishment unconstitutional. Despite strong evidence presented in the Georgia case—*McCleskey* v. *Kemp*—that killers of whites, especially black killers, were far more likely to be condemned to death than killers of blacks, the Court majority held that these statistics did not prove unconstitutional racial discrimination against any individual defendant.

In another 5-to-4 death penalty decision, *Tison* v. *Arizona*, the Court held that accomplices in crimes leading to death can be subject to capital punishment, even if there was no intent to kill on the accomplice's part. Another

*Federal appellate judge Robert Bork, nominated to replace Lewis Powell on the Supreme Court, discusses his judicial philosophy before an often hostile Senate Judiciary Committee. The committee—and then the full Senate—rejected the nomination.*

*Lillian Garland's employer replaced her with someone else when she left to have a baby. Her resulting lawsuit wound up before the Supreme Court, which upheld a California law requiring maternity leave for employees unable to work because of pregnancy. At her desk (in another job), facing a photo of her daughter, Garland smiles in victory on the day of the ruling.*

5-4 decision barred the use in sentencing hearings in capital cases of evidence regarding the impact of the crime on the victim's family (*Booth* v. *Maryland*).

*Abortion.* In December a 4-4 tie vote by the Court left standing a lower court ruling striking down an Illinois law on minors' access to abortions. Under the law, girls under 18 had to formally notify their parents and then wait 24 hours before obtaining an abortion, or else seek a court waiver of the requirement.

*Employment.* In *California Federal Savings and Loan Association* v. *Guerra,* the Supreme Court upheld a state law requiring unpaid leave for employees incapacitated by pregnancy, childbirth or related medical conditions. The Court also ruled in several cases that employers may favor women and minorities in hiring and promotion in order to remedy imbalances in their work forces and atone for past biases. In one noteworthy case, *Johnson* v. *Transportation Agency, Santa Clara County, Calif.,* the Court rejected the claim of a man who was denied promotion to a road-dispatcher's job when an allegedly less-qualified woman was chosen.

*Elections.* In a case involving free speech (*Federal Election Commission* v. *Massachusetts Citizens for Life*), the justices ruled that a federal prohibition against corporations' making "expenditures in connection with elections" could not be applied to a right-to-life group that urged voters to cast a "pro-life" ballot in an upcoming election. In another case, *Tashjian* v. *Republican Party of Connecticut,* the Court struck down a state law that limited voting in a party's primaries to people previously enrolled in the party.                                    C.J.S.

## FOREIGN AFFAIRS

U.S. foreign policy was shadowed by the unraveling Iran/contra affair. However, relations with the Soviet Union improved, culminating in an accord eliminating both sides' intermediate-range missiles worldwide; it was signed by the two nation's leaders at a summit meeting in Washington, D.C., in December.

**Iran/Contra Affair.** Revelation of U.S. arms sales to Iran and the diversion of profits to the Nicaraguan contras showed that the United States had violated two of its own emphatic policies: no arms for Iran and no dealing with terrorists. The presidentially appointed Tower Commission, in a February report, criticized the Reagan administration for conducting a secret operation of great consequence in a casual, ill-informed way. Among other observations, the report blamed Secretary of State George Shultz and Secretary of Defense Caspar Weinberger for opposing the project too mildly and then distancing themselves from events. The Senate and House committees investigating the affair held joint hearings in the spring and summer; Shultz testified indignantly that he had been stymied in efforts to make his dissent understood and effective. The joint report, issued in November, strongly criticized Reagan and asserted that a "cabal of zealots" had taken control of key areas of foreign policy.

Persian Gulf. The administration responded to the scandal by adopting an anti-Iranian posture and tilting toward Iraq in the continuing Persian Gulf war. This tilt toward Iraq survived an unintended attack by an Iraqi missile-firing plane on the U.S. warship *Stark* in the Gulf in May, which killed 37 sailors.

In May and June the United States engineered the transfer of 11 Kuwaiti oil tankers to the U.S. flag to protect them against Iranian attacks. Both the United States and the Soviet Union supported a UN Security Council resolution, passed in July, calling for a cease-fire in the Iran-Iraq war. Meanwhile, the first convoy of reflagged Kuwaiti tankers moved under U.S. naval escort through the Strait of Hormuz and into the Gulf. During the passage the tanker *Bridgeton* was damaged by a mine apparently laid by Iran. The United States asked for and got minesweeping help from friendly European nations and proceeded with the convoys. In September a U.S. helicopter attacked and disabled an Iranian vessel laying mines. The next month, U.S. helicopters inflicted casualties on Iranian gunboats. In subsequent Iranian missile attacks, two large tankers were struck—one American-owned but under the Liberian flag, the other a Kuwaiti vessel under the U.S. flag; in response, U.S. destroyers shelled two offshore Iranian oil platforms and boarded and disabled a third. Late in October President Ronald Reagan announced a ban on all Iranian imports and tighter curbs on U.S. exports to Iran.

The activity in the Gulf reopened a debate between the president and members of Congress demanding that he invoke the War Powers Act of 1973. That legislation requires the president to notify Congress within 48 hours of sending U.S. troops into combat or potential combat; the troops then must be withdrawn in 60–90 days unless Congress provides otherwise. The president declined to invoke the act.

Central America. The administration continued to clash with many members of Congress over U.S. funding of military operations against the government of Nicaragua. Despite growing opposition to funding, Congress during fiscal year 1987 allowed $70 million in military aid and $30 million in nonlethal aid. The military assistance was delivered to the contras from U.S. bases in Honduras, Nicaragua's northern neighbor. At the same time the United States rotated tens of thousands of U.S. troops through Honduras on training missions and maintained a formidable complex of bases and airfields as an implicit threat to Nicaragua. Contra forces, averaging about 12,000 during the year, operated in northern Nicaragua, attacking Sandinista troops, villages loyal to the Sandinistas, and economic targets.

A new ingredient in the situation arose in the summer, with the peace initiative of Costa Rican President Oscar Arias Sánchez. In August he and fellow presidents from Guatemala, Honduras, Nicaragua, and El Salvador signed a plan that called for a cease-fire between governments and irregular forces throughout the region, an end to all outside support for irregular forces, and the restoration of political and civil rights wherever they had been suspended. The plan overshadowed the nearly simultaneous announcement of a U.S. approach, developed by the administration and House Speaker Jim Wright (D, Texas) for Nicaragua, calling for a truce, direct Sandinista-contra negotiations, the restoration of civil liberties, internationally supervised elections, and an end to foreign aid for the contras and the Sandinistas.

President Reagan called the Arias plan "fatally flawed" because it did not treat the contras and the Sandinista government as equal parties. When Arias was named in October to receive the Nobel Peace Prize for his efforts, it became more difficult for Reagan to criticize the Arias plan (which Wright had already endorsed). However, Congress agreed to a temporary appropriation of $3.5 million in humanitarian aid to tide the contras over early November, when the peace plan was to go into effect. When that money ran out, Congress appropriated another $3.2 million, through mid-December.

The matter of further U.S. aid was complicated by revelation of Sandinista plans for a military buildup, with Soviet resources, even in the event that peace was achieved within Nicaragua. Partly because of this development, Congress approved $8.1 million in renewed nonmilitary aid to the contras, as part of its massive budget package passed just before adjournment in December. The aid was, however, strongly opposed by many liberals in Congress, and the issue of contra aid was set to meet a more decisive test when this interim aid ran out in early 1988. Meanwhile, Nicaraguan President Daniel Ortega Saavedra agreed to negotiate indirectly with the rebels; these negotiations broke down, however, and late in the year there was heavy fighting between the two sides. At one point, Ortega presented a detailed cease-fire proposal, worked out, to the annoyance of the Reagan administration, with the cooperation of House Speaker Wright; the plan was rejected by the contras.

**Soviet Union.** Early in the year, the Soviets continued to insist that the United States refrain from testing in space and deploying the anti-missile system known as the Strategic Defense Initiative (Star Wars), as a condition of any arms control agreement. President Reagan insisted on being free to proceed with SDI. In addition, the United States had, in late 1986, deployed bombers equipped to launch strategic nuclear weapons beyond the ceiling set by the unratified 1979 Strategic Arms Limitation Treaty (SALT II). The United States was also continuing with a series of underground nuclear tests, unmoved by a temporary Soviet moratorium on nuclear testing. The U.S.-Soviet negotiating climate brightened in February, when Gorbachev announced a readiness to consider the elimination of all Soviet and U.S. medium-range weapons from Europe within five years, without specifically making agreement conditional on U.S. suspension of SDI. In the months ahead the Soviets agreed to include the elimination of all shorter-range missiles in Europe as well, and they reversed their opposition to on-site inspection by each side to verify compliance. In July the Soviets agreed to eliminate their 100 intermediate-range nuclear weapons in Asia, and Gorbachev voiced acceptance of the U.S. "global double-zero" proposal, under which both countries would destroy all their intermediate-range nuclear missiles worldwide. The remaining obstacle was the existence of 72 aging Pershing 1A missiles under West German control. The Soviets said the Pershings would have to go and Bonn ultimately agreed. Soon afterward, on September 18, an "agreement in principle" was reached to "conclude a treaty."

A temporary setback occurred in late October, when Gorbachev unexpectedly insisted that conflicts over SDI be resolved before he would commit himself to a date for a summit.

But when Soviet Foreign Minister Eduard Shevardnadze visited Washington soon after, he brought a letter from Gorbachev in which the Soviet leader agreed to hold the summit, to begin in Washington on December 7 and to include the signing of a treaty eliminating intermediate-range nuclear weapons within three years. Shultz and Shevardnadze, meeting in Geneva beforehand, agreed on an elaborate set of procedures for verification of compliance with the pact, to be carried out during the three years in which the missiles were to be eliminated and for ten years afterward.

Enthusiasm was high during the three-day summit in Washington, which ended on a note of warmer personal relations between the two leaders. Their basic achievement consisted of signing the treaty already agreed upon. But they did lay some of the groundwork for progress toward a new pact limiting longer-range strategic weapons. Moreover, a new era of détente seemed to be emerging. Both sides had moderated their rhetoric. The Soviets appeared willing to withdraw some troops from Afghanistan; they also released some political prisoners and granted more exit permits to Jews. Just before the summit, on December 6, an estimated 200,000 persons had staged a massive demonstration in Washington, D.C. on behalf of Jewish emigration and related issues.

One negative note in U.S.-Soviet relations was the discovery that the newly built U.S. embassy in Moscow was filled with eavesdropping devices and would require considerable rebuilding. Meanwhile, members of Congress charged that the Soviets had selected the site of their new embassy in Washington— on a hill overlooking the city—so that they could spy on U.S. communications. Late in the year, in another incident, the United States quietly announced it was expelling a Soviet UN diplomat, Mikhail Katkov, for alleged espionage activities.

**Other Relations.** The United States voiced concern over destabilizing events in South Korea, the Philippines, and Panama (see KOREA, REPUBLIC OF; PHILIPPINES; PANAMA) and criticized Israel for harsh measures against Palestinian demonstrators (see ISRAEL). A trade treaty was negotiated with Canada and an immigration pact with Cuba was revived (see CANADA; CUBA). The United States continued to resist the idea of a full international peace conference on the Middle East with Soviet participation; Secretary Shultz pressed instead for direct talks

Late in the year, President Ronald Reagan and Soviet General Secretary Mikhail Gorbachev signed a major arms limitation accord, during a three-day summit meeting in Washington, D.C. At left, the two leaders, assisted by interpreters, confer in the Oval Office. At right, the president and First Lady Nancy Reagan (far right) bid farewell to Gorbachev and his wife, Raisa (at left).

between Israel and Jordan, under U.S. and Soviet sponsorship. In another area of diplomacy, Congress voted a significant sanction against South Africa, by denying tax credits to U.S. companies for taxes paid by subsidiaries in that country.                                    G.S.

**UPPER VOLTA.** See STATISTICS OF THE WORLD.

**URUGUAY.** Uruguay entered its third year of democratic rule in 1987 with a solid economic performance, but political storm clouds brewed over past human rights violations.

Reaction to the 1986 amnesty law, which protected members of the military accused of human rights violations, included demonstrations and street violence. Human rights groups, who had organized a petition drive to hold a plebiscite to annul the amnesty bill, claimed to have exceeded the number of signatures required to get the plebiscite on the ballot.

President Julio María Sanguinetti's government found itself opposed by both the military and the labor movement. Concerned about the unresolved amnesty issue, the military saw its forces reduced from 31,900 to 21,000 mem-

bers. For its part, labor protested the government's unilateral setting of wage levels and, in June, staged two strikes for higher pay and social legislation and against the amnesty. Sanguinetti resisted these demands, and another strike, of transport workers, followed.

A 2 to 4 percent increase in the gross domestic product was predicted. Unemployment dropped below 9 percent early in the year, and inflation was running at an annual rate of about 70 percent. Foreign debt was a heavy burden, and the government said it was limiting repayments to 8 percent of export earnings.

Regional economic integration proceeded slowly for Uruguay, as Argentina and Brazil chose to move ahead first with their own integration. Bilateral agreements were reached with both countries, however. Economic accords were signed with the Soviet Union, Egypt, Morocco, and India. Diplomatic relations were established with Angola and Qatar.

See STATISTICS OF THE WORLD.        J.F., Jr.

**UTAH.** See STATISTICS OF THE WORLD.

# V

**VANUATU.** See STATISTICS OF THE WORLD.

**VENEZUELA.** Venezuela's economy declined in 1987, largely because of falling oil prices. The government of President Jaime Lusinchi had to deal with violent student protests.

The main political parties moved to choose their candidates for the presidential election of 1988. In a primary in October, the ruling Democratic Action Party selected ex-President Carlos Andrés Pérez.

In Mérida, violent student protests followed an incident in March in which a student was shot and killed. The students caused more than $2 million in property damage, and over 100 of them were jailed. Over the next few months the protests spread to campuses throughout the country, causing more deaths and injuries. The government blamed the violence on a drug-trafficking conspiracy; observers cited as fac-

tors the denial of the right to assemble and the government's failure to curb inflation.

Finance Minister Manuel Azpúrua signed a rescheduling agreement in March on $20 billion owed by the government to private banks. A revised version, committing Venezuela to paying $250 million in principal during 1987, took effect later in the year; controversy over the agreements contributed to Azpúrua's resignation in October.

Venezuela entered into its first debt-for-equity exchange in September; the U.S.-based Morgan Bank agreed to finance half of a $600 million aluminum plant to be built by the public sector.

In June, Colombian gunmen, allegedly hired by drug traffickers, killed nine Venezuelan national guardsmen who were involved in destroying drug plantations along the Colom-

Hanoi shoppers storm the counter to buy sugar at the city's central marketplace. With a precarious food supply and one of the world's lowest per capita incomes, Vietnam was experimenting with a variety of economic reforms.

bian border. After two Colombian jets violated its air space in August, Venezuela placed its military on alert; on September 13, Venezuela closed its Colombian border.

Orlando Bosch, a Cuban exile accused of planning the 1976 bombing of a Cuban airliner, which took 73 Cuban lives, was acquitted in August by an appeals court. Cuba's official daily called the decision "abominable, immoral, and unjust."

See STATISTICS OF THE WORLD.          L.L.P.

**VERMONT.** See STATISTICS OF THE WORLD.

**VICE PRESIDENT OF THE UNITED STATES.** See PEOPLE IN THE NEWS: George Bush.

**VIETNAM.** The year 1987 saw potentially far-reaching changes in Vietnam's leadership and policies. At a congress of the Vietnamese Communist Party in December 1986, the three top officials had resigned from their posts, and Nguyen Van Linh, 71, often described as a reformer, had become party chief. Thousands of government and party bureaucrats were ousted. In February 1987, seven old ministries were combined into three new ones in an attempt to trim the huge bureaucracy, and there was a major shakeup in top ministerial posts. In June a newly elected 496-member National Assembly appointed Pham Hung, 75, as the country's premier and Vo Chi Chong,

73, as president. Because of the new leaders' ages and health problems, however, many observers concluded that these appointments were transitional moves.

To deal with its severe economic problems, Hanoi announced various reforms during the year that loosened state restraints over the economy. Then, in December, the government announced a sweeping new policy that appeared to jettison centralized planning in favor of decision-making at the factory level. The plan also provided worker incentives and tied wages to productivity. Meanwhile, inflation continued at an annual rate of close to 700 percent, and food production, affected by pests and drought, fell short of targets.

The stalemate in Cambodia continued between the estimated 140,000 Vietnamese occupying troops there and some 40,000 resistance guerrillas. Vietnamese and Thai troops fought a protracted battle in the spring at Chong Bok, a cluster of hills in northeastern Thailand that Vietnamese soldiers had occupied in an attempt to stop guerrilla infiltration in Cambodia. The Thai government claimed its forces had recaptured most of the territory.

As the number of refugees fleeing Vietnam increased substantially, the government agreed to resume the suspended Orderly Departure

Program, providing for legal emigration of Vietnamese refugees to the United States. Vietnam also promised to resume efforts to determine the fate of some 1,800 U.S. servicemen missing in action in Vietnam or off its shores since the Vietnam war. The United States, for its part, agreed to facilitate private charitable assistance to Vietnam.

On December 3, after a highly publicized trial, 17 people were sentenced to prison for an alleged attempt to stage a guerrilla invasion of Vietnam with U.S. and Thai support. The defendants were linked to a group called the Armed Forces of Resistance, said to have infiltrated Laos from Thailand in July with plans to invade Vietnam. Vietnam claimed that 100 members of the group, including a former South Vietnamese admiral, were killed in Laos in August.

See STATISTICS OF THE WORLD. M.H.

**VIRGINIA.** See STATISTICS OF THE WORLD.

**VIRGIN ISLANDS.** See STATISTICS OF THE WORLD.

# W

**WARSAW TREATY ORGANIZATION.** See COMMUNIST WORLD.

**WASHINGTON.** See STATISTICS OF THE WORLD.

**WESTERN SAHARA.** See AFRICA.

**WESTERN SAMOA.** See STATISTICS OF THE WORLD.

**WEST VIRGINIA.** See STATISTICS OF THE WORLD.

**WISCONSIN.** See STATISTICS OF THE WORLD.

**WOMEN.** In 1987 the U.S. Supreme Court reached important decisions on affirmative action for women and other issues involving women's rights. The Ontario legislature passed comparable worth legislation, and forced treatment of pregnant women became an issue.

**Politics.** In November elections, Houston Mayor Kathy Whitmire won a landslide victory against six opponents; Carrie Saxon Perry was the first black woman to be elected mayor of a major city in the Northeast—Hartford, Conn.; and Sue Myrick defeated the black male incumbent to become mayor of Charlotte, N.C. U.S. Representative Patricia Schroeder (D, Colo.), who had considered running for president, announced in September that she would not be a candidate, after falling at least $1 million short of her $2 million fund-raising goal.

In November, President Ronald Reagan named Ann Dore McLaughlin as U.S. secretary of labor. She became the only woman on the cabinet. Elizabeth Hanford Dole had resigned previously as secretary of transportation.

**Affirmative Action.** In the first U.S. Supreme Court case involving affirmative action for women, the Court upheld a voluntary affirmative action plan by a county transportation agency that led to the promotion of a woman over a man though the man appeared margin-

*Newly inducted Rotarians Maria Guillen, Katherine Lorenzi, Sylvia W. Whitington, and Ruth Koik Brodis look over the club manual after being voted in by the Chicago Pan-American Rotary Club in May. The four were the first women admitted to the group after the U.S. Supreme Court upheld a state law invalidating the Rotary's male-only policy.*

*Wilhelmina Holladay, founder of the new National Museum of Women in the Arts in Washington, D.C., poses before Suzanne Valadon's* The Abandoned Doll, *one of 500 works in the collection.*

ally better qualified. The case, *Johnson v. Transportation Agency, Santa Clara County, Calif.,* involved the job of road dispatcher, a position never before held by a woman.

**Pregnancy and Employment.** Existing federal law does not require special job protection for women who are pregnant; pregnancy and related medical problems are covered by disability leave rules applicable to other medical conditions. Nevertheless, the Supreme Court, in *California Federal Savings and Loan Association v. Guerra,* held that a state could legally require employers to provide unpaid maternity leave for four months and reinstate employees in similar jobs, even if such leaves were not granted for other disabilities. On the other hand, the Court, in *Wimberly v. Labor and Industrial Relations Commission of Missouri,* upheld a Missouri law denying unemployment compensation to women who leave their jobs because they are pregnant and are not rehired.

**Right of Association.** The Supreme Court held in *Board of Directors of Rotary International v. Rotary Club of Duarte* that a state could, without violating the First Amendment right of association, require Rotary Clubs to admit women. The Court found that the clubs were not sufficiently private to warrant denying women equal access to the business contacts

and community activities that characterize membership. Subsequently, the Lions Clubs and Kiwanis Clubs voted to end their ban on women members.

**Comparable Worth.** In June the Ontario provincial legislature passed the first so-called comparable worth measure in North America. The new measure required private companies with ten or more employees to upgrade low-paying jobs held by women and to end pay discrimination between men and women doing different jobs deemed to be of comparable value to the employer. Companies were given six years to implement the plan.

**Wage Gap.** A study released by the Women's Research and Education Institute, the research arm of the Congressional Caucus for Women's Issues, concluded that, while wage gaps still exist between men and women and there is still an overwhelming concentration of women in fields such as nursing, women's representation in most occupations—including law and medicine—was increasing. It was noted that women number nearly half of all workers in the formerly all-male bastions of bartending and bus driving.

**Reproductive Issues.** In August the Department of Health and Human Services proposed regulations that would require federally funded

431

family-planning services to omit any mention of abortion in presenting options to clients. The proposed rules would require abortion services financed by agencies that received federal as well as private funds, such as Planned Parenthood, to provide abortions at separate sites and forbid the use of federal funds for any program that encourages, promotes, or advocates abortion. The regulations were criticized by women's rights activists.

The rights of a pregnant woman in relation to her unborn child have become a growing source of controversy in hospitals and the courts. The *New England Journal of Medicine* reported that in at least 18 cases since 1981 hospitals had won court orders for cesarean sections or treatment of the fetus, over the objections of the mother, in an effort to protect the unborn life. In one recent case, George Washington University Hospital in Washington, D.C., secured a court order to perform a cesarean section and remove a 26-week-old fetus from a mother near death from cancer. Both the mother and the fetus died shortly after the surgery. In August the American College of Obstetricians and Gynecologists issued a statement opposing compulsory treatment of pregnant women.

**NOW.** Eleanor Smeal announced in early July that she would resign from the presidency of the National Organization for Women (NOW) in order to concentrate on efforts toward the election of more women to office. Molly Yard, NOW's political director, was elected as the new president later the same month. She indicated that, besides remaining active in demonstrations and other public activities, the organization would work energetically behind the scenes in such areas as filing lawsuits and lobbying for legislation favorable to women.

M.Gr. & K.P.

**WYOMING.** See STATISTICS OF THE WORLD.

# Y

**YEMEN, PEOPLE'S DEMOCRATIC REPUBLIC OF.** Serious divisions continued to plague the South Yemeni government in 1987, most significantly tribal and ideological splits within the ruling Yemen Socialist Party. The government also faced a continued threat from former president Ali Nasser Muhammad al-Hasani, who had been overthrown in a January 1986 coup, and an estimated 30,000 refugees in the neighboring Yemen Arab Republic (North Yemen). However, these exiles were themselves divided—between supporters of Muhammad, who continued publicly to support a Marxist South Yemen allied to the Soviet Union, and the National Alliance of the Patriotic Forces of South Yemen, which favored a non-Marxist, multiparty democratic system.

The Yemen Socialist Party met in June for the first party congress since 1985. The congress confirmed the government of President Haidar Abu Bakr al-Attas, reduced the number of Central Committee members, and reconfirmed close relations with the Soviet Union.

The effects of the coup continued to disrupt financial affairs and economic development. Nevertheless, agreements were signed with the Soviet Union and with two French companies to develop the country's oil resources. Discussions with North Yemen on unification and economic cooperation continued.

See STATISTICS OF THE WORLD.        C.H.A.

**YEMEN ARAB REPUBLIC.** With oil reserves estimated at 1 billion barrels, the Yemen Arab Republic began exporting oil in 1987; the amount per day was expected to range between 150,000 and 200,000 barrels. The country also began developing its natural gas reserves of about 50.8 billion cubic feet in order to meet local energy needs.

Former President Ali Nasser Muhammad al-Hasani of the People's Democratic Republic of Yemen (South Yemen) and an estimated 30,000 other political refugees from South Yemen continued to live in the YAR. Concern over these refugees and possible YAR support of an attempt by Muhammad to regain control in Aden were discussed during the July visit to Sana of Ali Salem al-Baith, head of the South Yemeni Socialist Party. The two countries also held talks on unity, with the South Yemenis most interested in economic and social cooperation while the YAR sought solutions to the refugee problem.

The $90 million Marib Dam project was inaugurated with ceremonies attended by Prime Minister Turgut Özal of Turkey, which built the dam, and Sheikh Zayed bin Sultan al-Nahayan, president of the United Arab Emirates, the principal financial backer of the project. The dam stores 1.4 billion cubic feet of water and supplies five irrigation channels serving a 17,300-acre area.

See STATISTICS OF THE WORLD.          C.H.A.

**YUGOSLAVIA.** Economic problems, nationality quarrels, and jurisdictional strife between federal and regional authorities continued to cause concern in Yugoslavia during 1987. In April the seventh plenum of the Central Committee of the League of Communists of Yugoslavia, meeting in Belgrade, again focused on these threats to the nation. An overhaul of the 1974 constitution was in the making; reforms were expected to be complete by 1988.

Following guidelines set by the International Monetary Fund, the government imposed a four-month wage freeze in March and pegged future wage increases to productivity. The action brought a wave of strikes throughout the country, the first time such concerted strike action had been staged against the Communist regime. A temporary price freeze followed, but labor unrest did not end. With inflation running at well over 100 percent and industrial output lagging behind goals, the government sharply increased the price of basic staples and froze wages again in mid-November. Soon afterward, the dinar was devalued by 25 percent.

A financial scandal at Agrokomerc, a large food-processing firm based in Bosnia-Herzegovina, exposed widespread fraud and led to a major political shakeup. The company was found to have issued as much as $400 million in worthless promissory notes to Yugoslav banks. The firm's chief executive was arrested, 50 officials were expelled from the province's party organization, and the country's vice president, Hamdija Pozderac, resigned.

Ethnic tensions remained a serious problem in the autonomous province of Kosovo, whose population is 80 percent Albanian and 13 percent Serb and Montenegrin. In late April between 10,000 and 15,000 Serbs and Montenegrins gathered at the little town of Kosovo Polje to protest what they called harassment by the Albanian majority. Growing unrest prompted the Yugoslav government to send federal riot police into the area.

See STATISTICS OF THE WORLD.          R.A.P.

**YUKON TERRITORY.** See STATISTICS OF THE WORLD.

# Z

**ZAIRE.** In 1987, Zaire's economic stress, aggravated by payments on its $5 billion foreign debt and the austerity measures imposed as a condition for further borrowing, continued to fall heavily on the poor and middle classes. Malnutrition and child mortality were reported on the rise. Little new private foreign investment was forthcoming; most financing took the form of international and bilateral loans for infrastructure and services. The U.S. government agreed to provide Zaire with a new loan of $126 million. The Paris Club of creditor governments subsequently agreed to reschedule $884 million of Zaire's debt on softer terms. The International Monetary Fund announced a new $370 million loan for 1987–1990.

Export-led growth, the basic premise of World Bank advice on African economic policy, failed to offer a solution to Zaire's long-term economic crisis. Prices of Zaire's main exports, copper and cobalt, remained depressed.

In fallout from the Iran/contra affair, Colonel

Oliver North revealed in congressional hearings that his U.S. National Security Council operation had attempted to secretly fund arms for Unita, the South African-supported rebel army in Angola, with some of the cash obtained by selling arms to Iran. Money was to be filtered through Saudi Arabia, and arms were to be sent through Zaire via the air base at Kamina in Shaba Province. Diplomats in Zaire said that the base was being used for sending arms to Unita as late as mid-1987.

A new border clash between Zairian and Congolese forces was reported from Mindouli, southwest of Brazzaville, in January. In the East, in the Ruwenzori Mountains along the frontier with Uganda and Rwanda, Zairian rebels formerly associated with Ugandan President Yoweri Museveni's guerrilla forces were said to be active. Another group of rebels claimed in July to have killed two soldiers and to have 17,500 men operating inside Zaire.

In June, Zaire officially launched an anti-AIDS education campaign in an effort to combat what was described as the propagation of a plague. The government also was distributing free condoms as part of its campaign.

See Statistics of the World.                B.S.

**ZAMBIA.** In 1987, Zambia faced its worst economic crisis since independence in 1964. Per capita income was falling fast, and the economy was in near collapse. The crisis was set in motion when the government removed subsidies on maize late in 1986, leading to a 120 percent increase in the price of "mealie" meal, the staple food, and to four days of rioting in which 15 people were killed. President Kenneth Kaunda then restored the subsidies. Similarly, Kaunda increased gasoline prices by 77 percent in April, then canceled the hike within 24 hours.

Early in the year, plans to start repaying arrears on the foreign debt collapsed because of a shortage of foreign exchange. Teachers, medical staff, and postal workers went on strike in March; Kaunda claimed the strikes were merely part of South Africa's plan to destabilize its neighbors.

On May 1, the president announced that Zambia would end its cooperation with the four-year-old International Monetary Fund reform program. The World Bank suspended disbursements of new funds because of arrears on existing loans, while Zambia limited payments on its $5 billion foreign debt to less than 10 percent of its declining export earnings. Also, Kaunda abolished the foreign exchange auction and fixed the new exchange rate at an unrealistically high rate. A price freeze and wage controls were imposed throughout the economy. The cabinet was reshuffled in May; Kaunda appointed a new finance minister and also fired high officials at the Bank of Zambia.

South Africa was assisting the Unita rebels in Angola against that country's government, and the fighting there had driven over 75,000 Angolans into two camps in Zambia's North Western province. The Angolan fighting had also closed the Benguela railway through Zambia, Zaire, and Angola to the Atlantic. In April, Zambia, Angola, and Zaire issued a declaration of intent to reopen the Benguela route. Earlier, Zambia announced that its rail shipments through South Africa had ended.

In February, Zambia sentenced a New Zealander based in Johannesburg to a two-year prison term for possession of a time bomb. Zambia released four young South African men said to have admitted to working for South African intelligence. On April 25, South African commandos killed four Zambian civilians in a raid on Livingstone. In July three members of the Zambian Air Force stationed at the Livingstone Air Base, as well as a businessman, were charged with spying for South Africa.

The death late in 1986 of one of President Kaunda's sons, who had suffered from AIDS, highlighted the epidemic in Zambia, where the AIDS virus was believed to have already infected one out of five adults living in urban areas. The president called for greater efforts against the disease.

See Statistics of the World.                K.W.G.

**ZIMBABWE.** During 1987, three years of talks between Zimbabwe's ruling party—the Zimbabwe African National Union-Patriotic Front (Zanu-PF)—and the other key black party, the Zimbabwe African People's Union (Zapu), culminated in a merger, despite their long-standing enmity, and the creation of a one-party state. Prior to this development, the constitution was amended to abolish special parliamentary seats for whites.

Negotiations toward the "national unity" pact between the two parties had broken down several times before agreement was finally reached on December 22, along the lines sought by Prime Minister Robert Mugabe. In accordance with the pact, he was inaugurated on December 31 as the country's first executive president, while remaining president of the merged party, which kept the Zanu name. Mugabe's longtime rival, Zapu leader Joshua Nkomo, became a vice president and second secretary of the merged party. Simon Muzenda was named as the party's other vice president and also as vice president of the nation. Western observers expected the merger to ease the country's ethnic tensions.

In April, former Prime Minister Ian Smith was suspended from Parliament for 12 months because of a speaking tour through South Africa in which he had encouraged South African whites to maintain their minority rule; in May, Smith resigned his leadership of the white Conservative Alliance party. The end to a guaranteed direct white political voice came in August and September, when the House of Assembly and the Senate voted to amend the constitution to abolish special parliamentary seats for whites.

Meanwhile, sporadic violence against whites continued. In one brutal incident that caused headlines around the world, 16 white Christian missionaries were hacked to death with axes by antigovernment rebels in late November, on two farms near Bulawayo. The victims, ranging from 40 years to six weeks in age, belonged to groups known as the Community of Reconciliation and the Brotherhood of Reconciliation; they had allocated portions of their land to black farmers and lived without armed guards. Authorities believed that squatters in the area may have called on the dissidents to attack them.

The specter of South African power in the region continued to alarm the government. The Mozambique National Resistance, a South African-supported army that seeks to overthrow the Mozambique government, raided border villages in Zimbabwe in May and June in retaliation for Zimbabwe's military aid to Mozambique. In October, 18 people were wounded when a car bomb exploded in a Harare suburb; the government blamed South Africa.

The frontline states—a group of nations bordering on or near South Africa—held a mini-summit in Lusaka in July, and agreed to continue efforts to reduce their dependence on South Africa; however, the Zimbabwe cabinet later rejected a proposal by the prime minister to impose trade sanctions on South Africa.

See STATISTICS OF THE WORLD.         K.W.G.

*Rebels in Matabeleland, a center of resistance to the Zimbabwean government, descended on this Pentecostal mission at Esogodini and another nearby on November 27, killing 16 missionaries and children in all and leaving the buildings burned-out ruins.*

# THE COUNTRIES OF THE WORLD

| Nation / Capital | Population | Area of Country (sq mi/ sq km) | Type of Government | Heads of State and Government | Currency: Value of U.S. Dollar | GNP (000,000): GNP Per Capita |
|---|---|---|---|---|---|---|
| **AFGHANISTAN** <br> Kabul | 14,200,000 <br> 2,000,000 | 250,000 <br> 647,497 | People's republic | President: Najibullah <br> Prime Minister: <br> Sultan Ali Keshtmand | Afghani <br> 50.60 | $ NA <br> NA |
| **ALBANIA** <br> Tiranë | 3,100,000 <br> 220,000 | 11,100 <br> 28,748 | People's socialist republic | Chairman, Presidium <br> of the People's Assembly: <br> Ramiz Alia <br> Chairman, Council of <br> Ministers (Premier): <br> Adil Çarçani | Lek <br> 5.537 | 1,930[1] <br> NA |
| **ALGERIA** <br> Algiers | 22,972,000 <br> 1,488,000 | 919,595 <br> 2,381,741 | Republic | President: <br> Chadli Benjedid <br> Premier: <br> Abdelhamid Brahimi | Dinar <br> 4.67 | 55,230 <br> 2,530 |
| **ANGOLA** <br> Luanda | 8,000,000 <br> 1,200,000 | 481,354 <br> 1,246,700 | People's republic | President: <br> José Eduardo dos Santos | Kwanza <br> 29.92 | NA <br> NA |
| **ANTIGUA AND BARBUDA** <br> St. Johns | 100,000 <br> 25,000 | 171 <br> 443 | Parliamentary state (C) | Governor-General: <br> Sir Wilfred E. Jacobs <br> Prime Minister: <br> Vere C. Bird, Sr. | East Caribbean dollar <br> 2.70 | 160 <br> 2,030 |
| **ARGENTINA** <br> Buenos Aires | 31,500,000 <br> 2,908,000 | 1,068,302 <br> 2,766,889 | Federal republic | President: <br> Raúl Alfonsín | Austral <br> 3.50 | 65,080 <br> 2,130 |
| **AUSTRALIA** <br> Canberra | 16,200,000 <br> 273,800[2] | 2,967,909 <br> 7,686,848 | Federal parliamentary state (C) | Governor-General: <br> Sir Ninian M. Stephen <br> Prime Minister: <br> Bob Hawke | Dollar <br> 1.401 | 171,170 <br> 10,840 |
| **AUSTRIA** <br> Vienna | 7,600,000 <br> 1,531,300 | 32,374 <br> 83,849 | Federal republic | President: <br> Kurt Waldheim <br> Chancellor: <br> Franz Vranitzky | Schilling <br> 11.49 | 69,060 <br> 9,150 |
| **BAHAMAS** <br> Nassau | 200,000 <br> 135,400 | 5,380 <br> 13,935 | Parliamentary state (C) | Governor-General: <br> Sir Gerald C. Cash <br> Prime Minister: <br> Lynden O. Pindling | Dollar <br> 1.00 | 1,670 <br> 6,710 |
| **BAHRAIN** <br> Manama | 400,000 <br> 122,000 | 240 <br> 622 | Emirate | Emir: <br> Isa bin Sulman al-Khalifah <br> Prime Minister: <br> Muhammad Khalifa <br> bin Sulman al-Khalifa | Dinar <br> 0.377 | 4,040 <br> 9,560 |
| **BANGLADESH** <br> Dacca | 107,100,000 <br> 3,605,000 | 55,598 <br> 143,998 | Republic (C) | President: <br> H. M. Ershad <br> Prime Minister: <br> Mizanur Rahman Choudhury | Taka <br> 31.14 | 14,770 <br> 150 |
| **BARBADOS** <br> Bridgetown | 300,000 <br> 7,500 | 166 <br> 431 | Parliamentary state (C) | Governor-General: <br> Hugh Springer <br> Prime Minister: <br> Erskine Sandiford | Dollar <br> 2.011 | 1,180 <br> 4,680 |
| **BELGIUM** <br> Brussels | 9,900,000 <br> 982,400[2] | 11,781 <br> 30,513 | Constitutional monarchy | King: <br> Baudouin <br> Prime Minister: <br> Wilfried Martens | Franc <br> 34.30 | 83,230 <br> 8,450 |

The section on countries presents the latest information available. All monetary figures are expressed in United States dollars. The symbol (C) signifies that the country belongs to the Commonwealth of Nations. NA means that the data were not available. * indicates that the category does not apply to the country under discussion. Footnotes at the end of the section contain more specialized information.

| Imports Exports | Revenue Expenditure | Elementary Schools: Teachers Students | Secondary Schools: Teachers Students | Colleges and Universities: Teachers Students |
|---|---|---|---|---|
| $ 999,000,000 566,000,000 | $ 675,600,000 988,800,000 | 35,364 1,115,993 | 7,827 143,346 | 1,226 12,868 |
| NA NA | 1,134,100,000 1,127,100,000 | 27,100 531,520 | 5,500 95,380 | 1,360 19,670 |
| 9,841,000,000 10,149,000,000 | 20,000,000,000 22,500,000,000 | 115,242 3,414,705 | 71,945 1,632,388 | 11,601 111,507 |
| 682,000,000 1,840,000,000 | 2,629,800,000 3,028,400,000 | 32,004 1,178,430 | NA 131,918 | 316 2,674 |
| 84,000,000 18,000,000 | 39,800,000 31,800,000 | 390 9,557 | 331 4,197 | NA NA |
| 3,814,000,000 8,396,000,000 | 8,276,600,000 11,190,000,000 | 212,932 4,315,752 | 193,551 1,466,424 | 33,450 416,571 |
| 23,450,000,000[3] 22,883,000,000 | 48,101,200,000 50,465,700,000 | 197,130[4] 3,006,169[4] | 197,130[4] 3,006,169[4] | 21,061 358,498 |
| 20,937,000,000 17,226,000,000 | 22,747,400,000 28,980,100,000 | 67,827 676,470 | NA 544,147 | 9,644 142,159 |
| 3,081,000,000 2,728,000,000 | 460,500,000 532,000,000 | 1,555 32,664 | NA 17,255 | NA NA |
| 3,159,000,000 2,863,000,000 | 1,415,100,000 1,349,600,000 | 2,774 46,364 | 1,196 29,602 | 148 835 |
| 2,170,000,000 927,000,000 | NA 1,250,000,000 | 189,884 8,915,442 | 115,751 3,083,643 | 2,626 40,527 |
| 607,000,000 352,000,000 | 324,900,000 324,300,000 | 1,317 30,907 | 1,368 27,715 | 200 1,664 |
| 56,210,000,000[5] 53,760,000,000[5] | 26,226,900,000 34,949,300,000 | 40,894 768,207 | NA 858,625 | NA 100,362 |

| Nation<br>Capital | Population | Area of<br>Country<br>(sq mi/<br>sq km) | Type of<br>Government | Heads of State and<br>Government | Currency:<br>Value of<br>U.S. Dollar | GNP<br>(000,000):<br>GNP<br>Per Capita |
|---|---|---|---|---|---|---|
| **BELIZE** . . . . . . . . .<br>Belmopan | 200,000. . .<br>4,500 | 8,867. .<br>22,965 | .Parliamentary<br>state (C) | Governor-General: . . . . . . .<br>Minita Gordon<br>Prime Minister:<br>Manuel Esquivel | .Dollar . . . . .$<br>2.00 | 180<br>1,130 |
| **BENIN** . . . . . . . .<br>Porto-Novo | 4,300,000. . .<br>144,000 | 43,484. .<br>112,622 | .People's.<br>republic | .President: . . . . . . . . . . . .<br>Ahmed Kérékou | .CFA franc[6]<br>276.6 | 1,080<br>270 |
| **BHUTAN** . . . . . . . .<br>Thimbu | 1,500,000. . .<br>35,000 | 18,147. .<br>47,000 | .Monarchy . . . | .King:<br>Jigme Singye<br>Wangchuk | .Ngultrum . . .<br>12.95 | 190<br>160 |
| **BOLIVIA** . . . . . . . .<br>Sucre<br>La Paz | 6,500,000. . .<br>80,000<br>881,400 | 424,165. .<br>1,098,581 | .Republic . . . | .President:<br>Víctor Paz Estenssoro | .Peso . . . . .<br>2.17 | 3,010<br>470 |
| **BOTSWANA** . . . . . .<br>Gaborone | 1,200,000. . .<br>59,700 | 231,805. .<br>600,372 | .Republic . .<br>(C) | .President:<br>Quett K. J. Masire | .Pula. . . . .<br>1.588 | 900<br>840 |
| **BRAZIL**. . . . . . . . .<br>Brasília | 141,500,000. . .<br>411,000 | 3,286,488. .<br>8,511,965 | .Federal . . .<br>republic | .President:<br>José Sarney | .Cruzado . . .<br>67.26 | 222,700<br>1,640 |
| **BRUNEI**. . . . . . . . .<br>Bandar Seri Begawan | 200,000. . .<br>49,900 | 2,226. .<br>5,765 | .Constitutional<br>monarchy (C) | Sultan: . . . . . . . . . . . .<br>Muda Hassanal<br>Bolkiah | .Dollar . . . . .<br>1.997 | 3,940[1]<br>17,580 |
| **BULGARIA** . . . . . . .<br>Sofia | 9,000,000. . .<br>1,070,400 | 42,823. .<br>110,912 | .People's. . . .<br>republic | .Chairman, Council of State: . . .<br>Todor Zhivkov<br>Chairman, Council of Ministers<br>(Premier):<br>Georgi Atanasov | .Lev . . . . . .<br>0.827 | 37,390[1]<br>NA |
| **BURMA**. . . . . . . . .<br>Rangoon | 38,800,000. . .<br>2,459,000 | 261,218. .<br>676,552 | .Socialist. . . .<br>republic | .President: . . . . . . . . .<br>U San Yu<br>Prime Minister:<br>U Maung Maung Kha | .Kyat. . . . . .<br>6.147 | 7,080<br>190 |
| **BURUNDI**. . . . . . . .<br>Bujumbura | 5,000,000. . .<br>151,000 | 10,747. .<br>27,834 | .Republic . . .<br> | .Head of State: . . . . . . . .<br>Pierre Buyoya | .Franc . . . . .<br>116.3 | 1,110<br>240 |
| **CAMBODIA**. . . . . .<br>**(PEOPLE'S REPUBLIC**<br>**OF KAMPUCHEA)**<br>Phnom Penh | 6,500,000. . .<br><br><br>700,000 | 69,898. . .<br>181,035 | .People's. . . .<br>republic | .President, Council of State: . . .<br>Heng Samrin<br>Chairman, Council of<br>Ministers (Premier):<br>Hun Sen | .New riel. . . .<br>100.0 | NA<br>NA |
| **CAMEROON** . . . . . .<br>Yaoundé | 10,300,000. . .<br>650,000[2] | 183,569. . .<br>475,442 | .Republic . . . | .President: . . . . . . . . . . . .<br>Paul Biya<br>Prime Minister:<br>Etecki Nbomou | .CFA franc[6]<br>276.6 | 8,300<br>810 |
| **CANADA** . . . . . . . .<br>Ottawa | 25,900,000. . .<br>309,800 | 3,831,033. . .<br>9,922,330 | .Federal . . . .<br>parliamentary<br>state<br>(C) | .Governor-General: . . . . . . . .<br>Jeanne Sauvé<br>Prime Minister:<br>Brian Mulroney | .Dollar . . . . .<br>1.31 | 347,360<br>13,670 |
| **CAPE VERDE** . . . . .<br>Praia | 300,000. . .<br>46,900 | 1,557. .<br>4,033 | .Republic . . . | .President: . . . . . . .<br>Aristides M. Pereira<br>Premier:<br>Pedro Rodrigues Pires | .Escudo . . . .<br>73.42 | 140<br>430 |
| **CENTRAL AFRICAN**<br>**REPUBLIC**<br>Bangui | 2,700,000. . .<br><br>473,800 | 240,535. . .<br>622,984 | .Republic . . . | .Chairman, Military Committee .<br>for National Recovery<br>(President):<br>Gen. André Kolingba | .CFA franc[6]<br>276.6 | 700<br>270 |
| **CHAD**. . . . . . . . . .<br>N'Djamena | 4,600,000. . .<br>303,000 | 495,755. . .<br>1,284,000 | .Republic . . . | .President: . . . . . . . . . . . .<br>Hissène Habré | .CFA franc[6]<br>276.6 | NA<br>NA |
| **CHILE**. . . . . . . . . .<br>Santiago | 12,400,000. . .<br>4,318,300[2] | 292,258. . .<br>756,945 | .Republic . . . | .President: . . . . . . . . . . . .<br>Gen. Augusto Pinochet Ugarte | .Peso . . . . . .<br>232.4 | 17,230<br>1,440 |
| **CHINA, PEOPLE'S.**<br>**REPUBLIC OF**<br>Peking | 1,062,000,000. . .<br><br>5,968,000 | 3,691,515. . .<br>9,560,980 | .People's. . . .<br>republic | .President: . . . . . . . . . . . .<br>Li Xiannian<br>Premier:<br>Li Peng | .Yuan . . . . . .<br>3.722 | 318,920<br>310 |
| **COLOMBIA**. . . . . . .<br>Bogotá | 29,900,000. . .<br>3,983,000 | 439,737. . .<br>1,138,914 | .Republic . . . | .President: . . . . . . . . . . . .<br>Virgilio Barco Vargas | .Peso . . . . . .<br>262.1 | 37,610<br>1,320 |
| **COMOROS** . . . . . . .<br>Moroni | 400,000. . .<br>20,100 | 838. .<br>2,171 | .Federal . . . .<br>Islamic<br>republic | .President: . . . . . . . . . . . .<br>Ahmed Abdallah Abderemane | .CFA franc[6]<br>276.6 | 110<br>280 |

| Imports Exports | Revenue Expenditure | Elementary Schools: Teachers Students | Secondary Schools: Teachers Students | Colleges and Universities: Teachers Students |
|---|---|---|---|---|
| $ 126,000,000<br>96,000,000 | $ 48,600,000<br>52,700,000 | 1,582<br>38,512 | 504<br>6,676 | NA<br>NA |
| 464,000,000<br>24,000,000 | 163,200,000<br>163,200,000 | 13,452<br>444,163 | 3,018<br>119,141 | 801<br>6,302 |
| NA<br>NA | 160,700,000<br>181,000,000 | 1,149<br>44,275 | 581<br>5,872 | NA<br>564 |
| NA<br>927,000,000 | NA<br>NA | 45,024<br>1,022,624 | NA<br>182,760 | 3,480<br>56,632 |
| 764,000,000<br>730,000,000 | 842,500,000<br>373,500,000 | 6,980<br>223,608 | 1,566<br>35,271 | 142<br>1,434 |
| 13,168,000,000<br>25,639,000,000 | 15,622,200,000<br>15,622,200,000 | 1,022,096<br>24,825,545 | 214,969<br>2,946,657 | 113,844<br>1,399,539 |
| 728,000,000<br>3,386,000,000 | 2,132,500,000<br>968,600,000 | 1,923<br>31,682 | 1,538<br>17,869 | 64<br>218 |
| 13,656,000,000[3]<br>13,348,000,000 | 19,269,700,000<br>19,259,000,000 | 61,819<br>1,063,329 | 25,201<br>318,201 | 13,205<br>88,637 |
| 283,000,000<br>315,000,000 | 1,104,400,000<br>943,700,000 | 95,435<br>4,541,900 | 40,272<br>1,195,400 | 2,260<br>27,830 |
| 186,000,000<br>110,000,000 | 128,600,000<br>147,100,000 | 6,192<br>337,329 | 1,567<br>22,061 | NA<br>2,090 |
| NA<br>NA | NA<br>NA | 37,914<br>1,540,335 | 4,772<br>153,064 | NA<br>NA |
| 1,151,000,000[7]<br>722,000,000[7] | 2,289,600,000<br>2,289,600,000 | 32,082<br>1,638,629 | 12,102<br>319,510 | 839<br>17,113 |
| 76,413,000,000[3]<br>87,479,000,000 | 64,210,000,000<br>85,080,000,000 | 142,283<br>2,251,535 | 130,551<br>2,323,105 | 34,965<br>795,400 |
| NA<br>NA | 181,100,000<br>237,100,000 | 1,459<br>50,000 | 175<br>4,115 | NA<br>NA |
| 109,000,000[7]<br>88,000,000[7] | 151,800,000<br>179,400,000 | 4,502<br>294,312 | 1,041<br>47,399 | 105<br>2,133 |
| 162,000,000<br>138,000,000 | 48,200,000<br>68,900,000 | 4,494<br>288,478 | NA<br>45,612 | 141<br>1,643 |
| 3,007,000,000<br>3,823,000,000 | 422,000,000<br>667,000,000 | 62,746<br>2,092,597 | NA<br>608,327 | 10,097<br>127,353 |
| 42,491,000,000<br>27,343,000,000 | 64,305,100,000<br>66,471,900,000 | 5,369,600<br>135,571,000 | 2,821,400<br>48,618,800 | 302,919<br>1,237,394 |
| 4,131,000,000<br>3,552,000,000 | 4,521,600,000<br>4,440,200,000 | 132,675<br>4,054,891 | 93,121<br>1,889,023 | 34,876<br>331,477 |
| NA<br>NA | 14,100,000<br>16,300,000 | 1,292<br>59,709 | NA<br>13,798 | NA<br>NA |

| Nation Capital | Population | Area of Country (sq mi/ sq km) | Type of Government | Heads of State and Government | Currency: Value of U.S. Dollar | GNP (000,000): GNP Per Capita |
|---|---|---|---|---|---|---|
| CONGO. . . . . . . . Brazzaville | 2,100,000. . . 456,400 | 132,047. . . 342,000 | . .People's. . . . republic | . .President: . . . . . . . . . . . . Col. Denis Sassou-Nguesso Premier: Ange Edouard Poungui | .CFA franc[6] 276.6 | $ 2,070 1,020 |
| COSTA RICA. . . . . . San José | 2,800,000. . . 241,500 | 19,575. . . 50,700 | . .Republic . . . | .President . . . . . . . . . . . . Oscar Arias Sánchez | .Colón. . . . . 68.25 | 3,340 1,290 |
| CUBA. . . . . . . . . Havana | 10,300,000. . . 2,003,600 | 44,218. . . 114,524 | . .Socialist. . . . republic | .President of the . . . . . . . . Councils of State and Ministers: Fidel Castro Ruz | .Peso . . . . . 0.733 | NA NA |
| CYPRUS . . . . . . . Nicosia | 700,000. . . 164,400 | 3,572. . . 9,251 | . .Republic . . (C) | .President:[8] . . . . . . . . . . Spyros Kyprianou | .Pound[8] . . . . 2,229 | 2,650 3,790 |
| CZECHOSLOVAKIA Prague | 15,600,000. . . 1,190,000 | 49,370. . . 127,869 | . .Federal . . . . socialist republic | .President: . . . . . . . . . . . Gustáv Husák Premier: Lubomir Štrougal | .Koruna . . . . 5.25 | NA NA |
| DENMARK[10] . . . . . Copenhagen | 5,100,000. . . 626,900 | 16,629. . . 43,069 | . .Constitutional monarchy | Queen: . . . . . . . . . . . . . Margrethe II Prime Minister: Poul Schlüter | .Krone . . . . . 6.29 | 57,330 11,240 |
| DJIBOUTI. . . . . . . Djibouti | 300,000. . . 210,000 | 8,495. . . 22,000 | . .Republic . . . | .President: . . . . . . . . . . . Hassan Gouled Aptidon Premier: Barkad Gourad Hamadou | .Djibouti . . . franc 176.8 | NA NA |
| DOMINICA . . . . . . Roseau | 100,000. . . 20,000 | 290. . . 751 | . .Republic . . (C) | .President: . . . . . . . . . . . Clarence A. Seignoret Prime Minister: (Mary) Eugenia Charles | .East. . . . . . Caribbean dollar 2.70 | 90 1,160 |
| DOMINICAN REPUBLIC Santo Domingo | 6,500,000. . . 1,300,000 | 18,816. . . 48,734 | . .Republic . . . | .President: . . . . . . . . . . . Joaquin Balaguer | .Peso . . . . . 4.845 | 5,050 810 |
| ECUADOR . . . . . . Quito | 10,000,000. . . 1,043,300 | 109,484. . . 283,561 | . .Republic . . . | .President: . . . . . . . . . . . Léon Febrés Cordero Rivadeneira | .Sucre . . . . . 211.5 | 10,880 1,160 |
| EGYPT . . . . . . . . Cairo | 51,900,000. . . 12,000,000[2] | 386,660. . . 1,001,450 | . .Republic . . . | .President: . . . . . . . . . . . Hosni Mubarak Prime Minister: Atef Sedki | .Pound . . . . . 0.70 | 32,220 680 |
| EL SALVADOR . . . . San Salvador | 5,300,000. . . 452,600 | 8,124. . . 21,041 | . .Republic . . . | .President: . . . . . . . . . . . José Napoleón Duarte | .Colón . . . . . 5.00 | 3,940 710 |
| EQUATORIAL GUINEA Malabo | 300,000. . . 10,000 | 10,831. . . 28,051 | . .Republic . . . | .President, Supreme Military . . Council: Lt. Col. Teodoro Obiang Nguema Mbasogo | .CFA franc[6] 276.6 | NA NA |
| ETHIOPIA . . . . . . . Addis Ababa | 46,000,000. . . 1,277,200 | 471,778. . . 1,221,900 | . .Socialist. . . state | .Head of State, Chairman,. . . . Provisional Military Administrative Council and Council of Ministers: Mengistu Haile Mariam | .Birr . . . . . 2.07 | 4,630 110 |
| FIJI . . . . . . . . . . Suva | 700,000. . . 71,300 | 7,056. . . 18,274 | . .Republic . . . | .President: . . . . . . . . . . . Penaia Ganilau Prime Minister: Kamisese Mara | .Dollar . . . . . 1,457 | 1,190 1,700 |
| FINLAND . . . . . . . Helsinki | 4,900,000. . . 485,800 | 130,129. . . 337,032 | . .Republic . . . | .President: . . . . . . . . . . . Mauno Koivisto Prime Minister: Harri Holkeri | .Markka . . . . 4.035 | 53,450 10,870 |
| FRANCE . . . . . . . Paris | 55,600,000. . . 2,360,000 | 211,208. . . 547,026 | . .Republic . . . | .President: . . . . . . . . . . . François Mitterrand Premier: Jacques Chirac | .Franc . . . . . 5.532 | 526,630 9,550 |
| GABON. . . . . . . . Libreville | 1,200,000. . . 350,000 | 103,347. . . 267,667 | . .Republic . . . | .President: . . . . . . . . . . . Omar Bongo Premier: Léon Mébiame | .CFA franc[6] 276.6 | 3,330 3,340 |

| Imports<br>Exports | Revenue<br>Expenditure | Elementary Schools:<br>Teachers<br>Students | Secondary Schools:<br>Teachers<br>Students | Colleges and Universities:<br>Teachers<br>Students |
|---|---|---|---|---|
| $  751,000,000[7] ........$<br>1,077,000,000[7] | NA ........<br>NA | 7,549 ........<br>458,237 | 5,437 ........<br>202,908 | 565<br>9,385 |
| 1,098,000,000 ........<br>989,000,000 | NA ........<br>NA | 12,223 ........<br>353,958 | NA ........<br>148,032 | 4,343<br>54,334 |
| 8,593,000,000 ........<br>8,567,000,000 | 13,992,400,000 ........<br>13,851,200,000 | 83,424 ........<br>1,282,999 | 89,826 ........<br>1,024,113 | NA<br>212,200 |
| 1,247,000,000[9] ........<br>476,000,000[9] | 723,400,000 ........<br>1,017,200,000 | NA ........<br>52,066[8] | 2,864[8] ........<br>41,417[8] | 252[8]<br>2,719[8] |
| 17,627,000,000[3] ........<br>17,541,000,000 | 46,344,900,000 ........<br>46,321,800,000 | 94,404 ........<br>2,037,121 | 26,050 ........<br>409,670 | 19,135<br>140,971 |
| 18,429,000,000[3] ........<br>16,699,000,000 | 28,257,900,000 ........<br>28,141,500,000 | NA ........<br>426,766 | NA ........<br>495,950 | NA<br>86,235 |
| NA ........<br>NA | 127,600,000 ........<br>127,600,000 | 559 ........<br>24,606 | 317 ........<br>6,311 | NA<br>NA |
| 58,000,000 ........<br>25,000,000 | 24,800,000 ........<br>22,700,000 | 665 ........<br>13,283 | 145 ........<br>3,234 | 59<br>284 |
| 1,247,000,000[3] ........<br>750,000,000 | 1,172,600,000 ........<br>1,172,600,000 | 20,607 ........<br>980,808 | NA ........<br>353,729 | NA<br>42,412 |
| 1,674,000,000 ........<br>2,780,000,000 | 1,522,500,000 ........<br>1,470,000,000 | 50,437 ........<br>1,677,364 | 39,909 ........<br>650,278 | 11,679<br>258,064 |
| 9,962,000,000 ........<br>3,714,000,000 | 17,695,100,000 ........<br>20,788,800,000 | 158,636 ........<br>5,349,579 | 149,437 ........<br>3,201,703 | 26,631<br>589,899 |
| 961,000,000 ........<br>679,000,000 | 764,400,000 ........<br>910,400,000 | 17,633 ........<br>851,895 | 3,390 ........<br>81,318 | 2,202<br>46,941 |
| 58,000,000 ........<br>26,000,000 | 23,400,000 ........<br>24,800,000 | NA ........<br>65,000 | NA ........<br>NA | 68<br>1,140 |
| 996,000,000 ........<br>333,000,000 | 901,500,000 ........<br>1,174,500,000 | 46,678 ........<br>2,497,114 | 13,474 ........<br>583,783 | 920<br>10,526 |
| 442,000,000 ........<br>236,000,000 | 311,400,000 ........<br>310,900,000 | 4,150 ........<br>116,318 | 2,749 ........<br>48,608 | NA<br>2,299 |
| 13,233,000,000 ........<br>13,617,000,000 | 21,554,300,000 ........<br>21,554,300,000 | 25,139 ........<br>369,047 | 37,356 ........<br>433,646 | 6,938<br>88,295 |
| 107,809,000,000 ........<br>97,726,000,000 | 122,000,000,000 ........<br>122,000,000,000 | 206,198 ........<br>4,387,003 | 318,452 ........<br>5,124,403 | NA<br>951,042 |
| 976,000,000[7] ........<br>1,920,000,000[7] | 934,400,000 ........<br>1,183,500,000 | 3,802 ........<br>172,201 | 2,135 ........<br>36,160 | 616<br>3,228 |

| Nation Capital | Population | Area of Country (sq mi/ sq km) | Type of Government | Heads of State and Government | Currency: Value of U.S. Dollar | GNP (000,000): GNP Per Capita |
|---|---|---|---|---|---|---|
| GAMBIA, THE . . . . . Banjul | 800,000. . . 44,200 | 4,361. . 11,295 | .Republic (C) | .President: . . . . . . . . . . . . Sir Dawda K. Jawara | .Dalasi. . . . . 7.271 | $ 170 230 |
| GERMAN . . . . . . . . . DEMOCRATIC REPUBLIC East Berlin | 16,700,000. . . 1,215,600 | 41,768. . 108,178 | .Socialist. . . . . republic | .Chairman, Council of State: . . Erich Honecker Chairman, Council of Ministers (Premier): Willi Stoph | .Mark . . . . . 1.632 | NA NA |
| GERMANY, FEDERAL REPUBLIC OF Bonn | 61,000,000. . . 292,600 | 95,976. . 248,577 | .Federal . . . . republic | .President: . . . . . . . . . . . Richard von Weizsäcker Chancellor: Helmut Kohl | .Deutsche . . . mark 1.632 | 667,970 10,940 |
| GHANA . . . . . . . . . . Accra | 13,900,000. . . 964,900 | 92,100. . 238,537 | .Republic (C) | .Chairman, Provisional. . . . National Defense Council (Head of State): Jerry J. Rawlings | .Cedi . . . . . 176.0 | 4,960 390 |
| GREAT BRITAIN. . . . London | 56,800,000. . . 6,767,000 | 94,227. . 244,046 | .Limited . . . . monarchy (C) | .Queen: . . . . . . . . . . . Elizabeth II Prime Minister: Margaret Thatcher | .Pound . . . . . 0.548 | 474,190 8,390 |
| GREECE . . . . . . . . . Athens | 10,000,000. . . 885,700 | 50,944. . 131,944 | .Republic . . . | .President: . . . . . . . . . . . Christos Sartzetakis Prime Minister: Andreas Papandreou | .Drachma . . . 129.6 | 35,250 3,550 |
| GRENADA . . . . . . . St. George's | 100,000. . . 10,000 | 120. . 311 | .Parliamentary state (C) | Governor-General: . . . . . . . . Sir Paul Scoon Prime Minister: Herbert A. Blaize | .East. . . . . . Caribbean dollar 2.70 | 90 970 |
| GUATEMALA . . . . . Guatemala City | 8,400,000. . . 1,300,000 | 42,042. . 108,889 | .Republic . . . | .President: . . . . . . . . . . . Marco Vinicio Cerezo Arévalo | .Quetzal . . . . 1.00 | 9,890 1,240 |
| GUINEA . . . . . . . . . Conakry | 6,400,000. . . 763,000 | 94,926. . 245,857 | .Republic . . . | .President: . . . . . . . . . . . Lansana Conté | .Franc . . . . . 340.0 | 1,950 320 |
| GUINEA-BISSAU. . . . Bissau | 900,000. . . 138,000 | 13,948. . 36,125 | .Republic . . . | .President, Council of . . . . . . the Revolution: João Bernardo Vieira | .Peso . . . . . 650.0 | 150 170 |
| GUYANA . . . . . . . . . Georgetown | 800,000. . . 187,600[2] | 83,000. . 214,969 | .Republic (C) | .President: . . . . . . . . . . . Desmond Hoyte Prime Minister: Hamilton Green | .Dollar . . . . . 10.00 | 460 570 |
| HAITI . . . . . . . . . . . Port-au-Prince | 6,200,000. . . 449,800 | 10,714. . 27,750 | .Republic . . . | .Head, military-civilian . . . . . . council: Henri Namphy | .Gourde . . . . 5.00 | 1,900 350 |
| HONDURAS . . . . . . Tegucigalpa | 4,700,000. . . 571,400 | 43,277. . 112,088 | .Republic . . . | .President: . . . . . . . . . . . José Azcona del Hoyo | .Lempira. . . . 2.00 | 3,190 730 |
| HUNGARY . . . . . . . Budapest | 10,600,000. . . 2,080,000 | 35,919. . 93,030 | .People's. . . . republic | .Chairman, Presidential Council: Pál Losonczi Chairman, Council of Ministers (Premier): Karoly Grosz | Forint . . . . . 46.89 | 20,720 1,940 |
| ICELAND . . . . . . . . Reykjavík | 200,000. . . 41,400 | 39,769. . 103,000 | .Republic . . . | .President: . . . . . . . . . . . Vigdís Finnbogadóttir Prime Minister: Thorsteinn Pálsson | .New króna 36.40 | 2,580 10,720 |
| INDIA . . . . . . . . . . . New Delhi | 800,300,000. . . 7,000,000 | 1,269,346. . 3,287,590 | .Federal . . . . republic (C) | .President: . . . . . . . . . . . Ramaswami Venkataraman Prime Minister: Rajiv Gandhi | .Rupee . . . . 12.95 | 194,820 250 |
| INDONESIA . . . . . . Jakarta | 174,900,000. . . 6,503,400 | 782,663. . 2,027,087 | .Republic . . . | .President: . . . . . . . . . . . Suharto | .Rupiah . . . . 1,650 | 86,590 530 |
| IRAN . . . . . . . . . . . Tehran | 50,400,000. . . 5,734,200 | 636,296. . 1,648,000 | .Islamic . . . . republic | .President: . . . . . . . . . . . Hojatolislam Sayed Ali Khamenei Prime Minister: Mir Hussein Moussavi | .Rial . . . . . . 66.68 | NA NA |

| Imports<br>Exports | Revenue<br>Expenditure | Elementary Schools:<br>Teachers<br>Students | Secondary Schools:<br>Teachers<br>Students | Colleges and Universities:<br>Teachers<br>Students |
|---|---|---|---|---|
| $    93,000,000<br>43,000,000 | $    40,100,000<br>62,700,000 | 2,640<br>66,257 | 737<br>14,450 | 179<br>1,489 |
| 23,433,000,000[3]<br>25,268,000,000 | 89,409,100,000<br>88,975,100,000 | 171,381<br>2,024,220 | NA<br>456,151 | 29,460<br>139,699 |
| 157,645,000,000<br>183,406,000,000 | 133,882,000,000<br>149,848,000,000 | 234,549<br>4,005,638 | 217,214<br>3,205,776 | 130,743<br>1,198,330 |
| 731,000,000<br>617,000,000 | 731,400,000<br>729,400,000 | NA<br>1,464,624 | NA<br>748,212 | NA<br>7,878 |
| 109,269,000,000<br>101,332,000,000 | 229,764,000,000<br>236,324,000,000 | 245,000<br>4,474,000 | NA<br>5,296,000 | NA<br>413,000 |
| 10,139,000,000<br>4,542,000,000 | 15,200,000,000<br>17,900,000,000 | 34,054<br>892,509 | 35,842<br>762,368 | 6,129<br>83,485 |
| NA<br>NA | 87,500,000<br>87,500,000 | 764<br>17,704 | NA<br>NA | 40<br>519 |
| 1,175,000,000<br>1,066,000,000 | 1,460,700,000<br>1,679,200,000 | 26,963<br>979,888 | 11,828<br>167,724 | NA<br>47,433 |
| 351,000,000<br>428,000,000 | 444,000,000<br>444,000,000 | 7,493<br>270,140 | 4,335<br>81,422 | 946<br>7,470 |
| 50,000,000<br>12,000,000 | 56,300,000<br>67,600,000 | 3,153<br>81,444 | 757<br>12,737 | NA<br>NA |
| 255,000,000<br>207,000,000 | 407,300,000<br>437,000,000 | 3,493<br>130,003 | NA<br>NA | 447<br>1,580 |
| 442,000,000<br>174,000,000 | 204,000,000<br>270,000,000 | 14,927<br>658,102 | NA<br>101,519 | 559<br>4,099 |
| 890,000,000<br>780,000,000 | 1,501,900,000<br>1,539,100,000 | 18,966<br>703,608 | 5,342<br>156,665 | 1,940<br>30,119 |
| 8,228,000,000<br>8,542,000,000 | 14,860,200,000<br>15,391,200,000 | 88,066<br>1,297,800 | 29,404<br>412,500 | 14,850<br>64,200 |
| 904,000,000<br>814,000,000 | 695,700,000<br>743,300,000 | NA<br>25,280 | NA<br>26,803 | NA<br>5,212 |
| 15,092,000,000<br>8,510,000,000 | 37,509,100,000<br>40,291,200,000 | 2,363,347<br>94,154,674 | 1,075,487<br>31,547,190 | 277,648<br>5,345,580 |
| 10,259,000,000[3]<br>18,590,000,000 | 19,493,700,000<br>19,493,700,000 | 10,564,470<br>29,108,580 | 403,422<br>6,320,013 | NA<br>570,392 |
| NA<br>12,378,000,000 | 36,826,500,000<br>41,000,800,000 | 297,298<br>5,994,403 | 196,541<br>2,832,841 | 7,214<br>113,993 |

| Nation Capital | Population | Area of Country (sq mi/ sq km) | Type of Government | Heads of State and Government | Currency: Value of U.S. Dollar | GNP (000,000): GNP Per Capita |
|---|---|---|---|---|---|---|
| **IRAQ** Baghdad | 17,000,000. 3,189,700[2] | 167,925. 434,924 | Republic | President and Chairman, Revolutionary Command Council: Saddam Hussein al-Takriti | Dinar 0.311 | $ NA NA |
| **IRELAND, REPUBLIC OF** Dublin | 3,500,000. 502,300 | 27,136. 70,283 | Republic | President: Patrick J. Hillery Prime Minister: Charles J. Haughey | Punt 1.630 | 17,250 4,840 |
| **ISRAEL** Jerusalem | 4,400,000. 477,000 | 7,992. 20,700 | Republic | President: Chaim Herzog Prime Minister: Yitzhak Shamir | Shekel 1.553 | 21,140 4,920 |
| **ITALY** Rome | 57,400,000. 2,815,500 | 116,304. 301,225 | Republic | President: Francesco Cossiga Prime Minister: Giovanni Goria | Lira 1,202 | 371,050 6,520 |
| **IVORY COAST** Abidjan | 10,800,000. 1,850,000 | 124,503. 322,462 | Republic | President: Félix Houphouët-Boigny | CFA franc[6] 276.6 | 6,250 620 |
| **JAMAICA** Kingston | 2,500,000. 516,000[2] | 4,244. 10,991 | Parliamentary state (C) | Governor-General: Florizel A. Glasspole Prime Minister: Edward P. G. Seaga | Dollar 5.49 | 2,090 940 |
| **JAPAN** Tokyo | 122,200,000. 8,354,000 | 145,824. 377,682 | Constitutional monarchy | Emperor: Hirohito Prime Minister: Noboru Takeshita | Yen 127.5 | 1,366,040 11,330 |
| **JORDAN** Amman | 3,700,000. 777,500 | 37,738. 97,740 | Constitutional monarchy | King: Hussein I Prime Minister: Zaid al-Rifai | Dinar 0.343 | 4,010[11] 1,560 |
| **KENYA** Nairobi | 22,400,000. 827,800 | 224,961. 582,646 | Republic (C) | President: Daniel arap Moi | Shilling 15.60 | 5,960 290 |
| **KIRIBATI (GILBERT ISLANDS)** Tarawa | 62,000. 21,000 | 342. 886 | Republic (C) | President: Ieremia T. Tabai | Dollar 1.401 | 30[1] NA |
| **KOREA, DEMOCRATIC PEOPLE'S REPUBLIC OF** P'yŏngyang | 21,400,000. 1,280,000 | 46,540. 120,538 | People's republic | President: Marshal Kim Il Sung Premier: Li Gun Mo | Won 0.94 | 17,040 NA |
| **KOREA, REPUBLIC OF** Seoul | 42,100,000. 9,645,800[2] | 38,025. 98,484 | Republic | President: Chun Doo Hwan Prime Minister: Kim Chung Yul | Won 795.1 | 88,440 2,180 |
| **KUWAIT** Kuwait | 1,900,000. 44,400 | 6,880. 17,818 | Constitutional emirate | Emir: Sheikh Jabir al-Ahmad al-Sabah Prime Minister: Sheikh Saad al-Abdullah al-Salem al-Sabah | Dinar 0.273 | 24,760 14,270 |
| **LAOS** Vientiane | 3,800,000. 377,400 | 91,429. 236,800 | People's republic | President: Phoumi Vongvichit Premier: Kaysone Phomvihan | New kip. 35.00 | NA NA |
| **LEBANON** Beirut | 3,300,000. 1,000,000 | 4,015. 10,400 | Republic | President: Amin Gemayel Prime Minister: Selim al-Hoss | Pound 466.0 | NA NA |
| **LESOTHO** Maseru | 1,600,000. 45,000 | 11,720. 30,355 | Constitutional monarchy (C) | King: Moshoeshoe II Prime Minister: Justin Lekhanya | Loti 1.941 | 730 480 |
| **LIBERIA** Monrovia | 2,400,000. 425,000 | 43,000. 111,369 | Republic | Head of State and Chairman, People's Redemption Council: Samuel K. Doe | Dollar 1.00 | 1,040 470 |

| Imports<br>Exports | Revenue<br>Expenditure | Elementary Schools:<br>Teachers<br>Students | Secondary Schools:<br>Teachers<br>Students | Colleges and Universities:<br>Teachers<br>Students |
|---|---|---|---|---|
| $ NA<br>9,785,000,000 | $ NA<br>NA | 112,428<br>2,698,542 | 42,374<br>1,068,224 | 4,907<br>84,751 |
| 10,028,000,000<br>10,360,000,000 | 10,609,000,000<br>12,373,000,000 | 20,933<br>566,289 | NA<br>212,342 | 2,897<br>33,982 |
| 8,021,000,000<br>6,080,000,000 | 43,864,400,000<br>43,864,400,000 | 42,536<br>609,071 | 35,508<br>348,262 | NA<br>60,610 |
| 90,994,000,000<br>76,957,000,000 | 169,591,000,000<br>247,343,000,000 | 276,716<br>4,204,272 | 532,264<br>5,319,934 | 48,590<br>1,112,487 |
| 1,742,000,000<br>2,939,000,000 | 2,059,100,000<br>2,059,100,000 | NA<br>1,179,456 | NA<br>245,342 | NA<br>12,755 |
| 1,110,000,000<br>564,000,000 | 664,600,000<br>985,400,000 | 10,374<br>341,748 | NA<br>NA | NA<br>4,884 |
| 109,700,000,000<br>211,200,000,000 | 349,000,000,000<br>349,000,000,000 | 461,256<br>11,095,372 | 551,932<br>11,167,864 | 181,286<br>1,935,033 |
| 2,656,000,000<br>838,000,000 | 2,840,000,000<br>2,970,000,000 | 15,179<br>487,890 | 14,443<br>311,402 | 1,011<br>22,305 |
| 1,437,000,000<br>958,000,000 | 2,307,900,000<br>2,215,100,000 | 96,202<br>4,702,414 | 14,275<br>529,396 | 1,800<br>10,000 |
| 36,000,000<br>3,000,000 | 10,900,000<br>10,900,000 | 471<br>13,194 | 130<br>1,901 | NA<br>NA |
| 1,390,000,000<br>1,340,000,000 | 14,269,300,000<br>14,198,100,000 | NA<br>NA | NA<br>NA | NA<br>NA |
| 31,136,000,000[12]<br>30,283,000,000 | 16,998,000,000<br>16,664,000,000 | NA<br>4,856,752 | NA<br>4,934,975 | NA<br>1,018,236 |
| NA<br>10,126,000,000 | 10,672,000,000<br>14,296,000,000 | NA<br>243,077 | NA<br>90,965 | 848<br>13,233 |
| NA<br>NA | 119,000,000<br>215,000,000 | 17,512<br>481,560 | 3,709<br>64,500 | 420<br>4,885 |
| NA<br>NA | 330,700,000<br>466,100,000 | 22,810<br>398,977 | NA<br>NA | 7,976<br>73,052 |
| NA<br>NA | 156,100,000<br>118,000,000 | NA<br>289,590 | NA<br>32,619 | 212<br>1,350 |
| 284,000,000<br>436,000,000 | 234,900,000<br>366,400,000 | 9,099<br>227,431 | NA<br>NA | NA<br>3,702 |

| Nation<br>Capital | Population | Area of<br>Country<br>(sq mi/<br>sq km) | Type of<br>Government | Heads of State and<br>Government | Currency:<br>Value of<br>U.S. Dollar | GNP<br>(000,000):<br>GNP<br>Per Capita |
|---|---|---|---|---|---|---|
| **LIBYA** . . . . . . . . .<br>Tripoli | 3,800,000. . .<br>990,700 | 679,362. .<br>1,759,540 | .Socialist . . . .<br>republic | .Head of State: . . . . . . . . .<br>Muammar al-Qaddafi<br>Secretary-General, General<br>People's Congress:<br>Omar al-Muntasser | .Dinar . . . . .$<br>0.277 | 27,000<br>7,500 |
| **LIECHTENSTEIN** . . . .<br>Vaduz | 26,700. . .<br>4,900 | 61. . .<br>157 | .Constitutional<br>monarchy | Sovereign: . . . . . . . . . . . .<br>Prince Francis Joseph II<br>Chief of Government:<br>Hans Brunhart | .Swiss franc<br>1.331 | NA<br>NA |
| **LUXEMBOURG** . . . .<br>Luxembourg | 400,000. . .<br>76,200 | 998. .<br>2,586 | .Constitutional<br>monarchy | Grand Duke: . . . . . . . . . . .<br>Jean<br>President:<br>Jacques Santer | .Franc . . . . .<br>34.14 | 4,900<br>13,380 |
| **MADAGASCAR** . . . .<br>Antananarivo | 10,600,000. . .<br>773,000 | 226,658. .<br>587,041 | .Socialist<br>republic | President: . . . . . . . . . . . . .<br>Cmdr. Didier Ratsiraka<br>Prime Minister:<br>Lt. Col. Désiré Rakotoarijaona | .Franc . . . .<br>1,237 | 2,510<br>250 |
| **MALAWI** . . . . . . . .<br>Lilongwe | 7,400,000. . .<br>186,800 | 45,747. .<br>118,484 | .Republic . . .<br>(C) | .President: . . . . . . . . . . . .<br>Hastings Kamuzu<br>Banda | .Kwacha . . . .<br>2.078 | 1,160<br>170 |
| **MALAYSIA** . . . . . . .<br>Kuala Lumpur | 16,100,000. . .<br>937,900 | 127,317. .<br>329,749 | .Federal . . . .<br>constitutional<br>monarchy<br>(C) | .Supreme Head of State: . . . . .<br>Sultan Mahmood Iskandar<br>Prime Minister:<br>Datuk Seri Mahathir bin<br>Mohamad | .Dollar . . . .<br>2.485 | 31,930<br>2,050 |
| **MALDIVES** . . . . . . .<br>Male | 200,000. . .<br>46,300 | 115. .<br>298 | .Republic . . . .<br>| .President: . . . . . . . . . . . .<br>Maumoon Abdul Gayoom | .Rufiyaa . . . .<br>10.10 | 50<br>290 |
| **MALI** . . . . . . . . . .<br>Bamako | 8,400,000. . .<br>404,000 | 478,767. .<br>1,240,000 | .Republic . . . .<br>| .President: . . . . . . . . . . . .<br>Moussa Traoré | .CFA Franc<br>276.6 | 1,070<br>140 |
| **MALTA** . . . . . . . . .<br>Valletta | 400,000. . .<br>9,340 | 122. .<br>316 | .Republic . . . .<br>(C) | .President: . . . . . . . . . . . . .<br>Paul Xuereb<br>Prime Minister:<br>Eddie Fenech Adami | .Pound . . . .<br>3.145 | 1,190<br>3,300 |
| **MAURITANIA** . . . . . .<br>Nouakchott | 2,000,000. . .<br>350,000 | 397,955. .<br>1,030,700 | .Islamic . . . .<br>republic | .President and Chairman, . . . .<br>Military Committee for<br>National Salvation:<br>Maaouiya Ould<br>Sidi Ahmed Taya | .Ouguiya . . .<br>75.31 | ˙700<br>410 |
| **MAURITIUS** . . . . . .<br>Port Louis | 1,100,000. . .<br>138,300 | 790. .<br>2,045 | .Parliamentary<br>state (C) | Governor-General: . . . . . . . .<br>Veerasamy Ringadoo<br>Prime Minister:<br>Aneerood Jugnauth | .Rupee . . . .<br>12.32 | 1,100<br>1,070 |
| **MEXICO** . . . . . . . .<br>Mexico City | 81,900,000. . .<br>10,500,000 | 761,604. .<br>1,972,547 | .Federal . . . .<br>republic | .President: . . . . . . . . . . . .<br>Miguel de la Madrid<br>Hurtado | .Peso . . . . .<br>2,199 | 163,790<br>2,080 |
| **MONACO**. . . . . . . .<br>Monaco | 27,000. . .<br> | 0.58. . .<br>1.49 | .Constitutional<br>monarchy | Prince: . . . . . . . . . . . . . . .<br>Rainier III<br>Minister of State:<br>Jean Ausseil | .French franc<br>5.532 | NA<br>NA |
| **MONGOLIAN** . . . . . .<br>**PEOPLE'S**<br>**REPUBLIC**<br>Ulan Bator | 2,000,000. . .<br>1,565,000<br><br>515,000 | 604,250. .<br> | .People's. . . .<br>republic | .Presidium Chairman: . . . . . .<br>Jambyn Batmönh<br>Premier:<br>Dumaagiyn Sodnom | .Tugrik. . . . .<br>3.356 | NA<br>NA |
| **MOROCCO** . . . . . . .<br>Rabat | 24,400,000. . .<br>566,900 | 172,414. .<br>446,550 | .Constitutional<br>monarchy | King:. . . . . . . . . . . . . . . .<br>Hassan II<br>Prime Minister:<br>Azzedine Laraki | .Dirham . . . .<br>7.82 | 13,390<br>610 |
| **MOZAMBIQUE** . . . . .<br>Maputo | 14,700,000. . .<br>903,660 | 309,496. .<br>801,590 | .People's. . . .<br>republic | .President: . . . . . . . . . . . .<br>Joaquim A. Chissano<br>Prime Minister:<br>Mário da Graça Machungo | .Metical . . . .<br>404.0 | 2,800<br>NA |
| **NAURU** . . . . . . . . .<br>Yaren | 8,000. . .<br>NA | 8. .<br>21 | .Republic . . . .<br>(C) | .President: . . . . . . . . . . . .<br>Hammer DeRoburt | .Australian. . .<br>dollar<br>1.401 | NA<br>NA |

| Imports Exports | Revenue Expenditure | Elementary Schools: Teachers Students | Secondary Schools: Teachers Students | Colleges and Universities: Teachers Students |
|---|---|---|---|---|
| $ NA | $ NA | 42,202 | 28,927 | NA |
| 10,841,000,000 | 3,790,000,000 | 741,502 | 351,778 | 27,535 |
| NA | 184,800,000 | 146 | 82 | NA |
| NA | 172,400,000 | 2,476 | 1,323 | NA |
| NA[5] | 1,740,200,000 | 1,685 | 2,020 | 318 |
| NA[5] | 1,739,100,000 | 22,826 | 24,341 | 982 |
| 402,000,000 | 452,200,000 | 42,462 | 11,685 | 1,059 |
| 274,000,000 | 589,800,000 | 1,625,216 | 299,584 | 37,746 |
| 284,000,000 | 153,900,000 | 14,499 | 1,238 | 229 |
| 252,000,000 | 289,200,000 | 847,157 | 24,657 | 1,961 |
| 13,987,000,000[13] | 8,260,000,000 | 81,664[14] | 54,787[14] | 4,020 |
| 13,917,000,000[13] | 9,050,000,000 | 2,120,050[14] | 1,173,202[14] | 31,018 |
| 61,000,000 | 19,500,000 | NA | NA | NA |
| 23,000,000 | 23,500,000 | 34,090 | 3,800 | NA |
| 410,000,000 | 258,200,000 | 7,932 | NA | 499 |
| 170,000,000 | 258,200,000 | 296,301 | 68,732 | 5,792 |
| 758,000,000 | 472,000,000 | 1,656 | 2,253 | 146 |
| 400,000,000 | 487,200,000 | 33,208 | 27,257 | 1,010 |
| 234,000,000 | 264,700,000 | 2,401 | 921 | NA |
| 374,000,000 | 264,700,000 | 107,390 | 26,727 | NA |
| 528,000,000 | 328,900,000 | NA | NA | NA |
| 441,000,000 | 365,100,000 | 135,012 | 71,219 | 458 |
| 14,015,000,000 | 72,000,000,000 | 437,408 | 343,431 | 92,338 |
| 21,822,000,000 | 107,000,000,000 | 15,219,245 | 6,130,824 | 1,121,252 |
| NA | 306,130,000 | NA | NA | NA |
| NA | 286,160,000 | 1,354 | 2,274 | NA |
| 824,000,000 | 2,069,700,000 | 4,700 | NA | 1,300 |
| 541,000,000 | 2,060,400,000 | 150,100 | 256,700 | 18,700 |
| 3,849,000,000 | 6,325,000,000 | NA | NA | NA |
| 2,165,000,000 | 7,746,300,000 | 2,279,887 | 1,200,383 | 119,920 |
| 424,000,000 | 139,000,000 | 29,634 | 3,751 | 352 |
| 80,000,000 | 214,000,000 | 1,402,541 | 126,602 | 1,106 |
| NA | 51,900,000 | NA | NA | NA |
| NA | 51,500,000 | 2,222 | 413 | NA |

| Nation Capital | Population | Area of Country (sq mi/ sq km) | Type of Government | Heads of State and Government | Currency: Value of U.S. Dollar | GNP (000,000): GNP Per Capita |
|---|---|---|---|---|---|---|
| **NEPAL** . . . . . . . . Kathmandu | 17,800,000. . . 350,000 | 54,362. . 140,797 | .Constitutional monarchy | King: . . . . . . . . . . . . . . Birendra Bir Bikram Shah Deva Prime Minister: Marich Man Singh Shrestha | .Rupee . . . .$ 21.00 | 2,610 160 |
| **NETHERLANDS, THE** Amsterdam | 14,600,000. . . 679,100 | 15,770. . 40,844 | .Constitutional monarchy | Queen: . . . . . . . . . . . . . Beatrix Prime Minister: Ruud Lubbers | .Guilder . . . . 1.837 | 132,920 9,180 |
| **NEW ZEALAND** . . . . Wellington | 3,300,000. . . 328,200 | 103,736. . 268,676 | .Parliamentary state (C) | Governor-General: . . . . . . . . Paul Reeves Prime Minister: David Lange | .Dollar . . . . . 1.549 | 23,720 7,310 |
| **NICARAGUA** . . . . . . Managua | 3,500,000. . . 1,216,000 | 50,193. . 130,000 | .Republic . . . | .President: . . . . . . . . . . . . Daniel Ortega Saavedra | .Córdoba . . . 70.00 | 2,760 850 |
| **NIGER** . . . . . . . . . Niamey | 7,000,000. . . 399,100 | 489,191. . 1,267,000 | .Republic . . | .President: . . . . . . . . . . . . Ali Seybou Prime Minister: Hamid Algabid | .CFA franc[6] 276.6 | 1,200 200 |
| **NIGERIA** . . . . . . . . Lagos | 108,600,000. . . 4,200,000 | 356,669. . 923,768 | .Federal . . . . republic (C) | .President: . . . . . . . . . . . . Ibrahim Babangida | .Naira . . . . . 4.192 | 75,940 760 |
| **NORWAY** . . . . . . . . Oslo | 4,200,000. . . 449,900 | 125,182. . 324,219 | .Constitutional monarchy | King: . . . . . . . . . . . . . . Olav V Prime Minister: Gro Harlem Bruntland | .Krone . . . . . 6.38 | 57,580 13,890 |
| **OMAN** . . . . . . . . . Masqat | 1,300,000. . . 50,000[2] | 82,030. . 212,450 | .Sultanate . . . | .Sultan and Prime Minister: . . . Qabus bin Sa'id | .Rial . . . . . . 0.385 | 8,360 7,080 |
| **PAKISTAN** . . . . . . . Islamabad | 104,600,000. . . 397,000 | 310,404. . 803,943 | .Federal . . . . republic | .President: . . . . . . . . . . . . Gen. Muhammad Zia ul-Haq Prime Minister: Muhammad Khan Junejo | .Rupee . . . . 17.49 | 36,230 380 |
| **PANAMA** . . . . . . . . Panamá | 2,300,000. . . 725,000 | 29,762. . 77,082 | .Republic . . . | .President: . . . . . . . . . . . . Eric Arturo Delvalle | .Balboa . . . . 1.00 | 4,400 2,020 |
| **PAPUA NEW GUINEA** Port Moresby | 3,600,000. . . 140,000 | 178,260. . 461,691 | .Parliamentary state (C) | Governor-General: . . . . . . . . Kingsford Dibela Prime Minister: Paias Wingti | .Kina . . . . . . 0.880 | 2,470 710 |
| **PARAGUAY** . . . . . . Asunción | 4,300,000. . . 457,200 | 157,048. . 406,752 | .Republic . . . | .President: . . . . . . . . . . . . Gen. Alfredo Stroessner | .Guarani . . . . 320.0 | 3,180 940 |
| **PERU** . . . . . . . . . . Lima | 20,700,000. . . 376,000 | 496,225. . 1,285,216 | .Republic . . . | .President: . . . . . . . . . . . . Alan García Pérez Prime Minister: Guillermo Larco Cox | .Inti . . . . . . 33.00 | 17,830 960 |
| **PHILIPPINES** . . . . . . Manila | 61,500,000. . . 1,630,500 | 115,830. . 300,000 | .Republic . . . | .President: . . . . . . . . . . . . Corazon C. Aquino Prime Minister: Salvador H. Laurel | .Peso . . . . 20.73 | 32,630 600 |
| **POLAND** . . . . . . . . Warsaw | 37,800,000. . . 1,659,400 | 120,725. . 312,677 | .People's. . . . republic | .Head of State: . . . . . . . . . Gen. Wojciech W. Jaruzelski Premier: Zbigniew Messner | .Złoty . . . . . 318.6 | 78,960 2,120 |
| **PORTUGAL** . . . . . . Lisbon | 10,300,000. . . 807,900 | 35,553. . 92,082 | .Republic . . . | .President: . . . . . . . . . . . . Mário Soares Prime Minister: Anibal Cavaco Silva | .Escudo . . . . 133.5 | 20,140 1,970 |
| **QATAR** . . . . . . . . . Doha | 300,000. . . 190,000 | 4,250. . 11,000 | .Constitutional emirate | Emir and Prime Minister: . . . . Sheikh Khalifa bin Hamad al-Thani | .Riyal . . . . . 3.641 | 5,110 15,980 |
| **ROMANIA** . . . . . . . Bucharest | 22,900,000. . . 1,961,200 | 91,699. . 237,500 | .Socialist. . . . republic | .Head of State and . . . . . . . President, State Council: Nicolae Ceauşescu Chairman, Council of Ministers (Premier): Constantin Dăscălescu | .Leu . . . . . . 8.59 | 57,030[1] NA |

| Imports / Exports | Revenue / Expenditure | Elementary Schools: Teachers / Students | Secondary Schools: Teachers / Students | Colleges and Universities: Teachers / Students |
|---|---|---|---|---|
| $ 765,000,000 | $ 279,800,000 | 38,016 | 15,910 | NA |
| 271,000,000 | 205,100,000 | 1,626,437 | 418,085 | 54,599 |
| 65,218,000,000 | 41,461,500,000 | 57,293 | NA | NA |
| 68,282,000,000 | 48,534,600,000 | 1,139,955 | 1,466,956 | 155,025 |
| 6,080,000,000 | 9,143,500,000 | 18,653 | 13,930 | NA |
| 5,736,000,000 | 10,162,900,000 | 425,771 | 214,518 | 59,868 |
| 826,000,000 | 1,140,300,000 | 17,969 | 6,014 | 1,423 |
| 385,000,000 | 1,424,000,000 | 534,317 | 161,745 | 31,537 |
| 324,000,000 | 302,200,000 | 6,940 | NA | 322 |
| 298,000,000 | 302,200,000 | 261,531 | NA | 2,450 |
| 6,205,000,000 | 4,669,400,000 | 359,701 | 98,487 | 7,759 |
| 13,134,000,000 | 4,376,700,000 | 14,383,487 | 3,561,207 | 83,357 |
| 15,560,000,000 | 37,880,000,000 | NA | NA | NA |
| 19,991,000,000 | 37,130,000,000 | 534,000 | 204,199 | 41,002 |
| 3,153,000,000 | 5,343,200,000 | 5,369 | 2,987 | NA |
| 4,972,000,000 | 5,438,800,000 | 155,389 | 39,892 | NA |
| 5,892,000,000 | 5,401,800,000 | 206,000 | 128,467 | 7,042 |
| 2,719,000,000 | 7,012,800,000 | 6,412,000 | 2,253,298 | 156,558 |
| 1,391,000,000 | 1,108,000,000 | 12,912 | 9,184 | 3,492 |
| 306,000,000 | 1,866,000,000 | 338,650 | 176,441 | 46,273 |
| 873,000,000[3] | 945,600,000 | 10,163 | 2,348 | 589 |
| 909,000,000 | 969,600,000 | 313,790 | 50,353 | 3,458 |
| 580,000,000 | 1,932,500,000 | 20,746 | NA | 1,945 |
| 290,000,000 | 1,932,500,000 | 539,889 | 164,464 | 20,496 |
| 2,048,000,000 | 3,249,500,000 | 89,370 | 55,959 | 16,913 |
| 2,705,000,000 | 4,160,000,000 | 3,343,631 | 1,429,219 | 305,390 |
| 5,261,000,000 | 4,331,800,000 | NA | NA | NA |
| 4,544,000,000 | 5,418,100,000 | 8,793,773 | 3,323,063 | 1,125,776 |
| 10,761,000,000[3] | 22,000,000,000 | 275,000 | 104,300 | 56,600 |
| 11,447,000,000 | 22,500,000,000 | 4,770,600 | 1,761,000 | 349,800 |
| 7,792,000,000 | 9,082,400,000 | 68,188 | 36,219 | 6,906 |
| 5,711,000,000 | 9,082,400,000 | 1,221,539 | 451,426 | 67,652 |
| 1,139,000,000 | 2,678,600,000 | 2,871 | NA | 401 |
| 3,541,000,000 | 4,689,900,000 | 31,844 | 19,506 | 4,624 |
| 7,565,000,000[3] | 75,955,600,000 | 150,539 | 49,208 | 13,344 |
| 10,735,000,000 | 75,955,600,000 | 3,067,446 | 1,272,245 | 174,042 |

# STATISTICS OF THE WORLD

| Nation Capital | Population | Area of Country (sq mi/ sq km) | Type of Government | Heads of State and Government | Currency: Value of U.S. Dollar | GNP (000,000): GNP Per Capita |
|---|---|---|---|---|---|---|
| **RWANDA** . . . . . . . . Kigali | 6,800,000 . . . 176,700 | 10,169 . . . 26,338 | . .Republic . . . | .President: . . . . . . . . . . . . Juvénal Habyarimana | .Franc . . . . . 74.20 | .$ 1,730 290 |
| **SAINT KITTS–** . . . . . **NEVIS** Basseterre | 50,000 . . . 14,700 | 65 . . 105 | .Parliamentary state (C) | Governor-General: . . . . . . . Sir Clement Arrindell Prime Minister: Kennedy Simmonds | .East. . . . . . Caribbean dollar 2.70 | 70 1,520 |
| **SAINT LUCIA** . . . . . Castries | 100,000 . . . 45,800 | 238 . . 616 | . Parliamentary state (C) | Governor-General: . . . . . . . . Allen Lewis Prime Minister: John G. M. Compton | .East. . . . . . Caribbean dollar 2.70 | 160 1,210 |
| **SAINT VINCENT** . . . . **AND THE GRENADINES** Kingstown | 100,000 . . . 33,700[2] | 150 . . 388 | .Parliamentary state (C) | Governor-General: . . . . . . . . Sir Joseph Lambert Eustace Prime Minister: James Mitchell | .East. . . . . . Caribbean dollar 2.70 | 100 840 |
| **SAN MARINO** . . . . . San Marino | 22,400 . . . 4,600 | 24 . . 61 | . .Republic . . . | .Co-Regents:. . . . . . . . . . . Renzo Renzi Germano de Biagi | .Italian lira . . . 1,202 | NA NA |
| **SÃO TOMÉ AND** . . . . **PRÍNCIPE** São Tomé | 100,000 . . . 35,000 | 372 . . 964 | . .Republic . . . | .President and Prime Minister: Manuel Pinto da Costa | .Dobra. . . . . 32.69 | 30 310 |
| **SAUDI ARABIA** . . . . Riyadh | 14,800,000 . . . 1,500,000 | 830,000 . . . 2,149,690 | . .Monarchy . . . | .King and Prime Minister: . . . . Fahd ibn Abdul-Aziz | .Riyal . . . . . 3.751 | 102,120 8,860 |
| **SENEGAL** . . . . . . . Dakar | 7,100,000 . . . 978,600 | 75,750 . . . 196,192 | . .Republic . . . | .President: . . . . . . . . . . . . Abdou Diouf Premier: Habib Thiam | .CFA franc[6] 276.6 | 2,400 370 |
| **SEYCHELLES** . . . . . Victoria | 100,000 . . . 23,300 | 108 . . 280 | . .Republic (C) | .President: . . . . . . . . . . . . France Albert René | .Rupee . . . . 5.226 | NA NA |
| **SIERRA LEONE** . . . . Freetown | 3,900,000 . . . 469,800 | 27,699 . . . 71,740 | . .Republic (C) | .President: . . . . . . . . . . . . Joseph Momoh | .Leone. . . . . 22.00 | 1,380 370 |
| **SINGAPORE** . . . . . . Singapore | 2,600,000 . . . 2,531,000 | 224 . . 581 | . .Republic (C) | .President: . . . . . . . . . . . . Wee Kim Wee Prime Minister: Lee Kuan Yew | .Dollar. . . . . 1.997 | 18,970 7,420 |
| **SOLOMON ISLANDS** Honiara | 300,000 . . . 26,000 | 10,983 . . . 28,446 | . .Parliamentary state (C) | Governor-General: . . . . . . . . Sir Baddeley Devesi Prime Minister: Ezekiel Alebua | .Dollar. . . . . 1.980 | 140 510 |
| **SOMALIA** . . . . . . . . Mogadishu | 7,700,000 . . . 500,000 | 246,201 . . . 637,657 | . .Republic . . . | .President and Chairman, . . . . Council of Ministers: Maj. Gen. Muhammad Siad Barre | .Somali . . . . 100.0 | 1,450 270 |
| **SOUTH AFRICA,**[16] . . . **REPUBLIC OF** Cape Town Pretoria | 34,300,000 . . . 213,800 528,400 | 471,445 . . . 1,221,037 | . .Republic . . . | .President: . . . . . . . . . . . . Pieter Willem Botha | .Rand . . . . . 3.030 | 65,320 2,010 |
| **SPAIN** . . . . . . . . . Madrid | 39,000,000 . . . 3,188,300 | 194,897 . . . 504,782 | . .Constitutional monarchy | King: . . . . . . . . . . . . . . Juan Carlos I Prime Minister: Felipe González Márquez | .Peseta . . . . 110.5 | 168,820 4,360 |
| **SRI LANKA** . . . . . . . **(CEYLON)** Colombo | 16,300,000 . . . 602,000 | 25,332 . . . 65,610 | . .Republic (C) | .President: . . . . . . . . . . . . Junius R. Jayewardene Prime Minister: Ranasinghe Premadasa | .Rupee . . . . 30.62 | 5,980 370 |
| **SUDAN** . . . . . . . . . Khartoum | 23,500,000 . . . 476,200 | 967,500 . . . 2,505,813 | . .Republic . . . | .Chairman of the Sovereign . . . Council: Ahmed al-Mirgani Prime Minister: Sadiq al-Mahdi | .Pound . . . . 2.93 | 7,350 330 |
| **SURINAME** . . . . . . . Paramaribo | 400,000 . . . 180,000 | 63,037 . . . 163,265 | . .Republic . . . | .President: . . . . . . . . . . . . Dési Bouterse Prime Minister: Jules Wijdenbosch | .Guilder . . . . 1.785 | 1,010 2,570 |
| **SWAZILAND** . . . . . . Mbabane | 700,000 . . . 38,600 | 6,704 . . . 17,363 | . .Monarchy . . . (C) | .King: . . . . . . . . . . . . . . Mswati III Prime Minister: Sotsha Dlamini | .Emalangeni . . 1.941 | 490 650 |

| Imports<br>Exports | Revenue<br>Expenditure | Elementary Schools:<br>Teachers<br>Students | Secondary Schools:<br>Teachers<br>Students | Colleges and Universities:<br>Teachers<br>Students |
|---|---|---|---|---|
| $ 343,000,000<br>112,000,000 | $ 164,600,000<br>187,900,000 | 14,005<br>790,198 | 1,082<br>45,158 | 186<br>1,527 |
| 51,000,000<br>17,000,000 | 26,900,000<br>27,100,000 | 357<br>8,070 | 289<br>4,060 | 8<br>40 |
| NA<br>NA | NA<br>79,700,000 | 1,084<br>32,107 | 350<br>5,314 | 105<br>537 |
| 61,000,000<br>32,000,000 | 64,400,000<br>64,400,000 | 1,184<br>21,497 | 320<br>5,123 | 41<br>259 |
| NA<br>NA | 107,100,000<br>107,100,000 | 165<br>1,456 | 155<br>1,266 | NA<br>NA |
| 26,000,000<br>13,000,000 | 22,000,000<br>23,400,000 | 517<br>16,013 | 325<br>6,436 | NA<br>NA |
| 23,622,000,000<br>NA | 31,300,000,000<br>45,300,000,000 | 72,615<br>1,161,096 | 35,947<br>496,778 | 8,631<br>82,369 |
| 620,000,000<br>402,000,000 | 1,450,800,000<br>1,450,800,000 | 11,513<br>583,507 | 4,141<br>92,417 | NA<br>13,450 |
| 88,000,000<br>20,000,000 | 82,000,000<br>91,200,000 | NA<br>14,663 | NA<br>3,973 | 28<br>144 |
| 156,000,000<br>112,000,000 | 115,300,000<br>176,100,000 | 10,451<br>350,161 | 4,235<br>86,653 | 296<br>2,445 |
| 26,285,000,000[15]<br>22,813,000,000[15] | 5,440,000,000<br>4,180,000,000 | 9,921<br>290,800 | 9,704<br>193,007 | 1,613<br>14,179 |
| 69,000,000<br>70,000,000 | NA<br>34,500,000 | 1,199<br>30,246 | 267<br>5,118 | NA<br>NA |
| 560,000,000<br>110,000,000 | 324,500,000<br>324,500,000 | 9,460<br>220,680 | 3,018<br>63,255 | NA<br>2,899 |
| 10,319,000,000[3]<br>9,326,000,000[17] | 19,400,000,000<br>23,400,000,000 | 277,426[4]<br>6,475,833[4] | —<br>— | 27,193<br>230,441 |
| 30,995,000,000<br>25,112,000,000 | 41,537,600,000<br>54,274,400,000 | 193,778<br>5,644,717 | 120,520<br>2,040,025 | NA<br>744,173 |
| 1,874,000,000<br>1,191,000,000 | 1,346,500,000<br>1,523,000,000 | 136,280<br>2,145,343 | NA<br>NA | 2,234<br>34,725 |
| 757,000,000<br>367,000,000 | 1,095,000,000<br>2,262,000,000 | 47,084<br>1,579,286 | 20,600<br>455,969 | 6,081<br>25,151 |
| 346,000,000<br>356,000,000 | 274,700,000<br>450,100,000 | NA<br>NA | NA<br>NA | 165<br>951 |
| 544,000,000<br>289,000,000 | 143,500,000<br>154,000,000 | 4,039<br>134,528 | 1,528<br>27,801 | 130<br>1,200 |

| Nation<br>Capital | Population | Area of<br>Country<br>(sq mi/<br>sq km) | Type of<br>Government | Heads of State and<br>Government | Currency:<br>Value of<br>U.S. Dollar | GNP<br>(000,000):<br>GNP<br>Per Capita |
|---|---|---|---|---|---|---|
| **SWEDEN** . . . . . . . .<br>Stockholm | 8,400,000. . .<br>659,000 | 173,732. . .<br>449,964 | .Constitutional<br>monarchy | King:. . . . . . . . . . . . .<br>Carl XVI Gustaf<br>Prime Minister:<br>Ingvar Carlsson | .Krona . . . . .$<br>5.940 | 99,050<br>11,890 |
| **SWITZERLAND** . . . .<br>Bern | 6,600,000. . .<br>144,000 | 15,941. . .<br>41,288 | .Federal . . . . .<br>republic | President:. . . . . . . . . . .<br>Pierre Aubert | .Franc . . . . .<br>1.331 | 105,180<br>16,380 |
| **SYRIA** . . . . . . . .<br>Damascus | 11,300,000. . .<br>2,083,000 | 71,500. . .<br>185,180 | .Socialist . . . . .<br>republic | President:. . . . . . . . . .<br>Hafez al-Assad<br>Prime Minister:<br>Mahmoud Zubi | .Pound . . . .<br>3.925 | 17,060<br>1,630 |
| **TAIWAN or** . . . . . . .<br>**FORMOSA**<br>**(REPUBLIC OF**<br>**CHINA)**<br>Taipei | 19,600,000. . .<br><br><br><br>2,500,000 | 13,900. . .<br>36,000 | .Republic . . . . | President:. . . . . . . . . .<br>Chiang Ching-kuo<br>Premier:<br>Yu Kuo-hua | .New Taiwan<br>dollar<br>28.75 | 38,200<br>NA |
| **TANZANIA** . . . . . . . .<br>Dar es-Salaam | 23,500,000. . .<br>757,300 | 364,900. . .<br>945,087 | .Republic . . . . .<br>(C) | President:. . . . . . . . . .<br>Ali Hassan Mwinyi<br>Prime Minister:<br>Joseph Warioba | .Shilling . . . .<br>78.33 | 5,840[18]<br>270 |
| **THAILAND** . . . . . . .<br>Bangkok | 52,600,000. . .<br>6,000,000 | 198,456. . .<br>514,000 | .Constitutional<br>monarchy | King:. . . . . . . . . . . . .<br>Bhumibol Adulyadej<br>Prime Minister:<br>Gen. Prem Tinsulanonda | .Baht . . . . .<br>25.19 | 42,100<br>830 |
| **TOGO.** . . . . . . . . . .<br>Lomé | 3,200,000. . .<br>366,500 | 21,925. . .<br>56,785 | .Republic . . . .<br> | President:. . . . . . . . . . .<br>Gen. Gnassingbé Eyadéma | .CFA franc[6]<br>276.6 | 750<br>250 |
| **TONGA** . . . . . . . . .<br>Nukualofa | 99,000. . .<br>27,700 | 270. . .<br>699 | .Constitutional<br>monarchy | King:. . . . . . . . . . . . .<br>Taufa'ahau Tupou IV<br>Prime Minister:<br>Prince Fatafehi Tu'ipelehake | .Pa'anga . . . .<br>1.401 | 70<br>730 |
| **TRINIDAD AND** . . . .<br>**TOBAGO**<br>Port of Spain | 1,300,000. . .<br><br>61,200 | 1,981. . .<br>5,130 | .Republic . . . .<br>(C) | President:. . . . . . . . . . .<br>Noor Muhammad Hassanali<br>Prime Minister:<br>Arthur N. Robinson | .Dollar . . . . . .<br>3.60 | 7,140<br>6,010 |
| **TUNISIA** . . . . . . . .<br>Tunis | 7,600,000. . .<br>596,700 | 63,170. . .<br>163,610 | .Republic . . . .<br> | President:. . . . . . . . . . .<br>Zine al-Abdine Ben Ali<br>Prime Minister:<br>Hebi Baccouche | .Dinar . . . .<br>0.782 | 8,730<br>1,220 |
| **TURKEY** . . . . . . . .<br>Ankara | 51,400,000. . .<br>2,251,500 | 301,382. . .<br>780,576 | .Republic . . . .<br> | President:. . . . . . . . . . .<br>Gen. Kenan Evren<br>Prime Minister:<br>Turgut Özal | .Lira . . . . .<br>987.8 | 56,060<br>1,130 |
| **TUVALU** . . . . . . . .<br>**(ELLICE ISLANDS)**<br>Funafuti | 8,200. . .<br><br>NA | 10. . .<br>26 | .Parliamentary<br>state (C) | Governor-General:. . . . . .<br>Tupua Leupena<br>Prime Minister:<br>Tomasi Puapua | .Australian. . .<br>dollar<br>1.401 | 5<br>NA |
| **UGANDA** . . . . . . . .<br>Kampala | 15,900,000. . .<br>458,000 | 91,134. . .<br>236,036 | .Republic . . . .<br>(C) | Head of state:. . . . . . . . . .<br>Yoweri Museveni<br>Prime Minister:<br>Samson Kisekka | .Shilling . . . .<br>59.81 | 3,290<br>NA |
| **UNION OF SOVIET** . .<br>**SOCIALIST**<br>**REPUBLICS**<br>Moscow | 284,000,000. . .<br><br><br>8,714,000 | 8,649,538. . .<br>22,402,200 | .Federal . . . . .<br>socialist<br>state | Chairman, Presidium . . . . . . .<br>of the Supreme Soviet:<br>Andrei Gromyko<br>Chairman, Council of Ministers<br>(Premier):<br>Nikolai Rhyzkov | .Ruble . . . . .<br>0.591 | 1,212,000[1]<br>NA |
| **UNITED ARAB** . . . . .<br>**EMIRATES**<br>Abu Dhabi | 1,400,000. . .<br><br>316,000 | 32,278. . .<br>83,600 | .Federal . . . .<br>state | President:. . . . . . . . . . . . .<br>Sheikh Zayed bin<br>Sultan al-Nahayan<br>Prime Minister:<br>Sheikh Rashid bin Saeed<br>al-Maktoum | .Dirham . . . . .<br>3.673 | 26,400<br>19,120 |
| **UNITED STATES.** . . . .<br>**OF AMERICA**<br>Washington, D.C. | 243,800,000. . .<br><br>627,400 | 3,618,770. . .<br>9,372,571 | .Federal . . . . .<br>republic | President:. . . . . . . . . . .<br>Ronald W. Reagan<br>Vice President:<br>George Bush | .Dollar . . . . .<br>* | 3,915,350<br>16,400 |

| Imports<br>Exports | Revenue<br>Expenditure | Elementary<br>Schools:<br>Teachers<br>Students | Secondary<br>Schools:<br>Teachers<br>Students | Colleges and<br>Universities:<br>Teachers<br>Students |
|---|---|---|---|---|
| $ 28,584,000,000<br>30,489,000,000 | $ 67,555,000,000<br>69,852,000,000 | 40,800<br>658,127 | 51,397<br>607,199 | NA<br>223,295 |
| 30,722,000,000<br>27,451,000,000 | 13,479,500,000<br>12,189,300,000 | NA<br>376,512 | NA<br>877,230 | 5,882<br>66,206 |
| 2,536,000,000<br>1,637,000,000 | NA<br>10,519,500,000 | 66,133<br>1,789,455 | 38,152<br>685,692 | NA<br>123,735 |
| 21,959,000,000<br>30,456,000,000 | 16,349,000,000<br>16,329,200,000 | 80,808<br>2,456,717 | 74,873<br>1,682,364 | 19,166<br>395,153 |
| 1,026,000,000<br>284,000,000 | 1,241,000,000<br>1,241,000,000 | 93,157<br>3,169,759 | 5,267<br>95,409 | 1,091<br>4,863 |
| 9,244,000,000<br>7,122,000,000 | 6,608,000,000<br>7,935,000,000 | 333,351<br>7,449,219 | NA<br>2,191,706 | 16,245<br>795,970 |
| 278,000,000<br>197,000,000 | 294,630,000<br>294,630,000 | 10,225<br>454,209 | 4,289<br>90,990 | 283<br>4,192 |
| 41,000,000<br>5,000,000 | 17,000,000<br>17,000,000 | 832<br>16,329 | NA<br>17,085 | 13<br>79 |
| 1,525,000,000<br>2,164,000,000 | 2,100,000,000<br>2,200,000,000 | 7,522<br>169,853 | 4,653<br>90,815 | NA<br>2,503 |
| 2,597,000,000<br>1,627,000,000 | 3,066,300,000<br>3,482,400,000 | 36,399<br>1,238,968 | 20,079<br>385,445 | 5,019<br>38,829 |
| 11,100,000,000<br>7,500,000,000 | 10,536,800,000<br>11,312,300,000 | 210,427<br>6,532,000 | 132,921<br>2,757,000 | 21,949<br>398,000 |
| 2,700,000<br>NA | NA<br>2,400,000 | 61<br>1,349 | NA<br>265 | NA<br>NA |
| NA<br>399,000,000 | NA<br>NA | 44,426<br>1,616,791 | 7,022<br>145,389 | 369<br>4,854 |
| 82,748,000,000[3]<br>87,041,000,000 | 657,881,000,000<br>657,620,000,000 | 2,839,200<br>27,461,900 | NA<br>23,774,400 | NA<br>6,382,300 |
| NA<br>14,337,000,000 | 3,540,100,000<br>4,537,500,000 | 5,691<br>137,700 | 3,660<br>56,773 | 599<br>6,856 |
| 387,081,000,000<br>217,304,000,000 | 854,143,000,000<br>1,002,147,000,000 | 1,432,000<br>27,945,000 | 1,057,000<br>17,060,000 | 700,000<br>12,242,000 |

| Nation Capital | Population | Area of Country (sq mi/ sq km) | Type of Government | Heads of State and Government | Currency: Value of U.S. Dollar | GNP (000,000): GNP Per Capita |
|---|---|---|---|---|---|---|
| UPPER VOLTA. . . . . (BURKINA FASO) Ouagadougou | 7,300,000. . . 375,000 | 105,869. . . 274,200 | .Republic . . . | .Head of State and Government: Blaise Compaoré | .CFA franc[6] 276.6 | $ 1,080 140 |
| URUGUAY . . . . . . . Montevideo | 3,100,000. . . 1,362,000 | 68,037. . . 176,215 | .Republic . . . | .President: . . . . . . . . . . . Julio María Sanguinetti Cairolo | .New peso. . . 273.3 | 4,980 1,660 |
| VANUATU (NEW. . . . HEBRIDES) Vila | 200,000. . . 15,000 | 5,700. . . 14,763 | .Republic (C) | .President: . . . . . . . . . . . Ati George Sokomanu Prime Minister: Rev. Walter H. Lini | .Vatu . . . . . 102.6 | 40 NA |
| VENEZUELA . . . . . . Caracas | 18,300,000. . . 3,184,958 | 352,144. . . 912,050 | .Federal republic | .President: . . . . . . . . . . . Jaime Lusinchi | .Bolivar . . . . 14.50 | 53,800 3,110 |
| VIETNAM . . . . . . . . Hanoi | 62,200,000. . . 3,000,000 | 127,242. . . 329,556 | .Socialist. . . . republic | .Chairman, Council of . . . . . . State (President): Vo Chi Cong Chairman, Council of Ministers (Premier): Pham Hung | .New dong . . 80.00 | 7,750 NA |
| WESTERN SAMOA . . Apia | 200,000. . . 33,200 | 1,097. . . 2,842 | .Constitutional monarchy (C) | Head of State: . . . . . . . . Malietoa Tanumafili II Prime Minister: Va'ai Kolone | .Talà . . . . . 2.043 | 110 660 |
| YEMEN, PEOPLE'S DEMOCRATIC REPUBLIC OF Aden | 2,400,000. . . 272,000 | 128,600. . . 333,000 | .People's. . . . republic | .President: . . . . . . . . . . . Haidar Bakr al-Attas Prime Minister: Yasin Said Numan | .Dinar . . . . . 0.343 | 1,130 540 |
| YEMEN ARAB . . . . . REPUBLIC Sana | 6,500,000. . . 427,000 | 75,300. . . 195,000 | .Republic . . . | .President: . . . . . . . . . . . Col. Ali Abdullah Saleh Prime Minister: Abdel Aziz Abdel Ghani | .Rial . . . . . . 10.00 | 4,140 520 |
| YUGOSLAVIA . . . . . Belgrade | 23,400,000. . . 1,470,100[2] | 98,766. . . 255,804 | .Federal . . . . socialist republic | .President: . . . . . . . . . . . Sinan Hassani President, Federal Executive Council (Prime Minister): Branko Mikulic | .Dinar . . . . . 1,262 | 47,900 2,070 |
| ZAIRE. . . . . . . . . . Kinshasa | 31,800,000. . . 1,700,000 | 905,568. . . 2,345,409 | .Republic . . . | .President: . . . . . . . . . . . Mobutu Sese Seko First State Commissioner (Prime Minister): Kengo wa Dondo | .Zaire . . . . . 128.1 | 5,220 170 |
| ZAMBIA . . . . . . . . Lusaka | 7,100,000. . . 641,000 | 290,586. . . 752,614 | .Republic . . . (C) | .President: . . . . . . . . . . . Kenneth D. Kaunda Prime Minister: Kebby Musokotwane | .Kwacha. . . . 8.045 | 2,620 400 |
| ZIMBABWE. . . . . . . (RHODESIA) Harare | 9,400,000. . . 656,000 | 150,804. . . 390,580 | .Republic . . . (C) | .Executive President: . . . . . . . Robert G. Mugabe Prime Minister: Robert G. Mugabe | .Dollar . . . . . 1.647 | 5,450 650 |

1. Figures are for gross domestic product.
2. Figure includes the whole metropolitan area.
3. Imports F.O.B.
4. These are combined figures for elementary and secondary education.
5. Figure for Belgium includes trade for Luxembourg.
6. "CFA" stands for Communauté Financière Africaine.
7. Excludes trade within Customs and Economic Union of Central Africa (Cameroon, Central African Republic, Congo, Gabon).
8. Information pertains to the Greek sector only. The president of the Turkish sector (Turkish Republic of Northern Cyprus) is Rauf Denktash; the prime minister is Dervis Eroğlu.
9. Unified figure, excludes military imports.
10. Entries include data for Greenland and the Faeroe Islands.

| Imports Exports | Revenue Expenditure | Elementary Schools: Teachers Students | Secondary Schools: Teachers Students | Colleges and Universities: Teachers Students |
|---|---|---|---|---|
| $    207,000,000 . . . . . . .$<br>79,000,000 | 251,600,000 . . . . . . . .<br>285,900,000 | 6,091 . . . . . . . .<br>351,807 | 1,940 . . . . . . . .<br>54,030 | 325<br>3,869 |
| 708,000,000 . . . . . . . .<br>854,000,000 | 563,700,000 . . . . . . . .<br>716,100,000 | 17,036 . . . . . . . .<br>350,178 | NA . . . . . . . .<br>197,890 | 4,349<br>50,151 |
| 71,000,000 . . . . . . . .<br>31,000,000 | NA . . . . . . . .<br>34,900,000 | 934 . . . . . . . .<br>22,244 | 188 . . . . . . . .<br>2,480 | NA<br>NA |
| 7,559,000,000[3] . . . . . . . .<br>7,418,000,000 | 13,595,300,000 . . . . . . . .<br>13,941,600,000 | 100,681 . . . . . . . .<br>2,660,440 | 63,303 . . . . . . . .<br>939,678 | 24,186<br>298,483 |
| 838,000,000 . . . . . . . .<br>430,000,000 | 5,104,400,000 . . . . . . . .<br>6,697,300,000 | 204,104 . . . . . . . .<br>7,887,439 | NA . . . . . . . .<br>NA | 17,242<br>114,701 |
| 51,000,000 . . . . . . . .<br>15,000,000 | 36,200,000 . . . . . . . .<br>51,700,000 | 1,502 . . . . . . . .<br>40,090 | NA . . . . . . . .<br>21,643 | 11<br>134 |
| 821,000,000 . . . . . . . .<br>27,000,000 | 582,500,000 . . . . . . . .<br>909,100,000 | 10,915 . . . . . . . .<br>238,004 | 1,444 . . . . . . . .<br>32,497 | 403<br>3,645 |
| 1,289,000,000 . . . . . . . .<br>10,000,000 | 805,000,000 . . . . . . . .<br>1,120,000,000 | 13,305 . . . . . . . .<br>731,989 | 3,952 . . . . . . . .<br>84,835 | 157<br>4,510 |
| 12,164,000,000 . . . . . . . .<br>10,641,000,000 | 7,049,400,000 . . . . . . . .<br>7,118,000,000 | 134,862 . . . . . . . .<br>2,823,248 | 62,643 . . . . . . . .<br>923,435 | 15,701<br>359,175 |
| 997,000,000 . . . . . . . .<br>591,000,000 | 677,300,000 . . . . . . . .<br>622,500,000 | 112,077 . . . . . . . .<br>4,654,613 | 43,459 . . . . . . . .<br>2,151,900 | NA<br>31,643 |
| 698,000,000[3] . . . . . . . .<br>539,000,000 | 533,400,000 . . . . . . . .<br>777,000,000 | 23,870 . . . . . . . .<br>1,121,769 | 5,682 . . . . . . . .<br>114,169 | 613<br>3,693 |
| 969,000,000[3] . . . . . . . .<br>1,053,000,000 | 1,794,000,000 . . . . . . . .<br>2,422,000,000 | NA . . . . . . . .<br>2,260,367 | NA . . . . . . . .<br>559,438 | NA<br>5,866 |

11. Figure for East Bank only.
12. Includes foreign aid.
13. Includes trade within constituent states.
14. Figures are for peninsular Malaysia only.
15. Figure includes transshipments to and from peninsular Malaysia.
16. Data generally exclude the homelands that have been granted independence. Estimated population of the following homelands, including homeland citizens residing in South Africa, in 1986 was: Bophuthatswana, 1,400,000; Ciskei, 721,000; Transkei, 2,500,000; Venda, 340,000. Presidents of the homelands were: Bophuthatswana, Lucas Mangope; Ciskei, Lennox Sebe; Transkei, K. D. Matanzima; Venda, Patrick Mphephu.
17. Figure excludes exports of gold.
18. Figure for mainland Tanzania only.

# THE STATES AND OUTLYING AREAS OF THE UNITED STATES

| State<br>Capital | Population | Area<br>(sq mi/<br>sq km) | Per<br>Capita<br>Personal<br>Income | Governor<br>Lieutenant-Governor | Revenue<br>Expenditure | Public<br>Roads<br>(Miles) |
|---|---|---|---|---|---|---|
| **ALABAMA** | 4,083,000 | 51,705 | $11,336 | Guy Hunt (R) | $ 6,601,000,000 | 87,979 |
| Montgomery | 195,200 | 133,915 | | Jim Folsom, Jr. (D) | 6,082,000,000 | |
| **ALASKA** | 525,000 | 591,004 | 17,796 | Steve Cowper (D) | 5,918,000,000 | 13,639 |
| Juneau | 27,000 | 1,530,693 | | Stephen McAlpine (D) | 4,950,000,000 | |
| **ARIZONA** | 3,386,000 | 114,000 | 13,474 | Evan Meacham (R) | 5,330,000,000 | 77,314 |
| Phoenix | 928,000 | 295,259 | | * | 4,599,000,000 | |
| **ARKANSAS** | 2,388,000 | 53,187 | 11,073 | Bill Clinton (D) | 3,342,000,000 | 77,050 |
| Little Rock | 178,100 | 137,754 | | Winston Bryant (D) | 3,018,000,000 | |
| **CALIFORNIA** | 27,663,000 | 158,706 | 16,904 | George Deukmejian (R) | 57,894,000,000 | 175,092 |
| Sacramento | 327,200 | 411,047 | | Leo T. McCarthy (D) | 51,840,000,000 | |
| **COLORADO** | 3,296,000 | 104,091 | 15,234 | Roy Romer (D) | 5,298,000,000 | 76,318 |
| Denver | 515,000 | 269,594 | | Mike Callihan (D) | 4,817,000,000 | |
| **CONNECTICUT** | 3,211,000 | 5,018 | 19,600 | William A. O'Neill (D) | 6,268,000,000 | 19,688 |
| Hartford | 135,700 | 12,997 | | Joseph L. Fauliso (D) | 5,429,000,000 | |
| **DELAWARE** | 644,000 | 2,044 | 15,010 | Michael N. Castle (R) | 1,682,000,000 | 5,332 |
| Dover | 22,500 | 5,295 | | S. B. Woo (D) | 1,335,000,000 | |
| **DISTRICT OF** | 622,000 | 67 | 19,397 | Mayor: | 3,407,000,000 | 1,102 |
| **COLUMBIA**<br>* | | 174 | | Marion S. Barry, Jr. (D) | 3,387,000,000 | |
| **FLORIDA** | 12,023,000 | 58,664 | 14,646 | Bob Martinez (R) | 13,798,000,000 | 99,074 |
| Tallahassee | 123,100 | 151,939 | | Bobby Brantley (R) | 12,854,000,000 | |
| **GEORGIA** | 6,222,000 | 58,910 | 13,446 | Joe Frank Harris (D) | 8,760,000,000 | 106,607 |
| Atlanta | 426,100 | 152,576 | | Zell B. Miller (D) | 7,618,000,000 | |
| **HAWAII** | 1,083,000 | 6,471 | 14,886 | John Waihee (D) | 2,677,000,000 | 4,040 |
| Honolulu | 380,000 | 16,760 | | Ben Cayetano (D) | 2,539,000,000 | |
| **IDAHO** | 998,000 | 83,564 | 11,223 | Cecil D. Andrus (D) | 1,610,000,000 | 71,544 |
| Boise | 116,800 | 216,430 | | C. L. (Butch) Otter (R) | 1,440,000,000 | |
| **ILLINOIS** | 11,582,000 | 56,345 | 15,586 | James R. Thompson, Jr. (R) | 17,573,000,000 | 134,778 |
| Springfield | 101,600 | 145,933 | | George H. Ryan (R) | 16,491,000,000 | |
| **INDIANA** | 5,531,000 | 36,185 | 13,136 | Robert D. Orr (R) | 7,917,000,000 | 91,462 |
| Indianapolis | 710,300 | 93,719 | | John M. Mutz (R) | 7,084,000,000 | |
| **IOWA** | 2,834,000 | 56,275 | 13,348 | Terry E. Branstad (R) | 4,697,000,000 | 112,498 |
| Des Moines | 190,800 | 145,752 | | Jo Ann Zimmerman (D) | 4,630,000,000 | |
| **KANSAS** | 2,476,000 | 82,277 | 14,650 | Mike Hayden (R) | 3,714,000,000 | 132,642 |
| Topeka | 118,900 | 213,096 | | Jack Walker (R) | 3,248,000,000 | |
| **KENTUCKY** | 3,727,000 | 40,409 | 11,238 | Martha Layne Collins (D) | 6,178,000,000 | 69,596 |
| Frankfort | 26,800 | 104,659 | | Steven Beshear (D) | 5,447,000,000 | |

The material in the following tables is the latest available. As before, it should be noted that the symbol * indicates that the category is not applicable to the area mentioned, and that NA means that the data were not available. The Office of Territorial Affairs was helpful in supplying some data for the table on Outlying Areas.

| Railways (Miles) | Aircraft Departures | English-language Daily Newspapers | Public Elementary Schools (K–8): Teachers Students | Public Secondary Schools (9–12): Teachers Students | Colleges and Universities: Institutions Students |
|---|---|---|---|---|---|
| 3,650 | 33,767 | 27 | NA 517,361 | NA 213,099 | 78 179,343 |
| NA | 62,993 | 8 | 3,323 76,472 | 3,491 30,134 | 15 27,479 |
| 1,698 | 120,297 | 19 | 19,975 386,057 | 7,960 162,195 | 31 216,854 |
| 2,594 | 12,115 | 32 | 11,520 303,536 | 12,051 129,874 | 36 77,958 |
| 6,287 | 529,945 | 121 | 109,603 2,926,705 | 74,548 1,328,849 | 290 1,650,439 |
| 3,369 | 199,063 | 26 | 15,829 377,086 | 14,065 171,907 | 48 161,314 |
| 466 | 49,344 | 24 | 11,868 317,793 | 15,890 140,823 | 48 159,348 |
| 212 | 605 | 3 | 2,691 62,795 | 3,054 29,819 | 8 31,883 |
| 47 | 129,177 | 3 | 2,952 59,085 | 2,392 24,598 | 19 78,868 |
| 3,085 | 329,700 | 47 | 43,884 1,082,885 | 35,459 476,622 | 87 451,392 |
| 5,031 | 296,795 | 33 | 30,684 756,752 | 19,584 322,842 | 80 196,826 |
| — | 115,561 | 5 | 3,946 111,294 | 3,141 52,605 | 12 49,937 |
| 2,256 | 32,596 | 11 | 4,870 149,380 | 4,551 59,289 | 10 42,668 |
| 7,960 | 394,768 | 88 | 57,279 1,225,311 | 29,848 579,982 | 162 678,689 |
| 4,813 | 63,747 | 71 | 23,588 653,554 | 23,499 312,045 | 75 250,567 |
| 3,503 | 26,430 | 37 | 15,312 323,358 | 15,651 161,000 | 59 152,897 |
| 7,376 | 11,782 | 46 | 13,312 285,671 | 10,607 124,558 | 52 141,359 |
| 2,846 | 33,626 | 24 | 22,017 448,768 | 11,489 195,065 | 45 141,724 |

457

| State Capital | Population | Area (sq mi/ sq km) | Per Capita Personal Income | Governor Lieutenant-Governor | Revenue Expenditure | Public Roads (Miles) |
|---|---|---|---|---|---|---|
| **LOUISIANA** Baton Rouge | 4,461,000 244,400 | 47,752 123,677 | $11,193 | Edwin W. Edwards (D) Robert L. Freeman (D) | $ 8,156,000,000 7,581,000,000 | 58,229 |
| **MAINE** Augusta | 1,172,000 22,000 | 33,265 86,156 | 12,790 | John R. McKernan (R) * | 2,137,000,000 1,948,000,000 | 21,968 |
| **MARYLAND** Annapolis | 4,535,000 31,700 | 10,460 27,091 | 16,864 | William Donald Schaefer (D) Melvin A. Steinberg (D) | 8,221,000,000 7,365,000,000 | 27,738 |
| **MASSACHUSETTS** Boston | 5,855,000 570,700 | 8,284 21,455 | 17,722 | Michael Dukakis (D) Evelyn F. Murphy (D) | 11,485,000,000 11,028,000,000 | 33,803 |
| **MICHIGAN** Lansing | 9,200,000 128,000 | 58,527 151,584 | 14,775 | James J. Blanchard (D) Martha W. Griffiths (D) | 17,262,000,000 15,634,000,000 | 117,664 |
| **MINNESOTA** St. Paul | 4,246,000 264,800 | 84,402 218,600 | 14,994 | Rudy Perpich (DFL) Marlene Johnson (DFL) | 9,378,000,000 8,121,000,000 | 132,644 |
| **MISSISSIPPI** Jackson | 2,625,000 208,800 | 47,689 123,514 | 9,716 | Bill Allain (D) Brad Dye (D) | 3,923,000,000 3,561,000,000 | 71,818 |
| **MISSOURI** Jefferson City | 5,103,000 33,600 | 69,697 180,514 | 13,789 | John Ashcroft (R) Harriet Woods (D) | 6,682,000,000 5,817,000,000 | 119,398 |
| **MONTANA** Helena | 809,000 23,900 | 147,046 380,847 | 11,803 | Ted Schwinden (D) George Turman (D) | 1,738,000,000 1,557,000,000 | 71,706 |
| **NEBRASKA** Lincoln | 1,594,000 180,400 | 77,355 200,349 | 13,742 | Kay Orr (R) William Nichols (R) | 2,144,000,000 2,137,000,000 | 92,199 |
| **NEVADA** Carson City | 1,007,000 36,000 | 110,561 286,352 | 15,437 | Richard Bryan (D) Bob Miller (R) | 1,909,000,000 1,643,000,000 | 43,438 |
| **NEW HAMPSHIRE** Concord | 1,057,000 31,900 | 9,279 24,032 | 15,911 | John Sununu (R) * | 1,361,000,000 1,195,000,000 | 14,491 |
| **NEW JERSEY** Trenton | 7,627,000 91,700 | 7,787 20,168 | 18,626 | Thomas H. Kean (R) * | 15,905,000,000 14,080,000,000 | 34,040 |
| **NEW MEXICO** Santa Fe | 1,500,000 52,000 | 121,593 314,924 | 11,422 | Garrey Carruthers (R) Jack Stahl (R) | 3,579,000,000 3,041,000,000 | 53,596 |
| **NEW YORK** Albany | 17,825,000 100,000 | 49,108 127,189 | 17,111 | Mario M. Cuomo (D) Stanley Lundine (D) | 46,762,000,000 40,106,000,000 | 110,136 |
| **NORTH CAROLINA** Raleigh | 6,413,000 212,000 | 52,669 136,412 | 12,438 | James G. Martin (R) Robert P. Jordan 3rd (D) | 9,879,000,000 8,492,000,000 | 93,630 |
| **NORTH DAKOTA** Bismarck | 672,000 44,500 | 70,702 183,117 | 12,472 | George Sinner (D) Lloyd Omdahl (D) | 1,651,000,000 1,541,000,000 | 86,173 |
| **OHIO** Columbus | 10,784,000 566,100 | 41,330 107,044 | 13,933 | Richard F. Celeste (D) Paul R. Leonard (D) | 21,242,000,000 17,568,000,000 | 113,288 |
| **OKLAHOMA** Oklahoma City | 3,272,000 443,200 | 69,956 181,185 | 12,283 | Henry Bellmon (R) Robert S. Kerr III (D) | 5,672,000,000 5,077,000,000 | 111,001 |
| **OREGON** Salem | 2,724,000 93,300 | 97,073 251,418 | 13,328 | Neil Goldschmidt (D) * | 5,337,000,000 4,812,000,000 | 94,578 |
| **PENNSYLVANIA** Harrisburg | 11,936,000 53,300 | 45,308 117,347 | 14,249 | Robert P. Casey (D) Mark Singel (D) | 20,337,000,000 18,067,000,000 | 115,663 |
| **RHODE ISLAND** Providence | 986,000 154,100 | 1,212 3,139 | 14,579 | Edward D. Di Prete (R) Richard Licht (D) | 2,129,000,000 2,010,000,000 | 5,997 |
| **SOUTH CAROLINA** Columbia | 3,425,000 98,600 | 31,113 80,582 | 11,299 | Carroll A. Campbell, Jr. (R) Nick Theodore (D) | 5,825,000,000 5,254,000,000 | 63,296 |
| **SOUTH DAKOTA** Pierre | 709,000 12,000 | 77,116 199,729 | 11,814 | William J. Janklow (R) Lowell C. Hansen (R) | 1,082,000,000 1,005,000,000 | 73,468 |

| Railways (Miles) | Aircraft Departures | English-language Daily Newspapers | Public Elementary Schools (K–8): Teachers Students | Public Secondary Schools (9–12): Teachers Students | Colleges and Universities: Institutions Students |
|---|---|---|---|---|---|
| 2,785 | 62,117 | 25 | 22,843 568,421 | 13,000 221,383 | 31 177,176 |
| NA | 6,941 | 8 | 8,546 139,909 | 5,615 65,688 | 30 52,201 |
| 849 | 59,345 | 16 | 18,140 437,611 | 20,293 225,239 | 56 231,649 |
| 1,079 | 101,984 | 46 | 18,420 555,630 | 31,887 285,273 | 121 421,175 |
| 3,451 | 155,748 | 48 | 42,623 1,096,013 | 19,830 585,859 | 92 507,293 |
| 5,092 | 122,469 | 24 | 20,081 462,752 | 21,233 237,183 | 69 221,162 |
| 1,510 | 12,527 | 21 | 14,567 329,981 | 11,535 141,214 | 42 101,180 |
| 5,823 | 209,667 | 45 | 24,416 544,197 | 23,253 250,910 | 92 241,146 |
| 3,274 | 27,282 | 10 | 6,562 107,710 | 3,143 45,951 | 16 35,958 |
| 4,426 | 25,477 | 19 | 9,433 183,016 | 8,254 81,523 | 28 97,769 |
| 1,451 | 80,291 | 7 | 3,520 107,070 | 3,254 47,878 | 8 43,656 |
| 355 | 1,496 | 8 | 6,063 106,912 | 4,041 54,062 | 28 52,283 |
| 1,194 | 146,887 | 25 | 37,656 734,468 | 28,342 375,697 | 60 297,658 |
| 2,062 | 32,909 | 19 | 8,139 187,479 | 4,482 90,072 | 20 68,295 |
| 3,453 | 337,064 | 72 | 74,058 1,687,415 | 68,354 917,948 | 301 1,000,000 |
| 3,217 | 157,404 | 53 | 37,265 749,451 | 19,538 336,714 | 128 327,288 |
| 4,472 | 13,366 | 11 | 4,656 83,097 | 2,643 34,868 | 19 37,939 |
| 6,102 | 160,735 | 90 | 51,816 1,206,138 | 46,448 587,637 | 142 514,745 |
| 4,024 | 50,616 | 48 | 16,247 412,008 | 15,916 178,048 | 47 169,173 |
| 2,865 | 76,132 | 20 | 12,981 304,359 | 10,828 142,109 | 46 137,967 |
| 5,113 | 198,437 | 93 | 43,829 1,092,558 | 47,362 590,663 | 206 533,198 |
| — | 10,653 | 7 | 3,874 89,589 | 3,845 43,484 | 13 69,927 |
| 2,533 | 34,630 | 18 | 22,212 424,125 | 12,433 182,518 | 63 131,902 |
| 1,277 | 13,769 | 13 | 5,531 87,288 | 2,737 36,647 | 18 32,772 |

| State Capital | Population | Area (sq mi/ sq km) | Per Capita Personal Income | Governor Lieutenant-Governor | Revenue Expenditure | Public Roads (Miles) |
|---|---|---|---|---|---|---|
| TENNESSEE Nashville | 4,855,000 462,500 | 42,144 109,152 | $12,002 | Lamar Alexander (R) John S. Wilder (D) | $ 6,142,000,000 5,439,000,000 | 83,851 |
| TEXAS Austin | 16,789,000 491,000 | 266,807 691,027 | 13,478 | William P. Clements (R) William P. Hobby (D) | 21,346,000,000 19,074,000,000 | 285,962 |
| UTAH Salt Lake City | 1,680,000 164,900 | 84,899 219,887 | 10,981 | Norman H. Bangerter (R) W. Val Oveson (R) | 3,133,000,000 2,818,000,000 | 49,938 |
| VERMONT Montpelier | 548,000 8,300 | 9,614 24,900 | 13,348 | Madeleine Kunin (D) Howard Dean (D) | 1,109,000,000 1,034,000,000 | 14,049 |
| VIRGINIA Richmond | 5,904,000 217,700 | 40,767 105,586 | 15,408 | Gerald Baliles (D) L. Douglas Wilder (D) | 9,030,000,000 7,833,000,000 | 65,802 |
| WASHINGTON Olympia | 4,538,000 29,600 | 68,139 176,479 | 15,009 | Booth Gardner (D) John A. Cherberg (D) | 9,781,000,000 9,012,000,000 | 80,478 |
| WEST VIRGINIA Charleston | 1,897,000 64,000 | 24,231 62,758 | 10,576 | Arch A. Moore, Jr. (R) * | 3,672,000,000 3,343,000,000 | 35,143 |
| WISCONSIN Madison | 4,807,000 176,000 | 56,153 145,436 | 13,909 | Tommy Thompson (R) Steve McCallum (R) | 9,740,000,000 8,718,000,000 | 108,667 |
| WYOMING Cheyenne | 490,000 47,300 | 97,809 253,324 | 12,781 | Mike Sullivan (D) * | 1,946,000,000 1,497,000,000 | 38,931 |

# OUTLYING AREAS OF THE UNITED STATES

| Area Capital | Population | Area (sq mi/ sq km) | Status | Governor Lieutenant-Governor | Revenue Expenditure | Roads (Miles) |
|---|---|---|---|---|---|---|
| AMERICAN SAMOA Pago Pago | 36,000 | 76 197 | Unorganized, unincorporated territory | A. P. Lutali Eni Hunkin | $ NA 91,600,000 | 95 |
| GUAM Agaña | 124,000 | 209 541 | Unincorporated territory | Joseph F. Ada Frank F. Blas | 169,000,000 NA | 419 |
| PUERTO RICO San Juan | 3,282,000 434,800 | 3,515 9,104 | Commonwealth | Rafael Hernández Colón * | 4,134,000,000 3,832,000,000 | 8,520 |
| TRUST TERRITORY OF THE PACIFIC ISLANDS[1] Capitol Hill, on Saipan Island | 156,000 | 708 1,834 | UN trust territory[1] | High Commissioner: Janet J. McCoy[1] | 125,137,000 118,869,000 | 362 |
| VIRGIN ISLANDS Charlotte Amalie | 111,000 | 133 344 | Unincorporated territory | Alexander A. Farrelly Derek M. Hodge | 235,000,000 245,400,000 | 641 |

1. Formal dissolution of the Trust Territory of the Pacific Islands has not been completed. In 1986 the Northern Mariana Islands became a U.S. commonwealth and the Federated States of Micronesia and the Republic of the Marshall Islands entered into compacts of free association with the United States. The legality of the vote in the Republic of Palau, in August 1987, to accept a compact of free association has been challenged.

| Railways (Miles) | Aircraft Departures | English-language Daily Newspapers | Public Elementary Schools (K–8): Teachers Students | Public Secondary Schools (9–12): Teachers Students | Colleges and Universities: Institutions Students |
|---|---|---|---|---|---|
| 2,537 | 126,632 | 27 | 25,008 573,591 | 15,015 239,236 | 80 194,845 |
| 12,802 | 529,643 | 103 | 86,557 2,225,791 | 87,390 871,026 | 158 769,692 |
| 1,483 | 57,660 | 6 | 8,656 298,760 | 6,150 104,635 | 14 103,994 |
| 102 | 6,856 | 8 | 2,857 62,485 | 3,488 27,454 | 22 31,416 |
| 3,729 | 54,959 | 36 | 31,539 663,423 | 25,358 302,953 | 72 292,416 |
| 3,562 | 129,891 | 25 | 17,040 504,972 | 15,645 242,816 | 53 231,553 |
| 3,156 | 8,464 | 21 | 10,859 284,549 | 8,377 108,889 | 29 76,659 |
| 3,647 | 59,155 | 33 | 23,531 490,721 | 18,049 266,832 | 63 275,069 |
| 1,993 | 8,156 | 9 | 4,187 73,988 | 2,120 28,791 | 8 24,204 |

| Railways (Miles) | Aircraft Departures | Daily Newspapers | Public Elementary and Secondary School Teachers | Public School Students: Elementary Secondary | Higher Education: Institutions Students |
|---|---|---|---|---|---|
| 0 | 1,820 | 0 | 616 | 7,535 2,589 | 1 758 |
| 0 | 3,500 | 1 | 1,329 | 18,886 6,777 | 2 4,601 |
| 60 | 11,195 | 4 | 32,683 | 507,973 178,921 | 41 155,917 |
| 0 | 6,156 | 0 | 2,539 | 37,320 6,802 | 2 1,042 |
| 0 | 6,125 | 2 | 1,631 | 18,599 6,787 | 1 2,572 |

461

# THE PROVINCES AND TERRITORIES OF CANADA

| Province Capital | Population | Area (sq mi/ sq km) | Per Capita Personal Income | Premier Lieutenant-Governor |
|---|---|---|---|---|
| **ALBERTA** Edmonton | 2,375,300 574,000 | 255,285 661,185 | $13,499 | Donald Getty Helen Hunley |
| **BRITISH COLUMBIA** Victoria | 2,889,200 66,300 | 366,255 948,596 | 13,192 | William N. Vander Zalm Robert Gordon Rogers |
| **MANITOBA** Winnipeg | 1,071,200 594,600 | 251,000 650,087 | 12,604 | Howard R. Pawley George Johnson |
| **NEW BRUNSWICK** Fredericton | 710,400 44,400 | 28,354 73,436 | 9,861 | Frank McKenna Gilbert Finn |
| **NEWFOUNDLAND** St. John's | 568,300 96,200 | 156,185 404,517 | 8,862 | Brian Peckford James A. McGrath |
| **NORTHWEST TERRITORIES** Yellowknife | 52,200 11,800 | 1,304,903 3,379,684 | 12,730[1] | Commissioner: John H. Parker |
| **NOVA SCOTIA** Halifax | 873,200 113,600 | 21,425 55,491 | 10,439 | John M. Buchanan Alan R. Abraham |
| **ONTARIO** Toronto | 9,113,500 612,300 | 412,582 1,068,582 | 14,031 | David Peterson Lincoln Alexander |
| **PRINCE EDWARD ISLAND** Charlottetown | 126,600 15,800 | 2,184 5,657 | 9,268 | Joseph Ghiz Robert Lloyd George MacPhail |
| **QUÉBEC** Québec | 6,540,300 164,600 | 594,860 1,540,680 | 11,690 | Robert Bourassa Gilles Lamontagne |
| **SASKATCHEWAN** Regina | 1,010,200 175,100 | 251,700 651,900 | 11,943 | Grant Devine Frederick Johnson |
| **YUKON TERRITORY** Whitehorse | 23,500 15,200 | 186,300 482,515 | 12,730[1] | Commissioner: Kenneth McKinnon |

1. Figure is the combined average for the Northwest Territories and Yukon Territory.
2. Figures include community and educational stations.

462

The material in this table has been prepared with the assistance of Statistics Canada. It should be noted that all dollar figures are in Canadian dollars.

| Revenue Expenditure | Motor Vehicle Registrations | Railways (Miles) | Radio and Television Stations[2] | Daily Newspapers | Elementary and Secondary Schools: Teachers Enrollment | Postsecondary Education: Institutions Enrollment |
|---|---|---|---|---|---|---|
| $ 8,600,000,000 10,600,000,000 | 1,729,287 | 3,035 | 153. 127 | 9. | 25,505. 475,300 | 25 70,830 |
| 9,370,000,000 10,220,000,000 | 2,175,032 | 3,922 | 300. 307 | 19. | 26,345. 525,700 | 26 59,090 |
| 3,374,000,000 3,941,000,000 | 739,488 | 1,649 | 71. 67 | 6. | 12,375. 219,500 | 16 23,430 |
| 2,975,000,000 3,407,000,000 | 416,805 | 684 | 55. 35 | 4. | 7,560. 139,400 | 12 17,360 |
| 2,316,000,000 2,489,000,000 | 257,693 | 149 | 90. 133 | 2. | 8,000. 136,140 | 11 14,610 |
| 633,000,000 681,000,000 | 23,271 | NA | 64. 79 | — | 700. 13,100 | 1 350 |
| 2,849,000,000 3,034,000,000 | 529,267 | 419 | 76. 58 | 6. | 10,210. 172,400 | 25 26,230 |
| 33,860,000,000 34,840,000,000 | 5,179,918 | 8,261 | 338. 325 | 46. | 99,040. 1,876,560 | 52 276,600 |
| 557,000,000 567,000,000 | 76,126 | NA | 9. 7 | 3. | 1,285. 24,660 | 3 2,950 |
| 25,600,000,000 28,700,000,000 | 2,974,099 | 3,451 | 304. 235 | 11. | 70,865. 1,154,720 | 87 278,800 |
| 3,200,000,000 3,800,000,000 | 697,160 | 2,495 | 55. 92 | 5. | 11,460. 215,470 | 7 25,170 |
| 280,000,000 291,000,000 | 20,479 | NA | 35. 17 | 1. | 300. 4,900 | 1 50 |

# KEY TO
# SIGNED ARTICLES

Here is a list of contributors to this Yearbook. The initials at the end of an article are those of the author or authors of that article.

**A.C.,** ALLEN CHEN, B.S., M.S.
Reporter, *Discover* Magazine.

**A.D.,** ALASDAIR DRYSDALE, PH.D.
Associate Professor, University of New Hampshire

**A.L.N.,** A. LIN NEUMANN, B.A.
Free-lance Journalist. Coeditor, *Bayanko: Images of the Philippine Revolt.*

**A.L.R.,** ARTHUR L. ROBINSON, PH.D.
Senior Writer, Research News Section, *Science* Magazine.

**B.B.R.,** BONNIE B. REECE, B.S., M.B.A., PH.D.
Associate Professor of Advertising, Michigan State University. Member, Editorial Review Board, *Journal of Public Policy and Marketing.*

**B.B.S.,** BONNIE BARRETT STRETCH, A.B., M.S.
Contributing Editor, *Art & Auction* Magazine. Critic, *Artnews.*

**B.D.J.,** BRIAN D. JOHNSON, B.A.
Senior Writer, *Maclean's* Magazine. Author, *Railway Country: Across Canada by Train.*

**B.J.,** BRUCE JUDDERY, A.B.
Canberra Correspondent, *Australian Business.*

**B.K.,** BOB KLAPISCH, B.A.
Baseball Reporter, New York *Post.*

**B.R.,** BEA RIEMSCHNEIDER, A.B., M.A.
Former Editor in Chief, *Archaeology.*

**B.R.M.,** BARBARA R. MUELLER
Editor, *The Essay-Proof Journalist.* Author, *Common Sense Philately.*

**B.S.,** BROOKE GRUNDFEST SCHOEPF, PH.D.
Anthropologist. Director, Project Connaissida, Zaire.

**B.V.,** BOB VERDI, A.B.
Columnist, Chicago *Tribune.*

**C.B.,** CHRISTIE BARTER, A.B.
Music Editor, *Stereo Review.*

**C.C.,** CRAIG COVAULT, B.A.
Senior Space Editor, *Aviation Week & Space Technology.*

**C.H.A.,** CALVIN H. ALLEN, JR., A.B.,M.A.,PH.D.
Professor of History, School of the Ozarks, Mo.

**C.J.S.,** CURTIS J. SITOMER, B.A.
Columnist, *Christian Science Monitor.*

**C.M.,** CHRISTINE MLOT, B.S.
Associate Editor, *Environment* Magazine. Free-lance Science Writer.

**C.S.J.W.,** CHARLES S. J. WHITE, B.A., M.A., PH.D.
Professor, Department of Philosophy and Religion, The American University. Former Director, Center for Asian Studies.

**D.D.B.,** DARALICE D. BOLES, A.B., M.ARCH.
Senior Editor, *Progressive Architecture.*

**D.E.S.,** DONALD E. SCHULZ, B.A., PH.D.
Assistant Professor of Political Science, University of Tampa.

**D.F.A.,** DONALD F. ANTHROP, PH.D.
Professor of Environmental Studies, San Jose State University, Author, *Noise Pollution.*

**D.H.,** DARRELL HAMMER, A.B., A.M., PH.D.
Professor of Political Science, Indiana University. Author, *The USSR: The Politics of Oligarchy.*

**D.L.L.,** DAVID L. LEWIS, B.S., M.S., M.A., PH.D.
Professor of Business History, Graduate School of Business Administration, University of Michigan.

**D.M.,** DALE MITCH, B.A.
Editor, *Skating* Magazine. Director of Publications and Public Relations, United States Figure Skating Association.

**D.M.P.,** DAVID M. PHILIPS, A.B.
Sports Writer, Providence *Journal.*

**D.P.,** DON PERETZ, A.B., M.A., PH.D.
Professor of Political Science, State Uni-

versity of New York at Binghamton. Author, *Middle East Today* and *The West Bank.*

**D.P.W.,** DAVID P. WERLICH, B.A., M.A., PH.D.
Professor of History, Southern Illinois University. Author, *Peru: A Short History.*

**D.R.W.,** DONALD R. WHITAKER, A.B.
Economist, Office of Industry Services, National Marine Fisheries Service. Contributor, *Fishing Gazette.*

**D.S.,** DAVID STAINES, A.B., A.M., PH.D.
Professor of English, University of Ottawa. Editor, *Journal of Canadian Poetry.*

**D.S.M.,** DONALD S. MACDONALD, PH.D.
Research Professor of Korean Studies, School of Foreign Service, Georgetown University. Former State Department Foreign Service Officer.

**E.C.R.,** EDWARD C. ROCHETTE
Retired Executive Director, American Numismatic Association. Numismatic Writer, Los Angeles *Times* Syndicate.

**E.J.F.,** ERIK J. FRIIS, B.S., M.A.
Editor and Publisher, *The Scandinavian-American Bulletin.* General Editor, *The Library of Nordic Literature.*

**E.S.K.,** ELAINE KNAPP, B.A.
Editor, Council of State Governments.

**F.D.S.,** FREDERICK D. SCHNEIDER, PH.D.
Professor Emeritus of History, Vanderbilt University.

**F.E.H.,** FREDERICK E. HOXIE, B.A., PH.D.
Director,D'Arcy McNickle Center for the History of the American Indian. Author, *A Final Promise: The Campaign to Assimilate the Indians.*

**F.L.,** FRANK LITSKY, B.S.
Sports Writer, New York *Times.* Author, *Superstars, The Winter Olympics* and *The New York Times Official Sports Record Book.*

**F.W.K.,** FRANKLIN W. KNIGHT, B.A., M.A., PH.D.
Professor of Latin American and Caribbean History, The Johns Hopkins University. Author, *Africa and the Caribbean: The Legacies of a Link.*

**G.B.H.,** GARY B. HANSEN, B.S., M.S., PH.D.
Professor of Economics, Utah State University. Director, Utah Center for Productivity and Quality of Working Life.

**G.D.L.,** GEORGE DE LAMA, B.S.
White House Correspondent, Chicago *Tribune.*

**G.M.H.,** GEOFFREY M. HORN, A.B., M.A.
Free-lance Writer.

**G.S.,** GADDIS SMITH, B.A., M.A., PH.D.
Larned Professor of History, Yale University. Author, *Morality, Reason, and Power: American Diplomacy in the Carter Years.*

**H.C.H.,** HAROLD C. HINTON, PH.D.
Professor of Political Science and International Affairs, George Washington Uni-

versity. Editor, *The People's Republic of China, 1949-1979: A Documentary Survey.*

**H.H.,** HERBERT HOWE, B.S., M.A., PH.D.
Acting Chairman, African Studies Program, School of Foreign Service, and Research Professor of African Politics, Georgetown University.

**H.W.H.,** HARRY W. HENDERSON, A.B.
Free-lance Writer. Former Writer-Economist, U.S. Department of Agriculture.

**I.C.B.,** IRIRANGI COATES BLOOMFIELD, A.B., M.A., PH.D.
Lecturer and Writer. Former Member, New Zealand United Nations Delegation.

**I.K.,** INDULIS KEPARS, B.A.
Chief Librarian, Australian Collections and Services, National Library of Australia.

**I.S.G.,** INEZ S. GLUCKSMAN, B.A., M.A.
Free-lance Writer and Editor.

**J.A.P.,** JOHN A . PETROPULOS, PH.D.
Professor of History, Amherst College. Author, *Politics and Statecraft in the Kingdom of Greece.*

**J.A.R.,** JAMES A. ROTHERHAM, A.B., M.A., M.A.L.D., PH.D.
Staff Director, Nutrition Subcommittee, U.S. House of Representatives.

**J.B.,** JOHN BEAUFORT
Contributing Drama Critic, *Christian Science Monitor.*

**J.D.,** JOHN DAMIS, PH.D.
Professor of Political Science, Portland State University. Author, *Conflict in Northwest Africa: The Western Sahara Dispute.*

**J.F.,** JAMES FANNING
Landscape Architect. Free-lance Writer. Former Author, "Gardener's Notes," *House and Garden* Magazine.

**J.F., Jr.** JOHN FORAN, JR., A.B., M.A.
Graduate Fellow and Doctoral Candidate in Sociology, University of California, Berkeley.

**J.F.A.,** JOANN FAGOT AVIEL, M.A., M.A.L.D., PH.D.
Professor of International Relations, San Francisco State University. Author, *Resource Shortages and World Politics.*

**J.F.J.,** JAMES F. JEKEL, M.D., M.P.H.
Professor of Epidemiology and Public Health, Yale University School of Medicine.

**J.F.S.,** JOANNE F. SCHNEIDER, A.B., M.A., PH.D.
Associate Professor of History, Wheaton College.

**J.G.D.,** JOHN G. DEEDY, A.B., M.A.
Former Managing Editor, *Commonweal.* Contributor, New York *Times.* Author, *Catholic Fact Book* and *American Catholicism: And Now Where?*

**J.H.,** JOHN HAY, A.B.
Editorial Board Member, Ottawa *Citizen.*

**J.H.B.,** JAMES H. BUDD
Free-lance Writer Based in Mexico. Correspondent, Murdoch Magazines and Gemini News Service.

**J.J.Z.,** JOSEPH J. ZASLOFF, A.B., M.A., PH.D.
Professor of Political Science, University of Pittsburgh. Specialist in Southeast Asian Affairs.

**J.L.,** JOHN LUTER, A.B.
Professor and Chairman, Journalism Department, University of Hawaii. Former Coordinator, Advanced International Reporting Program, Columbia University Graduate School of Journalism.

**J.M.,** JOHN MUTTER, B.A.
Senior Associate Editor, *Publishers Weekly* Magazine.

**J.M.L.,** JOEL M. LEE, A.B., A.M.
Senior Manager, Information Technology Publishing, American Library Association. Associate Editor, *ALA World Encyclopedia of Library and Information Services.*

**J.O.S.,** JAMES O. SAFFORD III, A.B., M.A., PH.D.
Former Instructor of History, The Shipley School, Bryn Mawr, Pa.

**J.Q.,** JOHN QUINN, B.F.A.
Senior Staff Artist, TFH Publications, Inc.

**J.R.S.,** JOHN SCHWARTZ, B.A., J.D.
Associate Editor, *Newsweek.*

**J.S.,** JOSEF SILVERSTEIN, B.A., PH.D.
Professor of Political Science, Rutgers University. Author, *Burmese Politics: The Dilemma of National Unity.*

**J.S.I.,** JACQUELINE S. ISMAEL, B.A., M.A., PH.D.
Professor of Social Welfare, University of Calgary. Author, *Kuwait: Social Change in Historical Perspective.*

**J.T.,** JACK THOMAS
Television Critic, Boston *Globe.*

**J.T.S.,** JAMES T. SHERWIN, A.B., LL.B.
Former New York State, Intercollegiate, and U.S. Speed Chess Champion and International Master.

**K.F.R.,** KARL F. REULING
American Editor, *Ballet International.*

**K.J.B.,** KIRK J. BEATTIE, A.B., M.A.
Assistant Professor of Government, Simmons College.

**K.M.,** KENT MULLINER, B.S., M.A.
Assistant to the Director, Ohio University Libraries.

**K.O.F.,** KIMBERLY OLSON FAKIH, B.A.
Contributing Editor, *Publishers Weekly.*

**K.P.,** KATHRYN PAULSEN, A.B.
Free-lance Writer and Editor.

**K.S.,** KAREN SPRINGEN, B.A., M.S.
Reporter and Researcher, *Newsweek.*

**K.T.,** KENNETH TERRY, B.A., M.A.
Senior News Editor, *Billboard.* Member of Grammy Screening Committee.

**K.W.G.,** KENNETH W. GRUNDY, A.B., M.A., PH.D.
Professor of Political Science, Case Western Reserve University.

**L.A.K.,** LAWRENCE A. KLETTER, A.B., M.A., J.D.
Certificate in Middle Eastern Studies, Columbia University. Associate, Fine & Ambrogne, Boston.

**L.B.A.,** LORI B. ANDREWS, B.A., J.D.
Research Fellow, American Bar Foundation. Author, *New Conceptions: A Consumer's Guide to the Newest Infertility Treatments Including In Vitro Fertilization, Artificial Insemination, and Surrogate Motherhood.*

**L.G.,** LOIS GOTTESMAN, A.B., M.A.
Free-lance Writer. Former Research Analyst, American Jewish Committee.

**L.J.M.,** LORUS J. MILNE, B.A., M.A., PH.D.
Professor of Zoology, University of New Hampshire.

**L.L.P.,** LARRY L. PIPPIN, A.B., M.A., PH.D.
Professor of Political Science, University of the Pacific.

**L.R.H.,** LINDLEY R. HIGGINS, P.E., B.S., M.S.
Consulting Engineer. President, Piedmont Publications. Author, *Cost Reduction From A to Z.*

**L.S.G.,** LOVETT S. GRAY, A.B.
Free-lance Writer and Consultant. Former Editor, National Council on Crime and Deliquency.

**L.W.G.,** LOWELL W. GUDMUNDSON, A.B., M.A., PH.D.
Assistant Professor of History, University of Oklahoma.

**L.Z.,** LAWRENCE ZIRING, B.S., M.I.A.,PH.D.
Director, Institute of Government and Politics, Professor of Political Science, Western Michigan University. Author, *Pakistan: The Enigma of Political Development* and *The Asian Political Dictionary.*

**M.C.,** MARK CURIALE, A.B.
Free-lance Writer and Editor.

**M.C.H.,** MICHAEL C. HUDSON, A.B., M.A., PH.D.
Professor of International Relations and Government; Director, Center for Contemporary Arab Studies, Georgetown University. President, Middle East Studies Association. Author, *Arab Politics: The Search for Legitimacy.*

**M.D.,** MICHAEL DIRDA, A.B., M.A., PH.D.
Staff Editor, *The Washington Post Book World.*

**M.D.H.,** M. DONALD HANCOCK, PH.D.
Professor of Political Science, Vanderbilt University.

**M.E.D.,** MARION E. DORO, B.A., M.A., PH.D.
Lucy Marsh Haskell Professor of Government, Connecticut College. Author, *Rhodesia/Zimbabwe: A Bibliographic Guide to the Nationalist Period.*

**M.G.,** MURIEL GRINDROD, A.B.
Author, *Italy, Rebuilding of Italy.*

**M.Gr.,** MILTON GREENBERG, A.B., M.A., PH.D.
Provost, The American University. Coauthor, *The American Political Dictionary; Political Science Dictionary.*

**M.G.G.,** M. GRANT GROSS, A.B., M.S., PH.D.
Director, Division of Ocean Sciences, National Science Foundation. Author, *Oceanography: A View of the Earth.*

**M.H.,** MURRAY HIEBERT, B.A., M.A.
Indochina Correspondent, *Far Eastern Economic Review.* Former Editor, *Indochina Issues.*

**M.M.,** MARGERY MILNE, B.A., M.A., PH.D.
Lecturer in Continuing Education, University of New Hampshire.

**M.S.B.,** MICHAEL S. BAKER, A.B., M.A.
Certificate in East Asian Studies, Columbia University.

**M.W.,** MARGARET WILLY, F.R.S.L.
Lecturer, Centre for Continuing Education, University of Sussex. Poetry Collected in *The Invisible Sun, Every Star a Tongue.*

**N.J.P.,** NEALE J. PEARSON, B.S., M.S., PH.D.
Professor of Political Science, Texas Tech University. Former Vice Consul, American Embassy in Tegucigalpa.

**N.M.R.,** NATHAN M. REISS, PH.D.
Associate Professor of Meteorology, Cook College, Rutgers University.

**N.P.N.,** NANCY PEABODY NEWELL, A.B.
Coauthor, *The Struggle for Afghanistan.*

**P.F.,** PHYLLIS FELDKAMP
Free-lance Writer, Editor, and Consultant. Coauthor, *The Good Life . . . Or What's Left of It.*

**P.G.,** PAUL GARDNER
Free-lance Writer. Author, *The Simplest Game* and *Nice Guys Finish Last.* Commentator, NBC Soccer Telecasts.

**P.H.C.,** PARRIS H. CHANG, PH.D.
Professor of Political Science, Chairman of Asian Area Studies, Pennsylvania State University. Author, *Elite Conflict in the Post-Mao China.*

**P.J.M.,** PAUL J. MAGNARELLA, A.M., PH.D.
Professor of Anthropology, University of Florida. Author, *Tradition and Change in a Turkish Town, The Peasant Venture.*

**P.J.S.,** PETER SCHWAB, B.A., M.A., PH.D.
Professor of Political Science, State University of New York at Purchase. Author, *Ethiopia: Politics, Economics, and Society.*

**P.M.F.,** PAMELA M. FESSLER, B.A., M.P.A.
News Editor, *Congressional Quarterly.* Former Budget Specialist, U.S. Office of Management and Budget.

**P.M.L.,** PETER LEWIS, B.A., M.A.
Fulbright Scholar in Political Science, Princeton University.

**P.S.,** PATRICIA STAMP, B.A., M.SC., PH.D.
Associate Professor of Social Science and Coordinator, African Studies Program, York University.

**P.W.,** PETER WINN, A.B., PH.D.
Associate Professor of History, Tufts University. Senior Research Fellow, Research Institute on Latin American and Iberian Studies, Columbia University.

**R.A.M.,** ROBERT A. MORTIMER, A.B., M.A., PH.D.
Professor of Political Science, Haverford College. Author. *The Third World Coalition in International Politics.*

**R.A.P.,** RICHARD A. PIERCE, PH.D.
Professor Emeritus of History, Queen's University, Ontario. Author, *Eastward to Empire: Exploration and Conquest on the Russian Open Frontier to 1750.*

**R.A.S.,** RONALD A. SCHORN, B.S., M.S., PH.D.
Technical Editor, *Sky and Telescope.* Former Chief, Ground-Based Planetary Astronomy, NASA.

**R.C.,** RAY CONLOGUE, B.A., M.A.
Theater Critic, Toronto *Globe and Mail.*

**R.C.O.,** ROBERT C. OBERST, B.A., M.A., PH.D.
Associate Professor of Political Science, Nebraska Wesleyan University. Coauthor, *Government and Politics in South Asia.*

**R.E.B.,** ROGER E. BILSTEIN, B.A., M.A., PH.D.
Professor of History, University of Houston at Clear Lake City. Author, *Stages to Saturn: A Technological History of the Apollo/ Saturn Launch Vehicles.*

**R.E.K.,** ROGER E. KANET, PH.B., A.B., M.A., A.M., PH.D.
Professor, Political Science Department, University of Illinois at Urbana-Champaign. Editor, *The Soviet Union, Eastern Europe, and the Third World* and *Soviet Foreign Policy in the 1980's.*

**R.H.C.,** RICHARD H. CAMER, B.A.
Associate Editor, *Psychology Today.*

**R.J.K.,** ROBERT J. KURSAR, A.B.
Assistant Managing Editor, *Traffic World* Magazine.

**R.J.L.,** ROBERT J. LaMARCHE, A.B.
Senior Editor, *Tennis* Magazine.

**R.J.M.,** R. J. MAY, M.E.C., D.PHIL.
Senior Fellow, Research School of Pacific Studies, Australian National University. Former Director, Institute of Applied Social and Economic Research, Papua New Guinea.

**R.J.W.,** RICHARD J. WILLEY, A.B., M.A., PH.D.
Professor of Political Science, Vassar College. Author, *Democracy in the West German Trade Unions.*

**R.L.F.,** RANDALL L. FRAME, B.A., M.A.
Associate News Editor, *Christianity Today.*

**R.O.,** ROXANNE ORGILL, B.A., M. MUSIC.
Music Critic, Hackensack (N.J.) *Record.*

466

**R.O.F.,** ROBERT O. FREEDMAN, PH.D. Dean and Professor of Political Science, School of Graduate Studies, Baltimore Hebrew College. Author, *Soviet Policy in the Middle East Since 1970.*

**R.P.C.,** RICHARD P. CRONIN, B.S., M.A., PH.D. Asian Affairs Specialist, Foreign Affairs and National Defense Division, Congressional Research Service, Library of Congress.

**R.T.,** ROBERT TIMBERG, B.S., M.A. White House Correspondent, Baltimore *Sun.*

**S.B.,** SARAH BARTLETT, B.A., M.PHIL. Money and Banking Editor, *Business Week.*

**S.C.,** STEVE COHEN, B.A. Executive Editor, *Ski* Magazine.

**S.D.H.,** STEVEN D. HELGERSON, M.D., M.P.H. Clinical Associate Professor of Epidemiology and Public Health, Yale University School of Medicine.

**S.E.,** SANFORD ELWITT, PH.D. Professor of History, University of Rochester. Author, *The Making of the Third Republic, The Third Republic Defended.*

**S.G.,** SHAV GLICK, A.B. Motor Racing Writer, Los Angeles *Times.*

**S.K.,** STANLEY KOCHANEK, B.A., M.A., PH.D. Professor of Political Science, Pennsylvania State University. Coauthor, *India: Government and Politics in a Developing Nation.*

**S.M.,** SIEGFRIED MANDEL, A.B., M.A., PH.D. Professor of English and Comparative Literature, University of Colorado at Boulder. Translator, *Lou Salome: Ibsen's Heroines, Friedrich Nietzsche: The Man in His Works.*

**S.M.G.,** SAM M. GOLDAPER Sports Reporter, New York *Times.* New York Area Chairman, Pro Basketball Writers' Association.

**T.D.,** THOMAS DEFRANK, B.A., M.A. Deputy Bureau Chief and White House Correspondent, *Newsweek.*

**T.H.M.,** THOMAS H. MAUGH, II, PH.D. Science Writer, Los Angeles *Times.* Coauthor, *Energy and the Future, Seeds of Destruction: The Science Report on Cancer Research.*

**T.I.,** TAREQ Y. ISMAEL, A.B., M.A., PH.D. Professor of Political Science, University of Calgary. Author, *The International Relations of the Contemporary Middle East.*

**T.J.O.H.,** T.J.O. HICKEY Former Member, Editorial Staff, *The Times* of London.

**T.McC.,** TOM McCOLLISTER, A.B. Sports Writer, Atlanta *Constitution.*

**W.C.C.,** WILLIAM C. CROMWELL, B.A., M.A., PH.D. Professor of International Relations, American University. Author, *The Eurogroup and NATO.*

**W.F.,** WILLIAM FREDERICK, PH.D. Assistant Professor of History, Ohio University.

**W.L.,** WILLIAM LEGGETT, A.B. Former Senior Writer, *Sports Illustrated.*

**W.M.,** WILLIAM MINTER, PH.D. Contributing Editor, Africa News Service. Author, *King Solomon's Mines Revisited: Western Interests and the Burdened History of South Africa.*

**W.N.,** WILLIAM NEIKIRK, A.B. Economics Correspondent, Washington Bureau, Chicago *Tribune.*

**W.S.,** WILLIAM SNIDER, A.B., M.S.J. Education Writer, *Education Week.* Author, *The Call For Choice: Competition in the Educational Marketplace.*

**W.W.,** WILLIAM WOLF, A.B. Film Critic. Lecturer, New York University and St. John's University. Author, *Landmark Films.*

467

# PICTURE CREDITS

# INDEX TO THE
# 1988 YEARBOOK
## EVENTS OF 1987

## INTRODUCTION

This Index is a comprehensive listing of persons, organizations, and events that are discussed in the 1988 Yearbook. Entries in **boldface** letters indicate subjects on which the Yearbook has an individual article. Entries in lightface type indicate individual references or sections within articles. In any entry, the letters a and b refer, respectively, to the left and right column of the page cited. If no letter follows a page number, the reference is to text that is printed in a different format. Usually only the first significant mention of a subject in a given article has been included in the Index.

In a main entry such as **Australia:** 81a, the first number refers to the page on which the article begins. The succeeding page numbers refer to other text discussions in the volume. The first number in lightface entries, when not in numerical order, will similarly provide the most extensive information on the subject. Subtitles following major entries refer to further references on the main subject, as in Congress of the United States: 414a; Agriculture, 64a. In the case of comprehensive articles such as the **United States of America,** reference is made to the page location of the beginning of the article. The discussion of foreign relations of the United States in that article may be augmented by reference to separate articles on the countries and international organizations concerned.

When an entry is designated by the abbreviation **illus.,** the reference is to a caption and picture on the page mentioned. When a text mention and an illustration of the same subject fall within the same article, usually only the text location is included in the Index.

### LIST OF ABBREVIATIONS USED IN THE INDEX

NATO   North Atlantic Treaty Organization
OPEC   Organization of Petroleum Exporting Countries
PLO   Palestine Liberation Organization
U.N.   United Nations
U.S.   United States
U.S.S.R.   Union of Soviet Socialist Republics

# A

Abbott, George: 304b, 395a
ABC. See AMERICAN BROADCASTING
    COMPANY
Abel, I.W.: 278a
Abenakis: 193a
abortion: 340b, 424a, 431b
Academy Awards: 262b
**Accidents and Disasters:** 55a, 135a,
    138a, 176b, 396b; Alberta tor-
    nado **illus.** 104
acid rain: 156b
acquired immune deficiency syn-
    drome. See AIDS
acquisitions. See MERGERS AND AC-
    QUISITIONS
actors and actresses. See MOTION
    PICTURES; TELEVISION AND RADIO
    BROADCASTING; THEATER
Adami, Eddie Fenech: 240a
Adams, John: 299a
**Advertising:** 58a; **illus.** 181
Aebi, Tania: 304b
affirmative action: 96a, 424a, 430b
**Afghanistan:** 58b, 252a, 436; Paki-
    stan, 294a; U.S.S.R., 405b
AFL-CIO: 214b
**Africa:** 60a, 65a, 252b. See also
    specific countries
African National Congress: 60b,
    195b, 348a
aged. See OLDER POPULATION
**Agriculture and Food Supplies:** 63a,
    158b, 421a; Africa, 60a, 67b,
    161a, 263b; biotechnology,
    221a; Europe, 161b
AIDS: 180a, 194b, 298b; Advertis-
    ing, 58b; Africa, 401b, 434a,
    434b; Belgium, 94b; drugs,
    182a, 223a; Education, 148a,
    237b, 380b, 434a; minorities,
    96b, 116b; testing, 117a,
    181a, 380b
air disasters: 212a, 396b
airlines: 396a, 106a, 420a
air pollution: 157a
Alabama: 456
Alaska: 138a, 153a, 159b, 456
**Albania:** 66a, 436
Alberta: 57a, 462
Alfonsín, Raúl: 72b
**Algeria:** 66b, 436
Alia, Ramiz: 66a
Allen, Woody: 302b, 257b
Alzheimer's disease: 185b, 223b
AMA. See AMERICAN MEDICAL ASSOCI-
    ATION
Amal movement: 68a, 216b, 249a
American Ballet Theatre: 132a
American Book Awards: 230b
American Broadcasting Company:
    386b
American Federation of Labor and
    Congress of Industrial Organi-
    zations. See AFL-CIO
American Indians. See INDIANS,
    AMERICAN

American Medical Association:
    117b, 181a
American Motors Corporation: 84b
American Samoa: 460
America's Cup: 83b, 374b
Anderson, Lindsay: 258a
Angleton, James Jesus: 278a
**Angola:** 67a, 60b, 65a, 434b, 436
animals. See PETS; ZOOLOGY
Anouilh, Jean: 278a
Antarctica: 136a, 158b
anthropology: 224a
Antigua and Barbuda: 436
apartheid: 60a, 237b, 347b
Apple Computer Corporation: 124a
Aquino, Corazon: 319a
**Arab League:** 68a, 149b, 248a, 384b
Arafat, Yasir: 208a, 249a
Aragon, Louis: 236a
**Archaeology:** 68b, 110b
**Architecture:** 70b, 330a
**Argentina:** 72b, 436; foreign debt,
    92a
Arias Sánchez, Oscar: 125a, 272b,
    292b, 328a, 425b
Arizona: 382a, 456
Arkansas: 128b, 456
armed forces. See MILITARY AND NA-
    VAL AFFAIRS
arms control: 251b, 122a, 295a,
    309a, 405a, 412a, 426a; and
    NATO, 171a, 275b; Washing-
    ton summit, 251b, 405b,
    427a; **illus.** frontispiece
arms sales: 252a; Bahrain, 317a;
    China, 246b, 252b; France,
    167a; Jordan, 208b; Saudi Ara-
    bia, 346b; Sweden, 383a; Yu-
    goslavia, 433b. See also IRAN/
    CONTRA ARMS AFFAIR
Arrington, Richard, Jr.: 149b
**Art:** 74a, 330a. See also MUSEUMS
asbestos: 148a
Ashbery, John: 230a
Asia: Agriculture, 65a; Asean sum-
    mit, 195b; Communist coun-
    tries, 123a. See also specific
    countries
Assad, Hafez al-: 248a, 384b
Association of Southeast Asian Na-
    tions: 195b
Astaire, Fred: 134a, 278a
Astor, Mary: 278a
**Astronomy:** 78b
Attas, Haidar Abu Bakr al-: 432a
Audi of America Corporation: 85a
**Australia:** 81a, 436; Agriculture,
    65a; Dogs, 42; Libya, 220b;
    Literature, 230b; South Africa,
    121a
**Austria:** 83b, 436; Israel, 201b; Lit-
    erature, 235b; Waldheim,
    Kurt, 149b, 201b, 310b, 339a
**Automobile Industry:** 84a, 212b,
    380a
automobile racing: 356a
avalanches: 55b

aviation: 396a, 420a; Accidents,
    55a
awards. See PRIZES AND AWARDS
Awolowo, Obafemi: 278b
Azcona del Hoyo, José: 189a
Azinger, Paul: 366a
AZT. See ZIDOVUDINE

# B

Babbitt, Bruce: 300a, 422a
Baby M: 188a, 303a, 382a
bacteria: 221a
Bahamas: 108a, 436
Bahrain: 317a, 436
Baird, Bil: 278b
Baker, Howard, Jr.: 304b, 410b
Baker, James A., III: 141a
Bakker, Jim: 300b, 305a, 336a
Bakker, Tammy: 300b, 305a, 336a
Balaguer, Joaquín: 108a
Baldrige, Malcolm: 278b, 297a
Baldwin, Dick: 360b
Baldwin, James: 279a
ballet. See DANCE
Ballet West: 132b
Baltimore: 149b
Banco Ambrosiano: 205a
**Bangladesh:** 86a, 56a, 436
**Banking and Finance:** 87b, 140b,
    419b; Canada, 105b; Switzer-
    land, 383b; Vatican, 205b.
    See also THIRD WORLD DEBT
Baptist churches: 338a
Barbados: 108a, 436
Barbie, Klaus: 165, 342a
Bardot, Brigitte: 301a
Barnes, Thomas V.: 150a
Barnett, Ross Robert: 279a
Barrow, Errol: 108a
Barth, John: 227b
Baryshnikov, Mikhail: 132a
baseball: 356b, 82a, 95a
basketball: 360a, 310a
Batts, Sharon: 303a
beagles, 45
Becker, Boris: 372a
Becker, Jurek: 235b
Bednorz, Johannes Georg: 323a, 328b
Bedrosian, Steve: 358a
**Behavioral Sciences:** 92b
Beirut: 216b, 384b
Belau. See PALAU
**Belgium:** 94a, 161a, 436; Acci-
    dents, 55b; Persian Gulf,
    247a, 251a, 406b
Belize: 438
Bell, Derek: 356b
Bell, George: 358a
Bellow, Saul: 228a
Ben Ali, Zine al-Abdine: 399b
Benin: 438
Benjedid, Chadli: 66b
Bennett, Michael: 279b, 298b, 395b
Bennett, William J.: 146b, 181a
Berlin: 74a, 169b
Bernstein, Leonard: 298b
Berry, Chuck: 304a

471

**Health and Medicine:** 180a, 380b; biotechnology, 221a, 327a; disease-prone personality, 93a; drugs, 222a; euthanasia, 271a; food hazards, 110a; Indians, American, 194a; insurance, 419b; radiation accident, 99a; synthetic bone, 110b. *See also* AIDS

heart disease: 184b

heart transplant, infant: 184a

heat wave (Greece): 57a, 177b

Heifetz, Jascha: 283a

Heller, Walter: 283a

hemophilia: 116b, 183b

herbicides: 159a, 221a

Herman, Woody: 283a

Hernández Colón, Rafael: 335a

Hess, Rudolf: 172a, 283a, 342b

Hextall, Ron: 368b

Hezbollah (Party of God): 216b, 385a

Higgins, George V.: 228b

Hinduism: 343a

Hirsh, Edward: 230b

Hitchcock, Henry-Russell: 72a, 283b

Hoban, Russell: 227b

hockey. *See* ICE HOCKEY

Hodel, Donald: 136a

Hodgins, Jack: 232b

Hoffman, Abbie: 299a

Holkeri, Harri: 164a

Holm, Peter: 302b

Holmes, Sherlock: 234b

homelands, South African: 455

homeless people: 187a, 420b

homosexuals: 118a, 183b. *See also* AIDS

**Honduras:** 188b, 70a, 274a, 442

Honecker, Erich: 123a, 168a

Honeyghan, Lloyd: 363a

Hong Kong: 90a, 115b, 140b

horse racing: 367a

hostages in Lebanon: 197b, 218a. *See also* IRAN/CONTRA ARMS AFFAIR

House of Representatives, U.S.: *See* CONGRESS OF THE U.S.

housing and construction: 420b

Houston: 132b, 150a, 333b, 430a; **illus.** 71

Houston Ballet: 132b

Howard Beach incident: 129a

Howser, Dick: 283b

Ho Ying-Chin: 283b

Hudnut, William H.: 150b

Hughes, Robert: 231b

humanities in education: 146b

human rights: Argentina, 72b; Cambodia, 101a; Chile, 112b; Colombia, 120b; Cuba, 129b; El Salvador, 151b; Guatemala, 178a; Haiti, 179a; Honduras, 189a; Kenya, 209a; Paraguay, 296b; Uruguay, 428a; U.S.S.R., 402a, 427a. *See also* CIVIL RIGHTS AND CIVIL LIBERTIES

**Hungary:** 189a, 442

Hun Sen: 100a

hurricane: 55a

Husák, Gustav: 122a, 131

Hussein, King: 208a, 248b; **illus.** 68a

Hussein, Saddam: 198b; **illus.** 68a

Huston, John: 258a, 283b

Hu Yaobang: 113b

hydroelectric power: 23

## I

IBM. *See* INTERNATIONAL BUSINESS MACHINES CORPORATION

Icahn, Carl C.: 143b

ice hockey: 368a

**Iceland:** 190a, 442

ice skating: 369b

Idaho: 456

illegal aliens: 104a. *See also* REFUGEES

Illinois: 456

immigration: 104a, 200b, 341b, 403b. *See also* REFUGEES

**India:** 190b, 442; Agriculture, 65a; China, 116a; Pakistan, 295a; Religion, 343a; Sri Lanka, 376a

Indiana: 57b, 456

Indianapolis: 150b

**Indians, American:** 193a, 24, 70a

**Indonesia:** 194a, 57b, 442

industries. *See* MANUFACTURING INDUSTRIES

inflation: 139b. *See also* articles on individual countries

insider-trading scandals: 91b, 126a

insurance: 419b

interest rates: 88b, 139b; Canada, 105b

International Bank for Reconstruction and Development. *See* WORLD BANK

International Business Machines Corporation: 124a

**International Conferences:** 194b, 144a; Arab League, 68a; Comecon, 123a; Commonwealth of Nations, 120b; European Communities, 161a; NATO, 276a; OPEC, 293a; Organization of African Unity, 62b; U.N., 405a; Warsaw Pact, 123a; World Bank, 92b. *See also* ARMS CONTROL

International Monetary Fund (IMF): 60a, 62b, 73b, 92b, 144a, 149a, 274b, 386a, 433a, 433b, 434a

Iowa: 128b, 456

IRA. *See* IRISH REPUBLICAN ARMY

**Iran:** 197a, 442; Arab League, 68a; Argentina, 74a; China, 115b; Egypt, 149b; France, 166b; OPEC, 293a; Religion, 344a; Saudi Arabia, 346a; U.N., 406a. *See also* IRAN/CONTRA

ARMS AFFAIR; IRAN-IRAQ WAR; IRAQ

Iran/contra arms affair: 412a; arms channels, 126b, 201a; Bush, George, 307a; congressional hearings, 300b, 314a, 419b; Costa Rica, 125a; Israel, 201a, 412a; money sources, 274a, 384a, 412b; North, Oliver, 300b, 314a, 434a; Poindexter, John, 256a, 412a; Switzerland, 384a

Iran-Iraq war: 245b, 250b, 68a, 212a, 317a, 346a, 406a. *See also* IRAN; IRAQ; PERSIAN GULF SHIPPING

**Iraq:** 198a, 444. *See also* IRAN; IRAN-IRAQ WAR

Ireland, Northern. *See* NORTHERN IRELAND

**Ireland, Republic of:** 199a, 161a, 444

Irish Republican Army: 199a

Irwin, John: 257a

Islam. *See* MUSLIMS

**Israel:** 200a, 248b, 252b, 444; Egypt, 149b; Iran/contra affair, 412a; Lebanon, 218a; U.N., 406b; U.S., 427b; U.S.S.R., 341b, 403b

**Italy:** 202b, 444; Accidents, 56a; Communism, 203a; European Communities, 161a; Literature, 236a; Persian Gulf, 247a, 251a, 406b

Ivory, James: 257b

Ivory Coast: 444

## J

Jackson, Jesse: 94a, 300b, 422a

Jackson, Michael: 303b

Jackson, Reggie: 358a

Jakes, Milos: 131b

Jamaica: 108b, 444

**James Bay Hydroelectric Project:** 23

**Japan:** 205a, 444; Agriculture, 65a; Automobiles, 84b; Banking, 87b; computer chips, 142a, 151a, 206b; fisheries, 66a; Korea, 209b; Literature, 236b; Military Affairs, 254a; Space Exploration, 354b; stock market, 140b; Toshiba case, 142b, 252b

Jaruzelski, Wojciech: 123a, 324b

Jarvik, Robert: 301a

Jazz Section: 131b

Jeantot, Philippe: 375a

jellyfish: 83b

Jochum, Eugen: 284a

Joffrey Ballet: 132a

John Paul II, Pope: 310a, 73b, 112b, 325a, 339a

Johnson, Ben: 373a

Johnson, Gus: 284a

Johnson, Howard: 357b

Jolley, Elizabeth: 231b

Nova Scotia: 103b, 462
NOW. See NATIONAL ORGANIZATION FOR WOMEN
Nuclear Non-Proliferation Treaty: 295a
nuclear power: 155b, 408b; Chernobyl, 405b
nuclear tests: 419a
nuclear waste: 159b
nuclear weapons: 251b, 309a, 405a, 412a, 426a; Communist World, 122a; Germany, 171a; NATO, 275b; Pakistan, 295a
Nudel, Ida: 301b
numismatics. See COINS AND COIN COLLECTING
Nureyev, Rudolf: 304a
Nyerere, Julius: 385b

## O

OAS. See ORGANIZATION OF AMERICAN STATES
Oates, Joyce Carol: 278b
OAU. See ORGANIZATION OF AFRICAN UNITY
Obando y Bravo, Miguel: 272b
**Obituaries:** 278a
oceanography: 138a
O'Connor, John Cardinal: 183b
Ohio: 128a, 458
oil. See PETROLEUM
Oklahoma: 458
older population: 185b, 223b; **illus.** 418
Olympics, 1988: 209b
Oman: 448
Ondaatje, Michael: 232a
O'Neill, Thomas P. ("Tip"), Jr.: 299a
Ontario: 106b, 431b, 462
OPEC. See ORGANIZATION OF PETROLEUM EXPORTING COUNTRIES
opera: 267a
Oppegard, Peter: 369b
Oppenheim, Bruce: 302b
Oregon: 458
organ donors and transplants: 184a
Organization of African Unity: 62b
**Organization of American States:** 292a
**Organization of Petroleum Exporting Countries:** 292a, 141a, 153a, 346a
Orser, Brian: 370a
Ortega Saavedra, Daniel: 272b, 292b, 425b
Orthodox churches: 336a
Özal, Turgut: 400a
Ozick, Cynthia: 228a
ozone: 136a, 158b, 408a

## P

**Pacific Islands:** 293a
Page, Geraldine: 288a, 395b
**Pakistan:** 294a, 59a, 448
Palau (Belau): 293b, 460

Palestine Liberation Organization: 248b, 149b, 208a, 217b
Palme, Olof: 383a
Pálsson, Thorsteinn: 190a
**Panama:** 295b, 448
pandas: 227a
Papandreou, Andreas: 177a
paper industry: 242
Papua New Guinea: 448
**Paraguay:** 296b, 448
Paris: Archaeology, 68b; Dance, 133b; opera, 267b
Paris Opera Ballet: 133b
Parkinson's disease: 186b
particle accelerators: 324a
Parti Québécois: 107a
Pavarotti, Luciano: 298b
Paz Estenssoro, Victor: 97a
Peabody awards. See GEORGE FOSTER PEABODY AWARDS
Peace Prize, Nobel: 328a
Pederson, Charles J.: 327a
Pell, Claiborne: 300a
Penn, Sean: 302b
Pennsylvania: 458
Pennsylvania Ballet: 132b
Pennzoil Corporation: 143b
**People in the News:** 297a
Pepper, Claude: **illus.** 418
Percy, Walker: 227b
Peres, Shimon: 200a, 248b
*perestroika* (restructuring): 121b, 308a
Pérez de Cuéllar, Javier: 197a, 198b, 405b
Perlmutter, Nathan: 288a
Perry, Carrie Saxon: 150a, 430a
Persian Gulf shipping: 246b, 153b, 194b, 317a; European nations, 167a, 175a, 205a, 247a, 251a, 271b, 406b; Iran, 197a; Iraq, 198a; Kuwait, 212a; U.N., 406a; U.S., 250b, 424b. See also IRAN-IRAQ WAR
**Persian Gulf States:** 317a. See also specific countries
**Peru:** 317a, 58a, 448; foreign debt, 92b
pesticides: 158b
Peterson, David: 106b
petroleum: 153a; Iran, 198a; Iraq, 199a; Kuwait, 212a; OPEC, 141a, 153a, 292a; Saudi Arabia, 346a; U.S., 141b. See also PERSIAN GULF SHIPPING
**Pets:** 317b, 36, 128b
Philadelphia: 95a, 149b
Philadelphia Flyers: 368a
**Philippines:** 319a, 252b, 255b, 448; Aquino, Corazon, 308b
**Photography:** 321a
**Physics:** 323a, 328b
Physiology or Medicine, Nobel Prize in: 328b
Pindling, Lynden O.: 108a
Pinochet Ugarte, Augusto: 112b
Piquet, Nelson: 356a
pit bulls: 128b, 317a

*Platoon:* 256a
Plaza Lasso, Galo: 288b
Poindexter, John: 256a, 412a
**Poland:** 324b, 56a, 236b, 340a, 448
Polisario Front: 256a
political parties: 421a
political prisoners: 130a, 272b, 402b
Pollard, Jonathan: 126b, 201b
Pollock, Sharon: 233a
pollution. See ENVIRONMENT
Pope John Paul II: 310a, 73b, 112b, 325a, 339a
popular music: 264a
population: 436
**Portugal:** 325b, 161a, 448; China, 115b
Pottle, Frederick A.: 288b
Powell, Lewis F., Jr.: 299b
Preakness: 367b
*Prensa, La:* 272b
president of the United States. See REAGAN, RONALD
Presley, Elvis: 266b
press, freedom of the: 333a; Nicaragua, 272b; South Africa, 347b
Preston, Robert: 288b
Price, Reynolds: 230b
Prince Edward Island: 462
prisons: 129b, 131a, 380b
privatization. See DENATIONALIZATION
**Prizes and Awards:** 327a, 72a, 230a, 262b, 269a, 358a, 389a, 395a
prospectors: 103a; **illus.** 98
Prost, Alan: 356b
protectionism: 107a, 142a, 241b
Protestant churches: 336a
psychology. See BEHAVIORAL SCIENCES
PTL scandal: 300b, 305a, 336a
**Publishing:** 331a, 227b, 327b
**Puerto Rico:** 335a, 460
Pulitzer Prizes: 328b, 230a, 269a, 395a
Punjab (India): 192a
Purdy, Al: 233b

## Q

**Qaddafi, Muammar al-:** 220a, 248a
Qatar: 448
quasars: 80a
Québec: 23, 107a, 194b, 462
Queensland, 81a

## R

radiation accident: 99a
radio. See TELEVISION AND RADIO BROADCASTING
radioactive waste: 159b, 99a
radon: 160a
Rahal, Bobby: 356a
railroads: 397a, 55a
Raines, Tim: 359a
Ramchandran, Marudur: 193a
Reagan, Maureen: 298a
Reagan, Michael: 298a
Reagan, Nancy: 186a, 297a

477

479

blacks, 94b; Bork, Robert, 422b; Bush, George, 306b; Canada, 107a, 144b, 156b; Caribbean, 130a; Central America, 188b, 272b; China, 116a; Civil Liberties, 116a; Coins, 119a; Crime, 126a; Economy, 87b, 139b; Education, 145a; Elections, 149b, 382a, 424a; Energy, 153a; Environment, 156b; Europe, 84a, 161a, 165b, 169b, 176b, 253a, 355a, 384a; India, 192b; Japan, 142a, 206b; Korea, 210a, 211b; Laos, 216a; Literature, 227b; Meese, Edwin, 311a; Mexico, 244a; Middle East, 197b, 198a, 201a, 208b, 212a, 221a, 346b, 384b, 400b; Military Affairs, 249b; NATO, 275a; North, Oliver, 314a; papal visit, 340a; Philippines, 320b; Reagan family, 297a; Religion, 336a; South America, 98a, 113a; Space Exploration, 351a; Stamps, 377b; State Government, 379a; Transportation, 396a; U.N., 406a; U.S.S.R., 405a; Venice summit, 194b, 204b; Washington summit, 251b, 405b; Women, 430a. *See also* IRAN/CONTRA ARMS AFFAIR.
United Steelworkers of America: 213a
Unruh, Jesse M.: 291a
UPI. *See* UNITED PRESS INTERNATIONAL
Upper Volta: 62a, 252b, 454
Urquhart, Jane: 232b
**Uruguay:** 428a, 454
U.S.S.R. *See* UNION OF SOVIET SOCIALIST REPUBLICS
USX Corporation: 213a, 241b
Utah: 55b, 136b, 460
U2: 264b, 304a, **illus.** 266a

## V

vaccines: 182a, 223a
Vachss, Andrew: 229a
Van Gogh, Vincent: 78b
Vanuatu: 55a, 294a, 454
Vargas, Virgilio Barco: 120a
Vatican: 78a, 205b. *See also* ROMAN CATHOLICISM
**Venezuela:** 428a, 57b, 454
Vermont: 460
Vernon, Jackie: 291b

Vernon Savings and Loan Association: 91a
Very Large Telescope: 81a
**Vietnam:** 429a, 123b, 454; Cambodia, 100a; China, 115b; Laos, 215b; Motion Pictures, 257a; Thailand, 391a
Viola, Frank: 359a
Virginia: 151a, 156a, 460
Virgin Islands: 460
volcanoes: 138a
Volcker, Paul A.: 91a, 139b
Vonnegut, Kurt: 228b
voting rights: 96a
Vranitzky, Franz: 83b

## W

Waite, Terry: 176b, 218a
Waldheim, Kurt: 84a, 149b, 201b, 310b, 339a
Walliser, Marie: 370b
Wall Street. *See* STOCK MARKET CRASH; STOCK MARKET SCANDALS
Walsh, Lawrence: 126b, 412a
Wampanoags: 193b
Warhol, Andy: 78b, 291b, 322a
Warsaw Pact: 123a, 276a
Washington: 460
Washington, D.C. *See* DISTRICT OF COLUMBIA
Washington, George: 11
Washington, Harold: 95a, 149b, 291b
Washington Redskins: 364b
Washington summit meeting: 251b, 309a, 405b, 427a; **illus.** frontispiece
wastes, hazardous. *See* HAZARDOUS WASTES
water pollution: 24, 160a, 420a
Watson, Jill: 369b
Watson, Tom: 366a
Wearne, Alan: 231b
weather. *See* CLIMATOLOGY
Wedtech Corporation: 127a, 312a
Weinberger, Caspar: 256a
Weldon, Fay: 234a
Western Samoa: 454
West Germany. *See* GERMANY, FEDERAL REPUBLIC OF
West Virginia: 460
White, Vanna: 300b, 388a
white-collar crime: 126a
Whitehead, Mary Beth: 188a, 303a, 382a
Whitmire, Kathy: 150a, 430a
Wiest, Dianne: 263a

Wilbur, Richard: 304a
Wilkinson, Wallace: 150b
Williams, Emlyn: 292a, 395b
Williams, Frank: 356b
Wilson, August: 391b
Wilson, Earle: 292a
Wimbledon: 373a
Win, Ne: 100a
Winans, R. Foster: 92a
winds: 176b
Winfrey, Oprah: **illus.** 387
Wisconsin: 460
Wittig, Georg: 292a
Wolfe, Gene: 227b
Wolfe, Tom: 228a
**Women:** 430a; AIDS, 180b; municipal elections, 150a; surrogate mothers, 188a, 382a; women's rights, **illus.** 20
World Bank (International Bank for Reconstruction and Development): 92b, 113a, 433b, 434a
World Series: 359a
World Wildlife Fund: 145a, 224b, 425b; **illus.** 414
Wright, Jim: 125b, 272b, 425b; **illus.** 414
Wyman, Jane: 298b
Wyoming: 460

## Y

yachting: 374b
Yard, Molly: 301a, 432a
Yeltsin, Boris: 122a, 309a, 403a
**Yemen, People's Democratic Republic of (South Yemen):** 432a, 454
**Yemen Arab Republic (North Yemen):** 432b, 454
Young, Andrew: 116b
Yourcenar, Marguerite: 292a
**Yugoslavia:** 433a, 454
Yukon Territory: 98, 462

## Z

Zaccaro, John: 299a
**Zaire:** 433a, 56b, 454
**Zambia:** 434a, 56b, 454
Zardari, Asif Ali: 301b
Zhao Ziyang: 113b, 123b
Zhivkov, Todor: 99b
Zhou Enlai: 299a
Zia ul-Haq, Muhammad: 294a
Zidovudine: 182a
**Zimbabwe:** 434b, 454
zoology: 225b; pets, 36, 128b, 317b
Zorinsky, Edward: 292a
Zurbriggen, Pirmin: 370a